PREFACE

We have great pleasure to present the FIRST EDITION of "**COMPUTER AIDED DRAFTING and MODELING LAB**". (Modeling is the American Spelling and Modelling is the British Spelling - Both are correct).

This book is written as per the latest syllabus of II Semester B.E. / B.Tech. of Civil & Mechanical (including Production & Automobile) Branches of **ANNA UNIVERSITY, Deemed Universities and various Autonomous Engineering Colleges.**

Computer Aided Drafting (CAD) is defined as an electronic tool employed to create and modify Engineering Drawings using a Drafting Software with a Compatible Computer Hardware. (Computer Aided Drafting is, sometimes, abbreviated as CADr, instead of CAD. CAD also means Computer Aided Design).

This CAD Lab Manual is a Teaching Companion to the Learned Faculty Members and Learning Companion to the Students.

We are immensely thankful to our Publishers Shri. V. Ramesh and Shri. Purushothaman, M/s. SCITECH Publications, Chennai, for their persistent efforts for bringing out the book in the present form with a nice getup.

Suggestions *or* comments to improve the usefulness of the book will receive a hearty welcome.

October , 2012 **AUTHORS**

☞ DEAR STUDENTS !

Computer Aided Drafting (CAD) is nothing but a technological advancement of " Basic Engineering Graphics".

- CAD has replaced the Drawing Instruments by various Softwares and Hardwares, *viz.*, the " ***Drawing Board***" by the "***Monitor***", the " ***Pencils***" by "***Mouse***", the " ***Manual Drafting***" by "***Key Board Operations***", etc. Obviously, it is " ***faster***" and more " ***accurate***" than Manual Drawing.

- Drafting Software Packages : AutoCAD – Developed by Autodesk Incorporation, USA, Unigraphics – Developed by Unigraphics, USA, I-DEAS – Developed by Structural Dynamics Research Corporation, USA and Pro/Engineer – Developed by Parametric Technology Corporation, USA.

- **AutoCAD - 2010 :** AutoCAD was first introduced in 1982 by Autodesk. It has hit the technical world like a shock wave, revolutionizing the manner of drawing preparation.

  Note : *This book is prepared using AutoCAD 2010. It is compatible with all the earlier AutoCAD versions.*

- This CADr Lab Manual is carefully designed to be Self-Explanatory and Self-Learning.
- It has Step-by-Step Command Sequences & Drawings for easy grasping of Drafting by the **Beginners.**
- Perhaps, too much is spoken about the book and it may be superfluous too, as *"The taste of pudding lies in eating".*

October . 2012

AUTHORS

"Wish you all the very best !"

ANNA UNIVERSITY SYLLABUS

COMPUTER AIDED DRAFTING AND MODELING LABORATORY

LIST of EXERCISES using SOFTWARE CAPABLE of DRAFTING and MODELING

1. Study of capabilities of software for Drafting and Modeling - Coordinate systems (Absolute, Relative, Polar, etc.) - Creation of simple figures like polygon and general multi-line figures.
2. Drawing of a Title Block with necessary text and projection symbol.
3. Drawing of Curves like Parabola, Spiral, Involute using Bspline or cubic Spline.
4. Drawing of Front View and Top View of Simple Solids like Prism, Pyramid, Cylinder, Cone, etc, and Dimensioning.
5. Drawing front view, top view and side view of objects from the given pictorial views (*e.g.* V – Block, Base of a Mixie, Simple Stool, Objects with Hole and Curves).
6. Drawing of a Plan of Residential Building (Two bed rooms, kitchen , hall , etc.)
7. Drawing of a Simple Steel Truss.
8. Drawing Sectional Views of Prism, Pyramid , Cylinder, Cone, etc.,
9. Drawing Isometric Projection of simple objects.
10. Creation of 3-D Models of simple objects and obtaining 2-D Multi-View drawings from 3-D models.

Note : Plotting of drawings must be made for each exercise and attached to the records written by students.

List of Equipments for a batch of 30 students :

1. Pentium IV computer or better hardware, with suitable graphics facility - 30 No.
2. Licensed software for Drafting and Modeling. - 30 Licenses
3. Laser Printer or Plotter to print / plot drawings - 2 No.

DETAILED CONTENTS

PART - I

ANNA UNIVERSITY

CAD LAB EXERCISES

WITH STEP-BY-STEP SOLUTIONS

PART-II 3-D MODELING

1

INTRODUCTION TO AutoCAD-2010

1. DRAFTING SOFTWARE

A general purpose Drafting Software must provide the user with a variety of functions for creating and manipulating the picture. The major functions of Drafting Software are :

1. Generation of Graphic Primitives *or* Elements, *e.g.*, Point, Line, Circle, etc.
2. Transformations, *e.g.*, Move, Rotate, Scale, etc.
3. Display Control and Windowing, *e.g.*, Zoom, Pan, Vpoint, etc.
4. Segmenting and Editing Functions, *e.g.*, Delete, Change, Trim, etc.

NOTE : Most CAD systems are menu driven. Commands can either be typed directly with the help of a Keyboard or can be picked up from the Screen Menu with the help of a Mouse. The effect of every command is immediately displayed on the Screen so that selection and correction can be done interactively and immediately.

1.1 APPLICATIONS OF CAD

Sl.No.	Engineering Branch	Applications
1.	Civil	Mapping, Contour plotting, Building plans, Structural drawings.
2.	Mechanical	Design of machine elements, CNC machine tools, Robotics, etc.
3.	Automobile	Kinematics, Hydraulics, Steering, etc.
4.	Electrical	Circuit Layout, Panel design, Control schematics.
5.	Electronics	Schematic diagrams of Printed Circuits, Integrated Circuits.
6.	Communication	Communication network, Satellite transmitting picture, T.V., etc.
7.	Architectural	Town planning, Interior decorations, Multi-storey complex.
8.	Aeronautical	Design of space-craft, Flight simulator, Lofting.
9.	Computer Science	Flow charts, Multimedia, etc.

NOTE: Computer Aided Drafting is, sometimes, abbreviated as CADr, instead of CAD. (CAD also means Computer Aided Design.)

2. AutoCAD - 2010

AutoCAD was developed by Autodesk Inc., U.S.A. It is the world-wide and most popular PC – CAD based system available in the market.

- The term *Auto* refers the company *Auto*desk Inc., and the term CAD is the acronym of Computer Aided Design or Drafting.
- AutoCAD's open architecture has allowed third party developers to write application software by using programming language like AutoLISP, etc., and that has significantly added to its popularity.

2.1 AutoCAD CAPABILITIES

- AutoCAD creates drawings from simple 2D drawings to 3D modeling of 3D objects.
- AutoCAD provides facilities that allow users to customize AutoCAD to make it more efficient and therefore increase their productivity.
- The built-in programming language AutoLISP helps to use AutoCAD commands while designing. The drawings can be linked with design or manufacturing packages such as ANSYS, IDEAS, PRO-ENGINEERS, UNIGRAPHICS, etc.

2.2 APPLICATIONS OF AutoCAD

- It is used by Civil Engineers in the design of buildings, dams, arches, etc.
- It is used by Mechanical / Production/ Automobile Engineers in the design of machine parts, assembly, automobile components, etc.
- It is used by electrical engineers in the design of electrical wiring circuits.
- It is used by electronics engineers in the design of PCBs.

2.3 MANUAL DRAFTING *Vs* AutoCAD DRAFTING

Criteria	**Manual Drafting Techniques**	**AutoCAD Drafting Techniques**
Scale	Scales are used as full size, reduced size or enlarged size.	All the dimensions you enter are input in real size, i.e., 1 : 1.
Drawing / Electronic sheet size	User may select a standard drawing sheet, *i.e.,* A2 or A3.	User can draw in real size, i.e., user set up an electronic paper on the computer big enough to hold the drawing at 1:1.
Drafting tools	Drafting tools such as mini-drafter, set-scale, etc., are used.	AutoCAD provides tools to help to draw accurately like toolbar, etc.
Accuracy	Accuracy of the drawing is relatively not that good.	Creating lines, circles and other shapes of exactly correct dimensions is easier.
Modifiability	Not easier.	Much easier to modify.

3. STARTING AutoCAD

- Switch on the Computer! *Windows XP* is loaded automatically!
- After a few seconds, the Screen, called Desktop Screen, appears and displays various *Icons* (*i.e., Graphic Images*) such as My Computer, AutoCAD 2010, etc.

How to start/run the AutoCAD software ?

Method 1

Double-click the **AutoCAD 2010** shortcut.

Method 2 : (Fig.1)

Click **Start** button from the **Taskbar** to display the **Programs Menu.**
Click **Programs** in the **Programs Menu** to display its **Submenu.**
Click **Autodesk** in the **Submenu** to display **AutoCAD 2010.**
Click **AutoCAD 2010** to display the software available in the **AutoCAD 2010.**
Click AutoCAD 2010 – English.

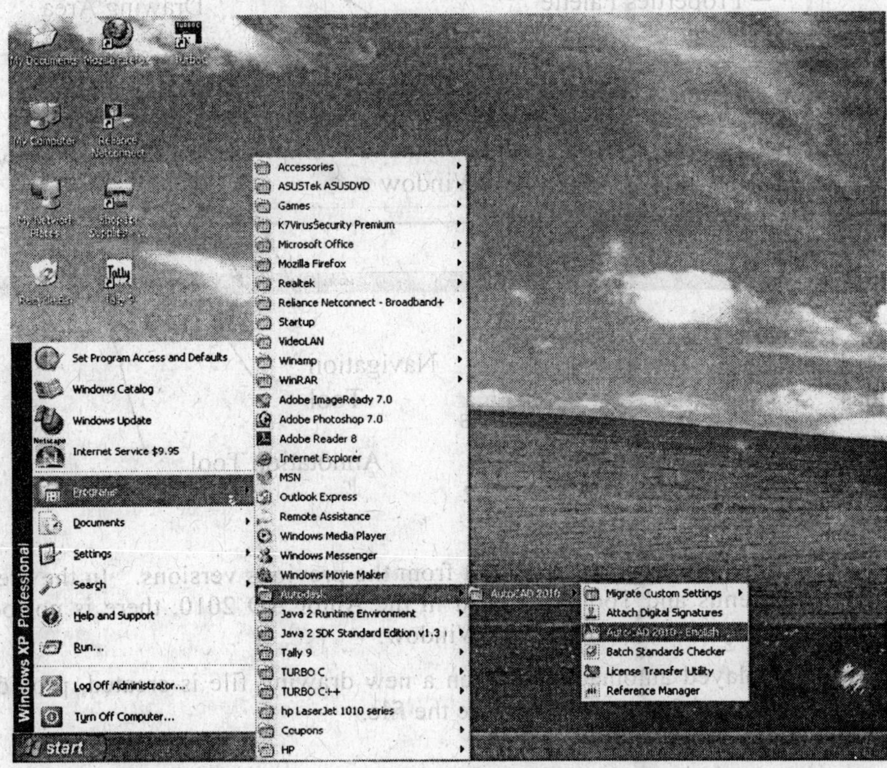

FIG. 1

After a few seconds, AutoCAD 2010 software is loaded in the main memory and AutoCAD 2010 window is displayed on the screen as shown in **Fig. 2.**

4. AN OVERVIEW OF AutoCAD WIDNOW

See Fig. 2. AutoCAD Window contains Title Bar, Standard Toolbar, Menu Bar, Tabs and Panels, Drawing Area, Cross Hair, Command Prompt Window, Status Bar, etc.

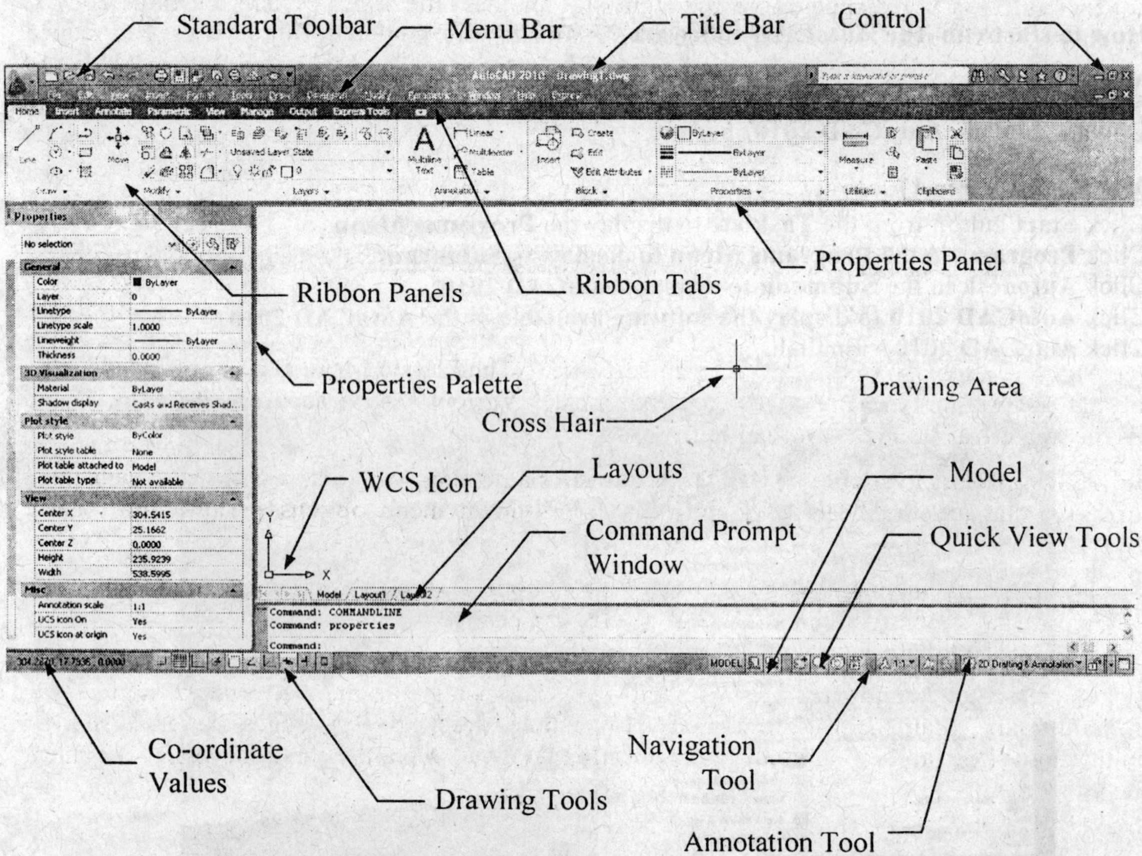

FIG. 2

NOTE : AutoCAD 2010 is a new version different from the previous versions. In the previous versions, AutoCAD has Menus and Toolbars. But in the AutoCAD 2010, there is no toolbar. Instead, the **Ribbon** is displayed on the AutoCAD Window.

The Ribbon is displayed automatically when a new drawing file is created, providing a compact palette of all of the tools necessary to create the file.

1. Title Bar

FIG. 3

See Fig. 3. The top line of the AutoCAD screen is the **Title Bar**. It lists the name of the software and the drawing file name.

Standard Toolbar is displayed on the left side of the Title Bar. In the Standard Toolbar, buttons such as New, Open, Save, Plot, etc., are displayed. The user can also customize the Standard Toolbar.

Control Buttons are displayed on the right side of the Title Bar. There are three control buttons, *viz.*, Minimize, Maximize and Close Buttons. The Minimize Button is used to reduce the AutoCAD screen as a rectangular icon on the Taskbar. The Maximize Button is used to **restore** a full screen of the AutoCAD screen. The Close Button is used to close the AutoCAD software.

2. Menu Bar

FIG. 4

See Fig. 4. AutoCAD is a menu driven software. The classic Menu Bar is displayed at the top but below the Title Bar of the drawing area. Various menus such as File, Edit, View, Insert, etc., are available from the Menu Bar.

Pull-Down Menus available on the Menu Bar offer a quicker way to access the commands and functions that are the heart of AutoCAD. Pull-down menu options perform three basic functions:

Display additional menu choices (options with ▶ symbol), called as *cascading menu*.
Display a Dialog Box that contains settings, user can change.
Issue a command that requires keyboard or drawing input.

As user select commands and options, AutoCAD flashes a single line help, called Status Line, in Status Bar. Status Line help messages are simple, descriptive messages that are displayed on the status line (at the bottom of the application window) when the cursor hovers over a menu item.

3. Status Bar

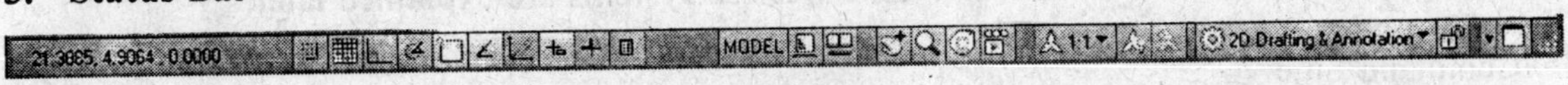

FIG. 5

See Fig. 5. The Status Bar displays the Coordinate Values of the cursor, Drawing Tools, Navigation Tools and Tools for Quick View and Annotation Scaling.

User can view the Drawing Tool buttons as icons or texts. Also, user can easily change the settings of snap, polar, osnap and otrack from the shortcut menus of these drawing tools.

User can preview and switch between open drawings and layouts in a drawing. Use the Navigation Tools to switch between open drawings and view a model in a drawing. User can also display tools for Scaling Annotations.

4. Ribbons – Tabs and Panels

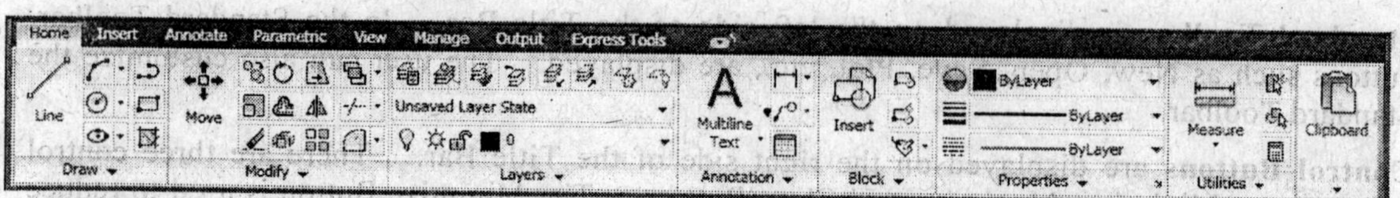

FIG. 6

See Fig. 6. Ribbons are interface element that displays panels made up of commands and controls that can be docked horizontally or vertically along the program's application window.

Ribbon Tabs control the display and order in which ribbon panels are displayed on the ribbon. Users add ribbon tabs to a workspace to control which ribbon tabs are displayed on the ribbon. Examples: Home Tab, Insert Tab, Annotate Tab, Parametric Tab, View Tab, etc.

Ribbon Panel is an organizational structure used to layout commands and controls for display on the ribbon or as a floating user interface. Panels in the Home Tab are: Draw Panel, Modify Panel, Layers Panel, Annotation Panel, etc.

Example: The DIMLINEAR command was once available on the dashboard's Dimensions control panel. On the ribbon, DIMLINEAR is located on the Annotation tab, in the Dimensions panel.

5. Cross-Hair Cursor
The cursor is a display indicating the current position of the pointer. The cursor is a pair of two crossed lines across the screen. When user selects an object, the drawing cursor changes into a small square. This square is called Selection Box or Selection Cursor. The cursor is controlled by the mouse.

6. Drawing Area
Drawing Area is the main area of the screen where entire drawing is drawn. It may be set in *Imperial* or *Metric* System. The limit for Metric System is 0,0 and 420,297. For setting the limits, use LIMITS command.

Co-ordinate System: All drawings are superimposed on an invisible grid or co-ordinate system, with a horizontal X-axis and a vertical Y-axis. These systems are explained later.

7. Command Line

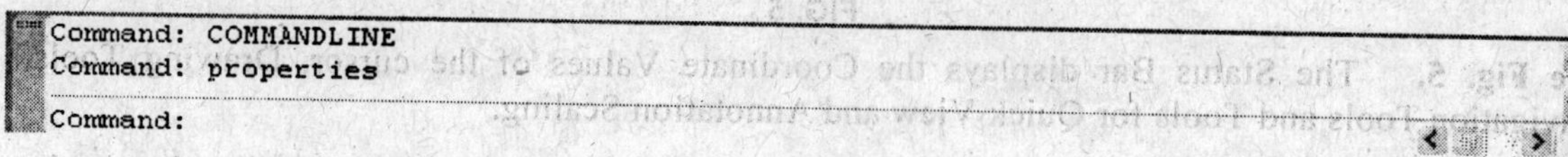

FIG. 7

See Fig. 7. User can enter a command by using the keyboard. Some commands also have abbreviated names called *Command Aliases*. To enter a command by using the keyboard, type the full command name on the command line and press Enter or Spacebar. Note that when **Dynamic Input** is on and is set to display dynamic prompts, user can enter many commands in tooltips near the cursor.

8. Layouts

FIG. 8

See Fig. 8. There are two distinct working environments or *spaces* in which user can create objects in a drawing. These are represented by the **Model** and **Layout** tabs.

Typically, a model composed of geometric objects is created in a three-dimensional space called **Model Space**. A final layout of specific views and annotations of this model is created in a two-dimensional space called **Paper Space**. These spaces are accessible on two or more tabs near the bottom of the drawing area: the Model tab and one or more layout tabs. Note that these tabs can be hidden, appearing instead as buttons on the status bar at the bottom-center of the application window.

Working on the Model tab, user draws a model of the subject at 1:1 scale. Working on a Layout tab, user can create one or more **Layout Viewports**, dimensions, notes and a title block to represent a drawing sheet.

Each layout viewport is like a picture frame containing a *photograph* of the model in model space. Each layout viewport contains a view that displays the model at the scale and orientation that user specified. User can also specify which layers are visible in each layout viewport.

After arranging the layout finished, user turn off the layer that contains the layout viewport objects. The views are still visible and user can plot the layout without displaying the viewport boundaries.

5. CO-ORDINATE SYSTEMS

Co-ordinate System is used to set orientation of the drawing and to locate points in the space. Co-ordinate system is classified into the following types:

1. **Classification based on Drawing Orientation**
   There are two coordinate systems: a fixed system called the World Coordinate System (WCS) and a movable system called the User Coordinate System (UCS). By default, these two systems are coincident in a new drawing.

   User Co-ordinate System
   User can relocate and rotate the User Coordinate System for convenient coordinate entry, grid display, grid snap, Ortho mode, and other drawing tools.

   Word Co-ordinate System

Normally in 2D views, the WCS *X* axis is horizontal and the *Y* axis is vertical. The WCS *origin* is where the *X* and *Y* axes intersect (0,0). All objects in a drawing file are defined by their WCS coordinates. However, it is usually more convenient to create and edit objects based on the movable UCS.

2. **Classification based on Method of Locating Points**

When a command prompts for a point, use the pointing device to specify a point, or enter a coordinate value at the command prompt. When dynamic input is on, user can enter coordinate values in tooltips near the cursor. User can enter two-dimensional coordinates as either Cartesian (*X*,*Y*) or Polar Coordinates.

Cartesian Coordinate System

A Cartesian Coordinate System has three axes, *X*, *Y*, and *Z*. When user enters coordinate values, user indicate a point's distance (in units) and its direction (+ or -) along the *X*, *Y*, and *Z* axes relative to the coordinate system origin (0,0,0).

In 2D, user specifies points on the *XY* plane, also called the *workplane*. The workplane is similar to a flat sheet of grid paper. The *X* value of a Cartesian coordinate specifies horizontal distance, and the *Y* value specifies vertical distance. The origin point (0,0) indicates where the two axes intersect.

Polar Coordinate System

Polar coordinates System uses a distance and an angle to locate a point. With both Cartesian and Polar coordinates, user can enter absolute coordinates based on the origin (0,0), or relative coordinates based on the last point specified.

Another method of entering a relative coordinate is by moving the cursor to specify a direction and then entering a distance directly. This method is called **Direct Distance Entry**.

User can enter coordinates in scientific, decimal, engineering, architectural, or fractional notation. User can enter angles in grads, radians, surveyor's units, or degrees, minutes and seconds. The UNITS command controls the unit format.

Display Coordinates on the Status Bar

The current cursor location is displayed as a coordinate value on the status bar. There are three types of coordinate display: static, dynamic, and distance and angle.

- *Static display:* Updates only when user specifies a point.
- *Dynamic display:* Updates as user moves the cursor.
- *Distance and angle display:* Updates the relative distance *(distance<angle)* as user moves the cursor. This option is available only when user draws lines or other objects that prompt for more than one point.

*

2

INVOKING COMMANDS IN AutoCAD

1. INVOKING COMMANDS IN AutoCAD

After loading the AutoCAD software, you need to invoke AutoCAD commands to perform any operation. For example, to draw a line, you need to invoke the **Line** command and then define the start point and the end point of the line. AutoCAD provides the following options to invoke the commands:

1. **Keyboard**
   User can invoke any AutoCAD command from the keyboard by typing the command name and then pressing the **Enter** key. If the **Dynamic Input** mode is on and the cursor is in the drawing area, by default, the command will be entered through the **Pointer Input** box. The **Pointer Input** box is a small box displayed on the right of the cursor.

2. **Ribbon**
   You can also invoke the AutoCAD command from the **Ribbon**. The tools for creating, modifying and annotating a 2D and 3D design are available in the panels instead of being spread out in the entire drawing area in different toolbars and menu. See Fig. 1.

FIG. 1

   In AutoCAD, by default the **Ribbon** is displayed horizontally below the **Quick Access Toolbar**. The **Ribbon** consists of various tabs. The tabs have different panels, which in turn, have tools arranged in rows. Some of the tools have small black down arrow. This indicates that the tools having similar functions are grouped together.

   To choose a tool, click on the down arrow, a drop-down will be displayed. Choose the required tool from the drop-down displayed. Note that if you choose a tool from the drop-down, the corresponding command will be invoked and the tool that you have chosen will be displayed in the panel.

3. **Application Menu**
   The **Application Menu** is available at the top-left of the AutoCAD window. It contains some of the tools that are available in the **Standard** toolbar. Click the down arrow on the **Application Menu** to display the tools. See Fig. 2.

To search a command, use the search field on the top of the **Application Menu**. To search a tool, enter the complete or partial name of the command in the search field, the possible tool list will be listed. Click on the required tool to activate the corresponding command.

By default, the **Recent Document** button is chosen in the **Application Menu**. The recently opened drawings will be listed. If multiple drawing files are opened, then choose the **Open Documents** button to list the documents that are opened in the **Application Menu**.

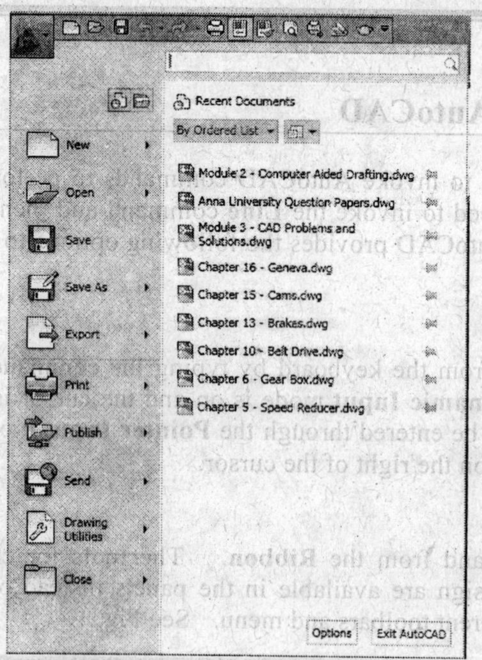

FIG. 2

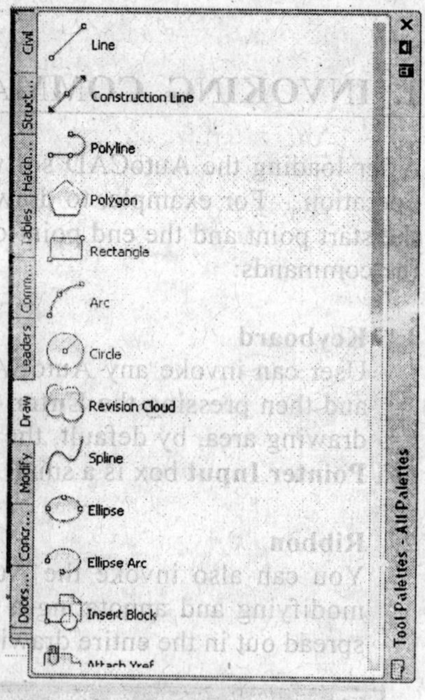

FIG. 3

Tool Palettes

AutoCAD provides **Tool Palettes** as an easy and convenient way of placing and sharing hatch patterns and blocks in the current drawing. By default, the **Tool Palettes** are not displayed. Choose the **Tool Palettes Windows** button from the **Palettes** panel in the **View** tab or choose the **CTRL+3** keys to display the **Tool Palettes** as a window on the right of the drawing area. See Fig. 3.

User can resize the Tool Palettes using the resizing cursor that is displayed when you place the cursor on the top or button extremity of the **Tool Palettes**.

5. **Menu bar**

User can also select commands from the **Menu Bar**. **Menu Bar** is also displayed by default. To display the menu bar, choose the down arrow in the **Quick Access Toolbar**, a flyout is displayed. Choose the **Show Menu Bar** option from it to display the **Menu Bar**. See Fig. 4.

A command can be invoked by left-clicking on a menu. Some of the menu items display an arrow on the right side, which indicates that they have a cascading menu. The cascading menu provides various options to execute the same AutoCAD commands.

FIG. 4

6. **Toolbar**

Toolbars are not displayed by default. To display a toolbar, choose the View tab in the **Ribbon** and click on **Toolbars** in the **Windows** panel, a flyout will be displayed. Move the cursor over the **AutoCAD** option to display a list of toolbars. Select the required toolbar. Alternatively, display the **Menu Bar** and then choose **Tools > Toolbars > AutoCAD** from it to display a list of toolbars. Select the required toolbar. Fig. 5 shows the **Draw** toolbar.

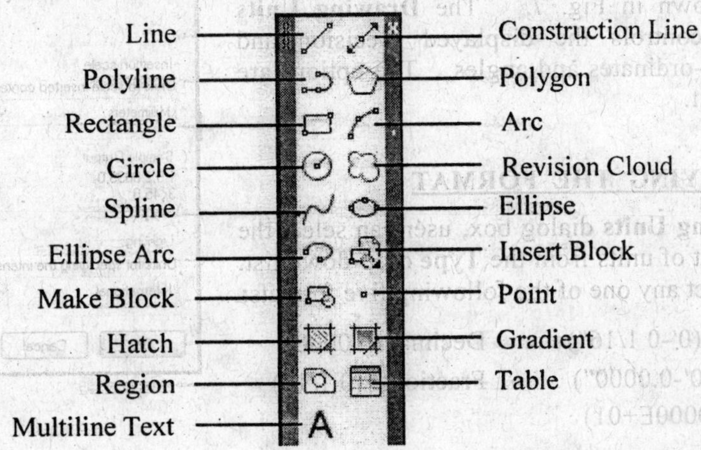

FIG. 5

In a **Toolbar**, the similar tools representing various AutoCAD commands are grouped together. When the cursor is moved over the button of a toolbar, the button gets lifted and a three-dimensional (3D) box encloses it. The tooltip (name of the tool and related information) is also displayed below the tool. Once you have located the desired tool, then left-click on it to invoke the corresponding command.

7. **Shortcut menu : (Fig.6)**

AutoCAD provides shortcut menus as an easy and convenient way of invoking the recently used tools. These shortcut menus are context-sensitive, which means that the tools present in them are dependent on the place/object for which they are displayed. A shortcut menu is invoked by right-clicking and is displayed at the cursor location. Right-click anywhere in the drawing area to displayed the general **Shortcut Menu**. It contains options to select the previously invoked tool again.

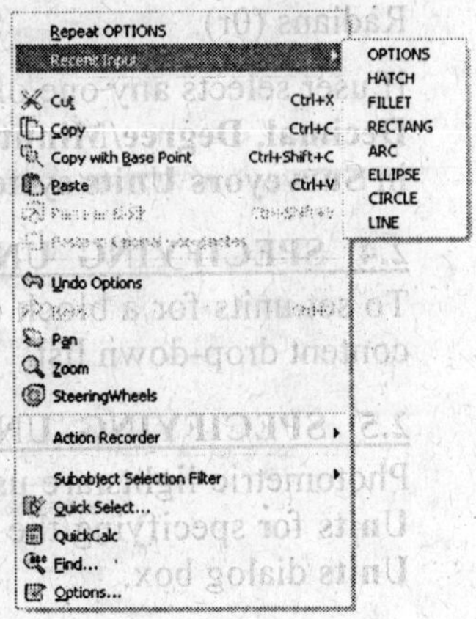

FIG. 6

2. SETTING UNITS TYPE AND PRECISION

Every object created is measured in drawing units. Before start to draw, user must decide what one drawing unit will represent based on what user plan to draw. Then create the drawing at actual size with that convention. For example, a distance of one drawing unit typically represents one millimeter, one centimeter, one inch or one foot in real-world units.

2.1 UNITS Command

UNITS command controls coordinate and angle display formats and precision. Enter **Units** at the Command Prompt and press the **Enter** key. Now, the **Drawing Units** dialog box is displayed on the screen as shown in Fig. 7. The **Drawing Units** dialog box controls the displayed precision and format for co-ordinates and angles. The options are explained next.

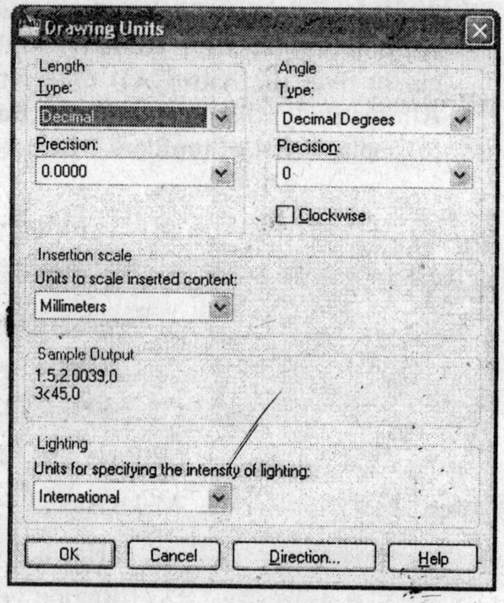

FIG. 7

2.2 SPECIFYING THE FORMAT

In the **Drawing Units** dialog box, user can select the desired format of units from the **Type** drop-down list. User can select any one of the following five formats:

Architectural (0′-0 1/16″) Decimal (0.0000)
Engineering (0′-0.0000″) Fractional (0 1/16)
Scientific (0.0000E+01)

2.3 SPECIFYING THE ANGLE FORMAT

In the Drawing Units dialog box, user can select the current angle format and the precision for the current angle display. User can select any one of the following five angle measuring formats:

Decimal Degrees (0) Deg/Min/Sec (0d) Grads (0g)
Radians (0r) Surveyor's Units (N 0d E)

If user selects any one of the first four measuring formats, then user can specify the angle in the **Decimal, Degree/Minute/Seconds, Grads** or **Radians** system. But, user cannot enter the angle in **Surveyors Units** system.

2.4 SPECIFYING UNITS FOR THE DRAWING

To set units for a block or a drawing to be inserted, select a unit from the **Units** to scale inserted content drop-down list.

2.5 SPECIFYING UNITS FOR LIGHTING

Photometric lights are used for the rendering of objects. Select the desired unit system from the **Units** for specifying the intensity of lighting drop-down list in the **Lighting** area of the **Drawing Units** dialog box.

3. SETTING LIMITS OF A DRAWING

In AutoCAD, limits represent the drawing area and it is endless. Therefore, user needs to define the drawing area before starting the drawing. This can be done using the **Limits** command.

3.1 LIMITS Command

The **Limits** command sets and controls the limits of the grid display in the current **Model** or **Layout** tab. Normally, the drawing area is set for A4 size (210 x 297) dimensions.

Problem 1: *Define the drawing area to A4 size (210 x 297) using the LIMITS command.*

Command: **LIMITS** ↵
Reset Model space limits:
Specify lower left corner or [ON/OFF] <0.0000,0.0000>: 0,0 ↵
Specify upper right corner <12.0000,9.0000>: **210,297** ↵
Command: *(Press F7)* <Grid on>
Command: **ZOOM** ↵
Specify corner of window, enter a scale factor (nX or nXP), or [All/Center/Dynamic/Extents/Previous/Scale/Window/Object] <real time>: **ALL** ↵
Regenerating model.

See Fig. 8.

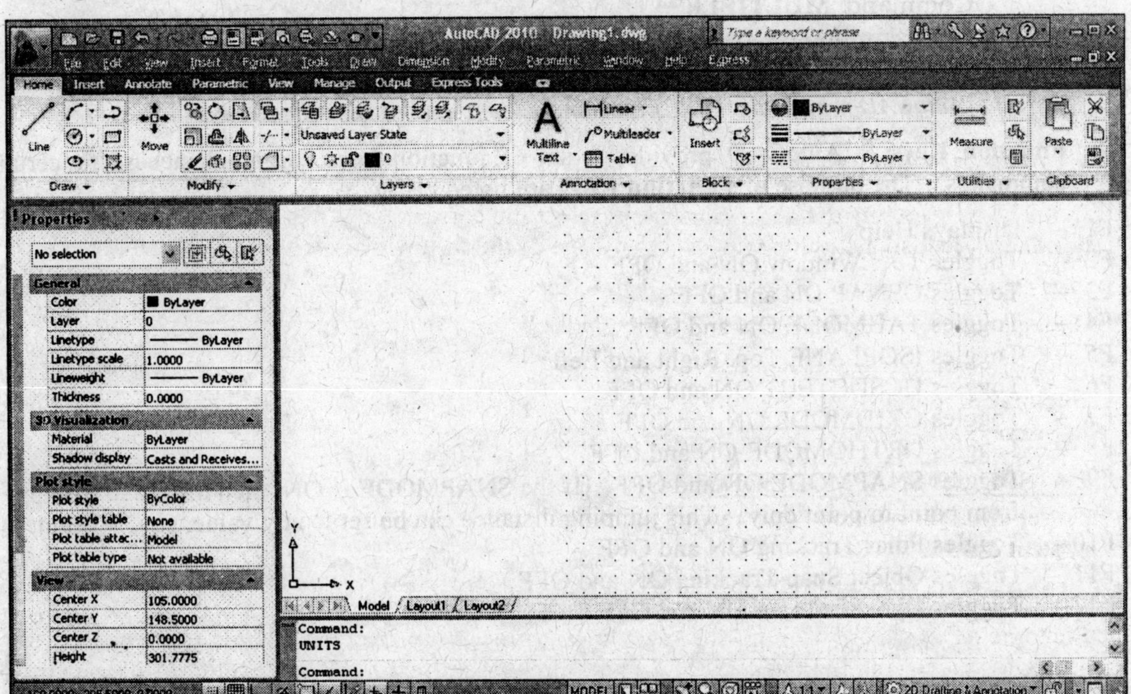

FIG. 8

4. TIPS FOR BEGINNERS

- **Backspace [←]:** If typing error is happened, then use the **Backspace** key to back up to the error and then retype the command. This key is in the upper right corner of the keyboard area.
- **Escape [Esc]:** Press the **Esc** key to quickly exit a dialog box without making changes. The **Esc** key is the upper left corner of the keyboard.
- **Undo:** If user accidently change something in the drawing and want to reverse that change, use the **Undo** command. To invoke the **Undo** command, enter **U** or **UNDO** at the command prompt. Each time user enters **Undo,** AutoCAD will undo one operation at a time, in reverse order.
- **Redo:** If user accidently **Undo** some operation in the drawing, use the **Redo** command to cancel the last **Undo** command. Note that the **Redo** command restores only one command.
- **Erase:** If objects are drawn by mistake, use the **Erase** command to erase the unwanted drawings.
- **Suppressing Dialog Boxes:** In AutoCAD, most of the commands are provided with both command line and dialog box execution. To suppress the dialog boxes, enter the command with a hyphen character preceding it. For example, enter **-UNITS** in the command prompt.
- **Repeat the last command:** To repeat the last command, press **Enter** key or **Spacebar** or right-click the drawing area and choose **Repeat.**
- **Repeat the same command for multiple times:** To repeat the same command for multiple times, enter **MULTIPLE** at the command prompt and press Enter key. For example, the commands sequence to repeat the **CIRCLE** command is as follows:

  Command: **MULTIPLE** ↵
  Enter command name to repeat: **CIRCLE** ↵
  Specify center point for circle or [3P/2P/Ttr (tan tan radius)]:
  [*AutoCAD repeats the CIRCLE command unit user presses the Esc key*]

- **Function Keys:** AutoCAD provides a set of function keys for quick access to certain commands. The purpose of **Function Keys** are listed below:

F1 – Displays Help
F2 – Toggles Text Window ON and OFF
F3 – Toggles OSNAP ON and OFF
F4 – Toggles TABMODE ON and OFF
F5 – Toggles ISOPLANE Top, Right and Left
F6 – Toggles UCSDETECT ON and OFF
F7 – Toggles GRIDMODE ON and OFF
F8 – Toggles ORTHOMODE ON and OFF
F9 – Toggles SNAPMODE ON and OFF [If the SNAPMODE is ON, then the cursor jumps from point to point only. This jumping distance can be set to any value, say, 0.1 unit.]
F10– Toggles Polar Tracking ON and OFF
F11– Toggles Object Snap Tracking ON and OFF
F12– Toggles Dynamic Input ON and OFF

*

3

FILE MANAGEMENT

1. STARTING A NEW DRAWING

A new drawing can be opened using the **NEW** tool in the **Quick Access Toolbar**. When you invoke the New command, by default, AutoCAD will display the **Select template** dialog box. **See Fig. 1.**

The **Select Template** dialog box displays a list of default templates available in AutoCAD 2010. The default template is **acad.dwt**, which starts the 2D drawing environment.

It is also possible to open any drawing without using any template either in metric or imperial system. To do so, choose the down arrow on the right of the **Open** button and select the **Open with no Template – Metric** option or the **Open with no Template – Imperial** option from the flyout.

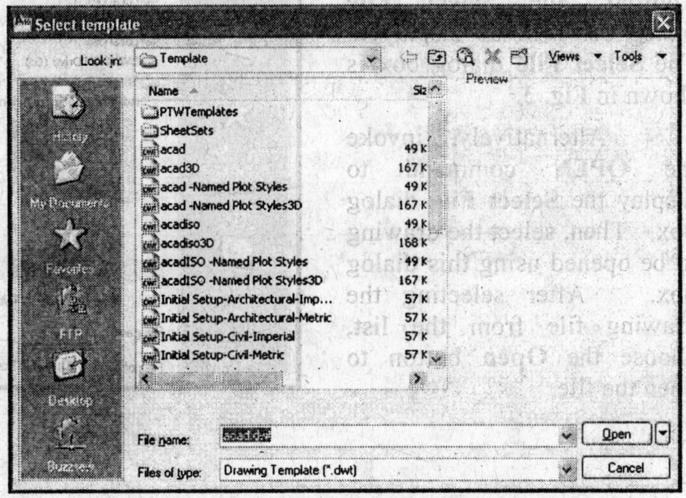

FIG. 1

You can also open a new drawing using the **Use a Wizard** and **Start from Scratch** options from the **Create New Drawing** dialog box. By default, this dialog box is not invoked.

To invoke the display of the **Create New Drawing** dialog box, enter **STARTUP** command in the command window and then enter **1** as the new value for this system variable.

After setting 1 as the new value for the system variable, whenever you invoke the New command, the **Create New Drawing** dialog box will be displayed. **See Fig. 2.**

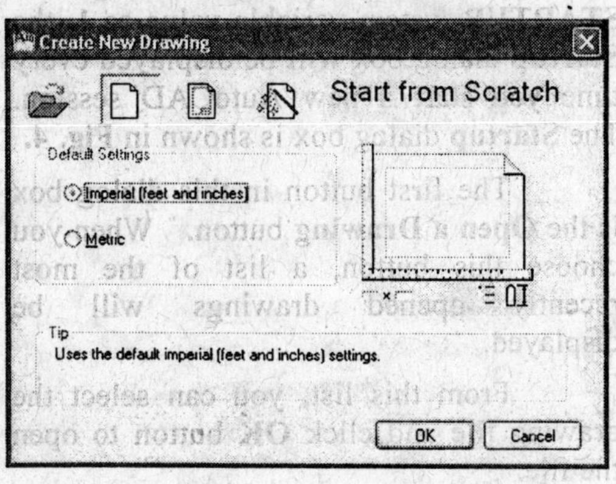

FIG. 2

2. OPENING AN EXISTING DRAWING

User can open an existing drawing file that has been saved previously. There are three methods that can be used to open a drawing file. They are: 1) using the **Select File** dialog box, 2) using the **Startup** dialog box and 3) Dragging **and Dropping**.

2.1 USING THE SELECT FILE DIALOG BOX

If you are in the drawing editor and you want to open a drawing file, choose the **Open** tool from the **Quick Access Toolbar**, the **Select File** dialog box will be displayed. The **Select File** dialog box is shown in **Fig. 3**.

Alternatively, invoke the **OPEN** command to display the **Select File** dialog box. Then, select the drawing to be opened using this dialog box. After selecting the drawing file from the list, choose the **Open** button to open the file.

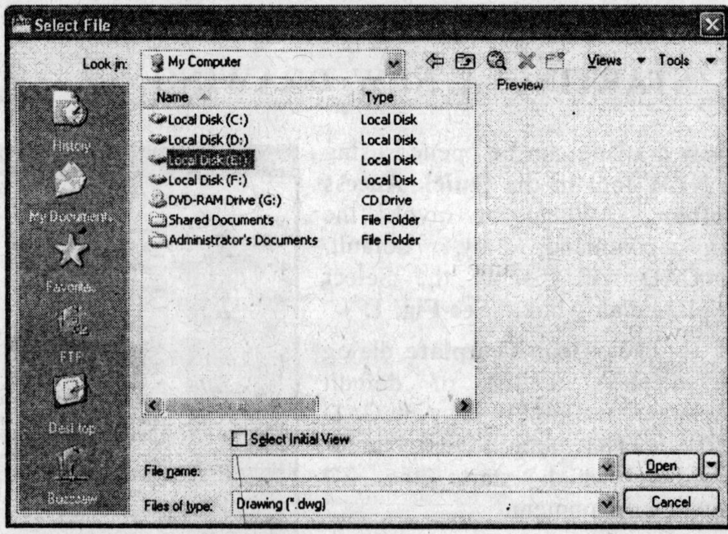

FIG. 3

2.2 USING THE STARTUP DIALOG BOX

If the setting is configured to show the **Startup** dialog box by setting the **STARTUP** system variable value as **1**, the **Startup** dialog box will be displayed every time you start a new AutoCAD session. The **Startup** dialog box is shown in **Fig. 4.**

The first button in this dialog box is the **Open a Drawing** button. When you choose this button, a list of the most recently opened drawings will be displayed.

From this list, you can select the drawing file and click **OK** button to open the file.

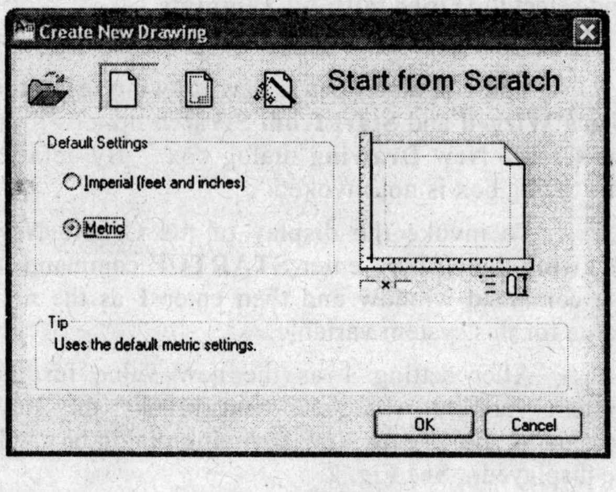

FIG. 4

2.3 DRAGGING AND DROPPING

User can also open an existing drawing in AutoCAD by dragging it from the Window Explorer and dropping it into AutoCAD. If you drop the selected drawing in the drawing area, the drawing will be inserted as a block and as a result you cannot modify it. But, if you draw the drawing from the **Window Explorer** and drop it anywhere other than the drawing area, AutoCAD opens the selected drawing.

3. SAVING A DRAWING

AutoCAD provides three commands, namely, **QSAVE, SAVEAS** and **SAVE,** to save your work. These commands allow the user to save drawings by writing it to a permanent storage device, such as a hard drive or in any removable drive.

When you choose the **Save** tool from the **Quick Access Toolbar** or the **Application Menu**, the **QSAVE** command is invoked. If the current drawing is unnamed and you save the drawing for the first time in the present session, the **SAVEAS** command will be invoked and you will be prompted to enter the file name in the **Save Drawing As** dialog box. Enter the name for the drawing and then choose the Save button.

When you choose **SAVEAS** from the **Application Menu** or choose the **Save As** tool from the **Quick Access Toolbar, Save Drawing As** dialog box will be displayed. Even if the drawing has been saved with a file name, this tool gives an option to save it with a different file name.

The **SAVE** command is the most rarely used command and can be invoked only from the command line by entering **SAVE** at the Command prompt. It is similar to the **SAVEAS** command and displays the **Save Drawing As** dialog box.

3.1 Save Drawing As dialog box

The **Save Drawing** As dialog box is shown in **Fig. 5.** This dialog box displays the information related to the drawing files on the system.

Place List: A column of icons is displayed on the left side of the dialog box. These icons contain the shortcuts to the folders that are frequently used. User can quickly save the drawings in one of these folders.

File name Edit Box: To save the work, enter the name of the drawing in the **File name** edit box by typing the file name or selecting it from the drop-down list.

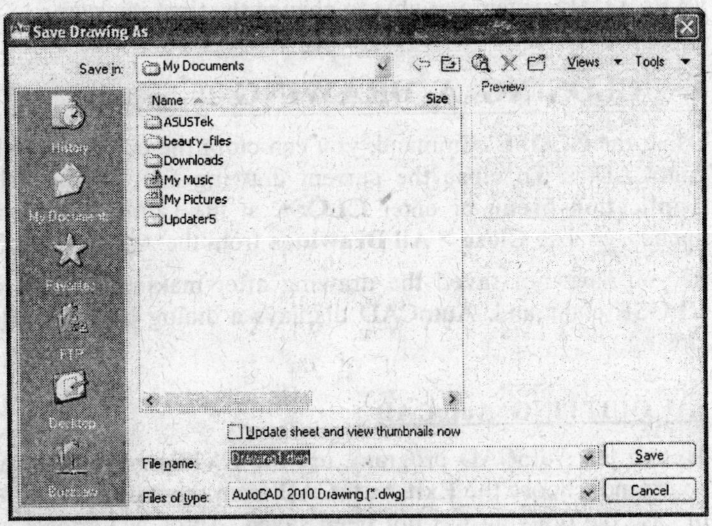

FIG. 5

Files of type Drop-Down List: The **Files of type** drop-down list is used to specify the drawing format in which user want to save file.

Save in Drop-down List: The current drive and path information is listed in the **Save in** drop-down list.

Views Drop-Down: The **Views** drop-down has the options for the type of listing of files and displaying the preview images. The Views drop-down is shown in Fig. 6.

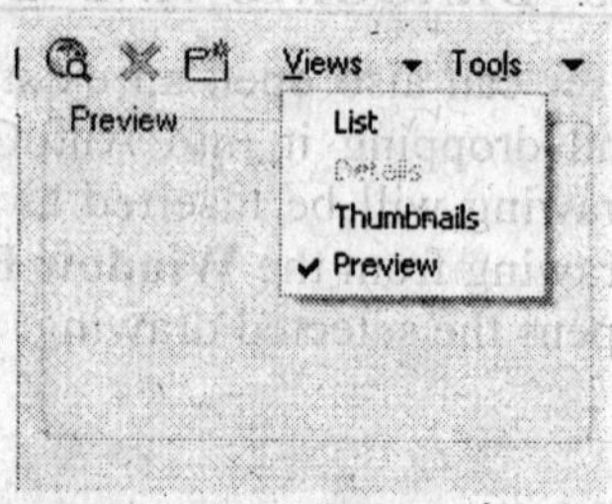

FIG. 6

Tools Drop-Down: The **Tools** drop-down has an option for adding or modifying the FTP sites. These sites can then be browsed from the FTP shortcut in the Places list. The **Tools** drop-down list is shown in Fig. 7.

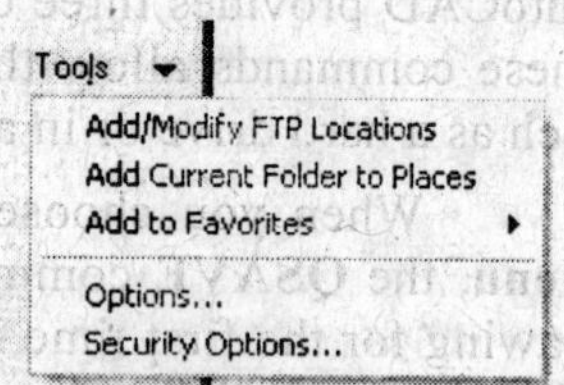

FIG. 7

Create New Folder Button: Choose the **Create New Folder** button to create a new folder under the name **New Folder**. The new folder is displayed in the **File** list box. You can accept the name or change the name to your requirement.

3.2 AUTOMATIC TIMED SAVE

AutoCAD allows you to save the work automatically at specific intervals. To change the time intervals, enter the intervals duration in minutes in the **Minutes between saves** text box in the **File Safety Precautions** area in the **Options** dialog box. The **Options** dialog box can be invoked by choosing the **Options** button from the **Application Menu**. Alternatively, use the **SAVETIME** system variable to change the time interval.

4. CLOSING A DRAWING

Using the **CLOSE** command, you can close the current drawing file without actually quitting the AutoCAD. To close the current drawing file, choose **Close > Current Drawing** from the **Application Menu** or enter **CLOSE** at the Command prompt. If multiple drawing files are opened, choose **Close > All Drawings** from the **Application Menu.**

If you have not saved the drawing after making the last changes and you have invoked the **CLOSE** command, AutoCAD displays a dialog box that allow you to save the drawing before closing.

4.1 QUITTING AutoCAD

To exit the AutoCAD program, use the **EXIT** or **QUIT** command. Even if you have an active command, choose the **Exit AutoCAD** from the **Application Menu** to quit the AutoCAD program. In case the drawing has not been saved, AutoCAD allows you to save the work first through a dialog box. Also, use the close button (**×**) of the main AutoCAD window to end the AutoCAD software.

5. DYNAMIC INPUT MODE

Turn on the **Dynamic Input Mode** to enter the commands through the pointer input and the dimensions using the dimensional input.

When this mode is turned on, all prompts are available at the tooltip as dynamic prompts and user can select the command options through the dynamic prompt.

The settings for the **Dynamic Input** mode are done using the **Dynamic Input** tab of the **Drafting Settings** dialog box.

Right-click on the **Dynamic Input** button in the **Status Bar**, a shortcut menu is displayed. Choose the **Settings** option from the **Shortcut Menu** to display the **Drafting Settings** dialog box as shown in **Fig. 8.**

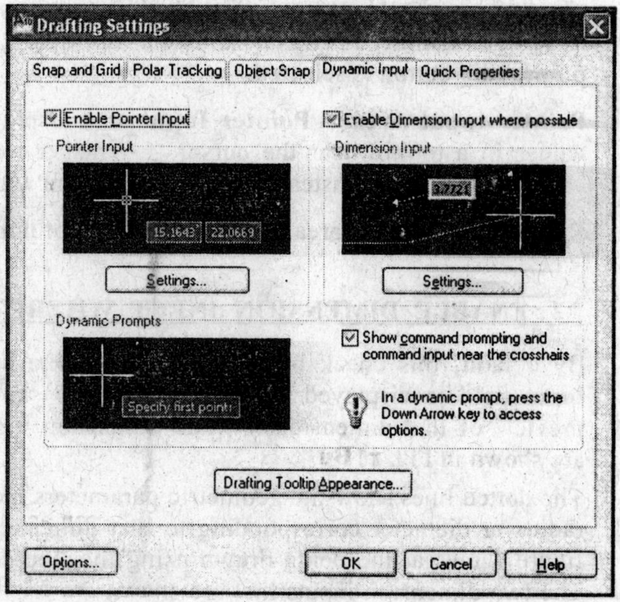

FIG. 8

5.1 ENABLE POINTER INPUT

Select the **Enable Pointer Input** check box to enter the commands through the pointer input. For example, Fig. 9 shows the **LINE** command entered through the **Pointer Input.**

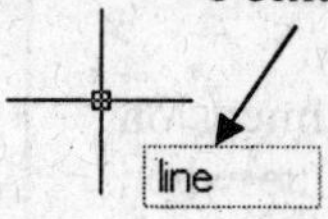

FIG. 9

Clear the **Enable Pointer Input** check box to turn off the **Dynamic Input**. Now, the commands have to be entered through the Command prompt, similar to the old releases of AutoCAD.

Settings: Choose the **Settings** button from the **Pointer Input** area to display the **Pointer Input Settings** dialog box as shown in Fig. 10. The radio buttons in the **Format** area of this dialog box are used to set the default settings for specifying the other points, after specifying first point.

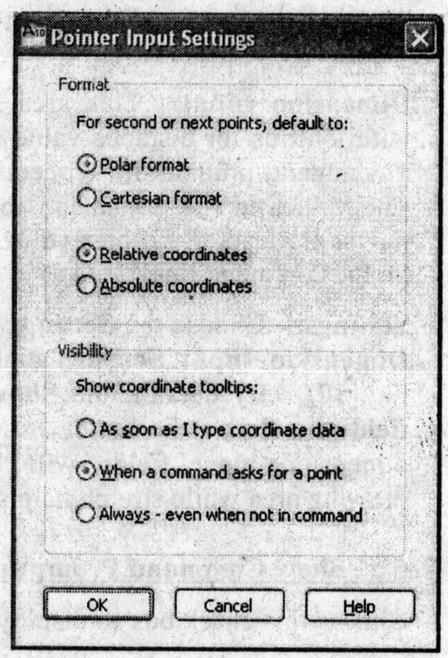

FIG. 10

By default, the **Polar format** and **Relative coordinates** radio buttons are selected. As a result, the coordinates will be specified in the polar form and with respect to the relative coordinates system.

Select the **Cartesian format** radio button to enter the coordinates in cartesian form. Select the **Absolute coordinates** radio button to measure the numerical entries with respect to the absolute coordinate system. The **Visibility** area in the **Pointer Input Settings** dialog box is used to set the visibility of the coordinate's tool tips. By default, the **When a command asks for a point** radio button is selected.

Pointer Input Area: **Pointer Input** area displays the location of the crosshairs as coordinate values in a tooltip near the cursor. When a command prompts for a point, enter coordinate values in the tooltip instead of in the Command window.

Preview Area: This area shows an example of pointer input.

5.2 ENABLE DIMENSION INPUT WHERE POSSIBLE

By default, this check box is selected. The dimension Input field is displayed in the graphics are showing the preview of that dimensions. The dimension input fields are shown in Fig. 11.

The dotted lines show the geometric parameters like length, radius or diameter corresponding to that dimension. The figure shows a line being drawn using the line command. The two dimension inputs that are shown are for the length of the line and the angle with a positive direction of X axis.

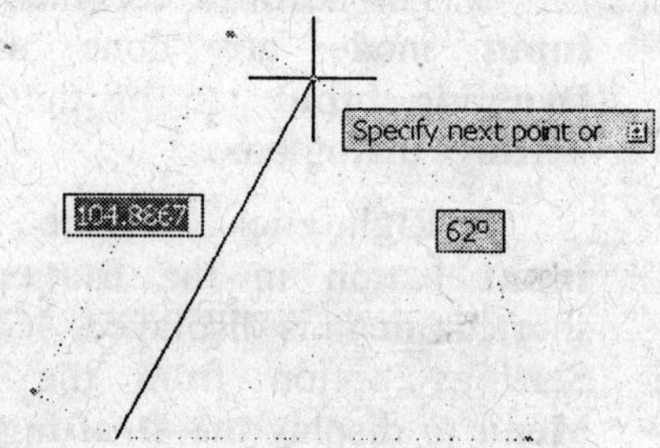

FIG. 11

Clear the **Enable Dimension Input where possible** check box so that the preview of dimensions will not be displayed.

Dimension Input: This area displays a dimension with tooltips for distance value and angle value when a command prompts for a second point or a distance. The values in the dimension tooltips change as user moves the cursor. Enter values in tooltip instead of on the command line.

Settings: Choose the **Settings** button to displays the **Dimension Input Settings** dialog box as shown in Fig. 12. By default, the **Show 2 dimension input field at a time** radio button is selected. So that, two dimension input fields will be displayed in the drawing area while stretching a sketched entity.

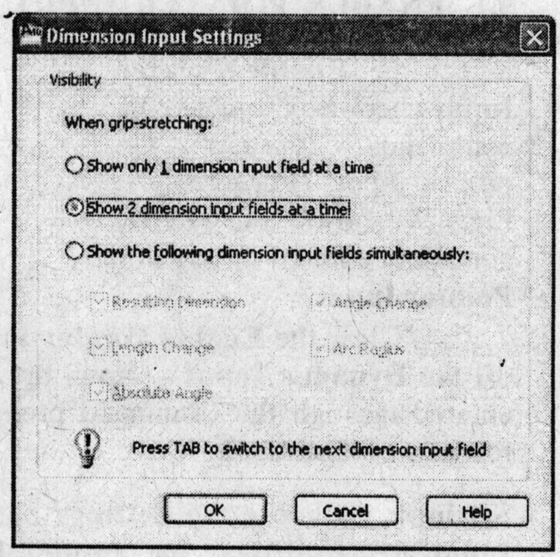

FIG. 12

5.3 Show Command Prompting and Command Input near the Crosshairs

Choose this check box to display the prompt sequences dynamically near the crosshairs.

Drafting Tooltip Appearance

Choose this button to display the **Tooltip Appearance** dialog box. This dialog box contains options to customize the tooltip appearance. Select **Color** button to change the color of tooltip.

6. PRINTING AND PLOTTING A DRAWING

Once a drawing is created on the screen, the next step is to get the hard copy of the drawing on a sheet of paper using a printer or plotter.

6.1 PLOTTING DRAWING

The **Plot** tool is used to plot a drawing. When the plot tool in invoked, the **Plot – Model** dialog box is displayed as shown in **Fig. 13.** The **Plot** tool can also be invoked by choosing **Plot** from the **Standard** toolbar.

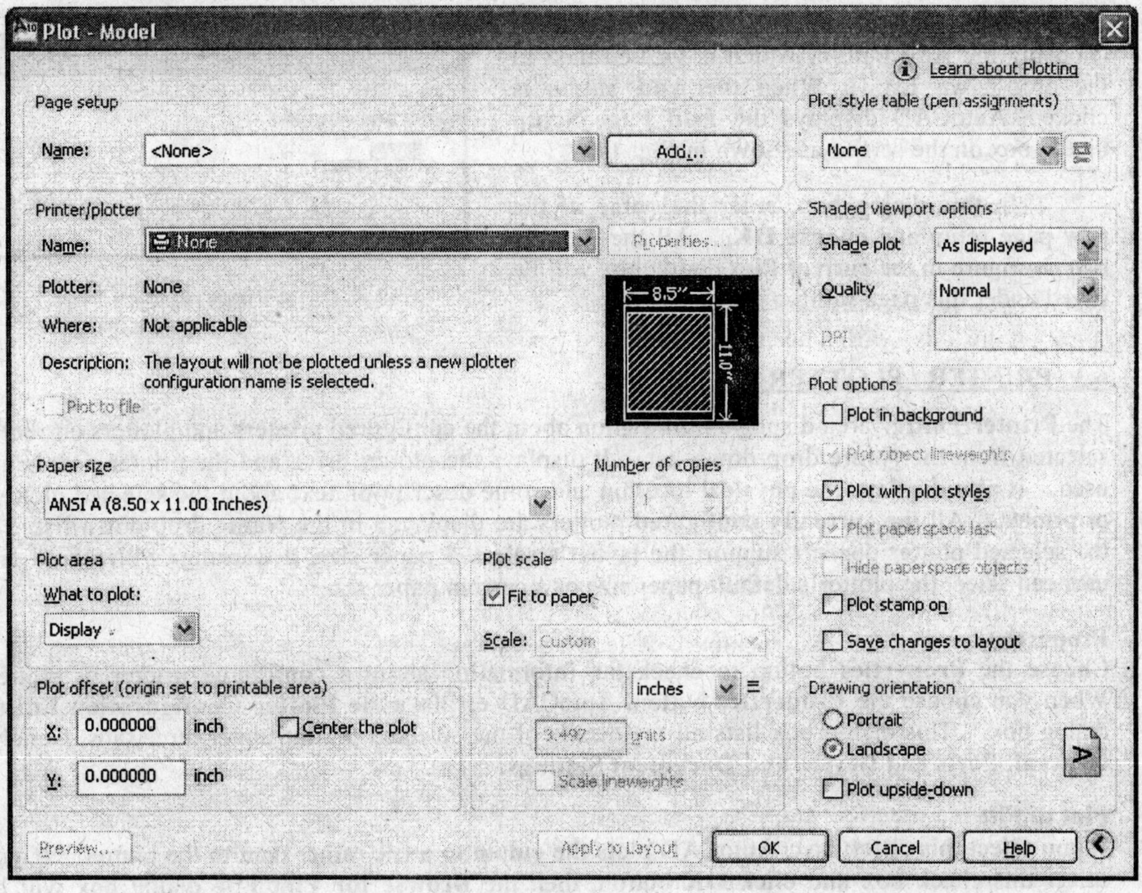

FIG. 13

The **Plot** dialog box specifies device and media settings and plots the drawing. The title of the **Plot** dialog box indicates the name of the current layout. User can examine these values and if they conform to your requirement, start plotting directly. Otherwise, you can alter these values to define plot specifications by using the options in the Plot dialog box. The options in the **Plot** dialog box are discussed next.

6.2 PAGE SETUP AREA

The **Page Setup** area displays a list of any named and saved page setups in the drawing. The Name dropdown list displays the name of the current page setup. From this list, select any one name. Also, user can create a new named page setup based on the current settings in the Plot dialog box by clicking Add.

A page setup contains the settings required to plot a drawing on a sheet of paper to create a layout. It consists of all the settings related to the plotting of a drawing including the plot devices used. If you select **Previous plot** from the drop-down list, the settings used for the last drawing plotted are applied to the current drawing. You can also import the existing page setup from the other files by selecting the **Import** option from the drop-down list.

You can add a new named page setup by choosing the **Add** button, which is located next to the drop-down list. When the **Add** button is clicked, AutoCAD displays the **Add Page Setup** dialog box on the screen as shown in **Fig. 14.**

In this dialog box, enter the name of the new page setup and choose **OK**. All the settings that configure in the current **Plot** dialog box will be saved under this page setup.

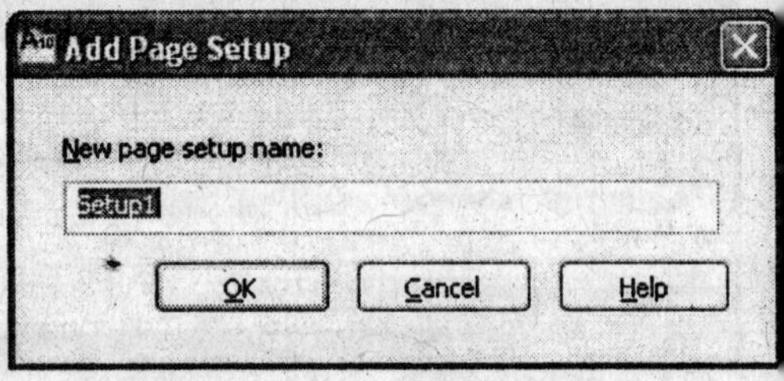

FIG. 14

6.3 PRINTER / PLOTTER AREA

The **Printer/Plotter** area displays information about the configured printers and plotters currently selected from the **Name** drop-down list. It displays the plotter drive and the printer port being used. It also displays the physical location and some description text about the selected plotters or printer. All the currently configured plotters are displayed in the **Name** drop-down list. If the selected plotter doesn't support the layout's selected paper size, a warning is displayed and user can select the plotter's default paper size or a custom paper size.

Properties

Choose the **Properties** button to check the information about a configured printer or plotter. When you choose the **Properties** button, AutoCAD displays the **Plotter Configuration Editor** dialog box. This dialog box lists all the details of the selected plotter under three tabs, namely, **General, Ports** and **Device and Document Settings.**

Plot to File

If you select this check box, AutoCAD plots the output to a file rather than to the plotter. If you select this check box and click **OK** button, then the **Browse for Plot File** dialog box will be displayed. In this dialog box, specify the name and its location.

6.4 PAPER SIZE AREA

The **Paper Size** drop-down list displays standard paper sizes that are available for the selected plotting device. Select the required paper size (say, A4). If no plotter is selected, the full standard paper size list is displayed and available for selection.

3.5 NUMBER OF COPIES AREA

The **Number of Copies** area specifies the number of copies to plot. Specify the required number of copies either by typing or using the spinner. By default, 1 copy is plotted.

3.6 PLOT AREA

The **Plot area** specifies the portion of the drawing to be plotted. Under **What to Plot** drop-down list, user can select an area of the drawing to be plotted. The options are:

Display

The **Display** option plots the view in the current viewport in the selected Model tab or the current paper space view in the layout.

Window

The **Window** option plots any portion of the drawing that specified. When user selects **Window**, the **Window** button becomes available. Click the **Window** button to use the pointing device to specify the two corners of the area to be plotted or enter coordinate values. The prompt is:

Specify first corner: *Specify a point*
Specify other corner: *Specify a point*

Layout

When plotting a layout, plots everything within the printable area of the specified paper size, with the origin calculated **from** 0,0 in the layout.

Limits

When plotting from the **Model** tab, plots the entire drawing area that is defined by the grid limits. If the current viewport does not display a plan view, this option has the same effect as the **Extents** option.

Extents

The **Extents** option plots the portion of the current space of the drawing that contains objects. All geometry in the current space is plotted. The drawing may be regenerated to recalculate the extents before plotting.

3.7 PLOT OFFSET (origin set to printable) AREA

The **Plot Offset** area specifies an offset of the plot area relative to the lower-left corner of the printable area or to the edge of the paper, depending on the setting made in the **Specify Plot Offset Relative To** option. The **Plot Offset** area of the **Plot** dialog box displays the specified plot offset option in parentheses.

3.8 PLOT SCALE AREA

The **Plot Scale** area controls the relative size of drawing units to plotted units. The default scale setting is 1:1 when plotting a layout. The default setting is **Fit to Paper** when plotting from the **Model** tab.

6.9 PREVIEW

The **Preview** button displays the drawing as it will appear when plotted on paper. To exit the print preview and return to the **Plot** dialog box, press **Esc**, press **Enter** or right-click and then click **Exit** on the shortcut menu. When the Preview button is clicked, the dialog boxes on the screen disappear and an outline of the paper size is shown. **See Fig. 15.**

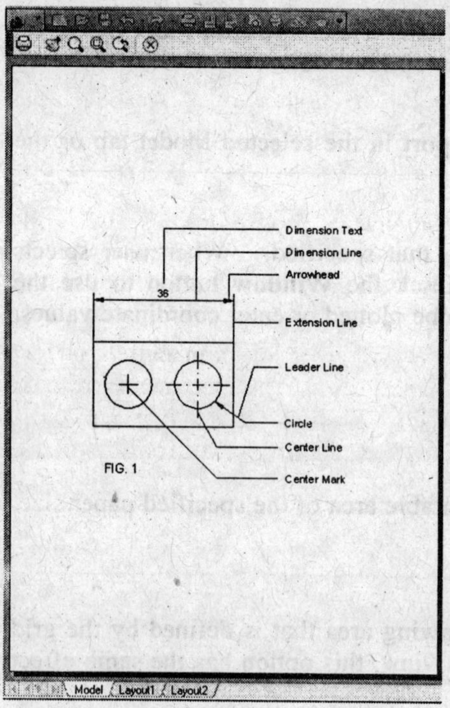

FIG. 16

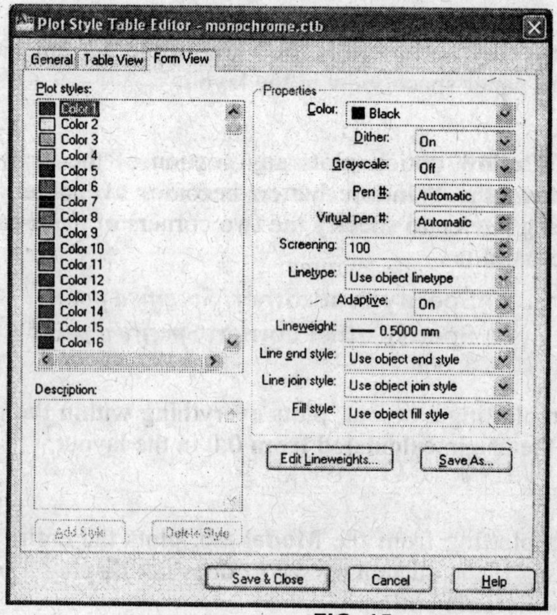

FIG. 15

6.10 PLOT STYLE TABLE (pen assignments) AREA

This area allow the user to view and select a plot style table, edit the current plot style table or creates a new plot style table. A **plot style table** is a collection of plot styles. A plot style is a group of pen settings that are assigned to an object or layer and that determine the color, line-type, thickness, line ending, line joining and the fill style of drawing objects while plotting.

Name (Unlabeled): Drop-down list displays the plot style table that is assigned to the current **Model** tab or layout tab and provides a list of the currently available plot style tables. If you select **New**, the **Add Plot Style Table** wizard is displayed, which you can use to create a new plot style table. The wizard that is displayed is determined by whether the current drawing is in color-dependent or named mode.

Edit: Choose **Edit** button to display **Plot Style Table Editor**, in which you can view or modify plot styles for currently assigned plot style table. **Plot Style Table Editor** is shown in **Fig. 16.**

*

4

BASIC AutoCAD COMMANDS

1. BASIC AutoCAD COMMANDS

Using the AutoCAD drawings tools, engineering graphics is formed by drawing *Geometric Primitives* like points, lines, circles, arcs, rectangles, polygons, etc. In general, we can draw objects either by specifying points with the pointing device or by entering values in the command line, at the command prompt.

AutoCAD commands are invoked from the **Menu Bars** or **Icons** in **Panels** or by typing command in the Command Prompt as explained in Chapter 2. In the Command Prompt, either the upper-case letters or the lower-case letters can be used. *Example*, `POINT` or `point`. Also, AutoCAD commands are abbreviated to one or two characters. *Example*: `L` or `l` for `line`.

2. LINE COMMAND

A **line** is defined as a straight curve. The most fundamental object in a drawing is line. In AutoCAD, a line is drawn between the two points by using the **LINE** command. The **LINE** command can be invoked by any one of the following five methods:

1. Choose **Line** tool from the **Draw** panel of the **Home** tab in the **Ribbon**. See Fig. 1.
2. Choose **Line** tool from the **Draw** tab of the **Tool Palettes**. To invoke the **Tool Palettes**, choose the **Tool Palettes** button from the **Palettes** panel in the **View** tab as in Fig. 2.
3. Choose **Line** tool from the **Draw** toolbar as shown in Fig. 3. To invoke the **Draw** toolbar, from the **Menu Bar**, choose **Tools > Toolbars > AutoCAD > Draw.**
4. Type **LINE** or **line** at the command prompt and press the Enter key.
5. Click **Line** from the **Draw** menu on the **Menu Bar**.

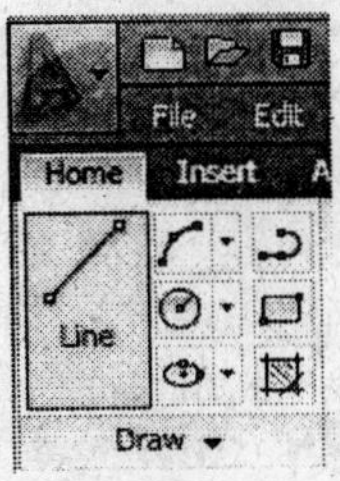

FIG. 1

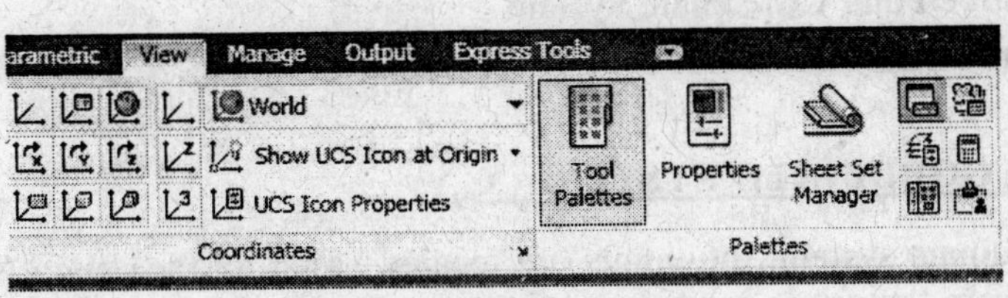

FIG. 2

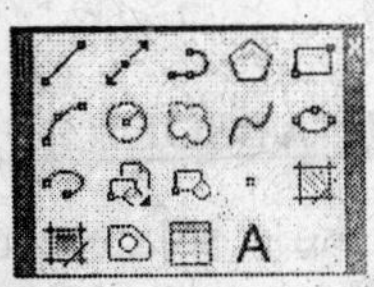

FIG. 3

If the **Line** tool is invoked, then you will be prompted to specify the starting point of the line. Select a point by using the mouse or by entering its coordinates at the command prompt. After specifying the first point, you will be prompted to specify the second point. Specify the second point. A line will be drawn on the drawing area. User can continue specifying points and draw lines or terminate the **Line** command by pressing Enter, Esc or Spacebar. After terminating the **Line** command, AutoCAD will again display the Command prompt.

Start a new file with the **Acad.dwt** template in the **2D Drafting & Annotation** or **AutoCAD Classic** workshop. The prompt sequence for the drawing shown in Fig. 4 is as follows:

Command: **LINE** ↵
Specify first point: *Specify the first point*
Specify next point or [Undo]: *Specify the second point*
Specify next point or [Undo]: *Specify the third point*
Specify next point or [Close/Undo]: ↵
(*Press Enter to exit the Line tool*)

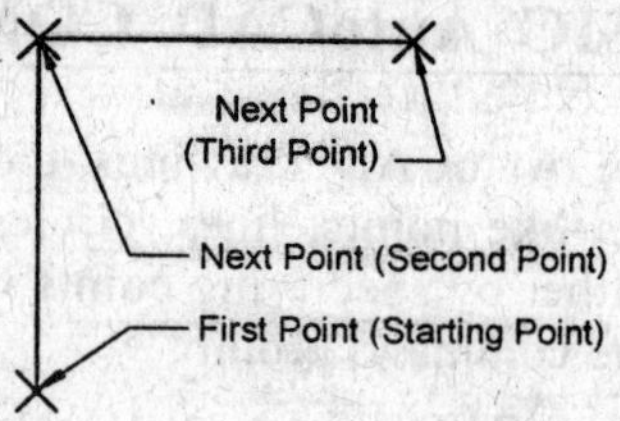

FIG. 4

The Line command has two options, namely, Undo and Close options.

Undo Option: While drawing a line, if a wrong endpoint is specified, then you can remove that line by using the **Undo** option of the **Line** tool. The **Undo** option can be used multiple times and many lines can be removed. To use the **Undo** option, type **Undo** or **U** at the **Specify next point or [Undo]** prompt.

Close Option: After drawing two continuous lines by using the Line command, the **Close** option is displayed at the Command prompt. The **Close** option is used to join the **current point** to the **start point** of the first line when two or more continuous lines are drawn. To use the **Close** option, type **Close** or **C** at the **Specify next point or [Close/Undo]** prompt.

Coordinate Systems

In AutoCAD, the default origin is located at the lower left corner of the drawing area. AutoCAD uses the following coordinate systems to locate a point in an XY plane:

1. Absolute Coordinate System
2. Relative Coordinate Systems
   - Rectangular or Relative Coordinate System
   - Relative Polar Coordinate System
3. Direct Distance Entry

2.1 ABSOLUTE COORDINATE SYSTEM (X, Y)

In the absolute coordinate system, the points are located based on the origin (0,0). If X and Y values of the point from the origin are known, then absolute coordinate system can be used. In AutoCAD, the absolute coordinates are specified at the Command prompt by entering the X and Y coordinates, separated by a comma.

Problem 1: *Draw a triangle on the point (60,60), (140,60) and (100,100).*

The command sequence to draw a triangle for the given points (60,60), (140,60) and (100,100) is as follows:

Command: **LINE** ↵
Specify first point: **60,60** ↵
Specify next point or [Undo]: **#140,60** ↵
Specify next point or [Undo]: **#100,100** ↵
Specify next point or [Close/Undo]: **C** ↵

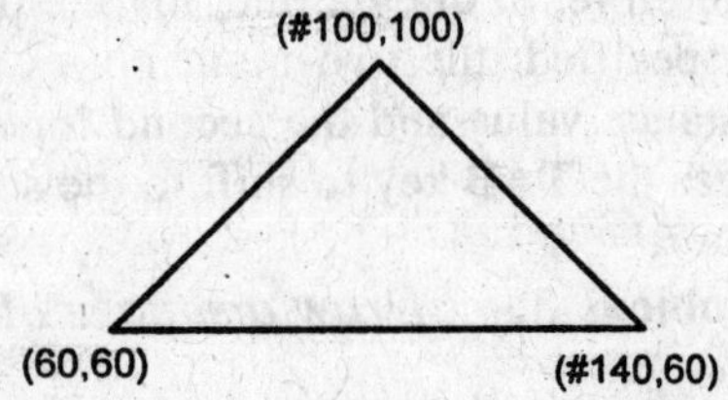

FIG. 5

See Fig. 5. Note that, to specify a point in an absolute coordinate system, add # as the prefix to the X coordinate value.

2.2 RELATIVE COORDINATE SYSTEMS

Relative Coordinate Systems are of two types, namely Relative Rectangular and Relative Polar.

1. Relative Rectangular Coordinate System

In **Relative Rectangular Coordinate** system, values are based on the very last point entered and not with respect to the origin. If the position of a point with respect to the previous points is known, then the relative rectangular co-ordinate system can be used.

To enter coordinate values in terms of the Relative Rectangular Coordinate system, check whether the **Dynamic Input** is on or not. If the **Dynamic Input** is turned on, then by default the profile will be drawn using the **Relative Rectangular Coordinate** system. To specify a point in this coordinate system, enter the X coordinate, type comma and then enter the y coordinate. By default, AutoCAD places the @ symbol in front of the X coordinate.

If the **Dynamic Input** is turned off, the coordinate values have to be prefixed by the @ symbol, so that the profile will be drawn using the Relative Rectangular Coordinate system.

Problem 2: *Draw a square of side 80 mm by Relative Rectangular Coordinate System.*

The command sequence to draw a square of 80 mm side using the LINE tool is as follows:

Command: **LINE** ↵
Specify first point: **60,60** ↵
Specify next point or [Undo]: **@80,0** ↵
Specify next point or [Undo]: **@0,80** ↵
Specify next point or [Undo]: **@-80,0** ↵
Specify next point or [Close/Undo]: **C** ↵

See Fig. 6.

Distance is measured +ve towards up and right.
Distance is measured –ve towards down and left.

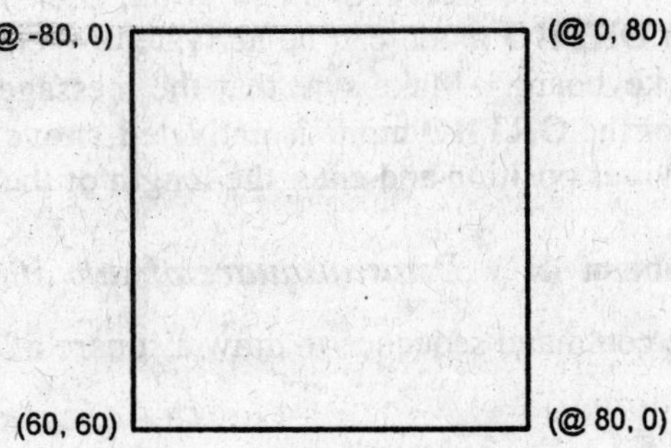

FIG. 6

2. Relative Polar Coordinate System

In the Relative Polar Coordinate system, a point is specified by defining the distance of the point from the current point and the angle between the two points with respect to the positive X axis. Angles are measured in anti-clockwise direction, taking 0° towards right.

If the **Dynamic Input** is turned on, then the relative polar coordinate mode is activated. Therefore, to draw a line, invoke the **LINE** tool and specify the start point. After the start point is specified, the two input boxes will be displayed on the screen. First input box shows the distance value and the second input box shows the angle value. Now, enter the distance value, press the **TAB** key to shift to the second input box and then enter the angle value.

Problem 3: *Draw a square of side 80 mm using the Relative Polar Coordinate System.*

The command sequence to draw a square of 80 mm side using the LINE command is as follows:

Command: **LINE** ↵
Specify first point: **60,60** ↵
Specify next point or [Undo]: **@80<0** ↵
Specify next point or [Undo]: **@80<90** ↵
Specify next point or [Undo]: **@80<180** ↵
Specify next point or [Close/Undo]: **C** ↵

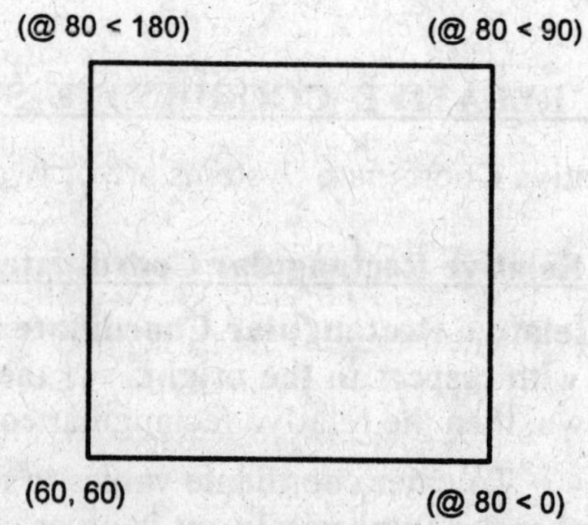

FIG. 7

See Fig. 7.

2.3 DIRECT DISTANCE ENTRY

In this method, a line is drawn easier by specifying only the length of the line. For this, first ensure that the **Dynamic Input** button is chosen in the **Status Bar**. Next, invoke the **Line** tool, you will be prompted to specify the first point. Specify the first point and press Enter. Now, you will be prompted to specify the next point. Now, enter the absolute length of the line and its angle with respect to the current position of the cursor in the corresponding text boxes.

Note that the user can use the **Tab** key to toggle between the text boxes. If the **Dynamic Input** is turned off, then user can enter the length of the line at the Command prompt.

If the **ORTHO** mode is on, user can position the cursor only along the X and Y axis. The **ORTHO** mode can be activated by clicking it in the **Status Bar** or by pressing **F8** key in the keyboard. Make sure that the message **<Ortho on>** is displayed on the Command prompt. After the **ORTHO** mode is activated, move the cursor to the required position with respect to the previous position and enter the length of the line.

Problem 4: *Draw a square of side 50 mm using the Direct Distance Entry method.*

The command sequence to draw a square of 50 mm side using the LINE command is as follows:

Command: **LINE** ↵

Specify first point: **80,80** ↵

Specify next point or [Undo]:

Press F8 <Ortho on>

(position the cursor to the right) **50** ↵

Specify next point or [Undo]:

(position the cursor to the up) **50** ↵

Specify next point or [Close/Undo]:

(position the cursor to the left) **50** ↵

Specify next point or [Close/Undo]: **C** ↵

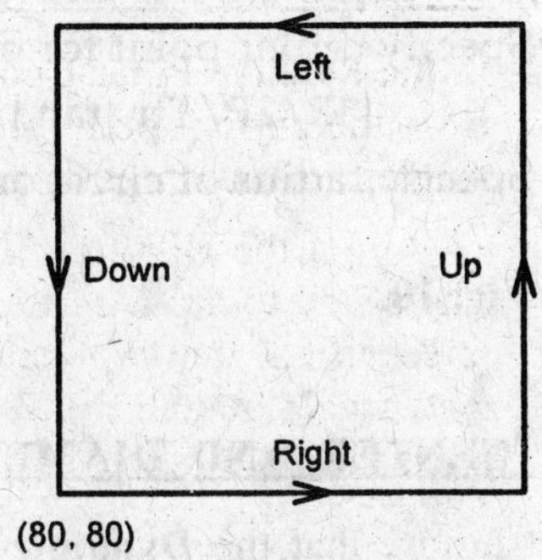

FIG. 8

See Fig. 8.

3. CIRCLE COMMAND

A circle can be drawn using the **CIRCLE** command. In AutoCAD, a circle can be drawn using six different tools. These tools are grouped together in the **Draw** panel of the **Ribbon**. To view these tools, choose the down arrow next to the **Center, Radius** tool in the **Draw** panel. All the tools are listed in a drop-down as shown in **Fig. 9.**

The tool chosen last will be displayed in the **Draw** panel. The **Circle** command can also be invoked by choosing the **Circle** tool from the **Draw** toolbar or from the **Tool Palettes**. Also, the **Circle** tool can be invoked by typing **CIRCLE** or **C** in the Command prompt or choosing **Circle** from the **Draw** Menu Bar.

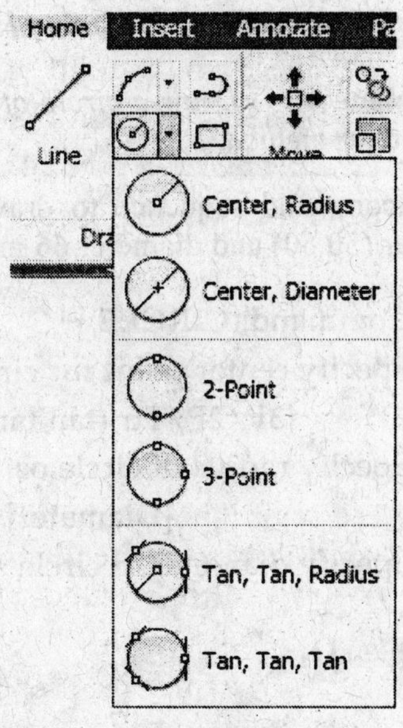

FIG. 9

3.1 CENTER AND RADIUS METHOD

First ensure that the **Dynamic Input** button is turned on. Choose the **Center, Radius** tool from the **Draw** panel. AutoCAD prompts to specify the center of the circle. Type the coordinates and press Enter or specify the center by using the left mouse button.

After specifying the center of the circle, move the cursor to define its radius, the current radius of the circle will be displayed in the dimension input box. This radius value will change as you move the cursor. Type a radius value in the dimension input box or click to define the radius. A circle of the specified radius value will be drawn in the graphics area.

Problem 5: *Draw a circle of 30 mm radius and 100,100 as the center point using the Center, Radius method.*

The command sequence to draw a circle with the center (100,100) and radius 30 mm is as follows:

Command: **CIRCLE** ↵
Specify center point for circle or
[3P/2P/Ttr (tan tan radius)]: **100,100** ↵
Specify radius of circle or [Diameter]: **30** ↵

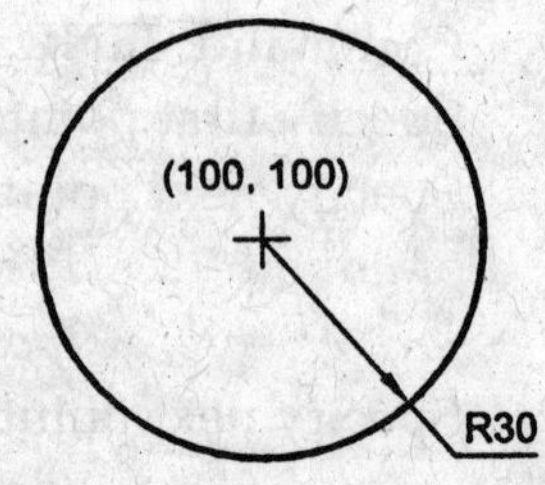

FIG. 10

See Fig. 10.

3.2 CENTER AND DIAMETER METHOD

First ensure that the **Dynamic Input** button is turned on. Choose the **Center, Diameter** tool from the **Draw** panel. AutoCAD prompts to specify the center of the circle. Type the coordinates and press Enter or specify the center by using the left mouse button.

After specifying the center of the circle, move the cursor to define its diameter, the current diameter of the circle will be displayed in the dimension input box. This diameter value will change as you move the cursor. Type a diameter value in the dimension input box or click to define the radius. A circle of the specified diameter value will be drawn in the graphics area.

Problem 6: *Draw a circle of 66 mm diameter and 50,50 as the center point using the Center, Diameter method.*

The command sequence to draw a circle with the center (50,50) and diameter 66 mm is as follows:

Command: **CIRCLE** ↵
Specify center point for circle or
[3P/2P/Ttr (tan tan radius)]: **50,50** ↵
Specify radius of circle or
[Diameter] <30.0000>: **D** ↵
Specify diameter of circle <60.0000>: **66** ↵

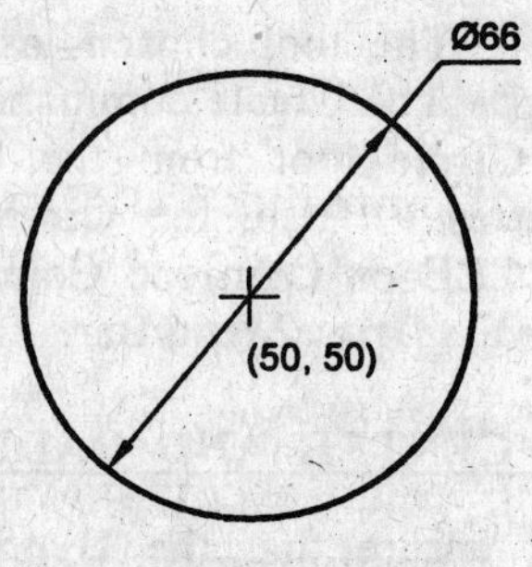

FIG. 11

See Fig. 11.

3.3 TWO POINTS (2P) METHOD

In this method, a circle can be drawn by specifying its two diametrical ends. For this, first ensure that the **Dynamic Input** button is turned on. Then choose the **2-Point** tool from the **Draw** panel. AutoCAD prompts to specify the first end of the diameter. Type the coordinates and press Enter or specify the center by using the left mouse button. After specifying the first end point of the circle, move the cursor to define the second end points of the circle's diameter. Now, you can type the coordinates or diameter in the dimension input box.

Problem 7: *Draw a circle with 50,50 as the first end point and 50,100 as the second end point using the 2-Points method.*

The command sequence to draw a circle using the two points (50,50) and (50,100) as its two end points is as follows:

Command: **CIRCLE ↵**
Specify center point for circle or
[3P/2P/Ttr (tan tan radius)]: **2p ↵**
Specify first end point of circle's diameter: **50,50 ↵**
Specify second end point of circle's diameter: **#50,100 ↵**

See Fig. 12.

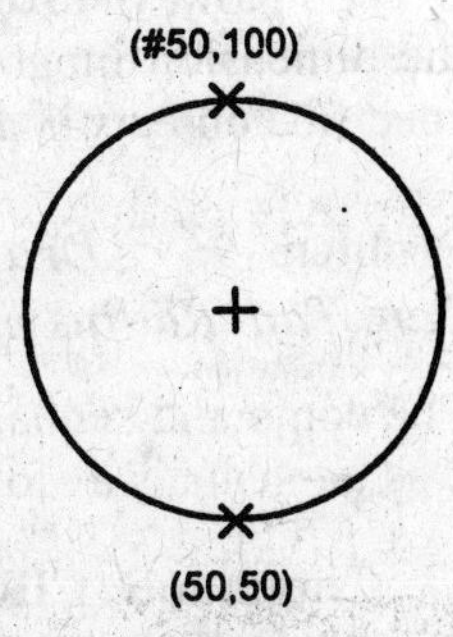

FIG. 12

3.4 THREE POINTS (3P) METHOD

A circle can be drawn by specifying three points on its periphery. To do so, choose the **3-Point** tool from the **Draw** panel. AutoCAD prompts to specify the first, second and third points of the circle. You can type the coordinates of the points or specify them by clicking the left mouse button.

Problem 8: *Draw a circle using the three points (50,50), (75,75) and (50,100) using the 3-Points method.*

The command sequence to draw a circle using the three points (50,50), (75,75) and (50,100) is as follows:

Command: **CIRCLE ↵**
Specify center point for circle or
[3P/2P/Ttr (tan tan radius)]: **3P ↵**
Specify first point on circle: **50,50 ↵**
Specify second point on circle: **#75, 75 ↵**
Specify third point on circle: **#50, 100 ↵**

See Fig. 13.

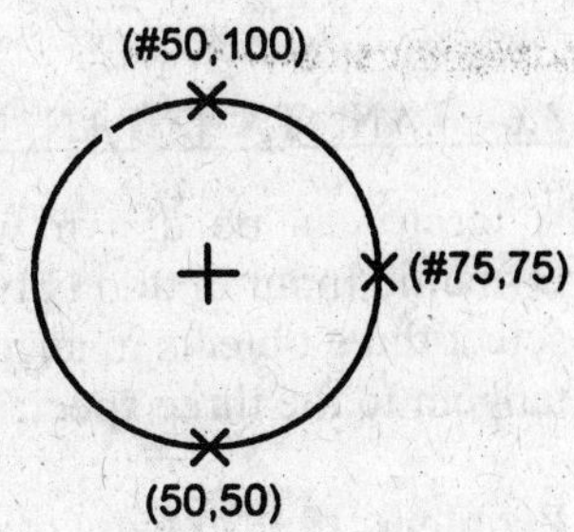

FIG. 13

3.5 TAN, TAN, RADIUS (Ttr) METHOD

An object is said to be tangent to a circle or an arc if it touches the circumference of the circle or the arc at only one point. The object may be a line, circle or an arc. A circle can be drawn with the specified radius and is tangent to two objects.

For this, first ensure that the Dynamic Input button is turned on. Choose the **Tan, Tan, Radius** tool from the **Draw** panel. AutoCAD prompts to specify a point on the first object to be tangent to the circle. Move the cursor near the object to be made tangent to the circle; a tangent symbol will be displayed. Specify the first point. Again, AutoCAD prompts to specify a point on the second object to be made tangent to the circle. Move the cursor near the second object that is to be tangent to the circle; a tangent symbol will be displayed. Specify the second point.

Now, the AutoCAD prompts to specify the radius of the circle. Type the radius value in the dimension input box and press enter. A circle with the specified radius and tangent to two specified objects is drawn in the graphics area of the AutoCAD.

Problem 9: *Draw a circle of 30 mm radius and two existing lines as tangents using the Tan, Tan, Radius method.*

The command sequence to draw a circle of radius 30 mm and two existing lines LINE-1 & LINE-2 as tangents is as follows:

Command: **CIRCLE** ↵
Specify center point for circle or
[3P/2P/Ttr (tan tan radius)]: **TTR** ↵
Specify point on object for first tangent of circle:
(Pick a point on LINE-1*)*
Specify point on object for second tangent of
circle: *(Pick a point on* LINE-2*)*
Specify radius of circle <15.0000>: **30** ↵

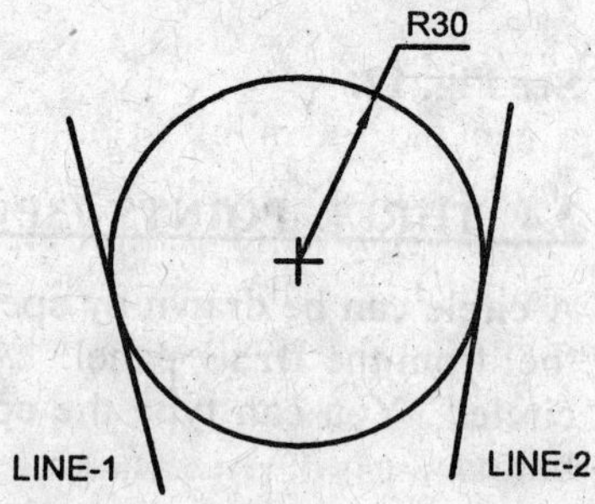

FIG. 14

See Fig. 14.

Sometimes more than one circle matches the specified criteria. The program draws the circle of the specified radius whose tangent points are closest to the selected points.

3.6 TAN, TAN, TAN METHOD

A circle can be drawn with the three objects as its tangent. For this, first ensure that the Dynamic Input button is turned on. Choose the **Tan, Tan, Tan** tool from the **Draw** panel. Then select three objects in succession to which the resulting circle is to be tangent. A circle, which is tangent to the three specified objects, is drawn in the graphics area of the AutoCAD.

Problem 10: *Draw a circle of three existing objects (one circle and two lines) as tangents using the Tan, Tan, Tan method.*

The command sequence to draw a circle of three existing objects as tangents is as follows:

Command: *(Select Tan, Tan, Tan tool from the Draw panel)*
_circle Specify center point for circle
or [3P/2P/Ttr (tan tan radius)]: _3p
Specify first point on circle: _tan to *(Pick a point on Circle)*
Specify second point on circle: _tan to *(Pick a point on L-1)*
Specify third point on circle: _tan to *(Pick a point on L-2)*

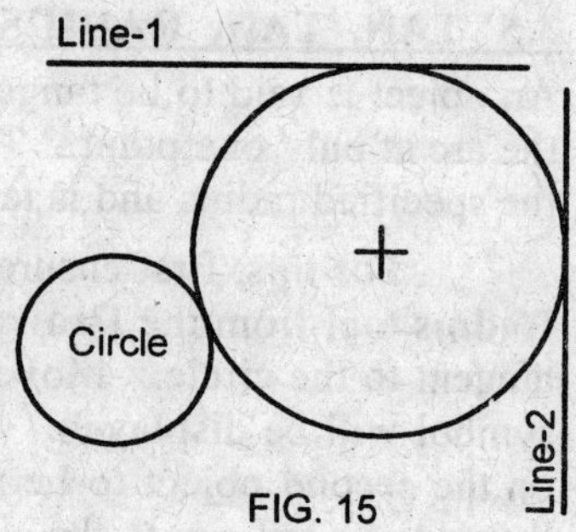

FIG. 15

See Fig. 15.

4. ARC COMMAND

An arc is a segment of a circle. The **Arc** tool is used to draw an arc segment. To draw an arc, user can specify various combinations of center, endpoint, start point, radius, angle, chord length, and direction values. Arcs can be drawn in eleven different tools. The tools to drawn an arc are grouped together in the **Arc** drop-down of the **Draw** panel in the **Ribbon**. See Fig. 16.

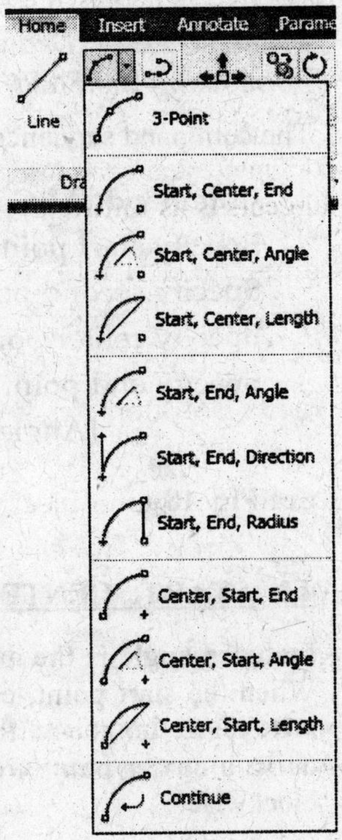

FIG. 16

4.1 3-POINTS

An arc can be drawn by specifying three points, start point, end point and another point on its periphery. In this method, the points can be specified either clockwise or counter-clockwise. Choose **3-Point** tool from the **Draw** panel. AutoCAD prompts to specify the start point. Specify the first point or enter the coordinates.

Now, AutoCAD prompts to specify the second point. Specify the second point using the left-clicking or entering the coordinates. Again, AutoCAD prompts to specify the end point of the arc. Specify the end point or enter the coordinates. An arc with the specified start point, second point and end point is drawn in the graphic area of the AutoCAD.

Problem 11: *Draw an arc using the three points, say, P1, P2 and P3 using the 3-point method.*

The command sequence to draw an arc using three points P1, P2 and P3 is as follows:

Command: **ARC** ↵
Specify start point of arc or [Center]: *(Pick P1)*
Specify second point of arc or [Center/End]: *(Pick P2)*
Specify end point of arc: *(Pick P3)*

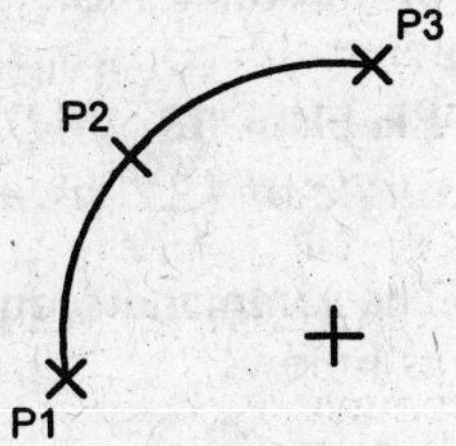

FIG. 17

See Fig. 17.

4.2 START, CENTER, END

When the start point, center point and end point are known, an arc can be drawn by specifying the start point, center point and end point. The center point is the center of a circle that the arc is part of. For this, choose **Start, Center, End** tool from the **Draw** panel. AutoCAD prompts to specify the start, center and end points is succession. Specify the start, center and ends point by clicking the left mouse button or enter the coordinates. An arc with the specified three points is drawn in the graphics area of the AutoCAD.

The radius of the arc is determined by the distance between the center point and the start point. So, the angle at which the arc ends is calculated using the end point.

Problem 12: *Draw an arc using the three points, start point, center point and end point using the Start, Center, End method.*

The command sequence to draw an arc using start point, center point and end point is as follows:

Command: **ARC** ↵
Specify start point of arc or [Center]: *(Pick P1)*
Specify second point of arc or [Center/End]: **C** ↵
Specify center point of arc: *(Pick P2)*
Specify end point of arc or
[Angle/chord Length]: *(Pick P3)*

See Fig. 18.

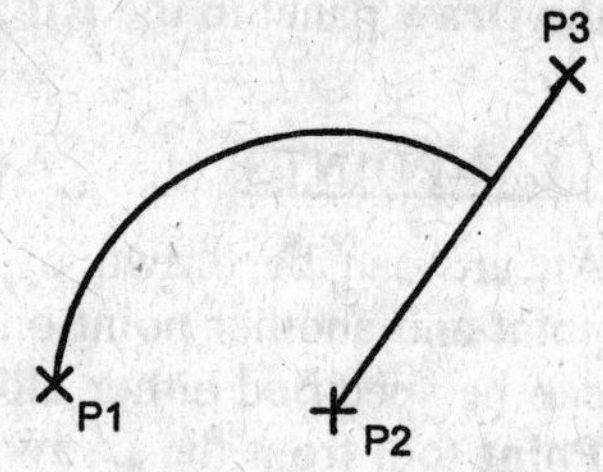

FIG. 18

4.3 START, CENTER, ANGLE

Included angle is the angle between the start and end points of an arc about the specified center. When the start point, center point and included angle are known, draw an arc by specifying the start/center point and the angle. Angle option draws an arc anti-clockwise from the start point using a center point with an included angle. If the angle is negative, AutoCAD draws an arc clockwise.

For this, choose the **Start, Center, Angle** tool from the **Draw** panel. AutoCAD prompts to specify the start point, center point and included angle. Specify these three points. An arc with the specified start point, center point and included angle is drawn in the graphics area of the AutoCAD.

Problem 13: *Draw an arc using the three points, start point, center point and included angle of 125° using the Start, Center, Angle method.*

The command sequence to draw an arc using start point, center point and included angle 125° is as follows:

Command: **ARC** ↵
Specify start point of arc or [Center]: *(Pick P1)*
Specify second point of arc or [Center/End]: C ↵
Specify center point of arc: *(Pick P2)*
Specify end point of arc or
[Angle/chord Length]: **A** ↵
Specify included angle: **125** ↵

See Fig. 19.

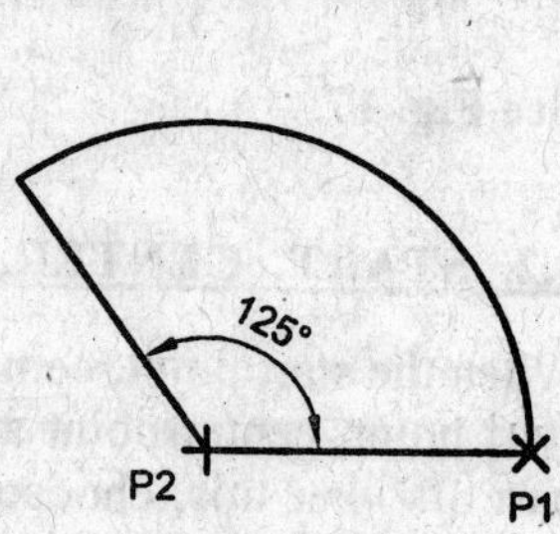

FIG. 19

4.4 START, CENTER, LENGTH

When the start point, the center point and the *chord* length are known, use the **Start-Center-Length** or the **Center-Start-Length** option to draw an arc. A *chord* is a straight line connecting the start point and end point of an arc. The length of the chord of the arc determines the included angle.

For this, choose the **Start, Center, Length** tool from the **Draw** panel. AutoCAD prompts to specify the **Start Point**, **Center Point** and **Length** of the chord in succession. Specify the start point and center point. Also, specify the length of the chord. AutoCAD calculates the include angle using the length of the chord. An arc is drawn in counter clockwise direction from the start point.

Problem 14: *Draw an arc with the start point, center point and 45 mm length of chord using the Start, Center, Length method.*

The command sequence to draw an arc using the start point, center point and chord length 45 mm is as follows:

Command: **ARC** ↵
Specify start point of arc or [Center]: *(Pick P1)*
Specify second point of arc or [Center/End]: **C** ↵
Specify center point of arc: *(Pick P2)*
Specify end point of arc or [Angle/chord Length]: **L** ←
Specify length of chord: **45** ↵

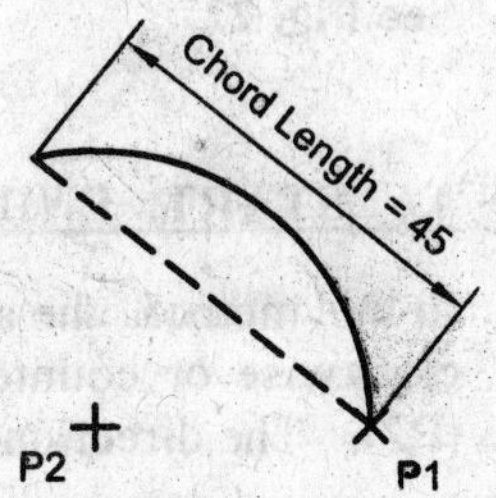

FIG. 20

See Fig. 20.

Chord Length option draws either a minor or a major arc. If the chord length is positive, AutoCAD draws minor arc counter clockwise from the start point P1 and uses the chord length to find the ending angle as shown in Fig. 20. The included angle in a minor arc is less than 180°.

If chord length is negative, major arc is drawn counter clockwise from the start point P1 as shown in Fig. 21. For this, enter –45 as the length of chord as shown below:

Specify length of chord: **–45** ↵

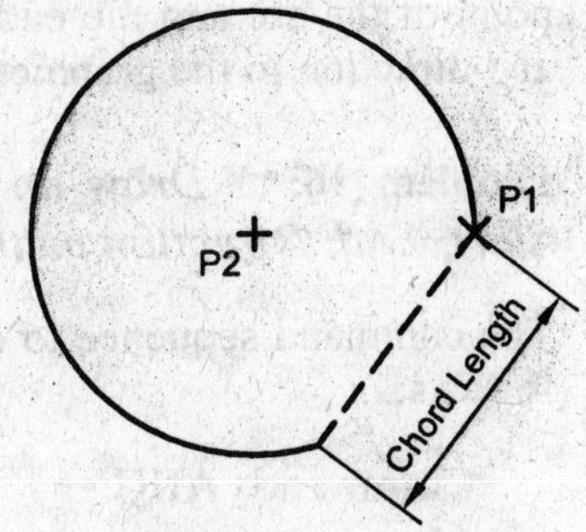

FIG. 21

4.5 START, END, ANGLE

When the start point, end point and included angle are known, draw an arc by specifying the start point, end point and the included angle. For this, choose the **Start, End, Angle** tool from the **Draw** panel. AutoCAD prompts to specify the start point, end point and included angle in succession. Specify these point to drawn an arc with the specified points. A positive included angle value draws an arc in the counter clockwise direction from the start point to the end point. Similarly, a negative included angle value draws the arc in clockwise direction.

Problem 15: *Draw an arc with the start point, end point and 55° as the included angle using the Start, End, Included Angle method.*

The command sequence to draw an arc using the start point, the end point and the included angle is as follows:

Command: **ARC** ↵
Specify start point of arc or [Center]: *(Pick P1)*
Specify second point of arc or [Center/End]: **E** ↵
Specify end point of arc: *(Pick P2)*
Specify center point of arc or
[Angle/Direction/Radius]: **A** ↵
Specify included angle: **55** ↵

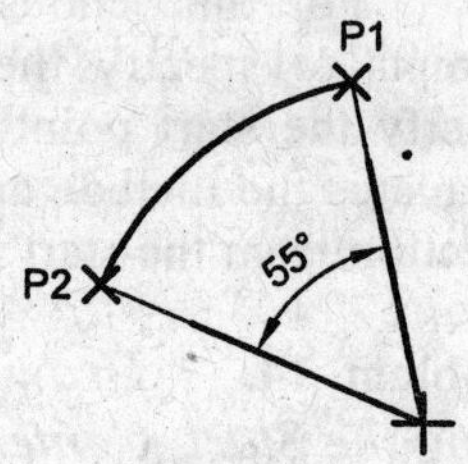

FIG. 22

See Fig. 22.

4.6 START, END, DIRECTION

In this method, the arc begins tangent to a specified direction. It creates any arc, major or minor, clockwise or counterclockwise, beginning with the start point (P1) and ending at an endpoint (P2). The direction is determined from the start point.

To drawn an arc using this method, choose **Start, End, Direction** tool from the **Draw** panel. AutoCAD prompts to specify the start point, end point and direction in succession. Specify a point on the line that is tangent to the start point or enter an angle between the start point of the arc and the end point of the tangent line. An arc is drawn with the specified points and direction in the graphics area of the AutoCAD.

Problem 16: *Draw an arc with the start point, end point and the direction using the Start, End, Direction method.*

The command sequence to draw an arc using the start point, the end point and the direction is as follows:

Command: **ARC** ↵
Specify start point of arc or [Center]: *(Pick P1)*
Specify second point of arc or [Center/End]: **E** ↵
Specify end point of arc: *(Pick P2)*
Specify center point of arc
or [Angle/Direction/Radius]: **D** ↵
Specify tangent direction for the start point of arc: **10** ↵

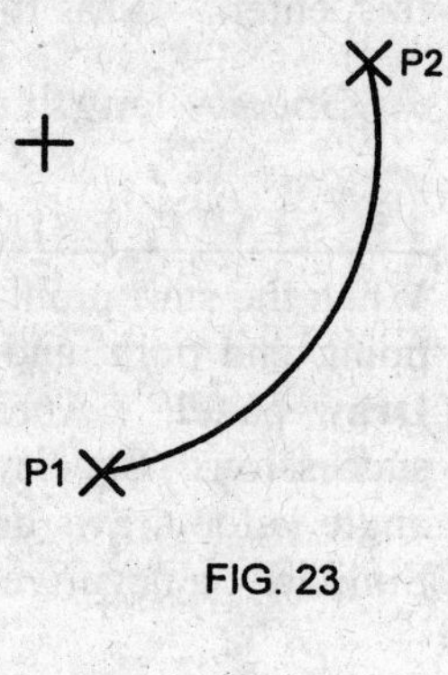

FIG. 23

See Fig. 23.

4.7 START, END, RADIUS

An arc can be drawn using the start point, end point and radius of an arc. For this, choose **Start, End, Radius** tool from the **Draw** panel. AutoCAD prompts to specify the start point, end point and radius in succession. Specify the start point, end point and radius of the arc. An arc is drawn with the specified data in the graphics area of the AutoCAD.

Here, the arc will be drawn in counter clockwise direction. That is, a negative radius value results in a major arc. Whereas, a positive radius value results in a minor arc.

Problem 17: *Draw an arc with the start point, end point and 16 mm as the radius using the Start, End, Radius method.*

The command sequence to draw an arc using the start point, the end point and the radius of the arc 16 mm is as follows:

Command: **ARC** ↵
Specify start point of arc or [Center]: *(Pick P1)*
Specify second point of arc or [Center/End]: **E** ↵
Specify end point of arc: *(Pick P2)*
Specify center point of arc or [Angle/Direction/Radius]: **R** ↵
Specify radius of arc: **16** ↵

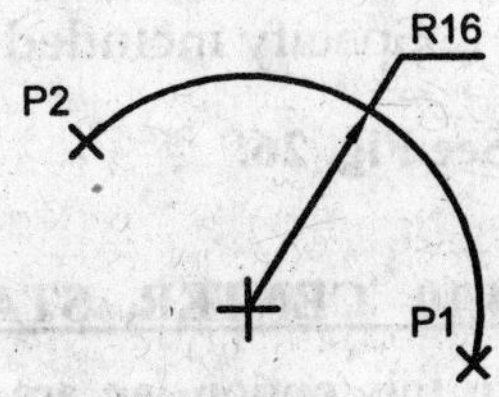

FIG. 24

See Fig. 24.

4.8 CENTER, START, END

In this method, an arc is drawn counterclockwise from the start point (P2) to an endpoint that falls on an imaginary ray drawn from the center point (P1) through a specified point (P3). For this, choose **Center, Start, End** tool from the **Draw** panel. AutoCAD prompts to specify the center point, start point and end point in succession. Specify the center point, start point and end point the arc. An arc is drawn with the specified data in the graphics area of the AutoCAD.

Problem 18: *Draw an arc with the center point, start point and end point using the Center, Start, End method.*

The command sequence to draw an arc using the center point, start point and the end point is as follows:

Command: **ARC** ↵
Specify start point of arc or [Center]: **C** ↵
Specify center point of arc: *(Pick P1)*
Specify start point of arc: *(Pick P2)*
Specify end point of arc or
[Angle/chord Length]: *(Pick P3)*

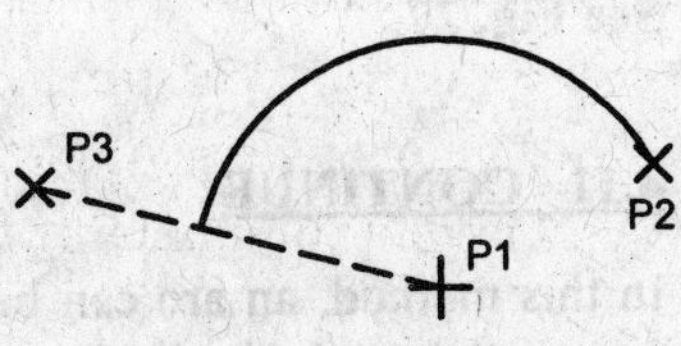

FIG. 25

See Fig. 25.

4.9 CENTER, START, ANGLE

In this method, an arc is drawn counterclockwise from the start point (P2) using a center point (P1) with a specified included angle. If the angle is negative, a clockwise arc is drawn.

Problem 19: *Draw an arc with the center point, start point and 120° included angle using the Center, Start, Angle method.*

The command sequence to draw an arc using the center point, start point and the included angle 125° is as follows:

Command: **ARC** ↵
Specify start point of arc or [Center]: **C** ↵
Specify center point of arc: *(Pick P1)*
Specify start point of arc: *(Pick P2)*
Specify end point of arc or [Angle/chord Length]: **A** ↵
Specify included angle: **125** ↵

See Fig. 26.

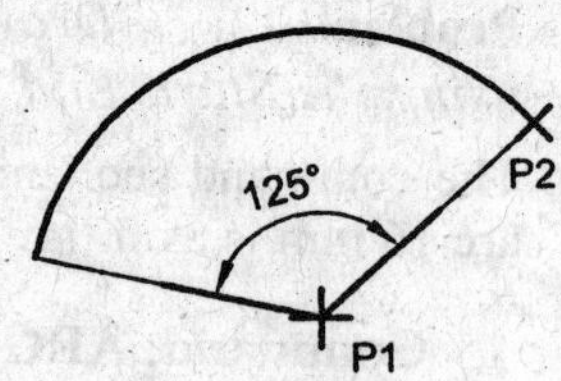

FIG. 26

4.10 CENTER, START, LENGTH

In this option, an arc is drawn using either a minor or a major arc based on the distance of a straight line between the start point and endpoint. If the chord length is positive, the minor arc is drawn counterclockwise from the start point. If the chord length is negative, the major arc is drawn counterclockwise.

Problem 20: *Draw an arc with the center point, start point and 35 mm chord length using the Center, Start, Length method.*

The command sequence to draw an arc using the center point, start point and the chord length 35 mm is as follows:

Command: **ARC** ↵
Specify start point of arc or [Center]: **C** ↵
Specify center point of arc: *(Pick P1)*
Specify start point of arc: *(Pick P2)*
Specify end point of arc or [Angle/chord Length]: **L** ↵
Specify length of chord: **35** ↵

See Fig. 27.

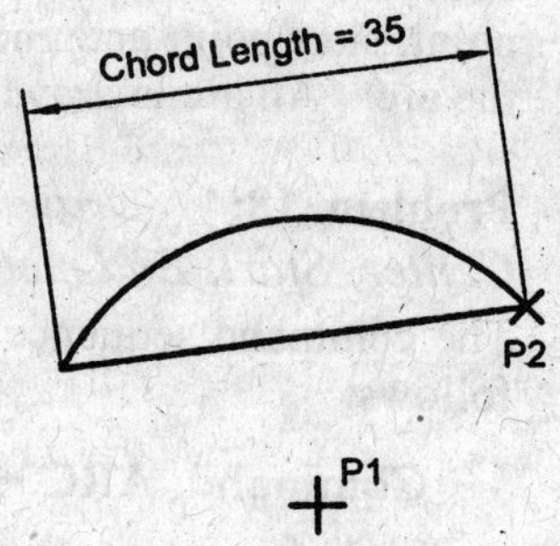

FIG. 27

4.11 CONTINUE

In this method, an arc can be drawn in continuation with the arc that is already drawn using any one of the methods discussed above. Immediately after an arc is drawn, user can start another arc tangent to the first arc at an endpoint by starting the **Arc** command and pressing **Enter** at the Specify start point of arc prompt. We need to specify only the endpoint of the arc.

Problem 21: *Draw an arc using the continue method.*

The command sequence to draw two arcs, first one is using the start point, center point and end point and the second one is using the Continue method, is as follows:

Command: **ARC** ↵
Specify start point of arc or [Center]: *(Pick P1)*
Specify second point of arc or [Center/End]: **C** ↵
Specify center point of arc: *(Pick P2)*
Specify end point of arc or [Angle/chord Length]: *(Pick P3)*

Command: **ARC** ↵
Specify start point of arc or [Center]: ↵
Specify end point of arc: *(Pick P4)*

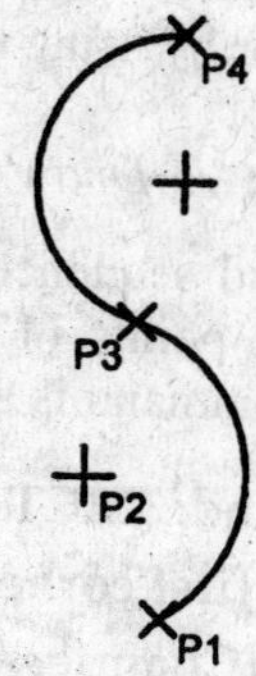

FIG. 28

See Fig. 28.

Immediately after an arc is drawn, we can start a line tangent to the arc at an endpoint by starting the **LINE** command and pressing **ENTER** at the **Specify First Point** prompt. Here, we need to specify only the line length. To draw a connected line, first draw an arc using any one of the methods discussed above and then activate the **LINE** command using the menu or using the shortcut menu.

Conversely, after a line is drawn, we can start an arc tangent to the line at an endpoint by starting the **ARC** command and pressing **ENTER** at the **Specify Start Point** prompt. Here, we need to specify only the endpoint of the arc. To draw a connected arc, first draw a line and then activate the **ARC** command using the menu or using the shortcut menu and use any one of the methods to draw an arc discussed above.

5. RECTANGLE COMMAND

A rectangle is a polyline based on two opposite corner points called **Diagonal Points.** A polyline is a connected sequence of line and arc segments. A rectangle or a square is drawn by choosing **Rectangle** tool from the **Draw** panel.

In AutoCAD, there are three methods to draw a rectangle. First one is by specifying the two opposite corners of the rectangle. Second one is by specifying the area and the size of one of the sides of the rectangle. The third one is by specifying the dimensions of the rectangle.

5.1 BY SPECIFYING TWO OPPOSITE CORNERS

First, ensure that the Dynamic Input button is turned on. Then, invoke the **Rectangle** tool by choosing **Rectangle** from the **Draw** panel. AutoCAD prompts to specify the first corner of the rectangle. Enter the coordinates of the first corner or specify the start point by using the mouse. The first corner can be any one of the four corners. Next, AutoCAD prompts to specify other corner. Specify the other corner diagonally opposite to the first corner by entering the coordinates or by using the left mouse button.

Problem 22: *Draw a rectangle defined by diagonal points (120,130) and (180,190).*

The command sequence to draw a rectangle defined by the diagonal points (120,130) and (180,190) using the Rectangle command is as follows:

Command: **RECTANG** ↵
Specify first corner point or
[Chamfer/Elevation/Fillet/
Thickness/Width]: **120,130** ↵
Specify other corner point or
[Area/Dimensions/Rotation]: **#180,190** ↵

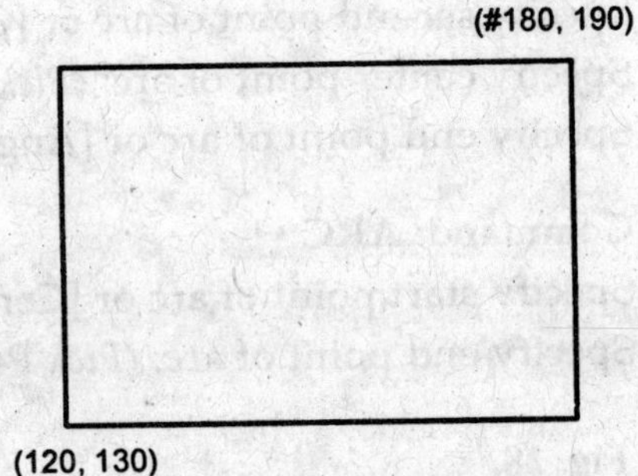

FIG. 29

See Fig. 29.

5.2 BY SPECIFYING AREA AND ONE SIDE

A rectangle can also be drawn by specifying its area and the length of one of its sides. For this, invoke the **Rectangle** tool from the **Draw** panel. Specify the first corner point. Next, invoke the shortcut menu by right-clicking and then choose the **Area** option. Next, specify the area and length (width) of the rectangle. If the area and length (width) of the rectangles is entered, then AutoCAD automatically calculates the width (length) of the rectangle using the formula **Area of the Rectangle = length × width.**

Problem 23: *Draw a rectangle of 1500 mm area and 50 mm length.*

The command sequence to draw a rectangle of 1500 mm area and 50 mm length using the Rectangle command is as follows:

Command: **RECTANG** ↵
Specify first corner point or [Chamfer/
Elevation/Fillet/Thickness/
Width]: (*Pick P1*)
Specify other corner point
or [Area/Dimensions/Rotation]: **A** ↵

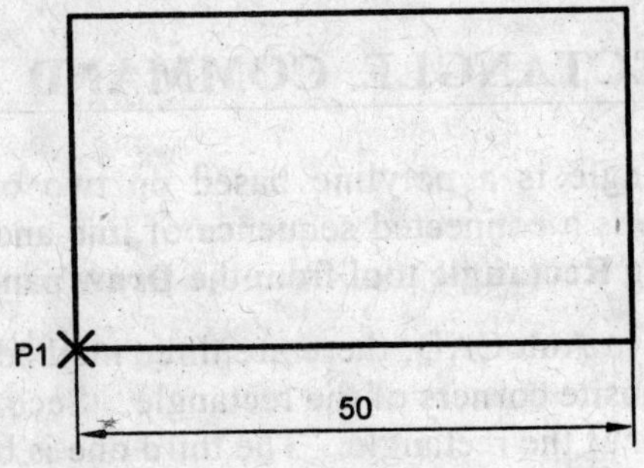

FIG. 30

Enter area of rectangle in current units <100.0000>: **1500** ↵
Calculate rectangle dimensions based on [Length/Width] <Length>: **L** ↵
Enter rectangle length <10.0000>: **50** ↵

See Fig. 30.

5.3 BY SPECIFYING THE DIMENSIONS

A rectangle can also be drawn by specifying its dimensions. This can be done by choosing the **Dimensions** option from the shortcut menu at the **Specify other corner point or [Area/Dimension/Rotation]** prompt and entering the length and width of the rectangle.

Problem 24: *Draw a rectangle of size 60 mm x 45 mm.*

The command sequence to draw a rectangle of size 60 mm x 45 mm using the Rectangle command is as follows:

Command: **RECTANG** ↵
Specify first corner point or [Chamfer/Elevation/
Fillet/Thickness/Width]: **50,50** ↵
Specify other corner point or
[Area/Dimensions/Rotation]: **D** ↵
Specify length for rectangles <10.0000>: **60** ↵
Specify width for rectangles <10.0000>: **45** ↵

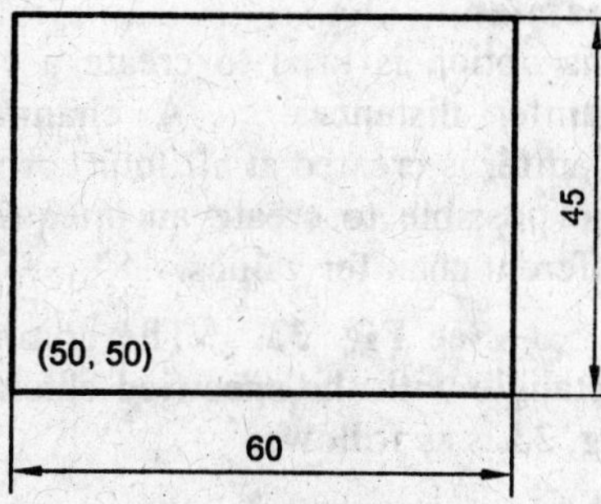

FIG. 31

See Fig. 31.

5.4 DRAWING RECTANGLE AT AN ANGLE

A rectangle can also be drawn at a specified angle. This can be done by choosing the **Rotation** option from the shortcut menu at **Specify other corner point or [Area/Dimension/Rotation]** prompt and entering the rotation angle. After entering the rotation angle, you can continue sizing the rectangle using any one of the above methods.

Problem 25: *Draw a rectangle at an angle of 35° rotation.*

The command sequence to draw a rectangle at an angle of 35° rotation using the Rectangle command is as follows:

Command: **RECTANG** ↵
Specify first corner point or [Chamfer/Elevation/
Fillet/Thickness/Width]: (*Pick P1*)
Specify other corner point or
[Area/Dimensions/Rotation]: **R** ↵

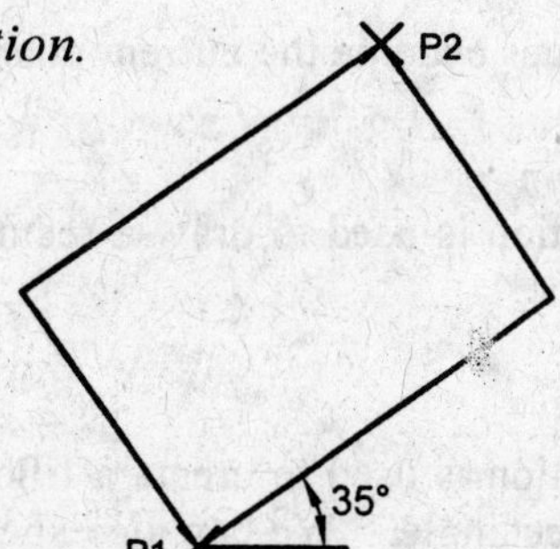

FIG. 32

Specify rotation angle or [Pick points] <0>: **35** ↵
Specify other corner point or [Area/Dimensions/Rotation]: *(Pick P2)*

See Fig. 32.

While specifying the other corner point, you can place the rectangle in any of the four quadrants. Move the cursor in the different quadrants and then select a point in the required quadrant.

5.5 OPTIONS IN THE RECTANGLE COMMAND

There are some parameters in a **Rectangle** tool before specifying the start point. These parameters are options in the Command. The options are: **Chamfer, Elevation, Fillet, Thickness** and **Width**.

1. Chamfer

This option is used to create a chamfer by specifying the chamfer distances. A chamfer is an angled corner. Chamfer is created at all four corners of the rectangle. It is also possible to create an unequal chamfer by giving two different chamfer values.

See Fig. 33. The command sequence to draw a rectangle with the specified chamfer distances as shown in **Fig. 33** is as follows:

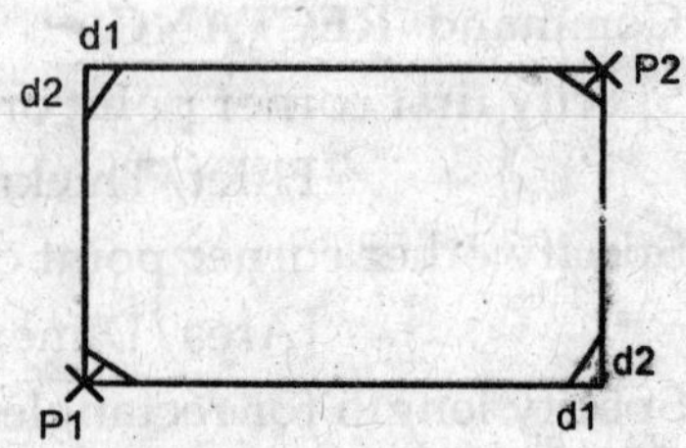

FIG. 33

Command: **RECTANG** ↵
Current rectangle modes: Chamfer=0.0000 x 0.0000
Specify first corner point or [Chamfer/Elevation/Fillet/Thickness/Width]: **C** ↵
Specify first chamfer distance for rectangles <0.0000>: **2** ↵
Specify second chamfer distance for rectangles <0.0000>: **3** ↵
Specify first corner point or
[Chamfer/Elevation/Fillet/Thickness/Width]: *(Pick P1)*
Specify other corner point or [Area/Dimensions/Rotation]: *(Pick P2)*

The values become the current chamfer distances for subsequent RECTANG commands.

2. Elevation

This option is used to draw a rectangle at a specified distance along the Z axis and from the XY plane.

3. Fillet

This option is used to create a filleted rectangle. Filleted rectangle means rounds the corner of the rectangle. We can also specify the radius of the fillet. **See Fig. 34.** The command sequence to draw a rectangle with the specified fillet radius as shown in **Fig. 34** is as follows:

Command: **RECTANG** ↵
Specify first corner point or [Chamfer/Elevation/
Fillet/Thickness/Width]: **F** ↵
Specify fillet radius for rectangles <2.0000>: **3** ↵
Specify first corner point or [Chamfer/Elevation/
Fillet/Thickness/Width]: (*Pick P1*)
Specify other corner point or
[Area/Dimensions/Rotation]: (*Pick P2*)

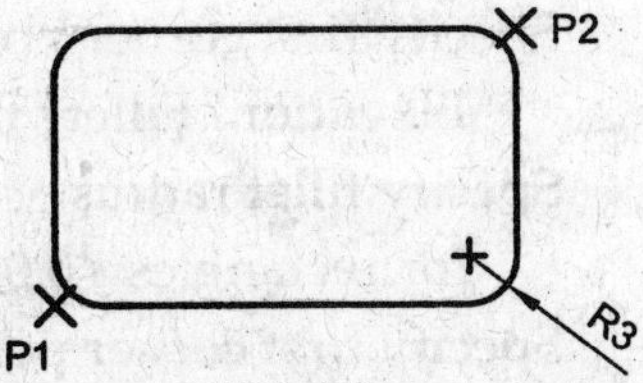

FIG. 34

The value becomes the current fillet radius for subsequent RECTANG commands.

4. Thickness

This option is used to draw a rectangle that is extruded in the Z direction by a specified value of thickness. The value becomes the current thickness for subsequent RECTANG commands.

5. Width

This option is used to draw a rectangle whose line segments have some specified width. **See Fig. 35.** The command sequence to draw a rectangle with the specified width as shown in **Fig. 35** is as follows:

Command: **RECTANG** ↵
Specify first corner point or [Chamfer/Elevation/
Fillet/Thickness/Width]: **W** ↵
Specify line width for rectangles <0.0000>: **1** ↵
Specify first corner point or [Chamfer/Elevation/
Fillet/Thickness/Width]: (*Pick P1*)
Specify other corner point or [Area/Dimensions/Rotation]: (*Pick P2*)

FIG. 35

The value becomes the current polyline width for subsequent RECTANG commands.

5. CAD EXERCISES - Step-by-Step Solutions

Example 1: Draw the diagram shown in **Fig. 36** using the Rectangle, Line, Circle and Arc commands.

The procedure and command sequence to draw the diagram shown in **Fig. 36** is given below:

STEP 1 : First draw the outer rectangle using the **Rectang** command with the fillet option in the Rectangle tool. The command sequence is given below:

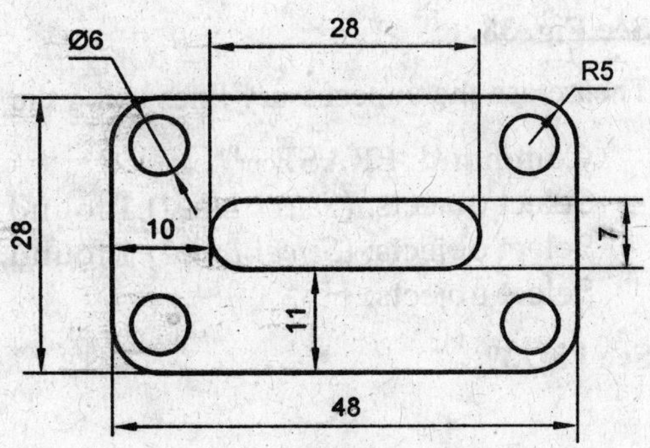

FIG. 36

Command: **RECTANG** ↵
Specify first corner point or [Chamfer/
Elevation/Fillet/Thickness/Width]: **F** ↵
Specify fillet radius
for rectangles <0.0000>: **5** ↵
Specify first corner point or
[Chamfer/Elevation/Fillet/
Thickness/Width]: (*Pick P1*)
Specify other corner point or [Area/Dimensions/Rotation]: **D** ↵
Specify length for rectangles <10.0000>: **48** ↵
Specify width for rectangles <10.0000>: **28** ↵
Specify other corner point or [Area/Dimensions/Rotation]: (*Pick P2*)

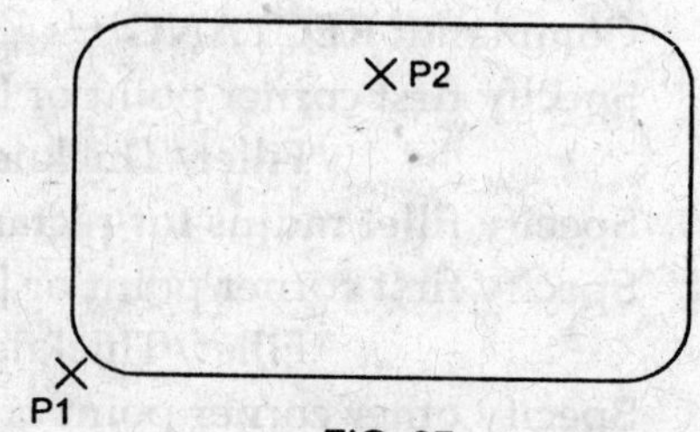

FIG. 37

See Fig. 37.

STEP 2 : Command sequence to draw the inner rectangle using the Line command is given below:

Command: **LINE** ↵
Specify first point: (*Pick P1*)
Specify next point or [Undo]: <Ortho on>
(*Move the cursor to right*) **10** ↵
Specify next point or [Undo]:
(*Move the cursor to up*) **11** ↵
Specify next point or [Close/Undo]:
(*Move the cursor to right*) **28** ↵
Specify next point or [Close/Undo]:
(*Move the cursor to up*) **7** ↵
Specify next point or [Close/Undo]: (*Move the cursor to left*) **28** ↵
Specify next point or [Close/Undo]: (*Move the cursor to down*) **7** ↵
Specify next point or [Close/Undo]: ↵

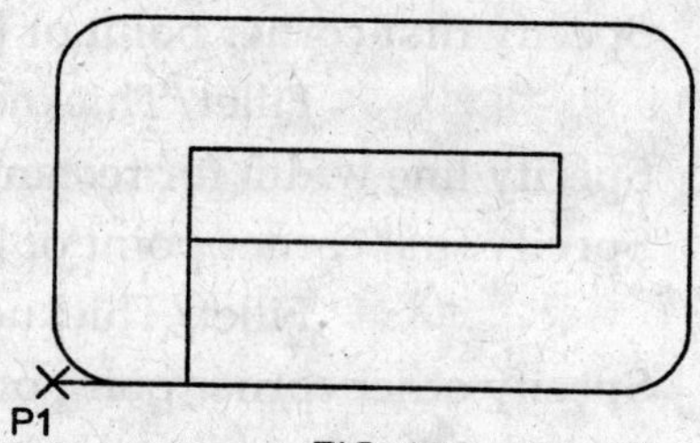

FIG. 38

See Fig. 38.

Then erase the unnecessary lines using the Erase command. The command sequence is:

Command: **ERASE** ↵
Select objects: (*Select Line1*) 1 found
Select objects: (*Select Line2*) 1 found, 2 total
Select objects: ↵

See Fig. 39.

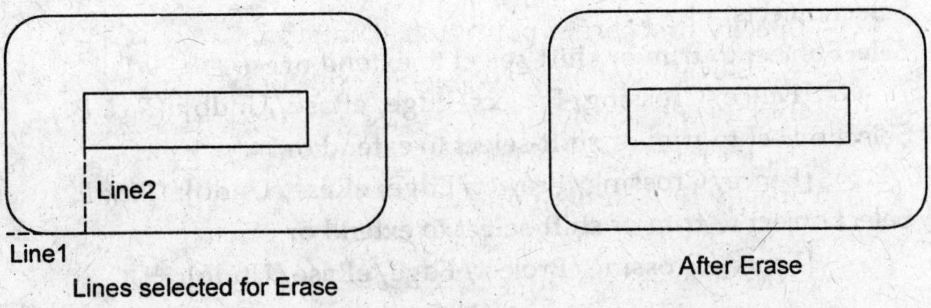

FIG. 39

STEP 3 : Command sequence to draw the arcs at the inner rectangle using the Arc command is given below:

Command: **ARC** ↵
Specify start point of arc or [Center]: (*Pick P1*)
Specify second point of arc or [Center/End]: **C** ↵
Specify center point of arc: (*Pick P2*)
Specify end point of arc or [Angle/chord Length]: (*Pick P3*)

Command: **MOVE** ↵
Select objects: (*Select the arc*) 1 found
Select objects: ↵
Specify base point or [Displacement] <Displacement>: (*Pick P4*)
Specify second point or <use first point as displacement>: (*Pick P2*)

See Fig. 40.

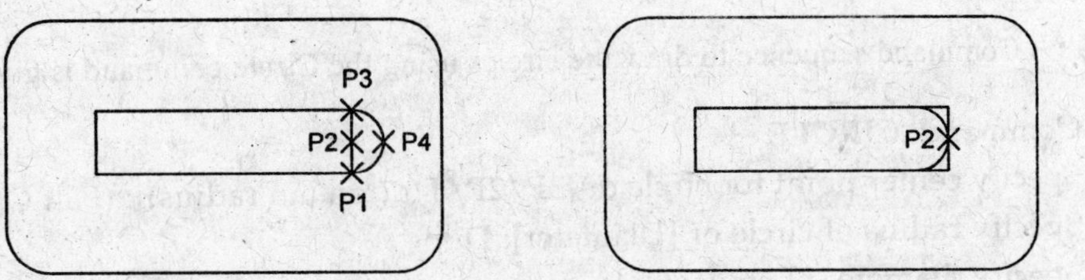

FIG. 40

STEP 4 : Command sequence to trim or delete the unwanted lines using the Trim and Erase command is given below:

Command: **TRIM** ↵
Current settings: Projection=UCS, Edge=None
Select cutting edges ...
Select objects or <select all>: (Select the arc) 1 found

Select objects: ↵
Select object to trim or shift-select to extend or
[Fence/Crossing/Project/Edge/eRase/Undo]: (*Pick P1*)
Select object to trim or shift-select to extend or
[Fence/Crossing/Project/Edge/eRase/Undo]: (*Pick P2*)
Select object to trim or shift-select to extend or
[Fence/Crossing/Project/Edge/eRase/Undo]: ↵

Command: **ERASE** ↵
Select objects: (*Select Line1*) 1 found
Select objects: ↵

See Fig. 41.

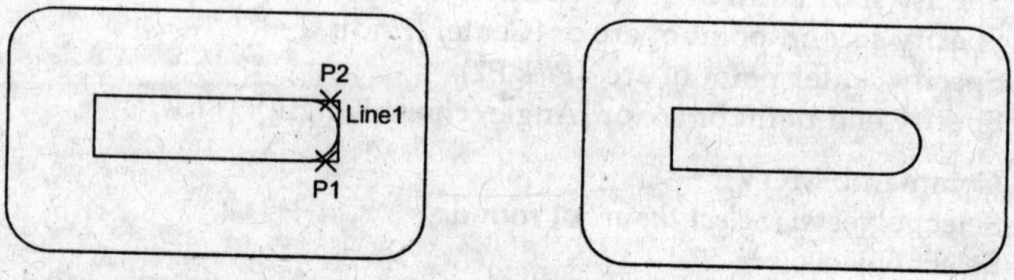

FIG. 41

STEP 5 : Similarly, draw the left arc and trim the unwanted lines as explained in the previous Steps 3 and 4.

STEP 6 : Command sequence to draw the circles using the Circle command is given below:

Command: **CIRCLE** ↵
Specify center point for circle or [3P/2P/Ttr (tan tan radius)]: (*Pick C1*)
Specify radius of circle or [Diameter]: **D** ↵
Specify diameter of circle: **6** ↵

Command: **CIRCLE** ↵
Specify center point for circle or [3P/2P/Ttr (tan tan radius)]: (*Pick C2*)
Specify radius of circle or [Diameter]: **D** ↵
Specify diameter of circle: **6** ↵

Command: **CIRCLE** ↵
Specify center point for circle or [3P/2P/Ttr (tan tan radius)]: (*Pick C3*)
Specify radius of circle or [Diameter]: **D** ↵
Specify diameter of circle: **6** ↵

Command: **CIRCLE** ↵
Specify center point for circle or
[3P/2P/Ttr (tan tan radius)]: (*Pick C4*)
Specify radius of circle or [Diameter]: **D** ↵
Specify diameter of circle: **6** ↵

See Fig. 42.

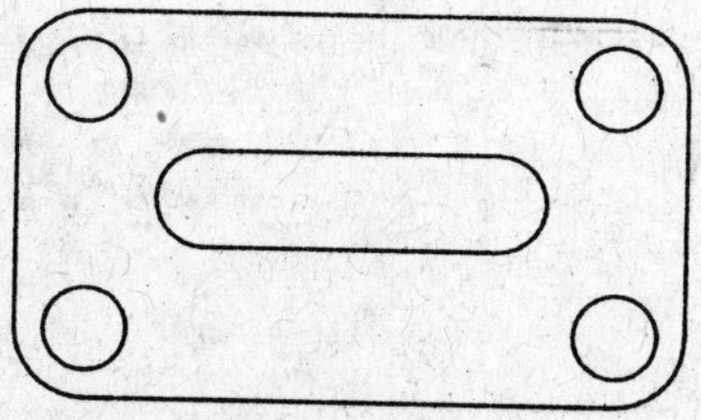

FIG. 42

STEP 7 : **Fig. 42** shows the final view of the diagram shown in **Fig. 36**. Finally, save the drawing.

The Trim and Erase tools are explained later.

6.1 EXERCISES

Draw the objects shown in Fig. 43, Fig. 44 and Fig. 45 using the draw commands such as Line, Arc, Circle and Rectangle.

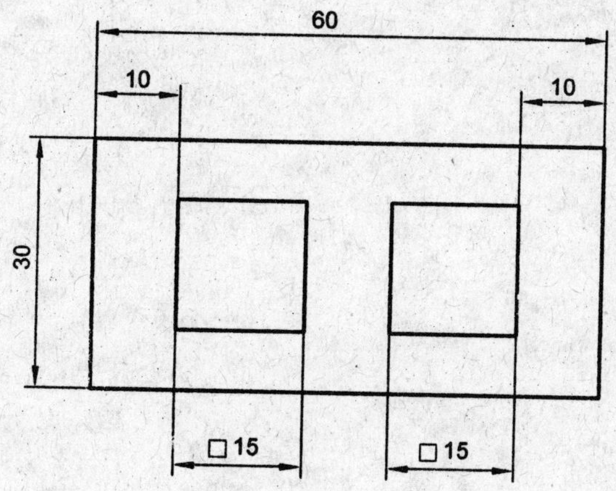

FIG. 43

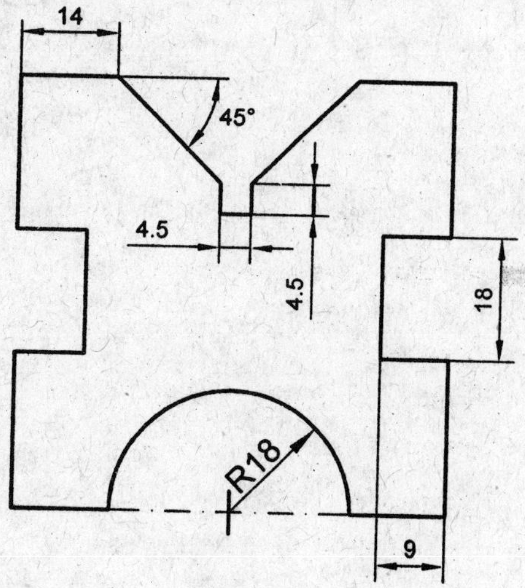

FIG. 44

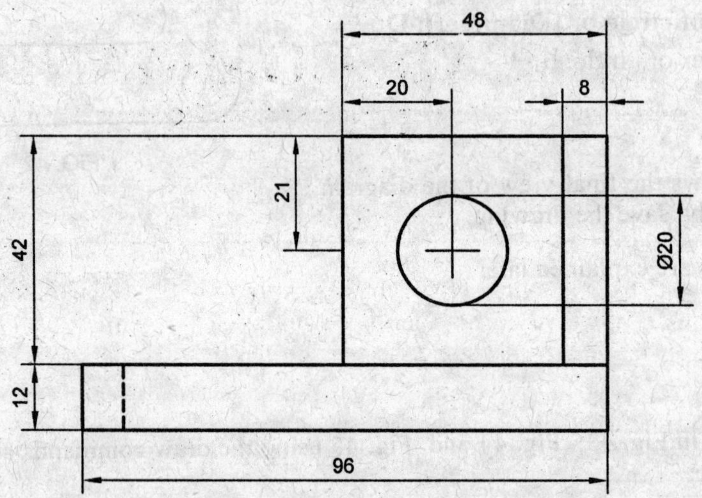

FIG. 45

5

ADVANCED AutoCAD COMMANDS

1. ELLIPSE COMMAND

An ellipse is a closed polyline composed of number of arc segments. The shape of an ellipse is determined by two axes that define its length and width. The longer axis is called the **Major Axis** and the shorter one is the **Minor Axis.**

An ellipse is drawn using the **ELLIPSE** command. An ellipse can be drawn using different methods. The tools to invoke these methods are grouped together in the **Draw** panel. See Fig. 1.

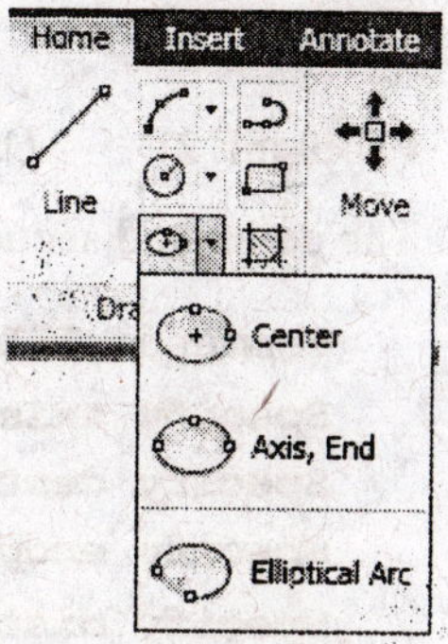

FIG. 1

Invoke the **Ellipse** tool by choosing **Ellipse** from the **Tool Palettes** or **Toolbar.** The **Ellipse** can also be invoked by entering **ELLIPSE** at the Command prompt or choosing an ellipse option from the **Draw** panel of the **Home** tab.

Once the Ellipse command is invoked, the **Specify axis endpoint of ellipse or [Arc/Center]** prompt is displayed. The next step depends on the option selected.

1.1 CENTER METHOD

An ellipse can be drawn by specifying the center point, end point of one axis and length of other axis. To do so, invoke the **Ellipse** tool by selecting **Center** option in from the **Draw** panel. AutoCAD prompts to specify the center of the ellipse.

The center of an ellipse is defined as the point of intersection of the major and minor axes. Specify the center point or enter coordinates. Now, AutoCAD prompts to specify the end point. Specify the end point of the major or minor axis. Now, AutoCAD prompts to specify the distance of the other axis. Specify the distance. An ellipse with the specified parameters is drawn in the graphics area of the AutoCAD.

Problem 1: *Draw an ellipse using the Center method.*

The command sequence to draw an ellipse using the center method is as follows:

```
Command: ELLIPSE ↵
Specify axis endpoint of ellipse or [Arc/Center]: C ↵
Specify center of ellipse: (Pick P1)
```

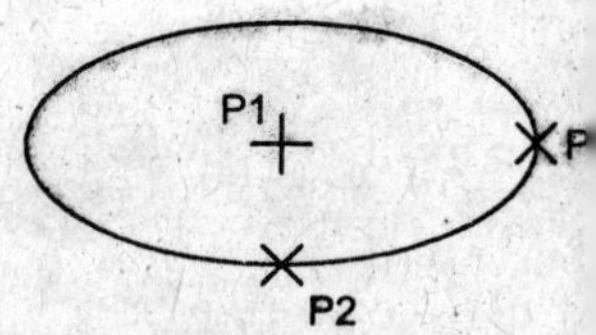

FIG. 2

```
Specify endpoint of axis: (Pick P2)
Specify distance to other axis or
                   [Rotation]: (Pick P3)
```

See Fig. 2. **Distance to other axis** defines the second axis as the distance from the center of the ellipse, or midpoint of the first axis, to the point you specify.

The **Rotation** option creates an ellipse by appearing to rotate a circle about the major axis. For this, enter **R** at the **Specify distance to the axis or [Rotation]** prompt. Here, the first axis specified is considered as the major axis. If you specify the rotation angle, the ellipse is draw at an angle with respect to the major axis. The range between the rotation angles is 0 to 89.4°.

Problem 2: *Draw an ellipse using the Rotation method.*

The command sequence to draw an ellipse using the center method is as follows:

```
Command: ELLIPSE ↵
Specify axis endpoint of ellipse or [Arc/Center]: C ↵
Specify center of ellipse: (Pick P1)
Specify endpoint of axis: (Pick P2)
Specify distance to other axis or [Rotation]: 75 ↵
```

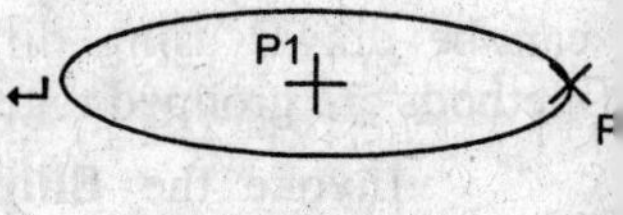

FIG. 3

See Fig. 3.

1.2 AXIS, END METHOD

An ellipse can be drawn by specifying its axes and the end point of the other axis. For this, choose **Axis, End** option of the **Ellipse** tool from the **Draw** panel. AutoCAD prompts to specify the axis end point. Specify the first end point of one axis of the ellipse. Next, AutoCAD prompts to specify the other end point of the axis. Specify the other end point of the axis. Now, AutoCAD prompts to specify the distance to other axis from the center. Specify the distance to other axis.

Problem 3: *Draw an ellipse using the Axis, End method.*

The command sequence to draw an ellipse using the axis, end method is as follows:

```
Command: ELLIPSE ↵
Specify axis endpoint of ellipse or
         [Arc/Center]: (Pick P1)
Specify other endpoint of axis: (Pick P2)
Specify distance to other axis or
         [Rotation]: (Pick P3)
```

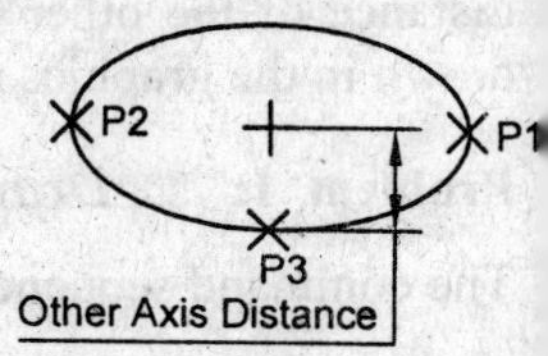

FIG. 4

See Fig. 4.

The Rotation option creates an ellipse by appearing to rotate a circle about the first axis. In the **Specify rotation around major axis:** prompt, specify a point or enter a positive angle value less than 90. Move the crosshairs around the center of the ellipse and click. If higher the value is entered, the eccentricity of the ellipse is greater. Entering 0 defines a circular ellipse.

Problem 4: *Draw an ellipse using the Axis, End method with the Rotation option.*

The command sequence to draw an ellipse using the rotation option and the rotation angle 60° is as follows:

```
Command: ELLIPSE ↵
Specify axis endpoint of ellipse or
                    [Arc/Center]: (Pick P1)
Specify other endpoint of axis:  (Pick P2)
Specify distance to other axis or [Rotation]: R ↵
Specify rotation around major axis:  60 ↵
```

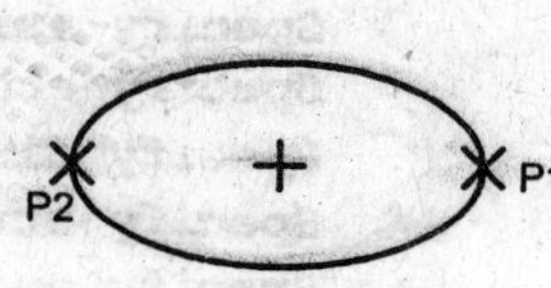

FIG. 5

See Fig. 5.

Problem 5: *Draw an ellipse using the Axis, End method with the Rotation option.*

The command sequence to draw an ellipse using the rotation option and the rotation angle 45° is as follows:

```
Command: ELLIPSE ↵
Specify axis endpoint of ellipse or
                    [Arc/Center]: (Pick P1)
Specify other endpoint of axis:  (Pick P2)
Specify distance to other axis or [Rotation]: R ↵
Specify rotation around major axis:  45 ↵
```

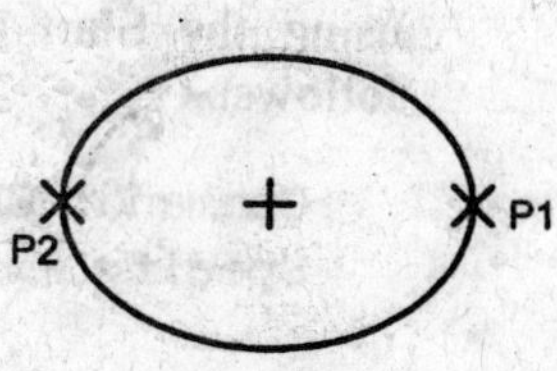

FIG. 6

See Fig. 6.

1.3 ARC METHOD

Using the **Elliptical Arc** tool from the **Draw** panel, an ellipse or an elliptical arc can be drawn. The angle of the first axis determines the angle of the elliptical arc. The first axis can define either the major or the minor axis of the elliptical arc.

If the **Arc** option of the Ellipse command is selected, you need to specify the end points of the axes, the distance to the other axis from the center and any one of the following information:

1. Start and End Angles of the arc
2. Start and Included Angles of the arc
3. Start and End parameters

Note that in the case of elliptical arc, angles are measured from the first point and in the counter-clockwise direction.

1. Start and End Angles of the arc

Problem 6: *Draw an ellipse by specifying Start and End Angles of the arc using the Elliptical Arc Method.*

The command sequence to draw an elliptical arc using the Start and End Angles option is as follows:

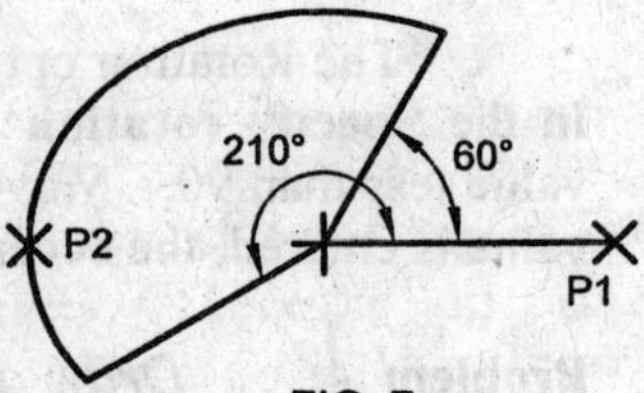

FIG. 7

```
Command: ELLIPSE ↵
Specify axis endpoint of ellipse or
                        [Arc/Center]: A ↵
Specify axis endpoint of elliptical arc or [Center]: (Pick P1)
Specify other endpoint of axis: (Pick P2)
Specify distance to other axis or [Rotation]: 16 ↵
Specify start angle or [Parameter]: 60 ↵
Specify end angle or [Parameter/Included angle]: 210 ↵
```

See Fig. 7.

2. Start and Included Angles of the arc

Problem 7: *Draw an ellipse by specifying the Start and Included Angles of the arc using the Elliptical Arc Method.*

The command sequence to draw an elliptical arc using the Start and Included Angles option is as follows:

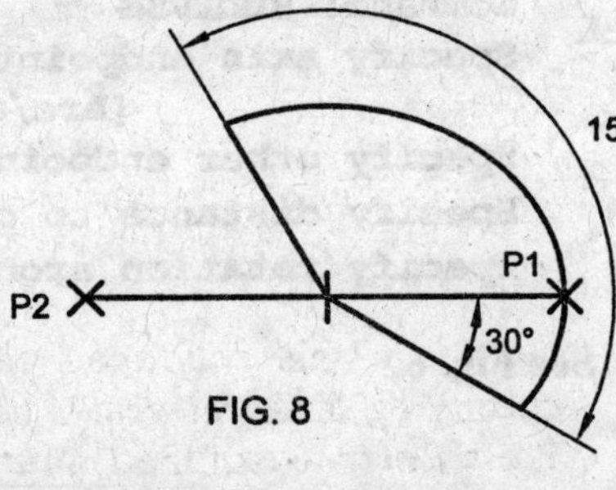

FIG. 8

```
Command: ELLIPSE ↵
Specify axis endpoint of ellipse or
                        [Arc/Center]: A ↵
Specify axis endpoint of elliptical arc or
                        [Center]: (Pick P1)
Specify other endpoint of axis: (Pick P2)
Specify distance to other axis or [Rotation]: 16 ↵
Specify start angle or [Parameter]: -30 ↵
Specify end angle or [Parameter/Included angle]: I ↵
Specify included angle of arc <current>: 150 ↵
```

See Fig. 8.

3. Start and End parameters

Problem 8: *Draw an ellipse by specifying the Start and End parameters of the arc using the Elliptical Arc Method.*

The command sequence to draw an elliptical arc using the Start and Included Angles option is as follows:

```
Command: ELLIPSE ↵
Specify axis endpoint of ellipse
     or [Arc/Center]: A ↵
Specify axis endpoint of elliptical
     arc or[Center]: (Pick P1)
Specify other endpoint of
     axis: (Pick P2)
Specify distance to other axis or
          [Rotation]: 16 ↵
Specify start angle or [Parameter]: P ↵
Specify start parameter or [Angle]: @1,0 ↵
Specify end parameter or    [Angle/Included angle]: @1<150 ↵
```

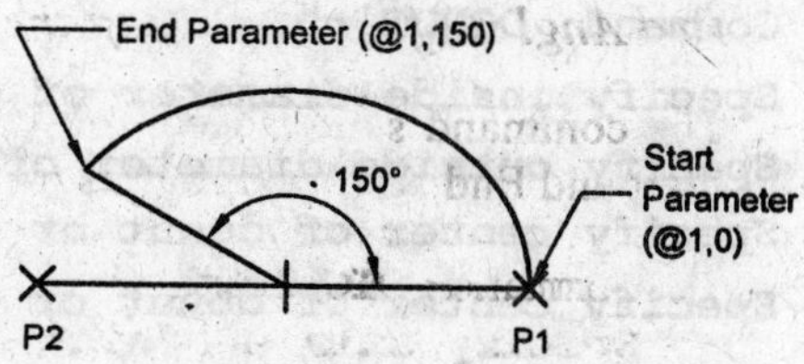

FIG. 9

See Fig. 9.

2. DONUT COMMAND

Donuts are filled rings or solid-filled circles that actually are closed polylines with width. The **DONUT** tool is used draw a thick circle. To draw a donut, specify its inside and outside diameters and its center.

For this, invoke the **Donut** tool by choosing the **Donut** from the **Draw** panel or entering **DONUT** at the Command prompt. AutoCAD prompts to specify the inside diameter of the donut. Specify the inside diameter. Now, AutoCAD prompts to specify the outside diameter of the donut. Specify the outside diameter. Next, AutoCAD prompts to specify the center of the donut. Specify the center point of the donut in the drawing area to place the donut.

In this way, you can create multiple copies of donuts with the same diameter by specifying different center points. The location of the donut is set based on the center point. Press **Enter** to exit the **Donut** command.

The interior of a donut is filled depends on the current setting of the **FILL** command. The command sequence to switch on/off the fill mode is as follows:

```
Command: FILL ↵
Enter mode [ON/OFF] <ON>: OFF ↵
```

The default values for the inside and outside diameters of donuts are saved in the **DONUTID** and **DONUTOD** system variables. A solid-filled circle is drawn by specifying the inside diameter as zero and if **FILLMODE** is on.

Problem 9: *Draw a donut with inside diameter 10 mm and outside diameter 20 mm with the fillmode off.*

The command sequence to draw a donut of inside diameter 10 mm and outside diameter 20 mm with the fill mode OFF is as follows:

```
Command: FILL ↵
Enter mode [ON/OFF] <ON>: OFF ↵
Command: DONUT ↵
Specify inside diameter of donut <0.5000>: 10 ↵
Specify outside diameter of donut <1.0000>: 20 ↵
Specify center of donut or <exit>: (Pick P1).
Specify center of donut or <exit>: ↵
```

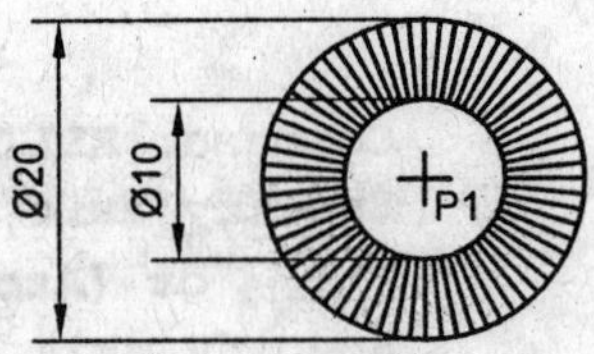

FIG. 10

See Fig. 10.

Problem 10: *Draw a donut with inside diameter 10 mm and outside diameter 20 mm with the fillmode on.*

The command sequence to draw a donut of inside diameter 10 mm and outside diameter 20 mm with the fill mode ON is as follows:

```
Command: FILL ↵
Enter mode [ON/OFF] <OFF>: ON ↵
Command: DONUT ↵
Specify inside diameter of donut <0.5000>: 10 ↵
Specify outside diameter of donut <1.0000>: 20 ↵
Specify center of donut or <exit>: (Pick P1)
Specify center of donut or <exit>: ↵
```

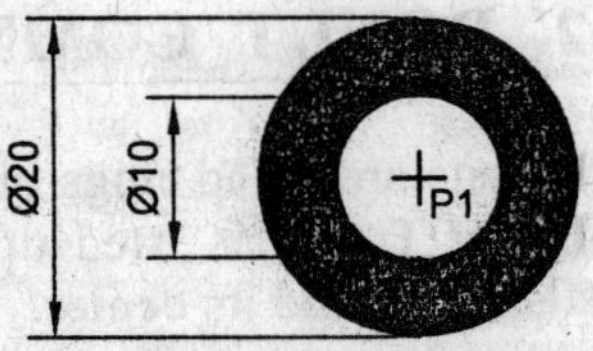

FIG. 11

See Fig. 11.

Problem 11: *Draw a donut with inside diameter 0 mm and outside diameter 20 mm with the fillmode on.*

The command sequence to draw a donut of inside diameter 0 and outside diameter 20 mm with the fill mode ON is as follows:

```
Command: FILL ↵
Enter mode [ON/OFF] <OFF>: ON ↵
Command: DONUT ↵
Specify inside diameter of donut <0.5000>: 0 ↵
Specify outside diameter of donut <1.0000>: 20 ↵
Specify center of donut or <exit>: (Pick P1)
Specify center of donut or <exit>: ↵
```

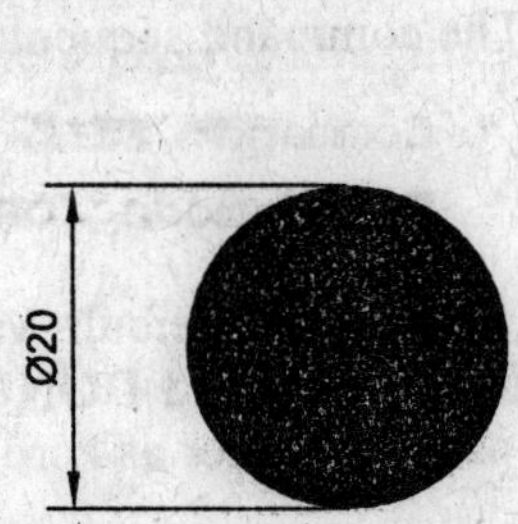

FIG. 12

See Fig. 12.

3. POINT COMMAND

A Point is one of the basic drawing objects and is specified as a dot (a period). A Point is defined as a geometric object that has no dimension and properties, except the location. A Point is drawn using the **Point** tool.

For this, invoke the **Point** tool, choose **Multiple Point** tool from the **Draw** panel by clicking it. A **Point** tool can also be invoked by choosing **Point** from the **Draw** menu or **Draw** toolbar. Another method to invoke the **Point** tool is type **POINT** in the Command prompt and press **Enter**. AutoCAD prompts to specify the location for the point. The location can be specified either by pointing device (Mouse) or by typing the co-ordinate values in the command prompt.

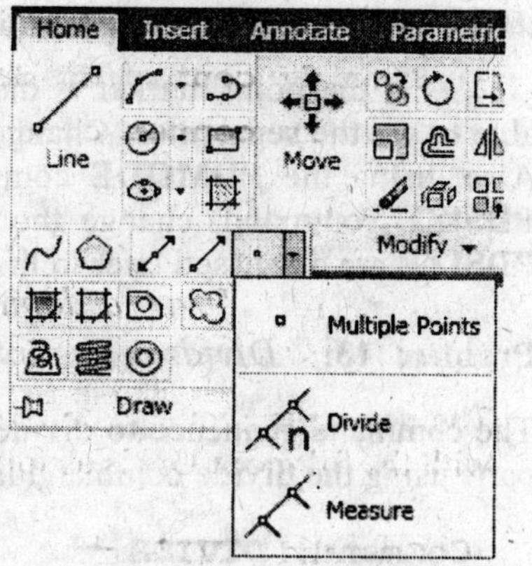

FIG. 13

AutoCAD provides various methods to place a point on the drawing area. Also, AutoCAD provides options to control the size and appearance of a point. The methods to place a point are grouped together in the **Draw** panel. **See Fig. 13.**

3.1 MULTIPLE POINTS

To draw/place multiples points in the drawing area, choose the **Multiple Points** tool from the **Draw** panel. AutoCAD prompts to specify a location to place the point. Specify the location by left-clicking or by entering the coordinates. Again, AutoCAD prompts to specify a location. Specify the location. In this manner, place as many points as needed. Press ESC to exit the command.

Problem 12: *Draw a point on the location 80,60 using the Point command.*

The prompt sequence to place a point on the location 80,60 is as follows:

```
Command: POINT ↵
Current point modes:
        PDMODE=0  PDSIZE=0.0000
Specify a point: 80,60 ↵
```

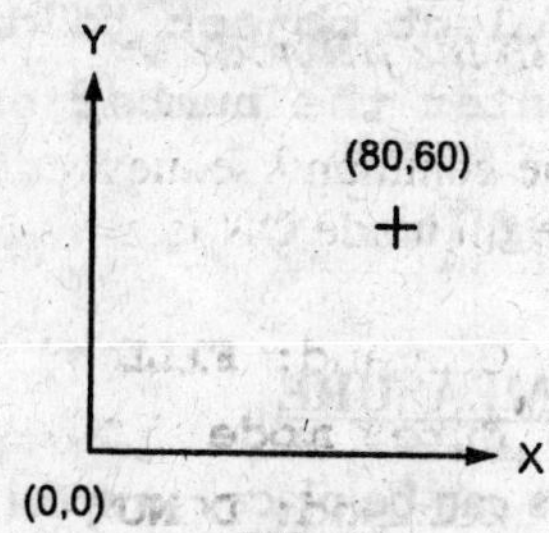

FIG. 14

See Fig. 14.

3.2 DIVIDE

Sometimes we may need to place points at an equal distance on an object. For this, choose the **Divide** tool from the **Draw** panel. AutoCAD prompts to select an object. Select an object. Now, AutoCAD prompts to specify the number of segments. Enter the number of segments. The specified numbers of points are placed on the selected object.

Note : The dividing operation does **not** actually break an object into individual objects; it only identifies the location of the divisions so that we can use them as geometric reference points.

The starting point for measurements or divisions varies with the object type. For lines or open polylines, the starting point is the endpoint closest to the selection point. For closed polylines, it is the polyline start point. For circles, it is at the angle from the center point that is equivalent to the current snap angle. For example, if the snap angle is 0, the circle starts at the three o'clock position and continues counterclockwise.

If the point marker is displayed as a single dot (the default setting), then it may not be able to see the segments. Change the style of the point markers using the **Point Style** dialog box. Also, using the **PDMODE** command, change the appearance of point markers and using the **PDSIZE** command, change the size of point. The **Point Style** dialog box, **PDMODE** and **PDSIZE** are discussed later in this chapter.

Problem 13: *Divide a line into 5 equal number of parts.*

The command sequence to divide a line into 5 equal parts using the divide command is as follows:

```
Command: DIVIDE ↵
Select object to divide: (Select the line)
Enter the number of segments or [Block]: 5 ↵
```

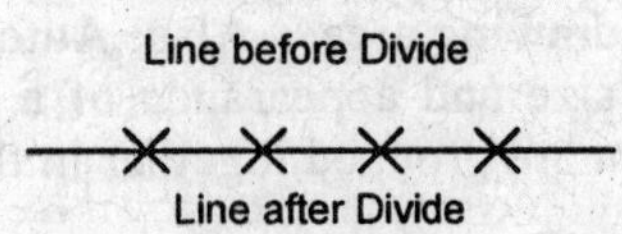

FIG. 15

See Fig. 15

Problem 14: *Divide an ellipse into 12 equal number of parts.*

The command sequence to divide an ellipse into 12 equal parts using the divide command is as follows:

```
Command: DIVIDE ↵
Select object to divide: (Select the ellipse)
Enter the number of segments or [Block]: 12 ↵
```

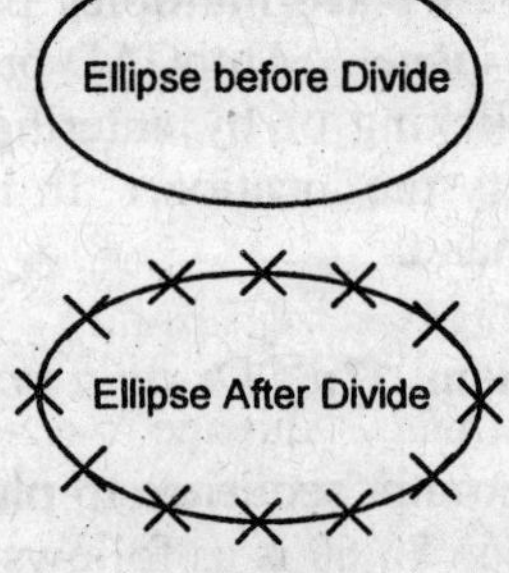

FIG. 16

See Fig. 16

3.3 MEASURE

Points can be placed at specified intervals on an object by selecting the object and specifying the length of the segment between two points. For this, choose the **Measure** tool from the **Draw** panel. AutoCAD prompts to select an object to measure. Select the object you needs to measure. Then, AutoCAD prompts to specify the length of the segment. Specify the length of the segment. Points are placed at the specified intervals.

The **MEASURE** command places point objects or blocks at measured intervals on an object. The points or blocks drawn by **MEASURE** are placed in the **Previous** selection set. For this, choose them all by entering **p** at the next **Select Objects** prompt. We can use the **Node** object snap to draw an object by snapping to the point objects. We can then remove the points by entering **erase previous.**

The last segment of a measured object may be shorter than the interval specified. The starting point for measurements or divisions varies with the object type. For lines or open polylines, the starting point is the endpoint closest to the selection point. For closed polylines, it is the polyline start point. For circles, it is at the angle from the center point that is equivalent to the current snap angle. For example, if the snap angle is 0, the circle starts at the three o'clock position and continues counterclockwise.

The markers are placed in the user coordinate system (UCS) of the object being measured (except for 3D polylines in the current UCS). Markers are always placed on the object, regardless of the elevation settings.

If the point objects are used for the markers, we can make the points easier to see by changing their appearance using the PDMODE system variable. Discussed later.

Problem 15: *Measure a line with 7 mm equal intervals.*

The command sequence to place points on a line in 7 mm equal intervals using the measure command is as follows:

Command: **MEASURE ↵**
Select object to measure: *(Select the line)*
Specify length of segment or [Block]: 7 ↵

See Fig. 17

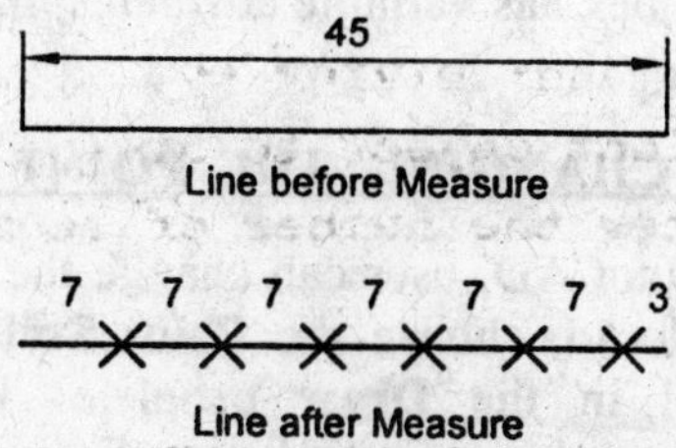

FIG. 17

Problem 16: *Measure a circle with 8 mm equal intervals.*

The command sequence to place points on a circle in 8 mm equal intervals using the measure command is as follows:

Command: **MEASURE ↵**
Select object to measure: *(Select the circle)*
Specify length of segment or [Block]: 8 ↵

See Fig. 18

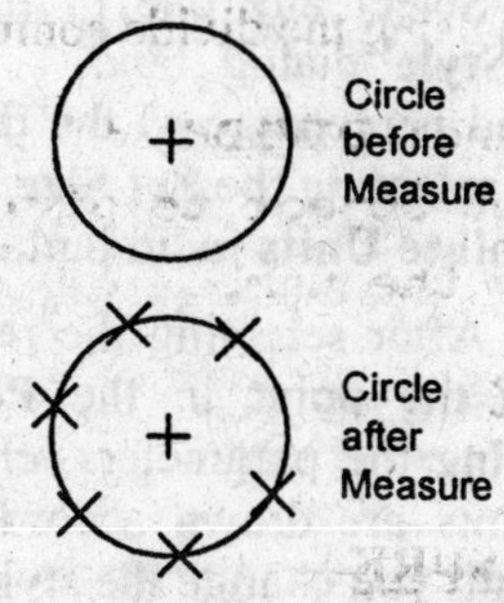

FIG. 18

Options in the Measure Command

Length of Segment: The Length of Segment option places point objects at the specified interval along the selected object, starting at the endpoint closest to the point user used to select the object. Measurement of closed polylines starts at their initial vertex (the first one drawn).

Measurement of circles starts at the angle from the center set as the current snap rotation angle. If the snap rotation angle is 0, then the measurement of the circle starts to the right of center, on its circumference.

Block: The Block option places blocks at a specified interval along the selected object. The prompt is:

`Enter name of block to insert:` *Enter the name of a block currently defined in the drawing*

`Align block with object? [Yes/No] <Y>:` *Enter* **y** *or* **n** *or press* ENTER

If **y** is entered, the block is rotated about its insertion point so that its horizontal lines are aligned with, and drawn tangent to, the object being measured. If **n** is entered, the block is always inserted with a 0 rotation angle.

`Specify length of segment:`

After the segment length is specified, the block is inserted at the specified interval. If the block has variable attributes, these attributes are not included.

3.4 CHANGING THE POINT STYLE AND SIZE

In AutoCAD, user can change the style and size of a point. To do so, choose the **Point Style** tool from the **Utilities** panel in the **Draw** panel or type **DDPTYPE** in the Command prompt and press Enter. The **Point Style** dialog box is displayed on the screen as shown in **Fig. 19.**

Select any one of the twenty point styles in the **Point Style** dialog box. Specify the point size as a specified percentage of the drawing area or as an absolute size by selecting the **Set Size Relative to Screen** or **Set size in Absolute Units** radio button respectively.

After selecting the required radio button, enter the size of the point in the **Point Size** edit box. After specifying the parameters, choose the **OK** button. Now, the points are drawn according to the selected style and size, until you change the style and size.

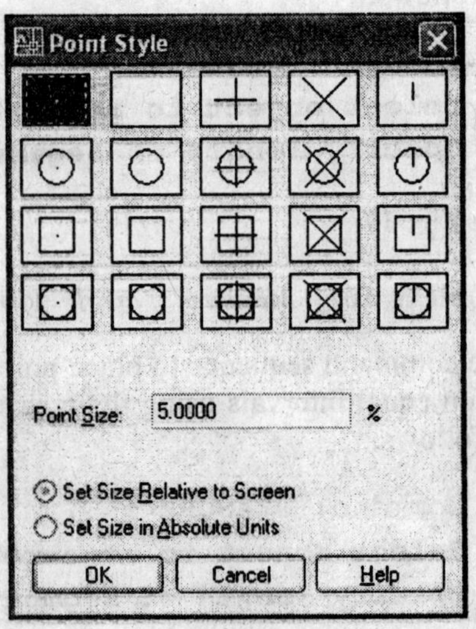

FIG. 19

The point style can be changed using the **PDMODE** system variable. Similarly, the point size can be changed using the **PDSIZE** system variable. The different values of **PDMODE** and the resulting style are shown in Table 1.

PDMODE

The point style can be changed using the **PDMODE** system variable. **PDMODE** values 0, 2, 3, and 4 specify a figure to draw through the point. A value of 1 specifies that nothing is displayed. **PDMODE** values and their symbols are shown in Table 1.

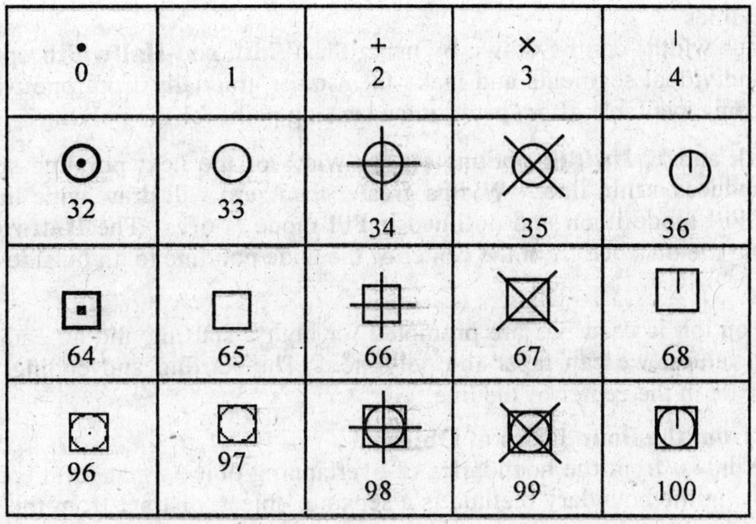

Table 1

Specifying the value 32, 64, or 96 selects a shape to draw around the point, in addition to the figure drawn through it.

PDSIZE

The point display size is changed using the PDSIZE system variable. PDSIZE controls the size of the point figures, except for PDMODE values 0 and 1. A setting of 0 generates the point at 5 percent of the drawing area height. A positive PDSIZE value specifies an absolute size for the point figures. A negative value is interpreted as a percentage of the viewport size. The size of all points is recalculated when the drawing is regenerated.

After changing PDMODE and PDSIZE, the appearance of existing points changes the next time the drawing is regenerated.

4. PLINE COMMAND

A **Polyline** is a connected sequence of line segments created as a single object. We can draw straight line segments, arc segments or a combination of the two. **PLINE** command draws two-dimensional polylines.

Multi-segmented lines provide editing capabilities unavailable for single lines. For example, we can adjust their width and curvature. After a polyline is drawn, we can edit it with **PEDIT** commands. Using the **EXPLODE** command a polyline can be converted into individual line and arc segments. Using the polyline, the following operations can be executed:

- Converting a spline-fit polyline into a true spline with **SPLINE** is possible.
- Using closed polylines, a polygon can be drawn.
- It is possible to draw a polyline from the boundaries of overlapping objects.

Create Wide Polylines

Polylines of various widths can be drawn by using the **Width** and **Halfwidth** options. We can set the width of individual segments and make them taper gradually from one width to another. These options become available after specifying a starting point for the polyline.

The **Width** and **Halfwidth** options set the width of the next polyline segments drawn. Zero (0) width produces a thin line. Widths greater than zero will draw wide lines. The wide lines are filled if Fill mode is on and outlined if **Fill** mode is off. The **Halfwidth** option sets width by specifying the distance from the center of the wide polyline to an outside edge.

Taper

When the **Width** option is used, we are prompted for both a starting and an ending width. By entering different values, we can taper the polyline. The starting and ending points of wide polyline segments are in the center of the line.

Create Polylines from the Boundaries of Objects

A polyline can be drawn from the boundaries of overlapping objects that form a closed area. A polyline created using the boundary method is a separate object, distinct from the objects used to create it. Edit it using the same methods used to edit other polylines.

To expedite the boundary selection process in large or complex drawings, specify a group of boundary candidates, called a **Boundary Set**. This set is created by selecting the objects we want to use define the boundary.

The **PLINEGEN** system variable controls the linetype pattern display around and the smoothness of the vertices of a 2D polyline. Setting **PLINEGEN** to 1 generates new polylines in a continuous pattern around the vertices of the completed polyline. Setting **PLINEGEN** to 0 starts and ends the polyline with a dash at each vertex. **PLINEGEN** does not apply to polylines with tapered segments.

PLINE command is activated by any one of the following methods:

1. Type **PLINE** or **PL** in the command prompt.
2. Choose the **Polyline** tool from the **Draw** panel of the **Home** tab. **See Fig. 20.**
3. Choose the **Polyline** from the **Draw** menu.

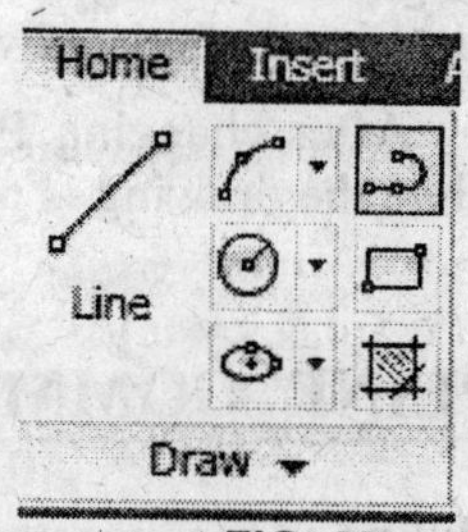

FIG. 20

To draw a polyline, invoke the **Polyline** tool using any one of the above methods. AutoCAD prompts to specify the start point. Specify the start point by left-clicking or entering coordinates. Now, AutoCAD prompts to specify the next point. You can continue specifying next point and draw a polyline depending on your requirements. Also, you can invoke the other options.

The **PLINE** command functions basically like the **LINE** command, except that some additional options are provided.

Problem 17: *Draw a rectangle of 50 mm side using the PLINE command.*

The command sequence to draw a rectangle of 50 mm side using the PLINE command is as follows:

```
Command: PLINE ↵
Specify start point: (Pick P1)
Current line-width is 0.0000
Specify next point or [Arc/Halfwidth/
          Length/Undo/Width]: @50<0 ↵
Specify next point or [Arc/Close/
          Halfwidth/Length/Undo/Width]:
>>Enter new value for ORTHOMODE <0>:
Resuming PLINE command.
Specify next point or [Arc/Close/Halfwidth/Length/Undo/Width]: @50<90 ↵
Specify next point or [Arc/Close/Halfwidth/Length/Undo/Width]: @50<180 ↵
Specify next point or [Arc/Close/Halfwidth/Length/Undo/Width]: C ↵
```

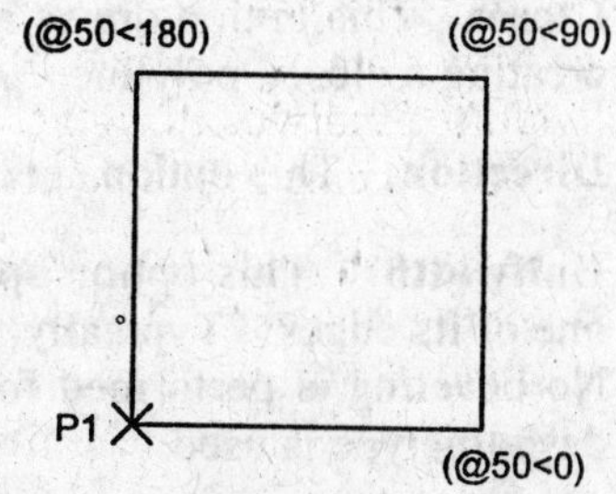

FIG. 21

See Fig. 21. The next point option draws a line segment to the specified point.

The options in the PLINE command are: Arc, Close, Halfwidth, Length, Undo and Width. These options are explained next.

4.1 ARC OPTION

When an arc segment in a polyline is drawn, the first point of the arc is the endpoint of the previous segment. We can specify the angle, center point, direction or radius of the arc. Also the arc can be completed by specifying a second point and an endpoint.

The **arc** option adds arc segments to the polyline. The prompt and options of the **arc** option is as follows:

Specify endpoint of arc or [Angle/CEnter/CLose/Direction/Halfwidth/ Line/Radius/Second pt/Undo/Width] : ***Specify a point or enter an option***

When **Endpoint of Arc** is specified, AutoCAD draws an arc segment with the specified end point. The arc segment is tangent to the previous segment of the polyline. The previous prompt is repeated.

Options in the Arc Option of the PLINE Command

1. **Angle:** The **Angle** option is used to specify the included angle of the arc segment from the start point. When a positive number is entered, AutoCAD draws counterclockwise arc segments. When a negative number is entered, AutoCAD draws clockwise arc segments. After entering an angle, AutoCAD prompts the user to specify endpoint/center/radius of the arc.

2. **Center:** Using this option, the center of the arc segment can be specified.

3. **Close:** This option draws an arc segment from the last point specified to the starting point, creating a closed polyline. At least two points must be specified to use this option.

4. **Direction:** This option specifies a starting direction for the arc segment.

5. **Halfwidth:** This option specifies the width from the center of a wide polyline segment to one of its edges. Typically, the intersections of adjacent wide polyline segments are beveled. No beveling is performed for non-tangent arc segments or very acute angles or when a dot-dash linetype is used.

6. **Line:** **Line** option exits the **Arc** option and returns to the initial **PLINE** command prompts.

7. **Radius:** The **Radius** option specifies the radius of the arc segment.

8. **Second Pt:** This option specifies the second point and endpoint of a three-point arc.

9. **Undo:** The **Undo** option removes the most recent arc segment added to the polyline.

10. **Width:** The **Width** option specifies the width of the next arc segment.

The command sequence to draw a diagram as shown in **Fig. 22** is as follows:

FIG. 22

```
Command: PLINE ↵
Specify start point: (Pick P1)
Current line-width is 0.0000
Specify next point or [Arc/Halfwidth/
        Length/Undo/Width]:  @20<0 ↵
Specify next point or [Arc/Close/Halfwidth/Length/Undo/Width]:A ↵
Specify endpoint of arc or  [Angle/CEnter/CLose/Direction/
     Halfwidth/Line/Radius/Second pt/Undo/Width]:  W ↵
Specify starting width <0.0000>: 0 ↵
Specify ending width <0.0000>: 2 ↵
Specify endpoint of arc or  [Angle/CEnter/CLose/Direction/
     Halfwidth/Line/Radius/Second pt/Undo/Width]:  @10<90 ↵
Specify endpoint of arc or [Angle/CEnter/CLose/Direction/
     Halfwidth/Line/Radius/Second pt/Undo/Width]: W ↵
Specify starting width <2.0000>: 2 ↵
Specify ending width <2.0000>: 0 ↵
Specify endpoint of arc or [Angle/CEnter/CLose/Direction/
     Halfwidth/Line/Radius/Second pt/Undo/Width]: @10<270 ↵
Specify endpoint of arc or [Angle/CEnter/CLose/Direction/
     Halfwidth/Line/Radius/Second pt/Undo/Width]: L ↵
Specify next point or [Arc/Close/Halfwidth/Length/Undo/Width]: @20<0 ↵
Specify next point or [Arc/Close/Halfwidth/Length/Undo/Width]: ↵
```

4.2 CLOSE OPTION

We can draw a closed polyline to create a polygon. The **Close** option in the **PLINE** command draws a line segment from the last point specified to the starting point, creating a closed polyline. At least two points must be specified to use this option. To close a polyline, specify the starting point of the last side of the object, enter **c** (Close), and press **Enter**.

4.3 HALFWIDTH OPTION

The **Halfwidth** option in the **PLINE** command specifies the width from the center of a wide polyline line segment to one of its edges. The prompt is:

Specify starting half-width <*current*>: *Enter a value or press* ENTER
Specify ending half-width <*current*>: *Enter a value or press* ENTER

The ***starting half-width*** becomes the default ending half-width. The ***ending half-width*** becomes the uniform half-width for all subsequent segments until the half-width is changed again. The starting and ending points of wide line segments are at the center of the line. Typically, the intersections of adjacent wide polyline segments are beveled. No beveling is performed for non-tangent arc segments or very acute angles or when a dot-dash linetype is used.

4.4 LENGTH OPTION

The **Length** option in the **PLINE** command draws a line segment of a specified length at the same angle as the previous segment. If the previous segment is an arc, the new line segment is drawn tangent to that arc segment. The prompt is:

Specify length of line: *Specify a distance*

4.5 UNDO OPTION

The **Undo** option removes the most recent line segment added to the polyline.

4.6 WIDTH OPTION

The **Width** option in the **PLINE** command specifies the width of the next line segment.

Specify starting width <*current*>: *Enter a value or press* ENTER
Specify ending width <*starting width*>: *Enter a value or press* ENTER

The ***starting width*** becomes the default ending width. The ***ending width*** becomes the uniform width for all subsequent segments until the width is changed again. The starting and ending points of wide line segments are at the center of the line.

Typically, the intersections of adjacent wide polyline segments are beveled. No beveling is performed for non-tangent arc segments or very acute angles or when a dot-dash linetype is used.

Problem 18: *Draw the diagram as shown in Fig. 23 using the PLINE command.*

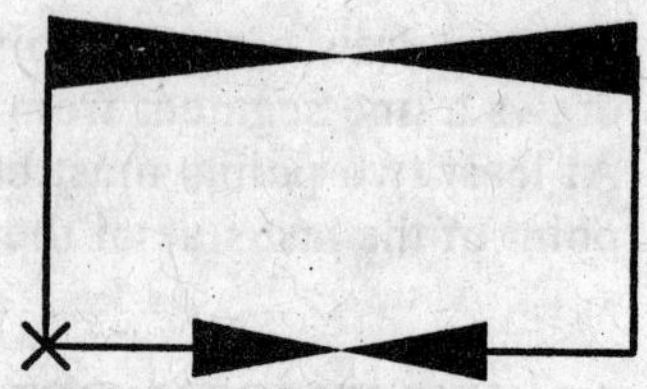

P1

FIG. 23

The command sequence to draw the **Fig. 23** using the PLINE command is as follows:

```
Command: PLINE ↵
Specify start point: (Pick P1)
Current line-width is 0.0000
Specify next point or [Arc/Halfwidth/Length/Undo/Width]: @10<0 ↵
Specify next point or [Arc/Close/Halfwidth/Length/Undo/Width]: W ↵
Specify starting width <0.0000>: 4 ↵
Specify ending width <4.0000>: 0 ↵
Specify next point or [Arc/Close/Halfwidth/Length/Undo/Width]: @10<0 ↵
Specify next point or [Arc/Close/Halfwidth/Length/Undo/Width]: W ↵
Specify starting width <0.0000>: 0 ↵
Specify ending width <0.0000>: 4 ↵
Specify next point or [Arc/Close/Halfwidth/Length/Undo/Width]: @10<0 ↵
Specify next point or [Arc/Close/Halfwidth/Length/Undo/Width]: W ↵
Specify starting width <4.0000>: 0 ↵
Specify ending width <0.0000>: 0 ↵
Specify next point or [Arc/Close/Halfwidth/Length/Undo/Width]: @10<0 ↵
Specify next point or [Arc/Close/Halfwidth/Length/Undo/Width]: @20<90 ↵
Specify next point or [Arc/Close/Halfwidth/Length/Undo/Width]: W ↵
Specify starting width <0.0000>: 5 ↵
Specify ending width <5.0000>: 0 ↵
Specify next point or [Arc/Close/Halfwidth/Length/Undo/Width]: @20<180 ↵
Specify next point or [Arc/Close/Halfwidth/Length/Undo/Width]: W ↵
Specify starting width <0.0000>: 0 ↵
Specify ending width <0.0000>: 5 ↵
Specify next point or [Arc/Close/Halfwidth/Length/Undo/Width]: @20<180 ↵
Specify next point or [Arc/Close/Halfwidth/Length/Undo/Width]: W ↵
Specify starting width <5.0000>: 0 ↵
Specify ending width <0.0000>: 0 ↵
Specify next point or [Arc/Close/Halfwidth/Length/Undo/Width]: C ↵
```

Problem 19: *Draw the diagram as shown in Fig. 24, using the Polyline tool.*

The command sequence to draw the **Fig. 24** using the PLINE command is as follows:

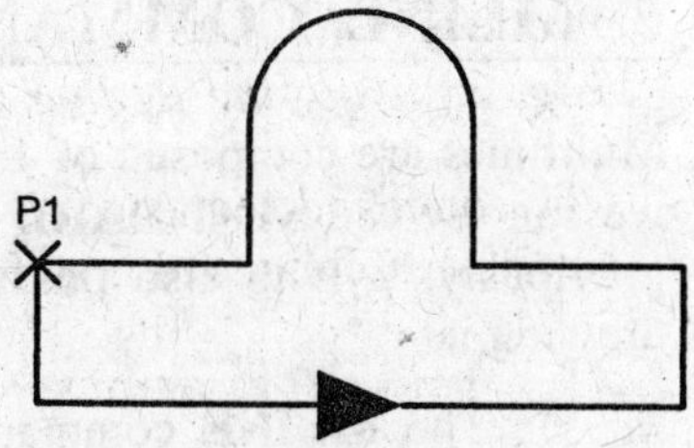

FIG. 24

```
Command: PLINE ↵
Specify start point: (Pick P1)
Current line-width is 0.0000
Specify next point or [Arc/Halfwidth/
   Length/Undo/Width]:
   (Move cursor to right) 15 ↵
Specify next point or [Arc/Close/
   Halfwidth/Length/Undo/Width]:
   (Move cursor to up) 10 ↵
Specify next point or [Arc/Close/Halfwidth/Length/Undo/Width]: A ↵
Specify endpoint of arc or [Angle/CEnter/CLose/Direction/
   Halfwidth/Line/Radius/Second pt/Undo/Width]:
   (Move cursor to right) 16 ↵
Specify endpoint of arc or [Angle/CEnter/CLose/Direction/
   Halfwidth/Line/Radius/Second pt/Undo/Width]: L ↵
Specify next point or [Arc/Close/Halfwidth/Length/
   Undo/Width]: (Move cursor to down) 10 ↵
Specify next point or [Arc/Close/Halfwidth/Length/
   Undo/Width]: (Move cursor to right) 15 ↵
Specify next point or [Arc/Close/Halfwidth/Length/
   Undo/Width]: (Move cursor to down) 10 ↵
Specify next point or [Arc/Close/Halfwidth/Length/
   Undo/Width]: (Move cursor to left) 20 ↵
Specify next point or [Arc/Close/Halfwidth/Length/Undo/Width]: W ↵
Specify starting width <0.0000>: 0 ↵
Specify ending width <0.0000>: 5 ↵
Specify next point or [Arc/Close/Halfwidth/Length/
         Undo/Width]: (Move cursor to left) 6 ↵
Specify next point or [Arc/Close/Halfwidth/Length/Undo/Width]: W ↵
Specify starting width <5.0000>: 0 ↵
Specify ending width <0.0000>: 0 ↵
Specify next point or [Arc/Close/Halfwidth/Length/
         Undo/Width]: (Move cursor to left) 20 ↵
Specify next point or [Arc/Close/Halfwidth/Length/Undo/Width]: C ↵
```

5. MLINE COMMAND

Multilines are composed of 1 to 16 parallel lines, called **Elements**. While drawing a multiline, we can use the **STANDARD** style, which has two elements or specify a style that have created previously. It is also possible to change the justification and scale of the multiline before drawing it.

The **MLINE** command draws multiple parallel lines. The **MLINE** command can be invoked by any one of the following methods:

1. Type **MLINE** or **ML** at the command prompt and press Enter.
2. Click the **Multiline** tool from the **Draw** menu.

If the **MLINE** command in invoked, then AutoCAD prompts to specify the start point. Specify the start point by left-clicking or entering coordinates. Now, AutoCAD prompts to specify the next point. Specify the next point. In this way, you can draw any number of lines as you required.

Problem 20: *Draw a multiline using the MLINE command.*

The command sequence to draw a multiline using the MLINE command is as follows:

```
Command: MLINE ↵
Current settings: Justification = Top,
Scale = 2.00, Style = STANDARD
Specify start point or [Justification/Scale/STyle]:  S ↵
Enter mline scale <2.00>:  5 ↵
Current settings: Justification = Top,
           Scale = 5.00, Style = STANDARD
Specify start point or [Justification/Scale/STyle]: (Pick P1)
Specify next point:  (Move cursor to right) 25 ↵
Specify next point or [Undo]:   (Move cursor to bottom) 20 ↵
Specify next point or [Close/Undo]:  (Move cursor to right) 20 ↵
Specify next point or [Close/Undo]:  (Move cursor to up) 20 ↵
Specify next point or [Close/Undo]:
           (Move cursor to right) 25 ↵
Specify next point or [Close/Undo]:
           (Move cursor to up) 20 ↵
Specify next point or [Close/Undo]:
           (Move cursor to left) 70 ↵
Specify next point or [Close/Undo]:  C ↵
```

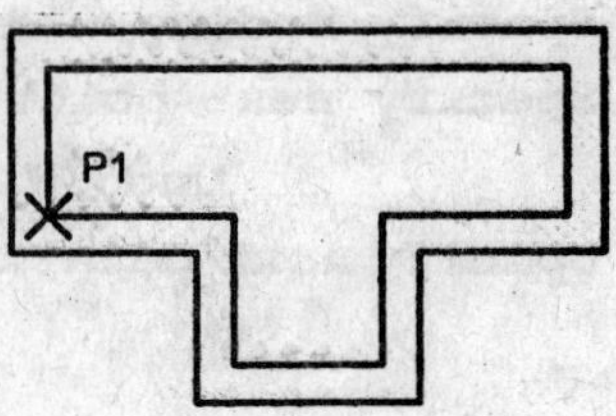

FIG. 25

See Fig. 25.

Options in the MLINE Command

1. **Start Point:** The **Start Point** specifies the next vertex of the multiline. If a multiline is created with two or more segments, the prompt includes the Close option. The **Next Point** option draws a multiline segment to the specified point using the current multiline style and continues to prompt for points. The **Undo** option undoes the last vertex point on the multiline. The previous prompt is displayed. The **Close** option closes the multiline by joining the last segments with the first segments.

2. **Justification:** Multiline **Justification** determines which side of the cursor that the multiline is drawn or whether it is centered on the cursor. In other words, *justification* option determines how the multiline is drawn between the points specified. The prompt is:

   `Enter justification type [Top/Zero/Bottom] <current>:`
   Enter an option or press ENTER

   The **Top** option draws the multiline below the cursor, so that the line with the most positive offset is at the specified points. The **Zero** option draws the multiline with its origin centered at the cursor, so that the **MLSTYLE** Element Properties offset of 0.0 is at the specified points. The **Bottom** option draws the multiline above the cursor, so that the line with the most negative offset is at the specified points.

3. **Scale:** Multiline **Scale** controls the overall width of the multiline using the current units. Multiline scale does not affect linetype scale. If the multiline scale is changed, we need to make equivalent changes to the linetype scale to prevent dots or dashes from being disproportionately sized.

4. **Style:** It is also possible to create named styles for multilines to control the number of elements and the properties of each element. We can add up to 16 elements to a multiline style. Elements with a positive offset appear on one side of the middle of the multiline; elements with a negative offset appear on the other side of the middle of the multiline. Using the Style option, we can specify a style to use for the multiline.

6. SPLINE COMMAND

A **spline** is a smooth curve that passes through or near a given set of points. We can control how closely the curve fits the points.

The **SPLINE** command draws a smooth curve to a sequence of points within a specified tolerance. It creates a particular type of spline known as a **Non-Uniform Rational B-spline** (NURBS) curve. A NURBS curve produces a smooth curve between control points. We can close the spline so that the start and endpoints are coincident and tangent.

Tolerance describes how closely the spline fits the set of fit points we specify. The lower the tolerance, the more closely the spline fits the points. At zero tolerance, the spline passes through the points. We can change the spline-fitting tolerance while drawing the spline to see the effect.

The following two methods are used for creating splines:

- Spline curves are drawn using the **Spline** option of **PEDIT** to smooth existing polylines created with **PLINE**. Such spline-fit polylines are created with uniform knot vectors and are more likely to be included in drawings created with earlier versions of the product.
- Splines are drawn using the **SPLINE** command. Drawings containing splines use less memory and disk space than those containing spline-fit polylines of similar shape.

It is also possible to convert spline-fit polylines into true splines with **SPLINE**. The **SPLINE** command can be activated by any one of the following methods:

1. Enter **SPLINE** or **SPL** in the command prompt and then press Enter.
2. Choose **Spline** tool from the **Draw** panel of the **Home**
3. Choose **Spline** tool from the **Draw** menu

Problem 21: *Draw a smooth curve as shown in Fig. 26.*

The command sequence to draw a spline using the **SPLINE** command is as follows:

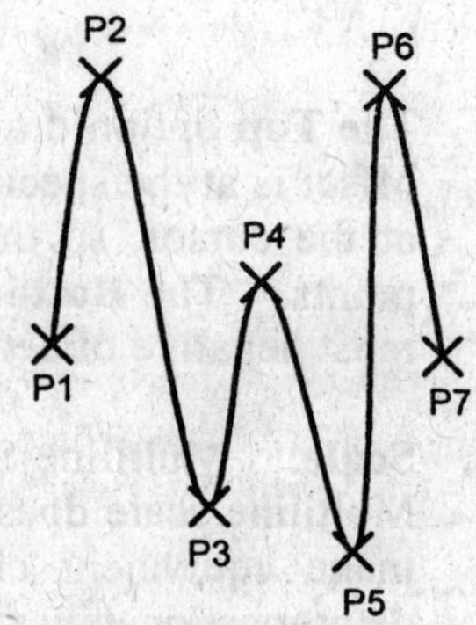

FIG. 26

```
Command: SPLINE ↵
Specify first point or [Object]: (Pick P1)
Specify next point: (Pick P2)
Specify next point or [Close/Fit tolerance]
              <start tangent>: (Pick P3)
Specify next point or [Close/Fit tolerance]
              <start tangent>: (Pick P4)
Specify next point or [Close/Fit tolerance] <start tangent>: (Pick P5)
Specify next point or [Close/Fit tolerance] <start tangent>: (Pick P6)
Specify next point or [Close/Fit tolerance] <start tangent>: (Pick P7)
Specify next point or [Close/Fit tolerance] <start tangent>: ↵
```

See Fig. 26.

Options in the SPLINE

1. **First Point:** It creates a spline using points specified, using **NURBS** (Non-Uniform Rational B-splines) mathematics.

2. **Object:** This option allow the user to convert 2D or 3D quadratic or cubic spline-fit polylines to equivalent splines and deletes the polylines.

3. **Next Point:** Continuing to enter points adds additional spline curve segments until **Enter** key pressed. Enter **undo** to remove the last point specified. Once **Enter** is pressed, we are prompted to specify the start tangent for the spline curve.

4. **Close:** This option closes the spline curve by defining the last point as co-incident with the first and making it tangent to the joint.

When the **Close** option is selected while drawing the spline as shown in Fig. 26, the command sequence for the last step instead of pressing Enter is:

```
Specify next point or [Close/
  Fit tolerance] <start tangent>: C ↵
Specify tangent: Specify a point or press ENTER
```

See Fig. 27.

Specify a point to define the tangent vector or use the **Tangent** and **Perpendicular** object snap modes to make the spline tangent or perpendicular to existing objects.

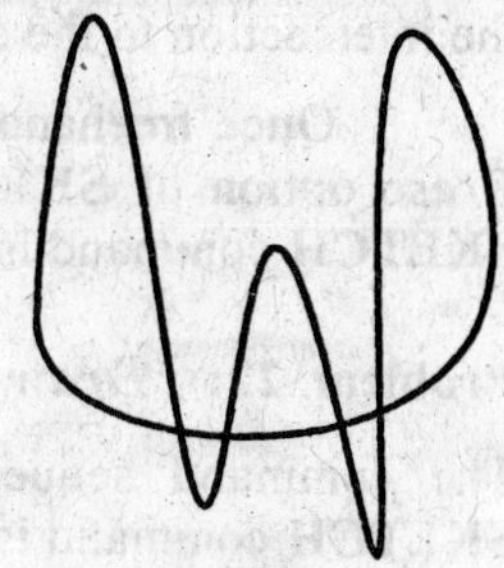

FIG. 27

5. **Fit Tolerance:** This option changes the tolerance for fitting of the current spline curve. The spline curve is redefined so that it fits through the existing points according to the new tolerance. We can repeatedly change the fit tolerance, but doing so changes the fit tolerance for all the control points regardless of the control point that is selected.

If the tolerance is set to 0, the spline curve passes through the fit points. If a tolerance greater than 0 is enters, then the spline curve to pass through the fit points within the specified tolerance. **SPLINE** returns to the previous prompt.

6. **Start Tangent:** This option defines the tangency for the first and last points of the spline curve. If tangency at both endpoints of the spline is specified, we can enter a point o **Tangent** and **Perpendicular** object snap modes to make the spline tangent or perpe to existing objects. Press **Enter** to calculate default tangents.

7. SKETCH COMMAND

Sketching is useful for creating irregular boundaries or for tracing with a digitizer. The **SKETCH** command is used to draw a series of freehand line segments. Sketching is useful for creating irregular boundaries or for tracing with a digitizer.

Create Sketches

To sketch, use the pointing device like a pen, clicking to put the *pen* down on the screen to draw and clicking again to lift it up and stop drawing. Freehand sketches comprise many line segments. Each line segment can be a separate object or a polyline. Set the minimum length or increment of the segments. Small line segments allow for greater accuracy, but they can greatly increase the drawing file size. For this reason, use this tool sparingly.

Before sketching, check the **CELTYPE** system variable to make sure the current linetype is **BYLAYER**. If we use a linetype with dots or dashes and set the sketch line segment shorter than the spaces or dashes, user won't see the spaces or dashes.

Erase Freehand Lines: Erase freehand lines by using the Erase option of the **SKETCH** command. In the Erase mode, wherever the cursor intersects the freehand line, everything from the intersection to the end of the line is erased.

Once freehand lines are recorded, it is not possible to edit them or erase them with the Erase option of **SKETCH**. Use the **ERASE** command after sketching is finished. The **SKETCH** command is invoked by typing **SKETCH** at the command prompt.

Problem 22: *Draw the Fig. 28 using freehand lines.*

The command sequence to draw freehand lines using the **SKETCH** command is:

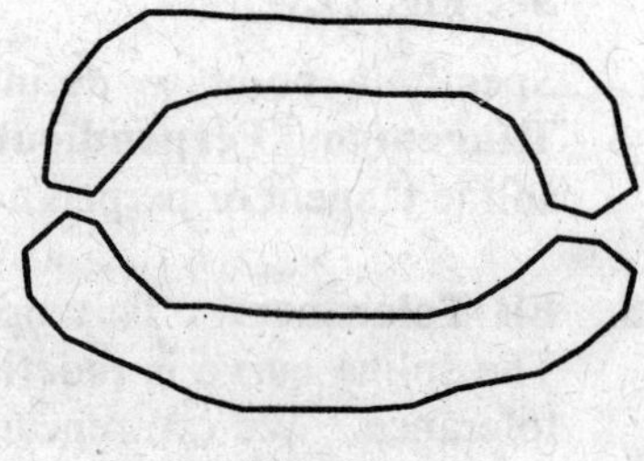

FIG. 28

Command: **SKETCH** ↵
Record increment <2.0000>: 3 ↵
Sketch. Pen eXit Quit Record Erase Connect.
(Click on the start point) **<Pen down>**
(Move the mouse and click at the end point) **<Pen up>**
(Click on the next start point) **<Pen down>**
(Move the mouse and click at the end point) **<Pen up>**
(Press X or Press ENTER to exit from sketching)
2 polylines with 56 edges recorded.

See Fig. 28. The record increment value defines the length of the line segments. The pointing device must be moved a distance greater than the increment value to generate a line.

After specifying the increment value, start sketching by clicking the mouse at the start point to make the pen *down* and move the mouse to the required positions. After finishing the particular segment of sketching, click the mouse at the end point to lift the pen *up*.

Sketching is captured as a series of independent lines. Setting the **SKPOLY** system variable to a nonzero value produces a polyline for each contiguous sequence of sketched lines rather than multiple line objects. The prompt is:

Sketch. Pen eXit Quit Record Erase Connect . *Enter an option or press a pointer button*

Options in the Sketch

1. **Pen (Pick Button):** This option raises and lowers the sketching pen. The pen must be raised before you can select menu items with the pointing device.

2. **Exit – ENTER (button 3):** This option records and reports the number of temporary lines sketched and ends the command.

3. **Quit (button 4):** This option discards all temporary lines sketched since the start of **SKETCH** or the last use of the **Record** option and ends the command.

4. **Record (button 2):** This option records temporary lines as permanent and does not change the pen's position. Reports the number of lines using the following prompt:

   nnn lines recorded.

5. **Erase (button 5):** This option erases any portion of a temporary line and raises the pen if it is down.

6. **Connect (button 6):** This option lowers the pen to continue a sketch sequence from the endpoint of the last sketched line or last Erase.

7. **(Period) (button 1):** This option lowers the pen, draws a straight line from the endpoint of the last sketched line to the pen's current location and returns the pen to the up position.

8. TRACE COMMAND

Traces are solid **filled** when Fill mode is **on.** When **Fill** mode is **off,** only the **outline** of a trace is displayed. The fill mode is controlled by **FILLMODE** system variable.

Fill mode is **on** when the value of **FILLMODE** is set to **1**. Fill mode is **off** when the value of **FILLMODE** is set to **0**. To display the changes, use **REGEN** system variable or click **View** menu and select Regen.

The **TRACE** command draws solid lines with specified width. To invoke the **Trace** command, type **TRACE** in the command prompt and press **Enter**.

Problem 23: *Draw the solid lines using the Trace command with the Fill mode is on.*
The command sequence to draw solid lines with the Fill mode is **on** using the **Trace** command is as follows:

```
Command: FILLMODE ↵
Enter new value for FILLMODE <0>: 1 ↵
Command: TRACE ↵
Specify trace width <2.0000>: 3 ↵
Specify start point: (Pick P1)
Specify next point: (Move the cursor to right) 25↵
Specify next point: (Move the cursor to up) 25↵
Specify next point: (Move the cursor to right) 25↵
Specify next point: ↵
```

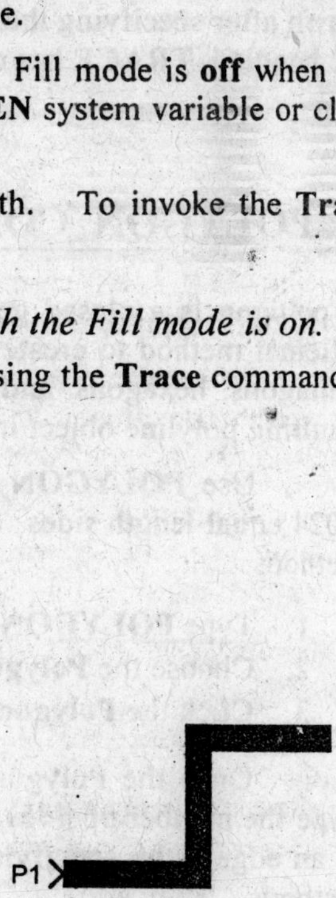

FIG. 29

See Fig. 29.

Problem 24: *Draw the solid lines using the Trace command with the Fill mode is off.*

The command sequence to draw solid lines with the Fill mode is **off** using the **Trace** command is as follows:

Command: **FILLMODE** ↵
Enter new value for FILLMODE <1>: 0 ↵
Command: TRACE ↵
Specify trace width <2.0000>: 3 ↵
Specify start point: ***(Pick P1)***
Specify next point: ***(Move the cursor to up)*** **25** ↵
Specify next point: ***(Move the cursor to right)*** **25** ↵
Specify next point: ***(Move the cursor to down)*** **25** ↵
Specify next point: ***(Move the cursor to left)*** **20** ↵
Specify next point: ↵

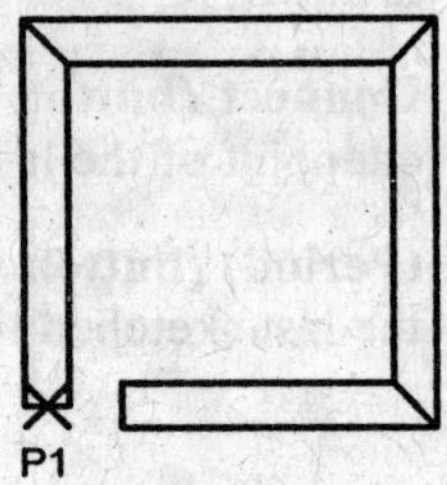

FIG. 30

See Fig. 30.

The endpoints of a trace are on the center line and are always cut square. **TRACE** automatically calculates the correct bevels for connection to adjacent segments. Each segment is drawn after specifying the next segment or pressing the **ENTER** key. Because of the way bevels are handled, **TRACE** has no undo option.

9. POLYGON COMMAND

A polygon is a closed geometric entity with equal sides. The **POLYGON** tool provides an efficient method to create rectangles and regular polygons such as equilateral triangles, squares, pentagons, hexagons, and so on. If necessary, use **EXPLODE** system variable to convert the resulting polyline object into lines.

Use **POLYGON** command to create equilateral closed polylines with between 3 and 1,024 equal-length sides. The **POLYGON** command can be invoked by any one of the following methods:

1. Type **POLYGON** or **POL** in the command prompt.
2. Choose the **Polygon** tool from the **Draw** panel of the **Home** tab.
3. Click the **Polygon** tool from the **Draw** menu.

Once the Polygon tool is invoked, AutoCAD prompts to specify the number of sides. Type the number of sides and press **Enter**. Now, you can draw polygon by specifying the length of an edge or by specifying the center of the polygon. The polygons are drawn using the three methods. They are:

1. Inscribed in Circle Method
2. Circumscribed about Circle Method
3. Edge Method

9.1 INSCRIBED IN CIRCLE METHOD

In this method, a polygon is drawn such that all vertices of the polygon lie on the circumference of an imaginary circle with the specified radius of a circle and center point.

Problem 25: *Draw a regular polygon with the number of sides 6 inside a circle of radius 25 mm.*

The command sequence to draw a polygon with the number of sides as 6 (called Hexagon) and radius of the circle as 25 mm using the **Polygon** command is as follows:

```
Command: POLYGON ↵
Enter number of sides <5>: 6 ↵
Specify center of polygon or [Edge]: (Pick P1)
Enter an option [Inscribed in circle/
   Circumscribed about circle] <I>: I ↵
Specify radius of circle: 25 ↵
```

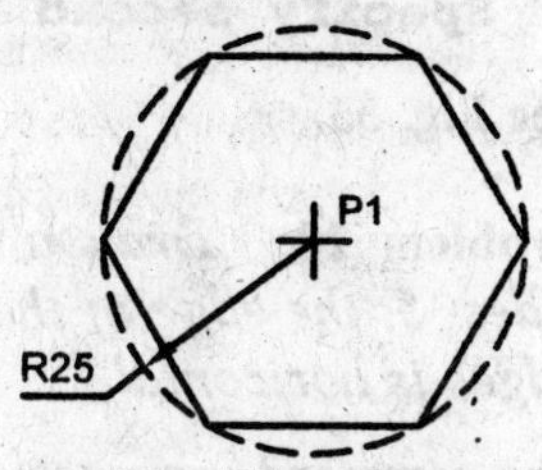

FIG. 31

See Fig. 31.

9.2 CIRCUMSCRIBED ABOUT CIRCLE METHOD

In this method, a polygon is drawn such that the sides of the polygon are tangential to an imaginary circle with the specified radius and center point.

Problem 26: *Draw a regular polygon with the number of sides 5 outside a circle of radius 20 mm.*

The command sequence to draw a polygon with the number of sides as 5 (called Pentagon) and radius of the circle as 20 mm using the **Polygon** command is as follows:

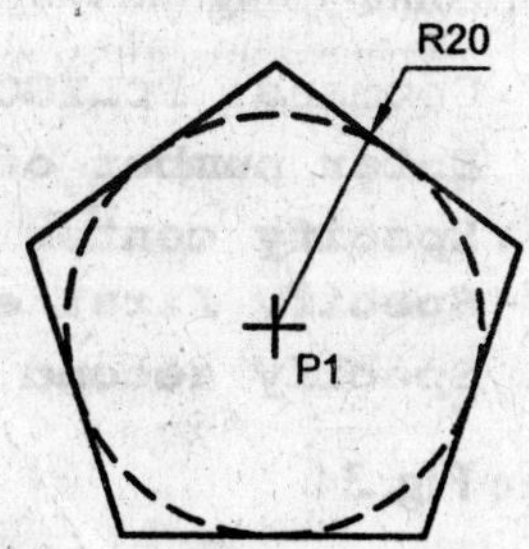

FIG. 32

```
Command: POLYGON ↵
Enter number of sides <6>: 5 ↵
Specify center of polygon or [Edge]: (Pick P1)
Enter an option [Inscribed in circle/Circumscribed about circle] <I>: C ↵
Specify radius of circle: 20 ↵
```

See Fig. 32.

9.3 EDGE METHOD

In this method, a polygon is drawn by specifying the two endpoints of the side of the polygon. AutoCAD constructs the rest of the polygon. Here, we can control the exact size and orientation of the polygon. In this method, AutoCAD prompts the user to specify the first and second endpoints of the edge.

Problem 27: *Draw a regular polygon with the number of sides 6, the edge of the polygon is 20 mm and one of the edges is vertical.*

The command sequence to draw a polygon with the number of sides as 6, edge of polygon as 20 mm and one of the edges vertical using the **Polygon** command is as follows:

```
Command: POLYGON ↵
Enter number of sides <5>: 6 ↵
Specify center of polygon or [Edge]: E ↵
Specify first endpoint of edge:   (Pick P1)
Specify second endpoint of edge: @20<90 ↵
```

See Fig. 33.

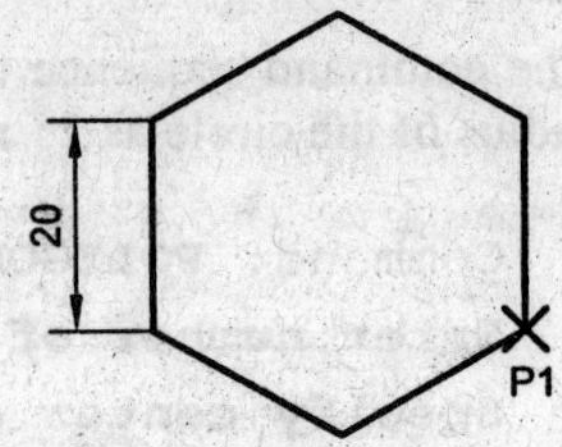

FIG. 33

Problem 28: *Draw a regular polygon with the number of sides 5, the edge of the polygon is 20 mm and one of the edges is horizontal.*

The command sequence to draw a polygon with the number of sides as 5, edge of polygon as 20 mm and one of the edges horizontal using the **Polygon** command is as follows:

```
Command: POLYGON ↵
Enter number of sides <6>: 5 ↵
Specify center of polygon or [Edge]: E ↵
Specify first endpoint of edge:   (Pick P1)
Specify second endpoint of edge: @20<0 ↵
```

See Fig. 34.

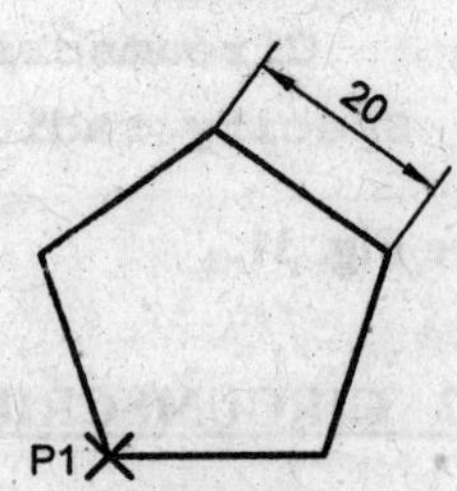

FIG. 34

10. CAD EXERCISES - Step-by-Step Solutions

Example 1: *Draw the diagram shown in Fig. 35 using the Pline, Line, Circle and Arc commands.*

Procedure and command sequence to draw the diagram shown in Fig. 35.

STEP 1 : First draw the outline of the diagram using the **Pline** command. The command sequence is given below:

```
Command: PLINE ↵
Specify start point: (Pick P1)
Current line-width is 0.0000
```

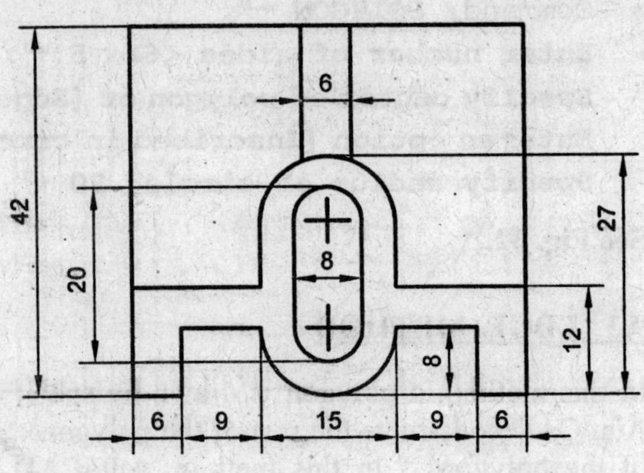

FIG. 35

Specify next point or [Arc/Halfwidth/
Length/Undo/Width]: <Ortho on>
(*Move the cursor to right*) **6** ↵
Specify next point or [Arc/Close/
Halfwidth/Length/Undo/Width]:
(*Move the cursor to up*) **8** ↵
Specify next point or [Arc/Close/
Halfwidth/Length/Undo/Width]:
(*Move the cursor to right*) **9** ↵
Specify next point or [Arc/Close/
Halfwidth/Length/Undo/Width]: A ↵
Specify endpoint of arc or
[Angle/CEnter/CLose/ Direction/
Halfwidth/Line/Radius/Second pt/Undo/Width]: CE ↵
Specify center point of arc: (*Move the cursor to right*) **7.5** ↵
Specify endpoint of arc or [Angle/Length]: (*Move the cursor to right*) **7.5**↵
Specify endpoint of arc or [Angle/CEnter/CLose/
Direction/Halfwidth/Line/Radius/Second pt/Undo/Width]: L ↵
Specify next point or [Arc/Close/Halfwidth/
Length/Undo/Width]: (*Move the cursor to right*) **9** ↵
Specify next point or [Arc/Close/Halfwidth/
Length/Undo/Width]: (*Move the cursor to down*) **8** ↵
Specify next point or [Arc/Close/Halfwidth/
Length/Undo/Width]: (*Move the cursor to right*) **6** ↵
Specify next point or [Arc/Close/Halfwidth/
Length/Undo/Width]: (*Move the cursor to up*) **42** ↵
Specify next point or [Arc/Close/Halfwidth/
Length/Undo/Width]: (*Move the cursor to left*) **45** ↵
Specify next point or [Arc/Close/Halfwidth/Length/Undo/Width]: C ↵

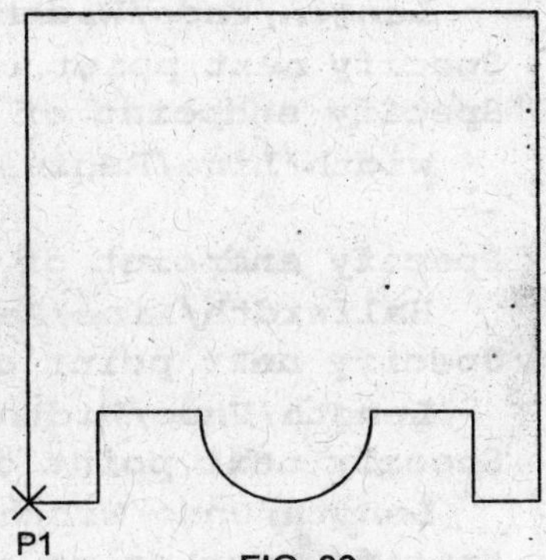

FIG. 36

See Fig. 36.

STEP 2 : Command sequence to draw another set of lines and arc using Pline command is given below:

Command: **PLINE** ↵
Specify start point: (***Pick P1***)
Current line-width is 0.0000
Specify next point or [Arc/Halfwidth/
Length/Undo/Width]: <Ortho on>
(*Move the cursor to up*) **12** ↵
Specify next point or [Arc/Close/
Halfwidth/Length/Undo/Width]:
(*Move the cursor to left*) **15** ↵

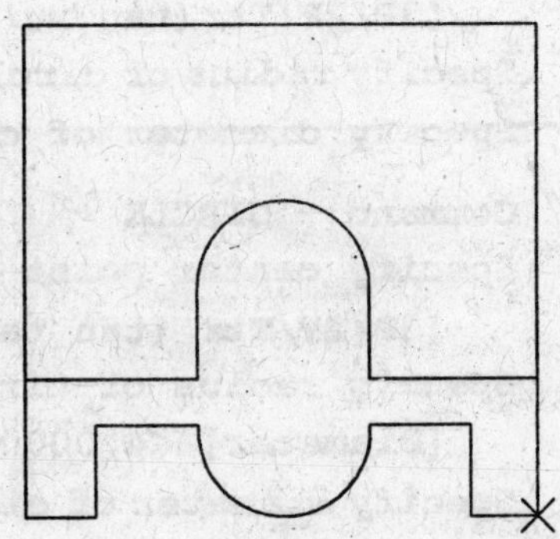

FIG. 37

Specify next point or [Arc/Close/Halfwidth/ Length/Undo/Width]: (*Move the cursor to up*) **8** ↵
Specify next point or [Arc/Close/Halfwidth/Length/Undo/Width]: A ↵
Specify endpoint of arc or [Angle/CEnter/CLose/Direction/Half-width/Line/Radius/Second pt/Undo/Width]: (*Move the cursor to left*) **15** ↵
Specify endpoint of arc or [Angle/CEnter/CLose/Direction/ Halfwidth/Line/Radius/Second pt/Undo/Width]: L ↵
Specify next point or [Arc/Close/Halfwidth/ Length/Undo/Width]: (*Move the cursor to down*) **8** ↵
Specify next point or [Arc/Close/Halfwidth/ Length/Undo/Width]: (*Move the cursor to left*) **15** ↵
Specify next point or [Arc/Close/ Halfwidth/Length/Undo/Width]: ↵

See Fig. 37.

STEP 3 : Mark the center point for both the arcs using the Dimcenter command. The command sequence is given below:

Command: **DIMCENTER** ↵
Select arc or circle: (*Select the Arc-1*)

Command: **DIMCENTER** ↵
Select arc or circle: (*Select the Arc-2*)

See Fig. 38.

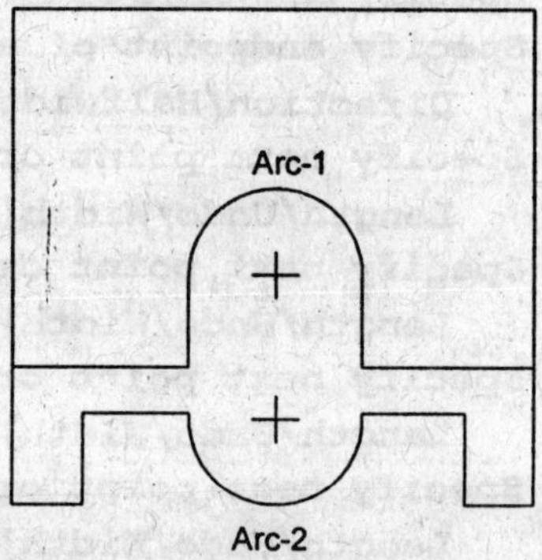

FIG. 38

STEP 4 : Using the center points of the arcs as center, draw two circles using the Circle command. The command sequence is given below:

Command: **CIRCLE** ↵
Specify center point for circle or [3P/2P/Ttr (tan tan radius)] : (*Pick C1*)
Specify radius of circle or [Diameter] : D ↵
Specify diameter of circle: 8 ↵

Command: CIRCLE ↵
Specify center point for circle or [3P/2P/Ttr (tan tan radius)] : (*Pick C2*)
Specify radius of circle or [Diameter] <4.0000>: D ↵
Specify diameter of circle <8.0000>: 8 ↵

See Fig. 39.

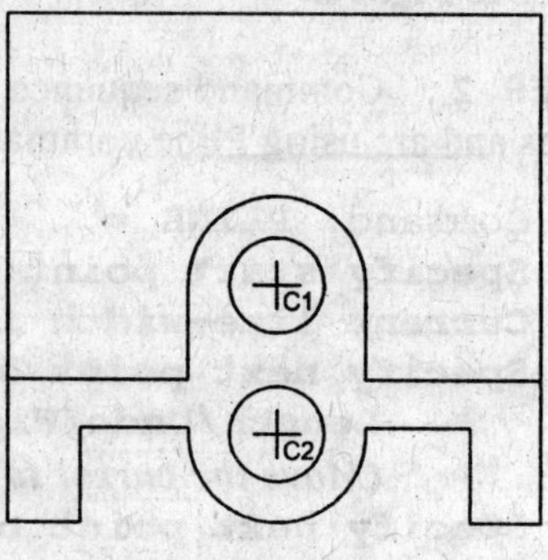

FIG. 39

STEP 5 : Draw two lines connecting the two ends points of the circle using the **Line** command. The command sequence is given below:

```
Command: LINE ↵
Specify first point: (Pick P1)
Specify next point or
   [Undo]: (Pick P2)
Specify next point or [Undo]: ↵
Command:  LINE ↵
Specify first point: (Pick P3)
Specify next point or
      [Undo]: (Pick P4)
Specify next point or [Undo]: ↵
```

See Fig. 40.

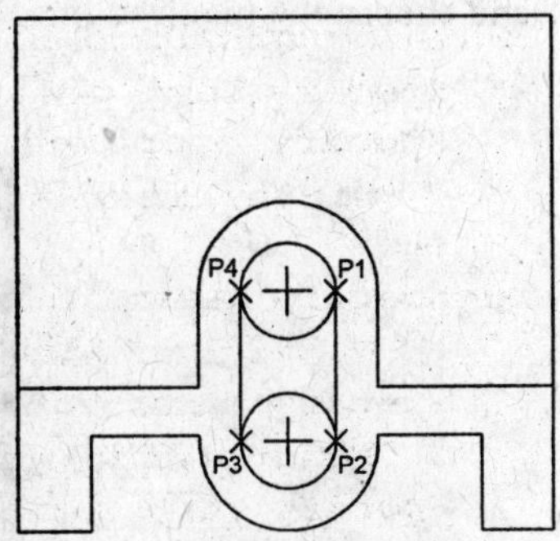

FIG. 40

STEP 6 : Trim the circles to obtain the required shape of the drawing using the **Trim** command. The command sequence is given below:

```
Command: TRIM ↵
Current settings: Projection=UCS, Edge=None
Select cutting edges ...
Select objects or <select all>: (Select L1) 1 found
Select objects: (Select L2) 1 found, 2 total
Select objects: ↵
Select object to trim or shift-select to extend or
      [Fence/Crossing/Project/Edge/eRase/Undo]: (Select C1)
Select object to trim or shift-select to extend or
      [Fence/Crossing/Project/Edge/eRase/Undo]: (Select C2)
Select object to trim or shift-select to extend or
      [Fence/Crossing/Project/Edge/eRase/Undo]: ↵
```

See Fig. 41.

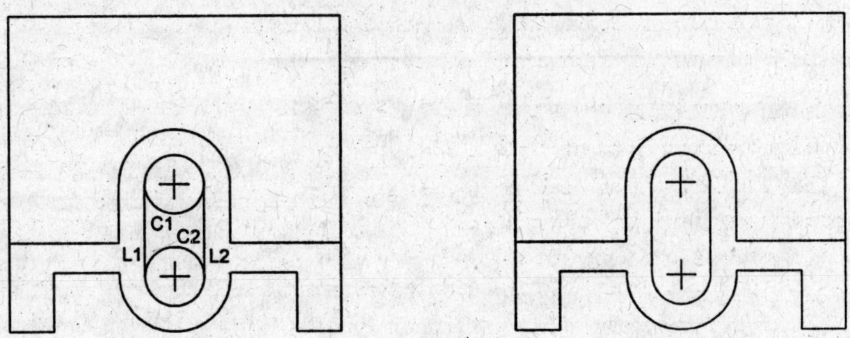

Before Trim

After Trim

FIG. 41

STEP 7 : Select the lines to darken and click the **Lineweight control** option on the **Properties** tool bar and choose the required line thickness.

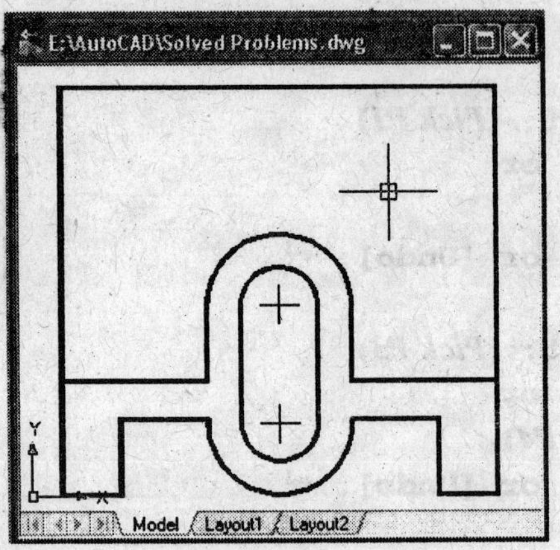

Fig. 42

Fig. 42 shows the final view of the diagram given in **Fig. 35.** Finally save the drawing.

6

OBJECT SELECTION METHODS

1. OBJECT SELECTION METHODS

We can control several aspects of selecting objects, such as whether a command is entered first or objects is selected first, the size of the pickbox cursor and how selected objects are displayed. For commands that use the **Select Objects** prompt, we can

- Enter a command first and then select objects
- Select the objects first and then enter a command

Select the Command First

When an editing command is invoked, a **Select Objects** prompt is displayed and the crosshairs is replaced with a **pickbox**. The **Select Objects** prompt can be responded by any one of the methods as follows:

- Select objects one at a time.
- Click an empty area. Drag the cursor to define a rectangular selection area.
- Enter a selection option. Enter *?* to display all selection options.
- Combine selection methods. For example, to select most of the objects in the drawing area, select all objects and then remove the objects that user do not want selected.
- Enter *filter* to use a named selection filter. The apostrophe runs the command transparently.

Select Objects First

Use one of two methods to select objects before starting a command:

- Use the **SELECT** command and enter *?* to display all selection options. All objects selected are put into the **Previous** selection set. To use the **Previous** selection set, enter *p* at the **Select Objects** prompt of any subsequent command.
- When noun/verb selection is turned on, select objects at the Command prompt before entering a command such as **MOVE, COPY** or **ERASE**. With this method, we can only select objects by clicking them individually or by using automatic selection.
- Enter *qselect* to filter the selection. Then enter *p* at the **Select Objects** prompt of any subsequent command.

Highlight Objects to Be Selected

Objects are highlighted when the **pickbox cursor rolls over them**, providing a **preview of which object will be selected** when we click. **When an area to select multiple objects is specified, the background of the area becomes transparent.**

These selection previewing **effects are turned on by default.** We can turn them off or change the appearance of selection **previewing.** For this, click **Options...** in the **Tools** menu to display the **Options** dialog box. On the **Options** dialog box, click the **Selection** tab and then click the **Visual Effect Settings...** button to display the **Visual Effect Settings** dialog box. The **Visual Effect Settings** dialog box shown in Fig. 1.

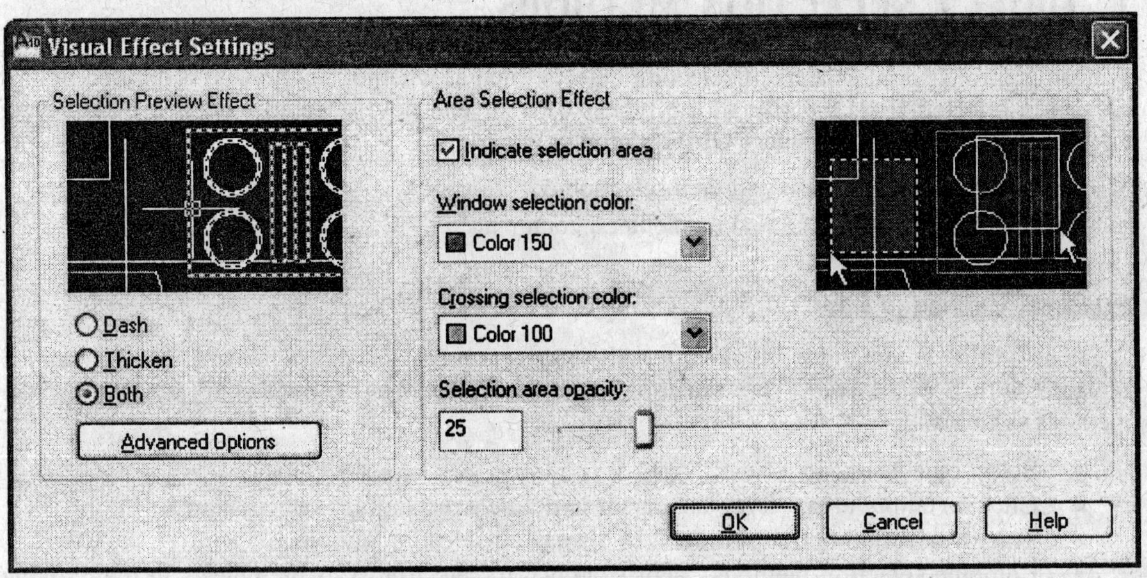

FIG. 1

When the **PICKBOX** system variable is set to 0, selection previewing of objects is not available.

Control the Appearance of Selected Objects

By default, selected objects are **displayed** with dashed lines. We can increase program speed by setting the **HIGHLIGHT** system variable to 0. Turning off selection highlighting does *not* affect grips on selected objects.

Set Up Default Selection Methods

Options on the **Selection** tab of the **Options** dialog box control default selection methods. Options on the **Selection** tab of the **Options** dialog box are:

- Use selection previewing and selection area effects to preview selection.
- Select objects before entering a command (noun-verb selection) or after entering a command.
- Press **SHIFT** to append objects to the selection set.
- Click and drag to create a selection window. Otherwise you must click twice to define the corners of a selection window.
- Start **Window** or **Crossing** selection automatically when you click an empty space. Otherwise, user must enter *c* or *w* to specify window crossing selection.
- Change the size of the pickbox using the **PICKBOX** system variable.
- Select all objects in a group when you select one object in that group.
- Include the boundary in the selection set when we select a hatch.

The **Selection** tab of **Options** dialog box is shown in **Fig. 2**.

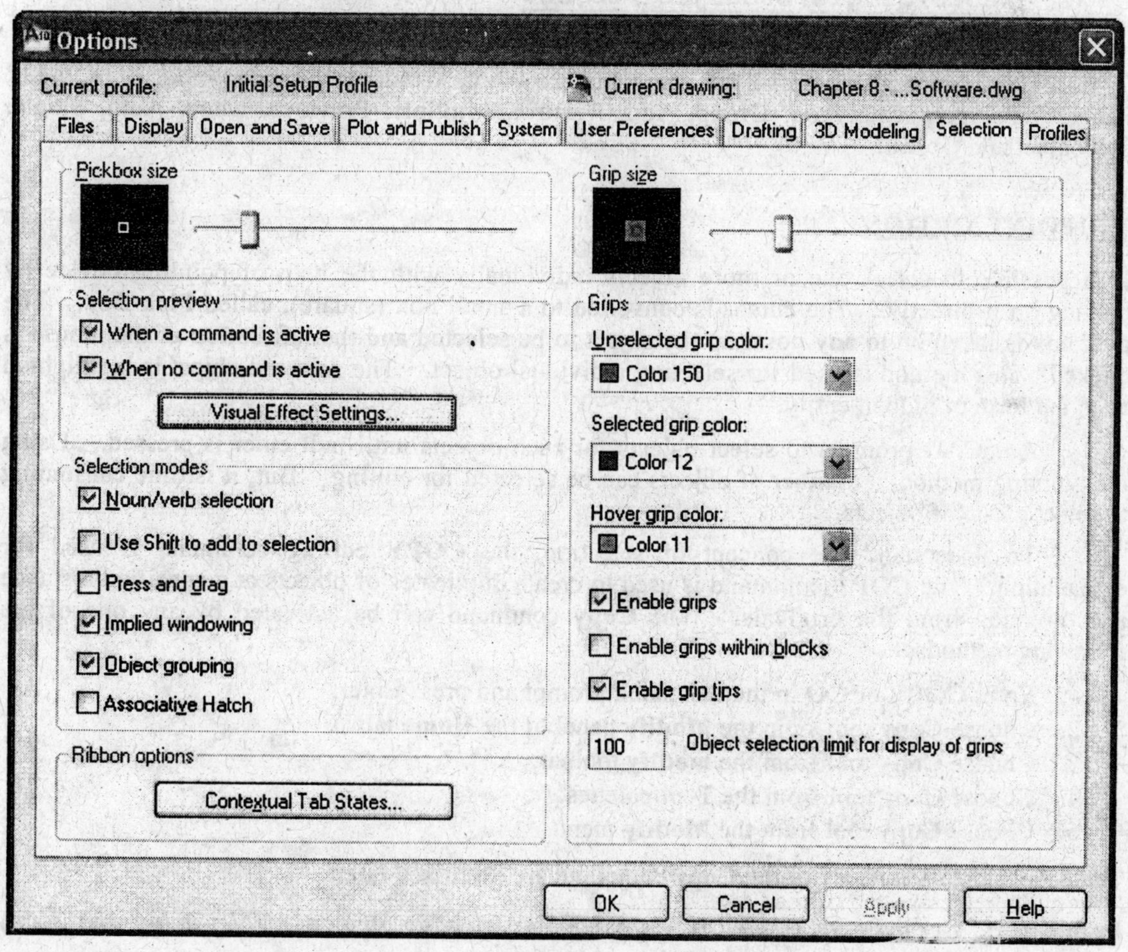

FIG. 2

2. SELECT COMMAND

To activate the **SELECT** command, type **SELECT** in the command prompt. The prompt is:

```
Command:    SELECT ↵
Select objects: Use an object selection method
```

A small box, called the **Object Selection Target**, replaces the crosshairs on the graphics cursor. Objects must be selected in order to be processed. The **Select Objects** prompt occurs after many commands, including the **SELECT** command itself. To view all options, enter *?* at the **Select objects** command prompt. The command sequence is:

```
Command:    SELECT ↵
Select objects: ? ↵
Expects a point or Window/Last/Crossing/BOX/ALL/Fence/
   WPolygon/CPolygon/Group/Add/Remove/Multiple/Previous/Undo/
   AUto/SIngle/SUbobject/Object
Select objects: Specify a point or enter an option
```

The options in the **SELECT** command are Point, Window, Last, Crossing, BOX, ALL, Fence, WPolygon, CPolygon, Group, Add, Remove, Multiple, Previous, Undo, Auto, Single, SUbobject and Object.

2.1 POINT OPTION

It is possible to select one or more objects individually with the help of pointing device by picking on it directly. The cursor is converted to a small box (square), called **Pick Box**. The pick box is taken on to any point on the object to be selected and the left button of the mouse is clicked. This method is used for selecting individual object. The selected object is highlighted as in the form of hidden entity.

AutoCAD prompts to select objects for each objects until null enter is pressed. Using the pointing method, a number of objects can be selected for editing. But, it is time consuming to select group of objects.

To understand the concept of selection, the **COPY** editing command is used for explanation. The **COPY** command is used to create duplicates of objects at a specified distance and direction from the originals. The **Copy** command can be activated by any one of the following methods:

1. Enter **COPY** or **CO** in the command prompt and press Enter.
2. Choose **Copy** tool from the **Modify** panel of the **Home** tab.
3. Choose **Copy** tool from the **modify** toolbar.
4. Choose Copy tool from the **Tool** palettes.
5. Choose **Copy** tool from the **Modify** menu.

The details and options about the **Copy** command are discussed later.

Problem 1: *Draw a circle by copying the already drawn circle using the Copy command and Point option in the Select command.*

The command sequence to copy the circle using the Copy command and Point option in the Select command is as follows:

Command: **COPY** ↵
Select objects: *(Move the Pick Box to the circle and click)* **1 found**
Select objects: *(Move the Pick Box to the horizontal center mark and click)* **1 found, 2 total**
Select objects: *(Move the Pick Box to the vertical center mark and click)* **1 found, 3 total**
Select objects: ↵
(The selected objects are highlighted as dashed lines.)
Current settings: Copy mode = Multiple
Specify base point or [Displacement/mOde] <Displacement>: *(Pick P1)*
Specify second point or <use first point as displacement>: *(Pick P2)*
Specify second point or [Exit/Undo] <Exit>: ↵

See Fig. 3. Note that whenever an editing command (here COPY command) is entered, the cursor turns into a small square (□) and prompts to select an object.

Also, the selected object turns into a dashed one.

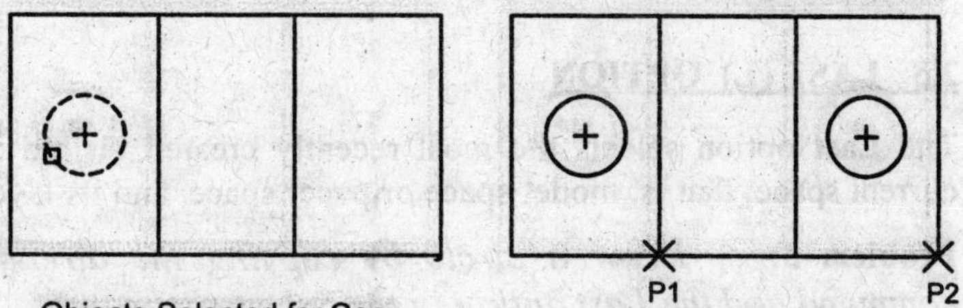

Objects Selected for Copy

Objects after Copy

FIG. 3

2.2 WINDOW (W) OPTION

The **Window** option selects all objects completely inside a rectangle defined by two points. Specifying the corners from left to right creates a window selection. (Specifying the corners from right to left creates a crossing selection.) The prompt is:

Specify first corner: ***Specify a point***
Specify opposite corner: ***Specify a point***

Problem 2: *Draw a circle by copying the already drawn circle using the Copy command and Window option in the Select command.*

The command sequence to copy the objects completely inside a rectangle using the Copy command and Window option in the Select command is as follows:

Command: **COPY** ↵
Select objects: W ↵
Specify first corner: *(Pick P1)*
Specify opposite corner: *(Pick P2)* **3 found**
Select objects: ↵
Current settings: Copy mode = Multiple

```
Specify base point or [Displacement/mOde] <Displacement>: (Pick P3)
Specify second point or <use first point as displacement>: (Pick P4)
Specify second point or [Exit/Undo] <Exit>: ↵
```

See **Fig. 4.** In the above example, a rectangular window is created by picking the first corner P1 and the diagonally opposite corner P2 so that a window like area surrounds the objects to be selected.

All the objects lying wholly within the window are selected.

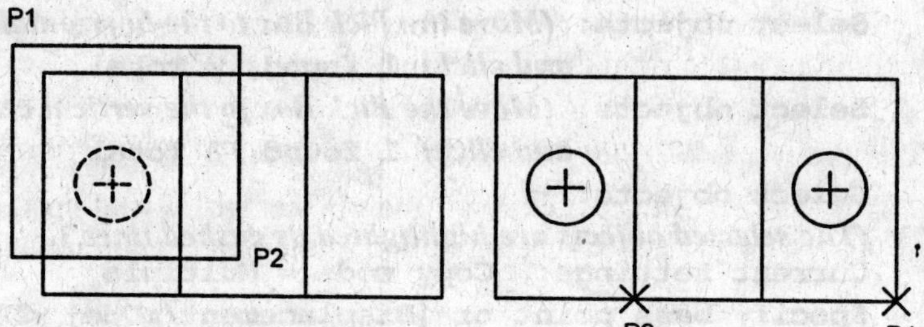

Objects Selected for Copy

Objects after Copy

FIG. 4

Note that the objects partly within and partly outside the window are **not** selected.

2.3 LAST (L) OPTION

The **Last** option selects the most recently created visible object. The object must be in the current space, that is, model space or paper space, and its layer must not be set to frozen or off.

Problem 3: *Draw a circle by copying the already drawn circle using the Copy command and the Last option in the Select command.*

See Fig. 5. The command sequence to copy the last object drawn using the Copy command and Last option in the Select command is as follows:

```
Command: CIRCLE ↵
Specify center point for circle or [3P/2P/Ttr(tan tan radius)]: (Pick P1)
Specify radius of circle or [Diameter] <3.0000>: 15 ↵
Command: CIRCLE ↵
Specify center point for circle or [3P/2P/Ttr
          (tan tan radius)]: (Pick P1)
Specify radius of circle or [Diameter] <15.0000>: 7 ↵

Command: COPY ↵
Select objects: L ↵
1 found
Select objects: ↵
Current settings: Copy mode = Multiple
Specify base point or [Displacement/mOde]
      <Displacement>: (Pick P2)
Specify second point or <use first point
      as displacement>: (Pick P3)
Specify second point or [Exit/Undo] <Exit>: ↵
```

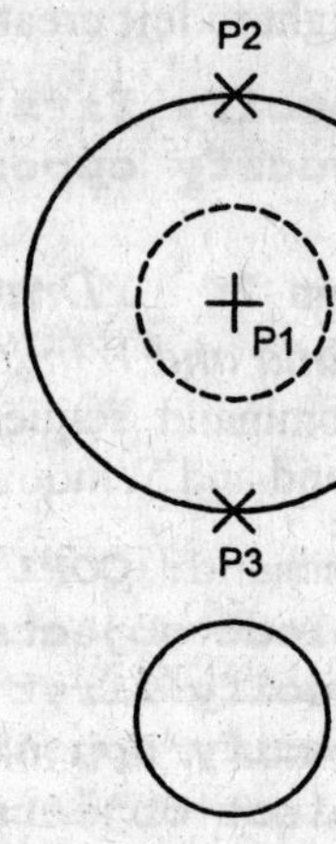

FIG. 5

2.4 CROSSING (C) OPTION

The **Crossing** option selects objects within and crossing an area defined by two points. A crossing selection is displayed as dashed or otherwise highlighted to differentiate it from window selection. Specifying the corners from right to left creates a crossing selection. (Specifying the corners from left to right creates a window selection.)

Problem 4: *Copy objects using Copy command and Crossing option in Select command.*

The command sequence to copy all the objects within and crossing an area of a rectangle using the **Copy** command and **Crossing** option in the **Select** command is as follows:

```
Command: COPY ↵
Select objects: C ↵
Specify first corner:   (Pick P1)
Specify opposite corner: (Pick P2) 11 found
Select objects: ↵
Current settings:  Copy mode = Multiple
Specify base point or [Displacement/mOde] <Displacement>: (Pick P3)
Specify second point or
   <use first point as
   displacement>: (Pick P4)
Specify second point or
   [Exit/Undo] <Exit>: ↵
```

See Fig. 6. In the above example, pick the first corner P1, a window made of dashed lines is displayed and pick the diagonally opposite corner P2.

It works like window, but select all the objects within the window and also objects crossing the boundary of the window.

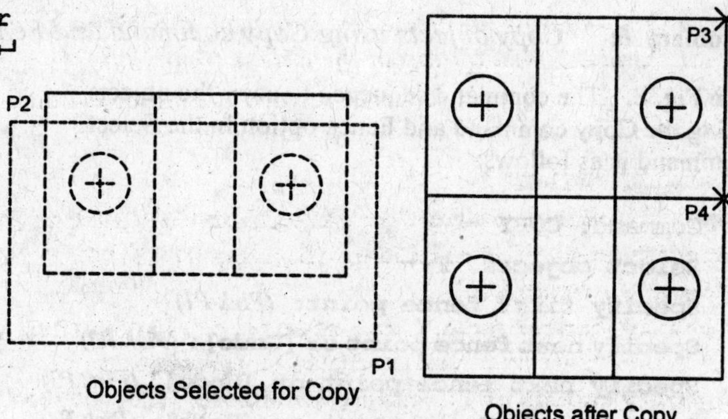

FIG. 6

2.5 BOX OPTION

The **BOX** option selects all objects inside or crossing a rectangle specified by two points. If the rectangle's points are specified from right to left, Box is equivalent to Crossing. Otherwise, Box is equivalent to Window.

2.6 ALL OPTION

The **All** option selects all objects in the file.

Problem 5: *Copy all the objects using the Copy command and the All option in the Select command.*

See Fig. 7. The command sequence to copy all the objects using the **Copy** command and **All** option in the **Select** command is as follows:

```
Command: COPY ↵
Select objects: ALL ↵
12 found
Select objects: ↵
Current settings:  Copy mode = Multiple
Specify base point or [Displacement/mOde]
       <Displacement>: (Pick P1)
Specify second point or <use first point as
       displacement>: (Pick P2)
Specify second point or [Exit/Undo] <Exit>: ↵
```

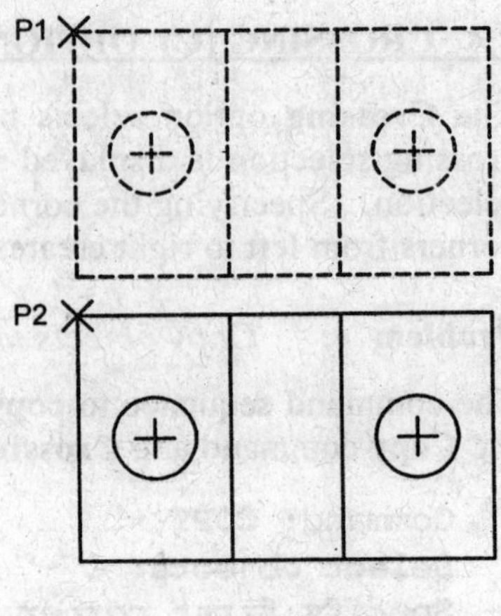

FIG. 7

2.7 FENCE (F) OPTION

A series of lines forming an open polygon is known as Fence. The Fence option selects all the objects through which it passes. The Fence method is similar to CPolygon except that the fence is not closed and a fence can cross itself. Fence is not affected by the PICKADD command.

Problem 6: *Copy objects using Copy command and Fence option in Select command.*

See Fig. 8. The command sequence to copy the objects using the Copy command and Fence option in the Select command is as follows:

```
Command: COPY ↵
Select objects: F ↵
Specify first fence point: (Pick P1)
Specify next fence point or [Undo]: (Pick P2)
Specify next fence point or [Undo]: (Pick P3)
Specify next fence point or [Undo]: (Pick P4)
Specify next fence point or [Undo]: ↵
9 found
Select objects: ↵
Current settings:  Copy mode = Multiple
Specify base point or [Displacement/mOde]
                    <Displacement>: (Pick P5)
Specify second point or
    <use first point as displacement>: (Pick P6)
Specify second point or [Exit/Undo] <Exit>: ↵
```

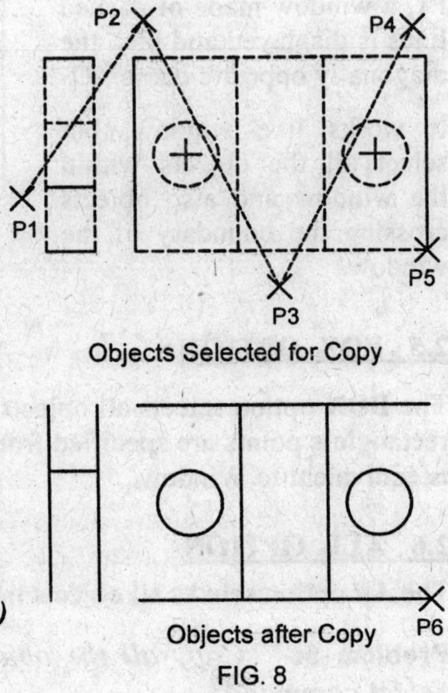

FIG. 8

2.8 WPOLYGON (WP) OPTION

The **WPolygon** option selects objects completely inside a polygon defined by points. The polygon can be any shape but cannot cross or touch itself. The last segment of the polygon is drawn so that it is closed at all times. WPolygon is not affected by the PICKADD system variable.

Problem 7: *Copy objects using Copy command and WPolygon option in Select command.*

See Fig. 9. The command sequence to copy objects within a polygon using the Copy command and WPolygon option in Select command is as follows:

```
Command: COPY ↵
Select objects: WP ↵
First polygon point: (Pick P1)
Specify endpoint of line or [Undo]: (Pick P2)
Specify endpoint of line or [Undo]: (Pick P3)
Specify endpoint of line or [Undo]: (Pick P4)
Specify endpoint of line or [Undo]: (Pick P5)
Specify endpoint of line or [Undo]: ↵ 15 found
Select objects: ↵
Current settings:  Copy mode = Multiple
Specify base point or [Displacement/mOde] <Displacement>: (Pick P6)
Specify second point or <use first point as displacement>: (Pick P7)
Specify second point or [Exit/Undo] <Exit>: ↵
```

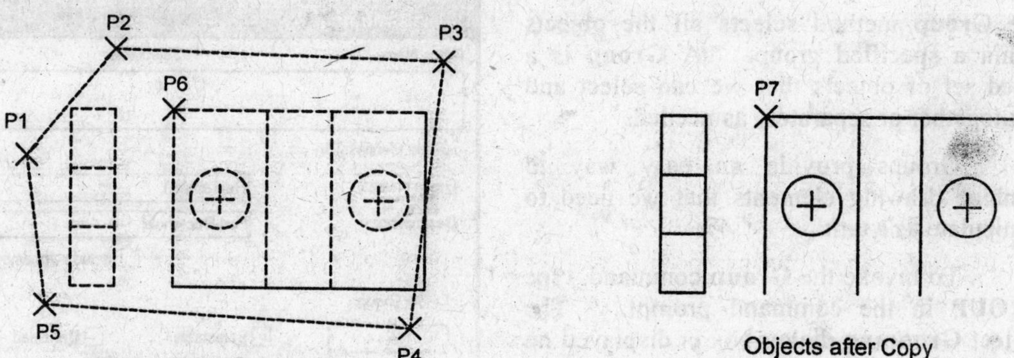

Objects Selected for Copy

Objects after Copy

FIG. 9

2.9 CPOLYGON (CP) OPTION

CPolygon option selects objects within and crossing a polygon defined by specifying points. The polygon is of any shape, but can't cross or touch itself. The last segment of the polygon is drawn so that it is closed all times. **CPolygon** is not affected by the **PICKADD** system variable.

Problem 8: *Copy objects using Copy command and CPolygon option in Select command.*

See Fig. 10. The command sequence to copy the objects within and crossing a polygon using the Copy command CPolygon option in Select command is as follows:

```
Command: COPY ↵
Select objects: CP ↵
First polygon point: (Pick P1)
Specify endpoint of line or [Undo]: (Pick P2)
Specify endpoint of line or [Undo]: (Pick P3)
Specify endpoint of line or [Undo]: (Pick P4)
Specify endpoint of line or [Undo]: (Pick P5)
Specify endpoint of line or [Undo]: ↵
17 found
Select objects: ↵
Current settings:  Copy mode = Multiple
Specify base point or [Displacement/mOde]
     <Displacement>: (Pick P6)
Specify second point or <use first point as
     displacement>: (Pick P7)
Specify second point or [Exit/Undo] <Exit>: ↵
```

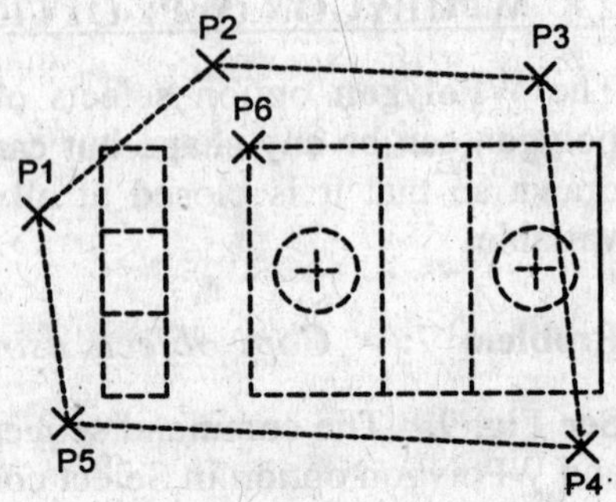

Objects Selected for Copy

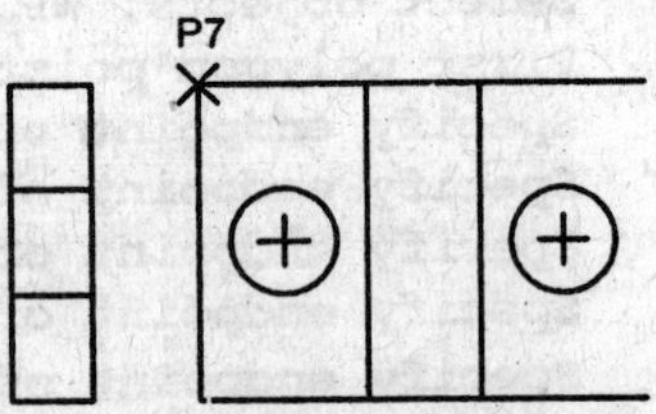

Objects after Copy

FIG. 10

2.10 GROUP (G) OPTION

The **Group** method selects all the objects within a specified group. A **Group** is a saved set of objects that we can select and edit together or separately as needed.

Groups provide an easy way to combine drawing elements that we need to manipulate as a unit.

To invoke the **Group** command, type **GROUP** in the command prompt. The **Object Grouping** dialog box is displayed on the screen as shown in **Fig. 11.**

In the **Object Grouping** dialog box, under **Group Identification**, enter a group name and a description.

In the **Create Group** area, click **New.** The dialog box closes temporarily. Select objects and press **Enter**.

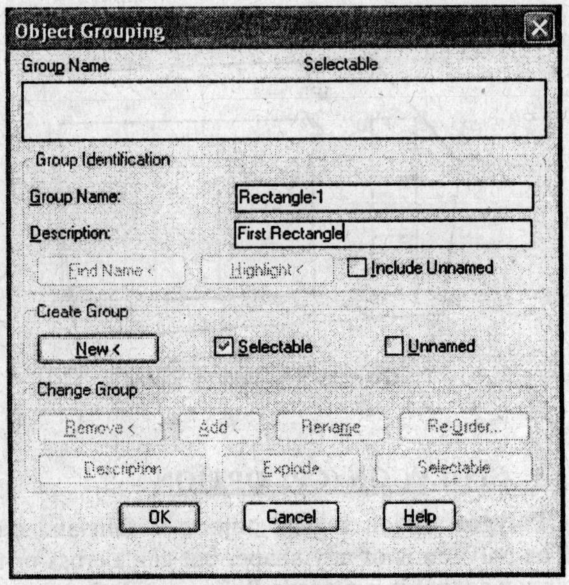

FIG. 11

Problem 9: *Convert a set of objects as a group using Group command. Copy objects in the group using the Copy command and the Group option in the Select command.*

See Fig. 12. The command sequence to save a set of objects using the GROUP command is as follows:

Command: **GROUP** ↵
(In the Object Grouping dialog box enter the Group Name as RECTANGLE-1 and Description. Click New button. The dialog box closes.)
Select objects for grouping:
Select objects: *(Pick line L1)* **1 found**
Select objects: *(Pick line L2)* **1 found, 2 total**
Select objects: *(Pick line L3)* **1 found, 3 total**
Select objects: *(Pick line L4)* **1 found, 4 total**
Select objects: ↵
(Now, the Object Grouping dialog box appears. Again, enter the Group Name as RECTANGLE-2 and Description and click New button. The dialog box closes.)
Select objects for grouping:
Select objects: *(Pick line L5)* **1 found**
Select objects: *(Pick line L6)* **1 found, 2 total**
Select objects: *(Pick line L7)* **1 found, 3 total**
Select objects: *(Pick line L8)* **1 found, 4 total**
Select objects: ↵
(Now, Object Grouping dialog box appears. Click OK to complete the grouping process.)

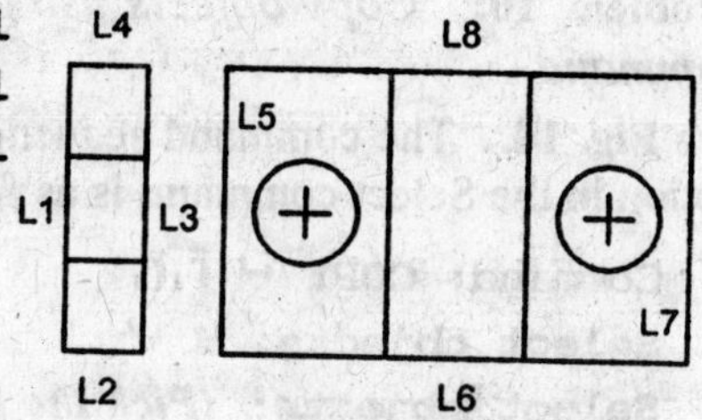

FIG. 12

The command sequence to copy the object in the group using the Copy command and Group option in the Select command is as follows:

Command: **COPY** ↵
Select objects: G ↵
Enter group name: RECTANGLE-1 ↵
4 found
Select objects: G ↵
Enter group name: RECTANGLE-2 ↵
4 found, 8 total
Select objects: ↵
Current settings: Copy mode = Multiple
Specify base point or [Displacement/mOde] <Displacement>: *(Pick P1)*
Specify second point or <use first point as displacement>: *(Pick P2)*
Specify second point or [Exit/Undo] <Exit>: ↵

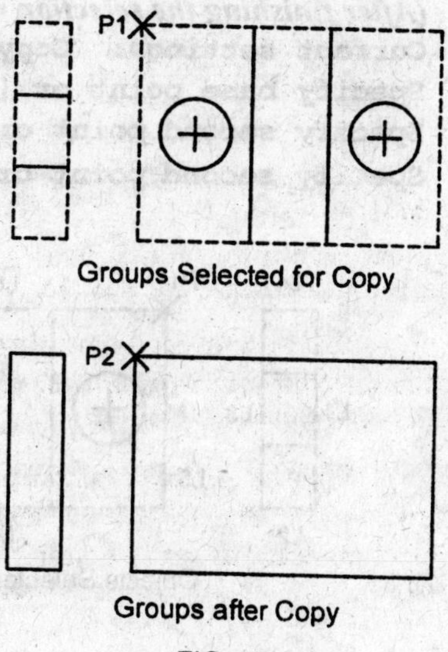

FIG. 13

See Fig. 13.

2.11 ADD (B) OPTION

The **Add** option switches to the Add method: selected objects can be added to the selection set by using any of the object selection methods. Auto and Add are the default methods.

2.12 REMOVE (R) OPTION

This method switches to the Remove method: objects can be removed from the current selection set using any object selection method. An alternative to Remove mode is to hold down SHIFT while selecting single objects or use the Automatic option. While working with the **Remove** option, if we want to add some more objects to the current select list, it can be done by using the **Add** option.

2.13 MULTIPLE (M) OPTION

The **Multiple** option specifies multiple points without highlighting the objects, thus speeding up the selection process for complex objects. The **Multiple** method also selects two intersecting objects if the intersection point is specified twice.

Problem 10: *Copy objects using the Copy command and CPolygon option in the Select command.*

See Fig. 14. The command sequence to copy the objects using the Copy command and Multiple option in the Select command is as follows:

Command: **COPY** ↵
Select objects: M ↵
Select objects: *(Pick the lines L1, L2, L3, L4, L5, L6, L7 and L8)* **8 selected, 8 found**
Select objects: ↵
(After finishing the selection option, the selected lines are highlighted as dashed lines)
Current settings: Copy mode = Multiple
Specify base point or [Displacement/mOde] <Displacement>: *(Pick P1)*
Specify second point or <use first point as displacement>: *(Pick P2)*
Specify second point or [Exit/Undo] <Exit>: ↵

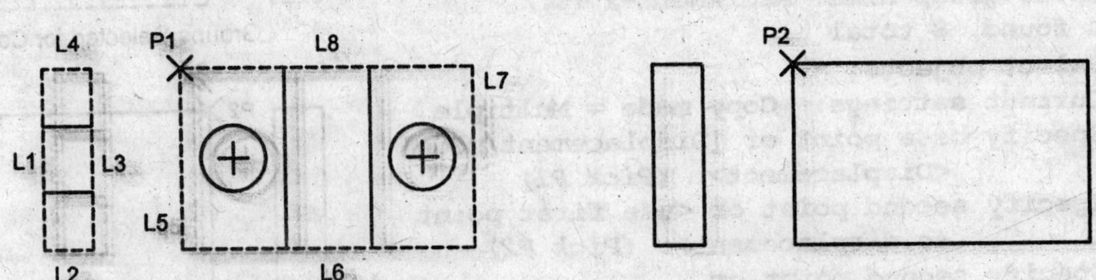

Objects Selected for Copy   Objects after Copy

FIG. 14

2.14 PREVIOUS (P) OPTION

The **Previous** option selects the most recent selection set. The **Previous** selection set is cleared by operations that delete objects from the drawing.

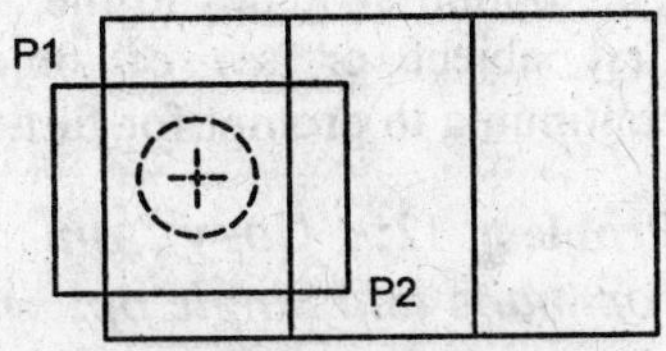

Objects Selected for Copy

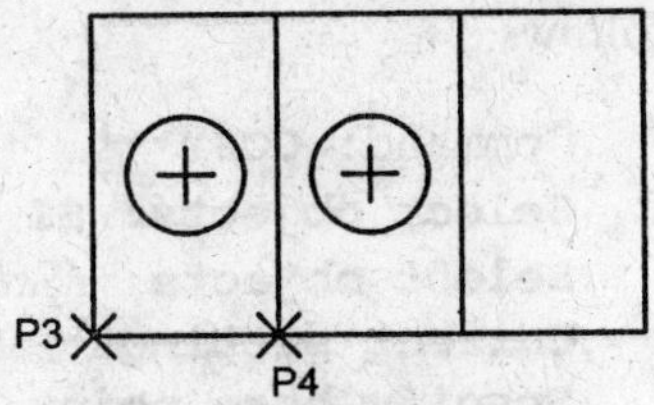

Objects after Copy

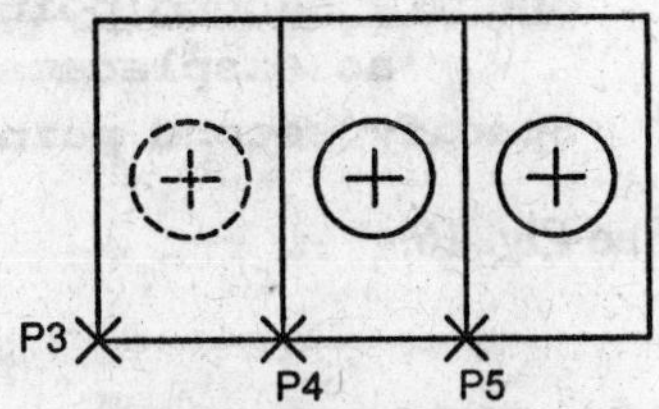

Previous selection set is Selected for Copy

FIG. 15

Problem 11: *Copy objects using the Copy command and Previous option in the Select command.*

The command sequence to copy objects using Copy command and Previous option in the Select command is as follows:

```
Command: COPY ↵
Select objects: W ↵
Specify first corner: (Pick P1)
Specify opposite corner: (Pick P2) 3 found
Select objects: ↵
Current settings:  Copy mode = Multiple
Specify base point or [Displacement/mOde]
      <Displacement>: (Pick P3)
Specify second point or <use first point
      as displacement>: (Pick P4)
Specify second point or [Exit/Undo] <Exit>: ↵

Command: COPY ↵
Select objects: P ↵
3 found
Select objects: ↵
Current settings:  Copy mode = Multiple
Specify base point or [Displacement/mOde] <Displacement>: (Pick P3)
Specify second point or <use first point as displacement>: (Pick P5)
Specify second point or [Exit/Undo] <Exit>: ↵
```

See Fig. 15. The program keeps track of whether each selection set was specified in model space or paper space. The **Previous** selection set is ignored if we switch spaces.

2.15 UNDO (U) OPTION

The **Undo** option cancels the selection of the object most recently added to the selection set.

2.16 AUTO (AU) OPTION

This option switches to automatic selection: pointing to an object selects the object. Pointing to a blank area inside or outside an object forms the first corner of a box defined by the Box method. Auto and Add are the default methods.

2.17 SINGLE (SI) OPTION

This option switches to the **Single method**. It selects the first object or set of objects designated rather than continuing to prompt for further selections.

Problem 12: *Copy an object using the Copy command and Single option in the Select command.*

Command sequence to copy an object using the Copy command and Single option in the Select command is as follows:

```
Command: COPY ↵
Select objects: SI ↵
Select objects: (Select the circle) 1 found
Current settings:  Copy mode = Multiple
Specify base point or [Displacement/mOde]
      <Displacement>: (Pick P1)
Specify second point or <use first point
      as displacement>: (Pick P2)
Specify second point or [Exit/Undo] <Exit>: ↵
```

See Fig. 16.

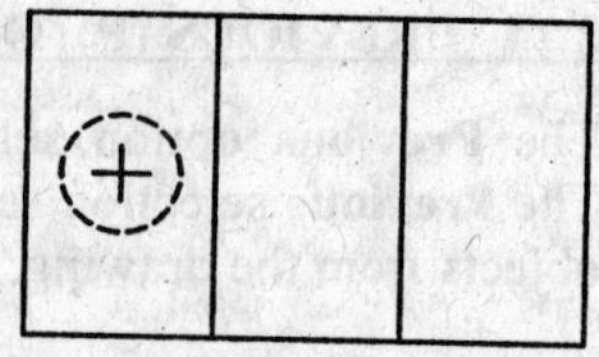

Circle Selected for Copy

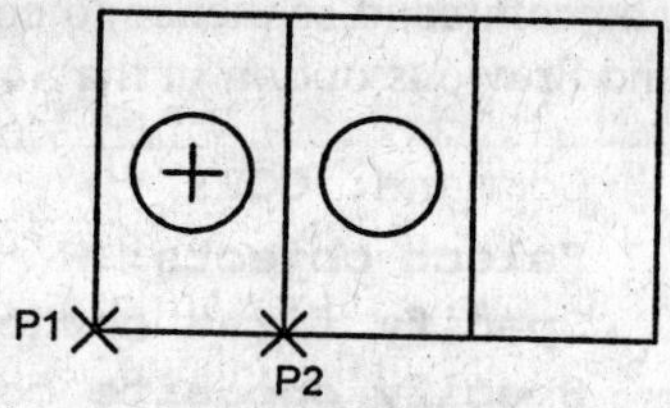

Circle after Copy

FIG. 16

2.18 SUBOBJECT (SU) OPTION

This option allows us to select original individual forms that are part of composite solids or vertices, edges, and faces on 3D solids. We can select one of these *subobjects* or create a selection set of more than one subobject. The selection set can include more than one type of subobject. The prompt is:

Select objects: *Select original individual forms that are part of composite solids or vertices, edges, and faces*

Pressing and holding the CTRL key is same as selecting the **SELECT** command's **Subobject** option.

2.19 OBJECT (O) OPTION

The **Object** option ends the ability to select subobjects. Also, this allows us to use object selection methods. The prompt is:

Select objects: *Use an object selection method*

*

7

CREATING TEXT

1. CREATING TEXT

The text in the drawings conveys a variety of information. It may be a complex specification, title block information, a label or even part of the drawing. In manual drafting, lettering is accomplished by hand using a lettering device, pen or pencil. This is a time-consuming and tedious job. AutoCAD has made this process extremely easy. Engineering Drawings invoke certain standards to be followed in connection with the placement of a text in a drawing.

In AutoCAD, there are two ways to create a text. They are, Single Line Text and Multiline Text. One of the new inclusions in AutoCAD is the Annotative Text option.

2. SINGLE LINE TEXT – TEXT COMMAND

The **Single Line** tool is most convenient for writing simple texts, such as labels, on a drawing. If you invoke the **Single Line** tool, AutoCAD prompts to specify the start point. Specify the start point either by left-clicking or by entering coordinates. By default text is left-justified along its baseline. Baseline is a line along which the text lie their bases. Then, AutoCAD prompts to specify the height and rotation angle of the text. Specify the height of the text. Also specify the rotation angle or press Enter.

Using the TEXT command, the user can create a single-line text object. The Text command can be activated using any one of the following methods:

1. Type **TEXT** in the command prompt and press Enter.
2. Choose **Single Line Text** tool on the **Annotation Panel** in the **Home** tab.
3. Choose **Single Line Text** tool from the **Text** in the **Draw** menu.

When the **Text** command is invoked, the next prompt displayed is as shown below:

Current text style: *<current>* **Current text height:** *<current>* **Annotative:** *<current>*
Specify start point of text or [Justify/Style]: *Specify a point or enter an option*

Use single-line text to create one or more lines of text, where each text line is an independent object that the user can relocate, reformat or otherwise modify.

The **TEXT** command creates a single-line text object. It displays a simplified version of the **In-Place Text Editor** that consists of a bounding box that is the height of the text and expands as the user types. Right-click to select options in the shortcut menu.

If the **DTEXTED** system variable is set to 1, text created using **TEXT** or **DTEXT** displays the **Edit Text** dialog box. The **Edit Text** dialog box is shown in **Fig. 1.**

FIG. 1

If **DTEXTED** is set to 2, the **In-Place Text Editor** is displayed. When creating text, the user can click anywhere in a drawing to create a new text block. The user can also use the keyboard to move among text blocks.

Note that text that would otherwise be difficult to read (if it is very small, very large or is rotated) is displayed at a legible size and is oriented horizontally so that user can easily read and edit it.

Problem 1: *Create a single line text using the Text command.*

The command sequence to create a single line text using the Text command is as follows:

```
Command: TEXT ↵
Current text style: "Standard" Text height: 0.2000  Annotative: No
Specify start point of text or [Justify/Style]: (Pick P1)
Specify height <0.2000>: 5 ↵
Specify rotation angle of text <0>: ↵
Enter text: TEXT EDITING ↵
Enter text: ↵
```

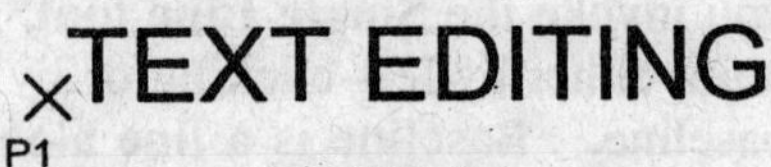

FIG. 2

See Fig. 2. The **Start Point** specifies a start point for the text object. The **Specify Height** prompt is displayed only if the current text style is not annotative and does not have a fixed height. The prompt is:

Specify height <*current*>: *Specify a point (1), enter a value or press* ENTER

The **Specify Paper Text Height** prompt is displayed only if the current text style is annotative. The prompt is:

Specify paper text height <*current*>: *Specify a height or press* ENTER

After displaying the **Specify Start Point** or **Specify Height** or **Specify paper text height** prompts, the next prompt displayed is the Specify rotation angle of text: as shown below:

Specify rotation angle of text <*current*>: *Specify an angle or press* ENTER

Enter text in the **In-Place Text Editor** for single-line text.

2.1 JUSTIFY OPTION

The **Justify** option controls justification of the text. If the user enters J in the Specify start point of text or [Justify/Style]: prompt, the next prompt displayed is:

`Enter an option [Align/Fit/Center/Middle/Right/TL/`
`TC/TR/ML/MC/MR/BL/BC/BR]` : *Specify an option or press* ENTER

The user can also enter any of these options at the Specify Start Point of Text prompt.

1. **Align:** The **Align** option specifies both text height and text orientation by designating the endpoints of the baseline. Enter text in the **In-Place Text Editor** for single-line text. The size of the characters adjusts in proportion to their height. The longer the text string, the shorter the characters.

2. **Fit:** The **Fit** option specifies that text fits within an area and at an orientation defined with two points and a height. The **Fit** option is available for horizontally oriented text only. Enter text in the In-Place Text Editor for single-line text. The longer the text string, the narrower the characters. The height of the characters remains constant.

3. **Center:** The **Center** option aligns text from the horizontal center of the baseline, which the users specify with a point. Enter text in the **In-Place Text Editor** for single-line text. The rotation angle specifies the orientation of the text baseline with respect to the center point. The text baseline runs from the start point toward the specified point. If the user specifies a point to the left of the center point, the text is drawn upside down.

4. **Middle:** The **Middle** option aligns text at the horizontal center of the baseline and the vertical center of the height the users specify. Middle-aligned text does not rest on the baseline. Enter text in the **In-Place Text Editor** for single-line text. The **Middle** option differs from the **MC** option in that it uses the midpoint of all text, including descenders. The **MC** option uses the midpoint of the height of uppercase letters.

5. **Right:** The **Right** option right-justifies the text at the baseline, which the users specify with a point. Enter text in the **In-Place Text Editor** for single-line text.

   See Fig. 3 for **Left, Center** and **Right** justifications.

FIG. 3

6. **TL (Top Left):** The **TL** option left-justifies text at a point specified for the top of the text. The **TL** option is available for horizontally oriented text only.

7. **TC (Top Center):** The **TC** option centers text at a point specified for the top of the text. The **TC** option is available for horizontally oriented text only.

8. **TR (Top Right):** The **TR** option right-justifies text at a point specified for the top of the text. The **TR** option is available for horizontally oriented text only.

9. **ML (Middle Left):** The **ML** option left-justifies text at a point specified for the middle of the text. The **ML** option is available for horizontally oriented text only.

10. **MC (Middle Center):** The **MC** option centers the text both horizontally and vertically at the middle of the text. The **MC** option is available for horizontally oriented text only. The **MC** option differs from the **Middle** option in that it uses the midpoint of the height of uppercase letters. The **Middle** option uses the midpoint of all text, including descenders.

11. **MR (Middle Right):** The **MR** option right-justifies text at a point specified for the middle of the text. The **MR** option is available for horizontally oriented text only.

12. **BL (Bottom Left):** The **BL** option left-justifies text at a point specified for the baseline. The **BL** option is available for horizontally oriented text only.

13. **BC (Bottom Center):** The **BC** option centers text at a point specified for the baseline. The **BC** option is available for horizontally oriented text only.

14. **BR (Bottom Right):** The **BR** option right-justifies text at a point specified for the baseline. The **BR** option is available for horizontally oriented text only.

See Fig. 4 for TL (Top Left), TC (Top Center), TR (Top Right), ML (Middle Left), MC (Middle Center), MR (Middle Right), BL (Bottom Left), BC (Bottom Center) and BR (Bottom Right) options.

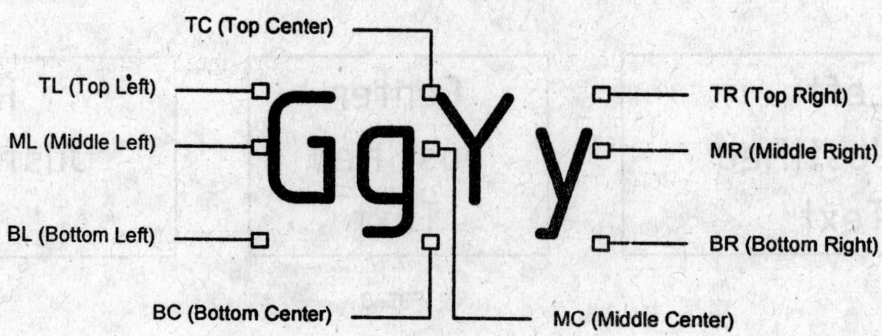

FIG. 4

2.2 STYLE OPTION

The **Style** option specifies the text style, which determines the appearance of the text characters. Text you create uses the current text style. If the **Style** option is selected, then the next prompt displayed is:

`Enter style name or [?] <current>:` *Enter a text style name or enter ? to list all text styles*

Enter *?* in the command prompt to list the current text styles, associated font files, height and other parameters. The options in the **Style** are defined in the **Text Style** dialog box.

3. STYLE COMMAND

By default, AutoCAD writes texts using the default text style called as **Standard**. To write a text using some other fonts and other parameters, the **Text Editor** is used. In the **Text Editor**, user can change the formatting and font of the text using this command only.

However, using the **Text Editor** every time to write the text and change its properties is a tedious job. To solve this tedious job, AutoCAD provides an option for modifying the default text style or creating a new text style using the Style tool. After creating a new text style, user can make it current. All the texts written after making the new style current will use this style.

The **STYLE** command is used to create, modify or set named text styles. The **Style** tool can be invoked by any one of the following methods:

1. Type **STYLE** or **ST** in the command prompt and press Enter.
2. Choose **Text Style** tool in the **Annotation Panel** in the **Home** tab.
3. Choose **Text Style** tool from the **Format** menu.

When the **Style** command is invoked, the **Text Style** dialog box is displayed on the screen as shown in **Fig. 5**. The options in the **Text Style** dialog box are explained below:

Current Text Style: This area lists the current text style.

Styles: The **Styles** area displays the list of styles in the drawing. The list contains defined style names and displays the current style that is selected by default. To change the current style, select another style from the list or choose New to create a new style.

Style names can be up to 255 characters long. They can contain letters, numbers and the special characters dollar sign ($), underscore (_) and hyphen (-).

Style List Filter: The **Style List Filter** drop-down list specifies whether all styles or only the styles in use are displayed in the styles list.

Preview: The **Preview** box displays sample text that changes dynamically as the user changes fonts and modifies the effects.

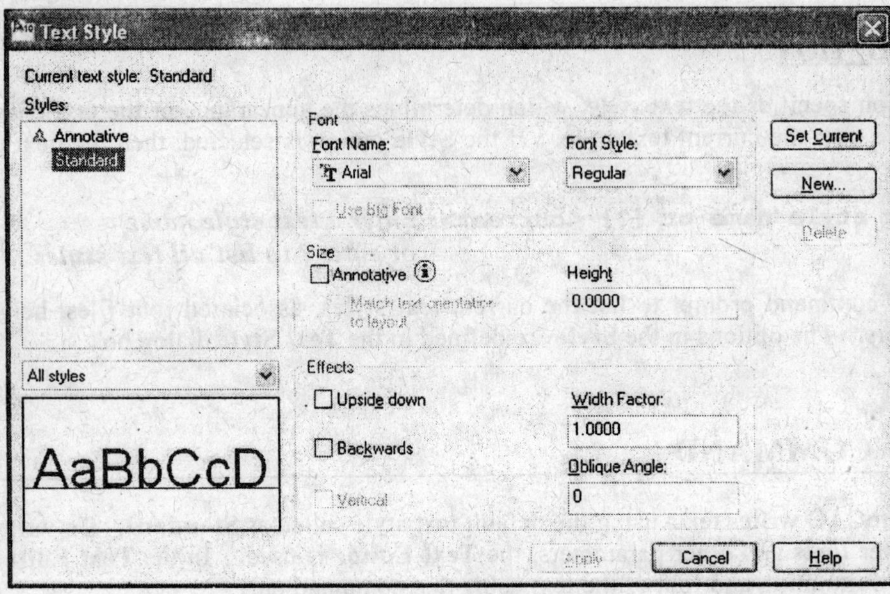

FIG. 5

Font: The **Font** area changes the style's font. Note that if the user changes the orientation or font file of an existing text style, all text objects with that style use the new values when the drawing is regenerated.

Font Name dropdown list specifies the font family name for all registered **TrueType** fonts and all compiled shape (SHX) fonts in the *Fonts* folder.

Font Style dropdown list specifies font character formatting, such as italic, bold or regular. When **Use Big Font** is selected, this option changes to **Big Font Name** and is used to select a **Big Font** file name.

Use Big Font checkbox specifies an Asian-language Big Font file. Use **Big Font** is available only if user specifies an SHX file under Font Name. Only SHX files are valid file types for creating **Big Fonts.**

Size: The **Size** area changes the size of the text.

Annotative checkbox specifies that the text is annotative. Click the information icon to learn more about the annotative objects.

Match Text Orientation to Layout checkbox specifies that the orientation of the text in paper space viewports matches the orientation of the layout. This option is unavailable if the **Annotative** option is cleared.

Height or Paper Text Height checkbox sets the text height based on the value user entered. If a height entered greater than 0.0 sets the text height for this style automatically. If user enters 0.0, the text height defaults to the last text height used or the value stored in the drawing template file.

Effects: The **Effects** area modifies characteristics of the font, such as its height, width factor and obliquing angle and whether it is displayed upside down, backwards or vertically aligned.

Upside Down checkbox displays the characters upside down.

Backwards checkbox displays the characters backwards.

Vertical checkbox displays the characters aligned vertically. Vertical is available only if the selected font supports dual orientation. Vertical orientation is not available for TrueType fonts.

Width Factor textbox sets the character spacing. Entering a value less than *1.0* condenses the text. Entering a value greater than *1.0* expands it.

Oblique Angle check box sets the obliquing angle of the text. Entering a value between *-85* and *85* italicizes the text.

Note that the **TrueType** fonts using the effects described in this section might appear bold on the screen. Onscreen appearance has no effect on plotted output. Fonts are plotted as specified by applied character formatting.

Set Current: The **Set Current** button sets the style selected under Styles to current.

New: The **New** button displays the **New Text** Style dialog box and automatically supplies the name 'style*n*' (where *n* is the number of the supplied style) for the current settings.

The user can accept the default or enter a name and choose **OK** to apply the current style settings to the new style name. The **New Text Style** dialog box is shown in **Fig. 6.**

FIG. 6

Delete: The **Delete** button deletes unused text styles.

Apply: The **Apply** button applies style changes made in the dialog box to the current style and to the text of the current style in the drawing.

See Fig. 7. It shows examples for various fonts, sizes and effects.

Style1 - Font Name Arial - Size 5

Style2 – Font Name Times – Size 3

Style3 – Font Name Times New Roman - Size 4

FIG. 7

4. MULTILINE TEXT – MTEXT COMMAND

The **Multiline Text** tool is used to create a multiline text object. The width of the multiline text is defined by two corners of the text boundary or by entering a width using the coordinate entry. The text created using the **Multiline Text** tool is a single object regardless of the number of lines it contains. The **Multiline Text** tool can be invoked by any one of the following methods:

1. Type **MTEXT** or **MT** in the command prompt and press Enter.
2. Choose **Multiline Text** tool in the **Annotation Panel** in the **Home** tab.
3. Choose **Multiline Text** tool from the **Text** on the **Draw** menu.

When the MTEXT command is activated, the next prompt displayed is as follows:

```
Current text style: <current> Text height: <current> Annotative: <current>
Specify first corner:
Specify opposite corner or [Height/Justify/Line spacing/
                                  Rotation/Style/Width/Columns]:
```

The user can create several paragraphs of text as a single multiline text (mtext) object. With the built-in editor, the user can format the text appearance, columns and boundaries.

After specifying the point for the opposite corner when the ribbon is active, the **MTEXT ribbon contextual tab** displays as shown in **Fig. 8.** If the ribbon is not active, the **in-place text editor** is displayed.

FIG. 8

Panels in the **Text Editor** tab are:

1. **Style Panel:** The **Style Panel** includes available list of Styles, Annotative and Text Height.
2. **Formatting Panel:** The **Formatting Panel** holds options such as Bold, Italic, Underline, Overline, Font, Color, Oblique Angle, Tracking and Width Factor.
3. **Paragraph Panel:** The **Paragraph Panel** possesses options such as Mtext justification, Paragraph Line Spacing, Numbering and Left, Center, Right, Justified & Distributed.
4. **Insert Panel:** The **Insert Panel** includes options such as Symbol, Insert Field and Columns.
5. **Options Panel:** The **Options Panels** contains options such as Find and Replace, Spell Check, Undo, Redo, Ruler and Options.
6. **Close Panel:** The **Close Panel** ends the MTEXT command and closes the MTEXT ribbon contextual tab.

If the user specifies one of the other options or if the user enters *-mtext* at the Command prompt, **MTEXT** bypasses the **In-Place Text Editor** and displays additional command prompts.

*

8

BASIC DISPLAY COMMANDS

1. BASIC DISPLAY COMMANDS

After creating drawings on the screen, it may be necessary to magnify a part or whole of the drawing for its close analysis or to shrink to bring more drawings into the graphics area. Magnifying the drawings is known as **Zooming in**. Shrinking the drawings is known as **Zooming out**.

This is done by using the **ZOOM** command. This command allows you to enlarge or reduce the size of the drawing displayed on the screen. Similarly, the user can slide the drawing view. This can be done by using the **PAN** tool.

2. ZOOM COMMAND

The ZOOM command is used to enlarge or reduce the view of a drawing on the screen, without affecting the actual size of entities. The Zoom tools are grouped together and are available in the Navigator bar. To invoke different Zoom tools, click on the down arrow next to the Zoom Extents tool in the Navigate panel on the View tab. All the options of the Zoom command will be displayed in the drop-down as shown in **Fig. 1.**

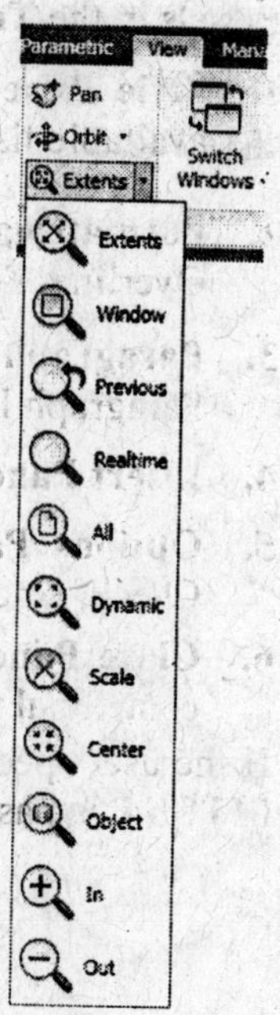

FIG. 1

The Zoom command can be invoked by any one of the following methods:

1. Type **Zoom** or **Z** in the command prompt and press Enter.
2. Choose **Zoom** in the Navigate panel in the View tab.
3. Choose **Zoom** from the View menu and then select Realtime.

User can change the magnification of a view by zooming in and out, which is similar to zooming in and out with a camera. Using ZOOM does not change the absolute size of objects in the drawing. It changes only the magnification of the view.

While working with the minute parts in the drawing, it may need to zoom out frequently to see an overview of the work. Use ZOOM Previous command to return quickly to the prior view.

When the Zoom command is activated, the next prompt displayed is:

Specify corner of window, enter a scale factor (nX or nXP) or [All/Center/Dynamic/Extents/Previous/Scale/Window/Object] <real time>:

Options in the Zoom command are: All, Center, Dynamic, Extents, Previous, Scale, Window and Object. There are two more options available in the drop-down list shown in **Fig. 1.** They are Zoom In and Out. These options are used to double the view of an image size or decrease the view of the image by half, respectively.

2.1 ALL OPTION

The All option zooms to display the entire drawing in the current viewport. In a plan view, All zooms to the grid limits or current extents, whichever is greater. In a 3D view, ZOOM All is equivalent to ZOOM Extents. The display shows all objects even if the drawing extends outside the grid limits.

Problem 1: *Display all the objects using the All option in the Zoom command.*

The command sequence to view all the objects using the All option in the Zoom command is as follows:

```
Command: ZOOM ↵
Specify corner of window, enter a scale factor (nX or nXP) or
                                [All/Center/Dynamic/Extents/ Previous/
                                Scale/Window/Object] <real time>: A ↵
```

See Fig. 2.

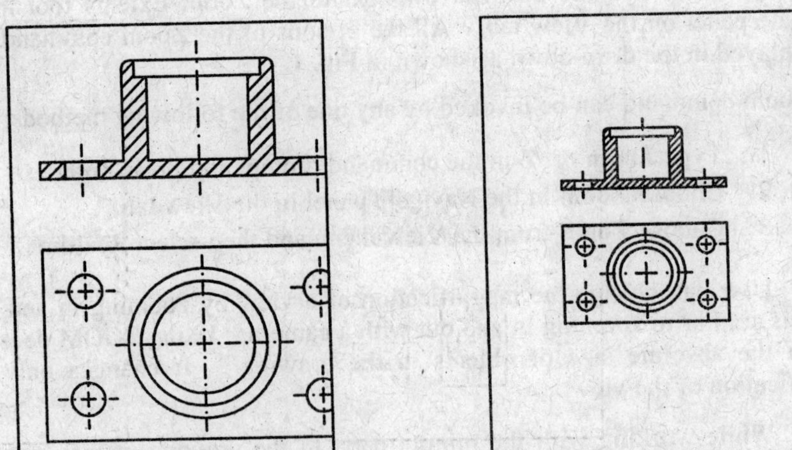

Before Zoom

After Zoom All

FIG. 2

2.2 CENTER OPTION

The Center option zooms to display a view defined by a center point and a magnification value or a height. A smaller value for the height increases the magnification. A larger value decreases the magnification. If the Center option of the Zoom command is selected, then the prompt displayed is:

Specify center point: *Specify a point*

Enter magnification or height <current>: *Enter a value or press* ENTER

2.3 DYNAMIC OPTION

The Dynamic options pans and zooms using a rectangular viewbox. The view box represents the view, which user can shrink or enlarge and move around the drawing. Positioning and sizing the view box pans or zooms to fill the viewport with the view inside the view box.

- To change the size of the view box, click, resize it and click again to accept the new size of the view box.
- To pan with the view box, drag it to the location user wants and press ENTER.

2.4 EXTENTS OPTION

The Extents option zooms in or out to display the extents of the drawing. This results in the largest possible display of all the objects.

Problem 2: *Display all the objects using the Extends option in the Zoom command.*

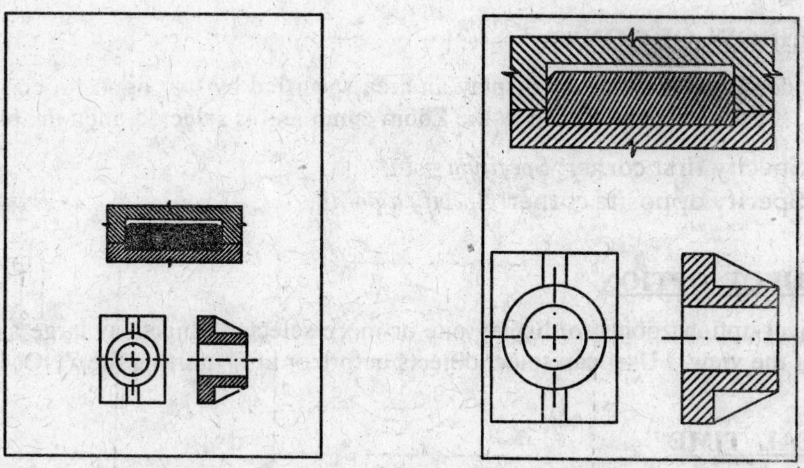

Before Zoom After Zoom Extend

FIG. 3

See Fig. 3. The command sequence to view all the objects using the Extends option in the Zoom command is as follows:

```
Command: ZOOM ↵
Specify corner of window, enter a scale factor (nX or nXP) or
                              [All/Center/Dynamic/Extents/Previous/
                              Scale/Window/Object] <real time>: E ↵
```

2.5 PREVIOUS OPTION

The Previous option zooms to display the previous view. User can restore up to 10 previous views. Note that if user changes the visual style, the view is changed. If user enters ZOOM Previous, it restores the previous view, which is shaded differently but not zoomed differently.

2.6 SCALE OPTION

The Scale option zooms to change the magnification of a view using a scale factor. If the Scale option in the Zoom command is selected, then the prompt displayed is:

Enter a scale factor (nX or nXP): *Specify a value*

- Enter a value followed by *x* to specify the scale relative to the current view.
- Enter a value followed by *xp* to specify the scale relative to paper space units.

For example, entering *.5x* causes each object to be displayed at half its current size on the screen. Entering *.5xp* displays model space at half the scale of paper space units. User can create a layout with each viewport displaying objects at a different scale.

Enter a value to specify the scale relative to the grid limits of the drawing. (This option is rarely used.) For example, entering *2* displays objects at twice the size they would appear if user were zoomed to the limits of the drawing.

2.7 WINDOW OPTION

The Window option zooms to display an area specified by two opposite corners of a rectangular window. If the Window option in the Zoom command is selected, then the prompt displayed is:

Specify first corner: *Specify a point*
Specify opposite corner: *Specify a point*

2.8 OBJECT OPTION

The Object option zooms to display one or more selected objects as large as possible and in the center of the view. User can select objects before or after starting the ZOOM command.

2.9 REAL TIME

The Real Time option zooms interactively to change the magnification of the view. If the Real Time option in the Zoom command is selected, then the prompt displayed is:

Press ESC or ENTER to exit or right-click to display the shortcut menu

The cursor changes to a magnifying glass with plus (+) and minus (-) signs. Holding down the pick button at the midpoint of the window and moving vertically to the top of the window zooms in to 100%. Conversely, holding the pick button down at the midpoint of the window and moving vertically to the bottom of the window zooms out by 100%.

When user reaches the zoom-in limit, the plus sign in the cursor disappears, indicating that user can no longer zoom in. When user reaches the zoom-out limit, the minus sign in the cursor disappears, indicating that user can no longer zoom out.

When user releases the pick button, zooming operation stops. User can release the pick button, move the cursor to another location in the drawing and then press the pick button again and continue to zoom the display from that location. To exit zooming, press ENTER or ESC.

3. PAN COMMAND

The **Pan** tool is used to move a view by sliding and placing it at the required position. The **Pan** tool can be invoked by any one of the following methods:

1. Type **PAN** or **P** in the command prompt and press Enter.
2. Choose **Pan** in the Navigate panel in the View tab.
3. Choose **Pan** from the View menu and then select Realtime.

When the **Pan** command is activated, the pointer (arrow) is changed as a hand image. Drag the cursor in any direction to move the drawing. To exit the Pan tool, press ESC or ENTER key.

With the Realtime option of PAN command, user can pan dynamically by moving the pointing device. Like panning with a camera, PAN does not change the location or magnification of objects on the drawing; it changes only the view.

If the user enters *-pan* at the Command prompt, PAN displays command prompts and user can specify a displacement to pan the drawing display.

4. BLIPMODE COMMAND

Blips are the temporary marks that appear on the screen, whenever a click is made on the screen. The blip marks are used only for reference points. The blip marks are not plotted.

The BLIPMODE command controls the display of blip marks. The blips can be made either ON or OFF using the Blipmode system variable.

When Blip mode is on, a temporary mark in the shape of a plus sign (+) appears where the user specifies a point. BLIPMODE is off by default.

The Blip mode can be made ON using the following prompt sequence:

```
Command: BLIPMODE ↵
Enter mode [ON/OFF] <OFF>: ON ↵
```

See Fig. 4.

The Blip mode can be made OFF using the following prompt sequence:

```
Command: BLIPMODE ↵
Enter mode [ON/OFF] <ON>: OFF ↵
```

To remove marker blips, use REDRAW, REGEN, ZOOM, PAN or other commands that redraw or regenerate the drawing.

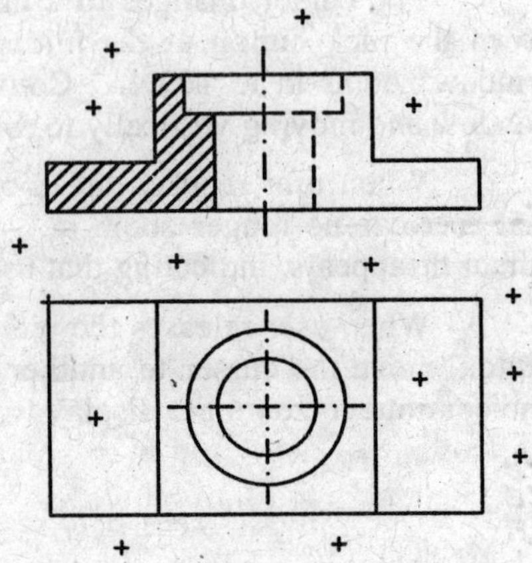

FIG. 4

5. REDRAW COMMAND

The REDRAW command refreshes the display in the current viewport. To activate the Redraw command, enter REDRAW or R in the command prompt.

When BLIPMODE is on, marker blips left by editing commands are removed from the current viewport.

6. REGEN COMMAND

The REGEN command regenerates the entire drawing from the current viewport. The Regen command can be invoked using any one of the following methods:

1. Type **REGEN** or **RE** in the command prompt.
2. Choose **Regen** tool from the View menu.

The Regen command regenerates the entire drawing and re-computes the screen coordinates for all objects in the current viewport. It also re-indexes the drawing database for optimum display and object selection performance.

If the Regen command is activated, then the prompt displayed is:

```
Command: REGEN ↵
Regenerating model.
```

*

9

BASIC DIMENSIONING

1. OVERVIEW OF DIMENSIONING

Dimensioning is the process of adding measurement annotation to a drawing. User can create dimensions for a variety of object types in many orientations. The basic types of dimensioning are, Linear, Radial (radius, diameter and jogged), Angular, Ordinate and Arc Length.

Linear dimensions can be horizontal, vertical, aligned, rotated, baseline or continued (chained). Note that to simplify drawing organization and dimension scaling, it is recommended that user creates dimensions on layouts rather than in model space.

2. PARTS OF A DIMENSION

Dimensions have several distinct elements. **See Fig. 1.** A list of the parts of a dimension along with their descriptions as listed below:

1. **Dimension Text:** Dimension Text is a text string that usually indicates the measurement value. The text can also include prefixes, suffixes and tolerances.

2. **Dimension Lines:** A Dimension Line indicates the direction and extent of a dimension. For angular dimensions, the dimension line is an arc.

3. **Arrowheads:** Arrowheads, also called Symbols of Termination, are displayed at each end of the dimension line. User can specify different sizes and shapes for arrowheads or tick marks.

4. **Extension Lines:** Extension Lines, also called Projection Lines or Witness Lines, extend from the feature to the dimension line.

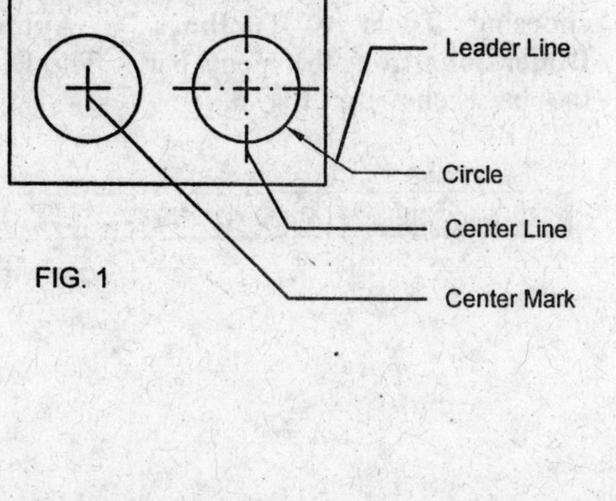

FIG. 1

Center Mark: A Center Mark is a small cross that marks the center of a circle or arc.

Centerlines: Centerlines are broken lines that mark the center of a circle or arc.

2.1 ASSOCIATIVE DIMENSIONS

Dimensions can be Associative, Nonassociative or Exploded. Associative dimensions adjust to changes in the geometric objects that they measure.

Dimension associativity defines the relationship between geometric objects and the dimensions that give their distance and angles. There are three types of associativity between geometric objects and dimensions.

1. **Associative Dimensions:** These dimensions automatically adjust their locations orientations and measurement values when the geometric objects associated with them are modified. Dimensions in a layout may be associated to objects in model space. The DIMASSOC system variable is set to 2.

2. **Nonassociative Dimensions:** These dimensions are selected and modified with the geometry they measure. Nonassociative dimensions do not change when the geometric objects they measure are modified. The dimension variable DIMASSOC is set to 1.

3. **Exploded dimensions:** These dimensions contain a collection of separate objects rather than a single dimension object. The DIMASSOC system variable is set to 0.

3. TYPES OF DIMENSIONS

The fundamental dimensioning types that the AutoCAD provides are: Quick dimensioning, Linear Dimensioning, Diameter dimensioning, Radius dimensioning, Angular Dimensioning, Ordinate dimensioning, Arc Length dimensioning, Aligned dimensioning, Jogged dimensioning. User can select the required command using any one of the following methods:

1. Select dimensioning tools from the **Dimensions** panel of the **Annotate** tab. **See Fig. 2.**

2. Select dimensioning tools from the **Dimension** toolbar. The dimension toolbar is displayed by choosing **Tools > Toolbars > AutoCAD > Dimensions** from the menu bar. The Dimension tool bar is shown in **Fig. 3.**

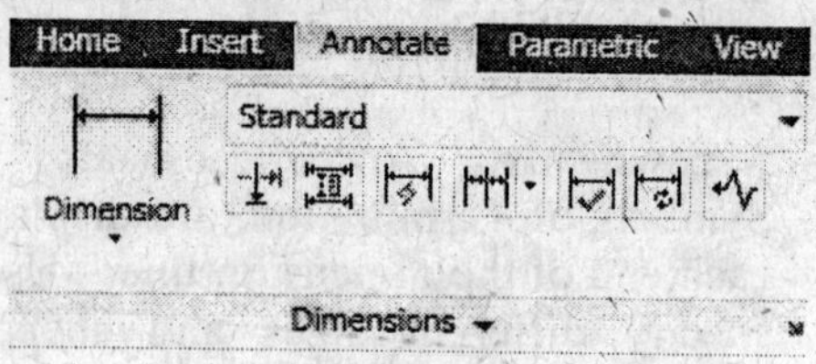

FIG. 2

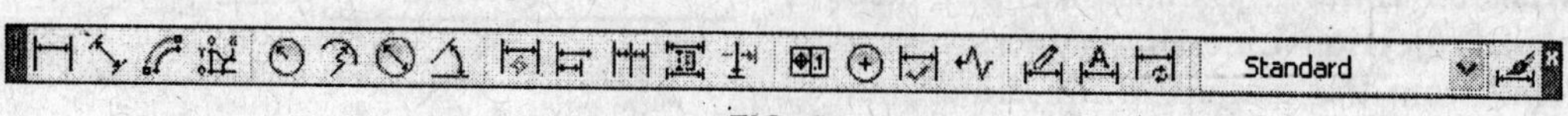

FIG. 3

Types of dimensions

In AutoCAD, types of dimensions are grouped together and are available in the Dimensions panel of the View tab. **See Fig. 4.** In this chapter, the types dimensions are explained in detail.

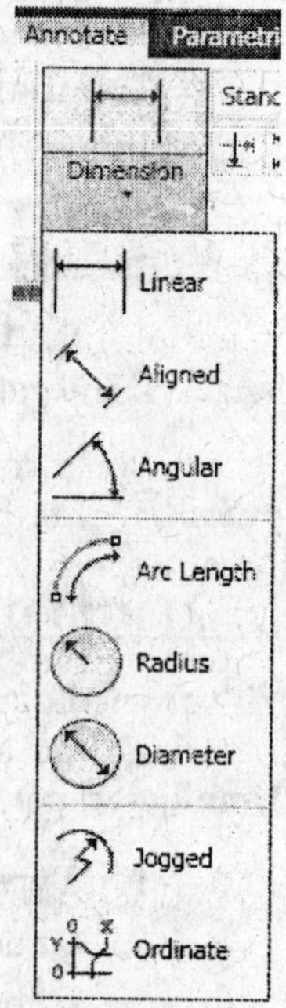

FIG. 4

3.1 LINEAR DIMENSIONS

Linear dimensions can be horizontal, vertical or aligned. These linear dimensions can also be stacked or they can be created end to end. While creating linear dimensions, user can modify the content of the text, the angle of the text or the angle of the dimension line.

User can create dimensions using only the horizontal or vertical components of the locations or objects that user specified. The **Dimlinear** command is used for this type of dimensions.

The **Linear** tool creates a linear dimension with a horizontal, vertical or rotated dimension line. The **Linear** tool can be activated using any one of the following methods:

1. Type **DIMLINEAR** or **DLI** in the command prompt and press Enter.
2. Choose **Linear** tool from the **Dimensions** panel of the Annotate tab.
3. Choose **Linear** tool from the **Dimension** menu.

Problem 1: *Create linear dimensions using the DIMLINEAR command.*

The command sequence to create linear dimensions using the DIMLINEAR command is given below:

Command: **DIMLINEAR** ↵
Specify first extension line origin or <select object>: *(Pick P1)*
Specify second extension line origin: *(Pick P2)*
Specify dimension line location or
[Mtext/Text/Angle/Horizontal/Vertical/Rotated]: *(Pick P3)*
Dimension text = 35

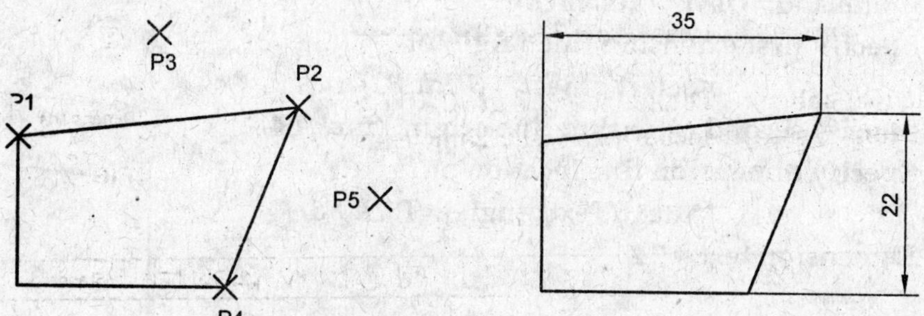

FIG. 5

Command: **DIMLINEAR** ↵
Specify first extension line origin or <select object>: *(Pick P2)*
Specify second extension line origin: ***(Pick P4)***
Specify dimension line location or
[Mtext/Text/Angle/Horizontal/Vertical/Rotated]: ***(Pick P5)***
Dimension text = 22

See Fig. 5.

3.2 ALIGNED DIMENSIONS

With aligned dimensions, the dimension line is parallel to the line (imaginary or real) between the extension line origins. The **DIMALIGNED** command creates aligned dimension. The **Dimaligned** command can be activated using any one of the following methods:

1. Type **DIMALIGNED** or **DAL** in the command prompt and press Enter.
2. Choose **Aligned** tool from the **Dimensions** panel of the **Annotate** tab.
3. Choose **Aligned** tool from the **Dimension** menu.

Problem 2: *Draw aligned dimensions using the DIMALIGNED command.*

The command sequence to create aligned dimension using the DIMALIGNED command is:

Command: **DIMALIGNED** ↵
Specify first extension line origin or
<select object>: ***(Pick P1)***
Specify second extension line origin: ***(Pick P2)***
Specify dimension line location or
[Mtext/Text/Angle]: ***(Pick P3)***
Dimension text = 35

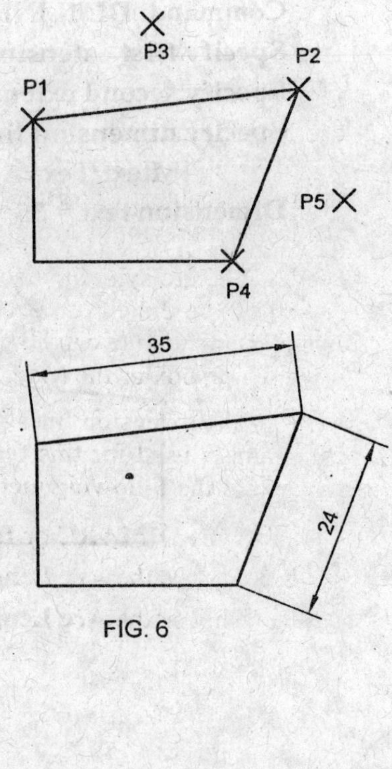

FIG. 6

Command: **DIMALIGNED** ↵
Specify first extension line origin or
<select object>: ***(Pick P2)***
Specify second extension line origin: ***(Pick P4)***
Specify dimension line location or
[Mtext/Text/Angle]: ***(Pick P5)***
Dimension text = 24

See Fig. 6.

3.3 ANGULAR DIMENSIONS

Angular dimensions measure the angle between two lines or three points. To measure the angle between two radii of a circle, select the circle and specify the angle endpoints. With other objects, select the objects and then specify the dimension location.

The **Dimangular** command is used for this type of dimensions. The Dimangular command can be activated using any one of the following methods:

1. Type **DIMANGULAR** or **DAN** in the command prompt and press Enter.
2. Click **Angular** on the Dimensions panel of the Annotate tab.
3. Select **Angular** from the Dimension menu.

Problem 3: *Draw an angular dimension using the DIMANGULAR command.*

The command sequence to create an angle using the Dimangular command is given below:

Command: **DIMANGULAR** ↵
Select arc, circle, line,
or <specify vertex>: *(Pick P1)*
Select second line: *(Pick P2)*
Specify dimension arc line location
or [Mtext/Text/Angle/
Quadrant]: *(Pick P3)*
Dimension text = 112

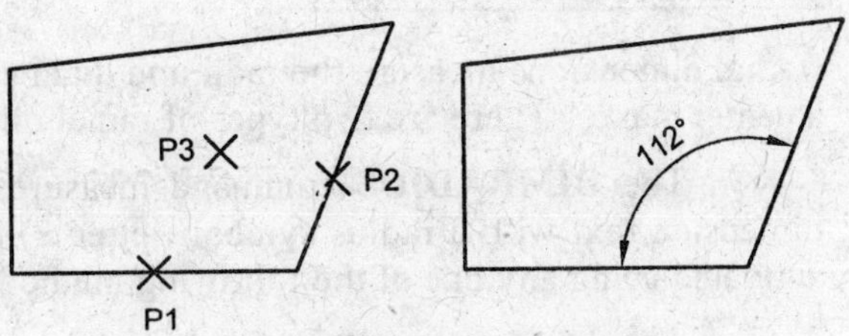

FIG. 7

See Fig. 7.

3.4 ARC LENGTH DIMENSIONS

Arc length dimensions measure the distance along an arc or polyline arc segment. Typical uses of arc length dimensions include measuring the travel distance around a cam or indicating the length of a cable. To differentiate them from linear or angular dimensions, arc length dimensions display an arc symbol by default.

The arc symbol, also called a Hat or Cap, is displayed either above the dimension text or preceding the dimension text. Specify the placement style using the Dimension Style Manager. The placement style can be changed on the Symbols and Arrows tab of either the New Dimension Style dialog box or the Modify Dimension Style dialog box.

The extension lines of an arc length dimension can be orthogonal or radial. The **Dimarc** command is used for this type of dimensions. The **DIMARC** command can be activated using any one of the following methods:

1. Type **DIMARC** or **DAR** in the command prompt and press Enter.
2. Choose the **Arc Length** tool from the **Dimensions** panel of the **Annotate** tab.
3. Choose the **Arc Length** tool from the **Dimension** menu.

Problem 4: *Draw the measurement of an arc using the DIMARC command.*

The command sequence to measure the length of an arc using the Dimarc command is given below:

Command: **DIMARC** ↵
Select arc or polyline arc segment: *(Select the arc)*
Specify arc length dimension location,
or [Mtext/Text/Angle/
Partial/Leader]: *(Pick a point)*
Dimension text = 28

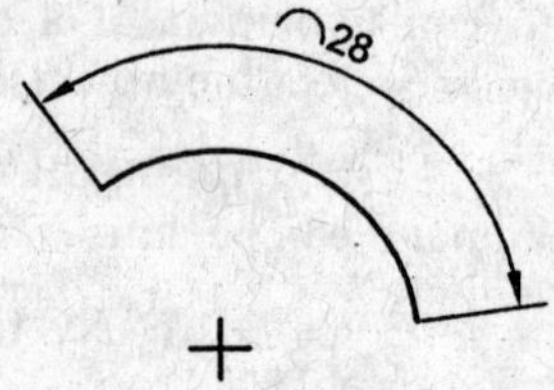

FIG. 8

See Fig. 8.

3.5 RADIUS DIMENSION

Radial dimensions measure the radii and diameters of arcs and circles with optional centerlines or a center mark. There are two types of radial dimensions: Dimradius and Dimdiameter.

The **DIMRADIUS** command measures the radius of an arc or circle and displays the dimension text with a radius symbol (letter *R*) in front of it. The **Dimradius** command can be activated using any one of the following methods:

1. Type **DIMRADIUS** or **DRA** in the command prompt and press Enter.
2. Choose **Radius** on the **Dimensions** panel of the **Annotate** tab.
3. Choose **Radius** from the **Dimension** menu.

Problem 5: *Draw a radius of a circle using the DIMRADIUS command.*

The command sequence to create a radius of the circle using the DIMRADIUS command is given below:

Command: **DIMRADIUS** ↵
Select arc or circle: *(Select the Circle)*
Dimension text = 10
Specify dimension line location or
[Mtext/Text/Angle]: *(Pick P1)*

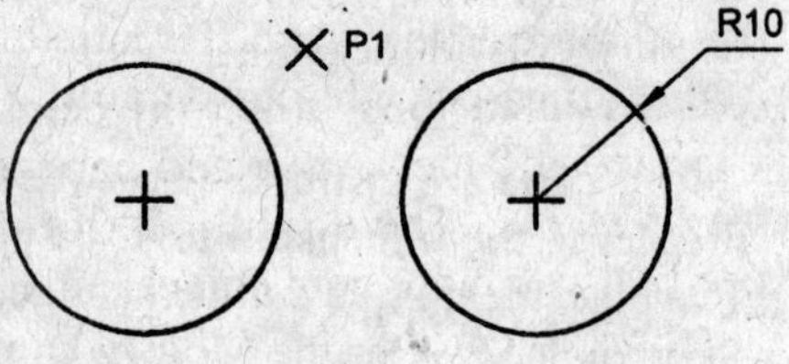

FIG. 9

See Fig. 9.

3.6 DIAMETER DIMENSION

The **DIMDIAMETER** command measures the diameter of an arc or circle and displays the dimension text with the diameter symbol (∅) in front of it.

The Dimdiameter command can be activated using any one of the following methods:

1. Type **DIMDIAMETER** or **DDI** in the command prompt and press Enter.
2. Choose the **Diameter** tool on the **Dimensions** panel of the **Annotate** tab.
3. Choose the **Diameter** tool from the **Dimension** menu.

Problem 6: *Draw the diameter of a circle using the DIMDIAMETER command.*

The command sequence to create a diameter of the circle using the Dimdiameter command is given below:

Command: **DIMDIAMETER** ↵
Select arc or circle: *(Select the Circle)*
Dimension text = 20
Specify dimension line location or
[Mtext/Text/Angle]: *(Pick P1)*

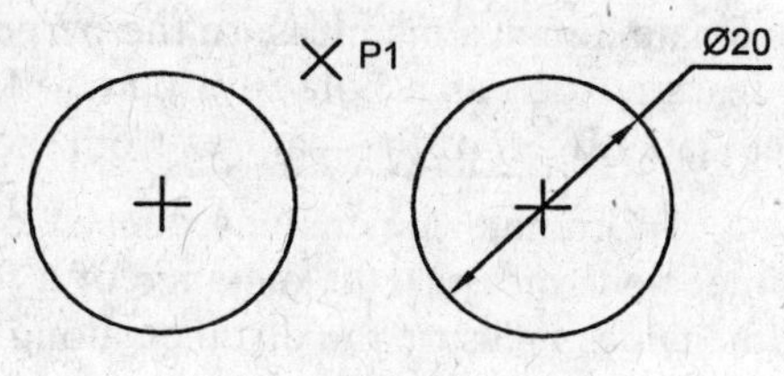

FIG. 10

See Fig. 10.

3.7 JOGGED DIMENSION

There are some instances when it is not possible to show the center of the circle in the sheet. In such situations, the jogged dimensions are used.

For example, see **Fig. 11.** In this figure, it may not be possible to mark the center of the circle. In such situations, the jogged dimensions are used. Note that, using the **Jogged** tool, it is possible to add only jogged radius dimensions.

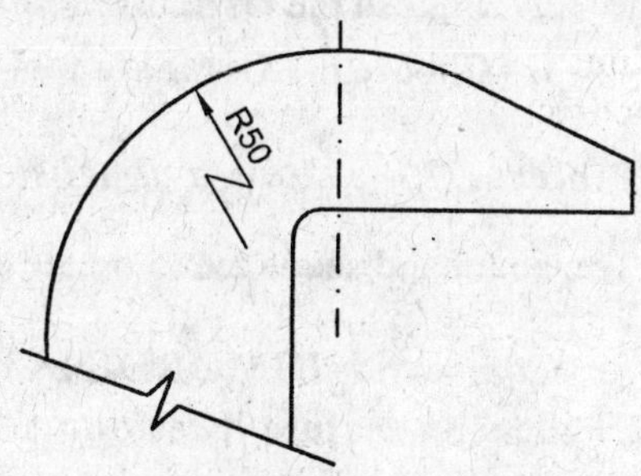

FIG. 11

With the DIMJOGGED command, you can create jogged radius dimensions, also called **Foreshortened Radius Dimensions**, when the center of an arc or circle is located off the layout and cannot be displayed in its true location. The origin point of the dimension can be specified at a more convenient location called the **Center Location Override.**

User can control the default angle of the jog in the **Modify Dimension Style** dialog box, **Symbols and Arrows** tab, under **Radius Dimension Jog.** These options are explained later in this chapter. The terminology of the Jogged dimension is shown in **Fig. 12.**

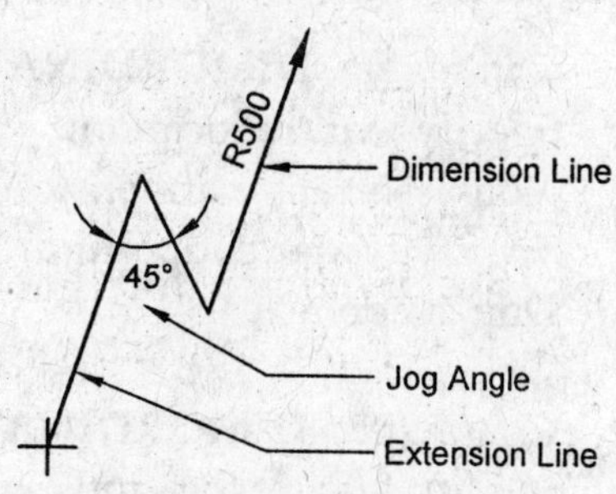

FIG. 12

Once a jogged radius dimension is created, modify the jog and the center location override by any one of the following methods:

1. Using grips to move the features
2. Changing the locations of the features with the Properties palette
3. Using STRETCH

Note that the Jogged radius dimensions can be viewed but not edited in versions previous to AutoCAD 2006. Also, if you make dramatic changes to the associated geometry, you may get unpredictable results for the jogged radius dimension.

3.8 ORDINATE DIMENSIONS

Ordinate dimensions measure the perpendicular distance from an origin point called the *datum* to a feature, such as a hole in a part. These dimensions prevent escalating errors by maintaining accurate offsets of the features from the datum.

Ordinate dimensions consist of an *X* or *Y* value with a leader line. *X*-datum ordinate dimensions measure the distance of a feature from the datum along the *X* axis. *Y*-datum ordinate dimensions measure the distance along the *Y* axis.

The **Dimordinate** command is used for this type of dimensions. The **Dimordinate** command can be activated using any one of the following methods:

1. Type **DIMORDINATE** or **DOR** in the command prompt and press Enter.
2. Choose the **Ordinate** tool from the **Dimensions** panel of the **Annotate** tab.
3. Choose the **Ordinate** tool from the **Dimension** menu.

Problem 7: *Draw a dimension using the DIMORDINATE command.*

The command sequence to create a dimension using the Dimordinate command is given below:

Command: **DIMORDINATE** ↵
Specify feature location:
Specify leader endpoint or [Xdatum/Ydatum/Mtext/Text/Angle]: *(Specify a point)*
Dimension text = 0

Command: **DIMORDINATE** ↵
Specify feature location:
Non-associative dimension created.
Specify leader endpoint or [Xdatum/Ydatum/Mtext/Text/Angle]: *(Specify a point)*
Dimension text = 0

Command: **DIMORDINATE** ↵
Specify feature location:
Specify leader endpoint or [Xdatum/Ydatum/Mtext/Text/Angle]: *(Specify a point)*
Dimension text = 11

Command: **DIMORDINATE** ↵
Specify feature location:
Specify leader endpoint or
[Xdatum/Ydatum/Mtext/
Text/Angle]: *(Specify a point)*
Dimension text = 13

Command: **DIMORDINATE** ↵
Specify feature location:
Specify leader endpoint or
[Xdatum/Ydatum/Mtext/
Text/Angle]: *(Specify a point)*
Dimension text = 33

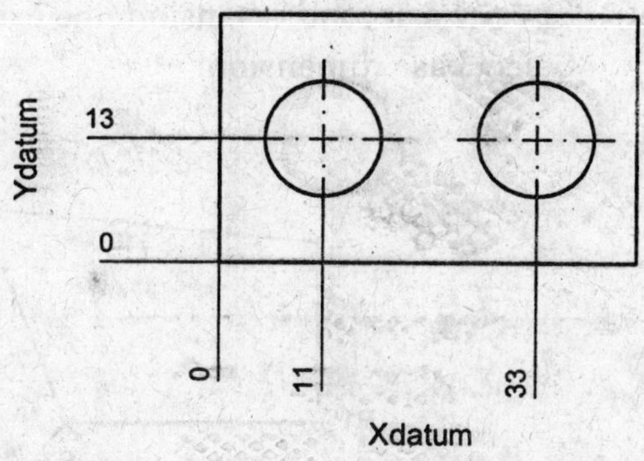

FIG. 13

See Fig. 13.

3.9 CREATE BASELINE AND CONTINUED DIMENSIONS

Baseline dimensions are multiple dimensions measured from the same baseline. Continued dimensions are multiple dimensions placed end to end. The **Dimbaseline** and **Dimcontinue** commands are used for this type of dimensions.

Baseline (or parallel) and continued (or chain) dimensions are series of consecutive dimensions that are based on a linear dimension. The DIMBASELINE command creates a linear, angular or ordinate dimension from the baseline of the previous or selected dimension. The Dimbaseline command can be activated using any one of the following methods:

1. Type **DIMBASELINE** or **DBA** in the command prompt and press Enter.
2. Choose the **Baseline** tool from the **Dimensions** panel of the **Annotate** tab.
3. Choose the **Baseline** tool from the **Dimension** menu.

Problem 8: *Draw a baseline dimension using the DIMBASELINE command.*

The command sequence to create baseline dimension using the DIMBASELINE command is given below:

Command: **DIMLINEAR** ↵
Specify first extension line origin or <select object>: *(Pick P1)*
Specify second extension line origin: *(Pick P2)*
Specify dimension line location or
[Mtext/Text/Angle/Horizontal/Vertical/Rotated]: *(Pick P3)*
Dimension text = 26

Command: **DIMBASELINE** ↵
Specify a second extension line origin or [Undo/Select] <Select>: *(Pick P4)*

Dimension text = 35

Specify a second extension line origin or [Undo/Select] <Select>: ↵

Select base dimension: ↵

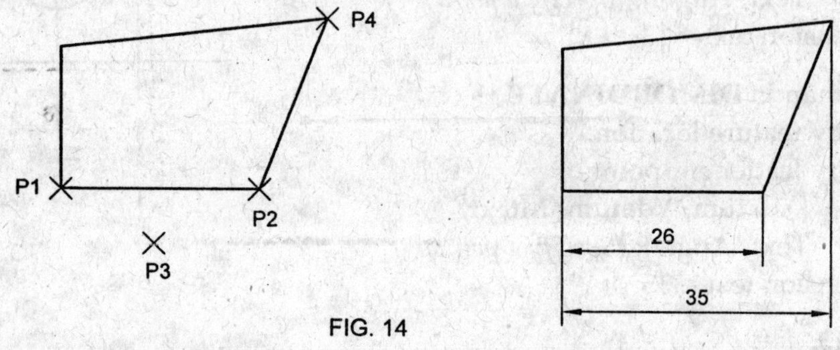

FIG. 14

See Fig. 14. The default spacing between baseline dimensions can be set from the Dimension Style Manager, Lines tab, Baseline Spacing.

The DIMCONTINUE command creates a dimension that starts from an extension line of a previously created dimension. The Dimcontinue command can be activated using any one of the following methods:

1. Type **DIMCONTINUE** or **DCO** in the command prompt and press Enter.
2. Click **Continue** on the Dimensions panel of the Annotate tab.
3. Select **Continue** from the Dimension menu.

Problem 9: *Draw a continued dimension using the DIMCONTINUE command.*

The command sequence to create continued dimension using the DIMCONTINUE command is given below:

Command: **DIMLINEAR** ↵

Specify first extension line origin or <select object>: *(Pick P1)*

Specify second extension line origin: *(Pick P2)*

Specify dimension line location or

[Mtext/Text/Angle/Horizontal/Vertical/Rotated]: *(Pick P3)*

Dimension text = 26

Command: **DIMCONTINUE** ↵

Specify a second extension line origin or [Undo/Select] <Select>: *(Pick P4)*

Dimension text = 9

Specify a second extension line origin or [Undo/Select] <Select>: ↵

Select continued dimension: ↵

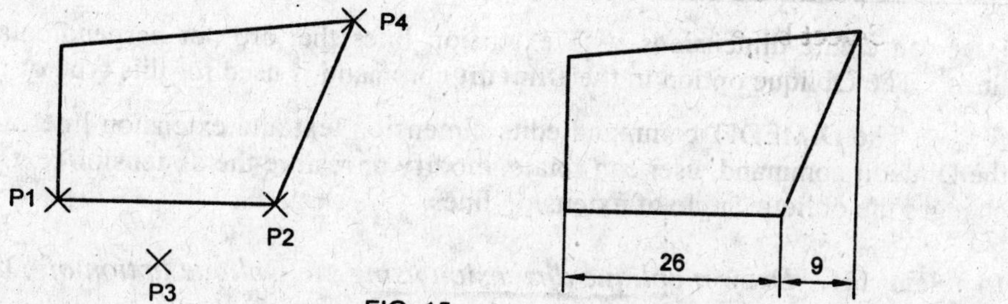

FIG. 15

See Fig. 15.

3.10 CREATE ROTATED DIMENSIONS

In rotated dimensions, the dimension line is placed at an angle to the extension line origins. The Rotation option of the DIMLINEAR command is used for this type of dimensions.

Problem 10: *Draw a rotated dimension using Rotate option of DIMLINEAR command.*

The command sequence to create a rotated dimension using the Rotated option of the Dimlinear command is as follows:

Command: **DIMLINEAR ↵**
Specify first extension line origin or <select object>: *(Pick P1)*
Specify second extension line origin: *(Pick P2)*
Specify dimension line location or
[Mtext/Text/Angle/Horizontal/Vertical/Rotated]: **R ↵**
Specify angle of dimension line <0>: **60 ↵**
Specify dimension line location or
[Mtext/Text/Angle/Horizontal/Vertical/Rotated]: *(Pick P3)*
Dimension text = 9

See Fig. 16.

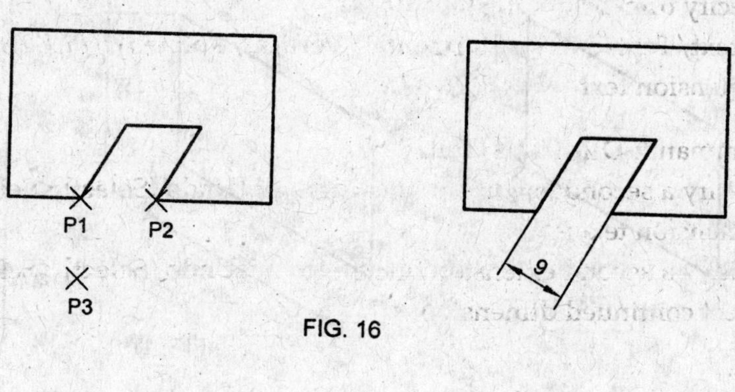

FIG. 16

3.11 CREATE DIMENSIONS WITH OBLIQUE EXTENSION LINES

User can create dimensions with extension lines that are not perpendicular to their dimension lines. The Oblique option in the **Dimedit** command is used for this type of dimensions.

The DIMEDIT command edits dimension text and extension lines. Using the options in the Dimedit command, user can rotate, modify or restore the dimension text. The Oblique option changes the oblique angle of extension lines.

Problem 11: *Draw a oblique dimension using the Oblique option of DIMEDIT command.*

The command sequence to create oblique dimension using the Oblique option of the Dimedit command is as follows:

Command: **DIMALIGNED** ↵
Specify first extension line origin or <select object>: *(Pick P1)*
Specify second extension line origin: *(Pick P2)*
Specify dimension line location or [Mtext/Text/Angle]: *(Pick P3)*
Dimension text = 30

Command: **DIMALIGNED** ↵
Specify first extension line origin or <select object>: *(Pick P2)*
Specify second extension line origin: *(Pick P4)*
Non-associative dimension created.
Specify dimension line location or [Mtext/Text/Angle]: *(Pick P5)*
Dimension text = 20

Command: **DIMEDIT** ↵
Enter type of dimension editing [Home/New/Rotate/Oblique] <Home>: **O** ↵
Select objects: *(Select dimension 30)* 1 found
Select objects:
Enter obliquing angle (press ENTER for none): **90** ↵

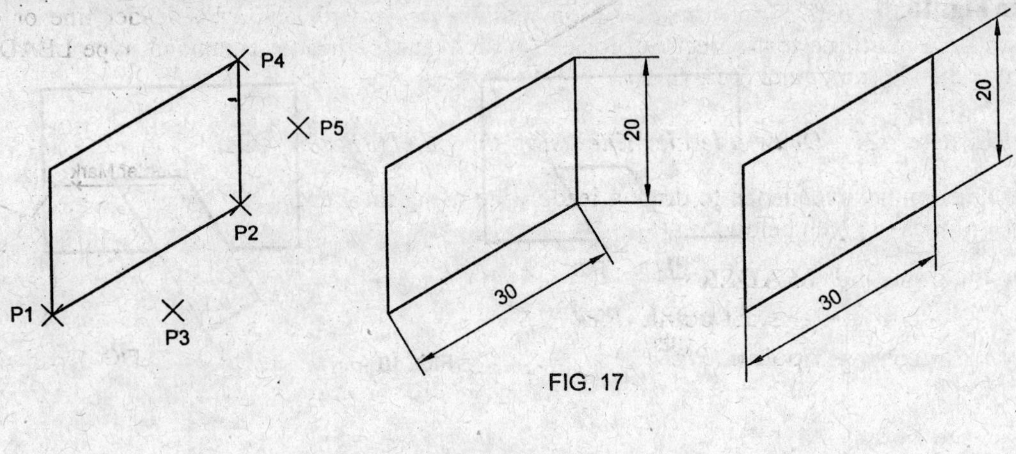

FIG. 17

Command: **DIMEDIT** ↵
Enter type of dimension editing [Home/New/Rotate/Oblique] <Home>: **O** ↵
Select objects: *(Select dimension 20)* 1 found
Select objects:
Enter obliquing angle (press ENTER for none): **30** ↵

See Fig. 17.

3.12 DIMCENTER COMMAND

The DIMCENTER command is used to mark the center point of the arcs or circles. The default sizes of the center mark components can be set from the Dimension Style Manager, Symbols & Arrows tab and Center Marks. The Dimcenter command can be activated using any one of the following methods:

1. Type **DIMCENTER** or **DCE** in the command prompt and press Enter.
2. Choose the **Center Mark** from the **Dimensions** panel of the **Annotate** tab.
3. Choose the **Center Mark** from the **Dimension** menu.

Problem 12: *Draw center point of a circle using the DIMCENTER command.*

The command sequence to mark the center point of the circle using the Dimcenter command is given below:

Command: **DIMCENTER** ↵
Select arc or circle: *(Select the Circle)*

See Fig. 18.

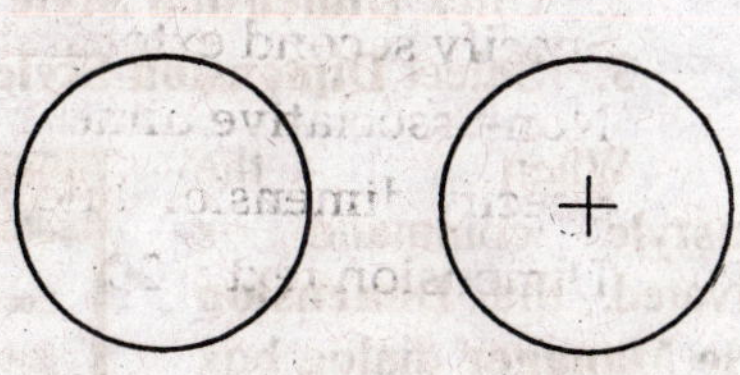

FIG. 18

3.13 LEADER COMMAND

The LEADER command creates a line that connects annotation to a feature. A leader object typically consists of an arrowhead, an optional horizontal landing, a leader line or curve and either a multiline text object or block. To activate the Leader command, type LEADER in the command prompt and press Enter.

Problem 13: *Draw a leader line using the LEADER command.*

The command sequence to draw a leader line using the Leader command is given below:

Command: **LEADER** ↵
Specify leader start point: *(Pick P1)*
Specify next point: *(Pick P2)*

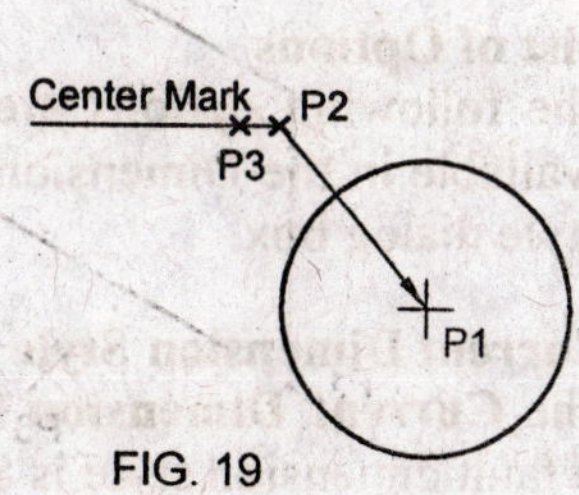

FIG. 19

Specify next point or [Annotation/Format/Undo] <Annotation>: *(Pick P3)*
Specify next point or [Annotation/Format/Undo] <Annotation>: ↵
Enter first line of annotation text or <options>: **Center Mark** ↵
Enter next line of annotation text: ↵

See Fig. 19.

4. DIMENSION STYLES

A **Dimension Style** is a named collection of dimension settings that controls the appearance of dimensions, such as arrowhead style, text location and lateral tolerances. User can create dimension styles to specify the format of dimensions quickly and to ensure that dimensions conform to standards. The options are stored in the DIMSTYLE system variable.

4.1 DIMSTYLE COMMAND

The DIMSTYLE command creates and modifies dimension styles. The Dimstyle command can be activated using any one of the following methods:

1. Type **DIMSTYLE or D** in the command prompt and press Enter.
2. Click **Dimension Style** in the Dimensions panel of the Annotate Tab.
3. Select **Dimension Style** in the Format menu.

When the **Dimstyle** command is activated, the **Dimension Style Manager** dialog box is displayed on the screen as shown in **Fig. 20.**

Using the Dimension Style dialog box, user can create New styles, Sets the Current style, Modifies styles, sets overrides on the current style and Compares styles.

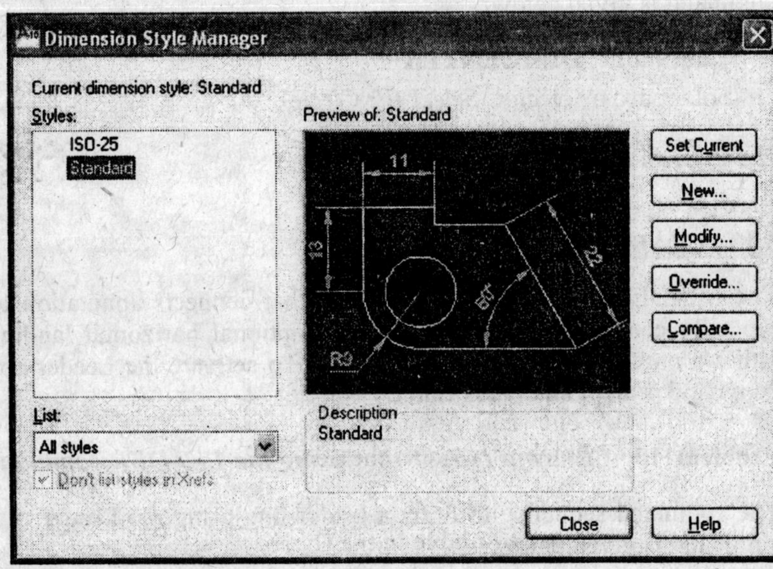

FIG. 20

List of Options
The following options are available in the Dimension Style dialog box.

Current Dimension Style
The **Current Dimension Style** displays the name of the dimension style that is current. The default dimension style is STANDARD. The current style is applied to dimensions user created.

Styles

The **Styles** box lists dimension styles in the drawing. The current style is highlighted. Right-click in the list to display a shortcut menu with options to set the current style, rename styles and delete styles. User cannot delete a style that is current or in use in the current drawing.

The item selected in List controls the dimension styles displayed. To make a style current, select it and click Set Current button.

List

The **List** drop-down list controls the display of styles in the Styles list. Select All Styles to see all dimension styles in a drawing. Select Styles in Use to see only the dimension styles currently used by dimensions in the drawing.

Don't List Styles in Xrefs

When this checkbox selected, suppresses display of dimension styles in externally referenced drawings in the Styles list.

Preview

The **Preview** area shows a graphic representation of the style selected in the Styles list.

Description

The **Description** area describes the style selected in the Styles list relative to the current style. If the description is longer than the space provided, click in the pane and use arrow keys to scroll down.

Set Current

The **Set Current** button sets the style selected under Styles to current. The current style is applied to dimensions user created.

4.2 NEW BUTTON

The **New** button displays the Create New Dimension Style dialog box, in which user can define a new dimension style. The Create New Dimension Style is shown in **Fig. 21.**

This dialog box is used to name the new dimension style, sets the style on which to start the new one and indicates the dimension types to which user wants the new style to apply.

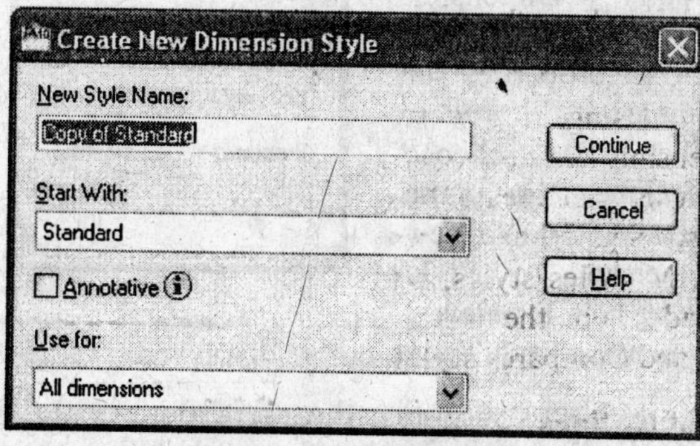

FIG. 21

The following options are available in the Create New Dimension Style dialog box.

New Style Name: This text box specifies the new dimension style name.

Start With: This drop-down list sets a style to use as a basis for the new one. For the new style, user can change only the properties that differ from the properties start with.

Annotative: This checkbox specifies that the dimension style is annotative. Click the information icon to learn more about annotative objects.

Use For: The Use For drop-down list creates a dimension substyle that applies only to specific dimension types.

Continue: The Continue button displays the New Dimension Style dialog box, in which user can define the new dimension style properties.

4.3 MODIFY BUTTON

The **Modify** button displays the **Modify Dimension Styles** dialog box, in which user can modify dimension styles.

This dialog box options are identical to those in the New Dimension Style dialog box. The **Modify Dimension Styles** dialog box is shown in Fig. 22.

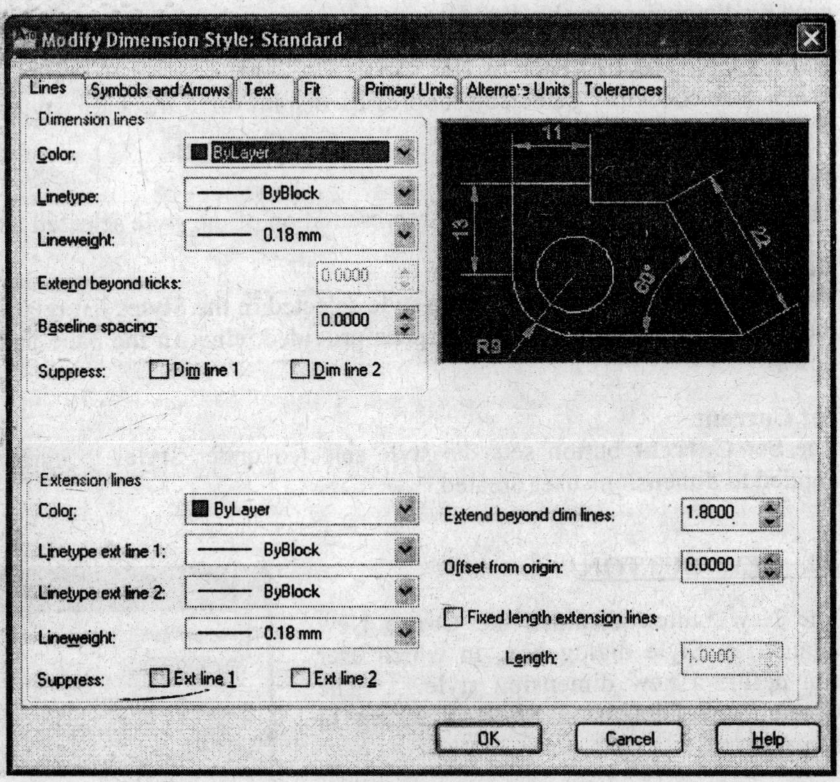

FIG. 22

Using the Modify Dimension Style dialog box, user can set properties for dimension styles. When choose Continue in the Create New Dimension Style dialog box, the New Dimension Style dialog box is displayed.

User can define the properties for the new style in this dialog box. The dialog box initially displays the properties of the dimension style that user selected to start the new style in the Create New Dimension Style dialog box.

Choose either Modify or Override in the Dimension Style Manager to display the Modify Dimension Style or the Override Dimension Style dialog box. The content of these dialog boxes is identical to the New Dimension Style dialog box, although user can modify or override an existing dimension style rather than creating a new one.

The sample image on each tab displays the effects of each option.

List of Tabs

The New, Modify and Override Dimension Style dialog boxes include the following tabs:

1. Lines
2. Symbols and Arrows
3. Text
4. Fit
5. Primary Units
6. Alternate Units
7. Tolerances

1. Lines Tab

The Lines tab sets the format and properties for dimension lines, extension lines, arrowheads and center marks. The options in the Lines tab are shown in **Fig. 22.**

Using the **Dimension Lines** area, Color, Linetype, Lineweight, Extend Beyond Ticks, Baseline Spacing and Suppress properties of the line are defined.

Using the **Extension Lines** area, user can control the appearance of the extension line such as Color, Linetype Ext 1, Linetype Ext 2, Lineweight, Suppress, Extend Beyond Dim Lines, Offset From Origin, Fixed Length Extension Lines and Length.

Preview area displays sample dimension images that show the effects of changes user makes to dimension style settings.

2. Symbols and Arrows Tab

The Symbols and Arrows tab sets the format and placement for arrowheads, center marks, arc length symbols and jogged radius dimensions.

The options in the Symbols and Arrows tab are shown in **Fig. 23.**

Using the **Arrowheads** area, user can controls the appearance of the dimension arrowheads such as arrowhead for First dimension line,. arrowhead for Second dimension line, arrowhead for Leader line and Arrow Size.

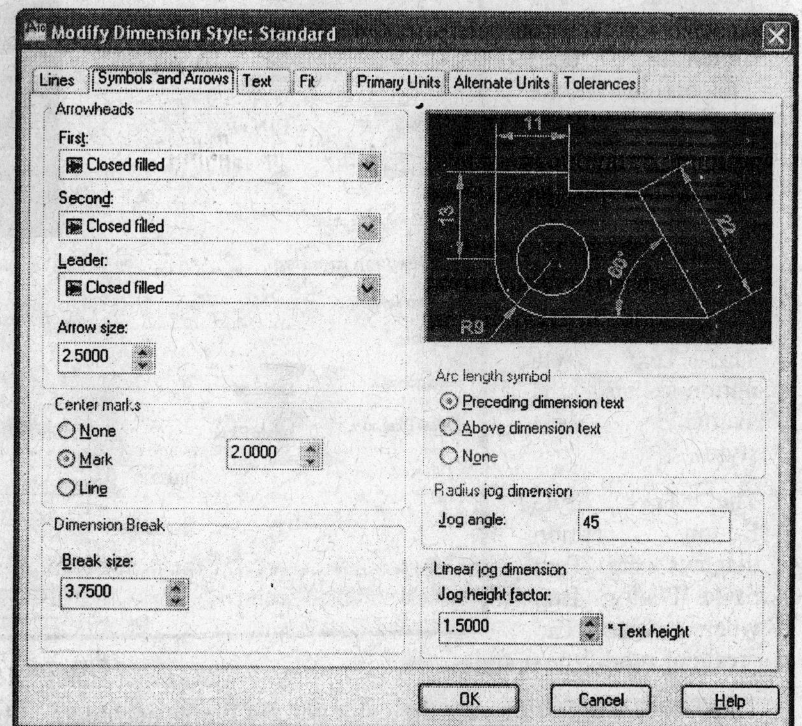

FIG. 23

Using the **Center Marks** area, user can control the appearance of center marks and centerlines for diameter and radial dimensions. The options are: *None* to create no center mark or centerline, *Mark* to create a center mark, *Line* to create a centerline and Size to display and set the size of the center mark or centerline.

Using the **Dimension Break** area, user can controls the gap width of dimension breaks.

Using the **Radius Jog Dimensions** area, user can control the display of jogged (zigzag) radius dimensions. Jogged radius dimensions are often created when the center point of a circle or arc is located off the page.

Using the **Linear Jog Dimensions** area, user can control the display of the jog for linear dimensions. Jog lines are often added to linear dimensions when the actual measurement is not accurately represent by the dimension. Typically the actual measurement is smaller than the desired value.

The **Preview** area displays sample dimension images that show the effects of changes make to dimension style settings.

3. Text Tab

The Text tab sets the format, placement and alignment of dimension text. The options in the Text tab are shown in **Fig. 24**.

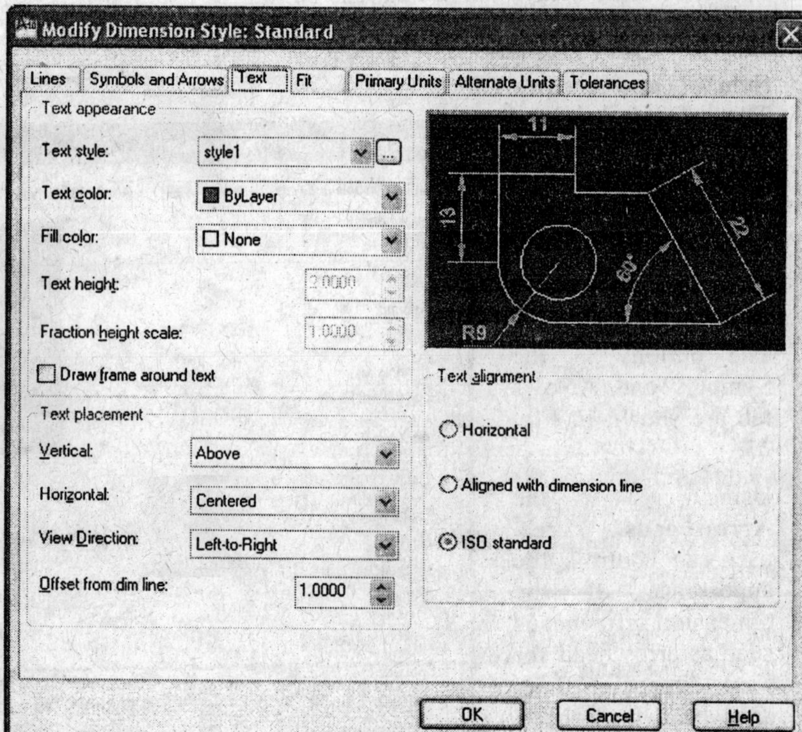

FIG. 24

Using the **Text Appearance** area, user can control the dimension text format and size. The Text Style option lists the available text styles.

The Text Style Button option displays the Text Style Dialog Box where user can create or modify text styles.

The Text Color option sets the color for the dimension text. The Fill Color option sets the color for the text background in dimensions.

The Text Height option sets the height of the current dimension text style. The Fraction Height Scale option sets the scale of fractions relative to dimension text. This is available only when Fractional is selected as the Unit Format on the Primary Units tab. The Draw Frame Around Text option draws a frame around dimension text.

Using the **Text Placement** area, user can controls the placement of dimension text. The options such as Vertical, Horizontal, View Direction and Offset from Dim Line are defined in this area.

Using the **Text Alignment** area, user can control the orientation of dimension text whether it is inside or outside the extension lines. The options such as Horizontal, Aligned with Dimension Line and ISO Standard are defined in this area.

The **Preview** area displays sample dimension images that show the effects of changes make to dimension style settings.

4. Fit Tab

The Fit tab controls the placement of dimension text, arrowheads, leader lines and the **dimension line. The options in the Fit tab are shown in Fig. 25.**

Using the **Fit Options** area, user can control the placement of text and arrowheads based on the space available between the extension lines. When space is available, text and arrowheads are placed between the extension lines. Otherwise, text and arrowheads are placed according to the Fit options.

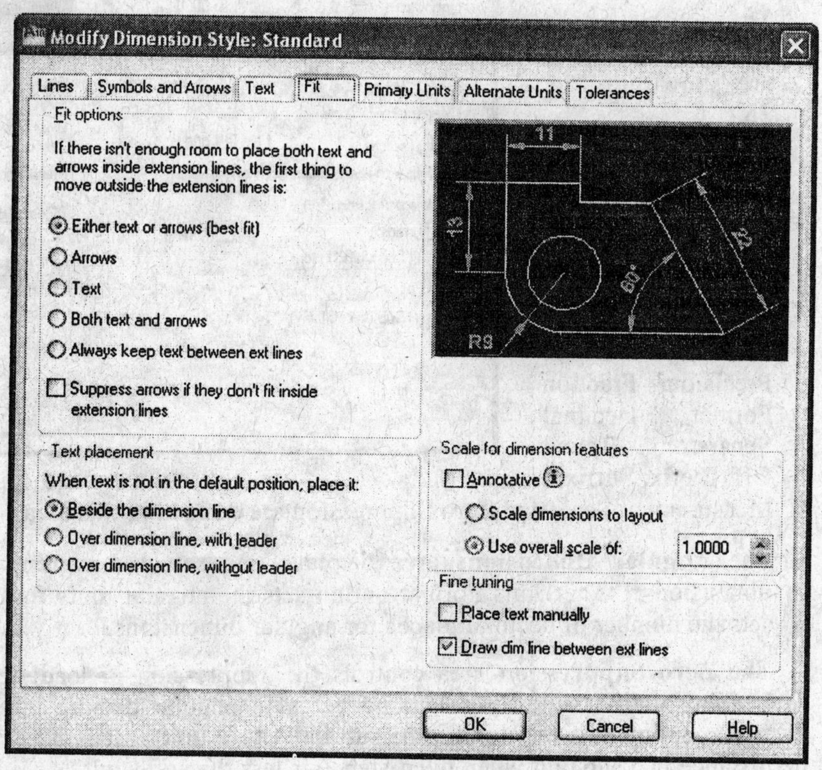

FIG. 25

Using the **Text Placement** area, user can sets the placement of dimension text when it is moved from the default position, that is, the position defined by the dimension style.

The **Preview** area displays sample dimension images that show the effects of changes make to dimension style settings.

Using the **Scale for Dimension Features** area, user can set the overall dimension scale value or the paper space scaling.

The **Fine Tuning** area provides additional options for placing dimension text. Options such as Place Text Manually and Draw Dim Line Between Ext Lines are available in this area.

5. **Primary Units Tab**

The Primary Units tab sets the format and precision of primary dimension units and sets prefixes and suffixes for dimension text.

The options in the Primary Units tab are shown in **Fig. 26.**

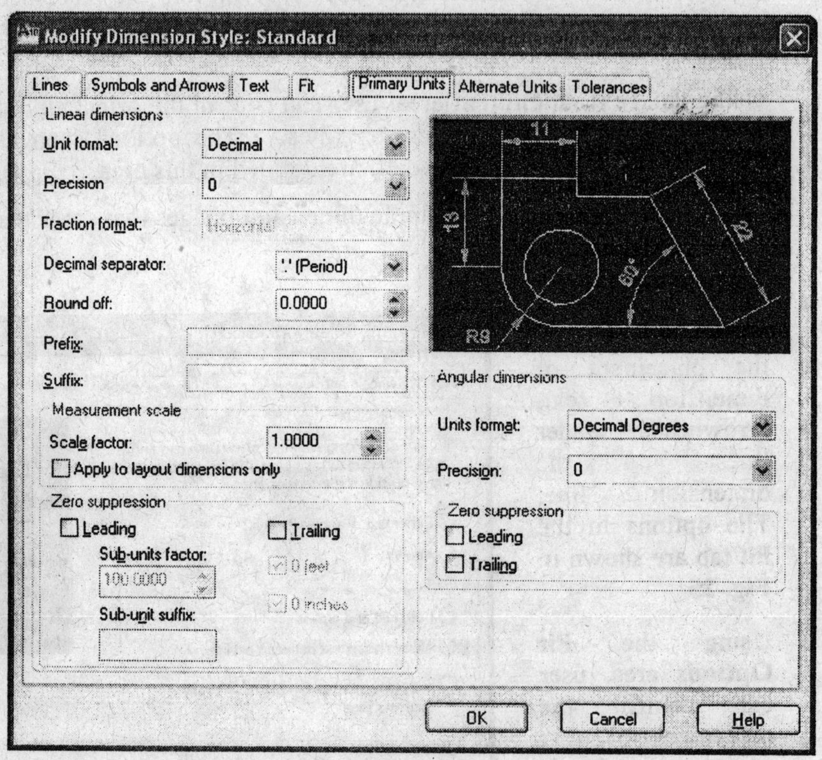

FIG. 26

The **Linear Dimensions** area sets the format and precision for linear dimensions. The options such as Unit Format, Precision, Fraction Format, Decimal Separator, Round Off, Prefix, Suffix, Measurement Scale and Zero Suppression are defined in this area.

The **Angular Dimensions** area displays and sets the current angle format for angular dimensions. The Units Format option sets the angular units format. The Precision option sets the number of decimal places for angular dimensions.

The **Zero Suppression** area controls the suppression of leading and trailing zeros. The Leading option suppresses leading zeros in angular decimal dimensions. The Sub-units factor option sets the number of sub units to a unit. It is used to calculate the dimension distance in a sub unit when the distance is less than one unit.

The Sub-unit suffix option includes a suffix to the dimension text sub unit. User can enter text or use control codes to display special symbols.

The Trailing option suppresses trailing zeros in angular decimal dimensions. The 0 Feet option suppresses the feet portion of a feet-and-inches dimension when the distance is less than 1 foot. The 0 Inches option suppresses the inches portion of a feet-and-inches dimension when the distance is an integral number of feet.

The **Preview** area displays sample dimension images that show the effects of changes make to dimension style settings.

6. **Alternate Units Tab**

The **Alternate Units** tab specifies display of alternate units in dimension measurements and sets their format and precision.

The options in the Alternate Units tab are shown in **Fig. 27.**

The **Display Alternate Units** checkbox adds alternate measurement units to dimension text.

The Alternate Units area displays and sets the current alternate units format for all dimension types except Angular.

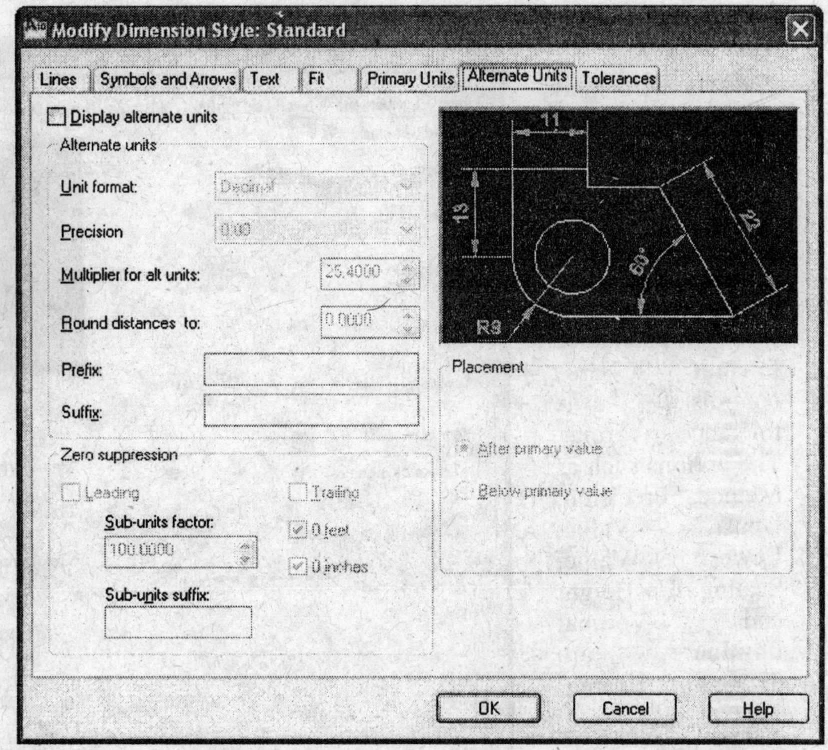

FIG. 27

The Unit Format option sets the unit format for alternate units. The Precision option sets the number of decimal places for alternate units. The other options such as Multiplier for Alternate Units, Round Distances To, Prefix and Suffix are also defined in this area.

The **Zero Suppression** area controls the suppression of leading and trailing zeros and of feet and inches that have a value of zero. The Leading option suppresses leading zeros in all decimal dimensions. The Sub-units factor option sets the number of sub units to a unit. The Sub-unit suffix option includes a suffix to the dimension value sub unit. User can enter text or use control codes to display special symbols.

The Trailing option suppresses trailing zeros in all decimal dimensions. The 0 Feet option suppresses the feet portion of a feet-and-inches dimension when the distance is less than 1 foot. The 0 Inches option suppresses the inches portion of a feet-and-inches dimension when the distance is an integral number of feet.

The **Placement** area controls the placement of alternate units in dimension text. The After Primary Value option places alternate units after the primary units in dimension text. The Below Primary Value option places alternate units below the primary units in dimension text.

The **Preview** area displays sample dimension images that show the effects of changes make to dimension style settings.

7. Tolerances Tab

The Tolerance tab controls the display and format of dimension text tolerances.

The options in the Tolerance tab are shown in **Fig. 28.**

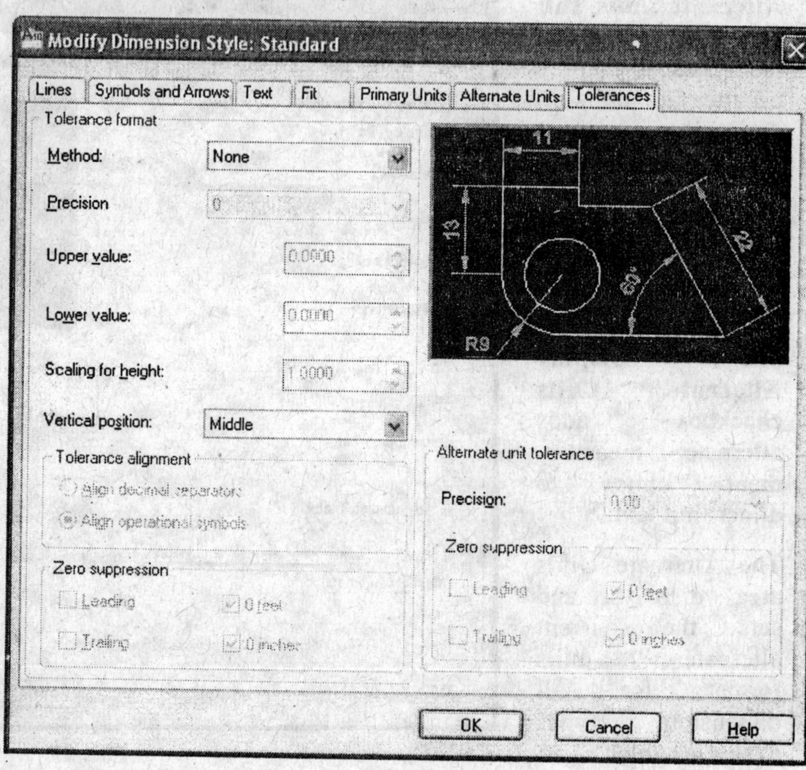

FIG. 28

The **Tolerance Format** area controls the tolerance format. The options such as Method, Precision, Upper Value, Lower Value, Scaling for Height and Vertical Position are defined in this area.

The **Tolerance Alignment** area controls the alignment of upper and lower tolerance values when stacked. The options are Align Decimal Separators and Align Operational Symbols.

The **Zero Suppression** area controls the suppression of leading and trailing zeros and of feet and inches that have a value of zero. The options are Leading, Trailing, 0 Feet and 0 Inches,

The **Alternate Unit Tolerance** area formats alternate tolerance units. The Precision option displays and sets the number of decimal places.

The **Zero Suppression** area controls the suppression of leading and trailing zeros and of feet and inches that have a value of zero. The options are Leading, Trailing, 0 Feet and 0 Inches.

The **Preview** area displays sample dimension images that show the effects of changes make to dimension style settings.

4.4 OVERRIDE BUTTON

The Override button displays the Override Current Style dialog box, in which user can set temporary overrides to dimension styles.

Dialog box options are identical to those in the New Dimension Style dialog box. Overrides are displayed as unsaved changes under the dimension style in the Styles list.

4.5 COMPARE BUTTON

The Compare button displays the Compare Dimension Styles dialog box, in which user can compare two dimension styles or list all the properties of one dimension style.

The **Compare Dimension Styles** dialog box is shown in **Fig. 29.**

The Compare Dimension Styles dialog box compares the properties of two dimension styles or displays all properties of one style.

User can print the results of the comparison to the Clipboard and then paste to other Microsoft Windows applications.

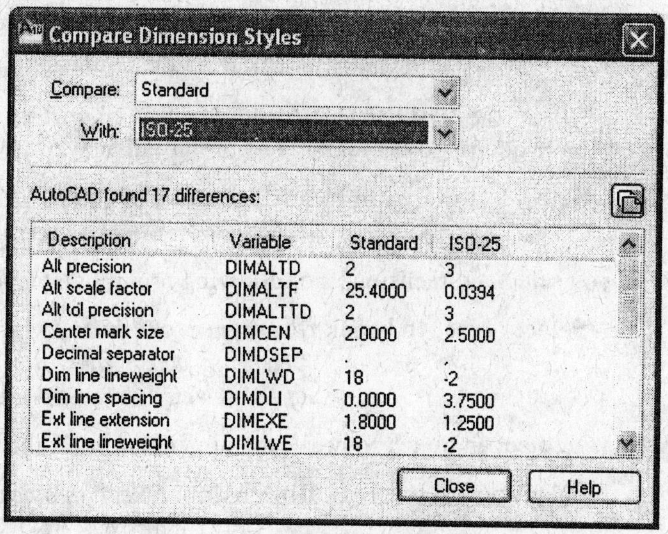

FIG. 29

Compare: The Compare drop-down list specifies the first dimension style for the comparison.

With: The With drop-down list specifies the second dimension style for the comparison. If user sets the second style to <none> or to the same style as the first, all the properties of the dimension style are displayed. Comparison results are displayed automatically under the following headings:

- Description of the dimension style property
- System variable that controls the property
- System variable values of style properties that differ for each dimension style

Results: The Result area displays the results of the dimension style comparison. If user compares two different styles, the properties that differ are displayed. If user sets the second style to <none> or to the same style as the first, all the properties of the dimension style are displayed.

Print to Clipboard button: This button copies the results of the comparison to the Clipboard. User can then paste the results to other Windows applications, such as word processors.

5. CREATING DIMENSION BREAKS

Breaks or restores dimension and extension lines where they cross other objects. Dimension breaks can be added to linear, angular, and ordinate dimensions, among others.

The **DIMBREAK** command is used for this purpose. The **DIMBREAK** command can be activated any one of the following methods:

1. Type DIMBREAK at the command prompt and press Enter.
2. Choose Break tool from the Dimension panel of the Annotate tab.
3. Choose Dimension Break tool from the Dimension menu.
4. Choose Dimension Break from the Dimension toolbar.

When the DIMBREAK command is invoked, AutoCAD prompts you to select a dimension to add/remove break. The prompt displayed is:

Select a dimension to add/remove break or [Multiple]:
Select a dimension, or enter m and press ENTER

After you select a dimension, the following prompt displayed is:

Select object to break dimension or [Auto/Manual/Remove] <Auto>:
Select an object that intersects the dimension or extension lines of the selected dimension, enter an option, or press ENTER

After you select an object to break the dimension with, the following prompt displayed is:

Select object to break dimension: *Select an object that passes through the dimension or press* ENTER *to end the command*

Note that Dimension breaks can be added to dimensions for objects that do not intersect the dimension or extension lines using the by Manual option. The options are explained next.

Multiple: The Multiple option specifies multiple dimensions to add breaks to or remove breaks from. The prompt displayed is:

Select dimensions: *Use an object selection method and press* ENTER
Select object to break dimensions or [Auto/Remove] <Auto>:
Enter an option or press ENTER

Auto: The Auto option places dimension breaks automatically at all the intersection points of the objects that intersect the selected dimension. Any dimension break created using this option is updated automatically when the dimension or an intersecting object is modified.

When a new object is drawn over the top of a dimension that has any dimension breaks, no new dimension breaks are automatically applied at the intersecting points along the dimension object. To add the new dimension breaks, must be run the command again.

Remove: The Remove option removes all dimension breaks from the selected dimensions.

Manual: The Manual option places a dimension break manually. You specify two points on the dimension or extension lines for the location of the break. Any dimension break that is created using this option is not updated if the dimension or intersecting objects are modified. You can only place a single manual dimension break at a time with this option.

6. CAD EXERCISES - Step-by-Step Solutions

***Example 1:** Draw the diagram shown in **Fig. 30** using the Polygon and Circle commands. Also, mark the dimensions and center point.*

The procedure and command sequence to draw the diagram shown in **Fig. 30** is given below:

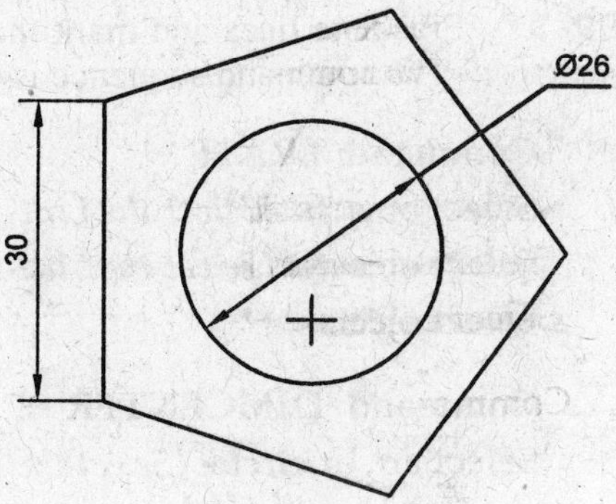

FIG. 30

STEP 1 : First draw the pentagon using the Polygon command. Also, locate the center point of the pentagon using the Line command. The command sequence is given below:

Command: **POLYGON** ↵
Enter number of sides <4>: **5** ↵
Specify center of polygon or [Edge]: **E** ↵
Specify first endpoint of edge:
Specify second endpoint of edge: **30** ↵

Command: **LINE** ↵
Specify first point: (*Pick P1*)
Specify next point or [Undo]: (*Pick P2*)
Specify next point or [Undo]: ↵

Command: **LINE** ↵
Specify first point: (*Pick P3*)
Specify next point or [Undo]: (*Pick P4*)
Specify next point or [Undo]: ↵

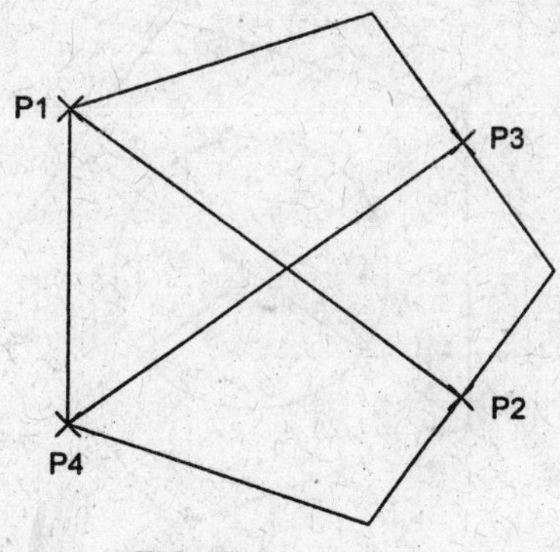

FIG. 31

See Fig. 31.

Note that the points P2 and P4 are the mid-point of the respective edges of the pentagon.

STEP 2 : Draw the circle with the meeting point of the two lines P1-P2 and P3-P4 as center and diameter as 26 mm using the Circle command. Also, mark the center point of the circle. The command sequence is given below:

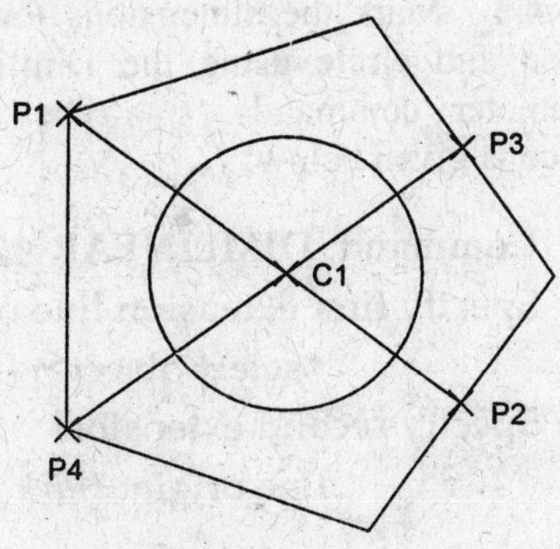

FIG. 32

Command: **CIRCLE** ↵
Specify center point for circle or
[3P/2P/Ttr (tan tan radius)]: (*Pick C1*)

Specify radius of circle or [Diameter]: **D** ↵
Specify diameter of circle: **26** ↵

See Fig. 32.

STEP 3 : Erase the lines and mark the center point of the circle using the Erase and Dimcenter commands. The command sequence is given below:

Command: **ERASE** ↵
Select objects: (*Select the Line-1*) 1 found
Select objects: (*Select the Line-2*) 1 found, 2 total
Select objects: ↵

Command: **DIMCENTER** ↵
Select arc or circle: (*Select the Circle*)

See Fig. 33.

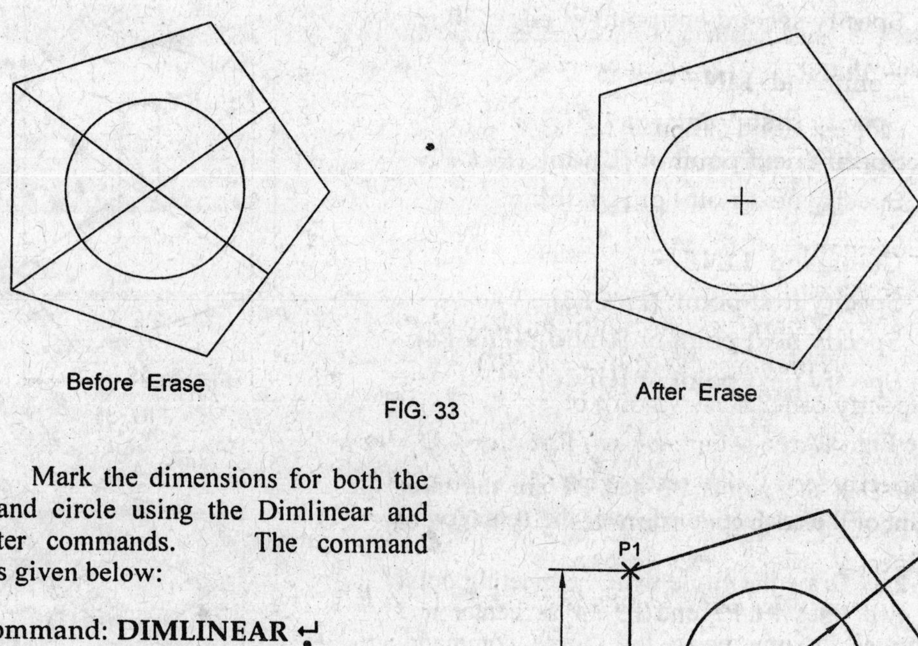

FIG. 33

STEP 4 : Mark the dimensions for both the pentagon and circle using the Dimlinear and Dimdiameter commands. The command sequence is given below:

Command: **DIMLINEAR** ↵
Specify first extension line origin or <select object>: (*Pick P1*)
Specify second extension line origin: (*Pick P2*)

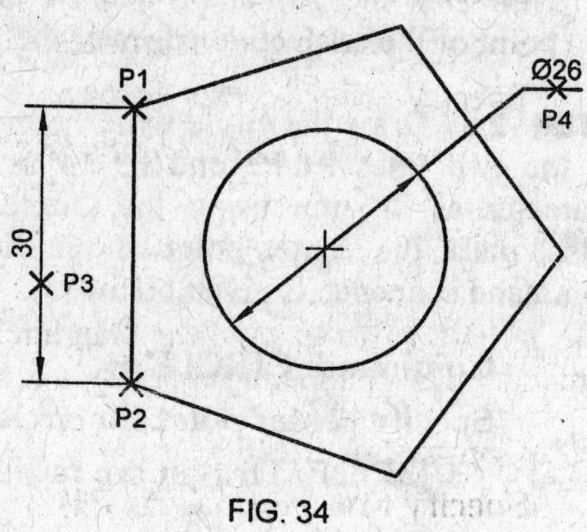

FIG. 34

Specify dimension line location or
[Mtext/Text/Angle/Horizontal/Vertical/Rotated]: (*Pick P3*)
Dimension text = 30

Command: **DIMDIAMETER** ↵
Select arc or circle: (*Select the Circle*)
Dimension text = 26
Specify dimension line location or [Mtext/Text/Angle]: (*Pick P4*)

See Fig. 34.

STEP 5 : Fig. 34 shows the final view of the diagram given in **Fig. 30.** Finally save drawing.

Example 2: *Draw the diagram shown in **Fig. 35** using the Rectang, Line, Arc and Circle commands. Also, mark the dimensions and center point.*

The procedure and command sequence to draw the diagram shown in Fig. 35 is given below:

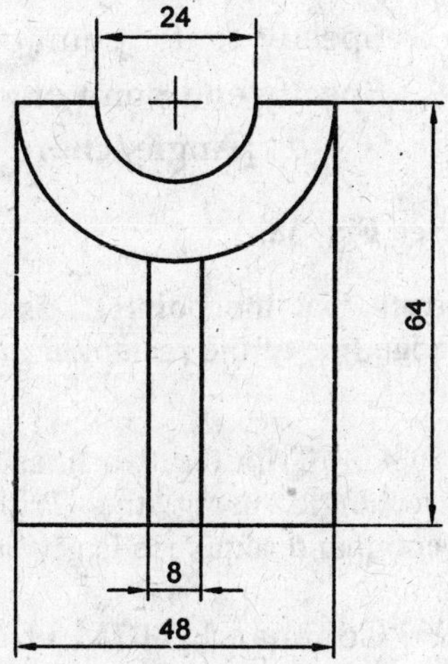

FIG. 35

STEP 1 : First draw the outer rectangle using the Rectang command. The command sequence is given below:

Command: **RECTANG** ↵
Specify first corner point or
[Chamfer/Elevation/Fillet/
Thickness/Width]: (*Pick P1*)
Specify other corner point or
[Area/Dimensions/Rotation]: **D** ↵
Specify length for rectangles <10.0000>: **48** ↵
Specify width for rectangles <10.0000>: **64** ↵
Specify other corner point or
[Area/Dimensions/Rotation]: (*Pick P2*)

See Fig. 36.

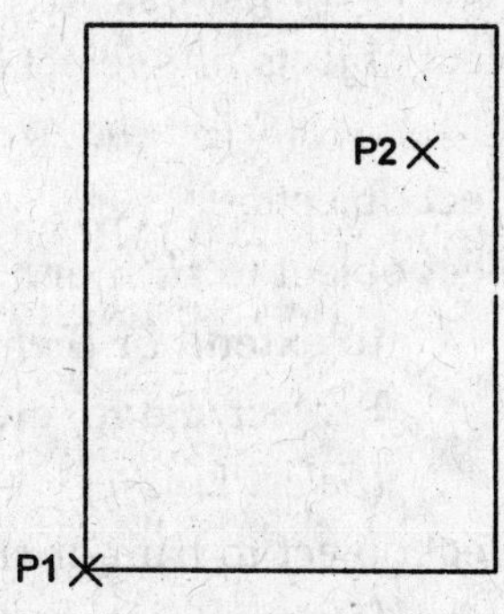

FIG. 36

STEP 2 : Draw two lines of the diagram using the Line command. The command sequence is given below:

Command: **LINE** ↵
Specify first point: (*Pick P1*)

Specify next point or [Undo]: **20** ↵
Specify next point or [Undo]: **64** ↵
Specify next point or [Close/Undo]: **8** ↵
Specify next point or [Close/Undo]: **64** ↵
Specify next point or [Close/Undo]: ↵

See **Fig. 37.**

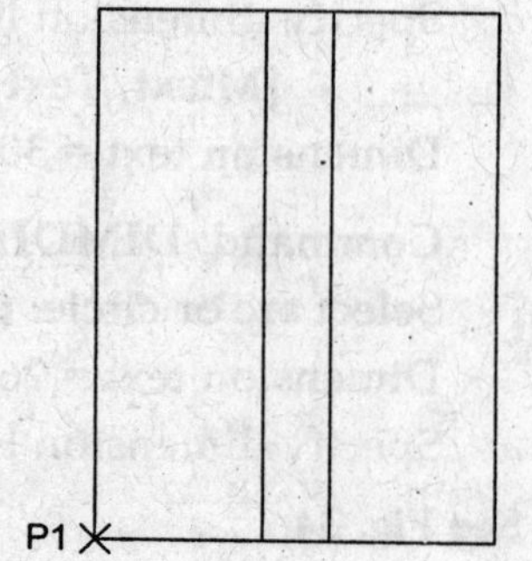

FIG. 37

STEP 3 : Draw the arc at the top edge line using the Arc command. The command sequence is given below:

Command: **ARC** ↵
Specify start point of arc or [Center]: (*Pick P1*)
Specify second point of arc or
[Center/End]: **C** ↵
Specify center point of arc: (*Pick P2*)
Specify end point of arc or
[Angle/chord Length]: (*Pick P3*)

See Fig. 38.

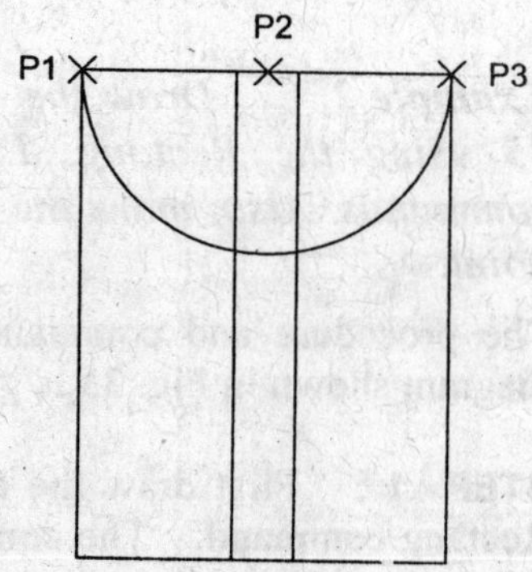

FIG. 38

Note that the point P2 is the mid-point of the top edge line of the rectangle.

STEP 4 : Trim the two lines drawn inside the rectangle using the Trim command. The command sequence is given below:

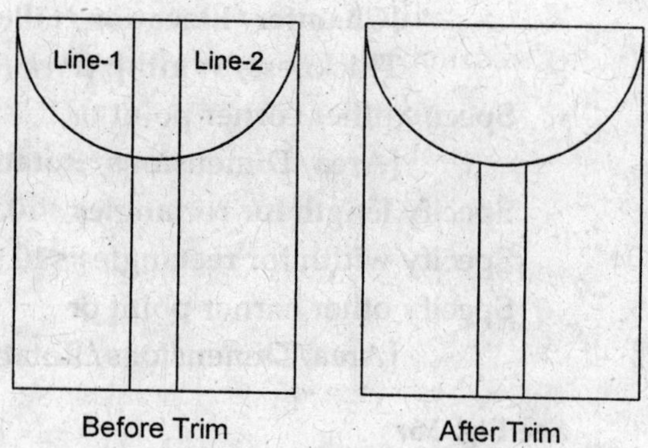

FIG. 39

Command: **TRIM** ↵
Current settings: Projection=UCS,
Edge=None
Select cutting edges ...
Select objects or <select all>:
(*Select the Arc*) 1 found
Select objects: ↵
Select object to trim or shift-select
to extend or [Fence/Crossing/
Project/Edge/eRase/Undo]:
(*Select Line-1*)
Select object to trim or shift-select to extend or
[Fence/Crossing/Project/Edge/eRase/Undo]: (*Select Line-2*)

Select object to trim or shift-select to extend or
[Fence/Crossing/Project/Edge/eRase/Undo]: ↵

See Fig. 39.

STEP 5 : To draw the inner arc, first draw circle using the Circle command and then trim the excess segment of the circle using the Trim command. The command sequence is given below:

Command: **CIRCLE** ↵
Specify center point for circle or
[3P/2P/Ttr (tan tan radius)]:
(*Pick P1*)
Specify radius of circle or
[Diameter]: **D** ↵
Specify diameter of circle: **24** ↵

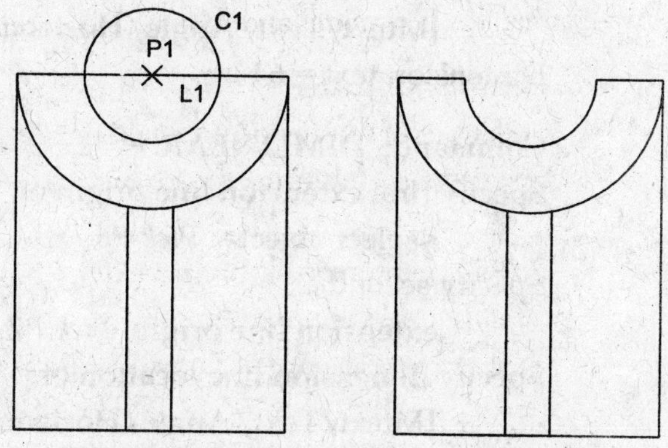

Before Trim After Trim

FIG. 40

Command: **TRIM** ↵
Current settings: Projection=UCS,
Edge=None
Select cutting edges ...
Select objects or <select all>:
(*Select C1*)1 found
Select objects: (*Select L1*) 1 found, 2 total
Select objects: ↵
Select object to trim or shift-select to extend or
[Fence/Crossing/Project/Edge/eRase/Undo]: (*Select C1*)
Select object to trim or shift-select to extend or
[Fence/Crossing/Project/Edge/eRase/Undo]: (*Select L1*)
Select object to trim or shift-select to extend or
[Fence/Crossing/Project/Edge/eRase/Undo]: ↵

See Fig. 40.

STEP 6 : Mark the center point of the circle and dimension of the drawing using the Dimcenter and Dimlinear commands. The command sequence is given below:

Command: **DIMCENTER** ↵
Select arc or circle: (*Select the arc*)

Command: **DIMLINEAR** ↵
Specify first extension line origin or <select object>: *Pick P1*

Specify second extension line origin: *Pick P2*
Specify dimension line location or
[Mtext/Text/Angle/Horizontal/Vertical/Rotated]: *Pick P3*
Dimension text = 48

Command: **DIMLINEAR** ↵
Specify first extension line origin or <select object>: *Pick P2*
Specify second extension line origin: *Pick P4*
Specify dimension line location or
[Mtext/Text/Angle/Horizontal/Vertical/Rotated]: *Pick P5*
Dimension text = 64

Command: **DIMLINEAR** ↵
Specify first extension line origin or
<select object>: *Pick P6*
Specify second
extension line origin: *Pick P7*
Specify dimension line location or
[Mtext/Text/Angle/Horizontal/
Vertical/Rotated]: *Pick P8*
Dimension text = 8

Command: **DIMLINEAR** ↵
Specify first extension line origin or
<select object>: *Pick P9*
Specify second
extension line origin: *Pick P10*
Specify dimension line location or
[Mtext/Text/Angle/Horizontal/
Vertical/Rotated]: *Pick P11*
Dimension text = 24

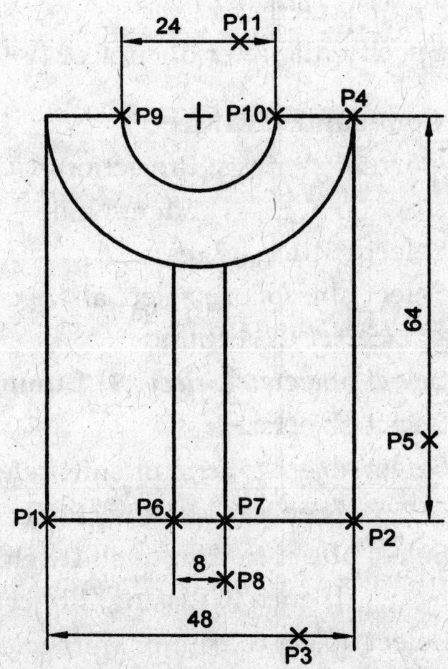

FIG. 41

See Fig. 41.

STEP 7 : **Fig. 41** shows the final view of the diagram given in **Fig. 35.** Finally save the drawing

*

10

EDITING AND MODIFICATION

1. INTRODUCTION

While drawing, it may not be possible to create drawings to the exact size and shape at the first instant itself. There are more chances of committing mistakes, which are to be rectified then and there. The process of correcting mistakes while drawing a design is known as *Editing* or *Modifying*.

AutoCAD provides a number of commands for Editing and Modifying. Examples: ERASE, MOVE, COPY, ROTATE, MIROR, etc. The editing commands will ask the user to *select* one or more object to execute the editing commands. Therefore, it is necessary to learn some of the selection methods.

1.1 MODIFY or EDIT COMMANDS

We can easily modify the size, shape and location of objects. Modification can be done by any one of the following methods:

- Enter a command first and then select the objects to modify.
- Select the objects first and then enter a command to modify them.
- Select and right-click an object to display a shortcut menu with relevant options.
- Double-click an object to display the Properties palette or in some cases, a dialog box or editor that is specific to that type of object.

List of Modify commands are:

1. ERASE
2. COPY
3. MIRROR
4. OFFSET
5. ARRAY
6. MOVE
7. ROTATE
8. SCALE
9. STRETCH
10. LENGTHEN
11. TRIM
12. EXTEND
13. BREAK
14. JOIN
15. CHAMFER
16. FILLET
17. EXPLODE

The **Modify** commands are invoked by any one of the following methods:

1. Type the required command at the command prompt and press Enter.
2. Choose the required tool from the **Modify** panel of the **Home** tab. See Fig. 1.
3. Choose the required tool from the **Modify** toolbar. **See Fig. 2.**
4. Choose the required tool from the **Modify** menu. **See Fig. 3.**

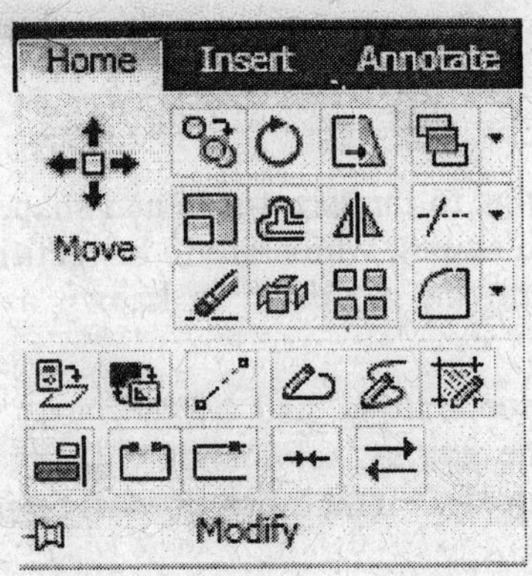

FIG. 1

FIG. 2

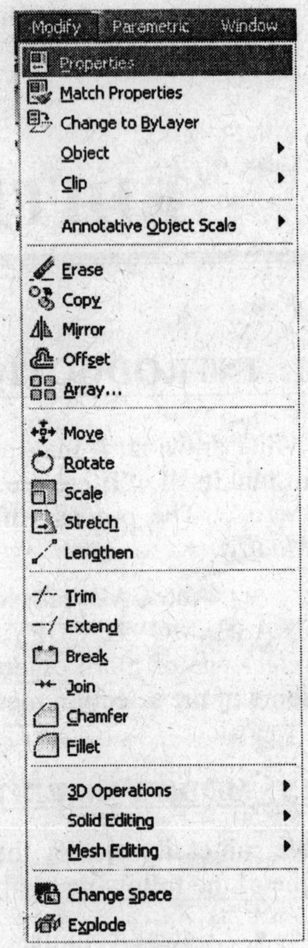

FIG. 3

2. ERASE TOOL

Sometimes you may need to erase the unwanted objects from the objects drawn. This can be done using the Erase tool. The Erase tool is used to delete/remove object/objects that are drawn on the screen. The Erase tool can be invoked by any one of the following methods:

1. Type the **ERASE** or **E** at the command prompt and press Enter.
2. Choose the **Erase** tool from the **Modify** panel of the **Home** tab.
3. Choose the **Erase** tool from the **Modify** menu.
4. Choose the **Erase** tool from the **Modify** toolbar.

When the **Erase** command is invoked, a small box, known as Pick Box, replaces the screen cursor. To erase an object, select it by using the pick box. The select object will be displayed in dashed lines and the **Select objects** prompt is displayed again. User can either continue selecting objects or press Enter to terminate the object selection process. Now, the selected objects are erased.

To erase all the objects in the drawing area, enter **All** at the **Select objects** prompt and press Enter. All the objects in the drawing area are selected and erased even if they are outside the display area.

To erase objects, you can also first select the objects to be erased and then choose the **Erase** option from this shortcut menu. The shortcut menu is displayed when you right-click in the drawing area.

Problem 1: *Erase an object using the ERASE command.*

The command sequence to erase an object using the Erase command is as follows:

Command: **ERASE** ↵
Select objects:
(Select the inner square) 1 found
Select objects: ↵

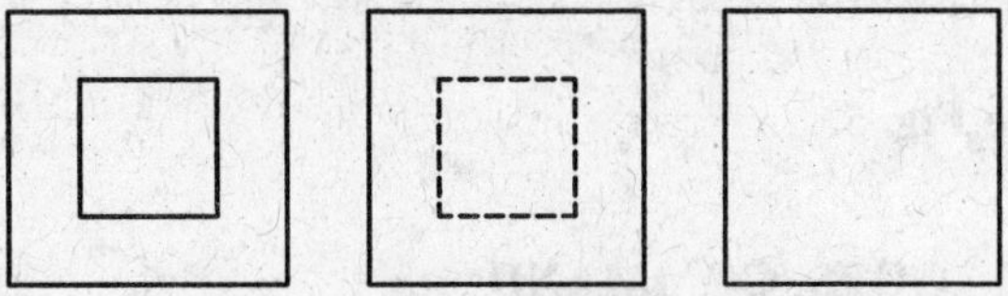

FIG. 4

See Fig. 4.

The Erase command is used exactly the same way as an eraser in manual drafting to remove unwanted portion of a drawing. We can restore accidentally erased objects using the UNDO command. The OOPS command restores all objects deleted by the most recent use of ERASE, BLOCK or WBLOCK.

2.1 UNDO (U or u) COMMAND

AutoCAD provides option to backtrack the recent actions using one of several methods. The simplest method of backtracking is to use Undo on the Standard toolbar or the UNDO command to undo a single action.

Many commands include their own Undo option so that user can correct mistakes without leaving the command. When user create lines and polylines, for example, enter **u** to undo the last segment.

If a wrong object is erased accidently, restore it using the UNDO command or the OOPS command. The OOPS command is discussed later. The UNDO command is invoked using any one of the three methods as follows:

1. Type the **UNDO** or **U** at the command prompt and press Enter.
2. Choose the **Undo** tool from the **Standard** toolbar.
3. Choose the **Undo** tool from the **Edit** menu bar.

Problem 2: *Restore an erased object using the UNDO command.*

The command sequence to restore an erased object using the Undo command is as follows:

Command: **ERASE** ↵
Select objects: *(Select the object)* 1 found
Select objects: ↵
Command: **UNDO** ↵
Current settings: Auto = On,
Control = All, Combine = Yes
Enter the number of operations to undo or
[Auto/Control/BEgin/End/Mark/Back] <1>: ↵
ERASE

See Fig. 5.

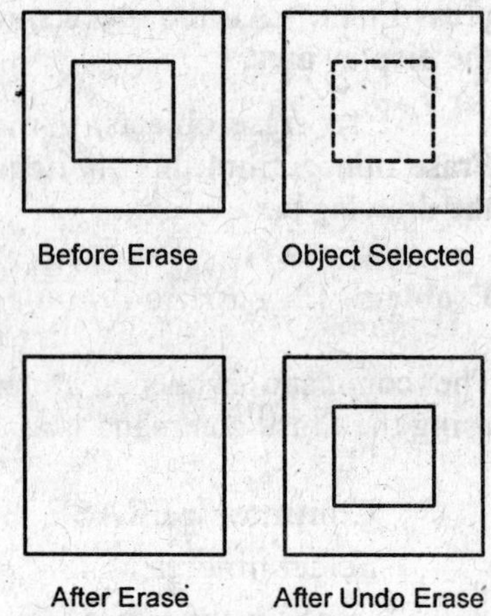

FIG. 5

2.2 OOPS COMMAND

The OOPS restores last objects erased by the ERASE command.
To activate the OOPS command, type OOPS or oops in the command prompt.

The OOPS command can also be used after BLOCK or WBLOCK because these commands can erase the selected objects after creating a block.

However, it is not possible to use OOPS to restore parameters, actions or grips in the Block Editor. It is also not possible to use OOPS to restore objects on a layer that has been removed with the PURGE command.

Problem 3: *Restore an erased object using the OOPS command.*

The command sequence to restore the erased object using the OOPS command is as follows:

Command: **ERASE** ↵
Select objects: *(Select the inner circle)* 1 found
Select objects: ↵
Command: **OOPS** ↵

See Fig. 6.

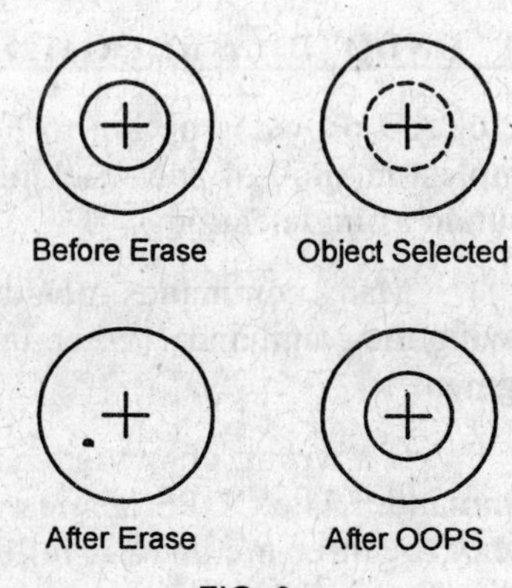

FIG. 6

3. COPY TOOL

Using the COPY tool, user can create duplicates of objects at a specified distance and direction from the originals. Use coordinates, grid snap, object snaps and other tools to copy objects with precision. We can also use grips to move and copy objects quickly.

The Copy tool can be invoked using any one of the following methods:

1. Type **COPY** or **CO** in the command prompt and press Enter.
2. Choose **Copy** tool from the **Modify** panel of the **Home** tab.
3. Choose **Copy** tool from the **Modify** menu.
4. Choose **Copy** tool from the **Modify** toolbar.

Problem 4: *Copy a rectangle using the COPY command.*

The command sequence to copy the rectangle using the Copy command is as follows:

Command: COPY ↵
Select objects: (*Select the rectangle*) 1 found
Select objects: ↵
Current settings: Copy mode = Multiple
Specify base point or [Displacement/mOde]
<Displacement>: *(Pick P1)*
Specify second point or
<use first point as displacement>: *(Pick P2)*
Specify second point or [Exit/Undo] <Exit>: ↵

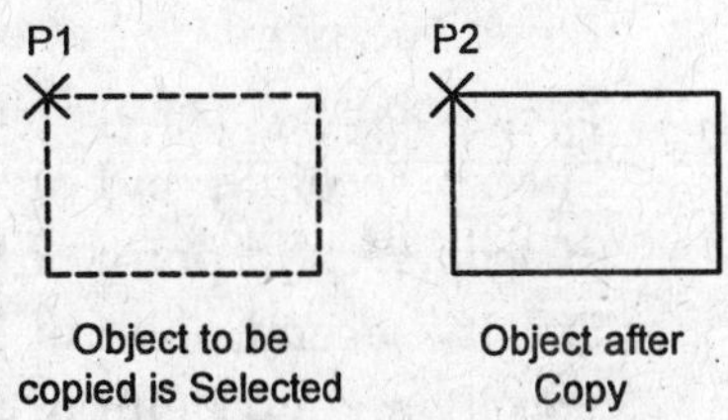

FIG. 7

See Fig. 7.

The two points specified define a vector that indicates how far the copied objects are to be moved and in what direction. The COPY command repeats automatically by default. To exit the command, press Enter. Options in the Copy command are explained next.

3.1 DISPLACEMENT OPTION

Using the Displacement option, user can specify a relative distance and direction using coordinates. When the Displacement option is selected, then the next prompt is:

Specify displacement <*last value*>: *Enter coordinates to represent a vector*

3.2 MODE OPTION

The Mode option controls whether the command repeats automatically. This setting is controlled by the COPYMODE system variable. When the Mode option is selected, then the next prompt displayed is:

Enter a copy mode option [Single/Multiple] <*current*>: *Enter s or m*

3.3 MULTIPLE OPTION

The Multiple option overrides the Single mode setting. The COPY command is set to repeat automatically for the duration of the command. This setting is controlled by the COPYMODE system variable. Note that this option is displayed only when copy mode is set to Single.

Problem 5: *Copy an object three times using the Multiple option of COPY command.*

The command sequence to create three copy of the objects using the Multiple option of Copy command is as follows:

Command: **COPY** ↵
Select objects: **C** ↵
Specify first corner: *(Pick P1)*
Specify opposite corner: *(Pick P2)* 2 found
Select objects: ↵
Current settings: Copy mode = Single
Specify base point or [Displacement/mOde] <Displacement>: **O** ↵
Enter a copy mode option [Single/Multiple] <Single>: **M** ↵
Specify base point or [Displacement/mOde] <Displacement>: *(Pick P3)*
Specify second point or <use first point as displacement>: *(Pick P4)*
Specify second point or [Exit/Undo] <Exit>: *(Pick P5)*
Specify second point or [Exit/Undo] <Exit>: *(Pick P6)*
Specify second point or [Exit/Undo] <Exit>: ↵

See Fig. 8.

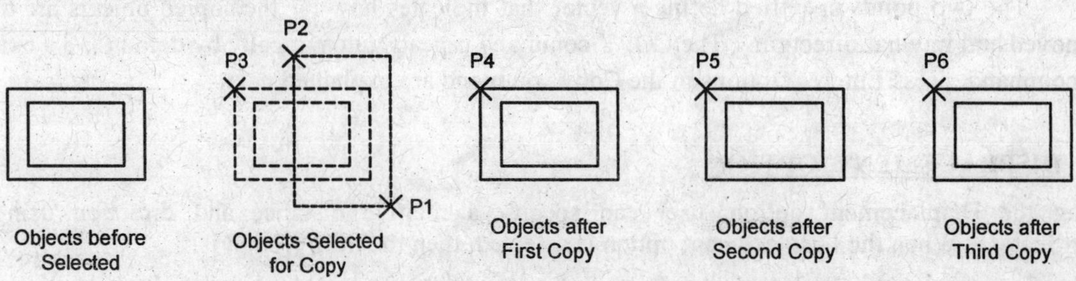

FIG. 8

3.4 COPYMODE COMMAND

The Copymode command controls whether the COPY command repeats automatically. If the COPYMODE command is invoked, AutoCAD prompts to enter new value for COPYMODE. The next prompt displayed is:

Enter new value for COPYMODE <0>: *Enter 0 or 1*

If 0 is entered, AutoCAD sets the COPY command to repeat automatically.

If 1 is entered, AutoCAD sets the COPY command to create a single copy.

4. MIRROR TOOL

User can flip objects about a specified axis to create a symmetrical mirror image. Mirroring is useful for creating symmetrical objects because user can quickly draw half the object and then mirror it instead of drawing the entire object.

The MIRROR tool is used to create a mirror copy of the selected objects. The objects can be mirrored at any angle. This tool is helpful for drawing symmetrical figures. The Mirror command can be invoked using any one of the following methods:

1. Type **MIRROR** or **MI** in the command prompt and press Enter.
2. Choose **Mirror** tool from the **Modify** panel in the **Home** tab.
3. Choose **Mirror** tool from the **Modify** menu.
4. Choose **Mirror** tool from the **Modify** toolbar.

If you invoke the Mirror command, AutoCAD prompts to select objects. If you select object or objects to be mirrored, AutoCAD prompts to enter the first point of the mirror line and then the second point of the Mirror Line. Mirror Line is an imaginary line about which the objects are mirrored. The mirror line can be specified at any angle. Specify the end points of the mirror line by specifying the points in the drawing area or by entering their coordinates. The two specified points become the endpoints of a line about which the selected objects are mirrored.

If the first point of the mirror line is specified, the preview of the mirrored objects will be displayed. Next, specify the second end point of the mirror line. After specifying the second point, AutoCAD prompts to specify whether you want to delete the source object or not. Enter **Yes** to delete the source object and **No** to retain the source object.

The prompt sequence that is displayed at the command prompt when the user choose the mirror command is as follows:

Select objects: *Use an object selection method and press* Enter *to finish*
Specify first point of mirror line: *Specify a point*
Specify second point of mirror line: *Specify a point*
Erase source objects? [Yes/No] <N>: *Enter y or n, or press* Enter

Problem 6: *Draw a mirror image of objects about Y axis using MIRROR command.*

The command sequence to mirror the objects about Y axis using the Mirror command is as follows:

Command: **MIRROR** ↵
Select objects: C ↵
Specify first corner: *(Pick P1)*
Specify opposite corner: *(Pick P2)* 6 found
Select objects: ↵
Specify first point of mirror line: *(Pick P3)*
Specify second point of mirror line: *(Pick P4)*
Erase source objects? [Yes/No] <N>: **N** ↵

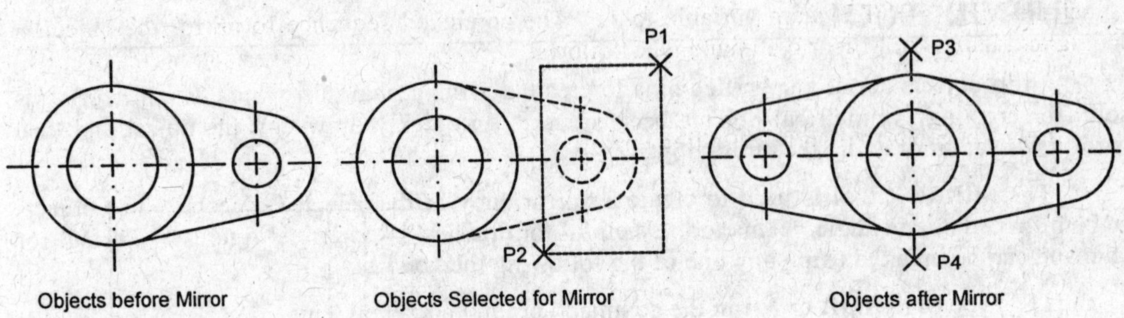

FIG. 9

See Fig. 9.

Problem 7: *Draw a mirror image of objects about X axis using the MIRROR command.*

The command sequence to mirror the objects about X axis using the Mirror command is as follows:

Command: **MIRROR** ↵
Select objects: **C** ↵
Specify first corner: *(Pick P1)*
Specify opposite corner:
(Pick P2) 7 found
Select objects: ↵
Specify first point of
mirror line: *(Pick P3)*
Specify second point of
mirror line: *(Pick P4)*
Erase source objects? [Yes/No] <N>: **N** ↵

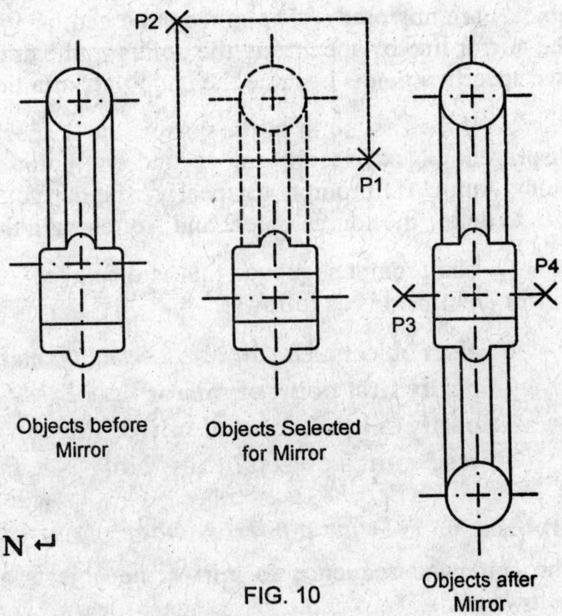

FIG. 10

See Fig. 10.

By default, when a text object is mirrored, the direction of the text is not changed. The text has the same alignment and justification as before the object was mirrored. Set the MIRRTEXT system variable to 1 if the text also to be reversed.

MIRRTEXT affects text that is created with the TEXT, ATTDEF or MTEXT commands; attribute definitions and variable attributes. Text and constant attributes that are part of an inserted block are reversed when the block is mirrored regardless of the MIRRTEXT setting.

Problem 8: *Draw a mirror image of objects including text using MIRROR command.*

First, set the MIRRTEXT system variable to 1. The command sequence to mirror the objects including text using the Mirror command is as follows:

Command: **MIRRTEXT** ↵
Enter new value for MIRRTEXT <0>: **1** ↵
Command: **MIRROR** ↵
Select objects: **W** ↵
Specify first corner: *(Pick P1)*
Specify opposite corner: *(Pick P2)* 6 found
Select objects: ↵
Specify first point of mirror line: *(Pick P3)*
Specify second point of mirror line: *(Pick P4)*
Erase source objects? [Yes/No] <N>: **N** ↵

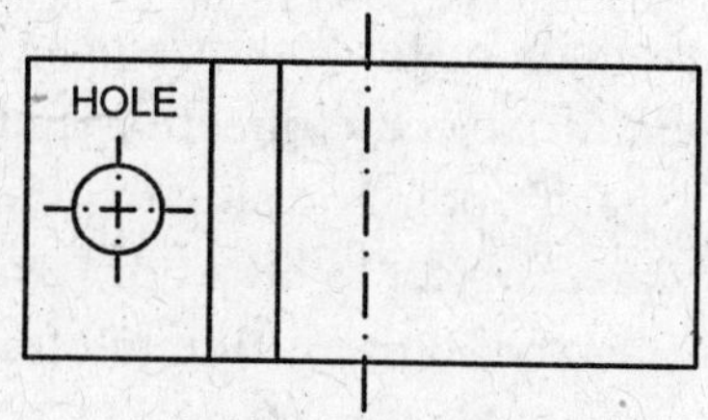

Objects before Mirror

See Fig. 11.

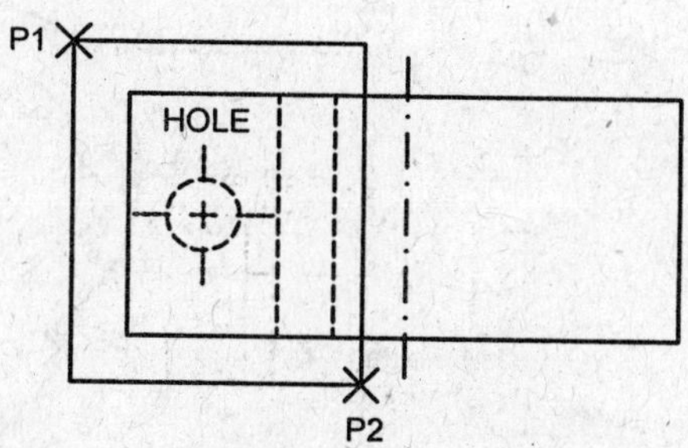

Objects Selected for Mirror

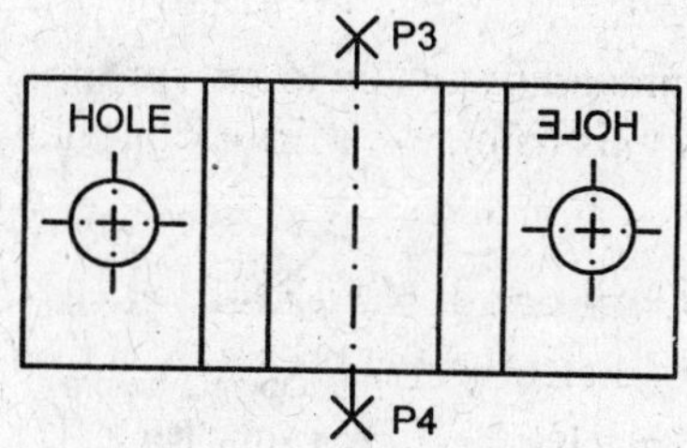

Objects after Mirror

FIG. 11

5. OFFSET TOOL

The OFFSET tool creates concentric circles, parallel lines and parallel curves. Offsetting a circle or an arc creates a larger or smaller circle or arc, depending on which side the offset is specified.

User can offset an object at a specified distance or through a point. After user offsets objects, user can trim and extend them as an efficient method to create drawings containing many parallel lines and curves.

The OFFSET command repeats for convenience. To exit the command, press Enter. The Offset command can be invoked using any one of the following methods:

1. Type **OFFSET** or **O** in the command prompt and press Enter.
2. Choose the **Offset** tool from the **Modify** panel in the **Home** tab.
3. Choose **Offset** tool from the **Modify** menu.
4. Choose **Offset** tool from the **Modify** toolbar.

Problem 9: *Draw the offset objects using the OFFSET command.*

The command sequence to set offset objects using the Offset command is as follows:

> Command: **OFFSET** ↵
> Current settings: Erase source=No Layer=Source OFFSETGAPTYPE=0
> Specify offset distance or [Through/Erase/Layer] <3.0000>: **5** ↵
> Select object to offset or [Exit/Undo] <Exit>: *(Select the Circle)*
> Specify point on side to offset or [Exit/Multiple/Undo] <Exit>: *(Pick P1)*
> Select object to offset or [Exit/Undo] <Exit>: *(Select the Square)*
> Specify point on side to offset or [Exit/Multiple/Undo] <Exit>: *(Pick P2)*
> Select object to offset or [Exit/Undo] <Exit>: ↵

See Fig. 12.

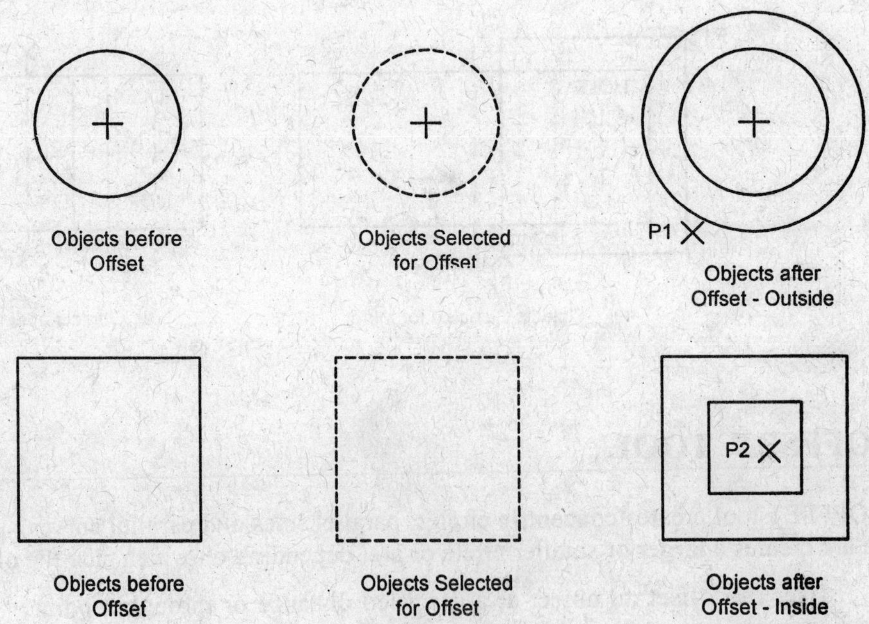

FIG. 12

5.1 OPTIONS IN THE OFFSET COMMAND

Offset Distance: The Offset Distance option creates an object at a specified distance from an existing object.

Exit: The Exit option exits the OFFSET command.

Multiple: The Multiple option enters the Multiple offset mode, which repeats the offset operation using the current offset distance.

Undo: The Undo option reverses the previous offset.

Through: The Through option creates an object passing through a specified point. Using this option, you can offset lines, arc, 2D polylines, xlines, circles, ellipses, elliptical arcs, rays and planar splines.

In the Through option, you need not specify a distance; you need to specify an offset point. The offset distance is stored in the OFFSETDIST system variable. A negative value indicates that the offset value is set to the Through option. If the Through option is invoked, then the prompt displayed is:

Select object to offset or <exit>: *Select one object or press* Enter *to end the command*

Specify through point or [Exit/Multiple/Undo] <exit or next object>:
Specify a point through which you want the offset object to pass or enter a distance

Note that for the best results when we offset a polyline with corners, specify the through point near the midpoint of a line segment, not near a corner.

Erase: The Erases option erases the source object after it is offset. The prompt is:

Erase source object after offsetting? [Yes/No] <*current*>: *Enter y or n*

Layer: The Layer option determines whether offset objects are created on the current layer or on the layer of the source object. The prompt is:

Enter layer option for offset objects [Current/Source] <*current*>: *Enter an option*

6. ARRAY TOOL

Sometimes, it may be needed to create an object multiple times in a rectangular or circular arrangement. This type of arrangement can be obtained by creating an array of objects. An **Array** is defined as a method of creating multiple copies of a selected object and arranging them in a rectangular or circular fashion.

The **Array** tool creates multiple copies of objects in a pattern. User can create copies of objects in a regularly spaced rectangular or polar array. The **Array** command can be invoked using any one of the following methods:

1. Type **ARRAY** or **AR** in the command prompt and press Enter.
2. Choose the **Array** tool from the **Modify** panel in the **Home** tab.
3. Choose the **Array** tool from the **Modify** menu.
4. Choose the Array tool from the **Modify** toolbar.

When the Array command is invoked, the Array dialog box is displayed on the screen. If *-array* is entered at the Command prompt, the options in the array are displayed. Each object in an array can be manipulated independently. If multiple objects are selected, the objects are treated as one item to be copied and arrayed.

User can create rectangular or polar arrays by choosing the appropriate options. Use the **Rectangular Array** option to create an array of rows and columns of copies of the selected object. Use the **Polar Array** option to create an array by copying the selected objects around a center point.

6.1 RECTANGULAR ARRAY

The **Rectangular Array** option creates an array of rows and columns of copies of the selected object. The **Array** dialog box is shown in **Fig. 13.** In this, the options/features in the Rectangular Array are displayed since, the Rectangular Array radio button is checked.

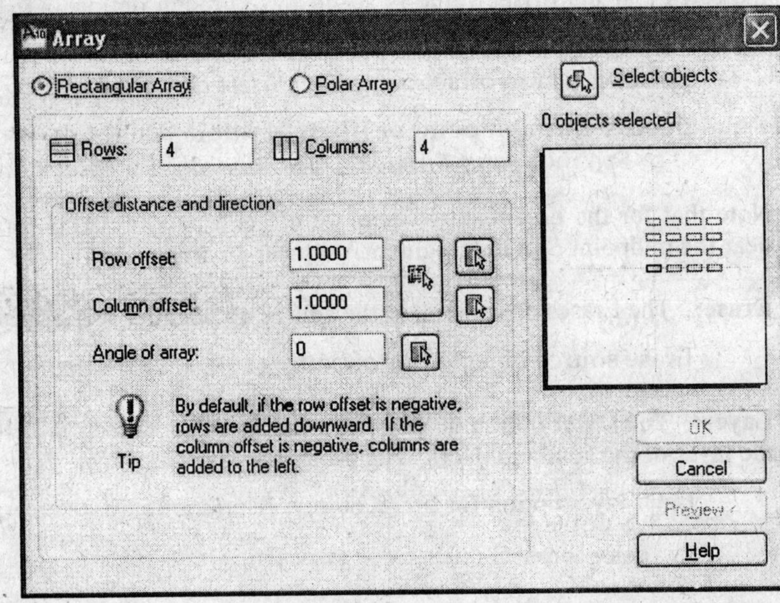

FIG. 13

Rows: The Rows edit box is used to specify the number of rows in the rectangular array. If one row is specified, user must specify more than one column. If a large number of rows and columns are specified for the array, it might take a while to create the copies.

Columns: The Columns edit box is used to specify the number of columns in the rectangular array. If one column is specified, we must specify more than one row. If a large number of rows and columns are specified for the array, it might take a while to create the copies.

Offset Distance and Direction: The Offset Distance and Direction area provides a space to specify the distance and direction of the array's offset.

Row Offset option specifies the distance (in units) between rows. To add rows downward, specify a negative value. To specify row spacing with the pointing device, use the Pick Both Offsets button or the Pick Row Offset button.

Column Offset option specifies the distance (in units) between columns. To add columns to the left, specify a negative value. To specify column spacing with the pointing device, use the Pick Both Offsets button or the Pick Column Offset button.

Angle of Array option specifies the angle of rotation. This angle is normally 0, so the rows and columns are orthogonal with respect to the *X* and *Y* drawing axes of the current UCS. The measurement conventions for angles is changed using the UNITS system variable.

Pick Both Offsets button temporarily closes the Array dialog box so that we can use the pointing device to set the row and column spacing by specifying two diagonal corners of a rectangle.

Pick Row Offset button temporarily closes the Array dialog box so that we can use the pointing device to specify the distance between rows. ARRAY prompts us to specify two points and uses the distance and direction between the points to specify the value in Row Offset.

Pick Column Offset button temporarily closes the Array dialog box so that we can use the pointing device to specify the distance between columns. ARRAY prompts us to specify two points and uses the distance and direction between the points to specify the value in Column Offset.

Pick Angle of Array button temporarily closes the Array dialog box so that we can specify the angle of rotation by entering a value or using the pointing device to specify two points. The measurement conventions for angles can be changed using the UNITS system variable. The ANGBASE and ANGDIR system variables affect the angle of arrays.

6.2 POLAR ARRAY

The Polar Array option creates an array by copying the selected objects around a specified center point.

The options in the Polar Array are displayed in the Array dialog box is show in **Fig. 14.**

Center Point: This text box specifies the center point of the polar array. Enter coordinate values for *X* and *Y* or choose Pick Center Point button to use the pointing device to specify the location.

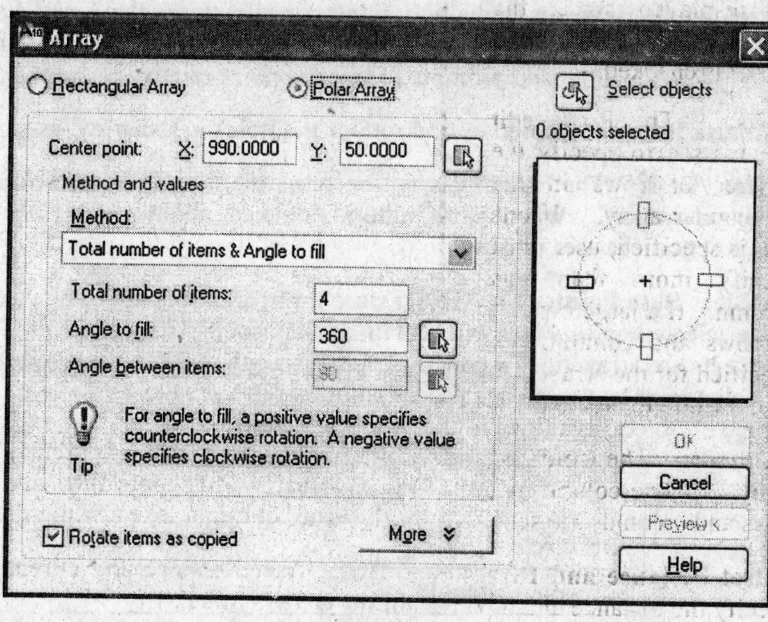

FIG. 14

Pick Center Point button temporarily closes the Array dialog box so that the pointing device can be used to specify the center point in the drawing area.

Method and Values: In the Method and Values area, the method and values used to position objects in the polar array are specified

Method textbox sets the method used to position objects. This setting controls which of the Method and Value fields are available for specifying values. For example, if the method is Total Number of Items & Angle to Fill, the related fields are available for specifying values; the Angle Between Items field is not available.

Total Number of Items textbox sets the number of objects that appear in the resultant array. The default value is 4.

Angle to Fill text box sets the size of the array by defining the included angle between the base points of the first and last elements in the array. A positive value specifies counterclockwise rotation. A negative value specifies clockwise rotation. The default value is 360. A value of 0 is not permitted.

Angle Between Items textbox sets the included angle between the base points of the arrayed objects and the center of the array. Enter a positive value. The default direction value is 90. Note that it is possible to choose the Pick buttons and use the pointing device to specify the values for Angle to Fill and Angle Between Items.

Pick Angle to Fill button temporarily closes the Array dialog box to define the included angle between the base points of the first and last elements in the array. The ARRAY command prompts to select a point relative to another point in the drawing area.

Pick Angle Between Items button temporarily closes the Array dialog box to define the included angle between the base points of the arrayed objects and the center of the array. The ARRAY command prompts to select a point relative to another point in the drawing area.

Rotate Items as Copied option rotates the items in the array, as shown in the preview area.

More/Less: The More/Less button turns the display of additional options in the Array dialog box on and off. When More button is clicked, additional options are displayed and the name of this button changes to Less.

Object Base Point: The Object Base Point area specifies a new reference (base) point relative to the selected objects that will remain at a constant distance from the center point of the array as the objects are arrayed. To construct a polar array, ARRAY determines the distance from the array's center point to a reference (base) point on the last object selected. The point used depends on the type of object, as shown in the following table.

Object Type	Default Base Point
Arc, circle, ellipse	Center point
Polygon, rectangle	First corner
Donut, line, polyline, 3D polyline, ray, spline	Starting point
Block, paragraph text, single-line text	Insertion point
Construction lines	Midpoint
Region	Grip point

Table 2 Base Point Settings by Object

Set to Object's Default option uses the default base point of the object to position the arrayed object. To manually set the base point, clear this option.

Base Point textbox sets a new *X* and *Y* base point coordinate. Choose **Pick Base Point** button to temporarily close the dialog box and specify a point. After a point is specified, the Array dialog box is redisplayed. Note that to avoid unexpected results, set the base point manually while constructing a polar array and do not want to rotate the objects.

6.3 OPTIONS COMMON TO RECTANGULAR ARRAY AND POLAR ARRAY

Select Objects: The Select Objects button specifies the objects used to construct the array. Objects can be selected before or after the Array dialog box is displayed.

To select objects when the Array dialog box is displayed, choose Select Objects button. The Array dialog box temporarily closes. When selecting objects are finished, press ENTER. The Array dialog box is redisplayed and the number of objects selected is shown below the Select Objects button.

Preview Area: The Preview Area shows a preview image of the array based on the current settings in the dialog box. The preview image is dynamically updated when we move to another field after changing a setting.

Preview: The Preview button closes the Array dialog box and displays the array in the current drawing.

Problem 10: *Draw multiple copies of objects in column wise using the ARRAY command.*

The command sequence to draw multiple copies of objects in column wise using the Rectangular Array option in the Array command is as follows:

Command: **ARRAY** ↵

(The Array dialog box is displayed on the screen. Enter 1 in the Rows text box and enter 4 in the Columns text box. Also, enter 24 in the Columns offset text box. Click the Select Objects button. The Array dialog box closes temporarily. Select the required objects using any one of the Selection Methods.)

Select objects: **W** ↵

Specify first corner: *(Pick P1)*

Specify opposite corner: *(Pick P2)* 4 found

Select objects: ↵

(The Array dialog box appears on the screen again. Click the Preview button to close the Array dialog box and to display the current objects array.)

Pick or press Esc to return to dialog or <Right-click to accept array>:

(Click anywhere in the drawing area. The Array dialog box appears on the screen. Click the OK button to accept the array.)

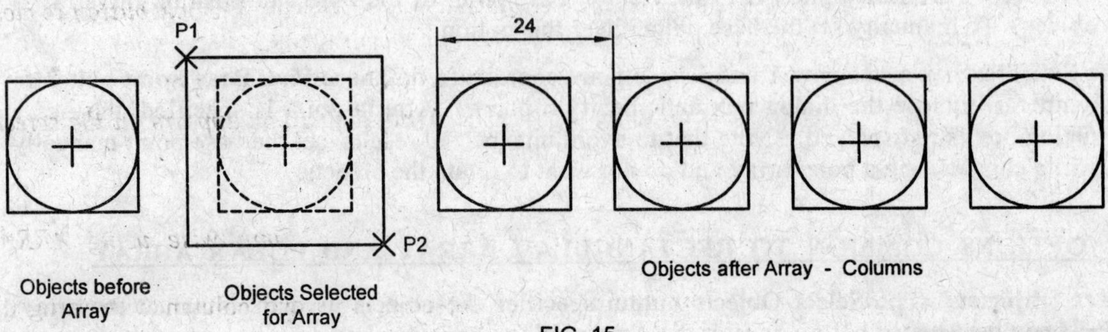

FIG. 15

See Fig. 15.

Problem 11: *Draw multiple copies of objects in row wise using the ARRAY command.*

The command sequence to draw multiple copies of objects in row wise using the Rectangular Array option in the Array command is as follows:

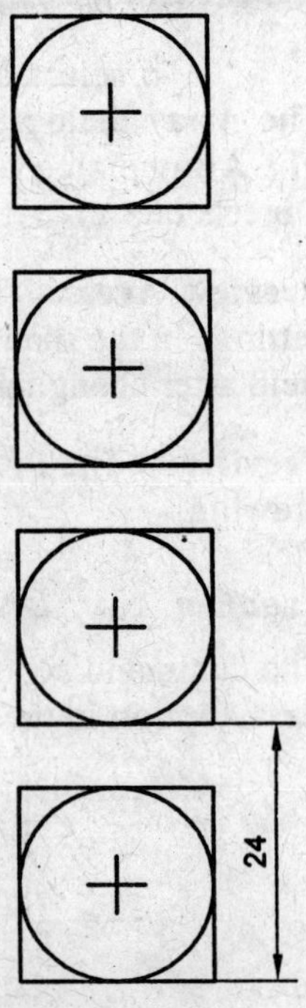
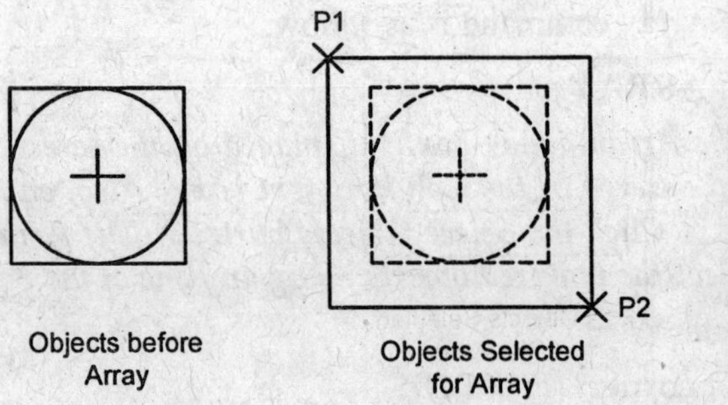

FIG. 16

Command: **ARRAY** ↵

(The Array dialog box is displayed on the screen. Enter 4 in the Rows text box and enter 1 in the Columns text box. Also, enter 24 in the Rows offset text box. Click the Select Objects button. The Array dialog box closes temporarily. Select the required objects using any one of the Selection Methods.)

Select objects: **W** ↵

Specify first corner: *(Pick P1)*

Specify opposite corner: *(Pick P2)* 4 found

Select objects: ↵

(The Array dialog box appears on the screen again. Click the Preview button to close the Array dialog box and to display the current objects array.)

Pick or press Esc to return to dialog or <Right-click to accept array>:

(Click anywhere in the drawing area. The Array dialog box appears on the screen. Click the OK button to accept the array.)

See Fig. 16.

Problem 12: *Draw multiple copies of objects in row and column wise using ARRAY command.*

The command sequence to draw multiple copies of objects in row and column wise using the Rectangular Array option in the Array command is as follows:

Command: **ARRAY** ↵

(The Array dialog box is displayed on the screen. Enter 3 in the Rows text box and enter 3 in the Columns text box. Enter 26 in the Columns offset text box and enter 26 in the Rows offset text box.

Click the Select Objects button. The Array dialog box closes temporarily. Select the required objects using any one of the Selection Methods.)

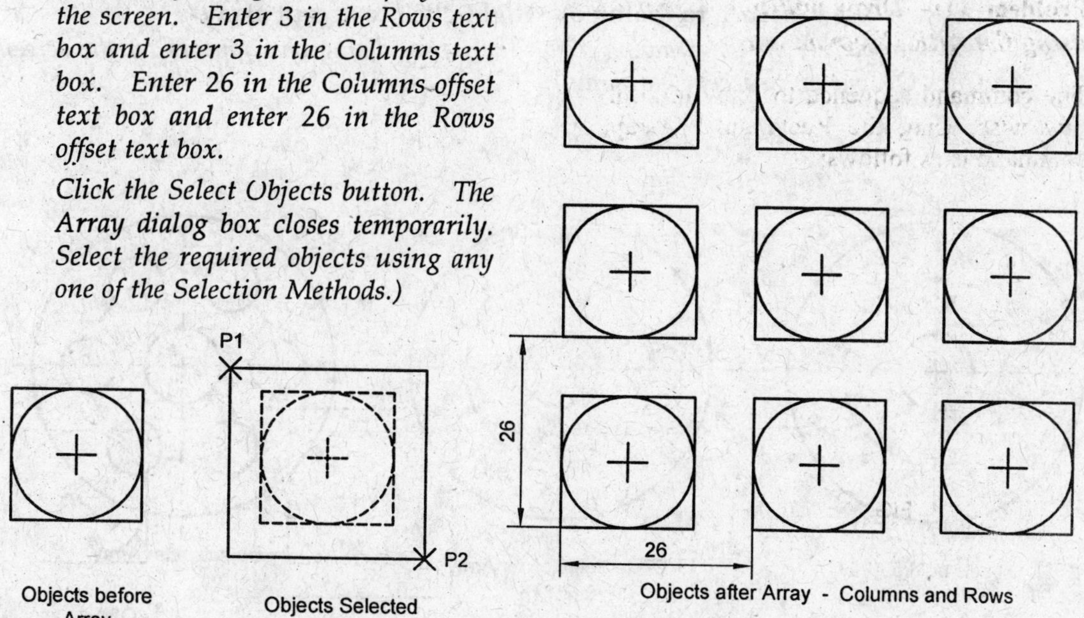

FIG. 17

Select objects: **W** ↵

Specify first corner: *(Pick P1)*

Specify opposite corner: *(Pick P2)* 4 found

Select objects: ↵ *(The Array dialog box appears on the screen again. Click the Preview button to close the Array dialog box and to display the current objects array.)*

Pick or press Esc to return to dialog or <Right-click to accept array>:

(Click anywhere in the drawing area. The Array dialog box appears on the screen. Click the OK button to accept the array.)

See Fig. 17.

Problem 13: *Draw multiple copies of an object using ARRAY command.*

See Fig. 18. The command sequence to draw multiple copies of an object using the Polar Array option in the Array command is as follows:

Command: **ARRAY** ↵

(The Array dialog box is displayed on the screen. Select the Polar Array option to display the options in the Polar Array. Click the Select Objects button. The Array dialog box closes temporarily. Select the required objects.)

Select objects: *(Select the small circle)*

Select objects: ↵

(The Array dialog box appears again. Click the Pick Center Point button to close the Array dialog box and click on the center point P1. The Array dialog box appears on the screen again. Enter 6 in the Total number of items text box. Click the Preview button to close the Array dialog box and to display the current objects array.)

Pick or press Esc to return to dialog or <Right-click to accept array>:

(Click anywhere in the drawing area. The Array dialog box appears on the screen. Click OK button to accept the array.)

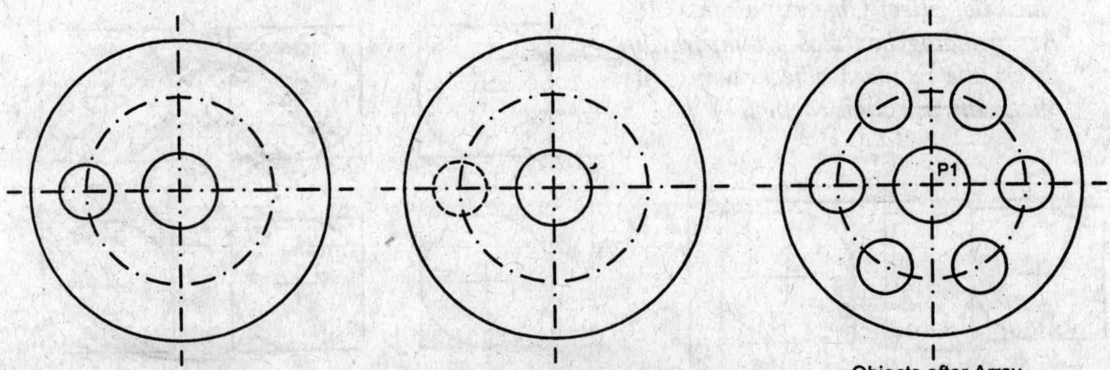

Objects before Array | Circle Selected for Array | Objects after Array

FIG. 18

7. MOVE TOOL

The MOVE tool is used to move objects from the current location to the new location without changing their size or orientation. Using coordinates, grid snap, object snaps and other tools objects are moved with precision. The MOVE command is invoked using any one of the following methods:

1. Type **MOVE** or **M** in the command prompt and press Enter.
2. Choose the **Move** tool from the **Modify** panel in the **Home** tab.
3. Choose the **Move** tool the **Modify** menu.
4. Choose the **Move** tool from the **Modify** toolbar.

When the Move command is invoked, AutoCAD prompts to select the objects to be moved. Select the objects by using any one of the selection methods discussed earlier. Now, AutoCAD prompts to specify the base point. Select the base point on the object that is selected to move. Then, AutoCAD prompts to specify the second point of displacement. Specify the new location where you want to move the object. The selected object is moved to this point.

Problem 14: *Move an object using the MOVE command.*

The command sequence to move the rectangle using the Move command is as follows:

Command: **MOVE** ↵
Select objects: *(Select the rectangle)* 1 found
Select objects: ↵
Specify base point or [Displacement]
<Displacement>: *(Pick P1)*
Specify second point or
<use first point as displacement>: *(Pick P2)*

See Fig. 19

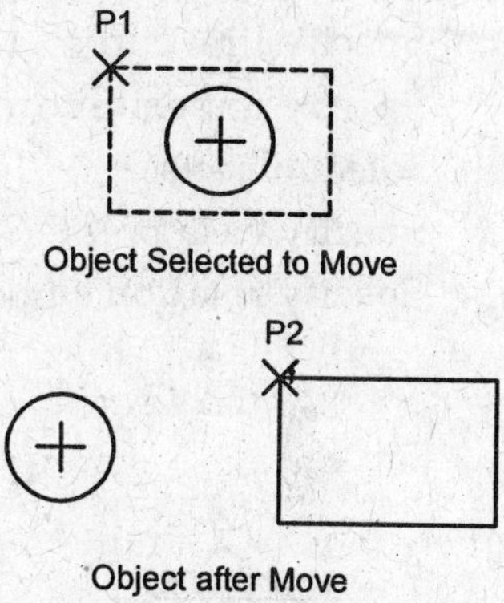

FIG. 19

The two points specified define a vector that indicates how far the selected objects are to be moved and in what direction.

Displacement option can be used to specify coordinates to represent a vector. If the Displacement option is selected, AutoCAD prompts the user to specify the coordinate value.

8. ROTATE TOOL

The **Rotate** tool rotates objects around a base point. The selected objects are rotated around a base point to an absolute angle. The Rotate command can be invoked using any one of the following methods:

1. Type **ROTATE** or **RO** in the command prompt and press Enter.
2. Choose the **Rotate** tool from the **Modify** panel in the **Home** tab.
3. Choose the **Rotate** tool from the **Modify** menu.
4. Choose the **Rotate** tool from the **Modify** toolbar.

When the Rotate command is invoked, AutoCAD prompts to select the objects and the base point about which the selected objects will be rotated. After specifying the base point, you need to specify the rotation angle.

Using the Rotate tool, it is possible to rotate objects counter clockwise and clockwise directions. During rotation, a positive angle value rotates the objects in counter clockwise direction. If a negative angle value is specified, the objects are rotated in clockwise direction.

Problem 15: *Rotate an object using the Rotate command.*

The command sequence to rotate an object using the Rotate command is as follows:

Command: **ROTATE** ↵
Current positive angle in UCS: ANGDIR=counterclockwise ANGBASE=0
Select objects: **W** ↵
Specify first corner: *(Pick P1)*
Specify opposite corner: *(Pick P2)* 3 found
Select objects: ↵
Specify base point: *(Pick P3)*
Specify rotation angle or [Copy/Reference] <60>: **25** ↵

See Fig. 20.

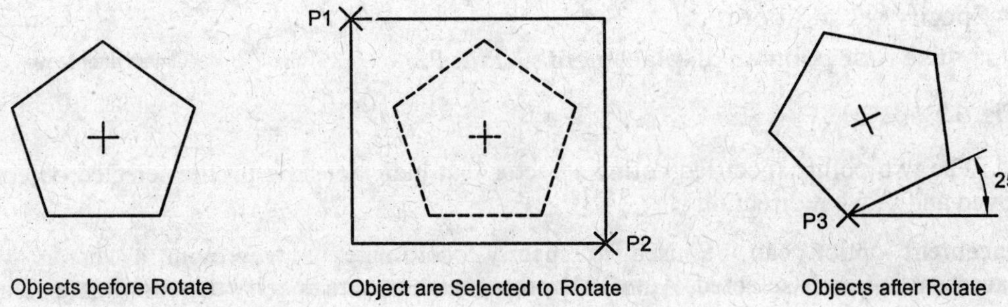

FIG. 20

8.1 OPTIONS IN THE ROTATE COMMAND

Rotation Angle: This option determines how far an object rotates around the base point.

Copy: The Copy option creates a copy of the selected objects for rotation.

Reference: The Reference option rotates objects from a specified angle to a new, absolute angle.

The value entered for the new angle is an absolute angle, **not** a relative value. Alternatively, if a point is specified, the reference angle will be rotated to that point.

For example, if the reference angle is 25° and the new angle is 60°, then the object will be rotated to 60° – 25° = **35°**.

Reference Angle = 25°;
New Angle = 60°
∴ Rotation Angle = 60° – 25° = 35°

9. SCALE TOOL

Sometimes, you may need to change the size of the object in a drawing. This can be done using the **Scale** tool. The **Scale** tool enlarges or reduces selected objects about a base point, keeping the proportions of the object the same after scaling. The Scale command can be invoked using any one of the following methods:

1. Type **SCALE** or **SC** in the command prompt and press Enter.
2. Choose the **Scale** tool from the **Modify** panel in the **Home** tab.
3. Choose the **Scale** tool from the **Modify** menu.
4. Choose the **Scale** tool from the **Modify** toolbar.

To scale an object, specify a base point and a scale factor. The base point acts as the center of the scaling operation and remains stationary. A scale factor greater than 1 enlarges the object. A scale factor between 0 and 1 shrinks the object.

Problem 16: *Enlarge the size of the objects using the Scale command.*
The command sequence to enlarge objects using the Scale command is as follows:

Command: **SCALE** ↵
Select objects: **W** ↵
Specify first corner: *(Pick P1)*
Specify opposite corner: *(Pick P2)* 2 found
Select objects: ↵
Specify base point: *(Pick P3)*
Specify scale factor or [Copy/Reference] <1.0000>: **1.5** ↵

See Fig. 21.

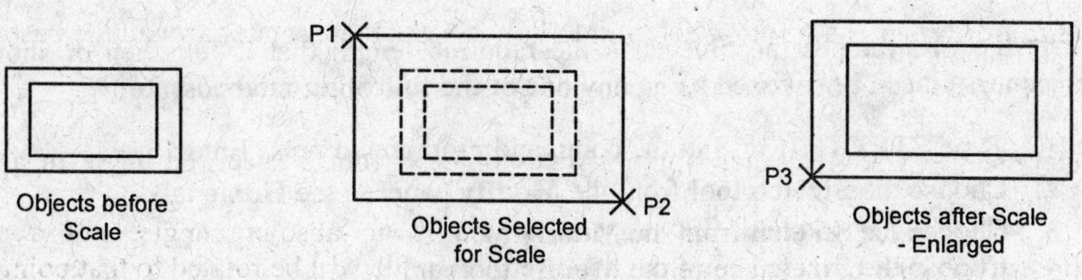

FIG. 21

9.1 OPTIONS IN THE SCALE COMMAND

Scale Factor: The Scale Factor multiplies the dimensions of the selected objects by the specified scale. A scale factor greater than 1 enlarges the objects. A scale factor between 0 and 1 shrinks the objects. We can also drag the cursor to make the object larger or smaller.
Copy: The Copy option creates a copy of the selected objects for scaling.

Reference: The Reference option scales the selected objects based on a reference length and a specified new length.

Problem 17: *Reduce the side of the objects using the Scale command.*

The command sequence to reduce objects using the Scale command is as follows:

Command: **SCALE** ↵
Select objects: **W** ↵
Specify first corner: *(Pick P1)*
Specify opposite corner: *(Pick P2)* 2 found
Select objects: ↵
Specify base point: *(Pick P3)*
Specify scale factor or [Copy/Reference] <1.0000>: **.75** ↵

See Fig. 22.

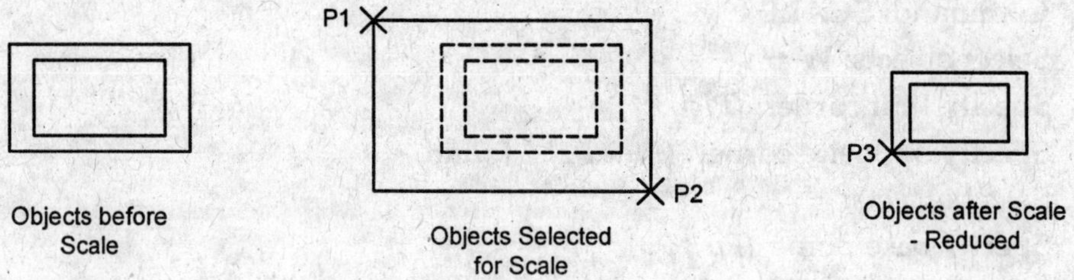

FIG. 22

10. STRETCH TOOL

The Stretch tool stretches the objects to the required length that is lengthen or shorten. The Stretch command can be invoked using any one of the following methods:

1. Type **STRETCH** or **S** in the command prompt and press Enter.
2. Choose the **Stretch** tool from the **Modify** panel in the **Home** tab.
3. Choose the **Stretch** from the **Modify** menu.
4. Choose the **Stretch** from the **Modify** toolbar.

When the Stretch tool is invoked, AutoCAD prompts to select objects. Use the Crossing or CPolygon selection method to select the objects to be stretched. After selecting the objects, AutoCAD prompts to specify the base point of displacement. Select the portion of the object that needs to be stretched. Now, AutoCAD prompts to specify the second point of displacement. Specify the new location. The selected object is lengthened or shortened.

When the Stretch Objects that are partially enclosed by a crossing window are stretched, objects that are completely enclosed within the crossing window or that are selected individually, are moved rather than stretched. Several objects such as circles, ellipses and blocks, cannot be stretched. Note that during the stretching process, select the objects by crossing-window or crossing-polygon methods *only*.

Problem 18: *Stretch the objects using the Stretch command.*

The command sequence to stretch objects using the Stretch command is as follows:

Command: **STRETCH** ↵
Select objects to stretch by crossing-window or crossing-polygon...
Select objects: *(Pick P1)*
Specify opposite corner: *(Pick P2)* 5 found
Select objects: ↵
Specify base point or [Displacement] <Displacement>: *(Pick P3)*
Specify second point or <use first point as displacement>:
(Move the cursor to the right) 5 ↵

See Fig. 23.

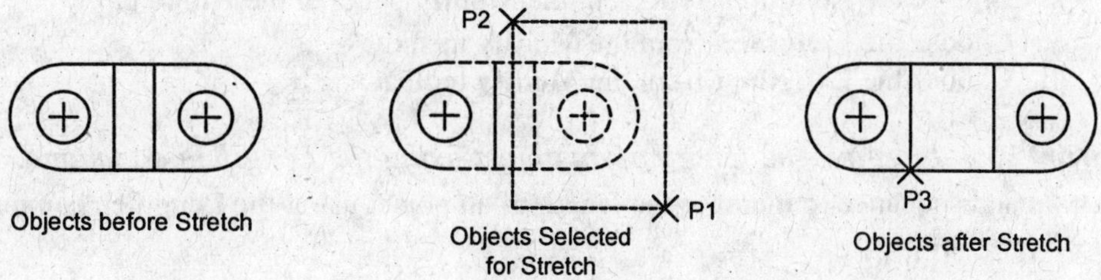

FIG. 23

If a second point is entered, the objects are stretched the vector distance from the base point to the second point. If *Enter* is pressed at the Specify Second Point of Displacement prompt, the first point is treated as an *X,Y,Z* displacement.

Problem 19: *Stretch the objects using the Stretch command.*

The command sequence to stretch objects using the Stretch command is as follows:

Command: **STRETCH** ↵
Select objects to stretch by crossing-window or crossing-polygon...
Select objects: *(Pick P1)*
Specify opposite corner: *(Pick P2)* 4 found
Select objects: ↵

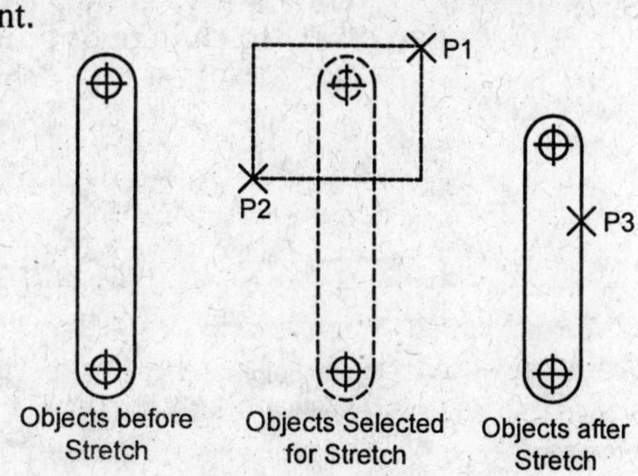

FIG. 24

Specify base point or [Displacement] <Displacement>: *(Pick P3)*
Specify second point or <use first point as
displacement>: *(Move the cursor to the down)* **6** ↵

See Fig. 24.

11. LENGTHEN TOOL

The Lengthen tool is used to change (increases/decreases) the length of objects and the included angle of arcs. The positive value will increase the length or angle. The negative value will decrease the length or angle. Changes can be specified as a percentage, an increment or as a final length or angle. LENGTHEN is an alternative to using TRIM or EXTEND.

The LENGTHEN command does not affect the closed objects. The extrusion direction of the selected object need not be parallel to the *Z* axis of the current User Coordinate System (UCS). The **Lengthen** command can be invoked using any one of the following methods:

1. Type **LENGTHEN** or **LEN** in the command prompt and press Enter.
2. Choose the **Lengthen** tool from the **Modify** panel in the **Home** tab.
3. Choose the **Lengthen** from the **Modify** menu.
4. Choose the **Lengthen** from the **Modify** toolbar.

Problem 20: *Increase the length of an object using the Lengthen command.*
The command sequence to increase the length of an object using the Lengthen command is:

Command: **LENGTHEN** ↵
Select an object or [DElta/Percent/Total/DYnamic]: *(Pick P1)*
Current length: 25.0000
Select an object or [DElta/Percent/Total/DYnamic]: **DE** ↵
Enter delta length or [Angle] <0.0000>: **10** ↵
Select an object to change or [Undo]: *(Pick P1)*
Select an object to change or [Undo]: ↵

See Fig. 25.

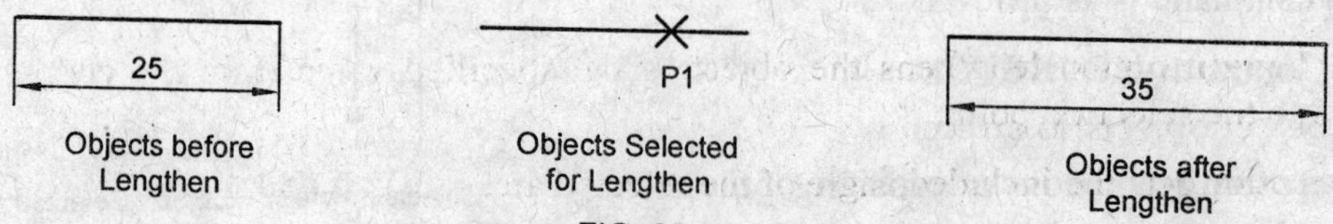

FIG. 25

Object Selection: The Object Selection displays the length and where applicable, the included angle of the object.

Delta: The Delta option changes the length of an object by a specified increment, measured from the endpoint that is closest to the selection point. Delta also changes the angle of an arc by a specified increment, measured from the endpoint that is closest to the selection point. A positive value extends the object; a negative value trims it.

Delta Length option changes the length of the object by the specified increment.

Angle option changes the included angle of the selected arc by the specified angle.

Percent: The Percent option sets the length of an object by a specified percentage of its total length. The current length or angle is taken as 100%. The value above 100% will increase the length or angle. The value below 100% will decrease the length or angle.

Problem 21: *Decrease the length of the object using the Percent option of the Lengthen command.*

See Fig. 26. The command sequence to decrease/reduce the length of the object using the Percent option of the Lengthen command is as follows:

Command: **LENGTHEN** ↵

Select an object or [DElta/Percent/Total/DYnamic]: **P** ↵

Enter percentage length <100.0000>: **75** ↵

Select an object to change or [Undo]: *(Pick P1)*

Select an object to change or [Undo]: ↵

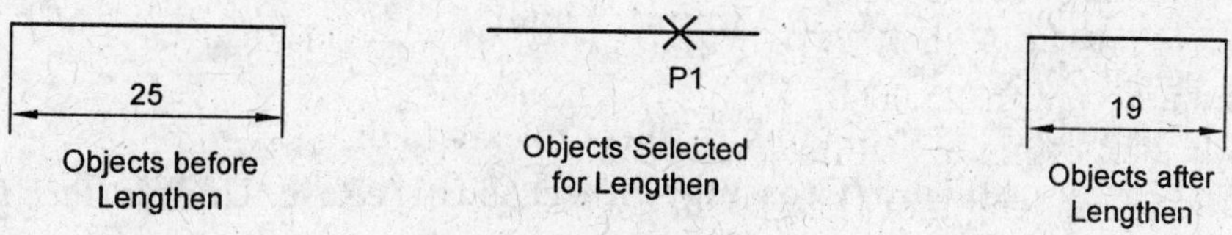

FIG. 26

Total: The Total option sets the length of a selected object by specifying the total absolute length from the fixed endpoint. Total also sets the included angle of a selected arc by a specified total angle.

Total Length option lengthens the object to the specified value from the endpoint that is closest to the selection point.

Angle option sets the included angle of the selected arc.

Dynamic: The Dynamic option turns on Dynamic Dragging mode. The length of a selected object is changed by dragging one of its endpoints. The other end remains fixed.

12. TRIM TOOL

Sometimes, you may need to trim the unwanted and extending edges in the drawing. The **Trim** tool trims the objects that extend beyond a required point of intersection. To trim objects, select the boundaries, then press ENTER and select the required objects to trim. To use all objects as boundaries, press ENTER at the first Select Objects prompt.

Note that to select cutting edges that include blocks, use only the single selection, Crossing, Fence, and Select All options. Specify an object selection method to select the objects to trim. If more than one trim result is possible, the location of the first selection point determines the result. The Trim command is invoked using any one of the following methods:

1. Type **TRIM** or **TR** in the command prompt and press Enter.
2. Choose the **Trim** tool from the **Modify** panel in the **Home** tab.
3. Choose the **Trim** tool from the **Modify** menu.
4. Choose the **Trim** tool from the **Modify** toolbar.

Problem 22: *Trim the objects using the Trim command.*

The command sequence to trim the objects that extend beyond required edges using the Trim command is as follows:

Command: **TRIM** ↵
Current settings: Projection=UCS, Edge=None
Select cutting edges ...
Select objects or <select all>: *(Pick L1)* 1 found
Select objects: *(Pick L2)* 1 found, 2 total
Select objects: ↵
Select object to trim or shift-select to extend or
[Fence/Crossing/Project/Edge/eRase/Undo]: *(Pick P1)*

Select object to trim or shift-select to extend or
[Fence/Crossing/Project/Edge/eRase/Undo]: *(Pick P2)*

Select object to trim or shift-select to extend or
[Fence/Crossing/Project/Edge/eRase/Undo]: *(Pick P3)*

Select object to trim or shift-select to extend or
[Fence/Crossing/Project/Edge/eRase/Undo]: *(Pick P4)*

Select object to trim or shift-select to extend or
[Fence/Crossing/Project/Edge/eRase/Undo]: ↵

See Fig. 27.

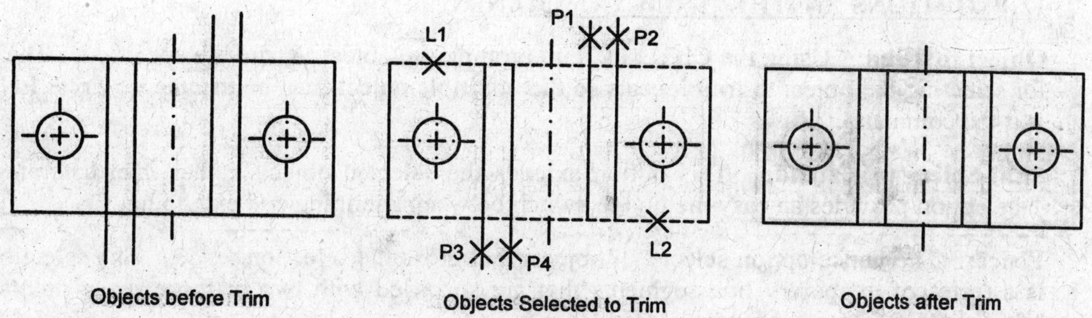

FIG. 27

Problem 23: *Trim all the objects using the Trim command.*

The command sequence to trim all the objects using the Trim command is as follows:

Command: **TRIM** ↵
Current settings: Projection=UCS, Edge=None
Select cutting edges ...
Select objects or <select all>: ↵
Select object to trim or shift-select to extend or
[Fence/Crossing/Project/Edge/eRase/Undo]: *(Pick P1)*
Select object to trim or shift-select to extend or
[Fence/Crossing/Project/Edge/eRase/Undo]: *(Pick P2)*
Select object to trim or shift-select to extend or
[Fence/Crossing/Project/Edge/eRase/Undo]: *(Pick P3)*
Select object to trim or shift-select to extend or
[Fence/Crossing/Project/Edge/eRase/Undo]: *(Pick P4)*
Select object to trim or shift-select to extend or
[Fence/Crossing/Project/Edge/eRase/Undo]: ↵

See Fig. 28.

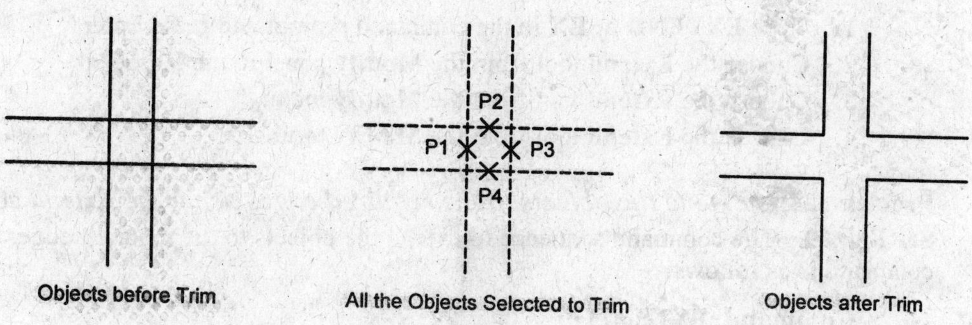

FIG. 28

12.1 OPTIONS IN THE TRIM COMMAND

Object to Trim: Using the Object to Trim prompt, the object to trim are specified. The prompt for selecting the object to trim repeats so that multiple objects can be trimmed. Press ENTER to exit the command.

Shift-Select to Extend: This option extends the selected objects rather than trimming them. This option provides an easy method to switch between trimming and extending.

Fence: The Fence option selects all objects that cross the selection fence. The selection fence is a series of temporary line segments that are specified with two or more fence points. The selection fence does not form a closed loop.

Crossing: The Crossing option selects the objects within and crossing a rectangular area defined by two points. Note that some crossing selections of objects to be trimmed are ambiguous. TRIM resolves the selection by following along the rectangular crossing window in a clockwise direction from the first point to the first object encountered.

Project: The Project option specifies the projection method used when trimming objects.

Edge: The Edge option determines whether an object is trimmed at another object's extrapolated edge or only to an object that intersects it in 3D space.

Erase: The Erase option deletes selected objects. This option provides a convenient method to erase unneeded objects without leaving the TRIM command.

Undo: The Undo option reverses the most recent change made by TRIM.

13. EXTEND TOOL

The **Extend** command extends objects to meet the edges of other objects. This command is similar to the Trim command, but it projects the in-completed end up to the defined boundary. The objects such as line, arc, elliptical arc, polyline and rays can be extended.

To extend objects, first select the boundaries. Then press Enter and select the objects that are required to extend. To use all objects as boundaries, press Enter at the first Select Objects prompt. The Extend command can be invoked using any one of the following methods:

1. Type **EXTEND** or **EX** in the command prompt and press Enter.
2. Choose the **Extend** tool from the **Modify** panel in the **Home** tab.
3. Choose the **Extend** tool from the **Modify** menu.
4. Choose the **Extend** tool from the **Modify** toolbar.

Problem 24: *Extend the objects to the required edges using the Extend command.*

See Fig. 29. The command sequence to extend the objects to the required edges using the Extend command is as follows:

Command: **EXTEND** ↵

Current settings: Projection=UCS, Edge=None
Select boundary edges ...
Select objects or <select all>: *(Pick C1)* 1 found
Select objects: ↵
Select object to extend or shift-select to trim or
[Fence/Crossing/Project/Edge/Undo]: *(Pick P1)*
Select object to extend or shift-select to trim or
[Fence/Crossing/Project/Edge/Undo]: *(Pick P2)*
Select object to extend or shift-select to trim or
[Fence/Crossing/Project/Edge/Undo]: ↵

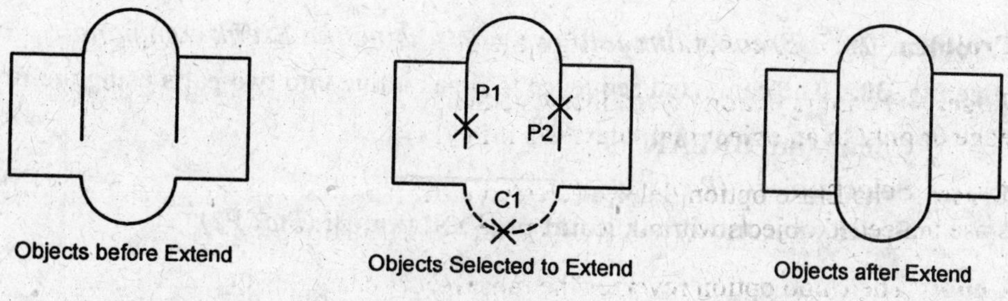

FIG. 29

13.1 OPTIONS IN THE EXTEND COMMAND

Boundary Object Selection: The Boundary Object Selection option uses the selected objects to define the boundary edges to which we want to extend an object.

Object to Extend: This option specifies the objects to extend. Press Enter to end the command.

Shift-Select to Trim: This option trims the selected objects to the nearest boundary rather than extending them. This is an easy method to switch between trimming and extending.

Fence: The Fence option selects all objects that cross the selection fence. The selection fence is a series of temporary line segments that can be specified with two or more fence points. The selection fence does not form a closed loop.

Crossing: This option selects objects within and crossing a rectangular area defined by two points.

Project: The Project option specifies the projection method used when extending objects.

Edge: The Edge option extends the object to another object's implied edge, or only to an object that actually intersects it in 3D space.

Undo: The Undo option reverses the most recent changes made by EXTEND.

14. BREAK TOOL

The **Break** tool breaks the selected object into two parts. A gap can be created between two specified points on an object, breaking it into two objects. If the points are off of an object, they are automatically projected on to the object.

The Break command is often used to remove a part of the selected objects or to break objects such as lines, arcs, circles, ellipses, xlines, rays, splines and polylines. The Break command can be invoked using any one of the following methods:

1. Type **BREAK** or **BR** in the command prompt and press Enter.
2. Choose the **Break** tool from the **Modify** panel in the **Home** tab.
3. Choose the **Break** tool from the **Modify** menu.
4. Choose the **Break** tool from the **Modify** toolbar.

Problem 25: *Break a line into two parts using the Break command.*

See Fig. 30. The command sequence to break a line into two parts using the Break command is:

Command: **BREAK** ↵
Select object: *(Pick P1)*
Specify second break point or [First point]: *(Pick P2)*

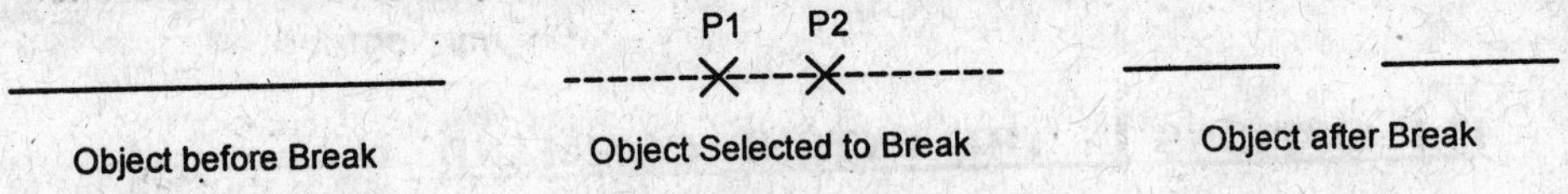

FIG. 30

In the Select object: prompt, if the object is selected by using the pointing device, the program both selects the object and treats the selection point as the first break point. At the next prompt we can continue by specifying the second point or overriding the first point.

Second Break Point option specifies the second point to use to break the object.

First Point option overrides the original first point with the specified new point.

The portion of the object is erased between the two points specified. If the second point is not on the object, the nearest point on the object is selected; therefore, to break off one end of a line, arc or polyline, specify the second point beyond the end to be removed.

To split an object in two without erasing a portion, enter the same point for both the first and second points. This can be done by entering @ to specify the second point.

Lines, arcs, circles, polylines, ellipses, splines, donuts and several other object types can be split into two objects or have one end removed. The program converts a circle to an arc by removing a piece of the circle starting counterclockwise from the first to the second point.

Problem 26: *Break a circle into two parts using the Break command.*

The command sequence to break a circle using the Break command is as follows:

Command: **BREAK** ↵
Select object: *(Pick C1 to select the circle)*
Specify second break point or [First point]: **F** ↵
Specify first break point: *(Pick P1)*
Specify second break point: *(Pick P2)*

See Fig. 31.

It is also possible to break selected objects at a single point with the Break at Point tool. Valid objects include lines, open polylines, and arcs. Closed objects such as circles cannot be broken at a single point.

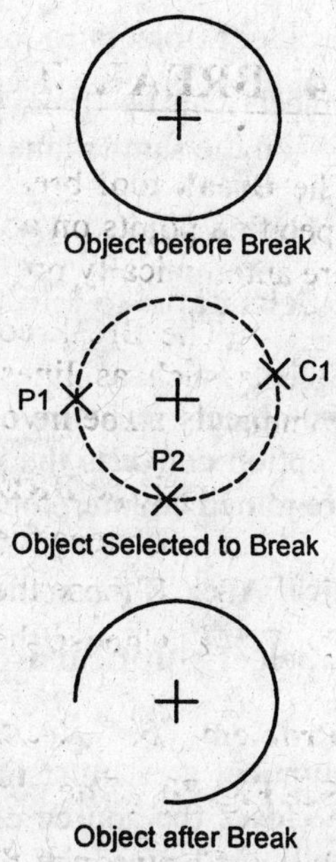

FIG. 31

15. JOIN TOOL

The JOIN tool is used to join similar objects to form a single, unbroken object. The Join command can be invoked using any one of the following methods:

1. Type **JOIN** or **J** in the command prompt and press Enter.
2. Choose the **Join** tool from the **Modify** panel in the **Home** tab.
3. Choose the **Join** tool from the **Modify** menu.
4. Choose the **Join** tool from the **Modify** toolbar.

Objects to be joined must be located in the same plane. Each type of object has additional restrictions. When the Join command is activated, AutoCAD prompts to select the source object. The prompt displayed is as follows:

Select source object: *Select a line, polyline, arc, elliptical arc, spline, or helix*

The source object is the one with which other objects will be joined. The next prompt depends on the source object selected.

Line: If the source object selected is a line, then the prompt displayed is:

Select lines to join to source: *Select one or more lines and press* ENTER

The line objects must be collinear (lying on the same infinite line), but can have gaps between them.

Polyline: If the source object selected is a polyline, then the prompt displayed is:

Select objects to join to source: *Select one or more objects and press* ENTER

The objects can be lines, polylines, or arcs. The objects cannot have gaps between them and must lie on the same plane parallel to the UCS *XY* plane.

Arc: If the source object selected is an arc, then the prompt displayed is:

Select arcs to join to source or [cLose]: *Select one or more arcs and press* ENTER, *or enter L*

The arc objects must lie on the same imaginary circle, but can have gaps between them. The Close option converts the source arc into a circle. Note that when joining two or more arcs, the arcs are joined counterclockwise beginning from the source object.

Elliptical Arc: If the source object selected is an elliptical arc, then the prompt displayed is:

Select elliptical arcs to join to source or [cLose]: *Select one or more elliptical arcs and press* ENTER, *or enter L*

The elliptical arcs must lie on the same ellipse, but can have gaps between them. The Close option closes the source ellipstical arc into a complete ellipse. Note that when joining two or more elliptical arcs, the elliptical arcs are joined counterclockwise beginning from the source object.

Spline: If the source object selected is a spline, then the prompt displayed is:

Select splines or helixes to join to source: *Select one or more splines or helixes and press* ENTER

The spline and helix objects must be contiguous (lying end-to-end). The resulting object is a single spline.

Helix: If the source object selected is a helix, then the prompt displayed is:

Select splines or helixes to join to source: *Select splines or helixes and press* ENTER

The helix objects must be contiguous (lying end-to-end). The resulting object is a single spline.

Problem 27: *Join two lines using the Join command.*

See Fig. 32. The command sequence to join two lines using the Join command is as follows:

Command: **JOIN** ↵
Select source object: *(Pick L1)*
Select lines to join to source: *(Pick L2)* 1 found
Select lines to join to source: ↵
1 line joined to source

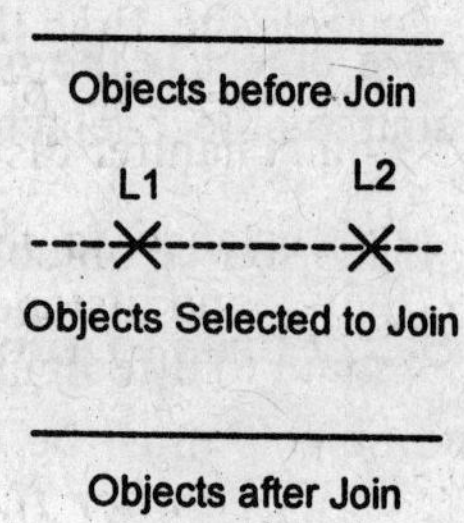

FIG. 32

Problem 28: *Join two splines using the Join command.*

The command sequence to join two splines using the Join command is as follows:

Command: **JOIN** ↵
Select source object: *(Pick P1)*
Select splines or helixes to join to source:
(Pick P2) 1 found
Select splines or helixes to join to source: ↵
1 spline joined to source

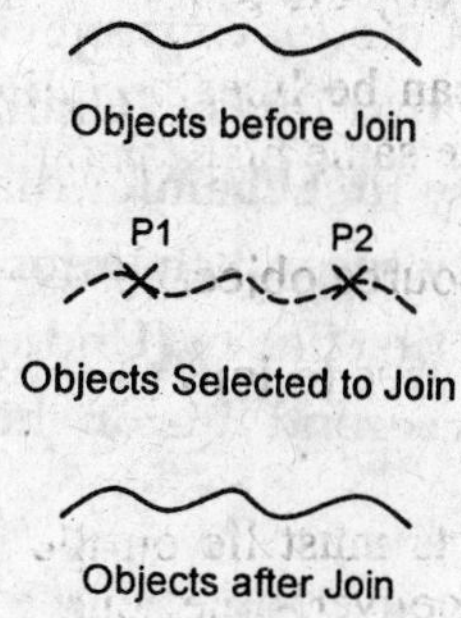

FIG. 33

See Fig. 33.

16. CHAMFER TOOL

Chamfering is the process of converting the sharp corners into beveled edges. The Chamfering connects two non-parallel objects by extending or trimming them to intersect or to join with a beveled line.

The **Chamfer** tool bevels the edges of objects to avoid sharp corners. Using this tool, we can increase or decrease the length of existing lines or arcs. The distances and angles that specified are applied in the order in which the objects selected.

We can chamfer lines, polylines, rays, and xlines. We can also chamfer 3D solids and surfaces. If a mesh to chamfer is selected, we can choose to convert it to a solid or surface before completing the operation. The **Chamfer** command can be invoked using any one of the following methods:

1. Type **CHAMFER** or **CHA** in the command prompt and press Enter.
2. Choose the **Chamfer** tool from the **Modify** panel in the **Home** tab.
3. Choose the **Chamfer** tool from the **Modify** menu.
4. Choose the **Chamfer** tool from the **Modify** toolbar.

When the Chamfer command is invoked, AutoCAD prompts to select the first line. Before selecting the first line, enter D at the **Select first line** prompt to invoke the Distance option. Now, AutoCAD prompts to specify the first and second chamfer distances. Specify the first and second chamfer distances using either by left-clicking or by entering coordinates.

The first distance is the distance of the corner calculated along the edge selected first. Similarly, the second distance is calculated along the edge that is selected last. The new chamfer distances remain in effect until user change them.

Problem 29: *Chamfer two lines using the Chamfer command.*

The command sequence to chamfer two lines using the Chamfer command is as follows:

Command: **CHAMFER** ↵
(TRIM mode) Current chamfer Dist1 = 10.0000, Dist2 = 10.0000
Select first line or [Undo/Polyline/Distance/Angle/Trim/mEthod/Multiple]: **D** ↵
Specify first chamfer distance <10.0000>: **5** ↵
Specify second chamfer distance <5.0000>: **7** ↵
Select first line or [Undo/Polyline/Distance/Angle/Trim/mEthod/Multiple]: *(Pick L1)*
Select second line or shift-select to apply corner: *(Pick L2)*

See Fig. 34.

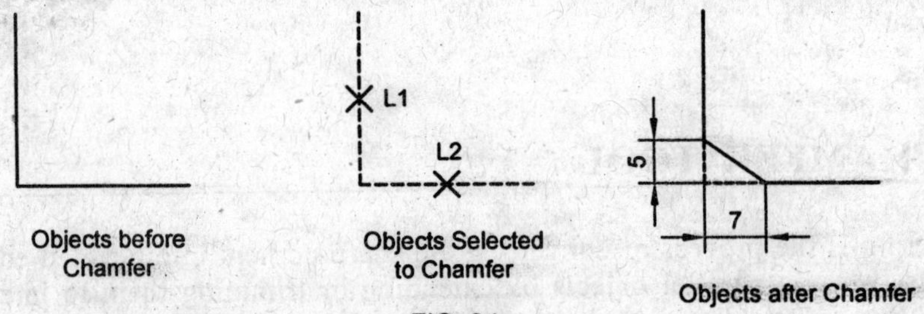

FIG. 34

16.1 OPTIONS IN THE CHAMFER COMMAND

First Line: Using the First Line, we can specify the first of two edges required to define a 2D chamfer, or the edge of a 3D solid to chamfer. If lines or polylines are selected, their lengths adjust to accommodate the chamfer line. We can hold down Shift while selecting the objects to override the current chamfer distances with a value of 0.

If the selected objects are line segments of a 2D polyline, they must be adjacent or separated by no more than one segment. If the selected objects are separated by another polyline segment, CHAMFER deletes the segment that separates them and replaces it with the chamfer.

Undo: The Undo option reverses the previous action in the command.

Polyline: The Polyline option chamfers an entire 2D polyline. The intersecting polyline segments are chamfered at each vertex of the polyline. Chamfers become new segments of the polyline. If the polyline includes segments that are too short to accommodate the chamfer distance, those segments are not chamfered.

Problem 30: *Chamfer the polyline lines using the Polyline option in Chamfer command.*

The command sequence to chamfer the polyline (here rectangle) using the Polyline option in the Chamfer command is as follows:

Command: **RECTANGLE** ↵
Specify first corner point or

[Chamfer/Elevation/Fillet/Thickness/Width]: *(Pick P1)*
Specify other corner point or [Area/Dimensions/Rotation]: **D** ↵
Specify length for rectangles <10.0000>: **30** ↵
Specify width for rectangles <10.0000>: **18** ↵
Specify other corner point or [Area/Dimensions/Rotation]: *(Pick P2)*

Command: **CHAMFER** ↵
(TRIM mode) Current chamfer Dist1 = 10.0000, Dist2 = 10.0000
Select first line or [Undo/Polyline/Distance/Angle/Trim/mEthod/Multiple]: **D** ↵
Specify first chamfer distance <10.0000>: **5** ↵
Specify second chamfer distance <5.0000>: **5** ↵
Select first line or [Undo/Polyline/Distance/Angle/Trim/mEthod/Multiple]: **P** ↵
Select 2D polyline: *(Select the rectangle)*
4 lines were chamfered

See Fig. 35.

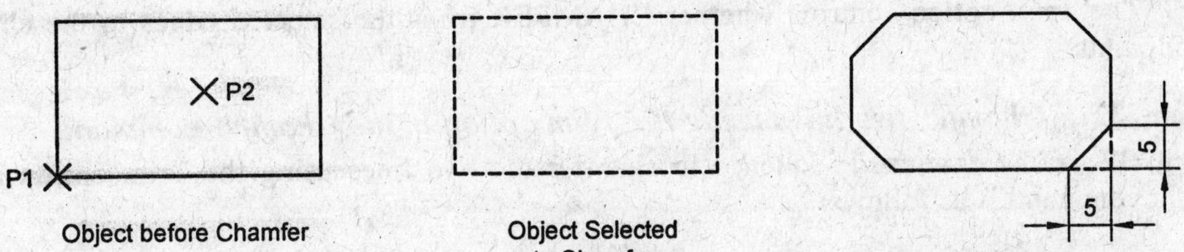

Object before Chamfer

Object Selected to Chamfer

Object after Chamfer

FIG. 35

Distance: The Distance option sets the distance of the chamfer from the endpoint of the selected edge. If both distances are set to zero, CHAMFER extends or trims the two lines so they end at the same point.

Angle: The Angle option sets the chamfer distances using a chamfer distance for the first line and an angle for the second line.

Problem 31: *Chamfer two lines using the Angle option in the Chamfer command.*

The command sequence to chamfer the two lines using the Angle option in the Chamfer command is as follows:

Command: **CHAMFER** ↵
(TRIM mode) Current chamfer Dist1 = 5.0000, Dist2 = 5.0000
Select first line or [Undo/Polyline/Distance/Angle/Trim/mEthod/Multiple]: **A** ↵
Specify chamfer length on the first line <10.0000>: **8** ↵

Specify chamfer angle from the first line <45>: **35** ↵
Select first line or [Undo/Polyline/Distance/Angle/
Trim/mEthod/Multiple]: *(Pick L1)*
Select second line or shift-select to apply corner: *(Pick L2)*

See Fig. 36.

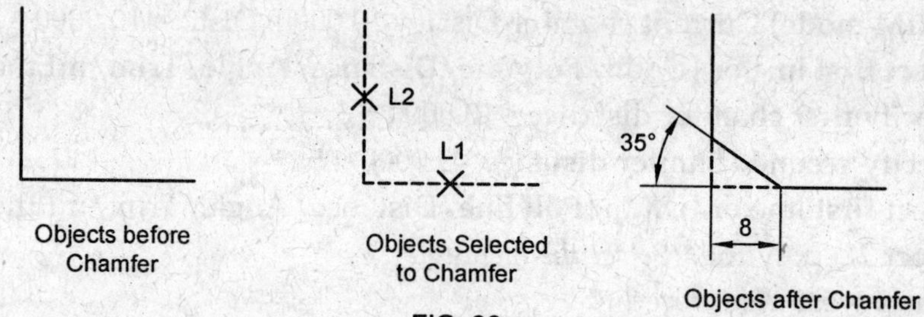

FIG. 36

Trim: The Trim option controls whether CHAMFER trims the selected edges to the chamfer line endpoints.

Problem 32: *Chamfer two lines using the Trim option in the Chamfer command.*
See Fig. 37. The command sequence to chamfer the two lines using the Trim option in the Chamfer command is as follows:

Command: **CHAMFER** ↵
(TRIM mode) Current chamfer Length = 8.0000, Angle = 35
Select first line or
[Undo/Polyline/Distance/Angle/Trim/mEthod/Multiple]: **D** ↵
Specify first chamfer distance <5.0000>: **8** ↵
Specify second chamfer distance <8.0000>: **8** ↵
Select first line or [Undo/Polyline/Distance/Angle/Trim/mEthod/Multiple]: **T** ↵
Enter Trim mode option [Trim/No trim] <Trim>: **NO** ↵

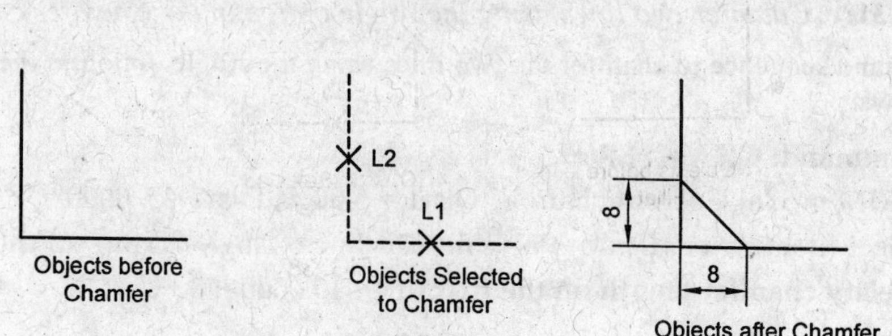

FIG. 37

Select first line or [Undo/Polyline/Distance/Angle/
Trim/mEthod/Multiple]: *(Pick L1)*
Select second line or shift-select to apply corner: *(Pick L2)*

Note that the chamfer is created without trimming the selected lines.

Method: The Method option controls whether CHAMFER uses two distances or a distance and an angle to create the chamfer.

Multiple: The Multiple option chamfers the edges of more than one set of objects. CHAMFER displays the main prompt and the Select Second Object prompt repeatedly until you press Enter to end the command.

17. FILLET TOOL

Filleting is the process of creating round corners at the sharp corners. The **Fillet** tool is used to rounds and fillets the edges of objects. This tool is same as **Chamfer** tool but radius is given instead of chamfer distance. The **Fillet** command can be invoked using any one of the following:

1. Type **FILLET** or **F** in the command prompt and press Enter.
2. Choose the **Fillet** tool from the **Modify** panel in the **Home** tab.
3. Choose the **Fillet** tool from the **Modify** menu.
4. Choose the **Fillet** tool from the **Modify** toolbar.

Problem 33: *Fillet two lines using the Fillet command.*
The command sequence to fillet two lines using the Fillet command is as follows:

Command: **FILLET** ↵
Current settings: Mode = TRIM, Radius = 10.0000
Select first object or [Undo/Polyline/Radius/Trim/Multiple]: *(Pick L1)*
Select second object or shift-select to apply corner: *(Pick L2)*

See Fig. 38.

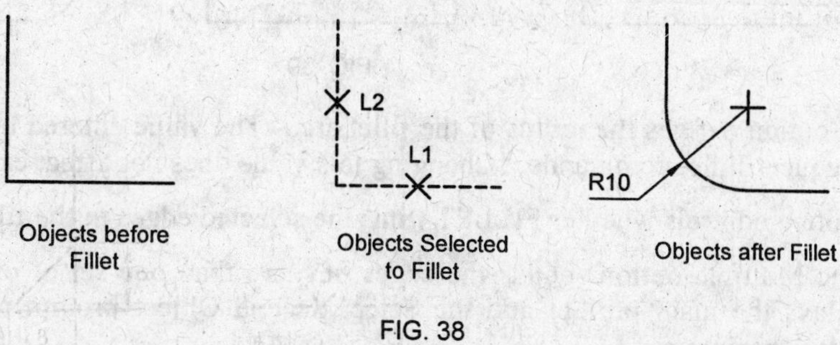

FIG. 38

17.1 OPTIONS IN THE FILLET COMMAND

First Object: Using the First Object option, we can select the first of two objects required to define a 2D fillet or selects the edge of a 3D solid to round or fillet the edge. After selecting the first object, the command prompts to select the second object.

Undo: The Undo option reverses the previous action in the command.

Polyline: The Polyline option inserts fillet arcs at each vertex of a 2D polyline where two line segments meet. If one arc segment separates two line segments that converge as they approach the arc segment, Fillet removes the arc segment and replaces it with a fillet arc.

Problem 34: *Fillet the rectangle using the Polyline option in the Fillet command.*

S **Fig. 39.** The command sequence to fillet the polyline (here rectangle) using the Polyline option in the Fillet command is as follows:

Command: **RECTANGLE** ↵
Specify first corner point or [Chamfer/Elevation/Fillet/Thickness/Width]: *(Pick P1)*
Specify other corner point or [Area/Dimensions/Rotation]: **D** ↵
Specify length for rectangles <10.0000>: **30** ↵
Specify width for rectangles <10.0000>: **14** ↵
Specify other corner point or [Area/Dimensions/Rotation]: *(Pick P2)*

Command: **FILLET** ↵
Current settings: Mode = TRIM, Radius = 10.0000
Select first object or [Undo/Polyline/Radius/Trim/Multiple]: **R** ↵
Specify fillet radius <10.0000>: **5** ↵
Select first object or [Undo/Polyline/Radius/Trim/Multiple]: **P** ↵
Select 2D polyline: *(Select the rectangle)*
4 lines were filleted

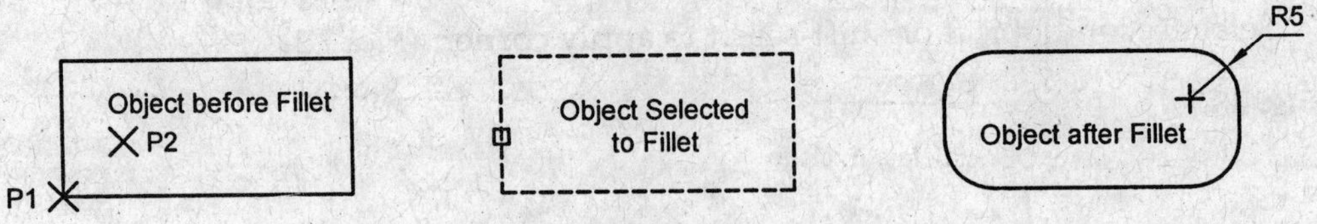

FIG. 39

Radius: This option defines the radius of the fillet arc. The value entered becomes the current radius for subsequent Fillet commands. Changing this value does not affect existing fillet arcs.

Trim: This option controls whether FILLET trims the selected edges to the fillet arc endpoints.

Multiple: The Multiple option rounds the edges of more than one set of objects. The Fillet command displays the main prompt and the Select Second Object prompt repeatedly until we press Enter to end the command.

18. EXPLODE TOOL

The **Explode** tool breaks a compound object into its component objects. We can convert a compound object such as a polyline, dimension, regions, hatch or block reference into individual elements. The **Explode** command can be invoked using any one of the following methods:

1. Type **EXPLODE** or **X** in the command prompt and press Enter.
2. Choose the **Explode** tool on the **Modify** panel in the **Home** tab.
3. Choose the **Explode** tool from the **Modify** menu.
4. Choose the **Explode** tool from the **Modify** toolbar.

Problem 35: *Explode the Polyline into lines using the Explode command.*

See Fig. 40. The command sequence to explode the polyline into lines using the Explode command is as follows:

Command: **RECTANGLE** ↵
Specify first corner point or
[Chamfer/Elevation/Fillet/Thickness/Width]: *(Pick P1)*
Specify other corner point or [Area/Dimensions/Rotation]: **D** ↵
Specify length for rectangles <10.0000>: **30** ↵
Specify width for rectangles <10.0000>: **18** ↵
Specify other corner point or [Area/Dimensions/Rotation]: *(Pick P2)*
Command: **EXPLODE** ↵
Select objects: *(Select the rectangle)* 1 found
Select objects: ↵

Object before Explode | Object Selected to Explode | Objects after Explode

FIG. 40

When the Explode command is invoked, AutoCAD prompts to select an object. Select the objects to be exploded. Select the objects and press Enter.

In the above example, a polyline, here rectangle, is exploded using the Explode command. Now, we can select and edit each of the four lines individually. To explode objects and change their properties at the same time, use XPLODE command.

The color, linetype, and lineweight of any exploded object might change. Other results differ depending on the type of compound object that are exploding.

19. CAD EXERCISE - Step-by-Step Solution

Problem 36 : *(Fig. 41) Create the drawing shown in Fig. 41 using AutoCAD.*

1. Start the **AutoCAD** Software. Open and setup a new drawing sheet to A4 size.
2. Draw the line AB of length 50 mm using the LINE command.
3. Draw the line BC of length 40 mm using the LINE command.
4. Draw the line CD of length 50 mm using the LINE command.
5. Join the points A and D using the LINE command.
6. Name the corners as A, B, C and D using the TEXT command. Name the center point of line AD as O using the TEXT command.

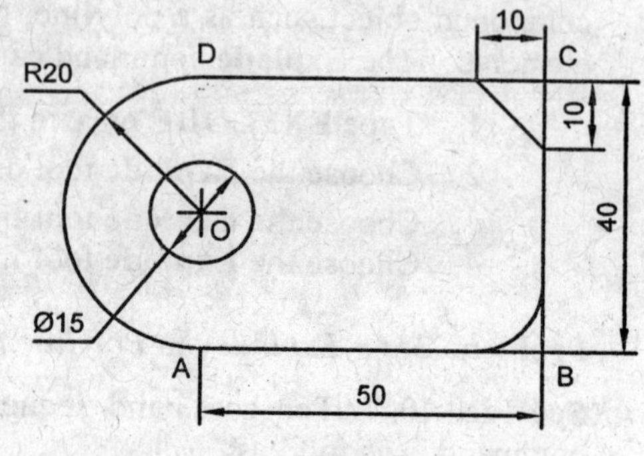

FIG. 41

7. Point O as center and 15 mm as diameter, draw a circle using the CIRCLE command.
8. Using the ARC command, draw the arc DA. The prompt sequence is:

   Command: **ARC**
   Specify start point of arc or [Center]: **(Pick point D)**
   Specify second point of arc or [Center/End]: **C**
   Specify center point of arc: **(Pick point O)**
   Specify end point of arc or [Angle/chord Length]: **(Pick point A)**
9. Mark the center of the arc using the CENTER command.
10. Delete the line AD using the ERASE command.
11. Using the CHAMFER command, draw chamfer of length 10 mm. The prompt sequence is:

    Command: **CHAMFER**
    (TRIM mode) Current chamfer Dist1 = 0.0000, Dist2 = 0.0000
    Select first line or [Undo/Polyline/Distance/Angle/Trim/mEthod/Multiple]: **D**
    Specify first chamfer distance <0.0000>: **10**
    Specify second chamfer distance <10.0000>: **10**
    Select first line or [Undo/Polyline/Distance/Angle/Trim/mEthod/Multiple]: **(Pick line BC)**
    Select second line or shift-select to apply corner: **(Pick line CD)**
12. Using the FILLET command, draw the fillet of radius 10 mm. The prompt sequence is:

    Command: **FILLET**
    Current settings: Mode = TRIM, Radius = 10.0000
    Select first object or [Undo/Polyline/Radius/Trim/Multiple]: **R**
    Specify fillet radius <5.0000>: **10**
    Select first object or [Undo/Polyline/Radius/Trim/Multiple]: **(Pick line AB)**
    Select second object or shift-select to apply corner: **(Pick line BC)**
13. Mark the dimensions using DIMLINEAR, DIMRADIUS and DIMDIAMETER commands.

*

11

OBJECT PROPERTIES

1. OBJECT PROPERTIES

The properties of a drawing entity are color, linetype, linetype scale, lineweight, plot style, thickness, etc. User can change these properties by using the **Properties** palette or the **Properties** panel in the **Home** tab of the **Ribbon.**

In AutoCAD, by default, the **By Layer** option is selected in the **Object Color, Lineweight** and **Linetype** drop-down lists of the **Properties** panel. Therefore, the properties set in the current layer are applied to the entities in it. The Layers are discussed in the next chapter.

1.1 CHANGING THE COLOR

Select the required object whose color needs to be changed. The current color of the object is displayed in the **Object Color** drop-down list. Select the down arrow in the **Object Color** drop-down list. A drop-down list is displayed with the available colors as shown in **Fig. 1.**

Select the required color from this list. If the required color is not available in this drop-down list, select the **Select Colors** option. The **Select Color** dialog box is displayed on the screen as shown in **Fig. 2.**

Select the desired color in this dialog box and then choose the **OK** button. The selected color is applied to the object.

Select a color from the **Object Color** drop-down list without selecting an object. Now, all new objects will be drawn in this color.

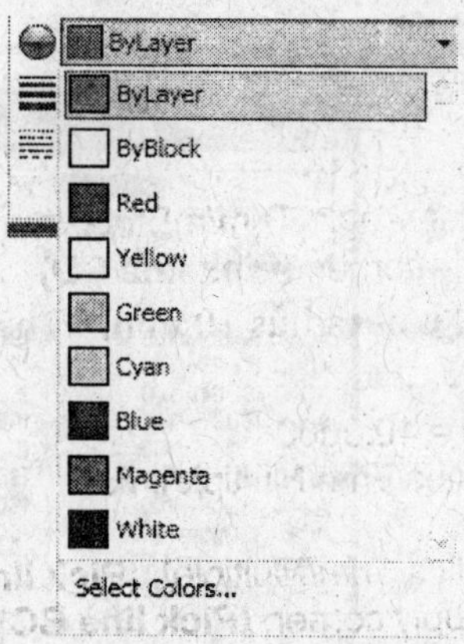

FIG. 1

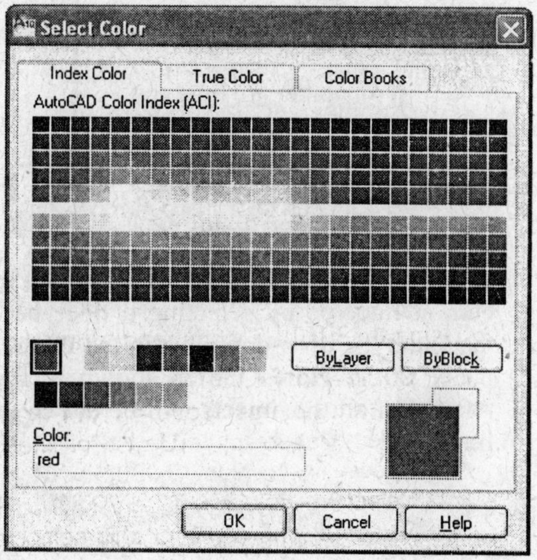

FIG. 2

1.2 CHANGING THE LINETYPE

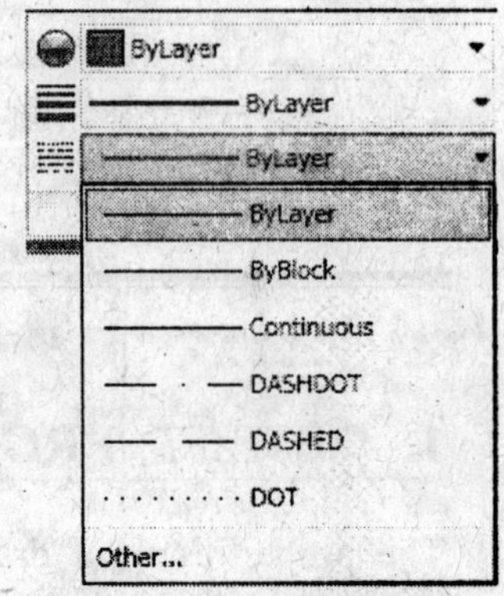

FIG. 3

Select the required object whose linetype needs to be changed. The current linetype of the object is displayed in the **Linetype** drop-down list. Select the down arrow in the **Linetype** list. A drop-down list is displayed with the available linetypes as shown in **Fig. 3.**

By default, By Layer, By Block and Continuous linetypes are listed in this drop-down list. However, the linetypes that are added by the user is also listed in this drop-down list.

Select the required linetype from this list. If the required linetype is not available in this drop-down list, select the **Other...** option. The **Linetype Manager** dialog box is displayed on the screen as shown in **Fig. 4.**

To load other linetypes, choose the **Load** button. The **Load or Reload Linetypes** dialog box is displayed on the screen as shown in **Fig. 5.**

Select a linetype in this dialog box. The selected linetype is displayed in the **Linetype Manager** dialog box. Next, select the required linetype from this dialog box and choose **OK.**

To make a linetype current, select the required linetype and choose the **Current** button in the **Linetype Manager** dialog box.

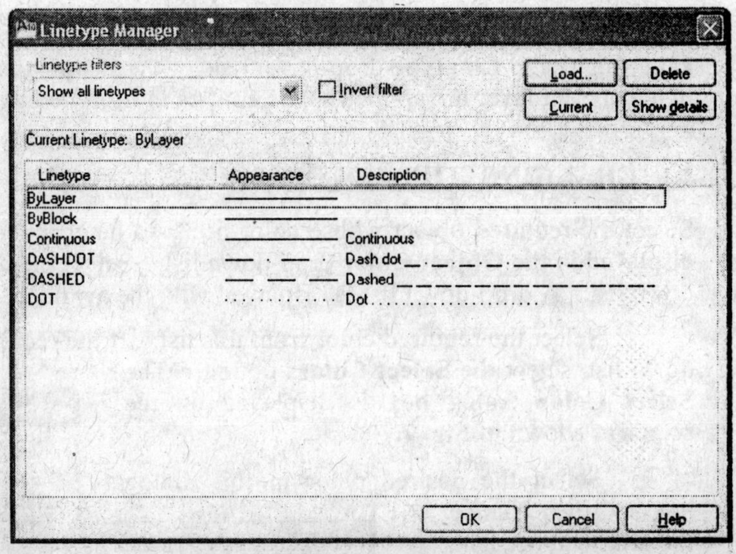

FIG. 4

Also, a linetype can be set as a current linetype by selecting a linetype from the **Linetype** drop-down list in the **Properties** panel of the **Home** tab as shown in **Fig. 3.** After this, all the objects will be drawn in this linetype.

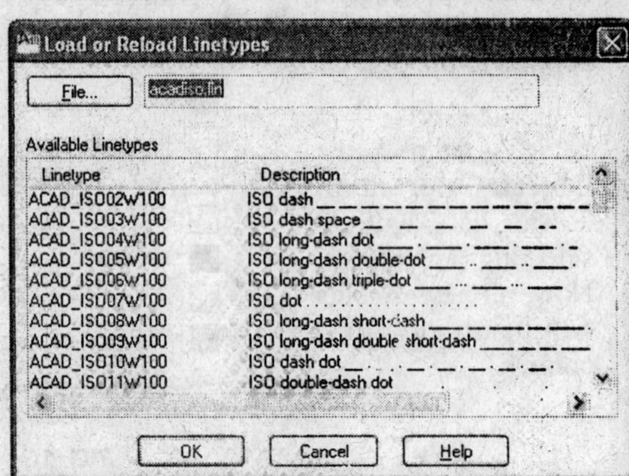

FIG. 5

1.3 CHANGING THE LINEWEIGHT

To change the lineweight of an object, select the required object. Select the required lineweight value from the **Lineweight** drop-down list in the **Properties** panel. The **Lineweight** drop-down list is shown in **Fig. 6.**

A new lineweight can be set as current by selecting a lineweight from this list without selecting any object.

To assign a lineweight value that is not listed in the drop-down list, select the **Lineweight Settings...** option from the **Lineweight** drop-down list. The **Lineweight Settings** dialog box is displayed on the screen as shown in **Fig. 7.**

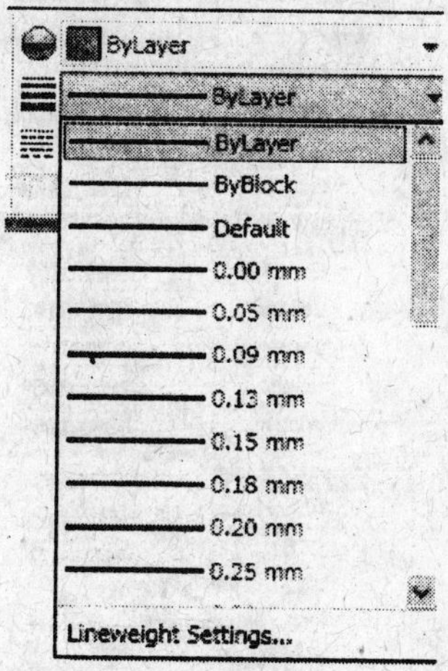

FIG. 6

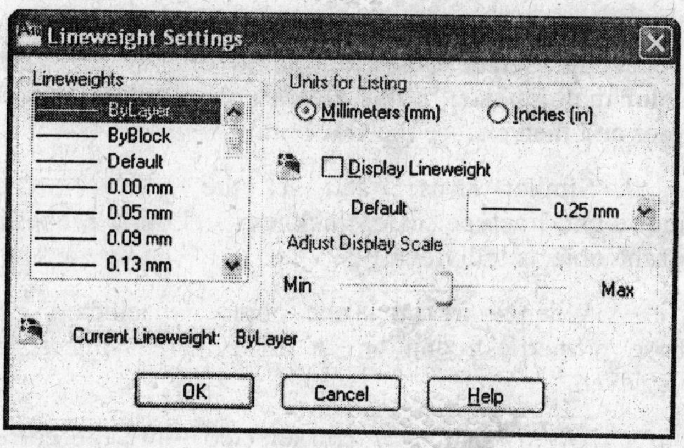

FIG. 7

In this dialog box, a lineweight for the objects can be set as current. The units for the lineweight can be changed. Also, the display of lineweight for the current drawing can be changed. Lineweights are displayed in pixel widths and depending on the lineweight value chosen, the lineweights are displayed if the **Display Lineweight** check box is selected.

1.4 CHANGING THE PLOT STYLE

The plot style drop-down list is available only if you are using the named plot style modes. To change the plot style, select a plot style from the **Plot Style** drop-down list in the **Properties** panel. A new plot style can be set as current by selecting it from the drop-down list.

2. PROPERTIES PALETTE

To change the general properties of the selected objects, the **Properties** palette is used. Choose the **Properties** button from the **Palettes** panel to display the **Properties** palette. The **Properties** palette is shown in **Fig. 8.** Also, right-click on an object and then choose the **Properties** option from the shortcut menu. Type **PROPERTIES** or **PR** at the command prompt and press Enter.

The **Properties** palette displays the properties of the selected object. Depending on the object selected, the properties differ. If the properties in the **Properties** palette is changed without selecting any object, the current properties in the **Properties** panel in the **Home** tab is also changed. Now, if an object is drawn, it will have the properties set in the **Properties** palette.

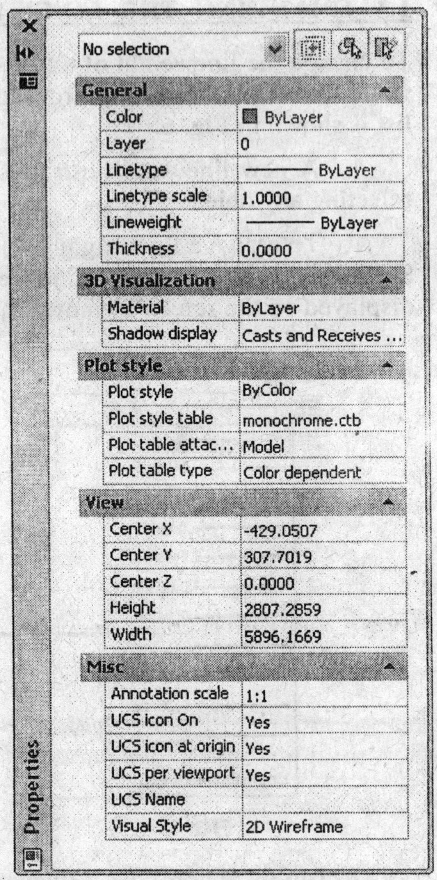

FIG. 8

The color of the selected object is displayed in the **Color** on the **General** list. When you select **Color** from the **General** list, a down arrow is displayed. Click the down arrow and select a color from the list to assign the color to the selected object.

To assign a color that is not displayed in the list, choose the **Select Color** option to display the **Select Color** dialog box. In this dialog box, select the desired color and then choose the **OK** button.

Similarly, user can set the layer, linetype, lineweight, linetype scale, thickness and other properties for the objects individually.

When more than one object is selected, only those properties common to all selected objects are displayed.

When no objects are selected, only the current settings of general properties are displayed. There are several **General Properties** common to all objects. All other object properties are specific to the type of object.

We can specify a new value to modify any property that can be changed. Click the value and use one of the following methods:

- Enter a new value.
- Click the down arrow at the right and select a value from the list.
- Click the **Pick Point** button to use the pointing device to change a coordinate value.
- Click the **QuickCalc** calculator button to calculate a new value.
- Click the left or right arrow to increase or decrease the value.
- Click the {...} button and change the property value in a dialog box.

2.1 OPTIONS IN THE PROPERTIES PALETTE

Object Type

The **Object Type** box displays the type of object that is selected.

Toggle Value of PICKADD Sysvar

The **Toggle Value** of PICKADD Sysvar option turns the PICKADD system variable on (1) and off (0). When PICKADD is on, each object selected, either individually or by windowing, is added to the current selection set. When PICKADD is off, selected objects replace the current selection set.

Select Objects

The **Select Objects** button selects desired objects using any selection method. The properties common to the selected objects are displayed in the **Properties** palette. User can then modify the properties of the selected objects in the **Properties** palette or user can make other changes to the selected objects by entering an editing command.

Quick Select

The **Quick Select** button displays the **Quick Select** dialog box. Use **Quick Select** dialog box to create selection sets based on filtering criteria.

The following shortcut menu options are available when right-click the title bar of the **Properties** palette:

Move: The **Move** option displays a four-headed arrow cursor that user can use to move the palette. The palette does not dock.

Size: The **Size** option displays a four-headed arrow cursor that user can use to drag an edge or a corner to make the palette smaller or larger.

Close: The **Close** option closes the **Properties** palette.

Allow Docking: The **Allow Docking** option toggles the ability to dock or anchor palette windows. If this option is selected, a window can be docked when user drags it over a docking area at the side of a drawing. A docked window adheres to the side of the application window and causes the drawing area to be resized. Selecting this option also makes **Anchor Right** and **Anchor Left** available.

Anchor Right / Anchor Left: The **Anchor Right / Anchor Left** option attaches the **Properties** palette to an anchor tab base at the right or left side of the drawing area. The palette rolls open and closed as the cursor moves across it. When an anchored palette is open, its content overlaps the drawing area. An anchored palette cannot be set to stay open.

Auto-hide: The **Auto-hide** option causes a floating palette to roll open and closed as the cursor moves across it. When this option is cleared, the palette stays open.

Transparency: The **Transparency** option displays the Transparency dialog box.

The following general properties are common to most objects and custom objects:

Color: The **Color** property specifies the color for objects. Select the **Select Color** in the color list to display the **Select Color** dialog box.

Use the **Select Color** dialog box to define the color of objects by selecting from the 255 AutoCAD Color Index (ACI) colors, true colors and color book colors.

Layer: The **Layer** property specifies the current layer of the object. The list shows all layers in the current drawing.

Linetype: The **Linetype** property specifies the current linetype of the object. The list shows all linetypes in the current drawing.

Linetype Scale: The **Linetype Scale** property specifies the linetype scale factor of the object.

Plot Style: The **Plot Style** property lists NORMAL, BYLAYER, BYBLOCK, plus any plot styles contained in the current plot style table.

Lineweight: The **Lineweight** property specifies the lineweight of the object. The list shows all available lineweights in the current drawing.

Hyperlink: The **Hyperlink** property attaches a hyperlink to a graphical object. If a description has been assigned to the hyperlink, the description is displayed. If no description has been assigned, the URL is displayed.

Thickness: The **Thickness** property sets the current 3D thickness. This property does not apply to all objects.

3. MATCH PROPERTIES

The **Match Properties** tool applies the properties of a selected object to other objects. The **Match Properties** tool can be invoked using any one of the following methods:

1. Type **MATCHPROP** or **MA** or **Painter** in the command prompt and press Enter.
2. Choose the **Match Properties** tool from the **Properties** panel in the **Home** tab.
3. Choose the **Match Properties** tool from the **Modify** menu.
4. Choose the **Match Properties** tool from the **Standard** toolbar.

The types of properties that can be applied include color, layer, linetype, linetype scale, lineweight, plot style and other specified properties. When the **Matchprop** command is invoked, AutoCAD prompts to select the source object. The prompt displayed is as follows:

Select source object: *Select the object whose properties want to copy*
Current active settings: *Currently selected matchprop settings*
Select destination object(s) or [Settings]: *Enter s or select one or more objects to copy properties to*

3.1 OPTIONS IN THE MATCHPROP COMMAND

Destination Object(s)
The **Destination Object(s)** option specifies the objects to which user wants to copy the properties of the source object. User can continue selecting destination objects or press Enter to apply the properties and end the command.

Settings
The **Settings** option displays the **Property Settings** dialog box, in which user can control which object properties to copy to the destination objects. By default, in the **Property Settings** dialog box all object properties are selected for copying.

Problem 1: *Apply the properties of a line to another line using the Matchprop command.*

The command sequence to apply the properties of a line to another line using the Matchprop command is as follows:

Command: **MATCHPROP** ↵
Select source object: *(Select C1)*
Current active settings: Color Layer Ltype Ltscale Lineweight Thickness PlotStyle Dim Text Hatch Polyline
Viewport Table Material
Shadow display Multileader
Select destination object(s)
or [Settings]: *(Select C2)*
Select destination object(s)
or [Settings]: *(Select C3)*
Select destination object(s)
or [Settings]: *(Select C4)*
Select destination object(s)
or [Settings]: *(Select C5)*
Select destination object(s)
or [Settings]: *(Select C6)*
Select destination object(s)
or [Settings]: *(Select C7)*
Select destination object(s)
or [Settings]: ↵

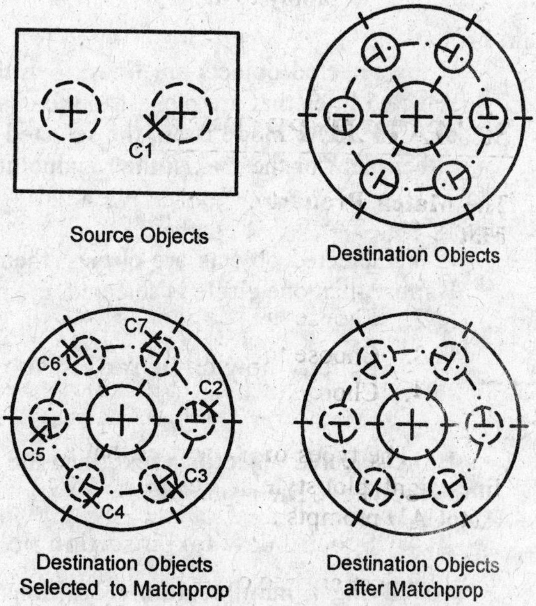

FIG. 9

See Fig. 9.

4. CHANGE TOOL

The **Change** tool changes the properties of existing objects. Using the **Change** command, user can change the color, layer, linetype, line type scale factor, line weight, thickness, material type and plot style of an existing objects.

The functions of the **Change** tool are the same as the **Properties** tool. The only difference is that in the **Properties** tool the **Properties** palette is displayed. Whereas, in the **Change** tool the properties are accessed through the command prompts only.

To activate the **Change** command, enter CHANGE in the command prompt. AutoCAD prompts to select objects. The prompt displayed is:

Select objects:

If user selects lines and other changeable objects in the same selection set, user gets varying results depending on the object selection sequence. The easiest way to use CHANGE is to select only lines in a selection set or select only objects other than lines in a selection set. fter selecting the object, the next prompt displayed is:

Specify change point or [Properties]:

Specify a new point or press Enter *to enter new values*

4.1 CHANGE POINT OR VALUES

The **Change Point or Values** option changes the selected objects. The result depends on the type of objects selected. The object may be any of the following:

Lines

If the selected objects are lines, then the **Change** command moves the endpoints of the selected lines that are closest to the change point to the new point, unless **Ortho** mode is on. If **Ortho** mode is on, the selected lines are modified so that they become parallel to either the *X* or the *Y* axis; their endpoints are not moved to the specified coordinate.

Circles

If the selected objects are circles, then the **Change** command changes the circle radius. If more than one circle is selected, the prompt is repeated for the next circle. The prompt is:

Specify new circle radius <no change>:

Text

If the selected object is a text, then the **Change** command changes text position and other properties. The prompt is:

Specify new text insertion point <no change>:

Specifying a new location repositions the text. Pressing Enter leaves the text in its original position. The next prompt is:

Enter new text style <*current*>:

If the text has a fixed height, the height prompt is not displayed. The prompt is:

Specify new height <*current*>:

Specify new rotation angle <*current*>:

Enter new text <*current*>:

The next object is highlighted and prompts are displayed.

Attribute Definitions

If the selected objects are attribute definitions, then the **Change** command changes the text and text properties of an attribute that is not part of a block. The prompt is:

Specify new text insertion point <no change>:

Specifying a new location repositions the text. Pressing Enter leaves the text at its original position. The next prompt is:

Enter new text style <*current*>:

If the text has a fixed height, the height prompt is not displayed. The prompt is:

Specify new height <*current*>:

Specify new rotation angle <*current*>:

Enter new tag <*current*>:

Enter new prompt <*current*>:

Enter new default value <*current*>:

Blocks

If the selected objects are blocks, then the **Change** command changes the location or rotation of a block. The prompt is:

Specify new block insertion point: *Specify a point or press* Enter

Specifying a new location repositions the block. Pressing Enter leaves the block in its original position. The next prompt is:

Specify new block rotation angle <*current*>:

The block is rotated about its insertion point to the specified angle.

4.2 PROPERTIES OPTION

The **Properties** option modifies properties of existing objects. If the **Properties** option is selected, the next prompt displayed is as follows:

Enter property to change [Color/Elev/LAyer/LType/ltScale/
LWeight/Thickness/Material/Annotative]:

Note that the **Plotstyle** option is displayed only when the named plot styles are used. If several objects are selected with different values for the property user wants to change, *varies* is displayed as the current value. It is possible to change several properties at a time. The **Enter Property to Change** prompt is redisplayed after each option is completed.

4.3 OPTIONS IN THE PROPERTIES OPTION OF THE CHANGE COMMAND

Color
The **Colour** option changes the color of the selected objects. For example, to change a color to red, enter *red* or *1*. If user enters *bylayer*, the object assumes the color of the layer on which it is located. If user enters *byblock*, the object inherits the color of the block of which it is a component.

True Color: The **True Colour** option specifies a true color to be used for the selected object.

Color Book: The **Color Book** option specifies a color from a loaded color book to be used for the selected object.

Elev
The **Elev** option changes the *Z*-axis elevation of 2D objects. We can change the elevation of an object only if all its points have the same *Z* value.

Layer
The **Layer** option **Changes** the layer of the selected objects.

Ltype
The **Ltype** option changes the linetype of the selected objects. If the new linetype is not loaded, the program tries to load it from the standard linetype library file, *acad.lin*. If this procedure fails, use LINETYPE system variable to load the linetype.

Ltscale
The **Ltscale** option changes the linetype scale factor of the selected objects.

Lweight
The **Lweight** option changes the lineweight of the selected objects. Lineweight values are predefined values. If user enters a value that is not a predefined value, the closest predefined lineweight is assigned to the selected objects.

Thickness
The **Thickness** option changes the *Z*-direction thickness of 2D objects. Changing the thickness of a 3D polyline, dimension or layout viewport object has no effect.

Material
The **Material** option changes the material of the selected objects if a material is attached.

Annotative
The **Annotative** option changes the Annotative property of the selected objects.

Problem 2: *Change the line type of a circle using the Ltype option in the Change command.*

The command sequence to change the line type of a circle using the Ltype options in the Change command is as follows:

```
Command: CIRCLE ↵
Specify center point for circle or
    [3P/2P/Ttr (tan tan radius)]: (Pick P1)
Specify radius of circle or [Diameter] <15.0000>: 10 ↵
Command: CHANGE ↵
Select objects: (Select the circle) 1 found
Select objects:  Specify change point or [Properties]: P ↵
Enter property to change [Color/Elev/LAyer/LType/
    ltScale/LWeight/Thickness/Material/Annotative]: LT ↵
Enter new linetype name <ByLayer>: DASHED ↵
Enter property to change [Color/Elev/LAyer/LType/ltScale/
    LWeight/Thickness/Material/Annotative]: ↵
```

See Fig. 10.

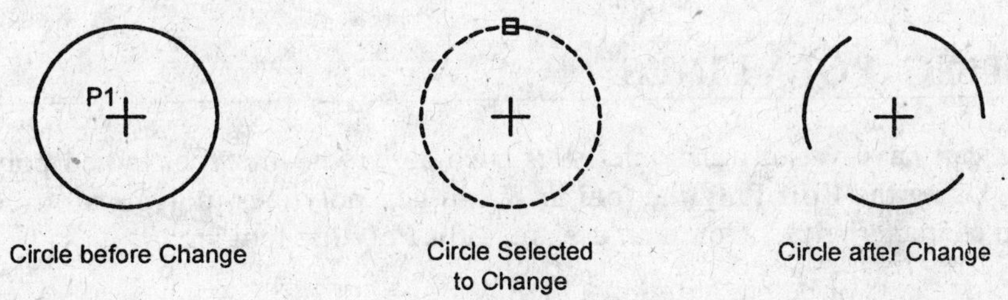

FIG. 10

In the above example, the line type of the circle is changed as dashed line. The line type of the circle is changed as dashed line. These dashed lines are wide lines. To increase the repetitions, reduce the line type scale factor. To decrease the repetitions, increase the line type scale factor.

Problem 3: *Change the line type scale factor of a circle using the Ltscale option in the Change command.*

The command sequence to change the line type scale factor of a circle using the Ltscale options in the Change command is as follows:

```
Command: CHANGE ↵
Select objects: (Select the circle) 1 found
```

```
Select objects:  Specify change point or [Properties]: P ↵
Enter property to change [Color/Elev/LAyer/LType/ltScale/
                    LWeight/Thickness/Material/Annotative]: S ↵
Specify new linetype scale <1.0000>: 0.2 ↵
Enter property to change [Color/Elev/LAyer/LType/ltScale/
                    LWeight/Thickness/Material/Annotative]: ↵
```

See Fig. 11.

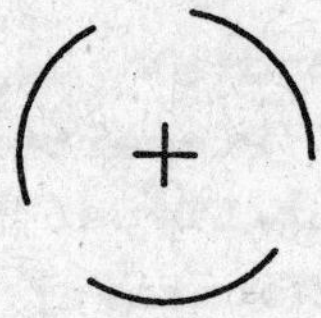

Circle before Change

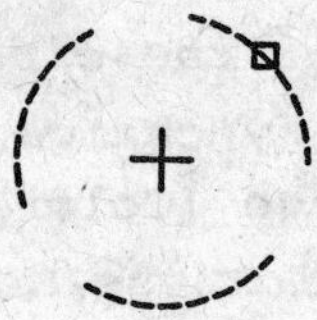

Circle Selected to Change

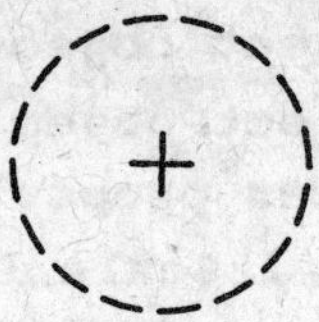

Circle after Change

FIG. 11

5. EDITING POLYLINES

A polyline can have various characteristics such as width, linetype, joined polyline, and closed polyline. Using the **Edit Polyline** tool, user can edit polylines, polygons or rectangles to attain the desired characteristics. Common uses for **Edit Polyline** tool are:

1. Move, add or delete individual vertices.
2. Individual polylines can be connected to one another can be joined into a single polyline.
3. Multiple polylines can be joined together to form a single polyline.
4. A polyline can be split into two or individual polylines or polyarcs.
5. A closed polyline can be opened and an opened one can be closed.
6. Multiple polylines can be edited at a time.
7. Set a uniform width for the entire polyline or control the width of each segment.
8. Create an approximation of a spline called a *spline-fit polyline*.
9. Display noncontinuous linetypes with or without a dash before and after each vertex.
10. Change the orientation of text in a linetype assigned to a polyline by reversing its direction.

5.1 EDITING SINGLE POLYLINE

Using the **Edit Polyline** tool, user can edit any type of polyline. The **Pedit** command can be invoked using any one of the following methods:

1. Type **PEDIT** or **PE** in the command prompt and press Enter.
2. Choose the **Edit Polyline** tool from the **Modify** panel in the **Home** tab.
3. Choose the **Polyline** from the **Object** in the **Modify** menu.
4. Choose the **Edit Polyline** from the **Modify II** toolbar.

When the **Pedit** command is invoked, AutoCAD prompts to select polyline. The prompt displayed is as follows:

`Select polyline or [Multiple]:`

If the selected object is a line, arc or a spline, the following prompt is displayed:

`Object selected is not a polyline.`
`Do you want it to turn into one? <Y>:` *Enter y or n or press* **ENTER**

If *y* is entered, the object is converted into a single-segment 2D polyline that user can edit. User can use this operation to join lines and arcs into a polyline. Before the selected spline is converted to a polyline, the following prompt is displayed:

`Specify a precision <10>:` ***Enter a new precision value or press*** **ENTER**

The precision value determines how accurately the resulting polyline is to fit to the source spline. Valid value is an integer between 0 and 99. Note that a high precision value may cause performance problems.

If you select a 2D polyline or after the object is converted into a polyline, the following prompt is displayed:

`Enter an option [Close/Join/Width/`
`Edit vertex/Fit/Spline/Decurve/Ltypegen/`
`Reverse/Undo]:` *Enter an option or press ENTER to end the command*

Note that user can select a single arc or line segment, also called a **Subobject**, within a polyline by pressing the Ctrl key when you click over it.

If the selected polyline is a closed polyline, **Open** replaces the **Close** option in the prompt. User can edit a 2D polyline if its normal is parallel to and in the same direction as the *Z* axis of the current UCS.

<u>Options in the Single Polyline Selection Method</u>

1. **Close Option:** The Close option creates the closing segment of the polyline, connecting the last segment with the first. The polyline is considered open unless you close it using the Close option.

Problem 4: *Draw a closing segment of a polyline using the Close option in the Pedit command.*

```
Command: PEDIT ↵
PEDIT Select polyline or [Multiple]: (Select the polyline)
```

```
Enter an option [Close/Join/Width/Edit vertex/Fit/Spline/
                        Decurve/Ltype gen/Reverse/Undo]: C ↵
Enter an option [Open/Join/Width/Edit vertex/Fit/Spline/
                       Decurve/Ltype gen/Reverse/Undo]: ↵
```

See Fig. 12.

Polyline before Close — Polyline Selected to Close — Polyline after Close

FIG. 12

2. **Open Option:** The **Open** option removes the closing segment of the polyline. The polyline is considered closed unless you open it using the **Open** option.

Problem 5: *Remove the closing segment of a polyline using the Open option in the Pedit command.*

```
Command: PEDIT ↵
Select polyline or [Multiple]: (Select the polyline)
Enter an option [Open/Join/Width/Edit vertex/Fit/Spline/
                       Decurve/Ltype gen/Reverse/Undo]: O ↵
Enter an option [Close/Join/Width/Edit vertex/Fit/Spline/
                       Decurve/Ltype gen/Reverse/Undo]: ↵
```

See Fig. 13.

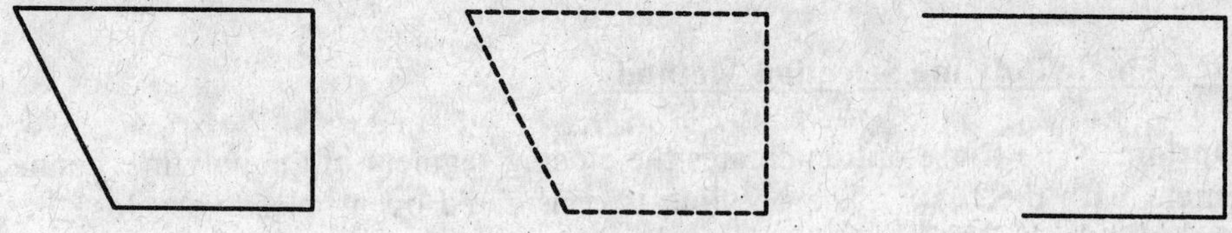

Polyline before Open — Polyline Selected to Open — Polyline after Open

FIG. 13

3. **Join Option:** The **Join** option adds lines, arcs, or polylines to the end of an open polyline and removes the curve fitting from a curve-fit polyline. For objects to join the polyline, their endpoints must touch unless you use the **Multiple** option at the first PEDIT prompt.

In this case, you can join polylines that do not touch if the fuzz distance is set to a value large enough to include the endpoints. If the Join option is selected, the next prompt displayed is:

`Select objects:` ***`Use an object selection method`***

If you previously selected multiple objects using the **Multiple** option, then the following prompt is displayed:

`Enter fuzz distance or [Jointype]<0.0000>:` ***`Enter a distance or j`***

Jointype option sets the method of joining selected polylines.

4. **Width Option:** The **Width** option specifies a new uniform width for the entire polyline. If the **Width** option is selected, the next prompt displayed is:

`Specify new width for all segments:`

Use the **Width** option of the **Edit Vertex** option to change the starting and ending widths of a segment.

Problem 6: *Change the width of a polyline using the Width option in the Pedit command.*

```
Command: PEDIT ↵
Select polyline or [Multiple]: (Select the polyline)
Enter an option [Close/Join/Width/Edit vertex/Fit/Spline/
                    Decurve/Ltype gen/Reverse/Undo]: W ↵
Specify new width for all segments: 2 ↵
Enter an option [Close/Join/Width/Edit vertex/Fit/Spline/
                    Decurve/Ltype gen/Reverse/Undo]: ↵
```

See Fig. 14.

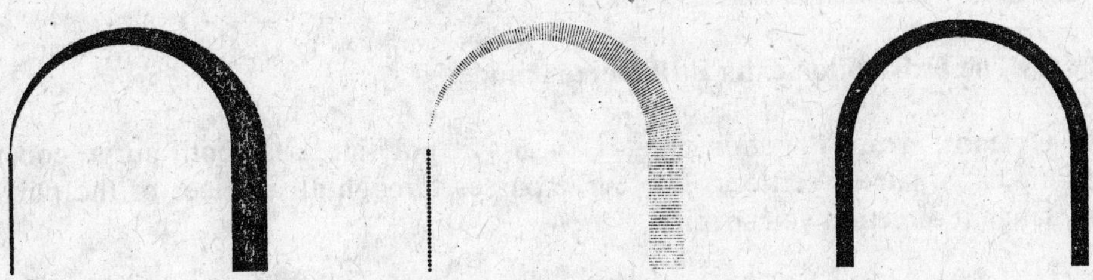

Polyline before changing Width   Polyline selected for changing Width   Polyline after changing Width

FIG. 14

5. **Edit Vertex Option:** The **Edit Vertex** option marks the first vertex of the polyline by drawing an X on the screen. If you have specified a tangent direction for this vertex, an arrow is also drawn in that direction. If the **Edit Vertex** option is selected, then the following prompt is displayed:

[Next/Previous/Break/Insert/Move/Regen/Straighten/Tangent/ Width/eXit] <*current*>: *Enter an option or press* ENTER

Pressing ENTER accepts the current default, which is either **Next** or **Previous.**

Next: The **Next** option moves the X marker to the next vertex. The marker does not wrap around from the end to the start of the polyline even if the polyline is closed.

Previous: The **Previous** option moves the X marker to the previous vertex. The marker does not wrap around from the start to the end of the polyline even if the polyline is closed.

Break: The **Break** option saves the location of the marked vertex while you move the X marker to any other vertex.

Insert: The **Insert** option adds a new vertex to the polyline after the marked vertex.

Move: The **Move** option moves the marked vertex.

Regen: The **Regen** option regenerates the polyline.

Straighten: The **Straighten** option saves the location of the marked vertex while you move the X marker to any other vertex. If you want to remove an arc segment that connects two straight segments of a polyline and then extend the straight segments until they intersect, use the **Fillet** command with a fillet radius of 0.

Tangent: The **Tangent** option attaches a tangent direction to the marked vertex for use later in curve fitting.

Width: The **Width** option changes the starting and ending widths for the segment that immediately follows the marked vertex.

Exit: The **Exit** option exits **Edit Vertex** mode.

6. **Fit Option:** The **Fit** option creates an arc-fit polyline, a smooth curve consisting of arcs joining each pair of vertices. The curve passes through all vertices of the polyline and uses any tangent direction you specify.

Problem 7: *Draw an arc-fit polyline using the Fit option in the Pedit command.*

Command: **PEDIT ↵**

Select polyline or [Multiple]: (*Select the polyline*)

Enter an option [Close/Join/Width/Edit vertex/Fit/Spline/ Decurve/Ltype gen/Reverse/Undo]: F ↵

Enter an option [Close/Join/Width/Edit vertex/Fit/Spline/ Decurve/Ltype gen/Reverse/Undo]: ↵

See Fig. 15.

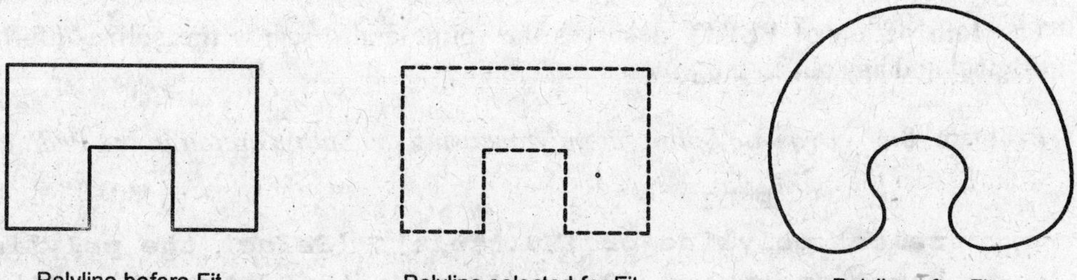

FIG. 15

7. **Spline Option:** The **Spline** option uses the vertices of the selected polyline as the control points, or frame, of a curve approximating a B-spline. This curve, called a **Spline-Fit Polyline**, passes through the first and last control points unless the original polyline was closed. The curve is pulled toward the other points but does not necessarily pass through them. The more control points you specify in a particular part of the frame, the more pull they exert on the curve. Quadratic and cubic spline-fit polylines can be generated.

   Spline-fit polylines are very different from the curves produced by the **Fit** option. Fit constructs pairs of arcs that pass through every control point. Both of these curves are different from true **B-splines** produced with the **Spline** command.

   When a spline-fit curve is fit to a polyline, the spline-fit curve's frame is stored so that it can be recalled by a subsequent decurving. You can turn a spline-fit curve back into its frame polyline by using the PEDIT Decurve option. This option works on fit curves in the same manner as it does on splines.

   Spline frames are not usually displayed on the screen. If you want to see them, set the SPLFRAME system variable to 1. Next time the drawing is regenerated, both the frame and the spline curve are drawn.

   Most editing commands act the same when applied to spline-fit polylines or fit curves. The editing commands and their operation are listed below:

   1. Editing tools, such as **Move, Erase, Copy, Mirror, Rotate** and **Scale**, operate on both the spline curve and its frame, whether the frame is visible or not.
   2. The **Extend** tool changes the frame by adding a new vertex where the initial or final line of the frame intersects the boundary geometry.
   3. The **Break** and **Trim** tools generate a polyline with only the fit spline, which is consistent with fit curves, where the curve fitting is permanent.
   4. The **Explode** tool deletes the frame and generates lines and arcs to approximate the spline-fit polyline.
   5. The **Offset** tool generates a polyline with only the fit spline, which is consistent with its behavior with fit curves.
   6. The **Divide** and **Measure** tools and the **Object** option of the **Area** and **Hatch** tools see only the fit spline, not the frame.

7. The **Stretch** tool refits the spline to the stretched frame after a spline is stretched.

The **Join** option of **PEDIT** decurves the spline and discards the spline information of the original and any added polylines.

Problem 8: *Draw an Spline-fit polyline using the Spline option in the Pedit command.*

```
Command: PEDIT ↵
Select polyline or [Multiple]: (Select the polyline)
Enter an option [Close/Join/Width/Edit vertex/Fit/Spline/
                    Decurve/Ltype gen/Reverse/Undo]: S ↵
Enter an option [Close/Join/Width/Edit vertex/Fit/Spline/
                    Decurve/Ltype gen/Reverse/Undo]: ↵
```

See Fig. 16.

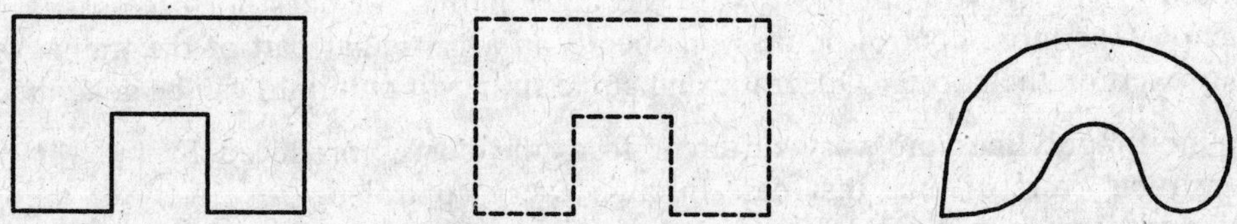

Polyline before Spline option   Polyline selected for Spline option   Polyline after Spline option

FIG. 16

The comparison between the smoothening the corners of a polyline using the **Fit** option and **Spline** option of the **Pedit** tool is shown in Fig. 17.

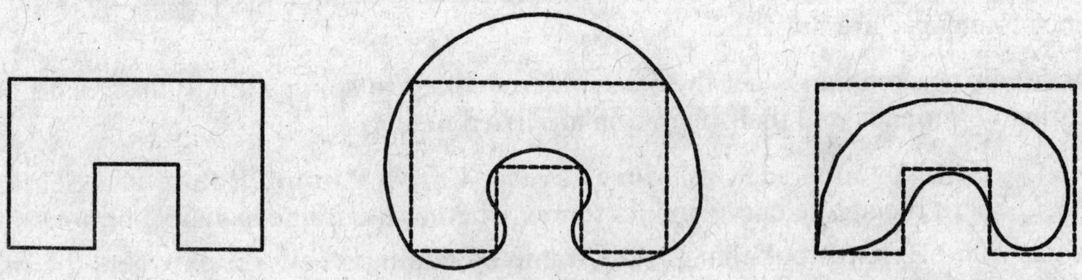

Original Polyline   Polyline after Fit option   Polyline after Spline option

FIG. 17

8. **Decurve Option:** The **Decurve** option removes extra vertices inserted by a fit or spline curve and straightens all segments of the polyline. Retains tangent information assigned to the polyline vertices for use in subsequent fit curve requests. If user edits a spline-fit polyline with a command such as **Break** or **Trim**, the **Decurve** option cannot be used.

Problem 9: *Straighten all the segments of a polyline using the Decurve option in the Pedit command.*

```
Command: PEDIT ↵
Select polyline or [Multiple]: (Select the polyline after Fit option)
Enter an option [Close/Join/Width/Edit vertex/Fit/Spline/
                    Decurve/Ltype gen/Reverse/Undo]: D ↵
Enter an option [Close/Join/Width/Edit vertex/Fit/Spline/
                    Decurve/Ltype gen/Reverse/Undo]: ↵

Command: PEDIT ↵
Select polyline or [Multiple]: (Select the polyline after Spline option)
Enter an option [Close/Join/Width/Edit vertex/Fit/Spline/
                    Decurve/Ltype gen/Reverse/Undo]: D ↵
Enter an option [Close/Join/Width/Edit vertex/Fit/Spline/
                    Decurve/Ltype gen/Reverse/Undo]: ↵
```

See Fig. 18.

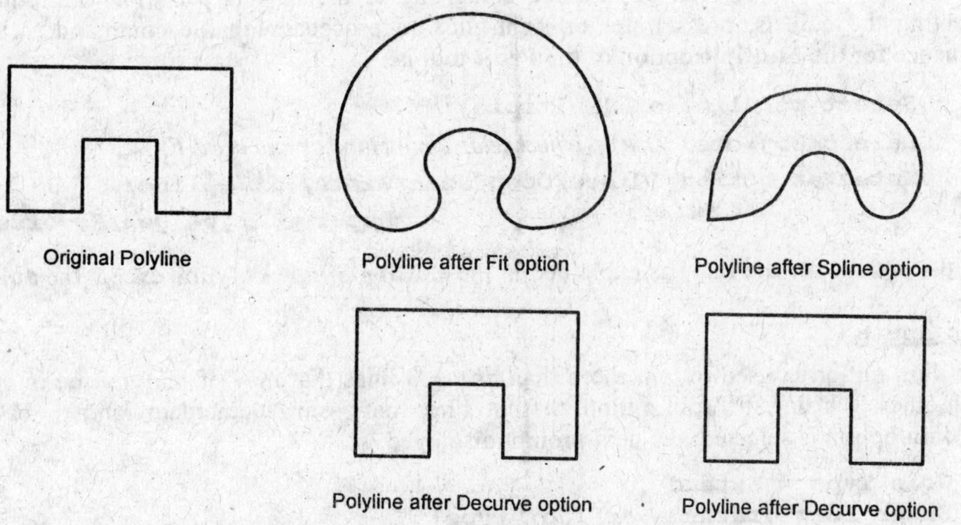

FIG. 18

9. Ltype Gen Option: The **Ltype Gen** option generates the linetype in a continuous pattern through the vertices of the polyline. When turned off, this option generates the linetype starting and ending with a dash at each vertex. **Ltype Gen** does not apply to polylines with tapered segments. If the **Ltype Gen** option is selected, the next prompt displayed is:

Enter polyline linetype generation option [ON/OFF] <*current*>: *Enter on or off, or press ENTER*

See Fig. 19. Fig. 19(i) shows a polyline with the **Ltype** gen option is set to ON.

Fig. 19(ii) shows a polyline with the **Ltype gen** option is set to OFF.

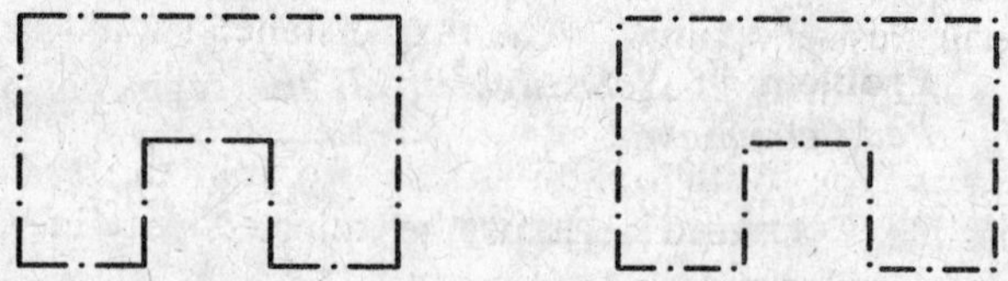

(i) Polyline with Ltype gen ON (ii) Polyline with Ltype gen OFF

FIG. 19

10. Reverse Option: The **Reverse** option reverses the order of vertices of the polyline. Use this option to reverse the direction of objects that use linetypes with included text. For example, depending on the direction in which a polyline was created, the text in the linetype might be displayed upside down.

11. Undo Option: The **Undo** option reverses operations as far back as the beginning of the PEDIT session.

5.2 EDITING MULTIPLE POLYLINES

If the **Multiple** option of the **Edit Polyline** tool is selected, you can select more than one polyline for editing. Polylines can be selected using any of the objects selection techniques. After selecting the objects, press Enter or right-click to proceed with the command. The prompt sequence for the **Multiple** option of the **Pedit** tool is:

Select polyline or [Multiple]: M ↵
Select objects: *Use an object selection method or and press Enter*
Enter an option [Close/Open/Join/Width/Fit/Spline/Decurve/Ltype gen/Reverse/Undo]:

All the options are the same as explained in the **Editing Single Polyline** except the **Join** option.

Join Option

The **Join** option is used to join more than one polylines that may or may not be in contact with each other. Using the **Join** option, the polylines that are not coincident can also be joined. If the **Join** option is selected, the next prompt displayed is:

Join Type = Extend
Enter fuzz distance or [Jointype]
<current>: *Enter a distance or J for changing Jointype*

The prompt sequence that follows when **Jointype** option selected is:

Enter join type [Extend/Add/Both] <Extend>: *Enter e, a or b*

Extend: The **Extend** option is used to join the selected polylines by extending or trimming the segments to the nearest endpoints. Remember that the segments of the selected polylines that are nearest to each other should not be parallel.

Add: The **Add** option is used to join the selected polylines by adding a straight segment between the nearest endpoints. The fuzz distance should be greater than the actual distance between the two endpoints to be joined.

Both: The **Both** option is used to join the selected polylines by extending or trimming if possible. Otherwise joins the selected polylines by adding a straight segment between the nearest endpoints.

Problem 10: *Join the lines into a polyline using the Join option in the Pedit command.*

See Fig. 20. The command sequence to join the lines into a polyline using the Join option in the PEDIT command is as follows:

```
Command: PEDIT ↵
Select polyline or [Multiple]: M ↵
Select objects: (Pick P1)
Specify opposite corner: (Pick P2) 8 found
Select objects: ↵
Convert Lines, Arcs and Splines to polylines [Yes/No]? <Y> Y ↵
Enter an option [Close/Open/Join/Width/Fit/Spline/
                 Decurve/Ltype gen/Reverse/Undo]: J ↵
Join Type = Extend
Enter fuzz distance or [Jointype] <0.0000>: ↵
7 segments added to polyline
Enter an option [Close/Open/Join/Width/Fit/Spline/
                 Decurve/Ltype gen/Reverse/Undo]: ↵
```

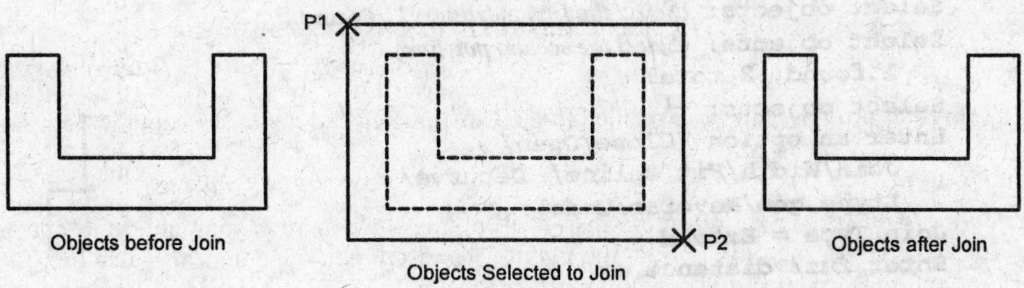

FIG. 20

Problem 11: *Join two polylines using the Extend option of the Join option in the Pedit command.*

See Fig. 21. The command sequence to join two polylines using the Extend option of the Join option in the PEDIT command is as follows:

```
Command: PEDIT ↵
Select polyline or [Multiple]: M ↵
```

```
Select objects: (Select polyline1) 1 found
Select objects:
   (Select polyline2) 1 found, 2 total
Select objects: ↵
Enter an option [Close/Open/Join/Width/
   Fit/Spline/Decurve/
   Ltype gen/Reverse/Undo]: J ↵
Join Type = Add segment
Enter fuzz distance or
   [Jointype] <0.0000>: J ↵
Enter join type
   [Extend/Add/Both] <Add>: E ↵
Join Type = Extend
Enter fuzz distance or
   [Jointype] <0.0000>: 10 ↵
5 segments added to polyline
Enter an option [Close/Open/Join/Width/Fit/Spline/
            Decurve/Ltype gen/Reverse/Undo]: ↵
```

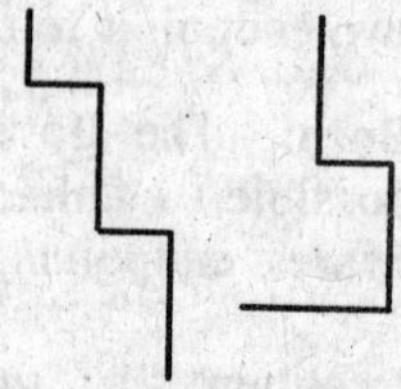

Before Joining

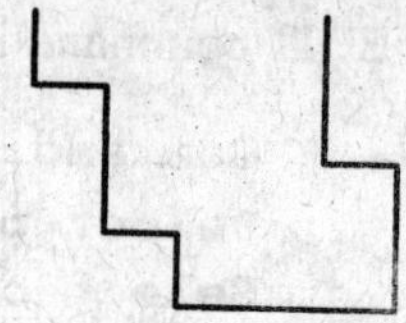

After Joining

FIG. 21

Problem 12: *Join two polylines using the Add option of the Join option in the Pedit command.*

See Fig. 22. The command sequence to join two polylines using the Add option of the Join option in the PEDIT command is as follows:

```
Command: PEDIT ↵
Select polyline or [Multiple]: M ↵
Select objects: (Select the first polyline) 1 found
Select objects: (Select the second polyline)
   1 found, 2 total
Select objects: ↵
Enter an option [Close/Open/
   Join/Width/Fit/Spline/ Decurve/
   Ltype gen/Reverse/Undo]: J ↵
Join Type = Extend
Enter fuzz distance or
   [Jointype] <0.0000>: J ↵
Enter join type
   [Extend/Add/Both] <Extend>: A ↵
Join Type = Add segment
Enter fuzz distance or
   [Jointype] <0.0000>: 10 ↵
6 segments added to polyline
Enter an option [Close/Open/
   Join/Width/Fit/Spline/Decurve/
   Ltype gen/Reverse/Undo]: ↵
```

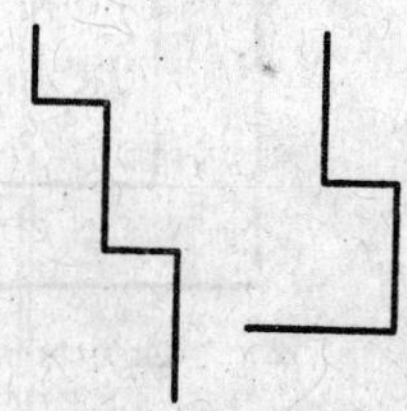

Before Joining

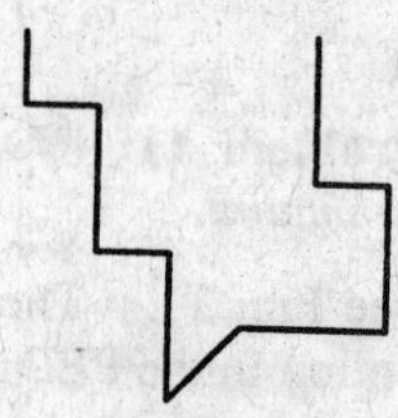

After Joining

FIG. 22

6. EDIT SPLINE

The **Edit Spline** tool edits a spline or spline-fit polyline. Using this tool, user can fit data in a selected spline, close or open a spline, move vertex points and refine or reverse a spline. The SPLINEDIT command can be invoked using any one of the following methods:

1. Type **SPLINEDIT** or **SPE** at the command prompt and press Enter.
2. Choose the **Edit Spline** tool from the **Modify** panel in the **Home** tab.
3. Choose the **Spline** tool from the **Object** in the **Modify** menu.
4. Choose the **Spline** tool from the **Modify II** toolbar.

When the **Splinedit** command is invoked, AutoCAD prompts to select a spline. The prompt sequence displayed is:

Select spline: *Select a spline*
Enter an option [Fit Data/Close/Move vertex/Refine/
rEverse/convert to Polyline/Undo]: *Enter an option or press* Enter

The prompt provides options to modify data such as the number and weight of control points, the fit tolerance and the start and end tangents. When a spline object or spline-fit polyline is selected, grips are appeared at the control points.

If the selected spline is closed, the **Close** option changes to **Open**. If the selected spline has no fit data, the **Fit Data** option is not available. Fit data consists of all fit points, the fit tolerance and tangents associated with splines created with the SPLINE command.

A spline can lose its fit data if user

- Uses the Purge option while editing fit data
- Refines the spline by elevating the order, adding a control point or changing the weight of a control point
- Changes the fit tolerance
- Moves a control point
- Trim, break, stretch or lengthen the spline

Note that the SPLINEDIT automatically converts splined polylines to spline objects. A splined polyline is converted even if user selects it and immediately exit SPLINEDIT.

6.1 OPTIONS IN THE SPLINEDIT COMMAND

1. **Fit Data**
While drawing a spline, the spline is fit to the specified points called **Data Points**. The **Fit Data** option allows the user to edit these data points. If the **Fit Data** option is selected, the next prompt displayed is:

Enter a fit data option [Add/Close/Delete/Move/Purge/
Tangents/toLerance/eXit] <eXit>: *Enter an option or press* Enter

Note that if the selected spline is closed, the **Close** option is replaced by the **Open** option. The options in the **Fit Data** option are explained next.

Add: The **Add** option adds fit points to a spline.

Close/Open: If the selected spline is closed, the **Close** option is replaced by the **Open** option. The purposes/functions of the **Close/Open** option are same as the **Close/Open** option in the SPLINEDIT command.

Delete: The **Delete** option removes fit points from a spline and refits the spline through the remaining points.

Move: The **Move** option moves fit points to a new location.

Purge: The **Purge** option removes a spline's fit data from the drawing database. After purging the spline's fit data, the main SPLINEDIT prompt is displayed without the **Fit Data** option.

Tangents: The **Tangents** option edits the start and end tangents of a spline.

Tolerance: The **Tolerance** option refits the spline to the existing points with new tolerance values.

Problem 13: *Refit the spline using the Tolerance option in the Splinedit command.*

The command sequence to refit the spline using the Tolerance option in the Splinedit command is as follows:

```
Command: SPLINEDIT ↵
Select spline: (Select the spline)
Enter an option [Fit data/Close/Move vertex/Refine/
    rEverse/convert to
    Polyline/Undo]: F ↵
Enter a fit data option
    [Add/Close/Delete/Move/
    Purge/Tangents/toLerance
    /eXit] <eXit>: L ↵
Enter fit tolerance
    <1.0000E-10>: 15 ↵
Enter a fit data option
    [Add/Close/Delete/Move/
    Purge/Tangents/tolerance
    /eXit] <eXit>: ↵
Enter an option [Fit data/
```

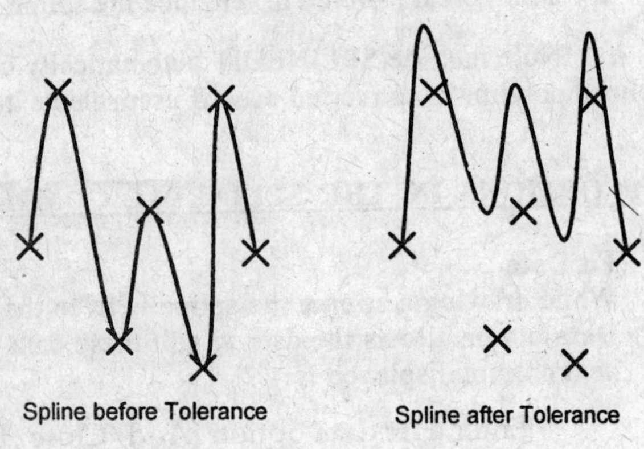

Spline before Tolerance   Spline after Tolerance

FIG. 23

```
Close/Move vertex/Refine/rEverse/convert to Polyline/Undo]: ↵
```

See Fig. 23.

Exit: The Exit option returns to the main Splinedit prompt.

2. **Close/Open**
If the selected spline is closed, the **Close** option changes to **Open**. The functions of the **Close** and **Open** options are:

Close: The **Close** option closes an open spline and makes it tangent continuous (smooth) at its endpoints. If the spline's start point and endpoint are the same, this option makes the spline tangent continuous at both points.

Open: The **Open** option opens a closed spline. If the spline's start point and endpoint were the same before using the **Close** option to make it tangent continuous at both points, the **Open** option returns the spline to its original state.

3. **Move Vertex**
The **Move Vertex** option relocates a spline's control vertices and purges the fit points. The functions of the options in the **Move Vertex** option are same as the functions of the options in the **Move** option.

4. **Refine**
The **Refine** option fine-tunes a spline definition.

Problem 14: *Add control points to change the shape of the spline using the Refine option in the Splinedit command.*

The command sequence to add control points to change the shape of the spline using the Refine option in the Splinedit command is as follows:

```
Command: SPLINEDIT ↵
Select spline: (Select the spline)
Enter an option [Fit data/Close/Move vertex/Refine/
                    rEverse/convert to Polyline/Undo]: R ↵
Enter a refine option [Add control point/
                    Elevate order/Weight/eXit] <eXit>: A ↵
Specify a point on the spline <exit>: (Pick P1)
Specify a point on the spline <exit>: (Pick P2)
Specify a point on the spline <exit>: (Pick P3)
Specify a point on the spline <exit>: (Pick P4)
Specify a point on the spline <exit>: ↵
Enter a refine option [Add control point/
                    Elevate order/Weight/eXit] <eXit>: ↵
```

```
Enter an option [Close/Move vertex/Refine/rEverse/
                        convert to Polyline/Undo/eXit] <eXit>: ↵
```

See Fig. 24.

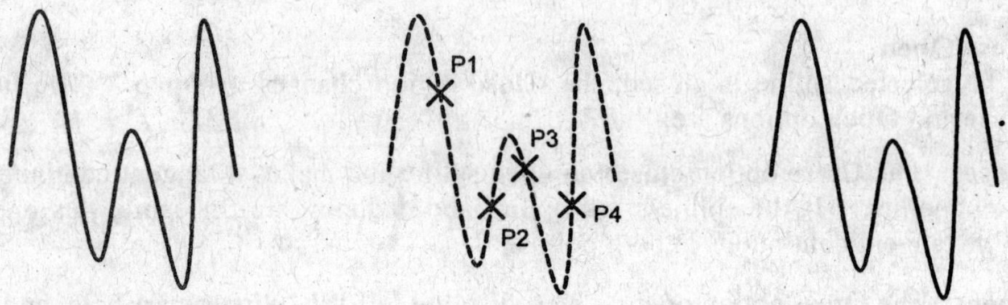

Spline before Refine   Spline Selected to Refine   Spline after Refine

FIG. 24

Now, user can change the shape of the spline using the newly added control points.

5. Reverse
The **Reverse** option reverses the spline's direction. This option is intended primarily for third-party applications.

6. Convert to Polyline
The **Convert to Polyline** option converts the spline to a polyline. When the **Convert to Polyline** option is selected, AutoCAD prompts to enter a new precision value. The precision value determines how accurately the resulting polyline is to fit to the source spline. Valid value is an integer between 0 and 99. Note that a high precision value may cause performance problems.

7. Undo
The **Undo** option cancels the last editing action.

*

12

DRAFTING SETTINGS

1. DRAFTING SETTINGS

AutoCAD provides a variety of precision drawing tools to help the user to produce accurate drawings quickly and without performing tedious calculations. **Drafting Settings** is the one of the most important facilities available in AutoCAD.

Enter **Drafting Settings** or **DS** in the command prompt or select the **Drafting Settings** in the **Tools** menu to display the **Drafting Settings** dialog box. See Fig. 1.

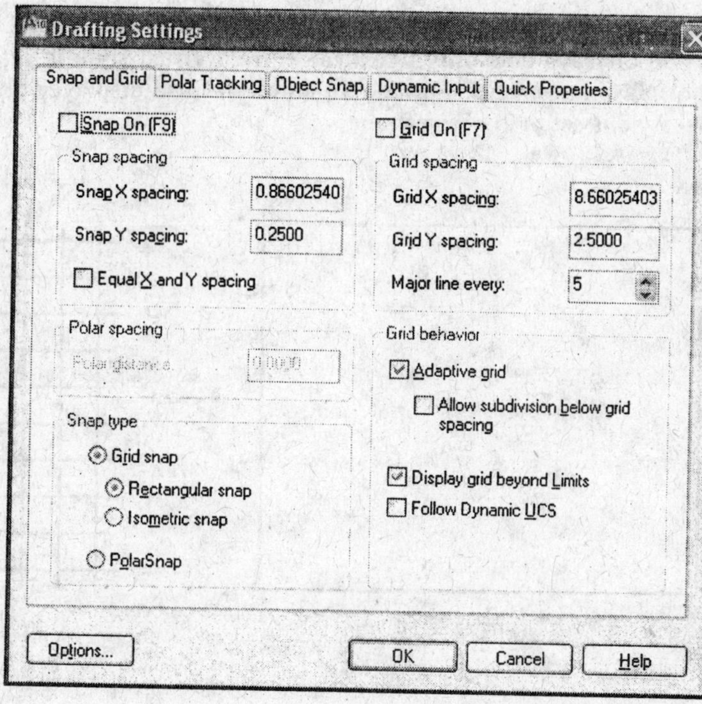

FIG. 1

Use the **Drafting Settings** dialog box to set the drawing modes such as Grid, Snap, Object Snap, Polar, Object Snap tracking and **Dynamic Input**. All the modes help to drawn accurately and also increase the drawing speed.

In the Drafting Settings dialog box, option specifies drafting settings organized for drawing aids in the following tabs:

1. Snap and Grid
2. Polar Tracking
3. Object Snap
4. Dynamic Input
5. Quick Properties

Options

The **Options** button displays the **Drafting** tab in the **Options** dialog box.

2. SNAP AND GRID TAB

The **Snap and Grid** tab specifies **Snap and Grid** settings. See Fig. 1.

The **Grid** is a rectangular pattern of dots or lines that extends over the specified area as the grid limits. Using the grid is similar to placing a sheet of grid paper under a drawing. The grid helps to align objects and visualize the distances between them. The grid is not plotted.

Snap mode restricts the movement of the crosshairs to specified intervals. When **Snap** mode is on, the cursor seems to adhere, or "snap," to an invisible rectangular grid. Snap is useful for specifying precise points with the arrow keys or the pointing device.

Grid mode and **Snap** mode are independent but are often turned on at the same time.

2.1 SETTING GRID

The grid can be displayed either as a rectangular pattern of dots or as rectangular pattern of lines. The grid displays dots only when the current visual style is set to 2D Wireframe, otherwise the grid displays lines. See Fig. 2. It shows the grid displayed as dots. That is, when the current visual style is set to 2D Wireframe.

FIG. 2

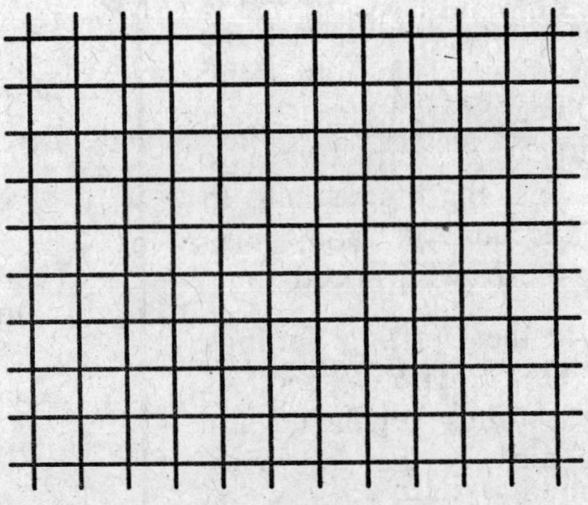

FIG. 3

A lined grid is displayed for all visual styles while working in 3D. See Fig. 3. It shows the grid displayed as lines. There are several methods to change the current visual style, including the VSCURRENT command

Grid On
The **Grid On** check box in the **Snap and Grid** tab of the **Drafting Settings** dialog box turns the grid on or off. Turn grid mode on or off by clicking **Grid** on the status bar, by pressing **F7** or by using the GRIDMODE system variable.

Grid Spacing

The **Grid Spacing** area in the **Snap and Grid** tab of the **Drafting Settings** dialog box controls the display of a grid that helps to visualize distances. Note that the limits of the grid are controlled by the LIMITS command and the GRIDDISPLAY system variable.

Grid X Spacing

This text box specifies the grid spacing in the *X* direction. If this value is 0, the grid assumes the value set for Snap X Spacing.

Grid Y Spacing

This text box specifies the grid spacing in the *Y* direction. If this value is 0, the grid assumes the value set for Snap Y Spacing.

Major Line Every

This text box specifies the frequency of major grid lines compared to minor grid lines. Grid lines rather than grid dots are displayed when the VSCURRENT is set to any visual style except 2D Wireframe.

Grid Behavior

The **Grid Behavior** area in the **Snap and Grid** tab of the **Drafting Settings** dialog box controls the appearance of the grid lines that are displayed when VSCURRENT is set to any visual style except 2D Wireframe.

Adaptive Grid

This checkbox limits the density of the grid when zoomed out.

Allow Subdivision Below Grid Spacing: This check box generates additional, more closely spaced grid lines when zoomed in. The frequency of these grid lines is determined by the frequency of the major grid lines.

Display Grid Beyond Limits

This check box displays the grid beyond the area specified by the LIMITS command.

Follow Dynamic UCS

This check box changes the grid plane to follow the XY plane of the dynamic UCS.

2.2 SETTING SNAP

The **Snap** points are invisible points that are created at the intersection of invisible horizontal and vertical lines. A snap point is independent of the grid spacing and the two can have equal or different values.

That is, when the snap mode is on, the cursor moves in specified intervals from one point to another. It is possible to turn on the snap mode even when the grid lines are invisible. To set snap spacing, enter the X and Y values in the corresponding edit boxes in the Snap spacing area of the **Snap and Grid** tab in the **Drafting Settings** dialog box.

Snap On

The **Snap On** checkbox in the **Snap and Grid** tab of the **Drafting Settings** dialog box turns Snap mode on or off. Turn **Snap** mode on or off by clicking **Snap** on the status bar, by pressing **F9** or by using the SNAPMODE system variable.

Snap Spacing

The **Snap Spacing** area in the **Snap and Grid** tab of the **Drafting Settings** dialog box controls an invisible, rectangular grid of snap locations that restricts cursor movement to specified *X* and *Y* intervals.

Snap X Spacing

This text box specifies the snap spacing in the *X* direction. The value must be a positive real number.

Snap Y Spacing

This text box specifies the snap spacing in the *Y* direction. The value must be a positive real number.

Equal X and Y Spacing

This checkbox forces the X and Y spacing to the same values for snap spacing and for grid spacing. The snap spacing intervals can be different from the grid spacing intervals.

Polar Spacing

The **Polar Spacing** area in the **Snap and Grid** tab of the **Drafting Settings** dialog box controls the **PolarSnap** increment distance.

Polar Distance

The **Polar Distance** text box sets the snap increment distance when **PolarSnap** is selected under **Snap Type & Style**. If this value is 0, the **PolarSnap** distance assumes the value for Snap X Spacing. The **Polar Distance** setting is used in conjunction with polar tracking and/or object snap tracking. If neither tracking feature is enabled, the **Polar Distance** setting has no effect.

Snap Type

The **Snap Type** area in the **Snap and Grid** tab of the **Drafting Settings** dialog box sets the snap style and snap type. There are two snap types. They are **PolarSnap** and **Grid snap**. The Grid snap is either of the **Rectangular snap** type or of the **Isometric snap**. **Rectangular snap** is the default snap.

Grid Snap

The **Grid Snap** radio button sets the snap type to **Grid**. When user specifies points, the cursor snaps along vertical or horizontal grid points.

Rectangular Snap: The **Rectangular Snap** sets the snap style to standard **Rectangular snap** mode. When snap type is set to **Grid** snap and **Snap** mode is on, the cursor snaps to a rectangular snap grid. See Fig. 4 for **Rectangular Snap**.

FIG. 4 RECTANGULAR SNAP GRID

FIG. 5 ISOMETRIC SNAP GRID

Isometric Snap: The **Isometric Snap** sets the snap style to **Isometric snap** mode. When the snap type is set to **Grid snap** and **Snap mode** is on, the cursor snaps to an isometric snap grid. See Fig. 5 for **Isometric Snap.**

In isometric drawing, the isometric axes are at angles 30°, 90° and 150°. The **Isometric snap/grid** displays the grid lines along these axes. Note that the X spacing is not available for this option. The vertical snap and grid spacing can be changed by entering values in the **Snap Y spacing** and **Grid Y spacing** edit boxes.

While drawing in isometric mode, the cursor orientation to the left, top or right plane of the drawing can be adjusted by using the **F5** key.

PolarSnap

The **PolarSnap** radio button sets the snap type to **Polar.** When **Snap** mode is on and user specifies points with polar tracking turned on, the cursor snaps along polar alignment angles set on the **Polar Tracking** tab relative to the starting polar tracking point.

3. POLAR TRACKING TAB

The **Polar Tracking** tab controls the **AutoTrack** settings. See Fig. 6. Polar tracking is used to locate points on an angular alignment path. Polar tracking constrains the movement of the cursor along a path that is based on the polar angle settings.

Polar Tracking On

The **Polar Tracking On** check box turns polar tracking on and off. Turn polar tracking on or off by pressing **F10** or by using the AUTOSNAP system variable.

3.1 POLAR ANGLE SETTINGS AREA

The **Polar Angle Settings** area sets the alignment angles for polar tracking.

Increment Angle

This drop-down list sets the polar increment angle used to display polar tracking alignment paths. User can enter any angle or select a common angle of 90°, 45°, 30°, 22.5°, 18°, 15°, 10° or 5° from the list.

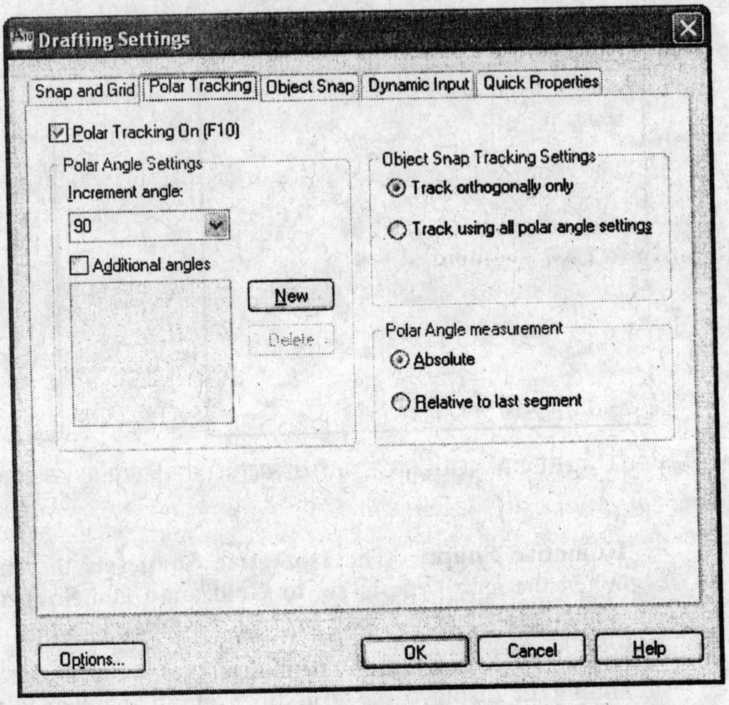

FIG. 6

Additional Angles

This check box makes any additional angles in the list available for polar tracking. Note that additional angles are absolute, not incremental.

List of Angles

If **Additional Angles** is selected, the **List of Angles** area lists the additional angles that are available. To add new angles, click **New**. To remove existing angles, click **Delete.**

New

The **New** button adds up to 10 additional polar tracking alignment angles.

Delete

The **Delete** button deletes selected additional angles.

3.2 OBJECT SNAP TRACKING SETTINGS AREA

The **Object Snap Tracking Settings** area sets options for object snap tracking.

Track Orthogonally Only

This radio button displays only orthogonal (horizontal/vertical) object snap tracking paths for acquired object snap points when object snap tracking is on.

Track Using All Polar Angle Settings

This radio button applies polar tracking settings to object snap tracking. When user uses object snap tracking, the cursor tracks along polar alignment angles from acquired object snap points.

3.3 POLAR ANGLE MEASUREMENT AREA

The **Polar Angle Measurement** area sets the basis by which polar tracking alignment angles are measured.

Absolute

This radio button bases polar tracking angles on the current user coordinate system (UCS).

Relative to Last Segment

This radio button bases polar tracking angles on the last segment drawn.

4. OBJECT SNAP TAB

The **Object Snap** tab controls running object snap settings. With running object snap settings, also called **Osnap,** user can specify a snap point at an exact location on an object.

When more than one option is selected, the selected snap modes are applied to return a point closest to the center of the aperture box. Press **TAB** to cycle through the options.

The options available in the **Object Snap** tab is shown in Fig. 7.

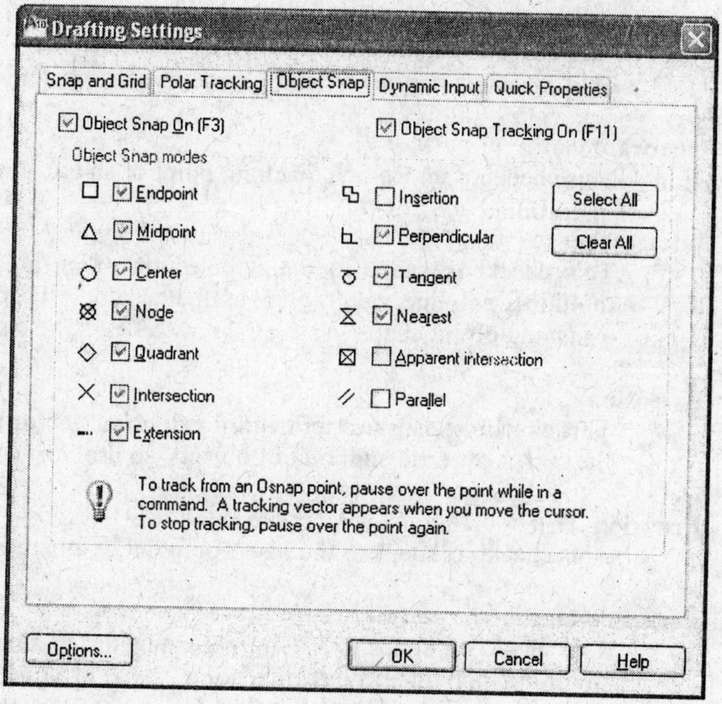

FIG. 7

Object Snap On

The **Object Snap On** checkbox turns running objects snaps on and off. The object snaps selected under **Object Snap Modes** are active while object snap is on.

Object Snap Tracking On

The **Object Snap Tracking On** checkbox turns objects snap tracking on and off. With object snap tracking, the cursor can track along alignment paths based on other object snap points when specifying points in a command. To use object snap tracking, user must turn on one or more object snaps.

4.1 OBJECT SNAP MODES AREA

The **Object Snap Modes** area lists object snaps that user can turn on as running object snaps.

Endpoint

This checkbox snaps to the closest endpoint of an arc, elliptical arc, line, multiline, polyline segment, spline, region or ray or to the closest corner of a trace, solid or 3D face.

Midpoint

This checkbox snaps to the midpoint of an arc, ellipse, elliptical arc, line, multiline, polyline segment, region, solid, spline or xline.

Center

This checkbox snaps to the center of an arc, circle, ellipse or elliptical arc.

Node

This checkbox naps to a point object, dimension definition point or dimension text origin.

Quadrant

This checkbox snaps to a quadrant point of an arc, circle, ellipse or elliptical arc.

Intersection

This checkbox snaps to the intersection of an arc, circle, ellipse, elliptical arc, line, multiline, polyline, ray, region, spline or xline. Extended Intersection is not available as a running object snap.

Extension

This checkbox causes a temporary extension line or arc to be displayed when user passes the cursor over the endpoint of objects, so user can specify points on the extension.

Insertion

This checkbox snaps to the insertion point of an attribute, a block, a shape or text.

Perpendicular

This checkbox snaps to a point perpendicular to an arc, circle, ellipse, elliptical arc, line, multiline, polyline, ray, region, solid, spline or xline.

Tangent

This checkbox snaps to the tangent of an arc, circle, ellipse, elliptical arc or spline.

Nearest

This checkbox snaps to the nearest point on an arc, circle, ellipse, elliptical arc, line, multiline, point, polyline, ray, spline or xline.

Apparent Intersection

This checkbox snaps to the visual intersection of two objects that are not in the same plane but may appear to intersect in the current view.

Parallel

This checkbox constrains a line segment, polyline segment, ray or xline to be parallel to another linear object. After specifying the first point of a linear object, specify the parallel object snap.

Select All

This button turns on all object snap modes.

Clear All

This button turns off all object snap modes.

4.2 AutoTrack Settings

The **AutoTrack** settings can be specified in the **Drafting** tab of the **Options** dialog box. Choose the **Options** button in the **Polar Tracking** tab of the **Drafting Settings** dialog box. The **Options** dialog box with the **Drafting** tab chosen is displayed.

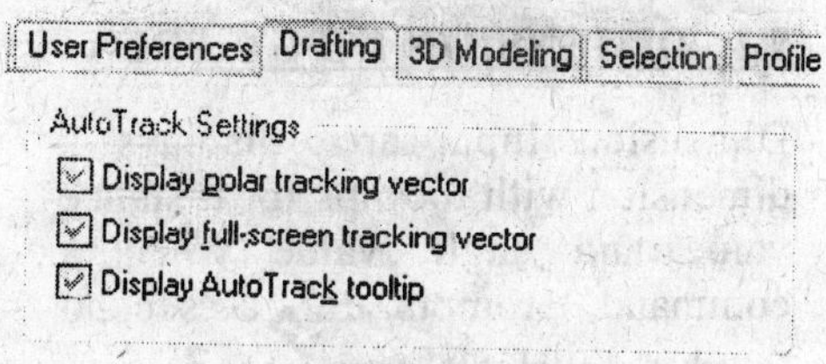

FIG. 8

The **AutoTrack Settings** area shows the AutoTrack settings. See Fig. 8. The **Display polar tracking vector** check box can be used to toggle the display of the angle alignment path for **Polar tracking.**

The **Display full-screen tracking vector** check box can be used to toggle the display of a full-screen construction line for **Otrack**. The **Display AutoTrack tooltip** check box can be used to toggle the display of tooltips with the paths. The TRACKPATH system variable can also be used to set the path display settings.

5. DYNAMIC INPUT TAB

The **Dynamic Input Tab** controls pointer input, dimension input, dynamic prompting and the appearance of drafting tooltips. See Fig. 9.

Enable Pointer Input

The **Enable Pointer Input** checkbox turns on pointer input. When pointer input and dimensional input are both turned on, dimensional input supersedes pointer input when it is available.

5.1 POINTER INPUT AREA

The **Pointer Input** area displays the location of the crosshairs as coordinate values in a tooltip near the cursor. When a command prompts for a point, enter coordinate values in the tooltip instead of in the Command window.

Preview Area: This area shows an example of pointer input.

Settings

The **Settings** button displays the **Pointer Input Settings** dialog box.

Enable Dimension Input

The **Enable Dimension Input** checkbox turns on dimensional input. Dimensional input is not available for some commands that prompt for a second point.

5.2 DIMENSION INPUT AREA

Dimension Input area displays a dimension with tooltips for distance value and angle value when a command prompts for a second point or a distance.

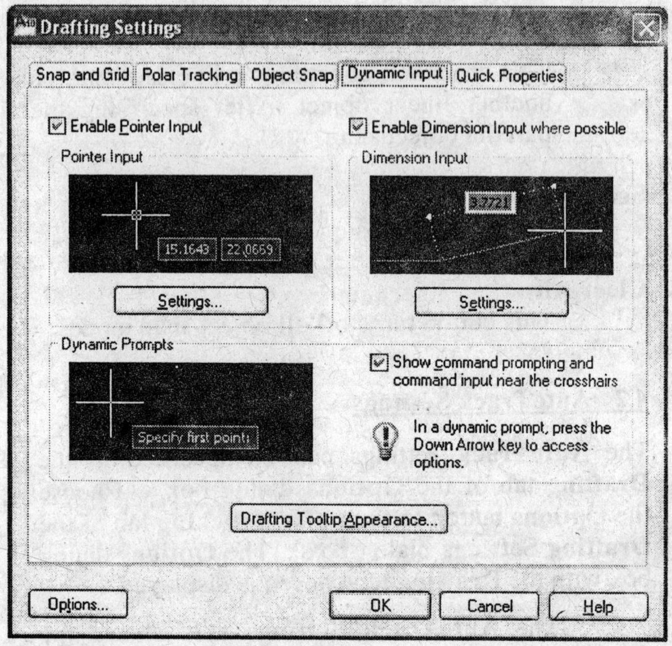

FIG. 9

The values in the dimension tooltips change as user moves the cursor. Enter values in the tooltip instead of on the command line.

Preview Area: This area shows an example of dimensional input.

Settings

The **Settings** button displays the **Dimension Input Settings** dialog box.

5.3 DYNAMIC PROMPTS AREA

The **Dynamic Prompts** area displays prompts in a tooltip near the cursor when necessary in order to complete the command. User can enter values in the tooltip instead of on the command line.

Preview Area: This area shows an example of dynamic prompts.

Show Command Prompting and Command Input near the Crosshairs

The **Show Command Prompting** and **Command Input** near the **Crosshairs** button displays prompts in **Dynamic Input** tooltips.

Drafting Tooltip Appearance

The **Drafting Tooltip Appearance** button displays the **Tooltip Appearance** dialog box.

6. QUICK PROPERTIES TAB

The **Quick Properties** tab specifies the settings for displaying the **Quick Properties** palette. See Fig. 10.

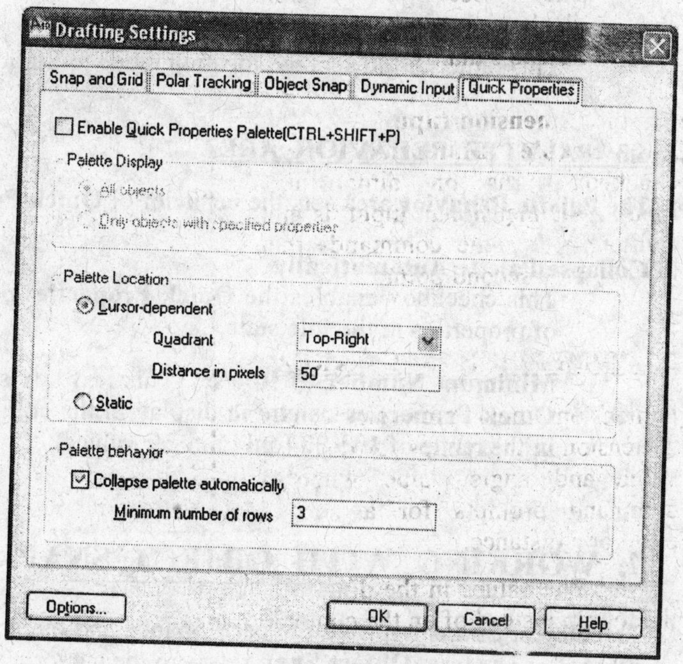

FIG. 10

Enable Quick Properties Palette
Depending on the object type, user can enable or disable **Quick Properties** palette using the **Enable Quick Properties Palette** check box.

The **Quick Properties** palette can also be turned on or off by clicking **Quick Properties** on the status bar or by using the QPMODE system variable.

6.1 PALETTE DISPLAY AREA

The **Palette Display** area sets the display settings of the **Quick Properties** palette.

All Objects
This radio button sets the **Quick Properties** palette to display for any selection of objects.

Only Objects with Specified Properties
This radio button sets the **Quick Properties** palette to display only for objects that are defined in the **Customize User Interface** (CUI) editor to display properties.

6.2 PALETTE LOCATION AREA

The **Plate Location** area sets the display position of the **Quick Properties** palette.

Cursor-Dependent
This radio button sets the **Palette Location** mode to **Cursor-dependent.** In cursor-dependent mode, the **Quick Properties** palette displays in a location relative to where user selected the object.

Quadrant: This drop-down list specifies the relative location to display the **Quick Properties** palette.

User can select one of the four quadrants top-right, top-left, bottom-right or bottom-left.

Distance in Pixels: This textbox sets the distance in pixels when **Cursor** is selected under the **Palette Location** modes. User can specify values in the range of 0 to 400 (only integer values).

Static

This radio button sets the location mode to Static.

6.3 PALETTE BEHAVIOR AREA

The **Palette Behavior** area sets the behavior of **Quick Properties** palette.

Collapse Palette Automatically

This checkbox enables the **Quick Properties** palette to display only a specified number of properties in the idle state.

Minimum Number of Rows: This text box sets the minimum number of rows for the **Quick Properties** palette to display in the collapsed idle state. User can specify values in the range of 1 to 30 (only integer values).

7. WORKING WITH OBJECT SNAP

The **Object Snaps** improve the performance and the accuracy of the drawing. The term **Object Snap** refers to the cursor's ability to snap exactly to a geometric point on an object. The advantage of using object snaps is that user need not specify an exact point.

For example, to snap the midpoint of a line, use the **Midpoint** object snap and move the cursor closer to the object. A marker is automatically displayed at the midpoint. Click to snap the midpoint.

The **Object Snap** toolbar can be invoked by selecting **Tools > Toolbars > AutoCAD > Object Snap**. The Object Snap toolbar is displayed as shown in Fig. 11.

While invoking a tool, object snaps can be invoked from the shortcut menu; that is press and hold the shift key and right-click. See Fig. 12. This shortcut menu can be invoked when you are inside any other sketching command.

The **Object Snap** modes available in AutoCAD software are: Endpoint, Midpoint, Center, Node, Quadrant, Intersection, Extension, Insertion, Perpendicular, Tangent, Nearest, Apparent Intersection and Parallel.

FIG. 11

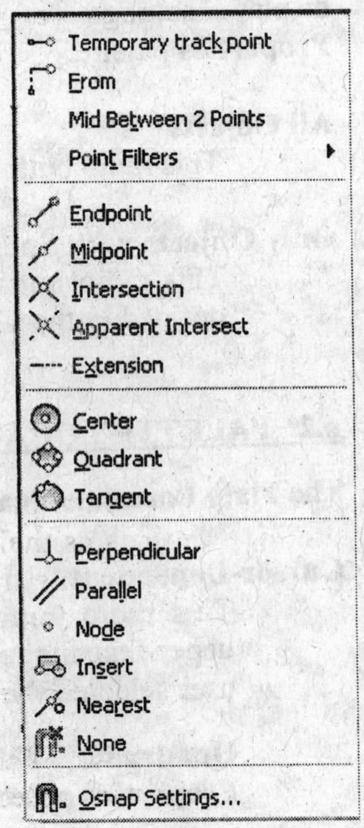

FIG. 12

7.1 AutoSnap Option

Object snaps include a visual aid called **AutoSnap**. It helps to see and use object snaps more efficiently. **AutoSnap** displays a marker and a tooltip when you move the cursor over an object snap location. The markers are displayed corresponding to the shapes shown in the **Object Snap** tab of the **Drafting Settings** dialog box.

AutoSnap settings, such as attaching a target box to the cursor when an object snap is invoked, or color and size of the marker, can be changed from the **Options** dialog box.

Invoke the **Options** dialog box from the **Application Menu** or by entering **OPTIONS** at the Command prompt. Choose the **Drafting** tab in the **Options** dialog box to display the **AutoSnap Settings.** The **AutoSnap Settings** are shown in Fig. 13.

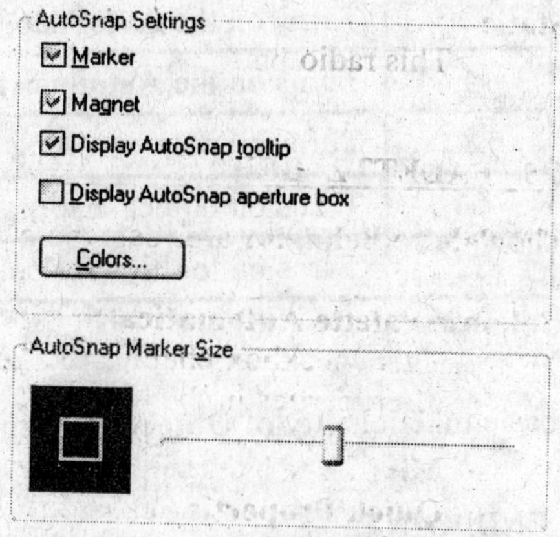

FIG. 13

AutoSnap Tools

AutoSnap Settings consists of the following snap tools:

- **Marker:** Select the **Market** check box to display the object snap location when the cursor moves over or near an object. Marker shape is dependent on the snap it is marking.
- **Magnet:** Select the **Magnet** check box to attract and lock the cursor onto the nearest detected snap points. Provides a visual cue, similar to snapping to a grid.
- **Display AutoSnap tooltip:** Select the **Display AutoSnap tooltip** check box to describe which part of the object you are snapping to in a small flag at the cursor location.
- **Display AutoSnap aperture box:** Select the **Display AutoSnap aperture box** check box to surround the crosshairs and define an area within which object snaps are evaluated. You can choose to display or not display the aperture box and you can change the aperture box size.
- **Colors:** Choose the **Colors...** button to display the **Drawing Window Colors** dialog box. In this dialog box, user can change the color of the AutoSnap marker.
- **AutoSnap Marker Size:** In the **AutoSnap Marker Size** area, user can adjust the size of the marker.

The AutoSnap markers, magnet and tooltips are turned on by default. User can change **AutoSnap** settings as their requirement on the **Drafting** tab in the **Options** dialog box. If you have set more than one running object snap, you can press **TAB** to cycle through all the object snap points available for a particular object.

The **AUTOSNAP** system variable controls the display of the **AutoSnap** marker, tooltip and magnet. It also turns on polar and object snap tracking, and controls the display of polar tracking, object snap tracking and **Ortho** mode tooltips. The setting is stored as a bitcode using the sum of the values shown in Table 1.

Bitcode Value	Functions
0	Turns off the AutoSnap marker, tooltips, and magnet. Also turns off polar tracking, object snap tracking, and tooltips for polar tracking, object snap tracking, and Ortho mode
1	Turns on the AutoSnap marker
2	Turns on the AutoSnap tooltips
4	Turns on the AutoSnap magnet
8	Turns on polar tracking
16	Turns on object snap tracking
32	Turns on tooltips for polar tracking, object snap tracking, and Ortho mode

Table 1

The basic functionality of **Object Snap** modes are explained next.

7.2 ENDPOINT

The **Endpoint** Object Snap mode is used to snap the cursor to the closest endpoint of an arc, elliptical arc, line multiline, polyline segment, spline, region or ray or to the closest corner of a trace, solid or 3D face.

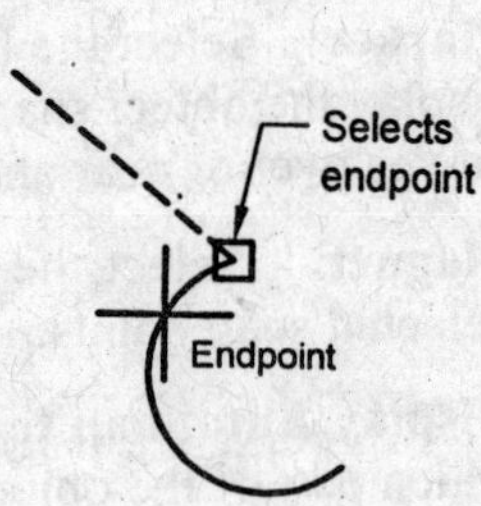

FIG. 14

Invoke a draw tool such as **Line** and select the **Endpoint** button from the **Object Snap** toolbar or from the **Object Snap** shortcut menu. Then move the cursor anywhere close to the end point of the object. A marker is displayed at the endpoint.

Click to select that point, the endpoint of the object is snapped. See Fig. 14. It shows the cursor snapping the endpoint of an arc. The dashed line is the proposed line to be drawn.

If there are several objects near the cursor crosshairs, the endpoint of the object that is closest to the crosshairs is snapped. Although, if the **Magnet** snap tool is on, user can move to grab the desired endpoint.

7.3 MIDPOINT

The **Midpoint** Object Snap mode is used to snap the cursor to the closest midpoint of an arc, ellipse, elliptical arc, line, multiline, polyline segment, spline, region, solid or xline.

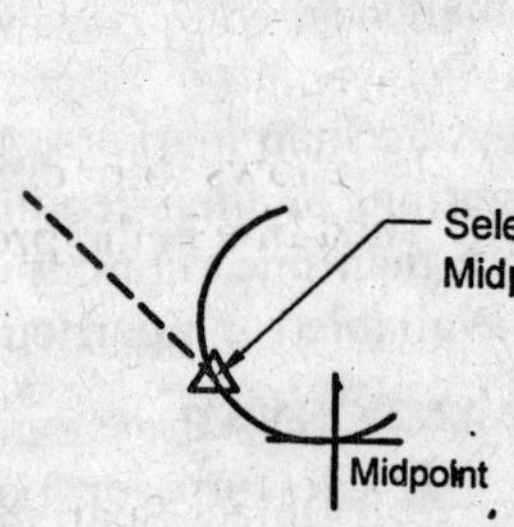

FIG. 15

To use this object snap, select the **Midpoint** option and select an object anywhere. The Midpoint of the object is snapped. Fig. 15 shows the cursor snapping the midpoint of an arc. The dashed line is the proposed line to be drawn.

7.4 CENTER

The **Center** Object Snap mode is used to snap the cursor to the center point of an arc, circle, ellipse or elliptical arc.

To use this object snap, select the **Center** option and move the cursor on the circumference of a circle or an arc. A marker is displayed at the center of the circle.

Left-click to snap the center point of the circle. See Fig. 16. It shows the cursor snapping the center point of a circle. The dashed line is the proposed line to be drawn.

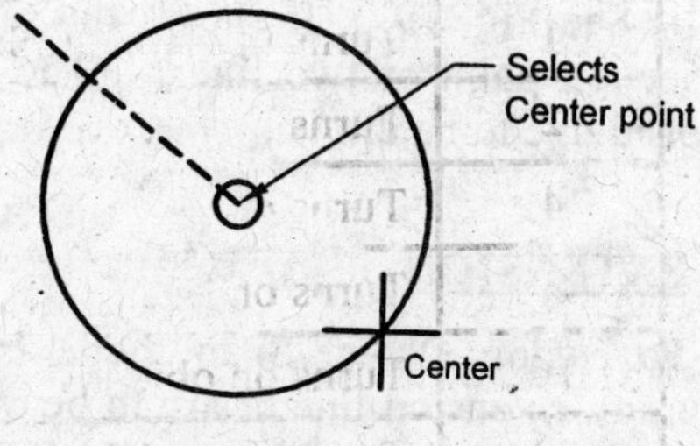

FIG. 16

7.5 NODE

The **Node** Object Snap mode is used to snap the cursor to the points placed by using the **Multiple Points, Divide** or **Measure** commands.

See Fig. 17. It shows three points placed by using the **Multiple Points** command. The dashed line is the proposed line to be drawn. When the cursor moves close to a point, the **Node** tooltip is displayed.

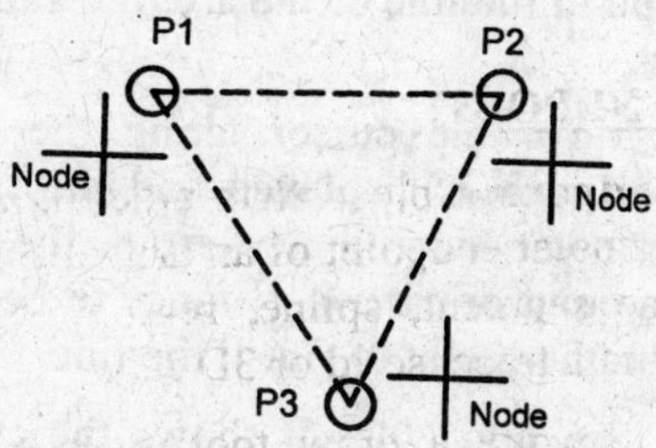

FIG. 17

7.6 QUADRANT

The **Quadrant** Object Snap mode is used to snap the cursor to the quadrant point of an arc, circle, ellipse or elliptical arc. A circle has four quadrants and each quadrant subtends an angle of 90°. Therefore, the quadrant points are located at 0°, 90°, 180° and 270° positions.

To use this object snap, select the **Quadrant** option and position the cursor on the circle or an arc closest to the desired quadrant. Left-click when the marker is displayed.

Fig. 18 shows the cursor snapping the fourth quadrant. Dashed line is the proposed line to be drawn.

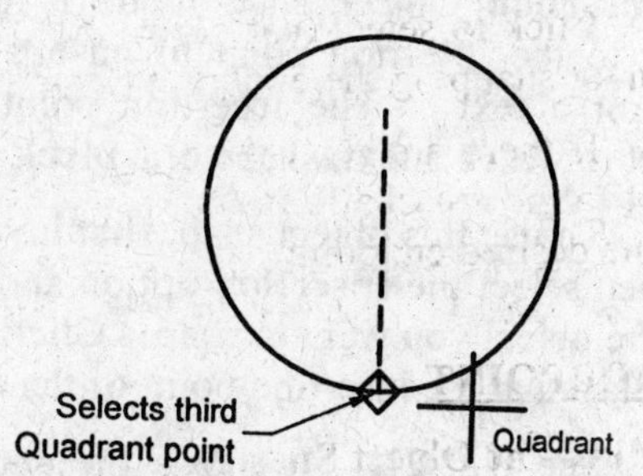

FIG. 18

7.7 INTERSECTION

The **Intersection** Object Snap mode is used to snap the cursor to the intersection of an arc, circle, ellipse, elliptical arc, line, multiline, polyline, ray, region, spline or xline. Extended Intersection is not available as a running object snap.

To use this object snap, select the **Intersection** option and move the cursor to the desired intersection point such that the intersection is within the target box. Click when the intersection marker is displayed.

See Fig. 19. It shows the cursor snapping the intersection point of two lines. The dashed line is the proposed line to be drawn.

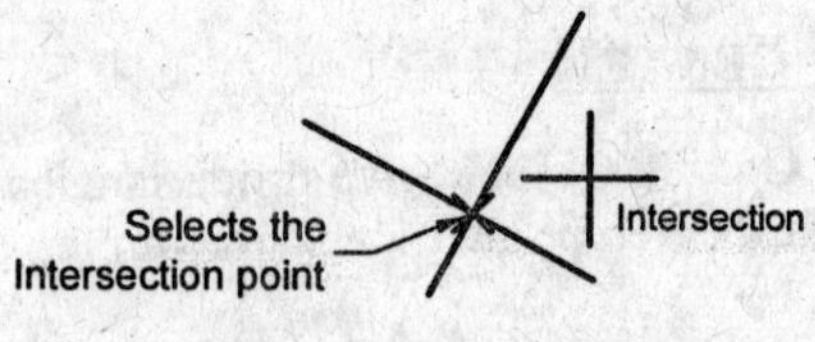

FIG. 19

7.8 EXTENSION

The **Extension** Object Snap mode is used to cause a temporary extension line or arc to be displayed when you pass the cursor over the end point of objects, so that user can specify points on the extension.

To use this object snap, first invoke the Line tool and then select the **Extension** option. Pause the cursor at the end of the line or the arc, indicating that it has been selected.

Move the cursor along the line, a temporary extension path is displayed and the tooltip displays the relative polar coordinates from the end of the line. Select a point or enter a distance to begin a line and then select another point to finish the line.

See Fig. 20. It shows the cursor snapping the **Extension** of a line.

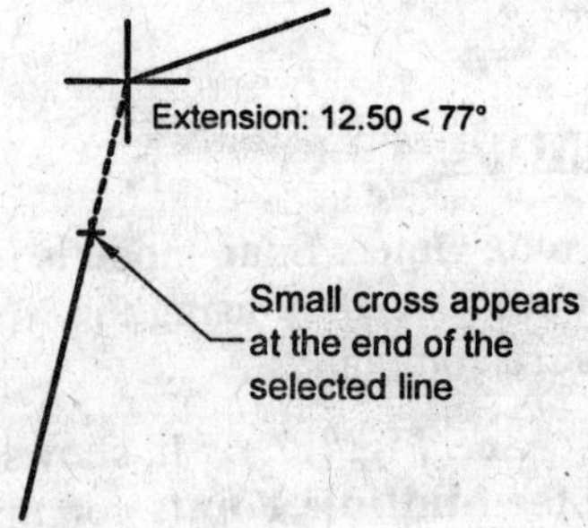

FIG. 20

7.9 INSERTION

The **Insertion** Object Snap mode is used to snap the cursor to the insertion point of an attribute, a block, a shape or a text. The insertion point is a point with respect to which a text, shape or a block is inserted.

To use this object snap, first invoke the **Line** tool and then select the **Insertion** option and move the cursor near the object you want to snap. Click when the marker is displayed at the insertion point of the object.

See Fig. 21. It shows the cursor snapping the insertion point of three objects. The dashed line is the proposed line to be drawn.

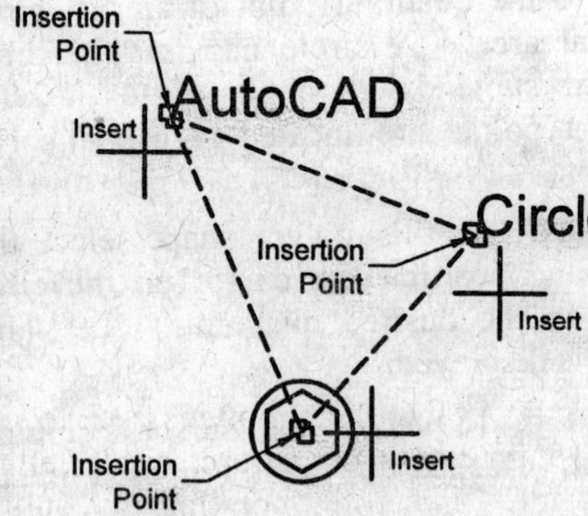

FIG. 21

7.10 PERPENDICULAR

The **Perpendicular** Object Snap mode is used to snap the cursor to a point perpendicular to an arc, circle, ellipse, elliptical arc, multiline, polyline, ray, region, solid, spline or xline.

To use this object snap, first invoke the **Line** tool and then select the **Perpendicular** option and select an object. A perpendicular line is attached to the cursor. Move the cursor and place the line. See Fig. 22. It shows the cursor snapping the perpendicular of a line. The dashed line is the proposed line to be drawn.

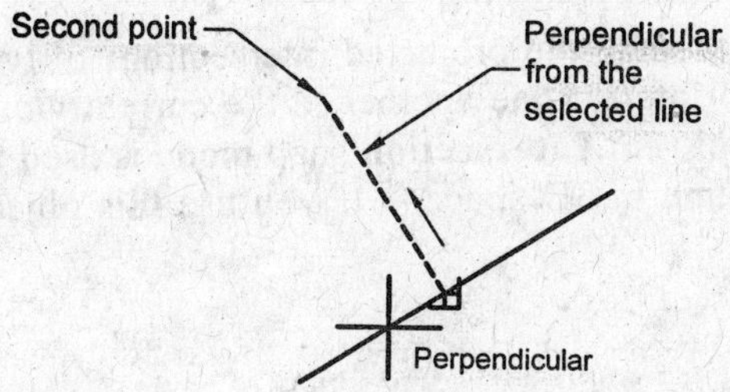

FIG. 22

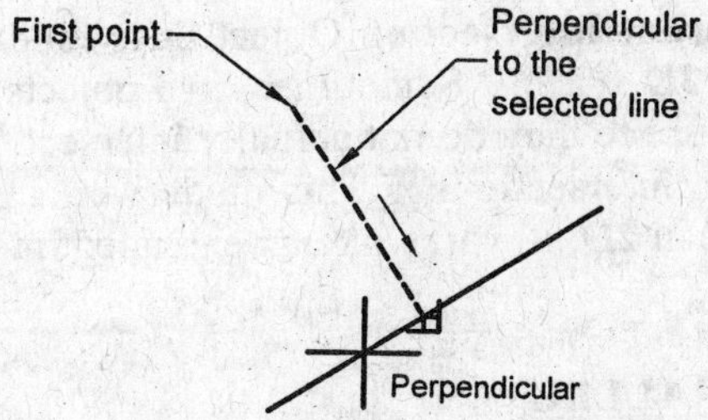

FIG. 23

After invoking the **Line** tool, the start point of the line is selected first and then the **Perpendicular** snap mode is selected, an object is needs to be selected. On doing so, AutoCAD selects a point such that the resulting line is perpendicular to the selected object. See Fig. 23.

7.11 TANGENT

The **Tangent** Object Snap mode is used to snap the cursor to the tangent of an arc, circle, ellipse, elliptical arc or spline.

To use this object snap, first invoke the **Line** tool and specify the first point. Then select the **Tangent** option and move the cursor on the circumference of a circle or an arc. Click when a tangent marker is displayed at the tangent point of the circle or arc.

See Fig. 24. It shows the cursor snapping the tangent point of a circle. The dashed line is the proposed line to be drawn.

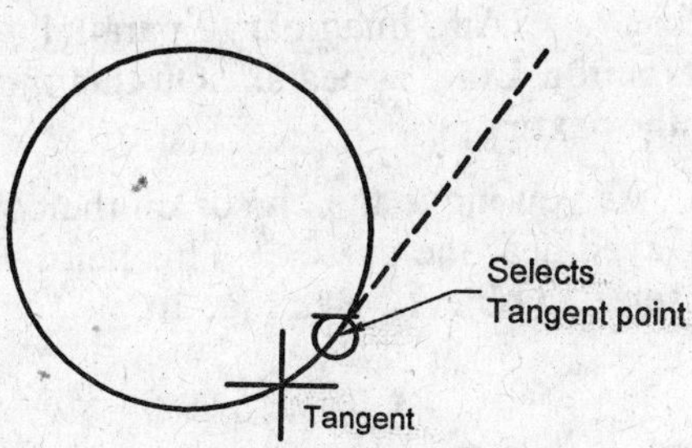

FIG. 24

7.12 NEAREST

The **Nearest** Object Snap mode is used to snap the cursor to the nearest point on an arc, circle, ellipse, elliptical arc, line, multiline, point, polyline, ray, spline or xline.

To use this object snap, first invoke the **Line** tool and then select the **Nearest** osnap and move the cursor near the intended point on the object. A marker is displayed at the nearest point. Click to snap that point.

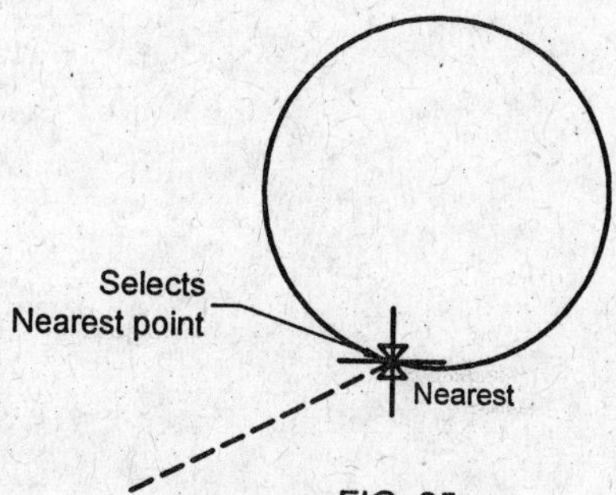

FIG. 25

See Fig. 25. It shows the cursor snapping the point in a circle. The dashed line is the proposed line to be drawn.

7.13 APPARENT INTERSECTION

The **Apparent Intersection** Object Snap mode is used to snap the projected intersections of two objects in 3D space. Sometimes, two objects appear to interest one another in the current view. But in 3D space they do not actually intersect. The **Apparent Intersection** snap mode is used to select such intersections. This mode works on wireframe in 3D space. If you use this object snap mode in 2D, it works like an extended intersection.

7.14 PARALLEL

The **Parallel** Object Snap mode is used when user needs to draw a line parallel to a line or a polyline.

To use this object snap, first invoke the Line tool and select the first point. Then select the **Parallel** osnap and move the cursor near the reference object and pause for a while. The **Parallel** tooltip appears on it indicating that the line has been selected.

Now, move the cursor at an angle parallel to the line. An imaginary parallel line, called **Construction Line**, appears. On this imaginary line, select the next point.

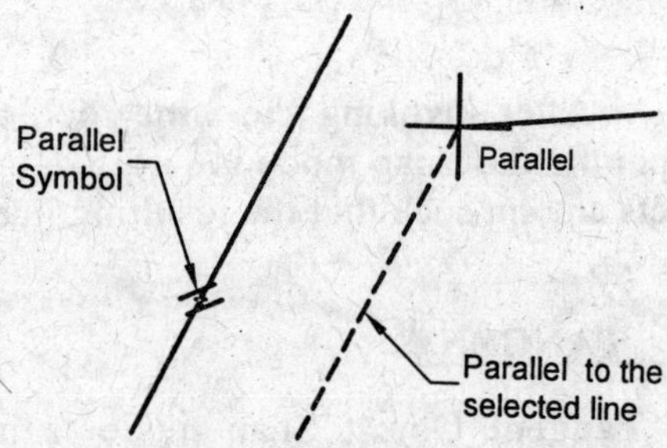

FIG. 26

As you move the cursor on the construction line, a tooltip with relative polar coordinates is displayed near the cursor. This helps to select the next point. Thus the line drawn is parallel to the selected object. See Fig. 26.

*

13

WORKING WITH LAYERS

1. CONCEPT OF LAYERS

Layers are like transparent overlays on which user can organize and group objects in a drawing. Layers are the equivalent of the overlays used in paper-based drafting. Layers are the primary organizational tool used in drawing. Use layers to group information by function and to enforce linetype, color and other standards.

By creating layers, user can associate similar types of objects by assigning them to the same layer. For example, user can put construction lines, text, dimensions and title blocks on separate layers.

See Fig. 1. The object lines are drawn in the first layer and the dimensions in the second layer. Place these two layers on top of each other and get a combined look of the drawing.

Using the layers, user can control the following:

- Objects on a layer are visible or dimmed in any viewports
- Whether and how the objects are plotted
- Color is assigned to all objects on a layer
- Default linetype and lineweight are assigned to all objects on a layer
- Objects on a layer can be modified or not
- Objects are displayed with different layer properties in individual layout viewports.

Every drawing includes a layer named 0. Layer 0 cannot be deleted or renamed. It has two purposes:

- Ensure that every drawing includes at least one layer
- Provide a special layer that relates to controlling colors in blocks

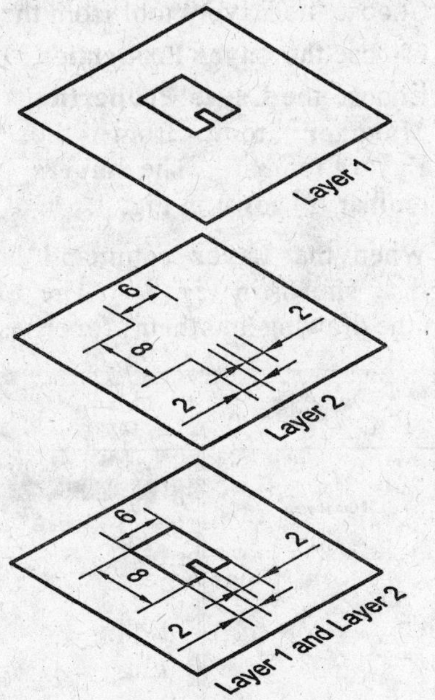

FIG. 1
DRAWING LINES AND DIMENSIONS IN DIFFERENT LAYERS

Use layers to control the visibility of objects and to assign properties such as color and linetype. Objects on a layer normally assume the properties of that layer. However, you can override any layer property of an object. For example, if an object's color property is set to BYLAYER, the object displays the color of that layer. If the object's color is set to Red, the object displays as red, regardless of the color assigned to that layer.

Note that it is recommended to create several new layers with which to organize the drawing rather than create the entire drawing on layer 0.

2. WORKING WITH LAYERS

Settings for layers, such as freeze, thaw, lock, unlock and so on can be specified using the **Layers** panel in the **Ribbon**. The **Layers** panel is shown in Fig. 2.

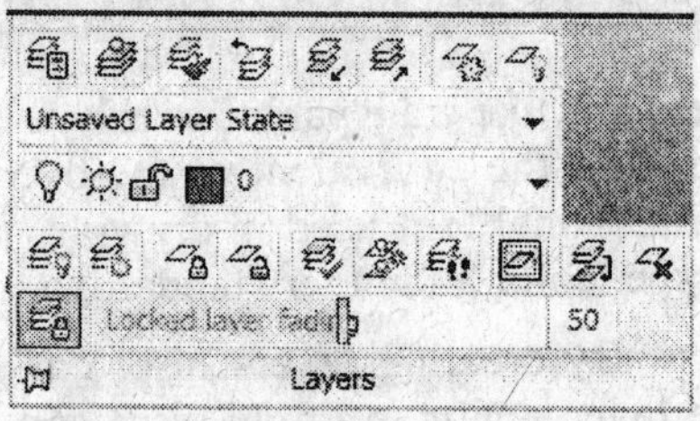

FIG. 2

The operations, such as add new layers, delete the existing layers or assign colors and linetype to layers, are performed using the **Layer Properties Manager** palette. The Layer Properties Manager palette can be invoked by using any one of the following methods:

1. Type **LAYER** at the command prompt and press Enter.
2. Choose the **Layers** tool from the **Format** menu.
3. Choose the **Layer Properties Manager** tool from the **Layers** panel at the **Home** tab.
4. Choose the **Layer Properties Manager** tool from the **Layers** toolbar. The **Layers** toolbar is shown in Fig. 3.

FIG. 3

When the **Layer** command is invoked, the **Layer Properties Manager** palette is displayed as shown in Fig. 4. The **Layer Properties Manager** palette displays a list of the layers in the drawing and their properties.

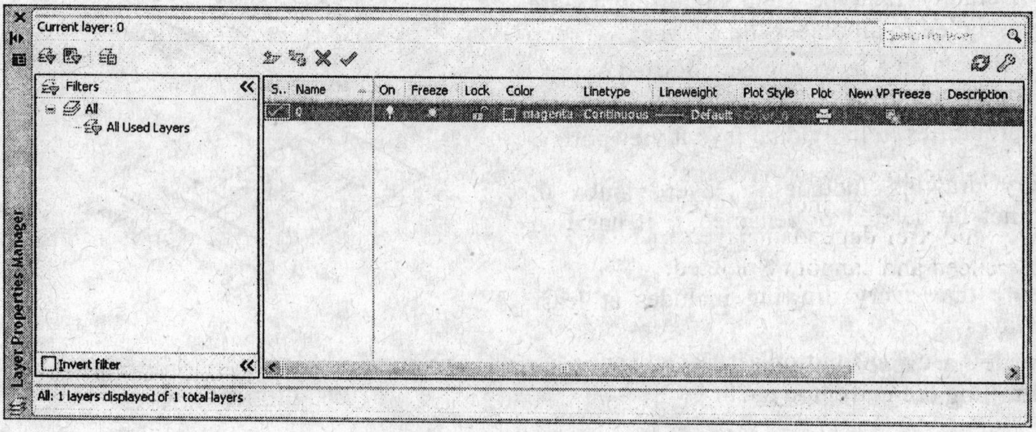

FIG. 4

User can add, delete and rename layers, change their properties, set property overrides for layout viewports or add layer descriptions and apply changes in realtime. User need not click OK button or Apply button to view property changes. Layer filters control which layers are displayed in the list and can also be used to make changes to more than one layer at a time.

When switching space (model space to layout space or layout to viewport), the **Layer Properties Manager** palette is updated and displays the current state of the layer properties and filter selection in the current space.

2.1 OPTIONS IN THE LAYER PROPERTIES MANAGER

New Property Filter

The **New Property Filter** button displays the **Layer Filter Properties** dialog box, where user can create a layer filter based on one or more properties of the layers.

New Group Filter

The **New Group Filter** button creates a layer filter that contains layers that user selects and adds to the filter.

Layer States Manager

The **Layer State Manager** button displays the Layer States Manager, in which user can save current property settings for layers in a named layer state and then restore those settings later.

New Layer

The **New Layer** button creates a new layer. The list displays a layer named LAYER1. The name is selected so that user can enter a new layer name immediately. The new layer inherits the properties of the currently selected layer in the layer list. The new layer is created below the last currently selected layer.

New Layer Frozen VP In All Viewports

This button creates a new layer and freezes it in all existing layout viewports. This button is accessible from the Model tab or layout tabs.

Delete Layer

The **Delete Layer** button deletes selected layers. User can delete only unreferenced layers. Referenced layers include layers 0 and DEFPOINTS, layers containing objects, the current layer and xref-dependent layers. Layers in a partially opened drawing are also considered referenced and cannot be deleted.

Set Current

The **Set Current** button sets the selected layer as the current layer. Objects that created are drawn on the current layer.

Current Layer

The **Current Layer** area displays the name of the current layer.

Status Line

The **Status Line** shows the name of the current filter, the number of layers displayed in the list view and the number of layers in the drawing.

Invert Filter

The **Invert Filter** checkbox displays all layers that do not meet the criteria in the selected layer property filter.

Indicate Layers in Use

This area displays icons in the list view to indicate whether layers are in use. In a drawing with many layers, clear this option to improve performance.

Refresh

The **Refresh** button refreshes the layer usage information by scanning all the entities in the drawing.

Settings

The **Settings** button displays the Layer Settings dialog box, in which user can set new layer notification settings, if layer filter changes are applied to the Layer toolbar and change the background color for layer property overrides.

Apply

The **Apply** button applies changes that have been made to layers and filters but does not close the dialog box.

3. CREATING NEW LAYERS

To create new layers, choose the **New Layer** button in the **Layer Properties Manager palette.** A new layer, named Layer1, with the same properties as that of the current layer will be created and listed. See Fig. 5.

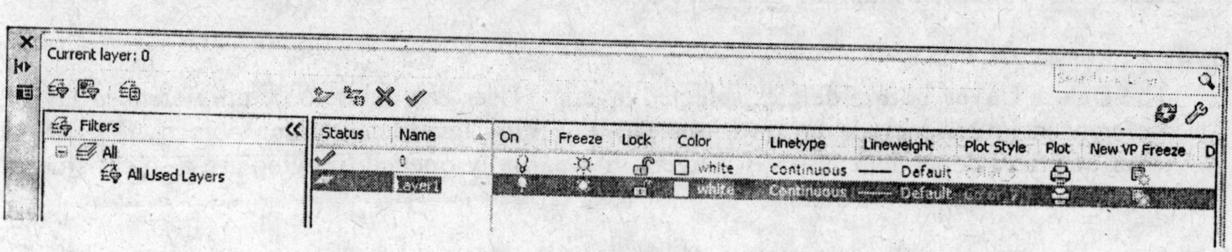

FIG. 5

Alternatively, right-click anywhere in the **Layers** list area of the **Layer Properties Manager** palette and then choose the **New Layer** option from the shortcut menu to create a new layer. If there are more layers and right-click on a layer other than the current layer and then choose **New Layer** from the shortcut menu. A new layer is created with the properties similar to the layer on which you right-clicked.

3.1 NAMING A NEW LAYER

New layers are created with the name layer1, layer 2 and so on. To change or edit the name of the layer, first select the layer. Then click once in the field corresponding to the **Name** column and then enter the name.

3.2 MAKING A LAYER CURRENT

To draw an object in a particular layer, you need to make it the current layer. There are different methods to make a layer current. They are:

1. Double-click on the name of a layer in the list box in the **Layer Properties Manager** palette. The selected layer is made current.
2. Select the layer from the **Layer** drop-down list in the **Layers** toolbar or from the **Layers** panel.
3. Select the name of the layer in the **Layer Properties Manager** and then choose the **Set Current** button in the **Layer Properties Manager**.
4. Right-click on a layer in the **Layer** list box in the **Layer Properties Manager** and choose the **Set current** option from the shortcut menu displayed. See Fig. 6.
5. Choose the **Make object's Layer Current** button from the **Layers** panel. AutoCAD prompts to select the object whose layer you want to make current. Select the required object. The layer associated with that object will become current.

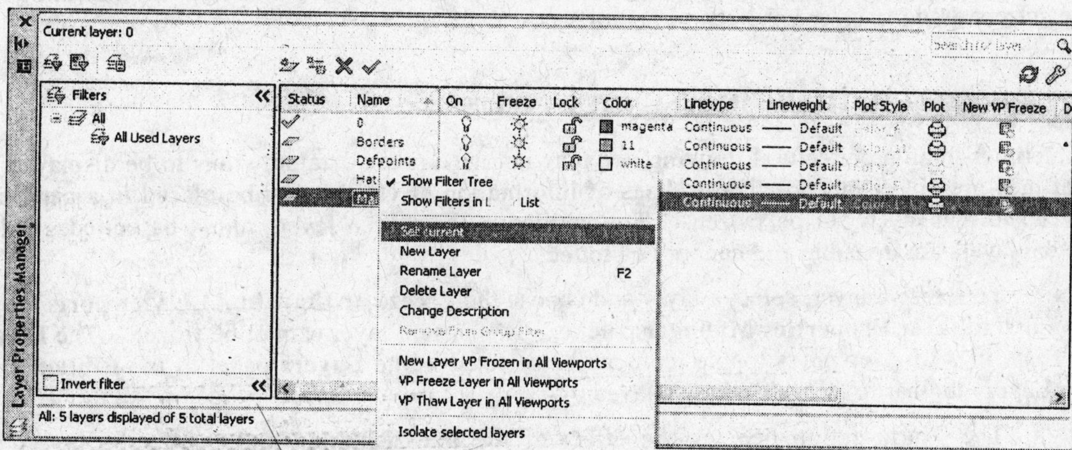

FIG. 6

When a layer is made current, a green color tick mark is displayed in the **Status** column of that layer. The name and properties of the current layer is displayed in the **Layers** toolbar and the name of the current layer is displayed at the upper-left corner of the **Layer Properties Manager** palette.

4. CONTROLLING THE DISPLAY OF LAYERS

The display of layers can be controlled by selecting the toggle buttons in the list box of any particular layer. In layers, you can control the following three operations:

1. Turn a layer On or Off
2. Freeze or Thaw in ALL Viewports
3. Lock or Unlock a Layer

4.1 TURN A LAYER ON OR OFF

To turn a layer on or off, choose the **Turn a layer On or Off** toggle icon (bulb). It is also possible to turn the layer on or off by clicking on the **On/Off** toggle icon from the **Layer** drop-down list in the **Layers** toolbar or the **Layers** panel. Turning a layer on or off using the **Layers** panel is shown in Fig. 7.

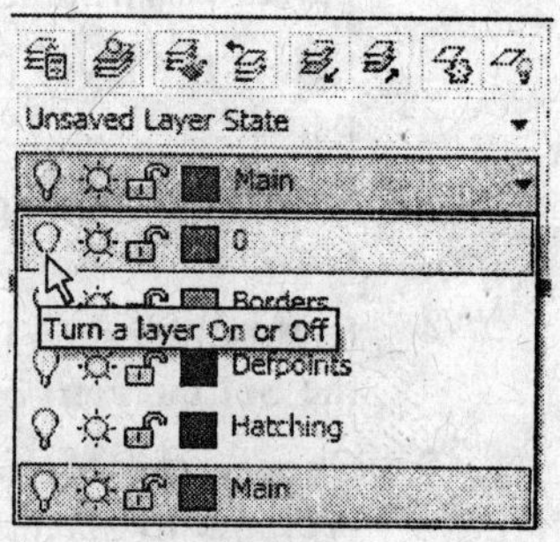

FIG. 7

The objects in the layers that are turned on are displayed and can be plotted. However, the objects in the layers that are turned off are not displayed and cannot be plotted. You can perform the operations such as drawing and editing of the objects in the layer that has been turned off.

The current layer can be turned off, but AutoCAD displays a message box informing that the current drawing layer has been turned off.

4.2 FREEZE OR THAW IN ALL VIEWPORTS

Sometimes in an architectural drawing, we may not need some data/drawings to be displayed, so that they are not changed. These types of information or entities can be placed in a particular layer and that layer can be frozen. The entities in the frozen layer cannot be edited. Also, frozen layers are invisible and cannot be plotted.

To freeze a layer, select a layer and choose the **Freeze or thaw in ALL viewports** toggle icon in the **Layer Properties Manager** palette. The current layer cannot be frozen. The **Freeze or thaw in ALL viewports** toggle icon can be selected in the **Layers** panel of the **Ribbon** or in the **Layers** toolbar to freeze or thaw a layer.

The **Thaw** option negates the effect of the **Freeze** option and the frozen layers are restored to normal. The difference between the **Off** option and the **Freeze** option is that the entities in the frozen layer are not regenerated and thus it saves time.

4.3 LOCK OR UNLOCK A LAYER

Sometimes it may be necessary to avoid editing some objects/drawings on a particular layer but still need to have them visible. In such situations, use the **Lock/Unlock** toggle icon to lock the layer. However, objects in the locked layer can be used for **Object Snaps** and inquiry commands.

Also, the locked layer can be set as the current layer and objects can be drawn on it. It is also possible to plot a locked layer. The **Unlock** option negates the **Lock** option and allows the user to edit objects on the layers that were previously locked.

5. CONTROLLING DEFAULT PROPERTIES OF LAYERS

By default, all the layers have some properties such as **Color, Linetype, Lineweight**, etc. These properties can be changed when required.

5.1 ASSIGNING COLOR TO A LAYER

To assign a color to a layer, choose the **Color** swatch in that layer in the **Layer Properties Manager** palette. The **Select Color** dialog box will be displayed. In this dialog box, select any one of the colors available and then click **OK** button to return to the **Layer Properties Manager** palette. The selected color is assigned to the layer.

5.2 ASSIGNING LINETYPE TO A LAYER

By default, all the layers have a **Linetype Continues.** To assign a new **Linetype** to a layer, click on the **Linetype** column of the required layer in the **Layer Properties Manager** palette. The **Select Linetype** dialog box is displayed.

The **Select Linetype** dialog box is shown in Fig. 8. In this dialog box, select a **Linetype** and then click **OK** button to return to the **Layer Properties Manager** palette. The selected linetype is assigned to the layer.

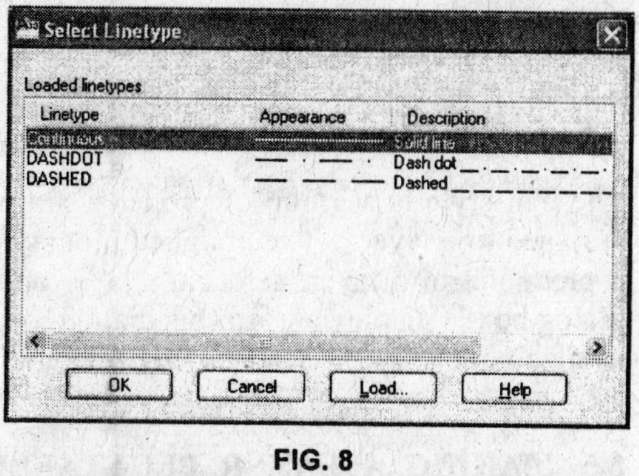

FIG. 8

If the **Select Linetype** dialog box is opened for the first time, only the **Continuous** linetype is displayed. User needs to load linetypes and then assign them to layers.

To load linetypes, choose the **Load** button in the **Select Linetype** dialog box. The **Load or Reload Linetypes** dialog box is displayed as shown in Fig. 9.

The **Load or Reload Linetypes** dialog box displays all linetypes in the *acadiso.lin* file. Select a line type in this dialog box. A number of linetypes can be selected by pressing and holding the SHIFT or CTRL key and then selecting the linetypes.

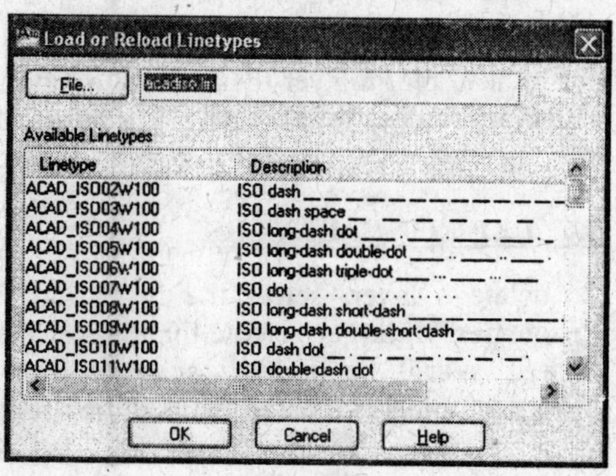

FIG. 9

After selecting the linetypes, choose the **OK** button. The selected linetypes are loaded in the **Select Linetype** dialog box. Now, select the desired linetype and choose **OK** button to return to the **Layer Properties Manager** palette. The selected linetype is assigned to the selected layer.

5.3 ASSIGNING LINEWEIGHT TO A LAYER

A **Lineweight** is used to give thickness to objects. For example, in Engineering Drawing, the objects such as Prism, Cube, etc., are drawn with a larger value of lineweight. However, the lines such as construction lines, dimension lines, etc., are drawn with a lesser value of lineweight.

As the **Linetype**, all the layers have a default **Lineweight**. To assign a new **Lineweight** of a layer, click the **Lineweight** column of the required layer to display the **Lineweight** dialog box. The **Lineweight** dialog box is shown in Fig. 10.

In this dialog box, select a **Lineweight** and then click **OK** button to return to the **Layer Properties Manager** palette.

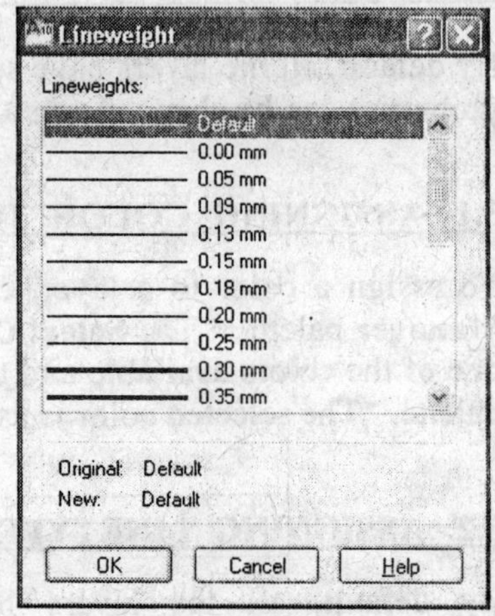

FIG. 10

5.4 ASSIGNING PLOT STYLE TO A LAYER

The plot style is a group of property settings such as color, linetype and lineweight that can be assigned to a layer. The assigned plot style affects the drawings while plotting only. To assign a plot style to a layer, select the layer and then click on its plot style. The **Select Plot Style** dialog box is displayed. In this dialog box, select a specific plot style from the **Plot styles** list of available plot styles. Choose **OK** button to return to the **Layer Properties Manager**.

5.5 MAKING A LAYER PLOTTABLE OR NON-PLOTTABLE

By default, all the layers are plotted, except the layers that are turned off or frozen. If user does not want to plot a layer that is not turned off or frozen, select the layer and choose the **Plot** icon. The **Plot** icon is a toggle icon. Therefore, user can choose this icon again to plot the layer.

5.6 DELETING LAYERS

To delete a layer, select the layer and then choose the **Delete Layer** button in the **Layer Properties Manager**. Note that a layer that contains any object cannot be deleted. Also, layers such as layer 0, Defpoints, Ashade, current layer and an Xref-dependent layer cannot be deleted. Layer Defpoints is created while dimensioning. Layer Ashade is created while rendering.

6. CAD EXERCISES - Step-by-Step Solutions

Example 1: *Fig. 11 shows an engineering object. In this object, the following elements are present:*

1. Object Lines (Continuous Wide Lines)
2. Hidden Lines (Dashed Lines)
3. Center Lines (Dashdot Lines)

Before start drawing lines, it is necessary to create layers and assign colors, linetypes and lineweight. Therefore, first set up three layers with the linetypes, lineweights and colors as shown in Table 1.

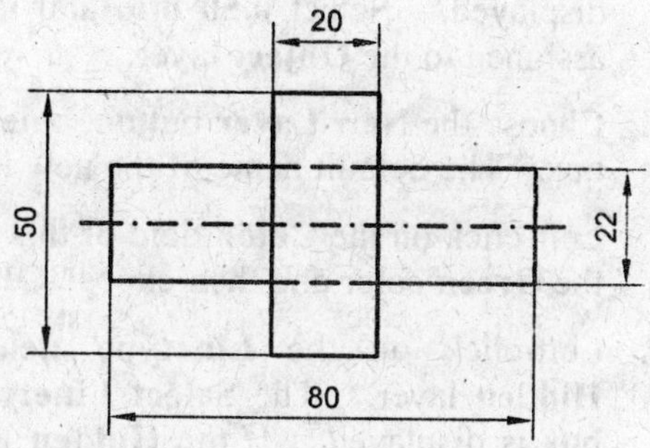

FIG. 11

Name of Layer	Color	Linetype	Lineweight
Object	Red	Continuous	0.50 mm
Hidden	Green	Hidden	0.30 mm
Center	Blue	Center	0.25 mm

Table 1

Depending on the object that you want to draw, you need to set a layer as the current layer. Here, create layers by using the **Layer Properties Manager** palette. Use the **Layer** drop-down list in the **Layers** panel to set a layer as the current layer and then draw the figure. The steps to draw the figure are:

1. In the above figure, the lineweights specified are in millimeters. Therefore, first change the units if they are in inches.

   For this, invoke the **Lineweight Settings** dialog box by right-clicking on the **Show/Hide Lineweight** button on the **Status Bar** and then choose the **Settings** option from the shortcut menu.

   Select the **Millimeters (mm)** radio button in the **Units for Listing** area of the dialog box and then choose the **OK** button. See Fig. 12.

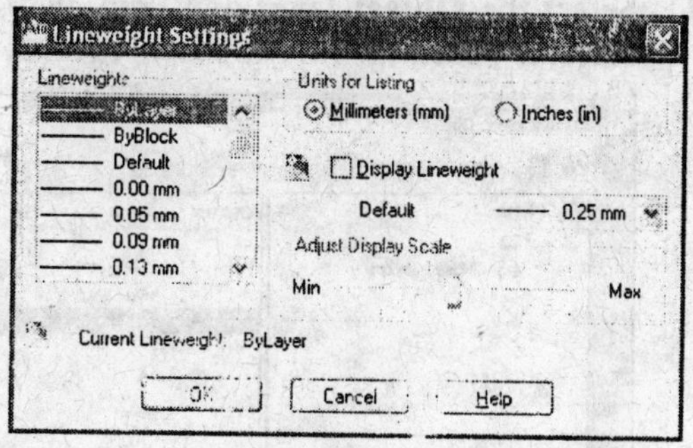

FIG. 12

2. Choose the **Layer Properties** button from the **Layers** panel in the **Home** tab of the **Ribbon** to display the **Layer Properties Manager** palette. The layer **0** with the default properties is displayed in the list box.
3. Choose the **New Layer** button, a new layer with the default properties is displayed in the list box. The default name of the new layer is **Layer1**. Change the default name to **Object**.

4. Left-click on the **Color** field of this layer. The **Select Color** dialog box is displayed. Select the **Red** color and then choose **OK** button. The **Red** color is assigned to the **Object** layer.

5. Left-click on the **Lineweight** field of the **Object** layer. The **Lineweight** dialog box is displayed. Select **0.50 mm** and then choose the **OK** button. The selected lineweight is assigned to the **Object** layer.

6. Choose the **New Layer** button, a new layer with the default properties is displayed in the list box. The default name of the new layer is **Layer1**. Change the default name to **Hidden**.

7. Left-click on the **Color** field of this layer. The **Select Color** dialog box is displayed. Select the **Green** color and then choose **OK** button. **Green** color is assigned to the **Hidden** layer.

8. Left-click on the **Linetype** field of the **Hidden** layer. The **Select Linetype** dialog box is displayed. If the **Hidden** linetype is not displayed in the dialog box, choose the **Load** button to display the **Load and Reload Linetypes** dialog box. Select the **HIDDEN** linetype from the list and then choose the **OK** button.

   Now, select **Hidden** linetype from the **Select Linetype** dialog box and then choose **OK** button. The selected linetype is assigned the **Hidden** layer. See Fig. 13.

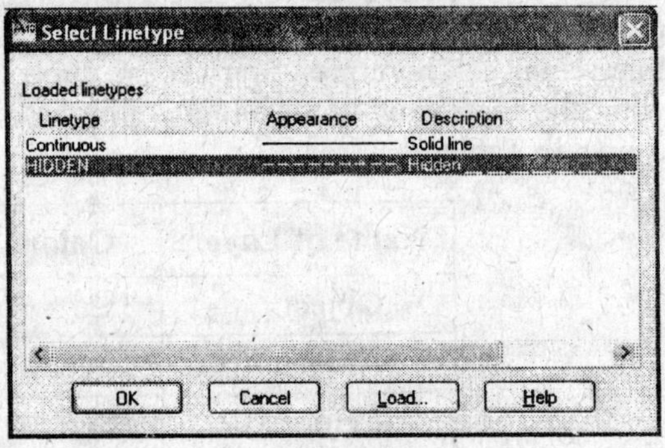

FIG. 13

9. Left-click on the **Lineweight** field of the **Hidden** layer. The **Lineweight** dialog box is displayed. Select **0.30 mm** and then choose the **OK** button. The selected lineweight is assigned to the **Hidden** layer.

10. Similarly, create the new layer **Center** and assign the color **Blue**. Also, for the **Center** layer, assign the **Linetype** as **Center** and assign the **Lineweight** as **0.25 mm**.

11. Select the **Object** layer and then choose the **Set Current** button to make the **Object** layer current. See Fig. 14. It shows the Layer Properties Manager palette with the layers created.

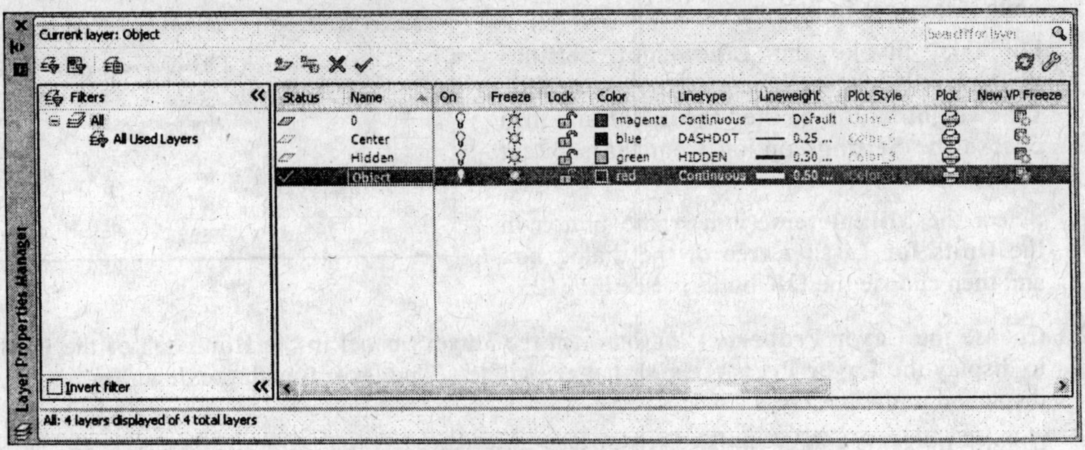

FIG. 14

12. Choose the **Show/Hide Lineweight** button from the **Status Bar** to turn on the display of the lineweights of the lines to be drawn.

13. Choose the **Dynamic Input** button from the **Status Bar** to turn it on.

14. Choose the **Line** tool from the **Draw** panel and draw solid lines in the drawing shown in Fig. 11. Note that a continuous line is drawn in red color. This is because the **Object** layer is the current layer and red color is assigned to it.

15. Click the down arrow in the **Layer** drop-down list available in the **Layers** panel to display the list of layers. Now, select the **Hidden** layer from the list to make it current. See Fig. 15.

16. Using the **Line** tool, draw the two hidden lines. The lines are drawn in **Green** color with hidden linetype.

    If the center line is drawn, the center line is displayed in the **Green** color with **Hidden** linetype. This is because the **Hidden** layer is the current layer.

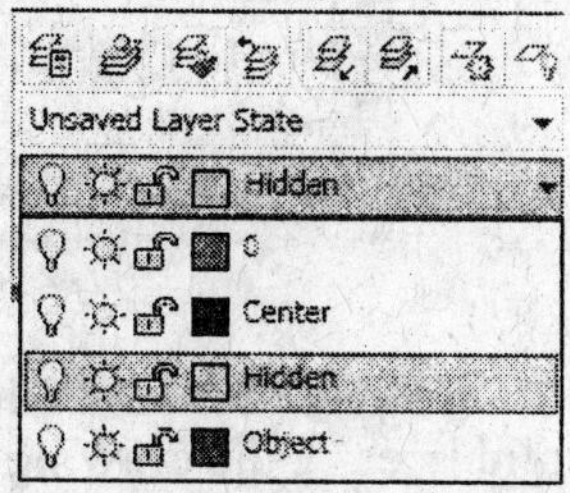

FIG. 15

17. Select the center line and then select the **Center** layer from the **Layer** drop-down list available in the **Layers** panel. The color and line type of the center line is changed. Now, the center line is displayed in **Blue** color and **Center** linetype.

Example 2: Fig. 16 shows the sectional view of an engineering object. In this diagram, the following elements are present:

1. Visible Outlines (Continuous Wide Lines)
2. Hidden Lines (Dashed Lines)
3. Center Lines (Dashdot Lines)
4. Dimension Lines (Continues Thin Lines)
5. Hatching Lines

Now, user can create separate layers for each of the elements. Each layer should have different layer name.

Activate the Layer command to display the **Layer Properties Manager** palette on the screen. Click on the **New** button to display the new layer with a name **Layer 1**. Rename this layer name as **CW Lines.**

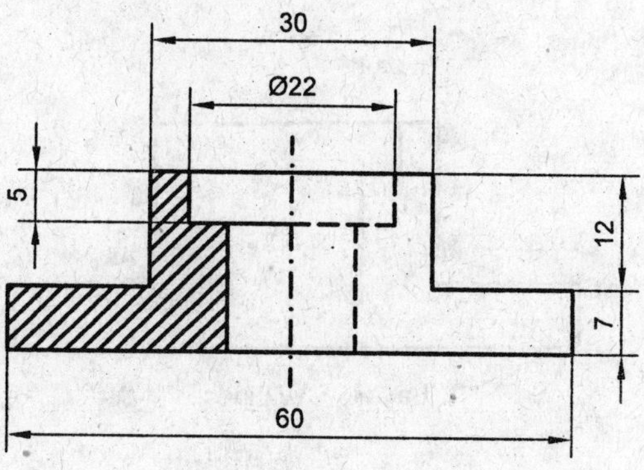

FIG. 16

Similarly, by clicking **New** button, create 4 more layers with the names **Dashdot, Dashed, Dimension** and **Hatching**. As explained in the **Example 1,** assign the necessary color, linetype and lineweight for each of the five layers. The result is shown in Fig. 17.

Choose the **Show/Hide Lineweight** button from the **Status Bar** to turn on the display of the lineweights of the lines to be drawn. Choose the **Dynamic Input** button from the **Status Bar** to turn it on.

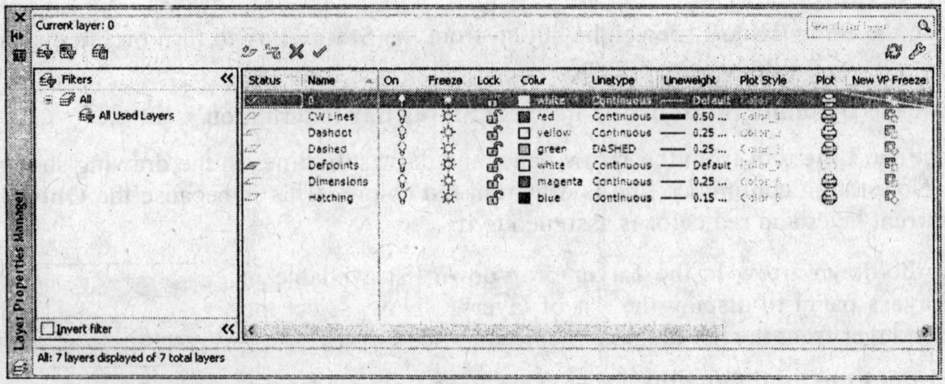

FIG. 17

Make the **CW Lines** layer current. Choose the **Line** tool from the **Draw** panel and draw solid lines in the drawing shown in Fig. 16. Similarly, draw the dashed lines and dashdot lines in the **Dashed** and **Dashdot** layers respectively. Also, draw the dimensions of the drawing in the **Dimensions** layer. Draw hatching lines in the **Hatching** layer.

<u>**Viewing Different Layers :**</u> Fig. 18

The objects drawn in each layer when the other layers are made OFF. For example, to view objects drawn in layer **CW Lines**, turn OFF all the other layers, namely, **Dashdot, Dashed**, **Dimension** and **Hatching**. Similarly, to view objects drawn in one layer, turn off all other layers

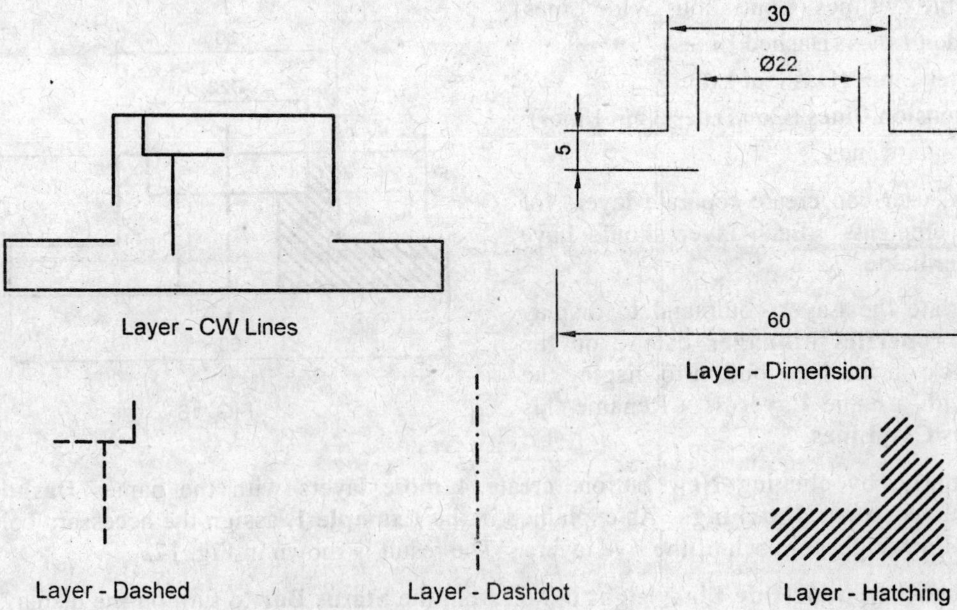

FIG. 18

ANNA UNIVERSITY

CAD LAB EXERCISES

FIG. 1

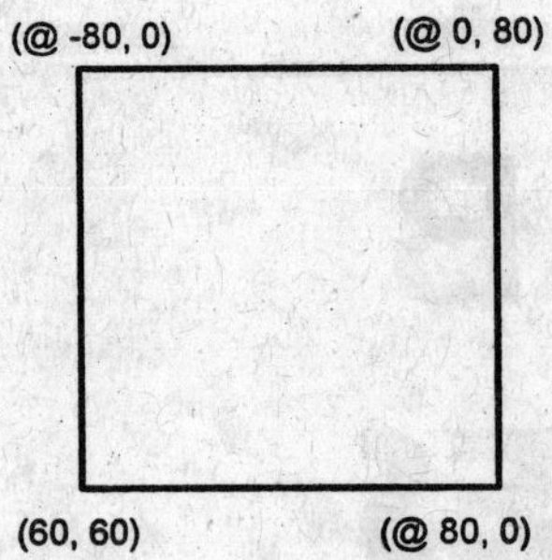

FIG. 2

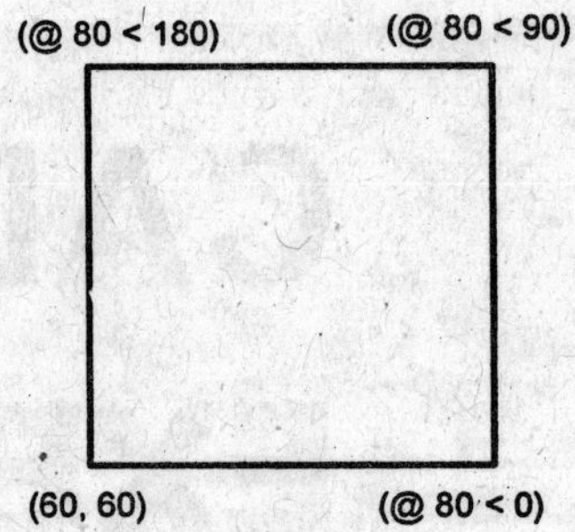

FIG. 3

ROLL No.	A.P.J. ABDUL KALAM
II Sem B.E. (M)	NAME OF THE INSTITUTION
SHEET No.	CO-ORDINATE SYSTEMS
DATE :	

Ex. No. : 1
Date :

Ch. 14 - CO-ORDINATE SYSTEMS

AIM : *To draw Lines using* ***Absolute Co-ordinate System, Relative Rectangular Co-ordinate System*** *and* ***Relative Polar Co-ordinate System*** *using AutoCAD.*

PROCEDURE: *(i) Draw a line on the points (60,60) and (140,60) :* ***See Fig.1.***

Absolute Co-ordinate System (X, Y) : Absolute co-ordinate values are based on the origin (0,0). Use absolute co-ordinate when you know X and Y values of the point from the origin.

```
Command: LINE ↵
Specify first point: 60,60 ↵
Specify next point or [Undo]: 140,60 ↵
Specify next point or [Undo]: ↵
```

(ii) Using **line** *command draw a square of side 80 units :* ***See Fig.2.***

Relative Rectangular Co-ordinate System (@ X distance, Y distance) : Use relative co-ordinates when we know the position of a point with respect to the previous points.

```
Command: LINE ↵
Specify first point: 60,60 ↵
Specify next point or [Undo]: @80,0 ↵
Specify next point or [Undo]: @0,80 ↵
Specify next point or [Undo]: @-80,0 ↵
Specify next point or [Close/Undo]: C ↵
```

Distance is measured +ve towards up and right. It is measured –ve towards down and left.

(iii) Using **line** *command draw a square of side 80 units :* ***See Fig.3.***

Relative Polar Co-ordinate System (@ distance < angle) : Polar co-ordinate system uses a distance and an angle with reference to the previous point to locate a point. Angles are measured in anti-clockwise direction, taking 0° towards right.

```
Command: LINE ↵
Specify first point: 60,60 ↵
Specify next point or [Undo]: @80<0 ↵
Specify next point or [Undo]: @80<90 ↵
Specify next point or [Undo]: @80<180 ↵
Specify next point or [Close/Undo]: C ↵
```

Undo means ***nullify.*** After drawing a line, say, we realize that we have made an error. We can remove line using `Undo` option. If we need to remove more than one line, we can use this option any number of times. We can either type `Undo` or just `U` at the **Specify next point or [Undo]:** prompt.

Ex. No. : 2 Date :	**CREATION of POLYGONS**

AIM

*Create a Regular Polygon of any number of sides, given the length of its side or edge equal to 25 mm, using CAD Software : **See Fig.1.***

COMMANDS USED : Snap, Grid, Limits, Polygon and Dimlinear.

PROCEDURE :

STEP 1 : Start the **AutoCAD** Software. Open and setup a new drawing sheet to A4 size.

STEP 2 : Limit Setting

Command : **LIMITS**

Specify lower left corner or [ON/OFF] <0.0000,0.0000> :
0.0

Specify upper right corner <420.0000,297.0000> : 100,100

Command : **ZOOM**

[All/Center/Dynamic/Extents/Previous/Scale/Window/Object] <real time> : All

STEP 3 : Draw a line of 25 mm length using the LINE command. Name it as AB using the TEXT command.

STEP 4 : Draw the polygons using the POLYGON command and Edge option and specifying the number of sides as 4, 5, 6, 7 & 8 as shown in Fig. 1.

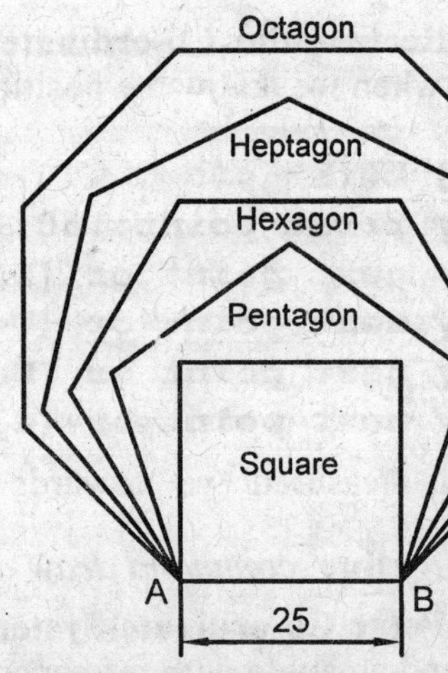

FIG. 1

Command: **POLYGON (Square)**

```
Enter number of sides <4>                 : 4
Specify center of polygon or[Edge]        : E ↵
Specify first endpoint of  Edge           : Pick point A
Specify second endpoint of  Edge          : Pick point B
```

Command: **POLYGON (Pentagon)**

```
Enter number of sides <4>                 : 5
Specify center of polygon or[Edge]        : E ↵
Specify first endpoint of  Edge           : Pick point A
```

```
Specify second endpoint of  Edge      : Pick point B
```

Command: **POLYGON (Hexagon)**

```
Enter number of sides <4>             : 6
Specify center of polygon or[Edge]    : E ↵
Specify first endpoint of  Edge       : Pick point A
Specify second endpoint of  Edge      : Pick point B
```

Command: **POLYGON (Heptagon)**

```
Enter number of sides <4>             : 7
Specify center of polygon or[Edge]    : E ↵
Specify first endpoint of  Edge       : Pick point A
Specify second endpoint of  Edge      : Pick point B
```

Command: **POLYGON (Octagon)**

```
Enter number of sides <4>             : 8
Specify center of polygon or[Edge]    : E ↵
Specify first endpoint of  Edge       : Pick point A
Specify second endpoint of  Edge      : Pick point B
```

STEP 5: Using the TEXT command, name the polygons as Square, Pentagon, Hexagon, Heptagon and Octagon.

Command : **TEXT**

```
Current text style:  "Standard"  Text height      : 2.5
Specify start point of text or [Justify/Style]  :
Specify rotation angle of text <0>                : 0
```

STEP 6 : Mark the dimension using the DIMLINEAR or DLI command.

Command : **DIMLINEAR ↵**

```
Specify first extension line origin or <select object> : (Pick A)
Specify second extension line origin                   : (Pick B)
Specify dimension line location or [Mtest/Text/Angle/Horizontal
/Vertical/ Rotated]          : (Select C to locate the position of dimension)
Dimension text =  25
```

Ex. No. : 3 Date :	MULTI - LINE FIGURES

*AIM: To draw the diagram shown in **Fig. 1** using Rectangle, Line, Circle and Arc commands.*

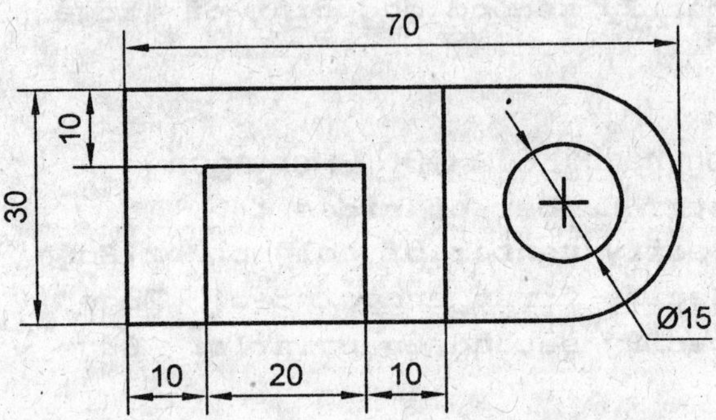

FIG. 1

The procedure and command sequence to draw the diagram shown in **Fig. 1** is given below:

COMMANDS USED : Snap, Grid, Limits, Rectangle, Arc and Dimlinear.

PROCEDURE :

STEP 1 : First draw the outer rectangle using the **Rectang** command. The command sequence is given below: ***(See Fig.2)***

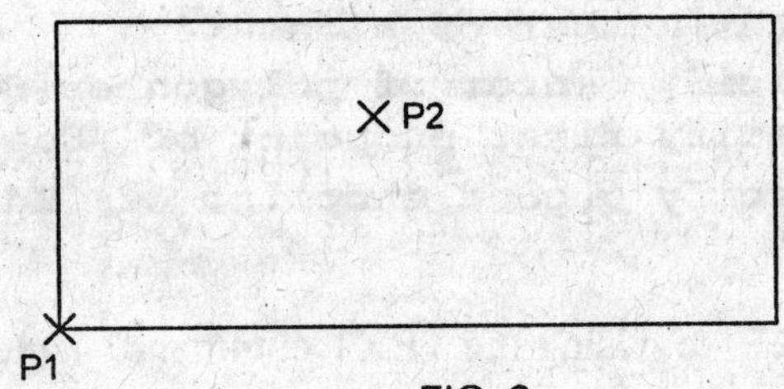

FIG. 2

Command: RECTANG ↵

```
Specify first corner point or
    [Chamfer/Elevation/Fillet/Thickness/Width]: (Pick P1)
Specify other corner point or [Area/Dimensions/Rotation]:D↵
Specify length for rectangles <10.0000>: 70 ↵
Specify width for rectangles <10.0000> : 30 ↵
Specify other corner point or [Area/Dimensions/Rotation]:(PickP2)
```

STEP 2 : Draw the arc using the Arc command and move the drawn arc to the correct position. The command sequence is given below: ***(See Fig. 3)***

Command: **ARC** ↵

```
Specify start point of arc or [Center]: C ↵
Specify center point of arc: (Pick P1)
Specify start point of arc: (Pick P2)
Specify end point of arc or [Angle/chord Length]: (Pick P3)
```

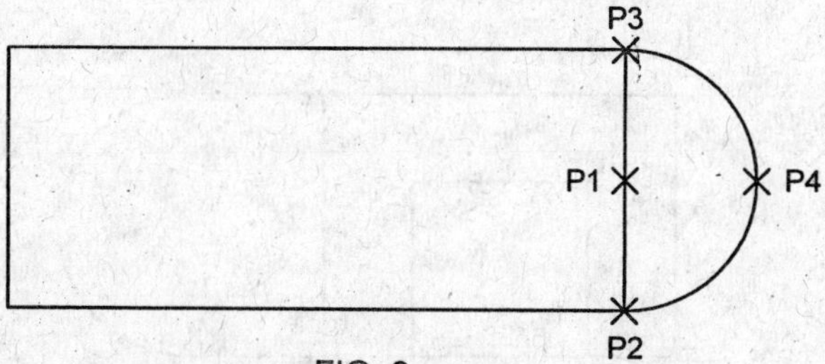

FIG. 3

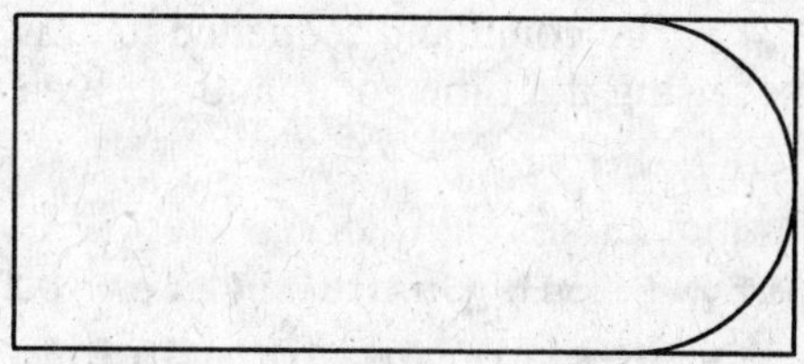

FIG. 4

Command: **MOVE** ↵

```
Select objects: (Select the Arc) 1 found
Select objects: ↵
Specify base point or [Displacement]<Displacement>:(Pick P4)
Specify second point or<use first point as displacement>:(Pick
P1)
```

See Fig. 4.

STEP 3

Command sequence to trim unwanted line segments using the Trim command is given below:

Command: **TRIM** ↵

```
Current settings: Projection=UCS, Edge=None
Select cutting edges ...
Select objects or <select all>:  (Select the arc) 1 found
Select objects: ↵
Select object to trim or shift-select to extend or
   [Fence/Crossing/Project/Edge/eRase/Undo]: (Pick P1)
Select object to trim or shift-select to extend or
   [Fence/Crossing/Project/Edge/eRase/Undo]: (Pick P2)
Select object to trim or shift-select to extend or
   [Fence/Crossing/Project/Edge/eRase/Undo]: ↵
```

See Fig. 5.

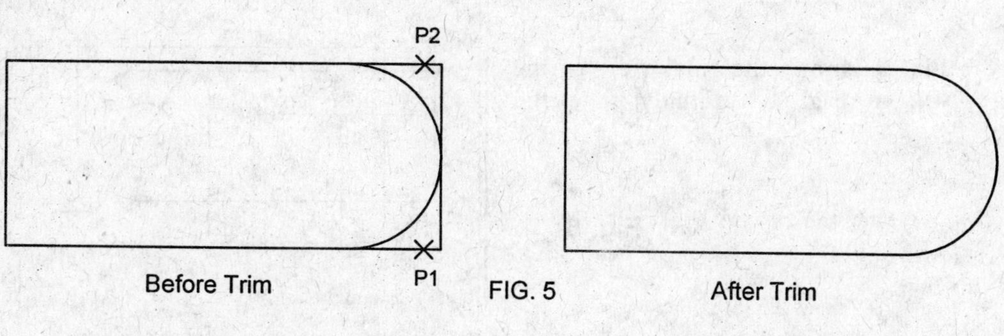

FIG. 5

STEP 4 : The command sequence to draw the lines using the Line command is given below:

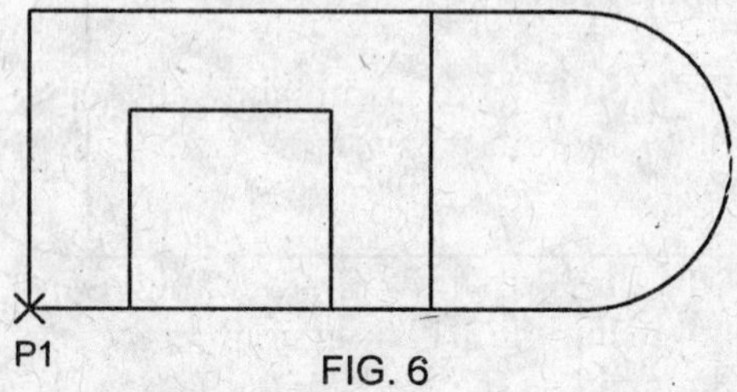

FIG. 6

Command: **LINE** ↵
Specify first point: (*Pick P1*)
Specify next point or [Undo]:
(*Move the cursor to right*) 10↵
Specify next point or [Undo]:
(*Move the cursor to up*) 20↵
Specify next point or [Close/Undo]: (*Move the cursor to right*) 20 ↵
Specify next point or [Close/Undo]: (*Move the cursor to down*) 20 ↵
Specify next point or [Close/Undo]: (*Move the cursor to right*) 10 ↵
Specify next point or [Close/Undo]: (*Move the cursor to up*) 30 ↵
Specify next point or [Close/Undo]: ↵
See Fig. 6.

STEP 5 : Mark the center of the arc using the **Dimcenter** command. With this point as the center point, draw a circle of diameter 15 mm using the **Circle** command. The command sequence is given below:

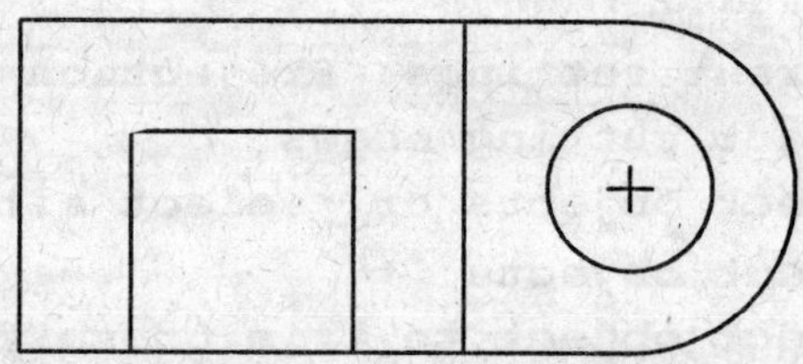

FIG. 7

Command: **DIMCENTER** ↵
Select arc or circle: (*Select the arc*)
Command: CIRCLE ↵
Specify center point for circle or [3P/2P/Ttr (tan tan radius)]:
Specify radius of circle or [Diameter] <15.00>: D ↵
Specify diameter of circle
<30.00>: 15 ↵

See Fig. 7.

STEP 6 : Fig. 8 shows the final view of the diagram given in **Fig. 1**. Finally save the drawing.

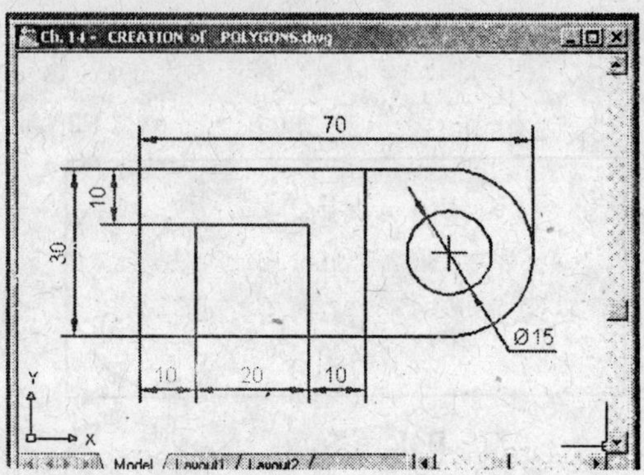

Fig. 8

Ex. No. : 4 *To draw the diagram shown in* ***Fig. 1*** *using the Rectang, Line, Circle and Arc commands.*

The procedure and command sequence to draw the diagram shown in **Fig. 1** is given below:

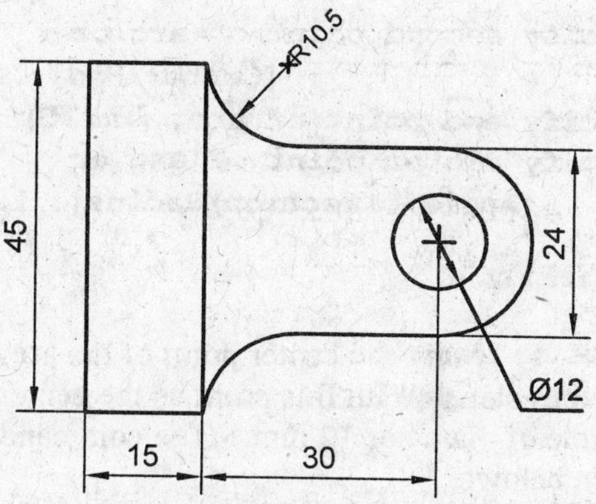

FIG. 1

STEP 1 : First draw the first rectangle of the diagram using the **Rectang** command. The command sequence is given below:

```
Command: RECTANG ↵
Specify first corner point or
   [Chamfer/Elevation/Fillet/
   Thickness/Width]: (Pick P1)
Specify other corner point or
   [Area/Dimensions/Rotation]:D ↵
Specify length for rectangles
        <10.0000>: 15 ↵
Specify width for rectangles
        <10.0000>: 45 ↵
Specify other corner point
   or [Area/Dimensions/
   Rotation]: (Pick P2)
```

See Fig. 2.

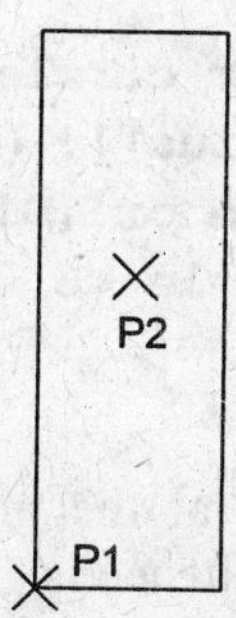

FIG. 2

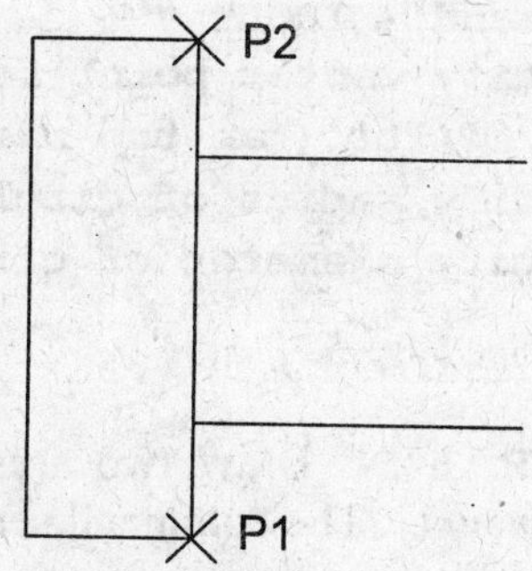

FIG. 3

STEP 2 : Draw the lines using the Line command. The command sequence is given below:

```
Command: LINE ↵
Specify first point: (Pick P1)
Specify next point or [Undo]:
   <Ortho on> (Move the cursor up) 10.5 ↵
Specify next point or [Undo]:
   (Move the cursor right) 30 ↵
Specify next point or [Close/Undo]: ↵
Command: LINE ↵
Specify first point: (Pick P2)
Specify next point or [Undo]: (Move the cursor down) 10.5 ↵
Specify next point or [Undo]: (Move the cursor right) 30 ↵
Specify next point or [Close/Undo]: ↵
```

See Fig. 3.

STEP 3 : Draw an arc joining the above two lines

using the Arc command. The command sequence is given below:

Command: **ARC** ↵
Specify start point of arc or [Center]: *(Pick P1)*
Specify second point of arc or [Center/End]: E ↵
Specify end point of arc: *(Pick P2)*
Specify center point of arc or [Angle/Direction/Radius]: 12 ↵

See Fig. 4.

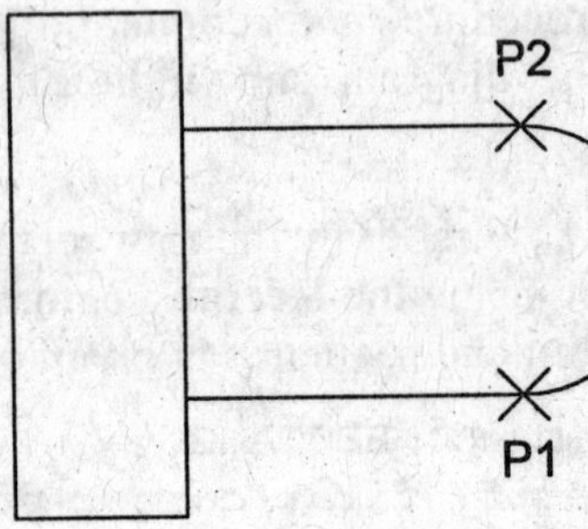

FIG. 4

STEP 4 : Mark the center point of the arc drawn in the previous step. With this point as the center point, draw a circle of diameter 12 mm. The command sequence is given below:

Command: **DIMCENTER** ↵
Select arc or circle: *(Select the arc)*

Command: CIRCLE ↵
Specify center point for circle or [3P/2P/Ttr (tan tan radius)]: *(Pick the center point)*
Specify radius of circle or [Diameter]<4>:D↵
Specify diameter of circle <8.0000>: 12 ↵

See Fig. 5.

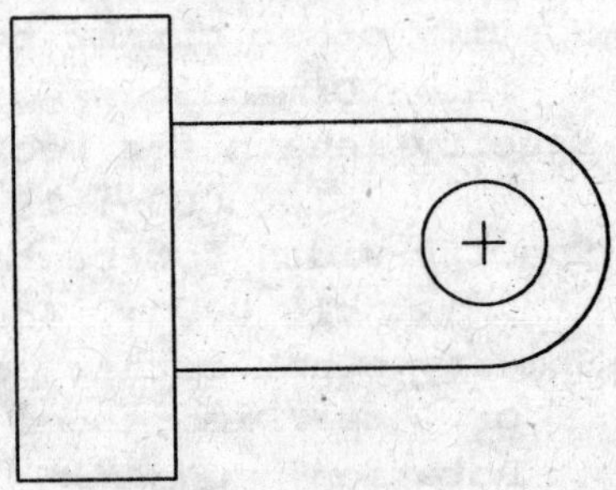

FIG. 5

STEP 5 : Draw two arcs at the meeting point of the rectangle and lines using the Arc command. The command sequence is given below:

Command: **ARC** ↵
Specify start point of arc or [Center]: *(Pick P1)*
Specify second point of arc or [Center/End]: C ↵
Specify center point of arc:
<Ortho on> *(Move the cursor to right)*
10.5 ↵
Specify end point of arc or [Angle/chord Length]:
(Move the cursor to down and Pick P2)

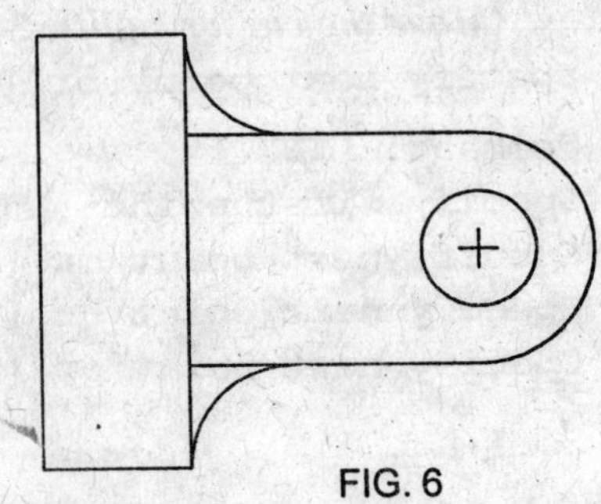

FIG. 6

Command: **LINE** ↵
Specify first point: *(Pick P3)*

Specify next point or [Undo]: 10.5 ↵
Specify next point or [Undo]: ↵

Command: ARC ↵
Specify start point of arc or [Center]: (*Pick the end point of the above line*)
Specify second point of arc or [Center/End]: C ↵
Specify center point of arc: <Ortho on> (*Move the cursor to down*) 10.5 ↵
Specify end point of arc or [Angle/chord Length]: (*Pick P4*)

See Fig. 6.

STEP 6 : Trim the unwanted lines using the Trim command. The details about the Trim command are explained later. Command sequence is given below:

Command: TRIM ↵
Current settings: Projection=UCS, Edge=None
Select cutting edges ...
Select objects or <select all>:
(*Select Arc-1*) 1 found
Select objects: (*Select Arc-2*) 1 found, 2 total
Select objects: ↵
Select object to trim or shift-select to extend or [Fence/Crossing/Project/Edge/eRase/Undo]: (*Select L1*)
Select object to trim or shift-select to extend or [Fence/Crossing/Project/Edge/eRase/Undo]: (*Select L2*)
Select object to trim or shift-select to extend or [Fence/Crossing/Project/Edge/eRase/Undo]: ↵

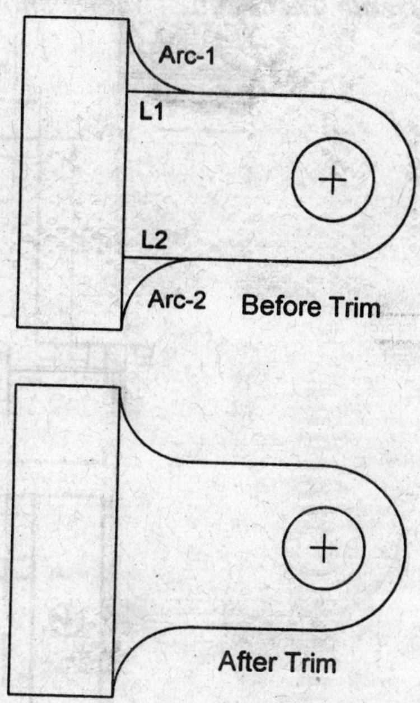

FIG. 7

See Fig. 7.

STEP 7 : Select the lines to darken and click the **Lineweight control** option on the **Properties** tool bar and choose the required line thickness.

STEP 8 : Mark dimensions using the **Dimlinear**, **Dimradius** and **dimdiameter** commands.

Fig. 8 shows the final view of the diagram given in **Fig. 1**. Finally save the drawing.

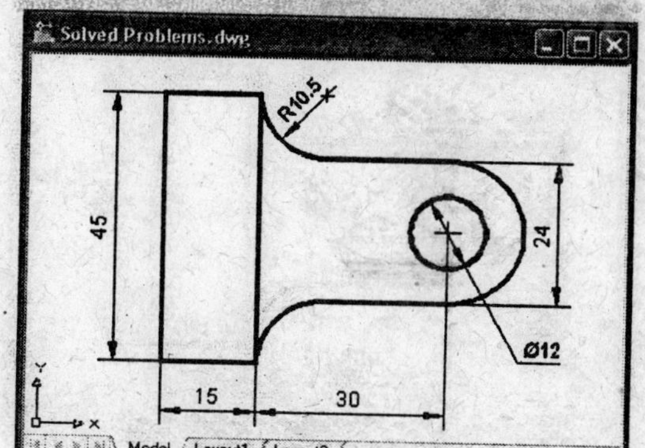

FIG. 8

EX. No. : 5

Create the Multi - Views shown in ***Fig.1*** *below, using CAD Software.*

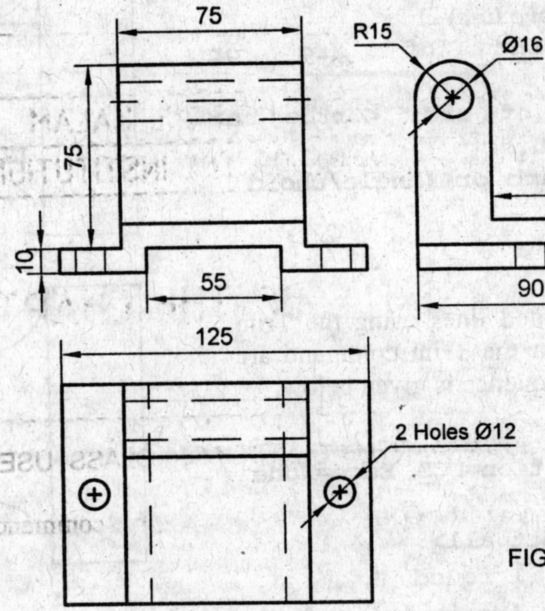

FIG. 1

Ex. No. : 1
Date :

Ch.15 - TITLE BLOCK

AIM : *To draw the Suggested Title Block for the Class Use shown in Fig.1.*

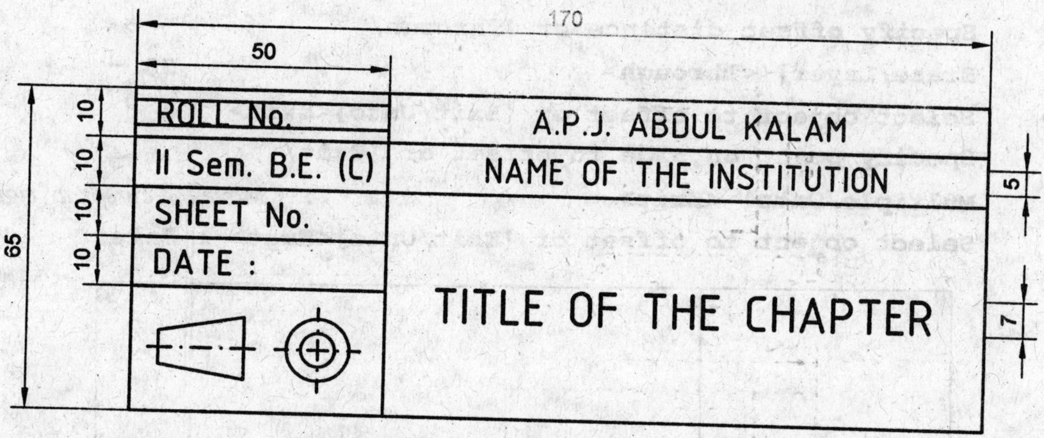

FIG. 1 SUGGESTED TITLE BLOCK FOR CLASS USE

STEP 1 : Command sequence to draw the Outer Line using the **Line** command : (**Fig.2**)

Command : **LINE**

Specify first point : *0*
Specify next point or [Undo] : < Ortho on > ↵
(*Move the cursor to right*) 170↵
Specify next point or [Undo] :
(*Move the cursor to up*) 65 ↵
Specify next point or [Undo] :
(*Move the cursor to left*) 170↵
Specify next point or [Undo] :
(*Move the cursor to down*) 65↵

FIG. 2

STEP 2 : Command sequence to modify the line using the **Offset** command : (**Fig.3**)

Command : **OFFSET**

```
Current settings: Erase source = No
Layer=Source OFFSETGAPTYPE=0
Specify offset distance or [Through/
Erase/Layer] <Through>                              : 50 ↵
Select object to offset or [Exit/Unto]<Exit> : A ↵
Specify point on side to offset or [Exit/
Multiple/Unto] <Exit>                       : (Move the cursor to right) ↵
Select object to offset or [Exit/Unto]<Exit> : Enter
```

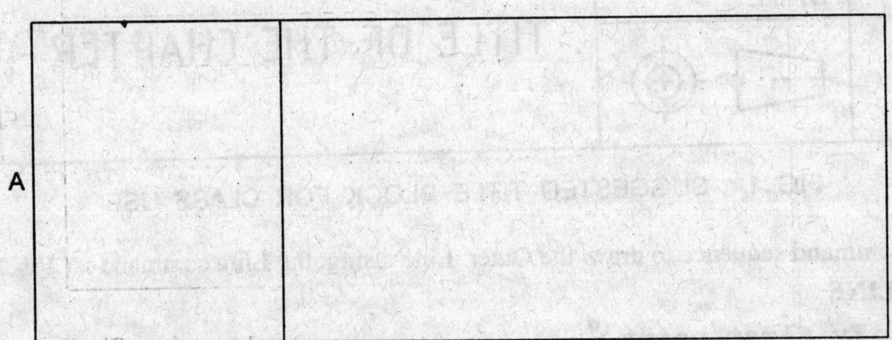

FIG. 3

STEP 3 : Command sequence to modify the line using the **Offset** command : (**Fig.4**)

Command : **OFFSET**

```
Current settings: Erase source = No
Layer=Source OFFSETGAPTYPE=0
Specify offset distance or [Through/
Erase/Layer] <Through>                              : 10 ↵
Select object to offset or [Exit/Unto]<Exit> : B ↵
```

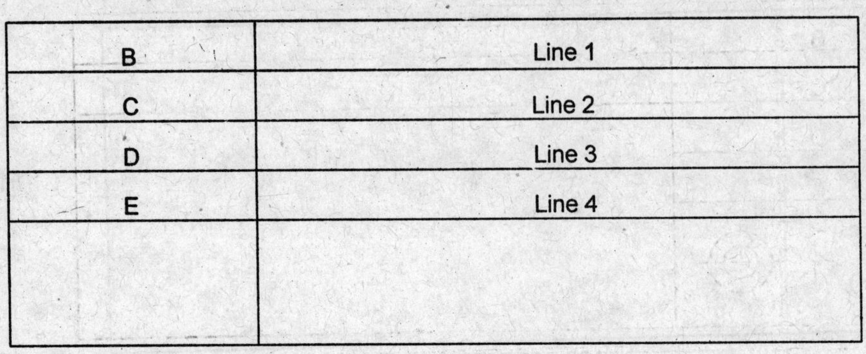

FIG. 4

Specify point on side to offset or [Exit/
Multiple/Unto] <Exit> : (*Move the cursor to down*)↵
Select object to offset or [Exit/Unto]<Exit> : **Enter**

Similarly, give Command Sequence to modify C,D and E as in : Fig.4, using ***Offset*** *command.*

STEP 4 : Then erase unnecessary lines using **Erase** command. Command sequence is: **(Fig.5)**

Command : **ERASE**

Select objects : (*Select Line 3*) **1 found**↵
Select objects : (*Select Line 4*) **1 found, 2 total**↵
Select objects : ↵

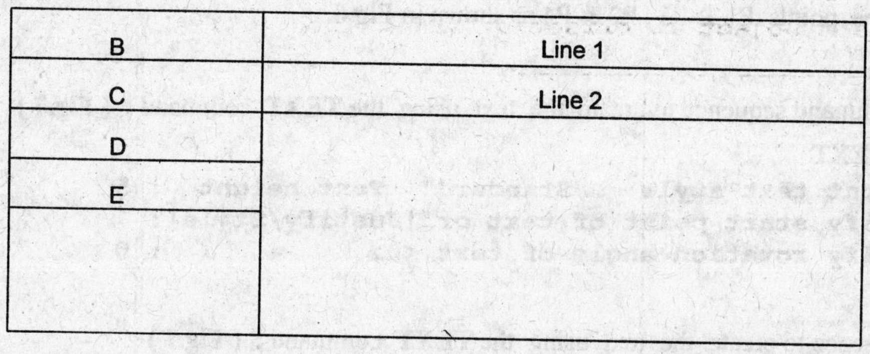

FIG. 5

STEP 5 : Command sequence to create **First Angle Projection Symbol** using **Circle and Line** commands : (**Fig.6**)

Command : **CIRCLE**

Specify center point for circle or
[3P/2P/Ttr (tan tan radius)] :
Specify radius of circle or [Diameter]: D
Specify diameter of circle : 8

Command : **CIRCLE**

Specify center point for circle or

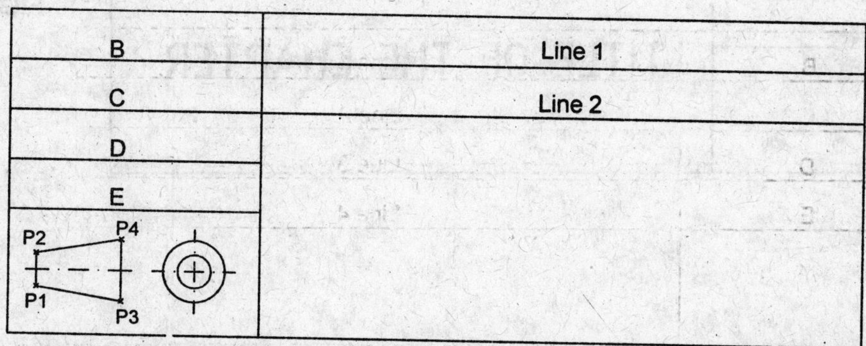

FIG. 6

[3P/2P/Ttr (tan tan radius)] :
Specify radius of circle or [Diameter] : D
Specify diameter of circle : 4

Command : **LINE**

Specify first point : (*Pick P1*)
Specify next point or [Undo] :
(*Move the cursor to up*) 4↵

Specify first point : (*Pick P3*)
Specify next point or [Undo] :
(*Move the cursor to up*) 8↵

Join the points P1 & P3 , P2 & P4 as shown in **Fig.6.**

STEP 6 : Command sequence to create the text using the **TEXT** command : **(Fig.7)**

Command : **TEXT**

Current text style: "Standard" Text height : 5
Specify start point of text or [Justify/Style] :
Specify rotation angle of text <0> : 0

Command sequence to create the text using the **TEXT** command : **(Fig.7)**

Command : **TEXT : (TITLE OF THE CHAPTER)**

Current text style: "Standard" Text height : 7
Specify start point of text or [Justify/Style] :
Specify rotation angle of text <0> : 0

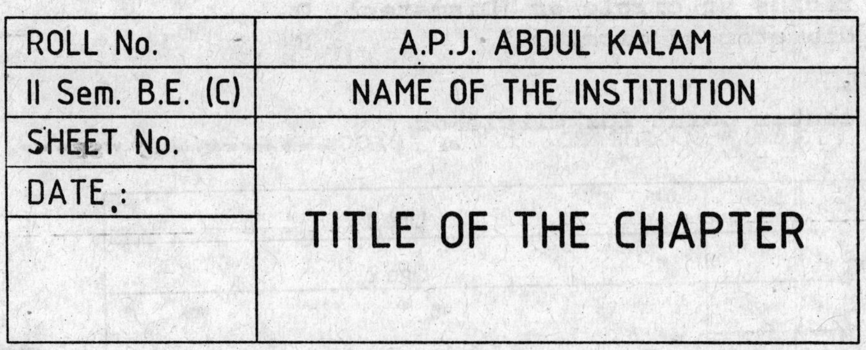

FIG.7

Mark the dimensions using the options available in the **Dimension** menu, or using the **dimlinear** or **dimaligned** commands : **(Fig.8)**

Command : **DIMLINEAR**

Specify first extension line origin or : Pick the two points, say, line points X and Y, drag and left click by mouse.

Note: ***Similarly, mark other dimensions of the given Title Block.***

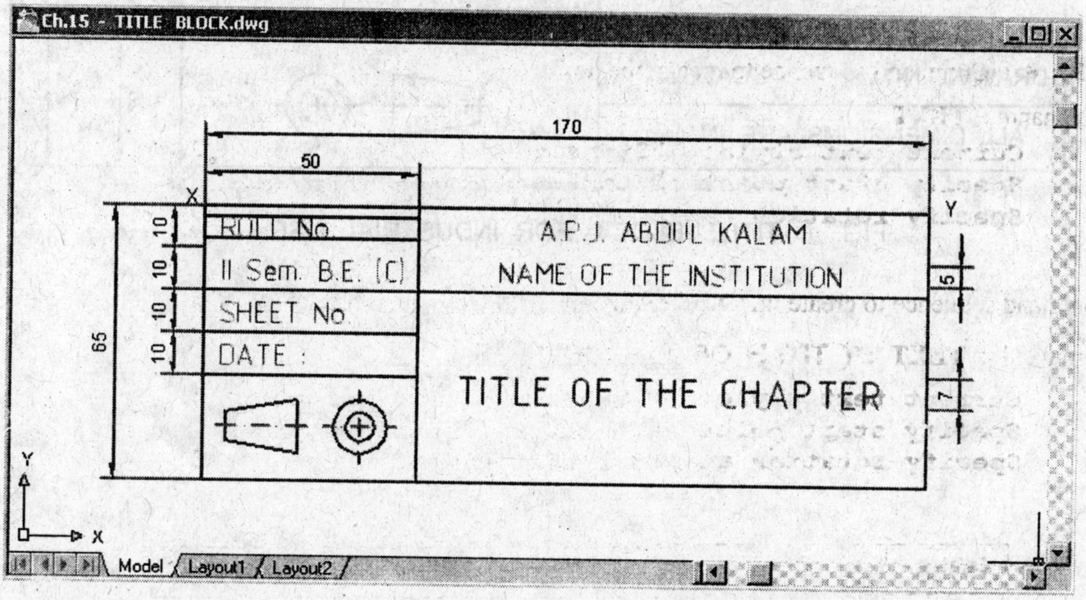

FIG. 8 SUGGESTED TITLE BLOCK FOR CLASS USE

<u>Ex. No. : 2</u> - *Create the Title Block shown in Fig.1, using Auto CAD.*

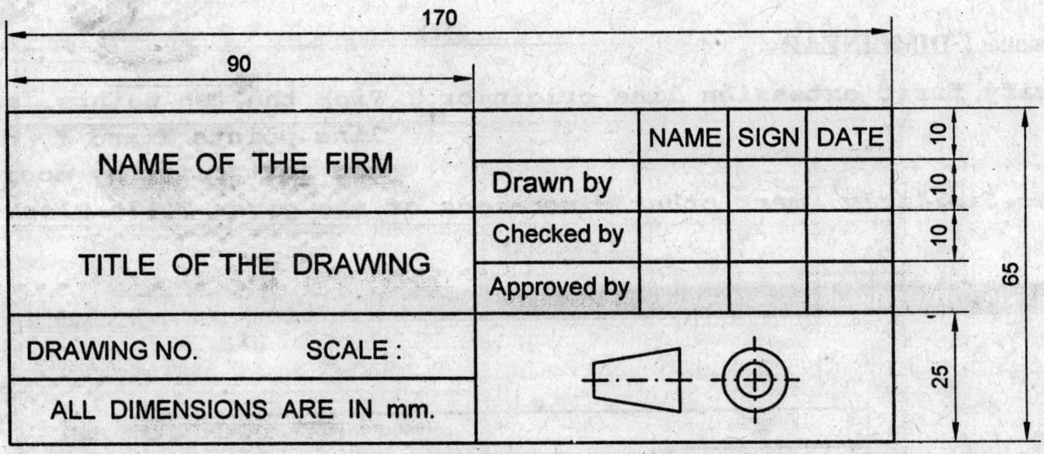

FIG. 1 TITLE BLOCK FOR INDUSTRIAL USE

Ex. No. : 1 Date :	*Ch.16* - **PARABOLA and SPIRAL CURVES**

<u>Ex. No. : 1</u>

AIM : *To draw a Parabola using Spline Command.*

Command : **SPLINE** (***See Fig . 1)***

```
Specify first point or [Object]: Pick  P1
Specify next point     : Pick P2
Specify next point or [Close/Fit tolerance]
<start tangent>        : Pick P3
Specify next point or [Close/Fit tolerance]
<start tangent>        : Pick P4
Specify next point or [Close/Fit tolerance]
<start tangent>        : Pick P5
Specify next point or [Close/Fit tolerance] <start tangent> : Enter
Specify start tangent : Enter
Specify end tangent   : Enter
```

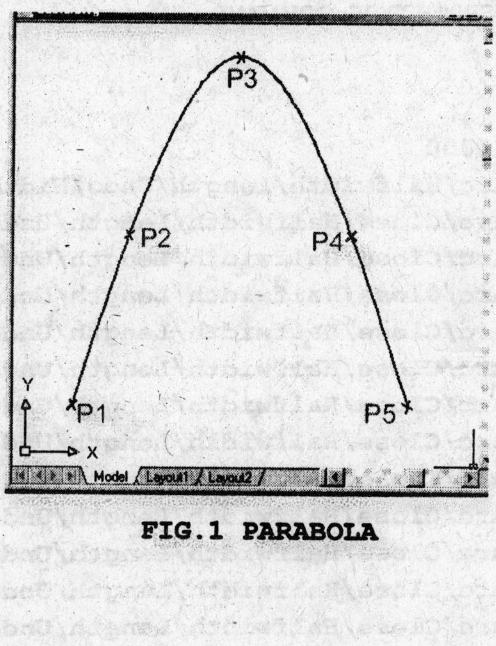

FIG.1 PARABOLA

Ex. No. : 2 - *To draw a Spiral Curve using B-Spline or Cubic Spline Command.*

STEP 1

Command : **SPLINETYPE** *(See Fig . 2)*

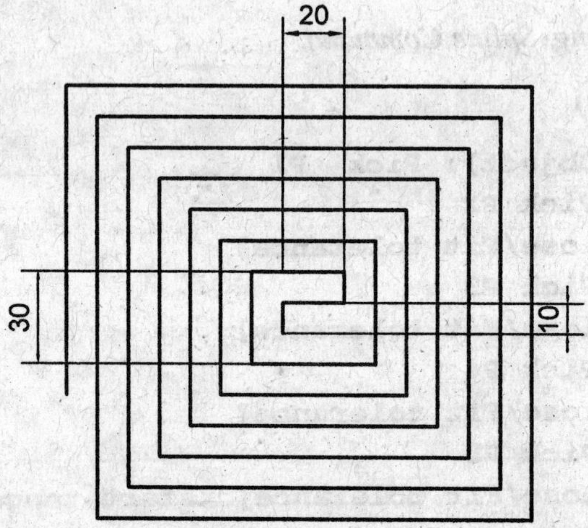

FIG.2

STEP - 1 SPIRAL using

SPLINETYPE COMMAND

```
Specify start point              :
Current line-width is 0.0000     :
Specify next point or [Arc/Halfwidth/Length/Undo/Width]        : 10
Specify next point or [Arc/Close/Halfwidth/Length/Undo/Width]  : 20
Specify next point or [Arc/Close/Halfwidth/Length/Undo/Width]  : 10
Specify next point or [Arc/Close/Halfwidth/Length/Undo/Width]  : 30
Specify next point or [Arc/Close/Halfwidth/Length/Undo/Width]  : 30
Specify next point or [Arc/Close/Halfwidth/Length/Undo/Width]  : 40
Specify next point or [Arc/Close/Halfwidth/Length/Undo/Width]  : 40
Specify next point or [Arc/Close/Halfwidth/Length/Undo/Width]  : 50
Specify next point or [Arc/Close/Halfwidth/Length/Undo/Width]  : 50
Specify next point or [Arc/Close/Halfwidth/Length/Undo/Width]  : 60
Specify next point or [Arc/Close/Halfwidth/Length/Undo/Width]  : 60
Specify next point or [Arc/Close/Halfwidth/Length/Undo/Width]  : 70
Specify next point or [Arc/Close/Halfwidth/Length/Undo/Width]  : 70
Specify next point or [Arc/Close/Halfwidth/Length/Undo/Width]  : 80
Specify next point or [Arc/Close/Halfwidth/Length/Undo/Width]  : 80
```

```
Specify next point or [Arc/Close/Halfwidth/Length/Undo/Width] : 90
Specify next point or [Arc/Close/Halfwidth/Length/Undo/Width] : 90
Specify next point or [Arc/Close/Halfwidth/Length/Undo/Width] : 100
Specify next point or [Arc/Close/Halfwidth/Length/Undo/Width] : 100
Specify next point or [Arc/Close/Halfwidth/Length/Undo/Width] : 110
Specify next point or [Arc/Close/Halfwidth/Length/Undo/Width] : 110
Specify next point or [Arc/Close/Halfwidth/Length/Undo/Width] : 120
Specify next point or [Arc/Close/Halfwidth/Length/Undo/Width] : 120
Specify next point or [Arc/Close/Halfwidth/Length/Undo/Width] : 130
Specify next point or [Arc/Close/Halfwidth/Length/Undo/Width] : 130
Specify next point or [Arc/Close/Halfwidth/Length/Undo/Width] :Enter
```

STEP 2 : To set B-Spline or Cubic Spline for creating a Spiral Curve

STEP 2 (a) To draw the B-Spline for creating Spiral Curve *[See Fig. 2 (a)]*

Command : **SPLINETYPE**

Enter new value for SPLINETYPE <6>: 5

Command : **PEDIT**

```
Select polyline or [Multiple]   : Select object (poly line object)
Enter an option [Close/Join/Width/Enter
vertex/Fit/Spline/Decurve/Ltype gen/Undo] :  spline
Enter an option [Open/Join/Width/Enter
vertex/Fit/Spline/Decurve/Ltype gen/Undo] :  enter
```

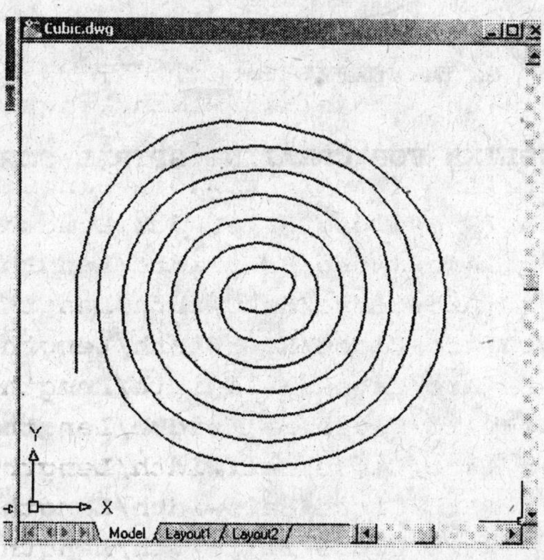

FIG.2(a) B-SPLINE FOR CREATING SPIRAL CURVE

STEP 2 (b) To draw the Cubic B-S pline for creating Spiral Curve [*See Fig. 2 (b)*]

Command : **SPLINETYPE**
Enter new value for SPLINETYPE <6>: 6

Command : **PEDIT**
Select polyline or [Multiple] : Select object (poly line object)
Enter an option [Close/Join/Width/Enter vertex/Fit/Spline/Decurve/Ltype gen/Undo] : spline
Enter an option [Open/Join/Width/Enter vertex/Fit/Spline/Decurve/Ltype gen/Undo] : enter

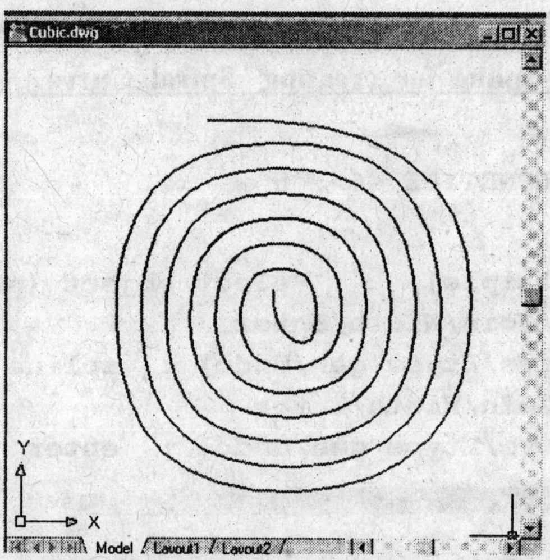

FIG.2 (b) B-SPLINE FOR CREATING SPIRAL CURVE

Ex. No. : 1 Date :	*Ch.17* - **TOP AND FRONT VIEWS OF SIMPLE SOLIDS**

Ex. No. : 1 - *To draw the Top and Front Views of a* ***Regular Pentagonal Prism*** *of side of base 30 mm and axis 55 mm long, resting with its base on HP such that one of its rectangular faces is perpendicular to VP.*

STEP 1 : Start the **AutoCAD Software**. Open and setup a new drawing sheet.

STEP 2 : To draw the 3-D view of the given Pentagonal Prism : (**Fig. 1**)

Command : **VPOINT**

```
Specify a view point or [Rotate]
<display compass and tripod>          :  1,-1,1
```

Command : **SHADEMODE**

```
Enter an option [2dwireframe/3dwire
frame/3dHidden/Realistic/Conceptual/
Other] <2dwireframe>                  : 3D
```

Command : **POLYGON**

```
Enter number of sides <4>             :  5
Specify center of polygon or [Edge]   :  0
Enter an option [Inscribed in
circle/Circumscribed about circle] <I> :  I
Specify radius of circle              :  30
```

Command : **EXTRUDE**

```
Select objects to extrude           :  1 found
Select objects to extrude             :
Specify height of extrusion or
[Direction/Path/Taper angle] <70.0000> :  55
```

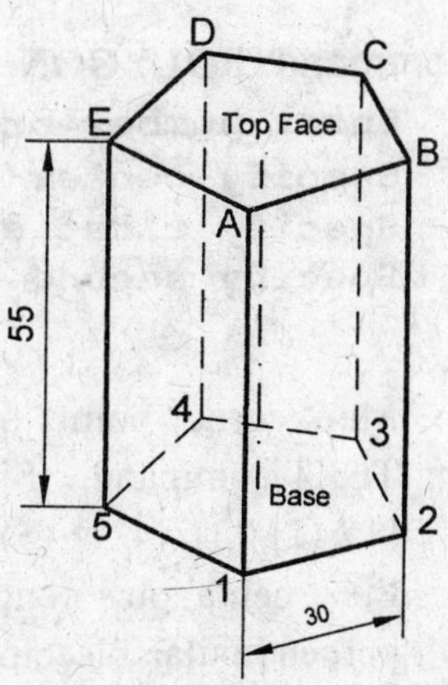

FIG.1
PENTAGONAL PRISM

Command : **SECTIONPLANE**

```
  Select face or any point to locate
  section line or [Draw section/
  Orthographic]                       : O
  Align section to:[Front/bAck/Top/Bottom/
  Left/Right]<Top>                    : T
```

STEP 2 : Then, draw the sectional front view for the remaining portion of the prism by *thick* lines (H). In this view, the cut surface is shown by hatching (*thin*) lines using 2H.

STEP 3 : (Fig. 2)

Draw a line arbitrarily using the LINE command. Name it as **XY** using the TEXT command. Mark VP above the XY line and HP below the XY line using the TEXT command.

STEP 4 : Top View (Fig. 2)

To draw the pentagon of side 30 mm and one of the sides perpendicular to the XY line, use the POLYGON command and Edge option. The prompt sequence is:

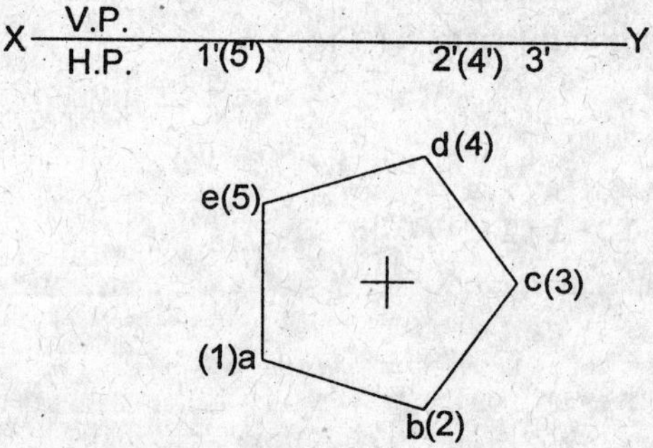

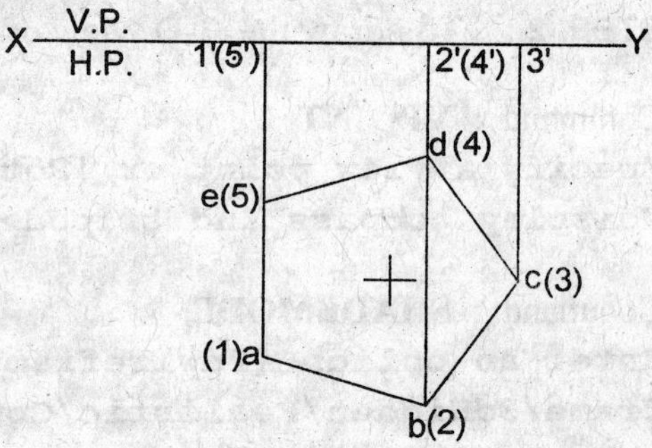

FIG.2

Command: **POLYGON** ↵

```
Enter number of sides <4>              : 5
Specify center of polygon or[Edge]     : E ↵
Specify first endpoint of  Edge       :(Pick a point below XY line)
Specify second endpoint of Edge      :(move
                        cursor to the up)30↵
```

Mark corner points of top face as a, b, c, d and e using TEXT command. Similarly, mark bottom face corners as (1), (2), (3), (4) & (5).

Fix pentagon center by the intersection of two perpendicular bisectors of any two sides of the pentagon using the LINE command.

Command : **TEXT**

```
Current text style:  "Standard"  Text
height                         : 2.5
Specify  start  point  of  text  or
[Justify/Style]                :
Specify rotation angle of text <0> : 0
```

STEP 5 : Front View (Fig. 3)

Using LINE command, draw the vertical projectors from top view to meet XY at the points 1′, (5′), 2′, (4′) and 3′.

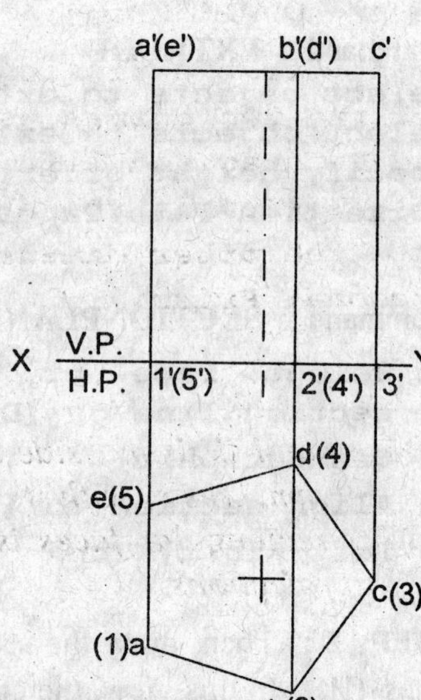

FIG.3

Command : **LINE**

```
Specify first point :

Specify next point or [Undo]   :
                    ( Move the cursor to right ) 30 ↵
Specify next  point or [Undo] :
                    ( Move the cursor to up ) 55 ↵
Specify next point or [Undo]   :
                    ( Move the cursor to left ) 30 ↵
Specify next point or [Undo]   :
                    ( Move the cursor to down ) 55 ↵
```

Mark these points using TEXT command and join them using the LINE command. At these points, draw vertical lines of 55 mm height using LINE command. Mark the points a′, (e′), b′, (d′), and c′ using TEXT command and join them using LINE command.

Draw the axis line of the pentagon using the LINE command. Select this line and choose the required **Linetype** from the **Properties** toolbar.

Note: (i) Use **narrow (thin)** lines for XY line, construction lines and dimension lines. Use **wide (thick)** lines for the top and front views. (ii) Use **dashed** lines for the invisible lines from the **Properties** toolbar. Choose appropriate line thicknesses.

STEP 6 : Dimensioning

Mark dimensions using the options available in the **Dimension** menu, or using the **dimlinear, dimaligned** or **dimangular** commands.To edit dimension text, select dimension and use DDEDIT or ED command. Finally, save the file.

Command : **DIMLINEAR**

```
Specify first extension line origin or
:Pick the two points, say, line points
A and B, drag and left click by mouse.
Note : Following the above procedure,
create the other dimensions given
Pentagonal Prism.
```

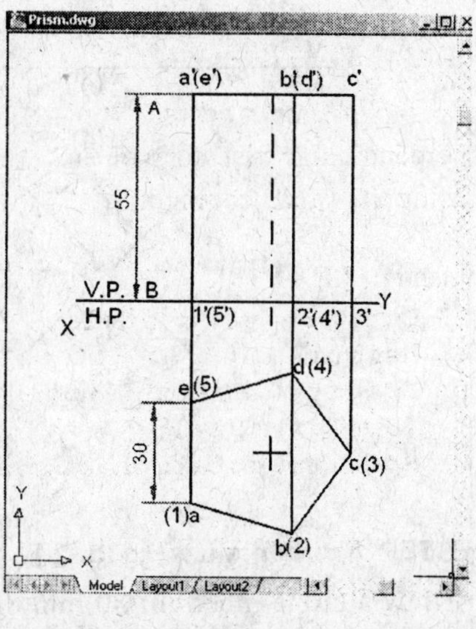

FIG.4 PENTAGONAL PRISM

Ex. No. : 2

A ***Hexagonal Prism***, *side of base 25 mm and height 50 mm, rests with its base on HP such that one of its rectangular faces is perpendicular to VP. Draw its projections.*

<u>Ex. No. 3 -</u> **AIM :** *A Cylinder of base 30 mm and axis 50 mm long, resting with its base on HP. Draw its top and front views, using CAD Software.*

STEP 1 : Start the **AutoCAD Software**. Open and setup a new drawing sheet.

STEP 2 : To draw the 3-D view of the given Cylinder : (**Fig. 1)**

Command : **VPOINT**

```
Specify a view point or [Rotate]
<display compass and tripod>          : 1,-1,1
```

Command : **SHADEMODE**

```
Enter an option [2dwireframe/3dwire
frame/3dHidden/Realistic/Conceptual/
Other] <2dwireframe>                  :   3D
```

Command : **CYLINDER**

```
Specify center point of base or [3P/2P/
Ttr/Elliptical]               : Pick any point
Specify base radius or [Diameter]        : D
Specify diameter                         : 30
Specify height or [2Point/Axis endpoint]:50
```

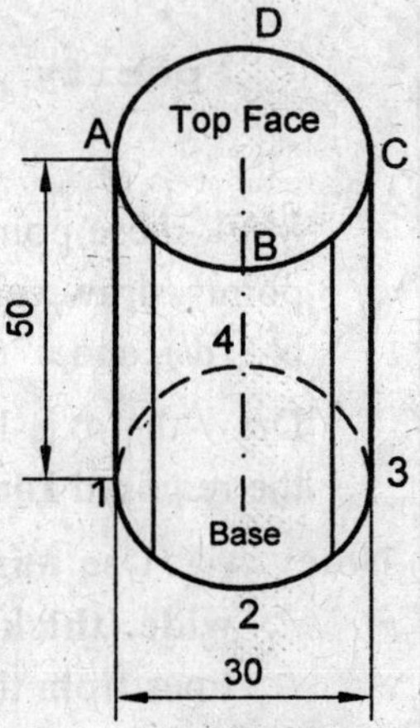

FIG.1
CYLINDER

STEP 3 : (Fig. 2)

Draw a line arbitrarily using the LINE command. Name it as **XY** using the TEXT command. Mark VP above the XY line and HP below the XY line using the TEXT command.

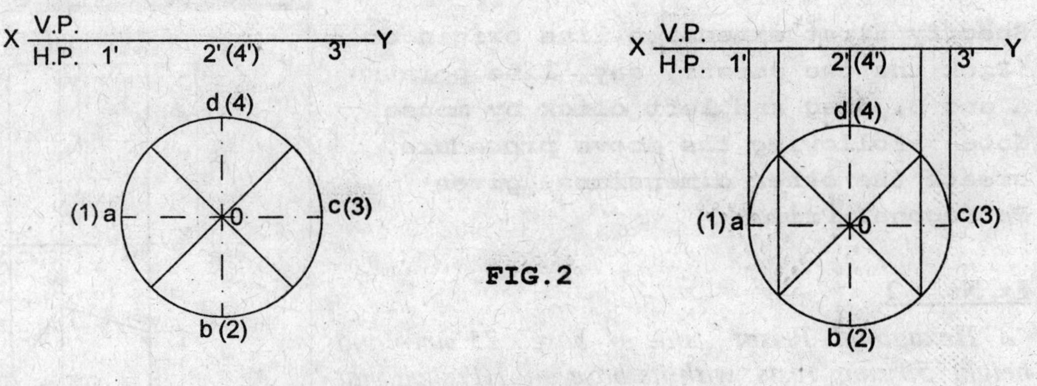

FIG.2

STEP 4 : Top View (Fig. 2)

Draw a circle abcd of 30 mm diameter such that center is 25 mm below XY to represent the top view of the top face. Base 1234 is hidden. Hence mark its top view as (1) (2) (3) (4) such that (1) and a coincide using TEXT command, etc. The prompt sequence is:

Command: **CIRCLE** ↵

```
Circle Specify center point for          :
Circle or [3P/2P/Ttr (tan tan radius)] : 0
Specify radius of circle or [Diameter]: D
Specify diameter of circle              : 30
```

Command : **TEXT**

```
Current text style:"Standard" Text
Height                               :2.5
Specify start point of text or
[Justify/Style]                      :
Specify rotation angle of text<0>:0
```

STEP 5 : Front View (Fig. 3)

Using LINE command, draw vertical projectors from top view to meet XY at the points 1′, 2′, (4′) and 3′.

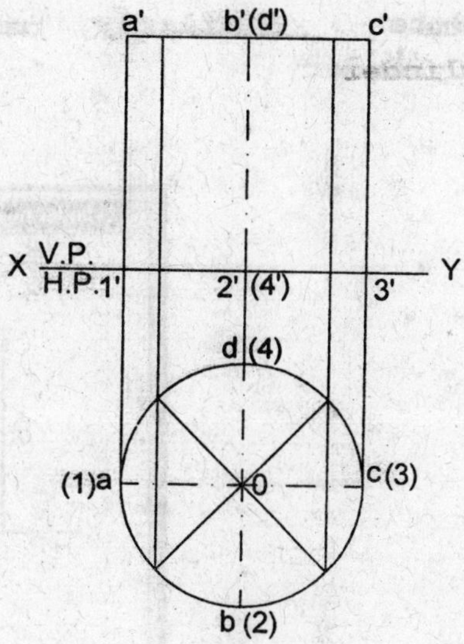

FIG.3

Command : **LINE**

```
Specify first point :
Specify next point or [Undo]   :
```
(Move the cursor to right) 30 ↵
```
Specify next  point or [Undo] :
```
(Move the cursor to up) 50 ↵
```
Specify next point or [Undo]   :
```
(Move the cursor to left) 30 ↵
```
Specify next point or [Undo]   :
```
(Move the cursor to down) 50 ↵

Mark these points using TEXT command and join them using the LINE command. At these points, draw vertical lines of 50 mm height using LINE command. Mark the points a′, b′ (d′), and c′ using TEXT command and join them using LINE command.

Draw the axis line of the pentagon using the LINE command. Select this line and choose the required **Linetype** from the **Properties** toolbar.

Note: (i) Use **narrow (thin)** lines for XY line, construction lines and dimension lines. Use **wide (thick)** lines for the top and front views. (ii) Use **dashed** lines for the invisible lines from the **Properties** toolbar. Choose appropriate line thicknesses.

STEP 6

Dimensioning: Mark the dimensions using the options available in the **Dimension** menu, or using the **dimlinear, dimaligned** or **dimangular** commands. To edit the dimension text, select the dimension and use the DDEDIT or ED command. Finally, save the file.

Command : **DIMLINEAR**

Specify first extension line origin or:Pick the two points, say, line points A and B, drag and left click by mouse.

Note : *Similarly, mark the other dimensions of the given Cylinder.*

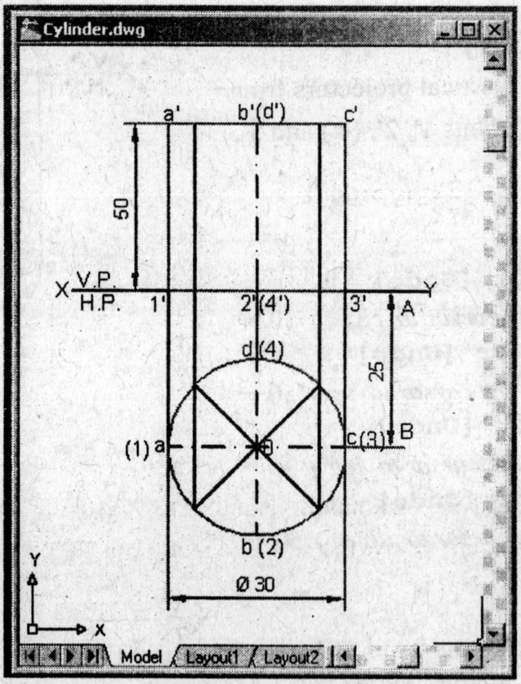

FIG. 4 CYLINDER

<u>Ex. No. 4</u>

Draw the projections of a ***Cylinder*** *75 mm diameter and 100 mm long, lying on the ground with its axis perpendicular to the Vertical Plane.*

Note: Divide the Front View of the Cylinder into 8 equal parts.

Ex. No. : 5 - *A* ***Hexagonal Pyramid****, side of base 30 mm and height 60 mm, rests with its base on HP such that one of the edges of the base is parallel to and 10 mm in front of VP. Draw its top and front views, using AutoCAD.*

STEP 1 : Start the **AutoCAD Software**. Open and setup a new drawing sheet.

STEP 2 : To draw the 3-D view of the given Pentagonal Prism : (**Fig. 1**)

Command : **VPOINT**
Specify a view point or [Rotate]
<display compass and tripod> :1,-1,1

Command : **SHADEMODE**
Enter an option [2dwireframe/3dwire frame/3dHidden/Realistic/Conceptual/ Other] <2dwireframe> : **3D**

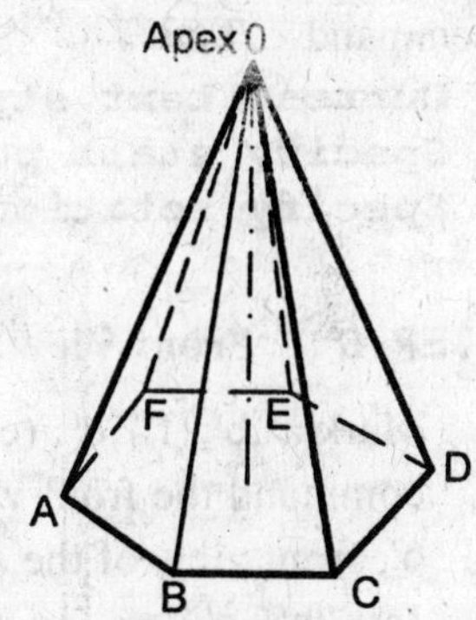

FIG. 1
HEXAGONAL PYRAMID

Command : **PYRAMID**
Specify center point of base or [Edge/Sides] : S
Enter number of sides <4> : 6
Specify center point of base : Pick any point
Specify base radius or [Inscribed] : I
Specify base radius or [Circumscribed] : 30
Specify height or [2Point /Top radius] : 60

STEP 3 : (Fig. 2)
Draw a line arbitrarily using the LINE command. Name it as **XY** using the TEXT command. Mark VP above the XY line and HP below the XY line using the TEXT command.

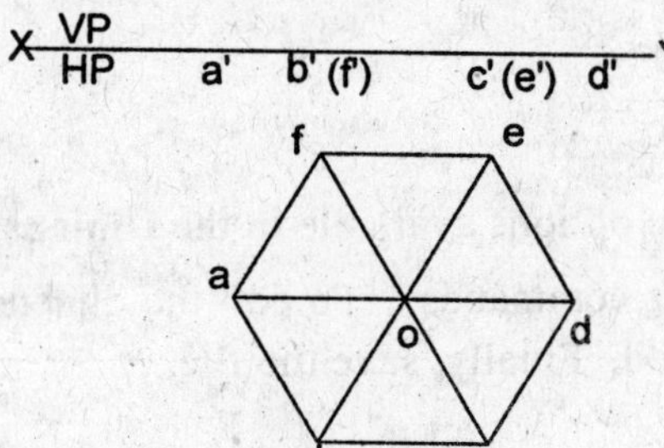

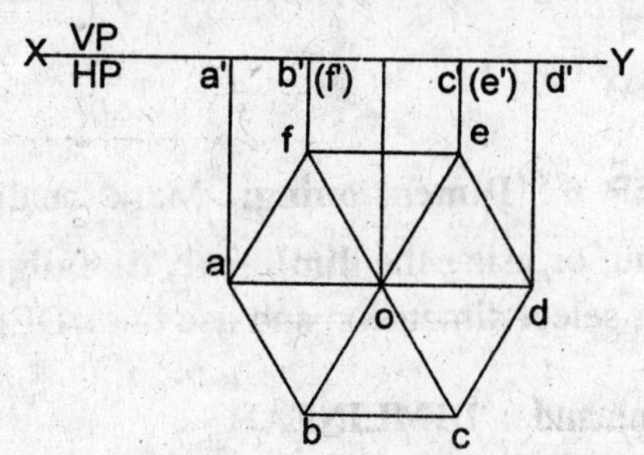

FIG. 2

STEP 4 : Top View (Fig. 2)
Draw hexagon a b c d e f of 30 mm side with ef parallel to and 10 mm below XY, use the POLYGON command and Edge option. The prompt sequence is:

Command: **POLYGON**

```
Enter number of sides <4>              : 6
Specify center of polygon or[Edge]  : E ↵
Specify first endpoint of  Edge      :(Pick a point below XY line)
Specify second endpoint of  Edge     :(move cursor to the up)30↵
```

Join the diagonals to fix o, the top view of the apex. Join oa, ob, etc., and complete the top view using LINE command. Similarly, mark bottom face corners as a, b, c, d, e and f using TEXT command.

Command : **TEXT**

```
Current text style: "Standard" Text height         : 2.5
Specify start point of text or [Justify/Style]  :
Specify rotation angle of text <0>              : 0
```

STEP 5 : Front View (Fig. 3)

Mark a′,b′,(f′),c′, (e′), and d′ using TEXT command the front view of base on XY. Mark o′, front view of the apex 60 mm above XY. Join o′ a′, etc., to represent front view of the slant edges using LINE command.

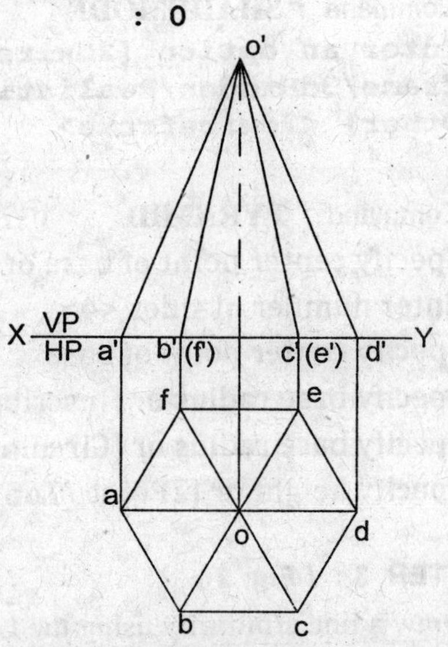

FIG.3

Command : **LINE**

```
Specify first point :
Specify next point or  [Undo]:  Hexagonal
                  edge one point (Ref. Fig.4.)
Specify next point or  [Undo]:  Hexagonal
                  edge another point
Specify next point or [Undo]  :  60
Specify next point or [Undo]  :  Enter
```

STEP 6 : Dimensioning: Mark the dimensions using the options available in the **Dimension** menu, or using the **dimlinear, dimaligned** or **dimangular** commands. To edit the dimension text, select dimension and use the DDEDIT or ED command. Finally, save the file.

Command : **DIMLINEAR**

```
Specify first extension line origin or : Pick the two points, say,
                                         line points A and B,
                                         drag and left click by
                                         mouse.
```

Note : Following the above procedure, mark the other dimensions of the given **Hexagonal Pyramid**.

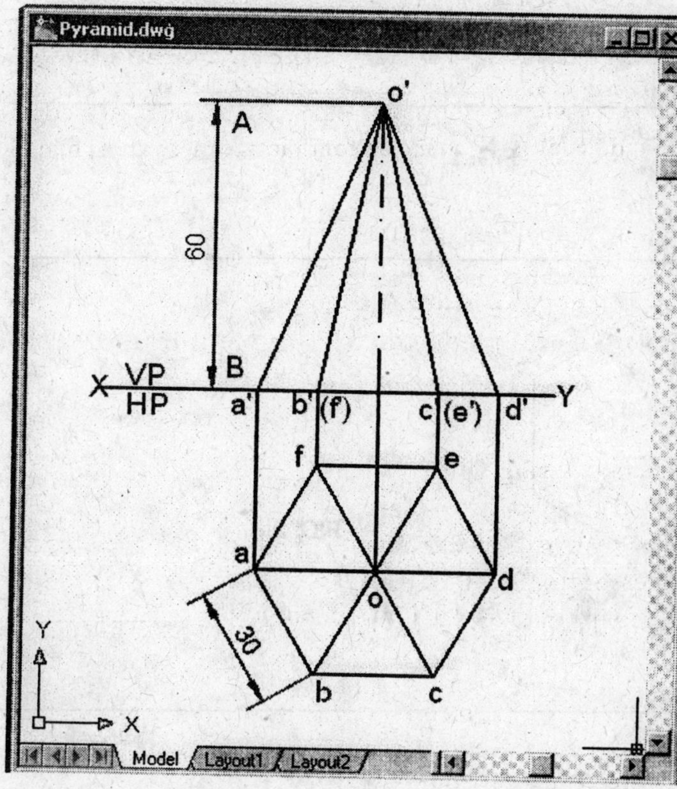

FIG.4 HEXAGONAL PYRAMID

x. No. : 6

Square Pyramid, side of base 30 mm and axis 50 mm long rests with its base on *dges of the base is parallel to and 10 mm in front of VP. Draw its projections.*

x. No. : 7

*raw the projections of a **Pentagonal Pyramid**, side of base 30 mm and height 60 m* *P such that one of the edges of the base is perpendicular to VP.*

Ex. No. : 8 - *A* ***Hexagonal Pyramid,*** *side of base 25 mm and axis 50 mm long, rests with one of the edges of its base on HP and its axis is inclined at 30° to HP and parallel to VP. Draw its projections using the CAD Software.*

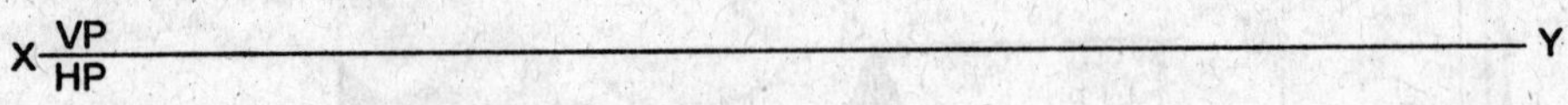

FIG. 1

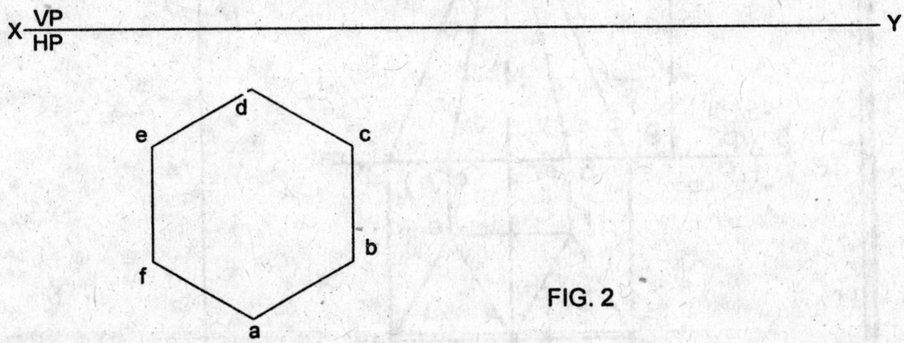

FIG. 2

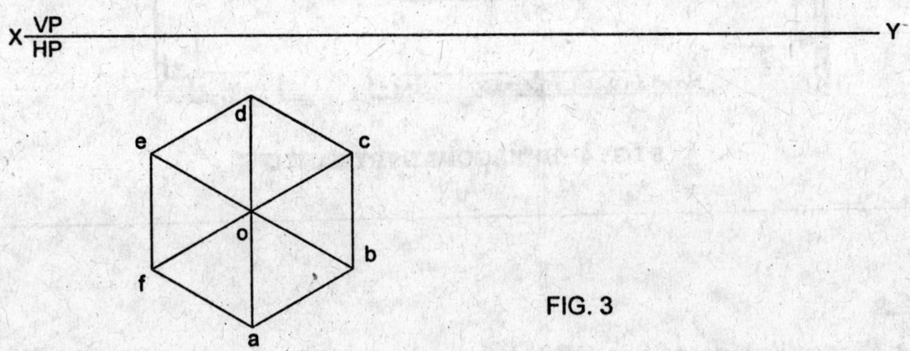

FIG. 3

STEP 1 : Draw XY line using the **Line** and **Text** commands. Using the **Text** command, place the texts VP and HP above and below the XY line respectively. **See Fig. 1.**

STEP 2 : Draw the top view hexagon of side 25 mm with one side vêrtical, using the **Polygon** command. Name the corners as a, b, ..., f using the **Text** command. **See Fig. 2.**

STEP 3 : Join the diagonals using the **Line** command. Name the center as o using the **Text** command. **See Fig. 3.**

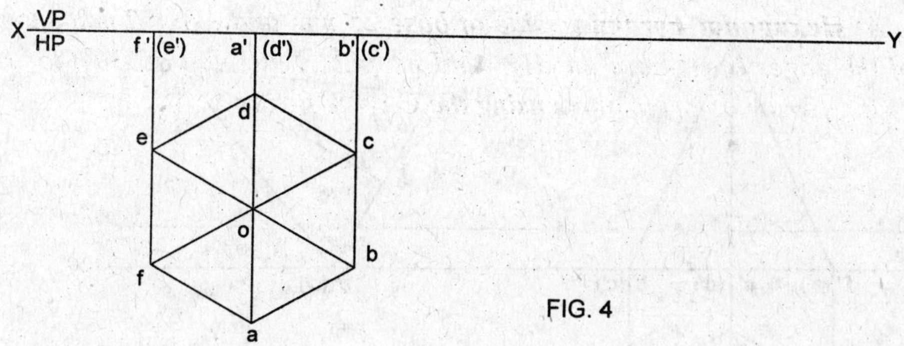

FIG. 4

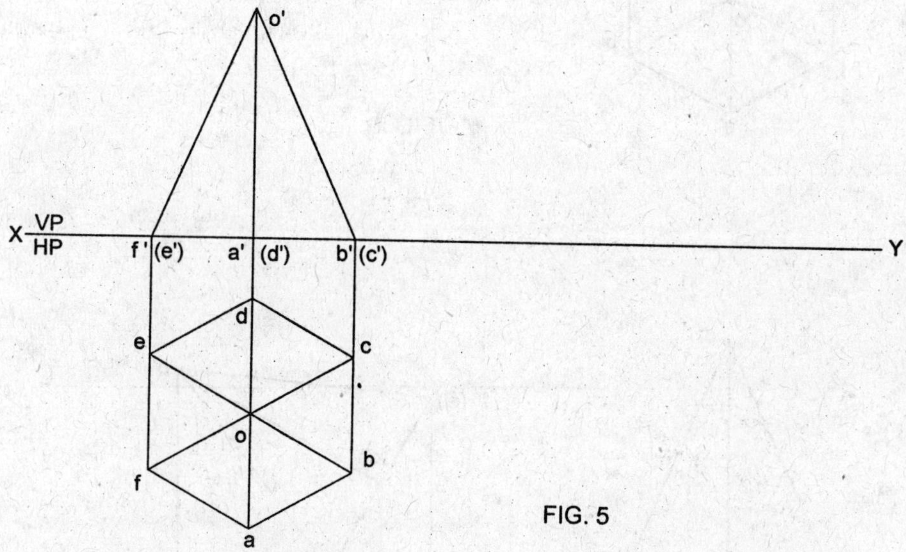

FIG. 5

STEP 4

Draw vertical projectors upwards from the corners of the top view of the hexagon to meet the XY line using the **Line** command. Name the meeting points as a′, b′, (c′), (d′), (e′) and f′ using the **Text** command. **See Fig. 4.**

STEP 5

Draw a vertical line of length 50 mm upwards from the point a′(d′) using the **Line** command. This is the top edge of the hexagonal pyramid. Name the top points of the line as o′ using the **Text** command.

Join the other corners of the base of the hexagon using the Line command. **See Fig. 5.** Thus, the first front view of the hexagonal pyramid is completed.

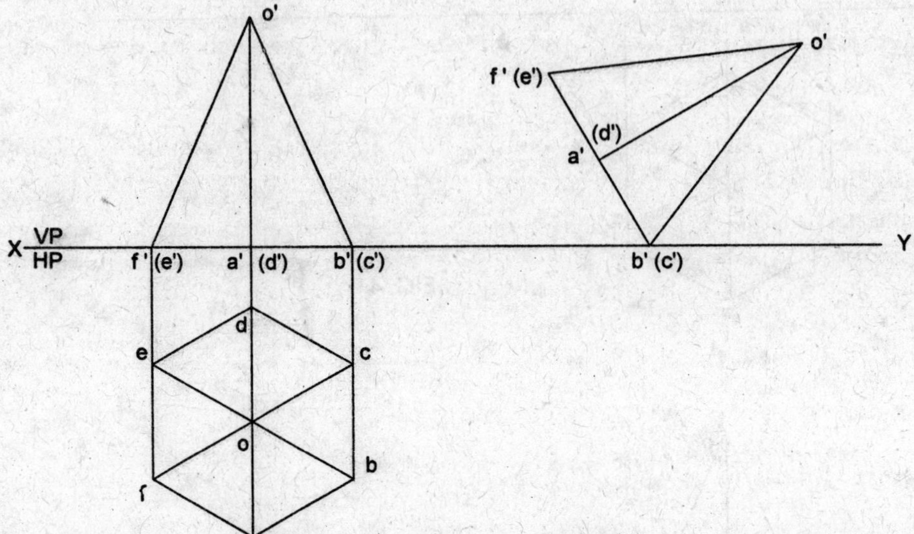

o'
f ' (e')
(d')
a'
o'
X
VP
HP
f ' (e')
a' (d')
b' (c')
b' (c')
Y
d
e
c
o
b
f
a

FIG. 6

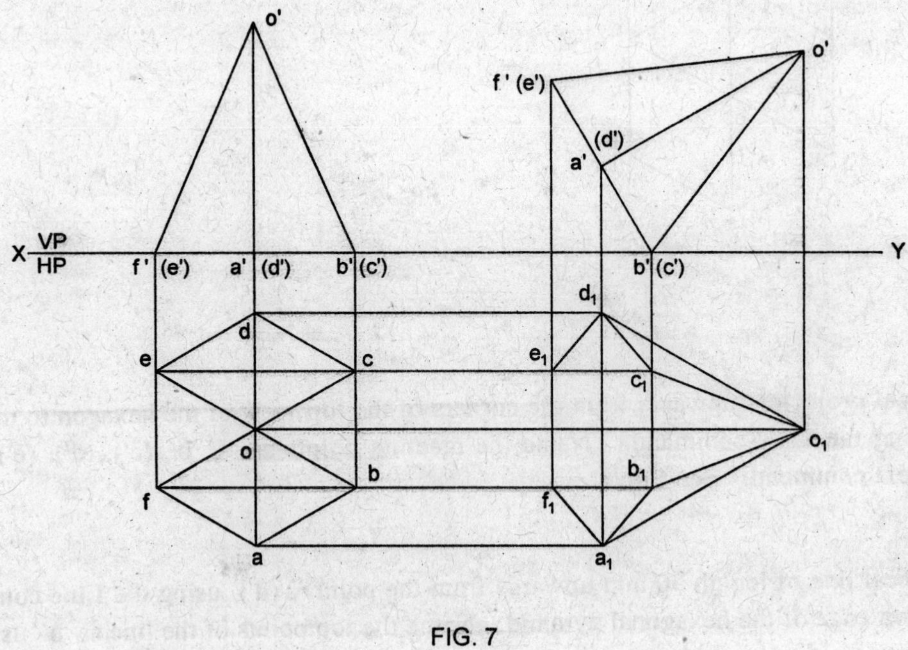

o'
o'
f ' (e')
(d')
a'
X
VP
HP
f ' (e')
a' (d')
b' (c')
b' (c')
Y
d
e
c
o
b
f
a
d_1
e_1
c_1
o_1
b_1
f_1
a_1

FIG. 7

STEP 6

Pyramid rests with an edge of its base on HP and its axis makes $\theta = 30^\circ$ to HP, *i.e.*, its base makes $(90 - \theta)$ to HP.

Draw a copy of the First Front View of the hexagonal pyramid using **Copy** command. Rotate the first front view of the Hexagonal Pyramid such that the edge b′(c′) is on XY and its base is inclined at 60° to XY using the **Rotate** command.

Fig. 6 shows the Final Front View.

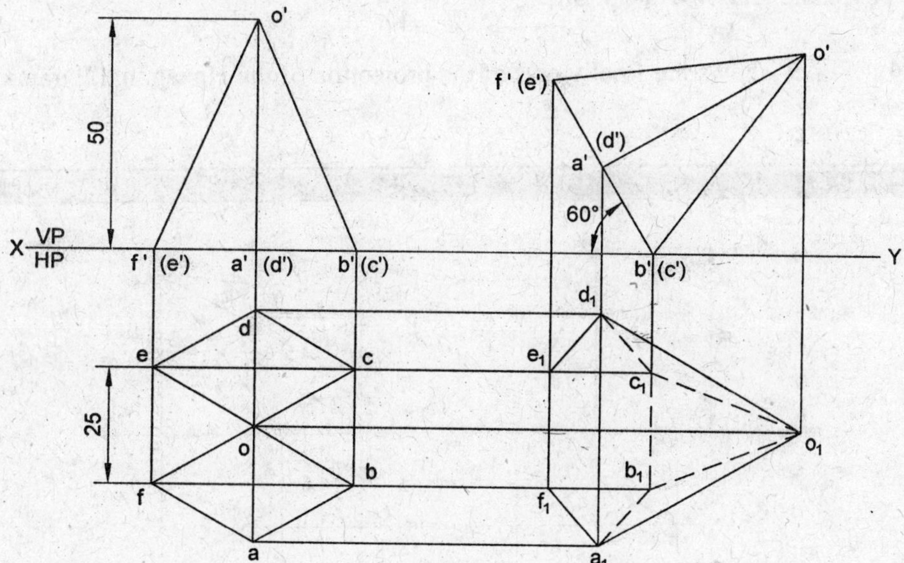

FIG. 8

STEP 7 : Draw projectors downwards from corners of the final front view to meet the horizontal projectors drawn from the corners of the first top view using the **Line** command.

STEP 8 : Name the meeting points as a_1, b_1, ..., f_1 and o_1 using the **Text** command.

STEP 9 : Using the **Line** command, join the base corners of pyramid to the apex to obtain the final top view of the Hexagonal Pyramid.

Fig. 7 shows the Final Top View of the Hexagonal Pyramid.

STEP 10 : Change the line type as **dashed** lines for the invisible edges of the pyramid. (**Fig. 8**)

STEP 11 : Use **narrow (thin)** lines for XY line, construction lines and dimension lines. Use **wide (thick)** lines for the top and front views.

STEP 12 : Mark the dimensions using the options available in the **Dimension** menu, or using the **dimlinear, dimaligned** or **dimangular** commands. To edit the dimension text, select the dimension and use the DDEDIT or ED command.

STEP 13 : Place texts I, II, III and IV using the **Text** command. For this, create a new text style using the Text Style dialog box. Draw an arrow at the bottom of the first top view using the **Pline** command and **Width** option.

STEP 14 : **Fig. 9** shows the final views of the projection of the Hexagonal Pyramid.

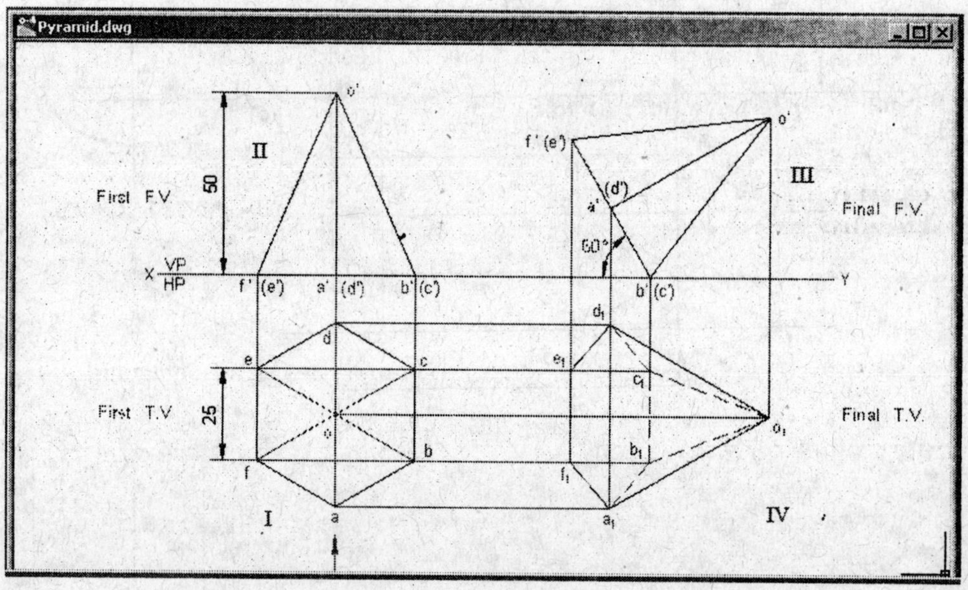

Fig. 9 Hexagonal Pyramid

Ex. No. : 9 - To *draw the top and front views of a* ***Cone*** *of base diameter 40 mm and height 60 mm lying with one of its generators on HP. The axis is parallel to VP. Use the CAD Software.*

STEP 1 : Start the **AutoCAD Software.** Open and setup a new drawing sheet.

STEP 2 : To draw the 3-D view of the given Pentagonal Prism : (**Fig. 1**)

Command : **VPOINT**

```
Specify a view point or [Rotate]
<display compass and tripod> : 1,-1,1
```

Command : **SHADEMODE**

```
Enter an option [2dwireframe/3dwire
frame/3dHidden/Realistic/Conceptual/
Other] <2dwireframe>                : 3D
```

Command : **CONE**

```
Specify center point of base or [3P/2P/
Ttr/Elliptical]          :Pick any point
Specify base radius or [Diameter]   :D
Specify diameter                    :40
Specify height or [2Point/Axis endpoint]:60
```

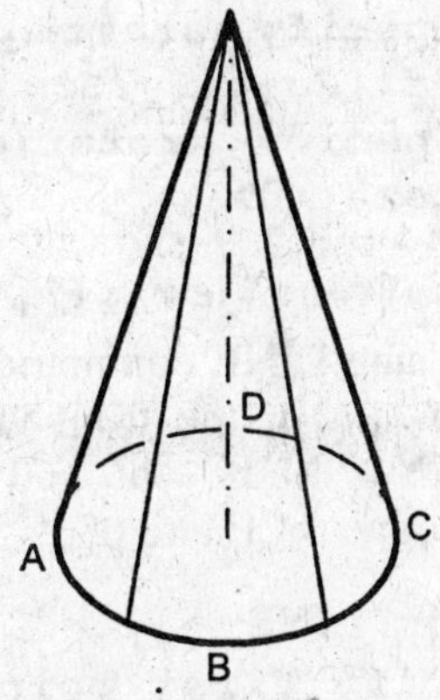

FIG.1 CONE

STEP 3 : (Fig. 2)

Draw a line arbitrarily using the LINE command. Name it as **XY** using the TEXT command. Mark VP above the XY line and HP below the XY line using the TEXT command.

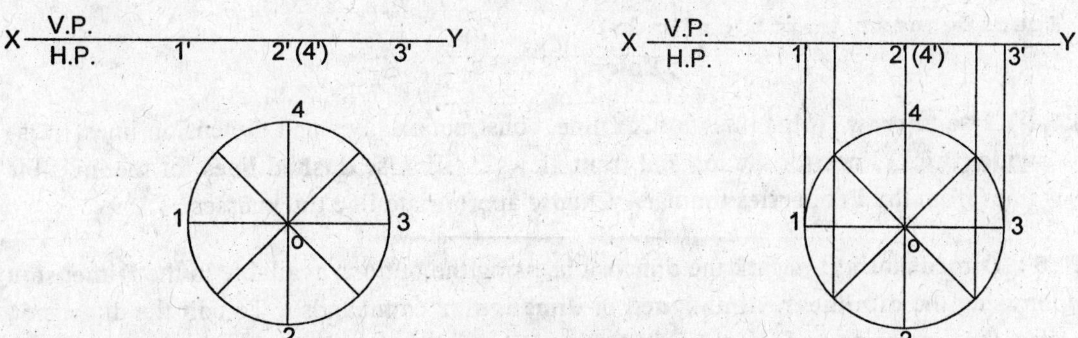

FIG.2

STEP 4 : Top View (Fig. 2)

Draw a circle 1234 of 40 mm diameter below XY. Center of the circle o is the top view of the apex and the axis using CIRCLE command.

Join o1, o2, o3 and o4 to represent the top view of the generators.

The prompt sequence is:

Command: **CIRCLE** ↵

```
CIRCLE Specify center point for
circle or [3P/2P/Ttr (tan tan radius)]   : O
Specify radius of circle or [Diameter]  : D
Specify diameter of circle              : 40
```

Command : **TEXT**

```
Current text style:
"Standard" Text height : 2.5
Specify start point of text
or [Justify/Style]            :
Specify rotation angle of
text <0>                      : 0
```

STEP 5 : Front View (Fig. 3)

Using LINE command, draw 1′ , 2′ , (4′) and (3′) the front view of the base on XY. Mark o′ 60 mm above XY. Draw o′ 1′ and o′ 3′.

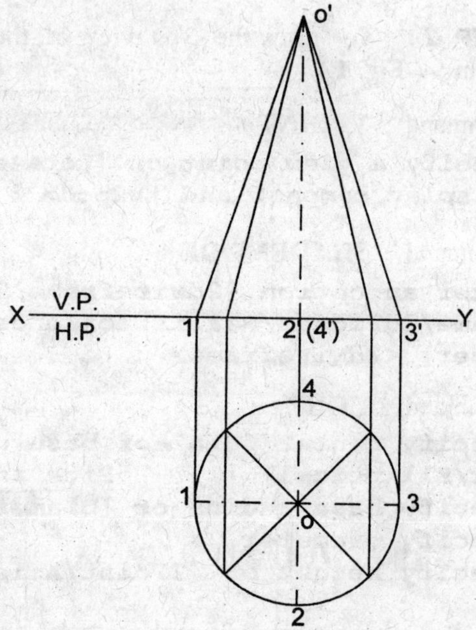

FIG.3

Command : **LINE**

```
Specify first point :
Specify next point or [Undo]
      : Cone edge one point (Ref Fig.4.)
Specify next point or [Undo]
      : Cone edge another point
Specify next point or [Undo]
                            : 60
Specify next point or[Undo]
                            : Enter
```

Note: (i) Use **narrow (thin)** lines for XY line, construction lines and dimension lines. Use **wide (thick)** lines for the top and front views. (ii) Use **dashed** lines for the invisible lines from the **Properties** toolbar. Choose appropriate line thicknesses.

STEP 6 : Dimensioning: Mark the dimensions using the options available in the **Dimension** menu, or using the **dimlinear, dimaligned** or **dimangular** commands. To edit the dimension text, select the dimension and use the DDEDIT or ED command. Finally, save the file.

Command : **DIMLINEAR**

```
Specify first extension line origin or:Pick the two points, say,
                                        line points A and B,
                                        drag and left click by
                                        mouse.
```

Note : *Following the above procedure, mark the other dimensions of the given Cone.*

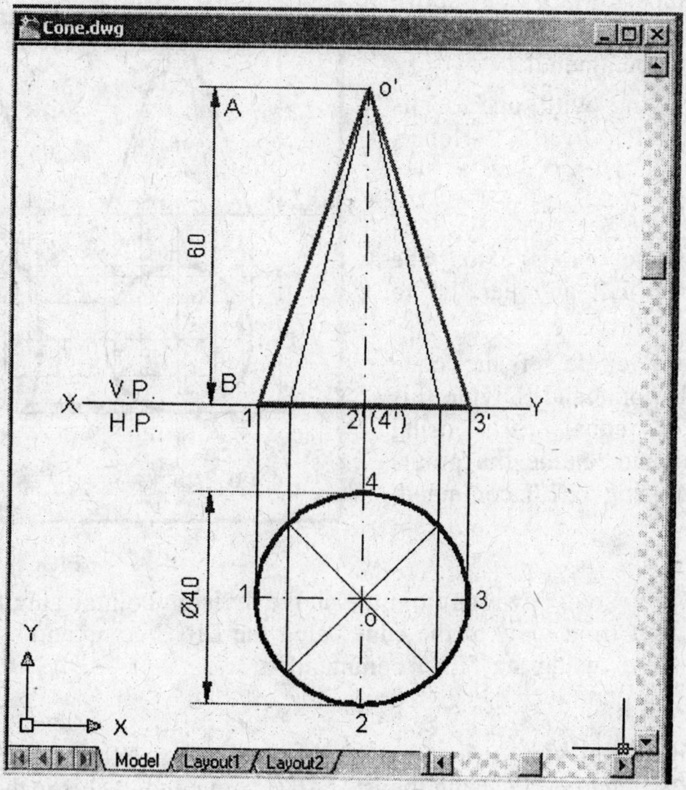

FIG. 4 CONE

Exercise : 10

*Draw the Front View and Top View of a **Cone** of base diameter = 30 mm and axis = 65 mm with its axis perpendicular to VP, keeping the vertex in front.*

Ex. No. : 11 - *Draw the top and front views of a* ***Cone*** *of base diameter 46 mm and height 65 mm lying with one of its generators on HP. The axis is parallel to VP. Use the CAD Software.*

1. Draw XY line using the LINE and TEXT commands. Mark VP above the XY line and HP below the XY line using the TEXT command.
2. The cone is lying with one of its generators on HP (*Given*). Hence, axis is inclined to HP.

Simple Position

Initially assume axis to be perpendicular to HP and parallel to VP.

3. Draw top view circle of the cone using CIRCLE command. Divide this circle into 12 equal parts using ARRAY command. Name the points 1, 2,.,12 and o using TEXT command.

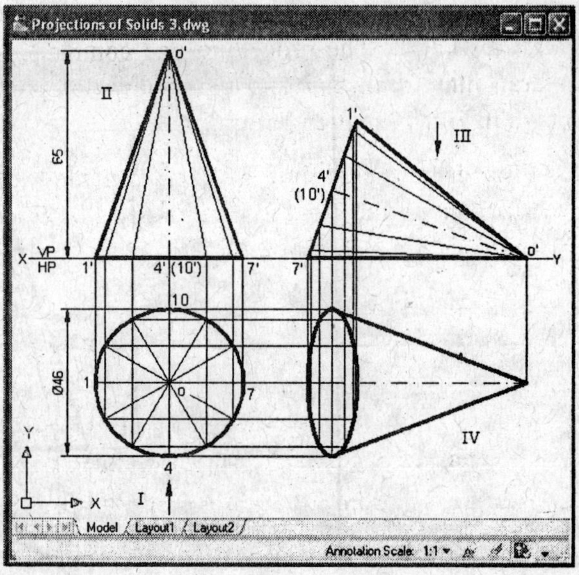

FIG. 1

4. Draw vertical projectors upwards from the above division points using the LINE command. Complete the first front view of the cone using the LINE command. Name the points as 1′, 2′, …, 12′ and o′ using the TEXT command.

Second Position

5. Redraw the first front view using the COPY command. Rotate the same such that the generator 7′o′ is lying on XY using the ROTATE command. This is the second front view.
6. Draw vertical projectors downwards from the second front view to meet the corresponding horizontal projectors drawn from the first top view using the LINE command.
7. Mark the intersecting points using the TEXT command. Complete the second top view by drawing ellipse for the base using the ELLIPSE command and by drawing lines for the generators using the LINE command.

Note: Use **narrow (thin)** lines for XY line, construction lines and dimension lines. Use **wide (thick)** lines for the top and front views. Choose appropriate line thicknesses.

8. **Dimensioning:** Mark the dimensions using the options available in the **Dimension** menu, or using the **dimlinear** or **dimaligned** commands. To edit the dimension text, select the dimension and use the DDEDIT or ED command.
9. Draw necessary arrows at the appropriate places to show the direction of views using the PLINE command and setting the width for arrowhead.
10. Finally, save the file.

Ex. No. : 1 Date :	*Ch.18* - ORTHOGRAPHIC VIEWS of PICTORIAL VIEWS

AIM : To draw the front view, top view and side view of the **V-Block** shown in **Fig. 1,** using AutoCAD.

PROCEDURE: The procedure and command sequence to draw the front, top and side views of the V-block shown in Fig. 1 is given below:

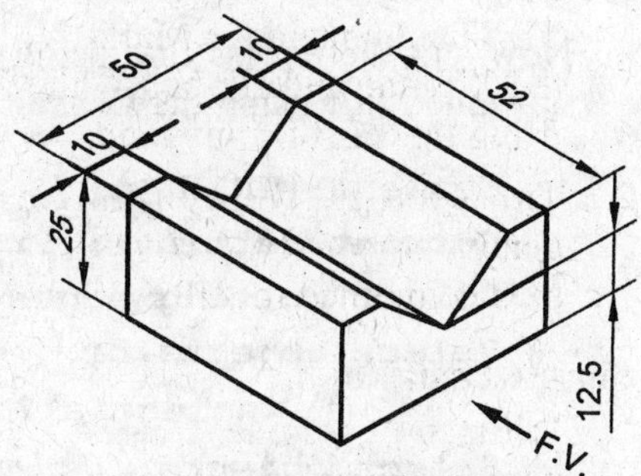

FIG. 1

1. First draw the outline of the front view of the V-block using the **Rectang** command. The command sequence is: **See Fig. 2**

```
Command: RECTANG ↵
Specify first corner point or
        [Chamfer/Elevation/Fillet/
        Thickness/Width]: (Pick P1)
Specify other corner point or
        [Area/Dimensions/Rotation]: D ↵
Specify length for rectangles <10.0000>: 50 ↵
Specify width for rectangles <10.0000>: 25 ↵
Specify other corner point or
        [Area/Dimensions/Rotation]: (Pick P2)
```

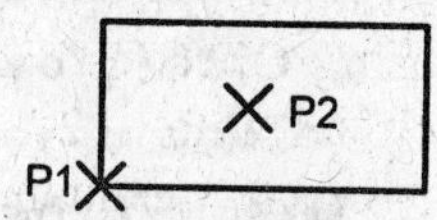

FIG. 2

2. Then, draw a horizontal line through the mid-points of the vertical edges of the rectangle. And then draw the remaining lines using the **Line** command. The command sequence is:

```
Command: LINE ↵
Specify first point: (Pick P1)
Specify next point or [Undo]: (Pick P2)
Specify next point or [Undo]: ↵
```

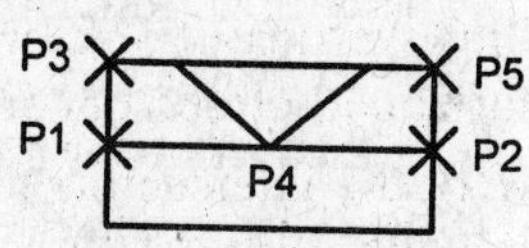

FIG. 3

```
Command: LINE ↵
Specify first point: (Pick P3)
Specify next point or [Undo]: <ortho on>(Move the cursor to right) 10 ↵
Specify next point or [Undo]: (Pick P4) (Point P4 is mid-point of the line P1-P2)
Specify next point or [Close/Undo]: ↵

Command: LINE ↵
Specify first point: (Pick P5).
```

```
Specify next point or [Undo]: (Move the cursor to left) 10 ↵
Specify next point or [Undo]: (Pick P4)
Specify next point or [Close/Undo]: ↵
```

See Fig. 3.

3. Now, cut the excess line using the **Trim** command. Also, remove the unwanted line using the **Erase** command. The command sequence is:

```
Command: TRIM ↵
Current settings: Projection=UCS, Edge=None
Select cutting edges ...
Select objects or
        <select all>: (Select Line L1) 1 found
Select objects: (Select Line L2) 1 found, 2 total
Select objects: ↵
Select object to trim or shift-select to extend or
[Fence/Crossing/Project/Edge/eRase/Undo]: (Select Line L3)
Select object to trim or shift-select to extend or
[Fence/Crossing/Project/Edge/eRase/Undo]: ↵

Command: ERASE ↵
Select objects: (Select Line L4) 1 found
Select objects: ↵
```

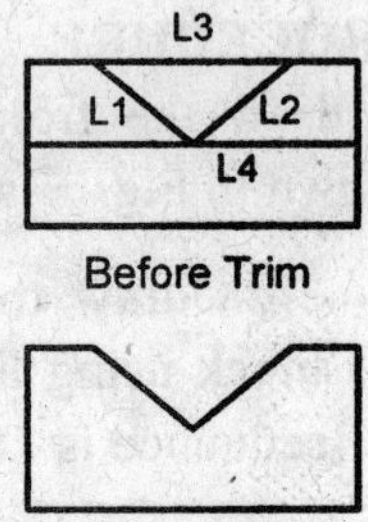

FIG. 4

See Fig. 4.

4. Draw the outline of the top view of the V-block using the **Rectang** command. The command sequence is:

```
Command: RECTANG ↵
Specify first corner point or [Chamfer/
   Elevation/Fillet/Thickness/Width]: (Pick P1)
Specify other corner point or
   [Area/Dimensions/Rotation]: D ↵
Specify length for rectangles <50.0000>: 50 ↵
Specify width for rectangles <25.0000>: 52 ↵
Specify other corner point or
   [Area/Dimensions/Rotation]: (Pick P2)
```

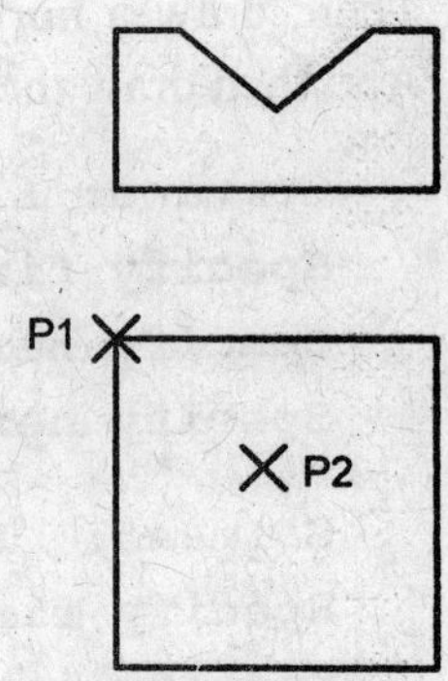

FIG. 5

See Fig. 5.

5. Now, draw the remaining lines using the **Line** command. Then, remove the excess lines using the **Erase** command. The command sequence is:

Command: **LINE** ↵
Specify first point: (*Pick P1*)
Specify next point or [Undo]: (*Pick P2*)
Specify next point or [Undo]: (*Pick P3*)
Specify next point or [Close/Undo]: ↵

Command: **LINE** ↵
Specify first point: (*Pick P4*)
Specify next point or [Undo]: (*Pick P5*)
Specify next point or [Undo]: (*Pick P6*)
Specify next point or [Close/Undo]: ↵

Command: LINE ↵
Specify first point: (*Pick P7*)
Specify next point or [Undo]: (*Pick P8*)
Specify next point or [Undo]: (*Pick P9*)
Specify next point or [Close/Undo]: ↵

Command: ERASE ↵
Select objects: (*Select Line L1*) **1 found**
Select objects: (*Select Line L2*) **1 found, 2 total**
Select objects: (*Select Line L3*) **1 found, 3 total**
Select objects: ↵

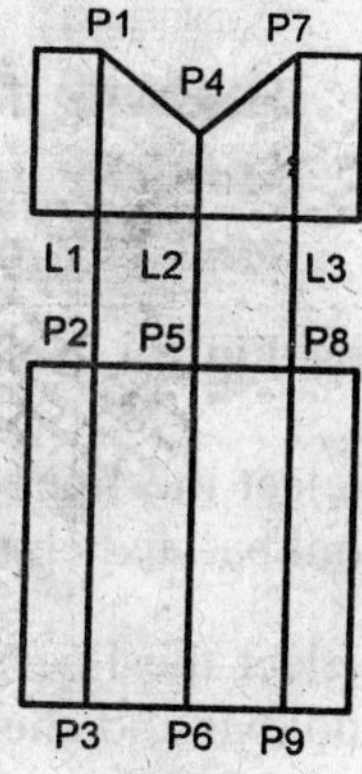

FIG. 6

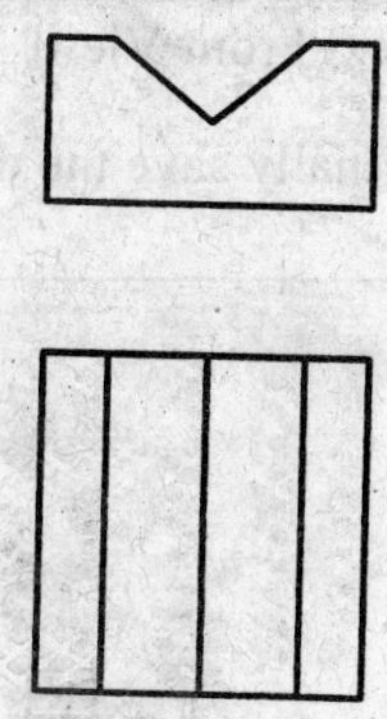
FIG. 7

See Fig. 6 and Fig. 7.

6. Draw the outline of the left side view of the V-block using the **Rectang** command. The command sequence is:

Command: **RECTANG** ↵
Specify first corner point or [Chamfer/Elevation/ Fillet/Thickness/Width]: (*Pick P1*)
Specify other corner point or [Area/Dimensions/Rotation]: D ↵
Specify length for rectangles <50.0000>: 52 ↵
Specify width for rectangles <52.0000>: 25 ↵
Specify other corner point or [Area/Dimensions/ Rotation]: (*Pick P2*)

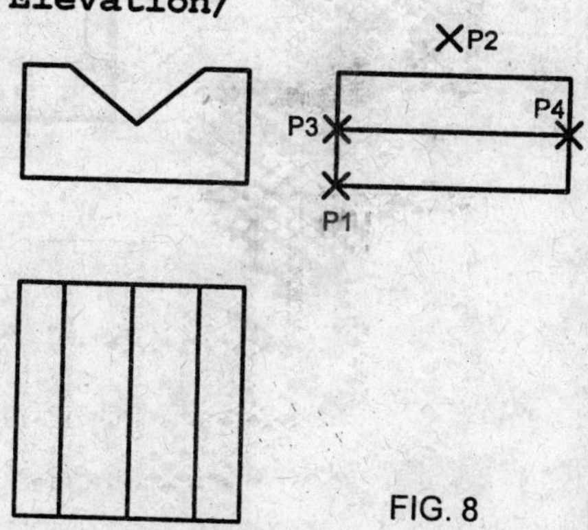

FIG. 8

```
Command: LINE ↵
Specify first point: (Pick P3)
Specify next point or [Undo]: (Pick P4)
Specify next point or [Undo]: ↵
```

See Fig. 8. Note that, the points P3 and P4 are the mid-points of the vertical lines.

7. Select the lines to be darkened and click the **Lineweight control** option on the **Properties** tool bar and choose the required line thickness.

8. Select the lines to be dashed one and click the **Linetype control** option on the **Properties** tool bar and choose the **Dashed** linetype.

9. Using the **Dimlinear** command, mark the dimension. Using the **Text** command, place the text Front View, Top View and Left Side View at the required positions.

10. Finally save the drawing. **Fig. 9** shows the final view of the diagram given in **Fig. 1.**

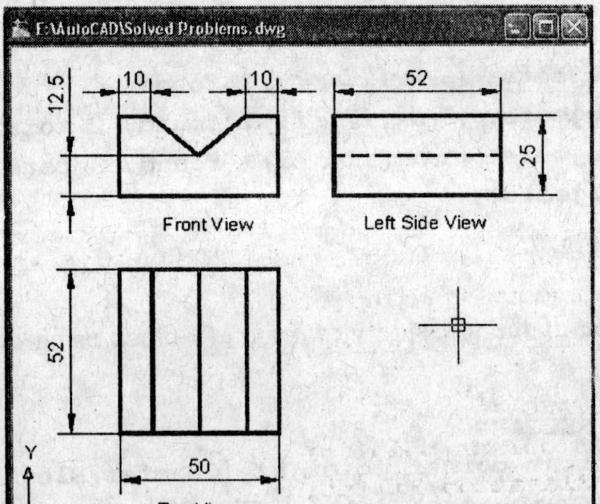

FIG. 9

Ex. No. : 2 Date :	MIXIE BASE

AIM : To draw the front view, top view and side view of the Mixie-Base shown in **Fig. 10.**

PROCEDURE: Command sequence to draw the front, top and side views of the Mixie-Base shown in **Fig. 10** is given below:

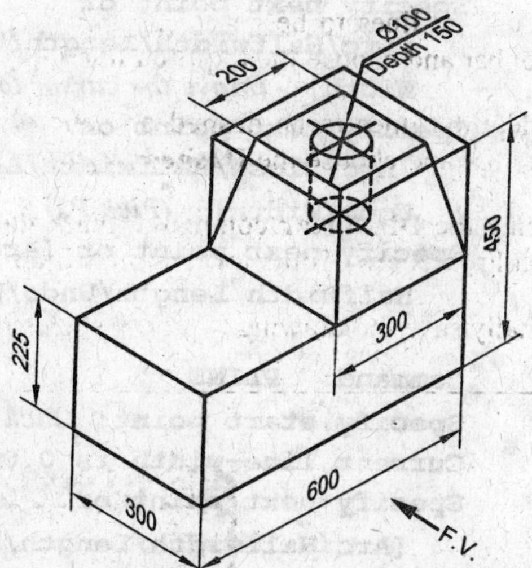

FIG. 10

1. First draw the outline of the front view of the Mixie-Base using the **Rectang** command. The command sequence is:

Command: **RECTANG ↵**
Specify first corner point or [Chamfer/Elevation/Fillet/ Thickness/Width] : *(Pick P1)*
Specify other corner point or [Area/Dimensions/Rotation] :D ↵
Specify length for rectangles <10.0000>: 600 ↵
Specify width for rectangles <10.0000>: 225 ↵
Specify other corner point or [Area/Dimensions/Rotation] : *(Pick P2)*

Command: **RECTANG ↵**
Specify first corner point or [Chamfer/Elevation/Fillet/ Thickness/Width] : *(Pick P3)*
Specify other corner point or [Area/Dimensions/Rotation] : D ↵
Specify length for rectangles <600.0000>: 300 ↵
Specify width for rectangles <225.000>: 225 ↵
Specify other corner point or [Area/Dimensions/Rotation] : *(Pick P4)*

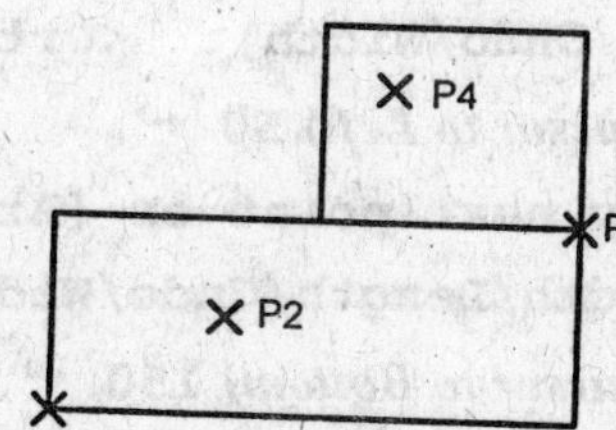

FIG. 11

See **Fig. 11.**

2. Now, draw the inner lines of the front view of the Mixie-Base using the **Pline** and **Line** commands. The command sequence is:

Command: **PLINE** ↵
Specify start point: *(Pick P1)*
Current line-width is 0.0000
Specify next point or
[Arc/Halfwidth/Length/Undo/
Width]: *(Move the cursor to Left)* **100** ↵
Specify next point or
[Arc/Close/Halfwidth/Length/
Undo/Width]: *(Pick P2)*
Specify next point or [Arc/Close/
Halfwidth/Length/Undo/Width]: ↵

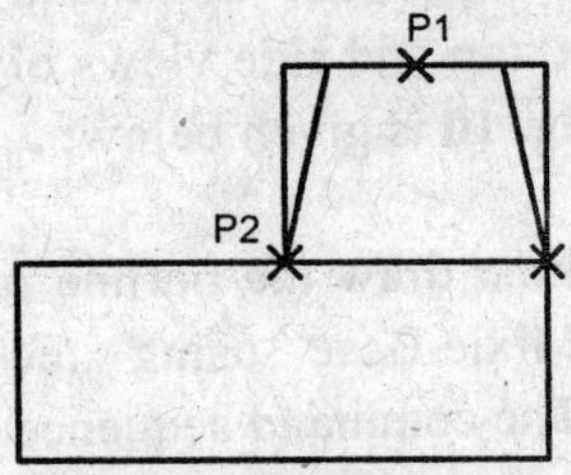

FIG. 12

Command: **PLINE** ↵
Specify start point: *(Pick P1)*
Current line-width is 0.0000
Specify next point or
[Arc/Halfwidth/Length/Undo/Width]: *(Move the cursor to Right)* **100** ↵
Specify next point or
[Arc/Close/Halfwidth/Length/Undo/Width]: *(Pick P3)*
Specify next point or [Arc/Close/Halfwidth/Length/Undo/Width]: ↵

See Fig. 12.

Command: **ERASE** ↵
Select objects: *(Select the upper rectangle)* **1 found**
Select objects: ↵

Command: **PLINE** ↵
Specify start point: *(Pick P1)*
Current line-width is 0.0000
Specify next point or [Arc/Halfwidth/
Length/Undo/Width]: **<Ortho on>**
(Move cursor to Left) **50** ↵
Specify next point or [Arc/Close/
Halfwidth/Length/Undo/Width]:
(Move cursor to Bottom) **150** ↵
Specify next point or [Arc/Close/

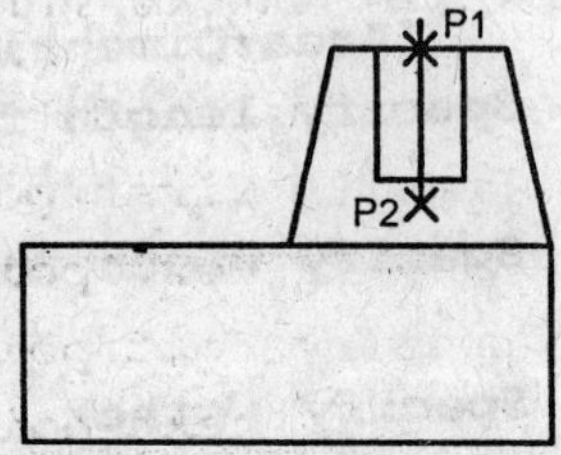

FIG. 13

Halfwidth/Length/Undo/Width]: *(Move cursor to Right)* 100 ↵
Specify next point or [Arc/Close/Halfwidth/
Length/Undo/Width]: *(Move cursor to Top)* 150 ↵

Specify next point or [Arc/Close/Halfwidth/
Length/Undo/Width]: ↵

Command: **LINE** ↵
Specify first point: *(Pick P2)*
Specify next point or [Undo]: *(Move cursor to Top)* 200 ↵
Specify next point or [Undo]: ↵

See Fig. 13.

3. Draw the outline of the top view of the Mixie-Base using the **Rectang** Command. The command sequence is:

Command: **RECTANG** ↵
Specify first corner point or
[Chamfer/Elevation/Fillet/
Thickness/Width]: *(Pick P1)*
Specify other corner point or
[Area/Dimensions/Rotation]: D ↵
Specify length for
rectangles <10.0000>: 600 ↵
Specify width for rectangles
<10.0000>: 300 ↵
Specify other corner point or
[Area/Dimensions/Rotation]: *(Pick P2)*

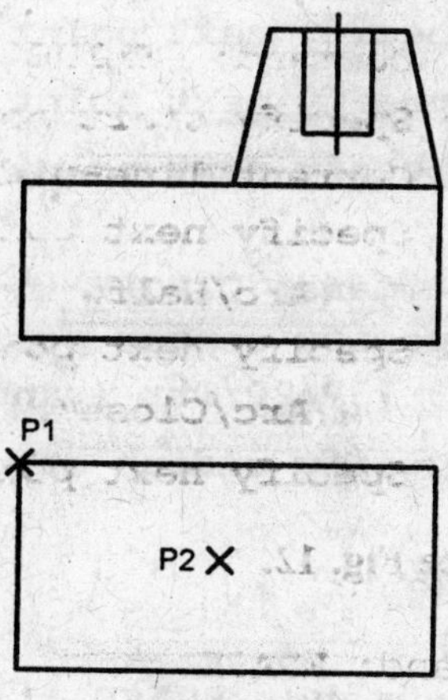

FIG. 14

See Fig. 14.

4. Draw the remaining inner lines of the top view of the Mixie-Base using the **Line** command. Then, remove the construction lines using the **Erase** command. The command sequence is:

Command: **LINE** ↵
Specify first point: *(Pick P1)*
Specify next point or [Undo]: *(Pick P2)*
Specify next point or [Undo]: *(Pick P3)*
Specify next point or [Close/Undo]: ↵

Command: **LINE** ↵
Specify first point: *(Pick P4)*
Specify next point or [Undo]: *(Pick P5)*
Specify next point or [Undo]:
<Ortho on> *(Move cursor to Down)* **50** ↵
Specify next point or
[Close/Undo]: *(Move cursor to Right)* **200** ↵
Specify next point or
[Close/Undo]: *(Move cursor to Down)* **200** ↵
Specify next point or
[Close/Undo]: *(Move cursor to Left)* **200** ↵
Specify next point or [Close/Undo]: **C** ↵

Command: **LINE** ↵
Specify first point: *(Pick P6)*
Specify next point or [Undo]: *(Pick P7)*
Specify next point or [Undo]: *(Pick P8)*
Specify next point or [Close/Undo]: ↵

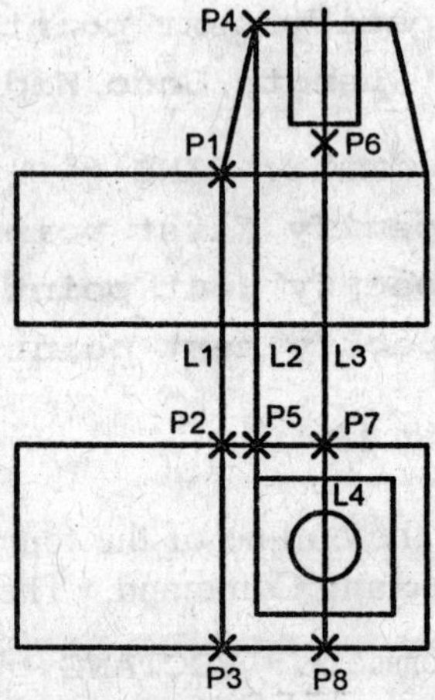

FIG. 15

Command: **CIRCLE** ↵
Specify center point for circle or
[3P/2P/Ttr (tan tan radius)]: *(Choose the mid-point of the Line P7-P8)*
Specify radius of circle or [Diameter]: **50** ↵

See Fig. 15.

Command: **ERASE** ↵
Select objects: *(Select line L1)* 1 found
Select objects: *(Select line L2)* 1 found, 2 total
Select objects: *(Select line L3)* 1 found, 3 total
Select objects: *(Select line L4)* 1 found, 4 total
Select objects: ↵

5. Complete the remaining portion of the top view of the mixie-base using the **Line** command. The command sequence is:

Command: **LINE** ↵
Specify first point: *(Pick P1)*
Specify next point or [Undo]: *(Pick P2)*

```
Specify next point or [Undo]: ↵

Command:  LINE ↵
Specify first point: (Pick P3)
Specify next point or [Undo]: (Pick P4)
Specify next point or [Undo]: ↵

Command:  LINE ↵
Specify first point: (Pick P5)
Specify next point or [Undo]: (Pick P6)
Specify next point or [Undo]: ↵

Command:  LINE ↵
Specify first point: (Pick P7)
Specify next point or [Undo]: (Pick P8)
Specify next point or [Undo]: ↵

Command: DIMCENTER ↵
Select arc or circle: (Select circle)
```

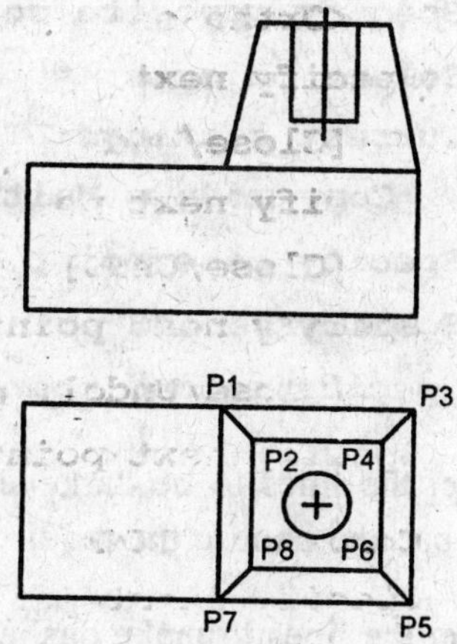

FIG. 16

See Fig. 16.

6. Draw the outline of the side view of the mixie-base using the **Rectang** command. The command sequence is:

```
Command: RECTANG ↵
Specify first corner point or
   [Chamfer/Elevation/Fillet/Thickness/Width]: (Pick P1)
Specify other corner point or [Area/
   Dimensions/Rotation]: D ↵
Specify length for rectangles
   <60.0000>: 300 ↵
Specify width for rectangles
   <30.0000>: 225 ↵
Specify other corner point or
   [Area/Dimensions/
   Rotation]: (Pick P2)
```

Here, the top portion of the side view of the mixie-base is same as the top portion of the front view. Therefore, it is not necessary to draw the top portion again.

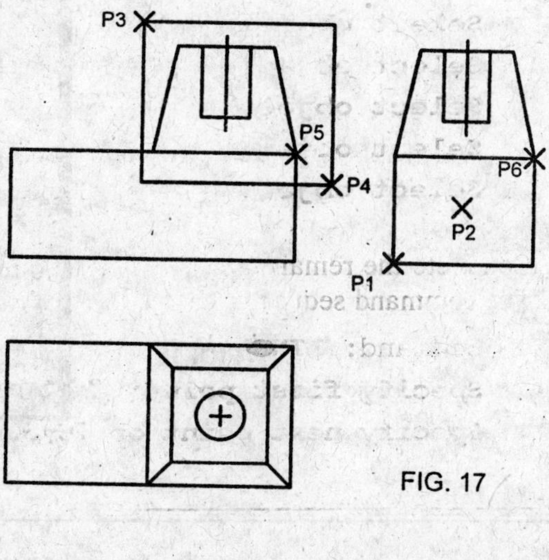

FIG. 17

Instead, reproduce the same using the **Copy** command. The command sequence is: **See Fig. 17.**

```
Command: COPY ↵
Select objects: (Pick P3)
Specify opposite corner: (Pick P4) 4 found
Select objects: ↵
Current settings:
   Copy mode = Multiple
Specify base point or [Displacement/mOde] <Displacement>:(Pick P5)
Specify second point or <use first point as displacement>:(Pick P6)
Specify second point or [Exit/Undo] <Exit>: ↵
```

7. Select the lines to be darkened and click the **Lineweight control** option on the **Properties** tool bar and choose the required line thickness.

8. Select the lines to make dashed one and click the **Linetype control** option on the **Properties** tool bar and choose the **Dashed** linetype.

9. Using the **Dimlinear** and **Dimdiameter** commands, mark the dimensions.

10. Using the **Text** command, place the text Front View, Top View and Left Side View at the required positions.

11. Finally save the drawing. **Fig. 18** shows the final view of the diagram given in **Fig. 10.**

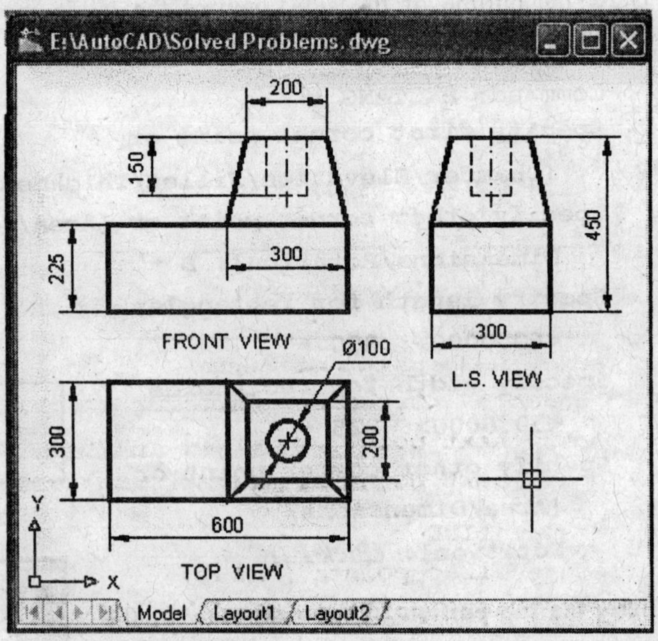

FIG. 18

Ex. No. : 3 Date :	STOOL

AIM : To draw the front view, top view and side view of the **Stool** shown in **Fig. 19.**

PROCEDURE : Command sequence to draw the front, top and side views of the Stool :

1. First draw the outline of the front view of the stool using the **Rectang** and **Line** commands. The command sequence is:

Command: **RECTANG ↵**
Specify first corner point
Or [Chamfer/Elevation/
Fillet/Thickness/
Width] : *(Pick P1)*
Specify other corner point
or [Area/Dimensions/
Rotation] : D ↵
Specify length for rectangles
<10.0000>: 120 ↵
Specify width for rectangles
<10.0000>: 8 ↵
Specify other corner point or
[Area/Dimensions/
Rotation] : *(Pick P2)*

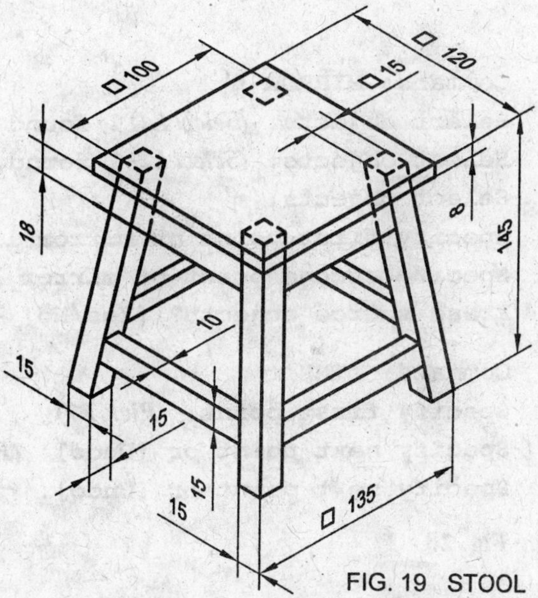

FIG. 19 STOOL

Command: **LINE ↵**
Specify first point:
(Select the Midpoint P3)
Specify next point or
[Undo] : <Ortho on> *(Move cursor to Down)* **145 ↵**
Specify next point or [Undo] : *(Move cursor to Right)* **67.5 ↵**
Specify next point or [Close/Undo] : ↵

Command: **LINE ↵**
Specify first point: *(Pick P3)*
Specify next point or [Undo] : *(Move the cursor to Right)* **50 ↵**
Specify next point or [Undo] : *(Pick P4)*
Specify next point or [Close/Undo] : ↵

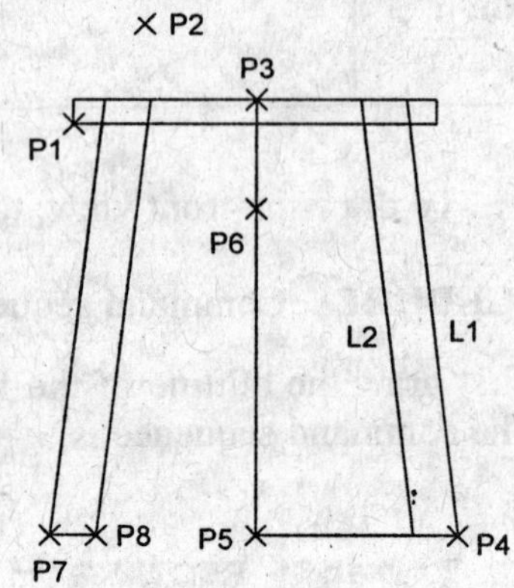

FIG. 20

Command: **COPY** ↵
Select objects: *(Select line L1)* **1 found**
Select objects: ↵
Current settings: Copy mode = Multiple
Specify base point or [Displacement/
mOde] <Displacement>: *(Pick P4)*
Specify second point or
<use first point as displacement>:
(Move cursor to Left) **15** ↵
Specify second point
or [Exit/Undo] <Exit>: ↵

Command: **MIRROR** ↵
Select objects: *(Select L1)* **1 found**
Select objects: *(Select L2)* **1 found, 2 total**
Select objects: ↵
Specify first point of mirror line: *(Pick P5)*
Specify second point of mirror line: *(Pick P6)*
Erase source objects? [Yes/No] <N>: ↵

Command: **LINE** ↵
Specify first point: *(Pick P7)*
Specify next point or [Undo]: *(Pick P8)*
Specify next point or [Undo]: ↵

See Fig. 20.

2. Now, draw the remaining lines of the front view of the stool using the **Line** command. Then, cut the unwanted lines using the **Trim** command. The command sequence is:

Command: **LINE** ↵
Specify first point: *(Pick P1)*
Specify next point or [Undo]: **<Ortho on>** *(Move cursor to Up)* **25** ↵
Specify next point or [Undo]: *(Move cursor to Right)* **150** ↵
Specify next point or [Close/Undo]: *(Move cursor to Up)* **15** ↵
Specify next point or [Undo]: *(Move cursor to Left)* **150** ↵
Specify next point or [Close/Undo]: ↵

Command: **LINE** ↵
Specify first point: *(Pick P2)*

Specify next point or [Undo]: <Ortho on> *(Move cursor to Down)* 18 ↵
Specify next point or [Undo]: *(Move cursor to Right)* 125 ↵
Specify next point or [Close/Undo]: ↵

Command: TRIM ↵
Current settings: Projection=UCS, Edge=None
Select cutting edges ...
Select objects or <select all>: *(Select line L1)* 1 found
Select objects: *(Select line L2)* 1 found, 2 total
Select objects: *(Select line L3)* 1 found, 3 total
Select objects: ↵
Select object to trim or shift-select to extend or
[Fence/Crossing/Project/Edge/eRase/Undo]: *(Select line L4)*
Select object to trim or shift-select to extend or
[Fence/Crossing/Project/Edge/eRase/Undo]: *(Select line L5)*
Select object to trim or shift-select
to extend or [Fence/Crossing/
Project/Edge/eRase/Undo]: *(Select line L6)*
Select object to trim or shift-select
to extend or[Fence/Crossing/Project/
Edge/eRase/Undo]: *(Select line L7)*
Select object to trim or shift-select
to extend or [Fence/Crossing/Project/
Edge/eRase/Undo]: *(Select line L8)*
Select object to trim or shift-select
to extend or [Fence/Crossing/Project/
Edge/eRase/Undo]: *(Select line L9)*
Select object to trim or shift-select
to extend or [Fence/Crossing/Project/
Edge/eRase/Undo]: *(Select line L10)*
Select object to trim or shift-select
to extend or [Fence/Crossing/Project/
Edge/eRase/Undo]: *(Select line L11)*
Select object to trim or shift-select
to extend or [Fence/Crossing/Project/

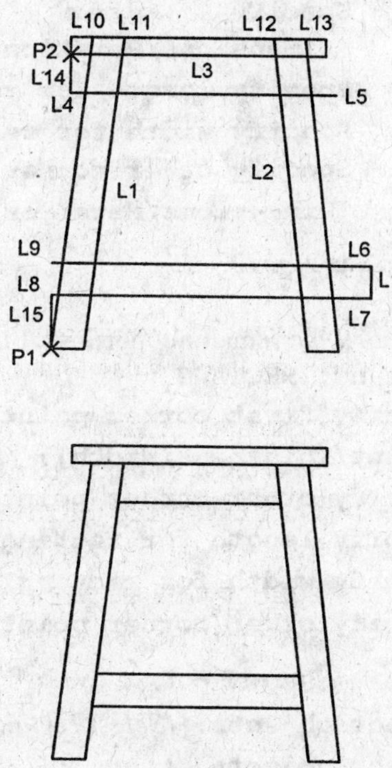

FIG. 21

```
Edge/eRase/Undo]: (Select line L12)
Select object to trim or shift-select to extend or [Fence/
Crossing/Project/Edge/eRase/Undo]          : (Select line L13)
Select object to trim or shift-select to extend or [Fence/
Crossing/Project/Edge/eRase/Undo]          : ↵

Command: ERASE ↵
Select objects: (Select line L14) 1 found
Select objects: (Select line L15) 1found, 2 total
Select objects: (Select line L16) 1found, 3 total
Select objects: ↵
```

See Fig. 21.

3. Draw the outline of the top view of the stool using the **Rectang** command. The command sequence is:

```
Command: RECTANG ↵
Specify first corner point or
[Chamfer/Elevation/Fillet/Width]: (Pick P1)
Specify other corner point or
[Dimensions/Rotation]          : D ↵
Specify length for rectangles <10>: 120 ↵
Specify width for rectangles <10> : 120 ↵
Specify other corner point or
[Dimensions/Rotation]          : (Pick P2)
```

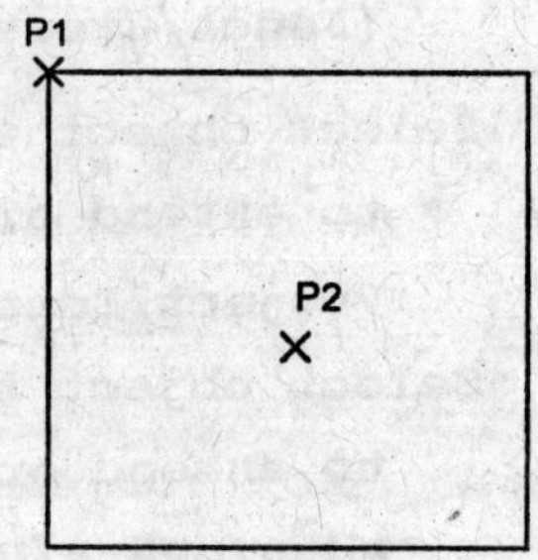

FIG. 22

See Fig. 22.

4. Draw the remaining portion of the top view of the stool using the **Line** command.

```
Command: RECTANG ↵
Specify first corner point or [Chamfer/Elevation/
Fillet/Thickness/Width]: (Pick P1)
Specify other corner point or [Area/Dimensions/Rotation]: D ↵
Specify length for rectangles <120.0000>: 135 ↵
Specify width for rectangles <120.0000>: 135 ↵
Specify other corner point or [Area/Dimensions/Rotation]: (Pick P2)

Command: MOVE ↵
Select objects: (Select rectangle R) 1 found
Select objects: ↵
```

Specify base point or [Displacement]
<Displacement>: <Ortho on> *(Pick P3)*
Specify second point or <use first point
as displacement>: *(Move cursor to Down)* **7.5** ↵

Command: **MOVE** ↵
Select objects: *(Select rectangle R)* **1 found**
Select objects: ↵
Specify base point or [Displacement]
<Displacement>: *(Pick P4)*
Specify second point or <use first point
as displacement>: *(Move cursor to Left)* **7.5** ↵

Command: **LINE** ↵
Specify first point: *(Pick P5)*
Specify next point or [Undo]: *(Pick P6)*
Specify next point or [Undo]: ↵

Command: **LINE** ↵
Specify first point: *(Pick P7)*
Specify next point or [Undo]: *(Pick P8)*
Specify next point or [Undo]: ↵
See Fig. 23.

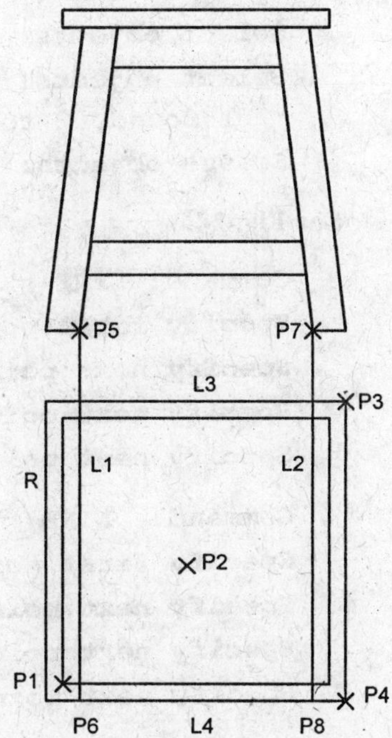

FIG. 23

Command: **TRIM** ↵
Select objects or <select all>: *(Select L1)*
Select objects : *(Select L2)*
Select objects: ↵
Select object to trim or shift-select
to extend or [Fence/Crossing/Project/
Edge/eRase/Undo] : *(Select L3)*
Select object to trim or shift-select
to extend or [Fence/Crossing/Project/
Edge/eRase/Undo] : *(Select L4)*
Select object to trim or shift-select
to extend or [Fence/Crossing/Project/
Edge/eRase/Undo] : ↵

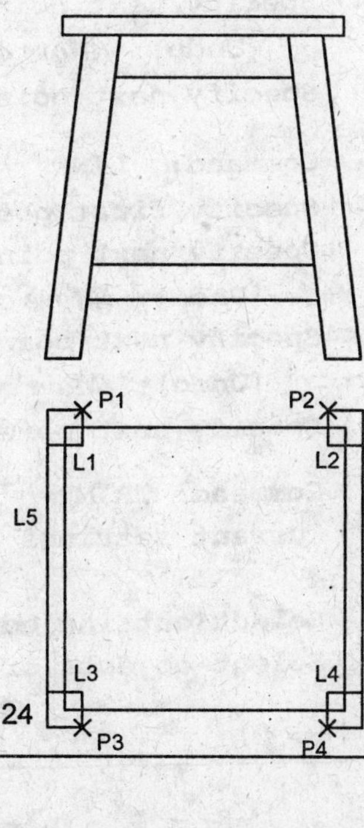

FIG. 24

Command: ERASE ↵
Select objects: *(Select L1)* 1 found
Select objects: *(Select L2)*
1 found, 2 total
Select objects: ↵

See Fig. 24.

Command: **LINE** ↵
Specify first point: *(Pick P1)*
Specify next point or [Undo]: <Ortho on> *(Move cursor to Down)* 15 ↵
Specify next point or [Undo]: *(Move cursor to Left)* 15 ↵
Specify next point or [Close/Undo]: ↵

Command: LINE ↵
Specify first point: *(Pick P2)*
Specify next point or [Undo]: *(Move cursor to Down)* 15 ↵
Specify next point or [Undo]: *(Move cursor to Right)* 15 ↵
Specify next point or [Close/Undo]: ↵

Command: **LINE** ↵
Specify first point: *(Pick P3)*
Specify next point or
[Undo]: *(Move cursor to Up)* 15 ↵
Specify next point or
[Undo]: *(Move cursor to Left)* 15 ↵
Specify next point or [Close/Undo]:↵

Command: LINE ↵
Specify first point: *(Pick P4)*
Specify next point or
[Undo]: *(Move cursor to Up)* 15 ↵
Specify next point or
[Undo]: *(Move cursor to Right)* 15 ↵
Specify next point or [Close/Undo]:↵

Command: TRIM ↵
Current settings: Projection=UCS,
Edge=None
Select cutting edges ...
Select objects or <select all>
: *(Select L1)* 1 found

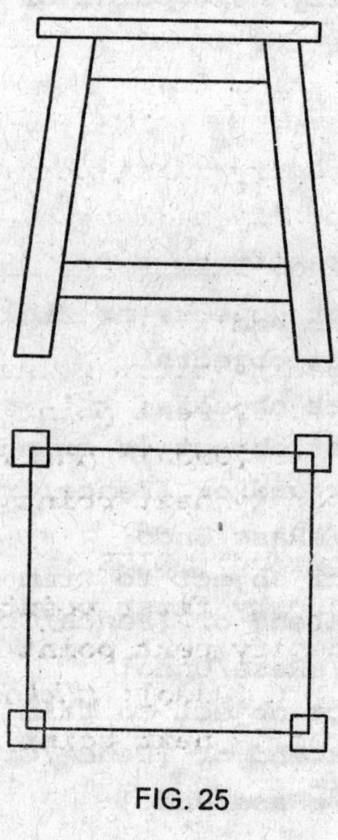

FIG. 25

Select objects: *(Select L2)* 1 found, 2 total
Select objects: *(Select L3)* 1 found, 3 total
Select objects: *(Select L4)* 1 found, 4 total
Select objects: ↵
Select object to trim or shift-select
  to extend or [Fence/Crossing/
  Project/Edge/eRase/Undo]: *(Select L5)*
Select object to trim or shift-select
  to extend or [Fence/Crossing/
  Project/Edge/eRase/Undo]: *(Select L6)*
Select object to trim or shift-select
  to extend or [Fence/Crossing/
  Project/Edge/eRase/Undo]: ↵

See Fig. 25.

Command: LINE ↵
Specify first point: *(Pick P1)*
Specify next point or [Undo]: *(Pick P2)*
Specify next point or [Undo]: ↵

Command: LINE ↵
Specify first point: *(Pick P3)*
Specify next point or [Undo]: *(Pick P4)*
Specify next point or [Undo]: ↵

Command: LINE ↵
Specify first point: *(Pick P5)*
Specify next point
  or [Undo]: *(Pick P6)*
Specify next point or [Undo]: ↵

Command: LINE ↵
Specify first point: *(Pick P7)*
Specify next point
  or [Undo]: *(Pick P8)*
Specify next point or [Undo]: ↵

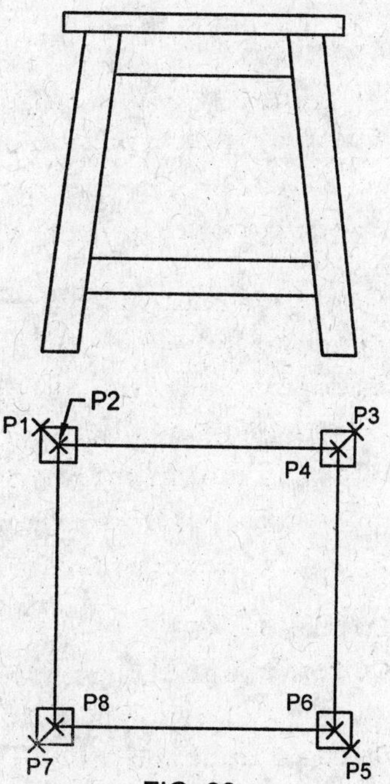

FIG. 26

See Fig. 26.

5. Draw the invisible lines in both the front and top views of the stool using the **Line** command.

6. Select the lines to be dashed one and click the **Linetype control** option on the **Properties** tool bar and choose the **Dashed** linetype.

7. Select the lines to be darkened and click the **Lineweight control** option on the **Properties** tool bar and choose the required line thickness.

8. Using the **Dimlinear** command, mark the dimension.

9. Using the **Text** command, place the text Front View and Top View at the required positions.

10. Finally save the drawing. **Fig. 27** shows the final view of the diagram given in **Fig. 19.**

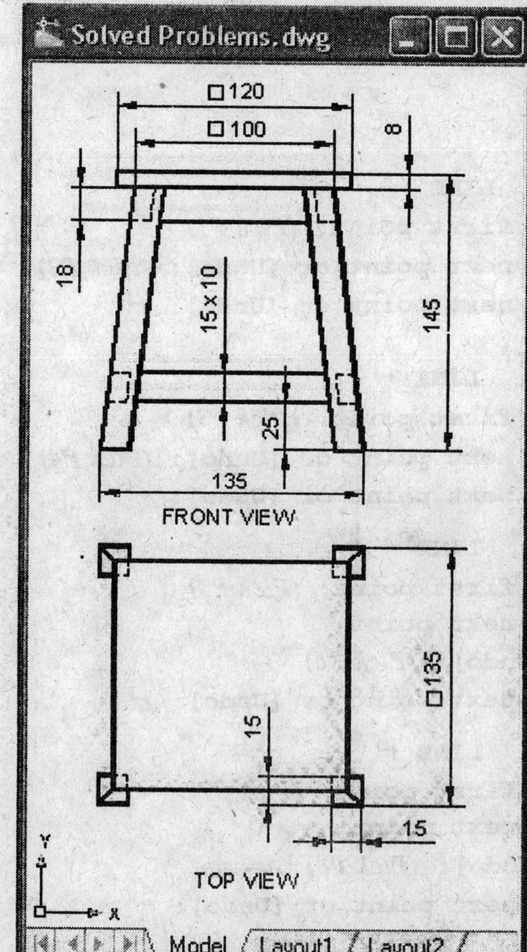

FIG. 27

Ex. No. : 4
Date :

OPEN BEARING

AIM : To draw front view, top view and side view of the **Open Bearing** shown in **Fig. 28.**

PROCEDURE : Command sequence to draw the front, top and side views of the Open Bearing shown in **Fig. 28** is given below:

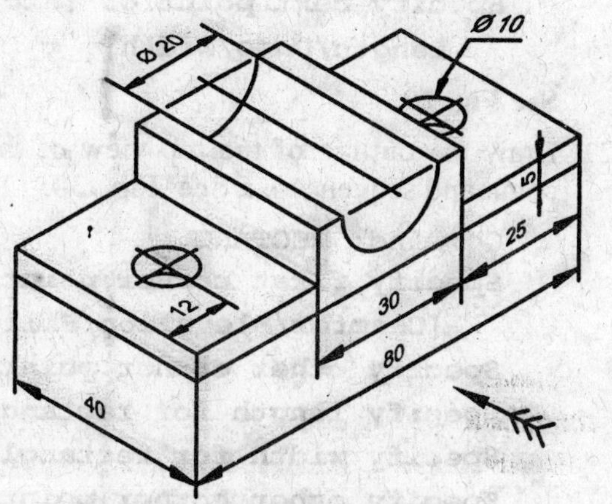

FIG. 28 OPEN BEARING

1. First draw the outline of the front view of the open bearing using the **Line** command. The command sequence is:

```
Command: PLINE ↵
Specify start point: (Pick P1)
Current line-width is 0.0000
Specify next point or
   [Arc/Halfwidth/Length/Undo/
   Width]: (Move cursor to Right) 5 ↵
Specify next point
   or [Arc/Close/Halfwidth/
   Length/Undo/Width]: A ↵
Specify endpoint of arc or
   [Angle/CEnter/CLose/Direction/
   Halfwidth/Line/Radius/
   Second pt/Undo/Width]: R ↵
Specify radius of arc: 10 ↵
Specify endpoint of arc or
   [Angle]: (Move cursor to Right) 20 ↵
Specify endpoint of arc or [Angle/
CEnter/CLose/Direction/Halfwidth/
Line/Radius/Second pt/Undo/Width]: L ↵
Specify next point or [Arc/Close/Halfwidth/
   Length/Undo/Width]: (Move cursor to Right) 5 ↵
Specify next point or [Arc/Close/Halfwidth/
   Length/Undo/Width]: (Move cursor to Down) 10 ↵
Specify next point or [Arc/Close/Halfwidth/
   Length/Undo/Width]: (Move cursor to Right) 25 ↵
Specify next point or [Arc/Close/Halfwidth/
   Length/Undo/Width]: (Move cursor to Down) 5 ↵
Specify next point or [Arc/Close/Halfwidth/
   Length/Undo/Width]: (Move cursor to Left) 80 ↵
```

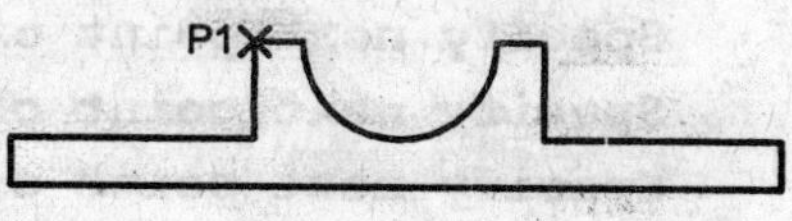

FIG. 29

```
Specify next point or [Arc/Close/Halfwidth/
   Length/Undo/Width]: (Move cursor to Up) 5 ↵
Specify next point or [Arc/Close/Halfwidth/
   Length/Undo/Width]: (Move cursor to Right) 25 ↵
Specify next point or [Arc/Close/Halfwidth/
   Length/Undo/Width]: (Move cursor to Up) 10 ↵
Specify next point or [Arc/Close/Halfwidth/
   Length/Undo/Width]: ↵
```

See Fig. 29.

2. Draw the outline of the top view of the open bearing using the **Rectang** command. The command sequence is: **See Fig. 30.**

```
Command: RECTANG ↵
Specify first corner point or
   [Chamfer/Elevation/Fillet/Thickness/Width]: (Pick P1)
Specify other corner point or [Area/Dimensions/Rotation]: D ↵
Specify length for rectangles <10.0000>: 80 ↵
Specify width for rectangles <10.0000>: 40 ↵
Specify other corner point or [Area/Dimensions/Rotation]: (Pick P2)

Command: LINE ↵
Specify first point: (Pick P3)
Specify next point or [Undo]: (Pick P4)
Specify next point or [Undo]: (Pick P5)
Specify next point or [Close/Undo]: ↵

Command: LINE ↵
Specify first point: (Pick P6)
Specify next point or [Undo]: (Pick P7)
Specify next point or [Undo]: (Pick P8)
Specify next point or [Close/Undo]: ↵

Command: LINE ↵
Specify first point: (Pick P9)
Specify next point or [Undo]: (Pick P10)
Specify next point or [Undo]: (Pick P11)
Specify next point or [Close/Undo]: ↵

Command: LINE ↵
Specify first point: (Pick P12)
Specify next point or [Undo]: (Pick P13)
Specify next point or [Undo]: (Pick P14)
Specify next point or [Close/Undo]: ↵
```

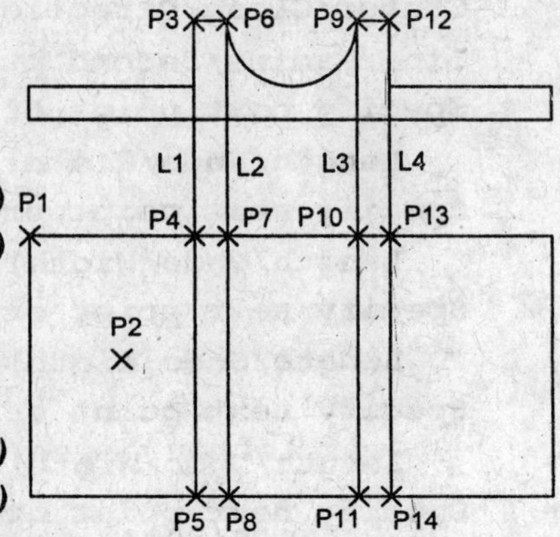

FIG. 30

Command: **ERASE** ↵
Select objects: *(Select line L1)* **1 found**
Select objects: *(Select line L2)* **1 found, 2 total**
Select objects: *(Select line L3)* **1 found, 3 total**
Select objects: *(Select line L4)* **1 found, 4 total**
Select objects: ↵

Command: LINE ↵
Specify first point: *(Pick P1)*
Specify next point or [Undo]: <Ortho on> *(Move cursor to Right)* **12** ↵
Specify next point or [Undo]: ↵

Command: C ↵
CIRCLE Specify center point for circle or [3P/2P/Ttr (tan tan radius)]: *(Pick P2)*
Specify radius of circle or [Diameter]: D ↵
Specify diameter of circle: 10 ↵

Command: MIRROR ↵
Select objects: *(Select Circle)* **1 found**
Select objects: ↵
Specify first point of mirror line: *(Pick P3 – the mid-point)*
Specify second point of mirror line: *(Pick P4 – the mid-point)*
Erase source objects? [Yes/No] <N>: ↵

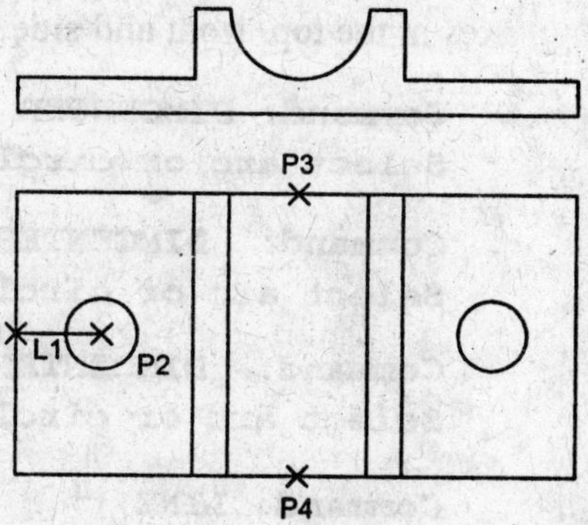

FIG.

Command: ERASE ↵
Select objects: *(Select line L1)* **1 found**
Select objects: ↵

See Fig. 31.

3. Draw outline of the side view of the open bearing using the **Rectang** and **Line** commands.

Command: RECTANG ↵
Specify first corner point or [Chamfer/Elevation/Fillet/Thickness/Width]: *(Pick P1)*
Specify other corner point or [Area/Dimensions/Rotation]:D

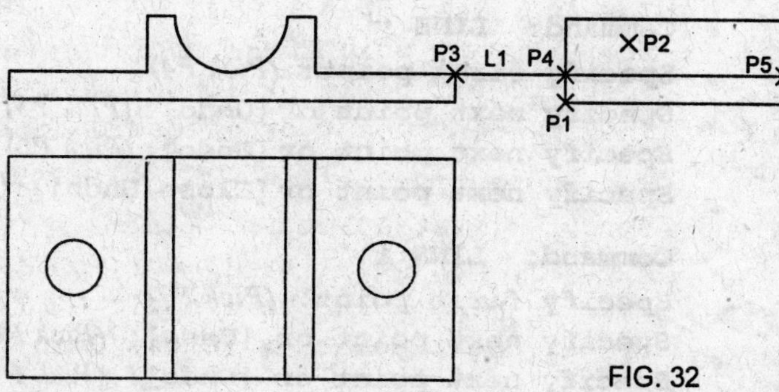

FIG. 32

Specify length for rectangles <10.0000>: 40 ↵
Specify width for rectangles <10.0000>: 15 ↵
Specify other corner point or [Area/Dimensions/Rotation]: *(Pick P2)*

Command: LINE ↵
Specify first point: *(Pick P3)*
Specify next point or [Undo]: *(Pick P4)*
Specify next point or [Undo]: *(Pick P5)*
Specify next point or [Close/Undo]: ↵

Command: ERASE ↵
Select objects: *(Select line L1)* **1 found**
Select objects: ↵

See Fig. 32.

4. Draw the center point (axis) of the two circles in the top view and one half-circle in the front view of the open bearing using the **Dimcenter** command. Also, draw the hidden lines and axes in the top, front and side views. The command sequence is:

Command: DIMCENTER ↵
Select arc or circle: *(Select circle C1)*

Command: DIMCENTER ↵
Select arc or circle: *(Select circle C2)*

Command: DIMCENTER ↵
Select arc or circle: *(Select arc A1)*

Command: LINE ↵
Specify first point: *(Pick P1)*
Specify next point or [Undo]: *(Pick P2)*
Specify next point or [Undo]: *(Pick P3)*
Specify next point or [Close/Undo]: ↵

Command: LINE ↵
Specify first point: *(Pick P4)*
Specify next point or [Undo]: *(Pick P5)*
Specify next point or [Undo]: *(Pick P6)*
Specify next point or [Close/Undo]: ↵

Command: LINE ↵
Specify first point: *(Pick P7)*
Specify next point or [Undo]: *(Pick P8)*
Specify next point or [Undo]: *(Pick P9)*
Specify next point or [Close/Undo]: ↵

```
Command: LINE ↵
Specify first point: (Pick P10)
Specify next point or [Undo]: (Pick P11)
Specify next point or [Undo]: (Pick P12)
Specify next point or [Close/Undo]: ↵

Command: LINE ↵
Specify first
   point: (Pick P13)
Specify next
   point or
   [Undo]: (Pick P14)
Specify next
   point or
   [Undo]: (Pick P15)
Specify next
   point or
   [Close/Undo]: ↵
Command: LINE ↵
Specify first point: (Pick P16)
Specify next point or [Undo]: (Pick P17)
Specify next point or [Undo]: (Pick P18)
Specify next point or [Close/Undo]: ↵
Command: LINE ↵
Specify first point: (Pick P19)
Specify next point or [Undo]: (Pick P20)
Specify next point or [Undo]: (Pick P21)
Specify next point or [Close/Undo]: ↵
```

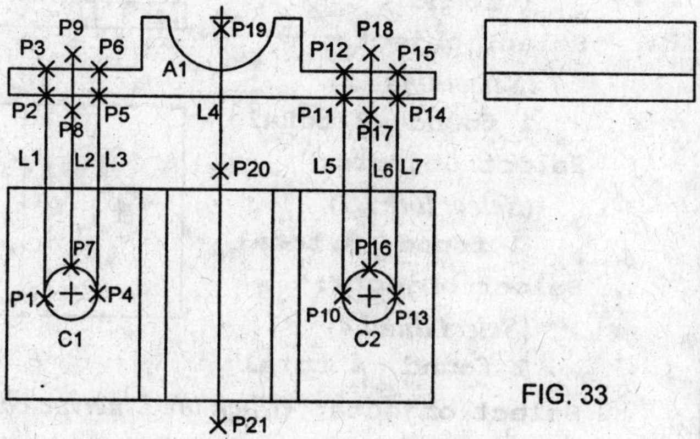

FIG. 33

See Fig. 33.

```
Command: ERASE ↵
Select objects: (Select line L1) 1 found
Select objects: (Select line L2) 1 found, 2 total
Select objects: (Select line L3) 1 found, 3 total
Select objects: (Select line L4) 1 found, 4 total
Select objects: (Select line L5) 1 found, 5 total
Select objects: (Select line L6) 1 found, 6 total
Select objects: (Select line L7) 1 found, 7 total
Select objects: ↵
```

5. Select the lines to be dashed one and click the **Linetype control** option on the **Properties** tool bar and choose the **Dashed** linetype.

The properties of the line can be changed using the **Chprop** command.

Command: **SELECT** ↵
Select objects:
(*Select line L1*)
1 found
Select objects:
(*Select line L2*)
1 found, 2 total
Select objects:
(*Select line L3*)
1 found, 3 total
Select objects:
(*Select line L4*)
1 found, 4 total
Select objects: (***Click the Linetype control option on the Properties tool bar and choose the Dashed linetype.***)

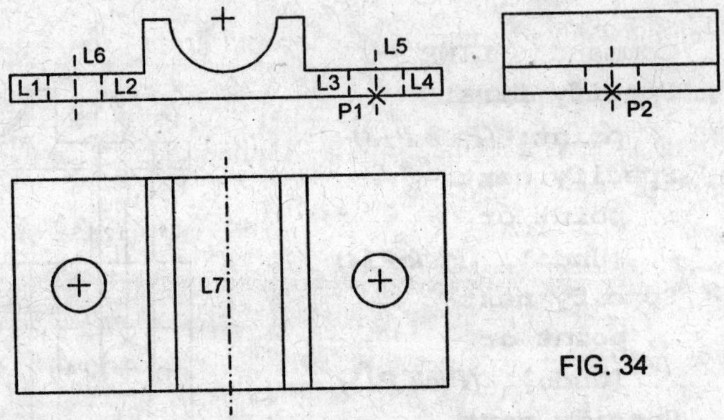

FIG. 34

Command: **CHPROP** ↵
Select objects: (*Select line L5*) **1 found**
Select objects: (*Select line L6*) **1 found, 2 total**
Select objects: (*Select line L7*) **1 found, 3 total**
Select objects: ↵
Enter property to change [Color/LAyer/LType/ltScale/LWeight/Thickness/Material/Annotative]: LT ↵
Enter new linetype name <DASHDOT>: DASHDOT ↵
Enter property to change [Color/LAyer/LType/ltScale/LWeight/Thickness/Material/Annotative]: ↵

Command: **COPY** ↵
Select objects: (*Select line L3*) **1 found**
Select objects: (*Select line L4*) **1 found, 2 total**
Select objects: (*Select line L5*) **1 found, 3 total**
Select objects: ↵
Current settings: Copy mode = Multiple
Specify base point or [Displacement/mOde] <Displacement>:(***Pick P1***)
Specify second point or <use first point as displacement>:(***Pick P2***)
Specify second point or [Exit/Undo] <Exit>: ↵

See Fig. 34.

6. Select the lines to be darkened and click the **Lineweight control** option on the **Properties** tool bar and choose the required line thickness.

   Select the lines to be dashed one and click the **Linetype control** option on the **Properties** tool bar and choose the **Dashed** linetype.

7. Using the **Dimlinear, Dim-aligned** and **Dim-diameter** command, mark the dimensions.
8. Using the **Text** command, place the text Front View and Top View at the required positions.
9. Finally save the drawing.

Fig. 35 shows the final required Orthographic Views of the **Open Bearing** diagram given in **Fig. 28.**

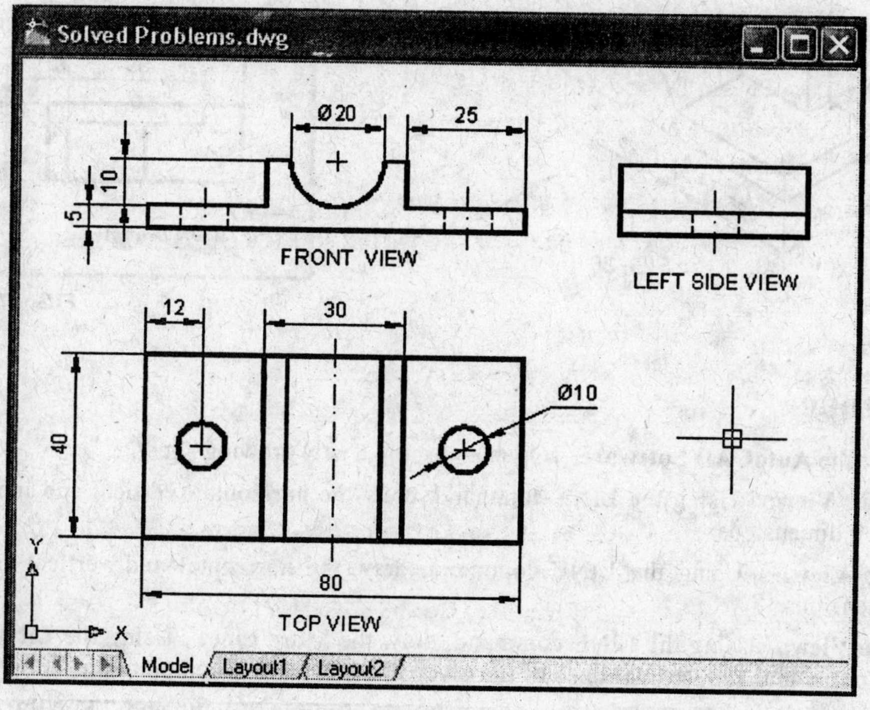

FIG. 35

Ex .No. : 5 - To draw the front, top and left side views for the given isometric view shown in Fig. 36 using the CAD software.

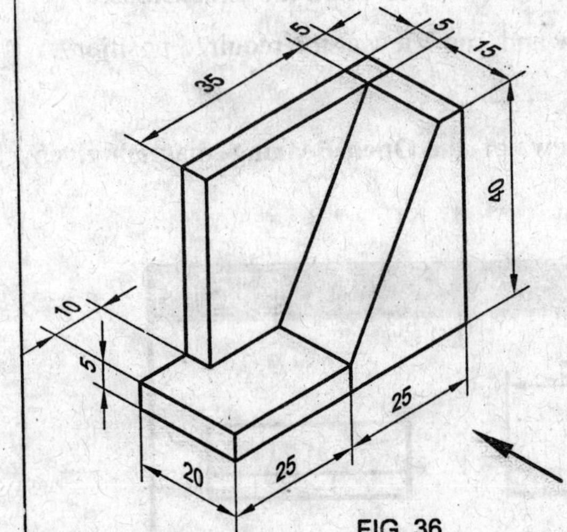

FIG. 36

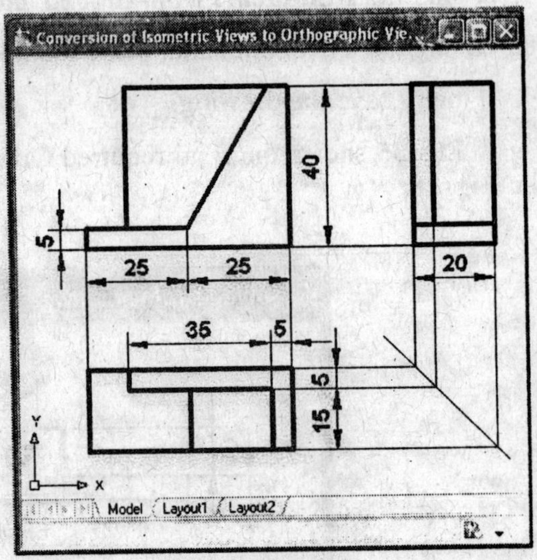

FIG. 37

PROCEDURE

1. Start the **AutoCAD Software**. Open and setup a new drawing sheet.
2. **Front View:** Using the LINE command, draw the horizontal, vertical and inclined lines of the given dimensions.
3. **Top View:** Using the LINE command, draw the horizontal and vertical lines of the given dimensions.
4. **Side View:** Using the LINE command, draw the Mitre Line. Using the LINE command, draw the horizontal and vertical lines of the given dimensions and complete the side view.
5. **Dimensioning:** Mark the dimensions using the **dimlinear** command. Finally, save the file.

Ex. No. : 1 Date :	*Ch.19* - PLAN OF TWO BED ROOM RESIDENTIAL BUILDING

THEORY

"A house is built of bricks and cement!
A home is built of love and affection!!"

1. BUILDING DRAWING – AN INTRODUCTION

Building Plans

Building Plans are important legal documents. Correct drawings save cost, labour and time in the office as well as on the site.

Any Engineer, be it Civil, Mechanical, Electrical or Electronics, etc., will be involved at some stage or the other in the construction of Residential, Office or Factory Building.

Residential Buildings

Various rooms in a residential building are: Verandah, Sit-out, Hall, Living Room, Drawing Room, Dining Room, Bed Room with attached Toilet, Kitchen-cum-Store Room, Bath Room, Toilet (Water Closet), Study Room, Pooja Room, Portico, etc.

Office Buildings

Various rooms in a small office building are: Verandah, Waiting Hall / Reception, Manager's Room, Office Room, Store Room, Toilet, etc.

Building Drawing

The main aim of building drawing is to give sufficient information by the Civil Engineer to the client.

In order to give sufficient information about the building, the following views are generally drawn:

i) Top View (Plan)
ii) Front View (Elevation) and
iii) Section at a particular plane or several planes.

2. HOW TO DRAW THE PLAN (TOP VIEW)?

Top View (Plan) : A Top View drawn by viewing the building from the top shows only the outer shape of the building and terrace. But the details required from the point of view of construction such as size of rooms, thickness of walls, positions of doors, windows, etc., are not known.

Hence, in order to show these details, the building [Fig.1(a)] is imagined to be ***cut*** by a ***Horizontal Plane at the Sill Level of the Window*** [Fig. 1(b)].*

The upper portion is removed. Now, the remaining portion (i.e., lower portion) is seen from the top. Top view [Fig. 1(b)] is drawn by projecting the remaining portion on a Horizontal Plane (HP) below the building.

Sunshade is seen above the Horizontal Cutting Plane (HCP). It should be shown by *dashed line*.

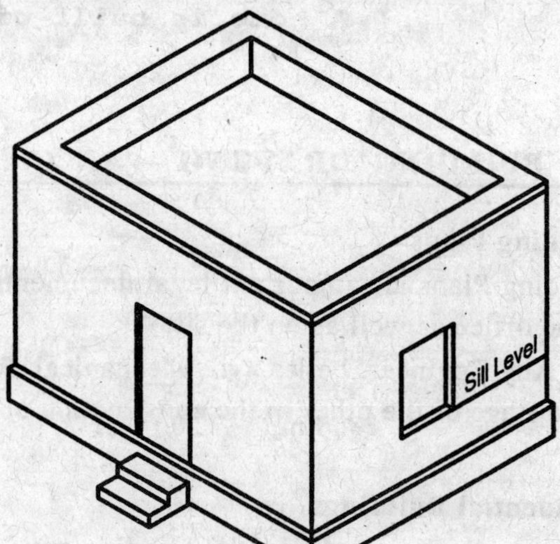

(a)

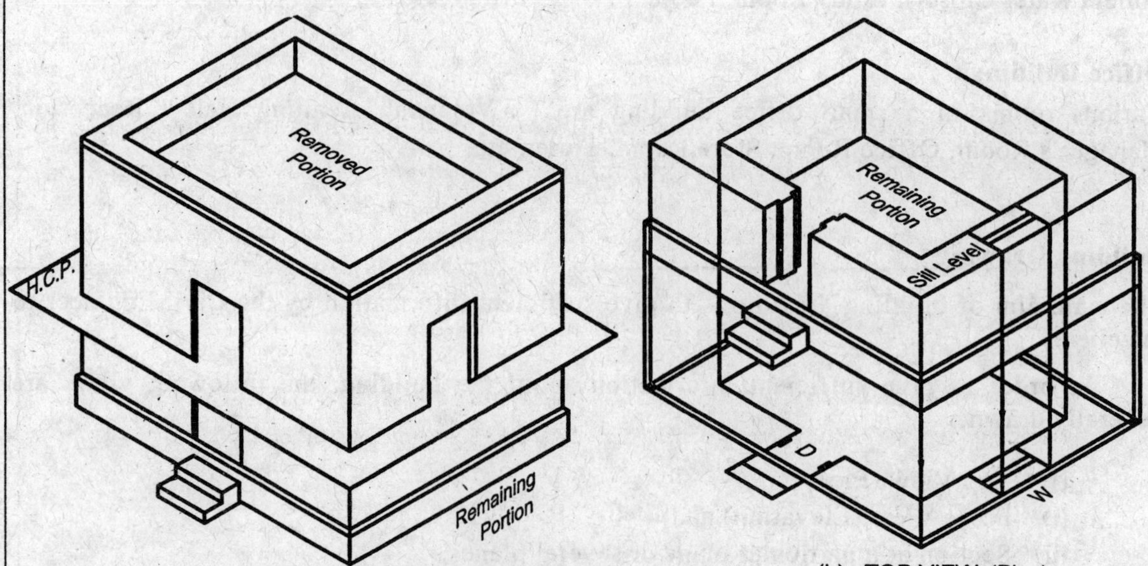

H.C.P. - Horizontal Cutting Plane at Window Sill Level

(b) TOP VIEW (Plan)

FIG. 1

1.1 LINE SKETCH or LINE PLAN or LINE DIAGRAM

The Civil Engineer should, to start with, study the plot size and get the requirements from clients regarding the number, size and location of rooms, etc. Based on the above, he prepares the Line Sketch or Line Plan of the building. It is a *skeleton drawing* showing number of rooms and their inside dimensions, locations, positions of doors, windows, etc.

Note: *The size of a room in the line sketch represents only the internal measurement.*

1.2 SPECIFICATIONS OF BUILDING COMPONENTS

1. Walls : Thickness of 1 ½ brick wall above plinth level using C.M. 1:5 =300 mm
Thickness of Partition wall in brick work using C.M. 1:5 = 100 mm

2. Doors (D and D_1)

Sl.No.	*Types of Buildings*	*Size of Doors in mm*
1.	Office Buildings	1200 x 2100 / 900 x 2100
2.	Residential Buildings	1100 x 2100 / 800 x 2100
3.	Door for Bath and Water Closet (W.C.)	800 x 2000

3. Windows

Sill Level = 900 mm
W = 1500 mm x 1200 mm
W_1 = 1000 mm x 1200 mm / 1200 mm x 1200 mm

4. Ventilator

V = 600 mm x 450 mm / 800 mm x 600 mm, placed at 1500 mm above floor level.

Unit of Dimensioning: Dimensioning shall be done in millimeters. The abbreviation *mm* may be omitted. A note stating "ALL DIMENSIONS IN mm ONLY" may be added.

AIM : To create the Plan of a Two Bedroom Residential Building shown in Fig. 2.

PROCEDURE : Command sequence to draw the plan as shown in **Fig. 2** is given below:

1. First draw the outline of the plan using the **Rectang** command. Then draw the inner border line using the **Line** command. Then remove the construction lines using **Erase** command.

```
Command: RECTANG ↵
Specify first corner point or
   [Chamfer/Elevation/Fillet/Thickness/Width]: (Pick P1)
Specify other corner point or [Area/Dimensions/Rotation]: D ↵
Specify length for rectangles <10.0000>: 93.25 ↵
Specify width for rectangles <10.0000>: 112.5 ↵
Specify other corner point or
   [Area/Dimensions/Rotation]: (Pick P2)
```

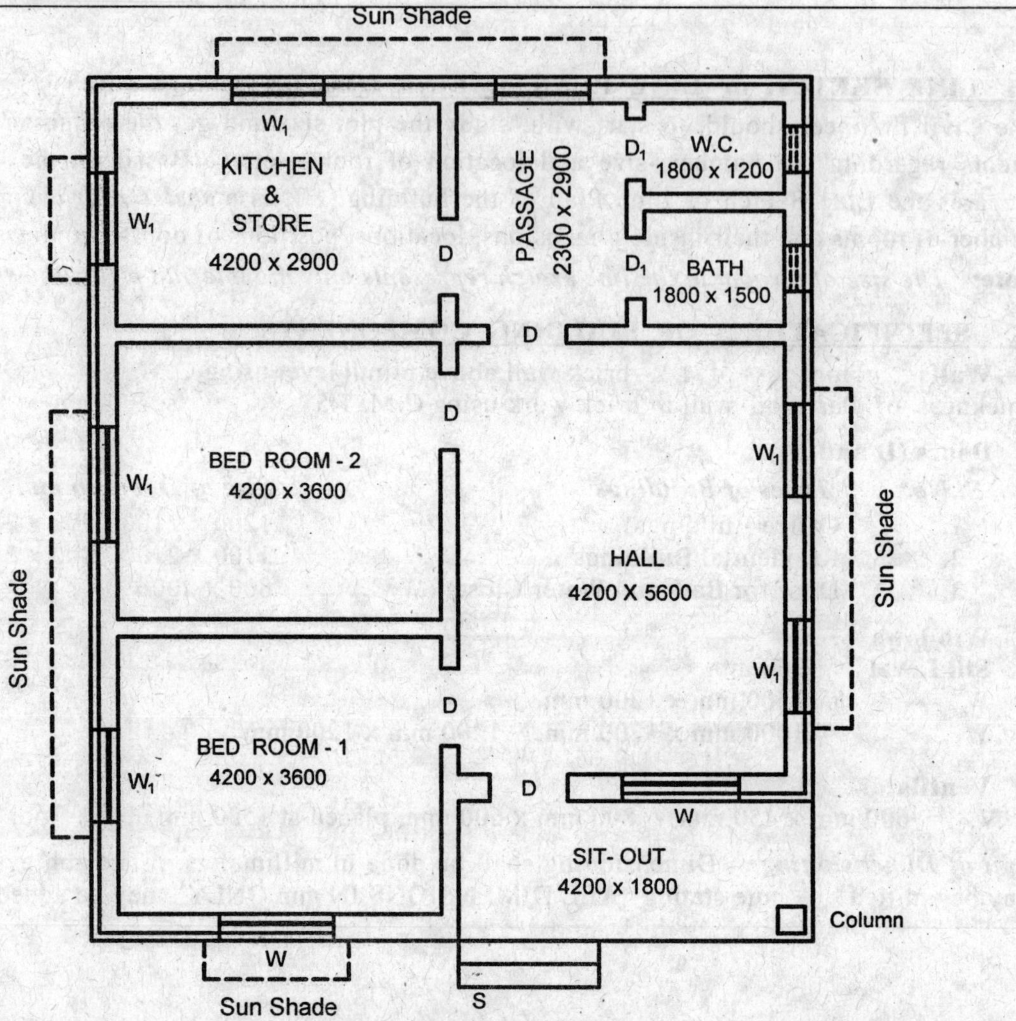

S - STEPS

D - DOOR 1000 x 2100

D_1 - DOOR 800 x 2100

W - WINDOW 1500 x 1200

W_1 - WINDOW 1200 x 1200

V - VENTILATOR 600 x 450

FIG. 2

ALL DIMENSIONS ARE IN mm ONLY

Command: **LINE** ↵

Specify first point: (*Pick P1*)

Specify next point or [Undo]: **<Ortho on>** (*Move cursor to Right*) **1** ↵

Specify next point or [Undo]: (*Move cursor to Up*) **1** ↵

```
Specify next point or [Close/Undo]: (Move cursor to Up) 110.5 ↵
Specify next point or [Close/Undo]: (Move cursor to Right) 91.25 ↵
Specify next point or [Close/Undo]: (Move cursor to Down) 92.25 ↵
Specify next point or [Close/Undo]: (Move cursor to Left) 44.5 ↵
Specify next point or [Close/Undo]: ↵

Command: LINE ↵
Specify first point: (Pick P3)
Specify next point or [Undo]: (Move cursor to Right) 45 ↵
Specify next point or [Undo]: ↵
```

See Fig. 3.

FIG. 3

2. Now, draw the inner walls of the plan using the **Line** command. Then, remove the construction lines using the **Erase** command. The command sequence is:

```
Command: LINE ↵
Specify first point: (Pick P1)
Specify next point or [Undo]:<Ortho on> (Move cursor to Right) 3.5 ↵
Specify next point or [Undo]: (Move cursor to Up) 3.5 ↵
Specify next point or [Close/Undo]: (Move cursor to Right) 42 ↵
Specify next point or [Close/Undo]: (Move cursor to Up) 36 ↵
Specify next point or [Close/Undo]: (Move cursor to Left) 42 ↵
Specify next point or [Close/Undo]: (Move cursor to Bottom) 36 ↵
Specify next point or [Close/Undo]: ↵
```

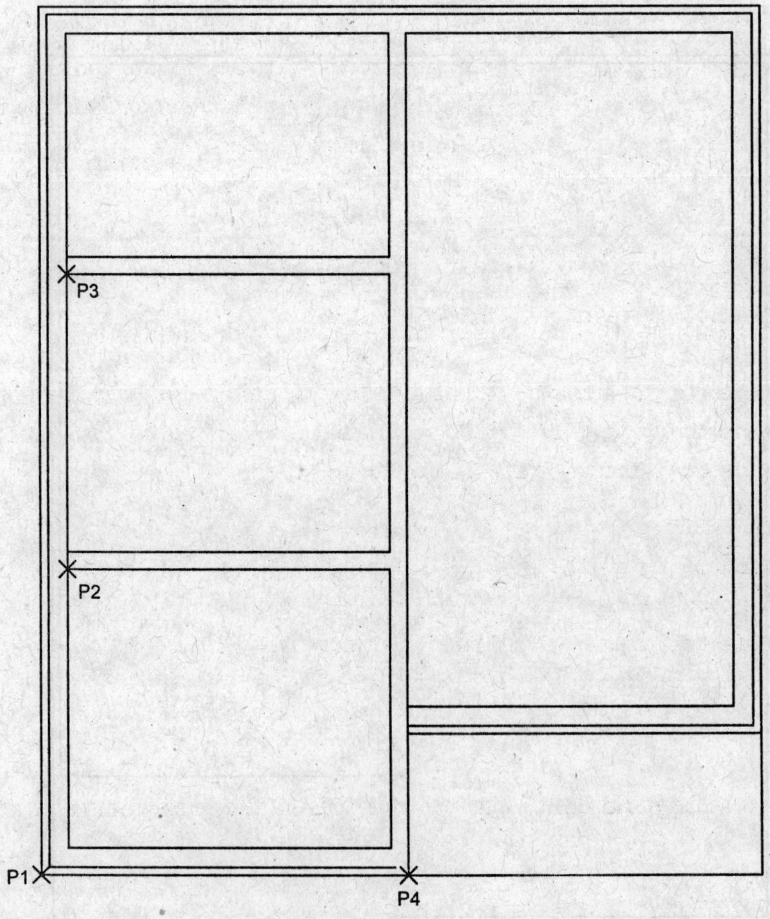

FIG. 4

Command: **LINE** ↵
Specify first point: (*Pick P2*)
Specify next point or [Undo]: (*Move cursor to Up*) 2.25 ↵
Specify next point or [Undo]: (*Move cursor to Right*) 42 ↵
Specify next point or [Close/Undo]: (*Move cursor to Up*) 36 ↵
Specify next point or [Close/Undo]: (*Move cursor to Left*) 42 ↵
Specify next point or [Close/Undo]: (*Move cursor to Bottom*) 36 ↵
Specify next point or [Close/Undo]: ↵

Command: **LINE** ↵
Specify first point: (*Pick P3*)
Specify next point or [Undo]: (*Move cursor to Up*) 2.25 ↵
Specify next point or [Undo]: (*Move cursor to Right*) 42 ↵
Specify next point or [Close/Undo]: (*Move cursor to Up*) 29 ↵
Specify next point or [Close/Undo]: (*Move cursor to Left*) 42 ↵
Specify next point or [Close/Undo]: (*Move cursor to Bottom*) 29 ↵
Specify next point or [Close/Undo]: ↵

Command: **LINE** ↵
Specify first point: (*Pick P1*)
Specify next point or [Undo]:<Ortho on> (*Move cursor to Right*) 47.75↵
Specify next point or [Undo]: (*Move cursor to Up*) 109 ↵
Specify next point or [Close/Undo]: (*Move cursor to Right*) 42 ↵
Specify next point or [Close/Undo]: (*Move cursor to Bottom*) 87.25 ↵
Specify next point or [Close/Undo]: (*Move cursor to Left*) 42 ↵
Specify next point or [Close/Undo]: ↵

Command: **LINE** ↵
Specify first point: (*Pick P4*)
Specify next point or [Undo]: <Ortho on> (*Move cursor to Up*) 18.25↵
Specify next point or [Undo]: (*Move cursor to Right*) 45.5 ↵
Specify next point or [Close/Undo]: ↵

See Fig. 4.

3. Now, draw the passage and bath room wall lines using the **Line** command. The command sequence is:

Command: **LINE** ↵
Specify first point: (*Pick P1*)
Specify next point or [Undo]: <Ortho on> (*Move cursor to Bottom*) 29 ↵

Specify next point or [Undo]: (*Move cursor to Left*) **42** ↵
Specify next point or [Close/Undo]: (*Move cursor to Bottom*) **2.25** ↵
Specify next point or [Close/Undo]: (*Move cursor to Right*) **42** ↵
Specify next point or [Close/Undo]: ↵

Command: **LINE** ↵
Specify first point: (*Pick P2*)
Specify next point or [Undo]: **<Ortho on>** (*Move cursor to Left*) **18** ↵
Specify next point or [Undo]: (*Move cursor to Up*) **29** ↵
Specify next point or [Close/Undo]: (*Move cursor to Left*) **2.25** ↵
Specify next point or [Close/Undo]: (*Move cursor to Bottom*) **29** ↵
Specify next point or [Close/Undo]: ↵

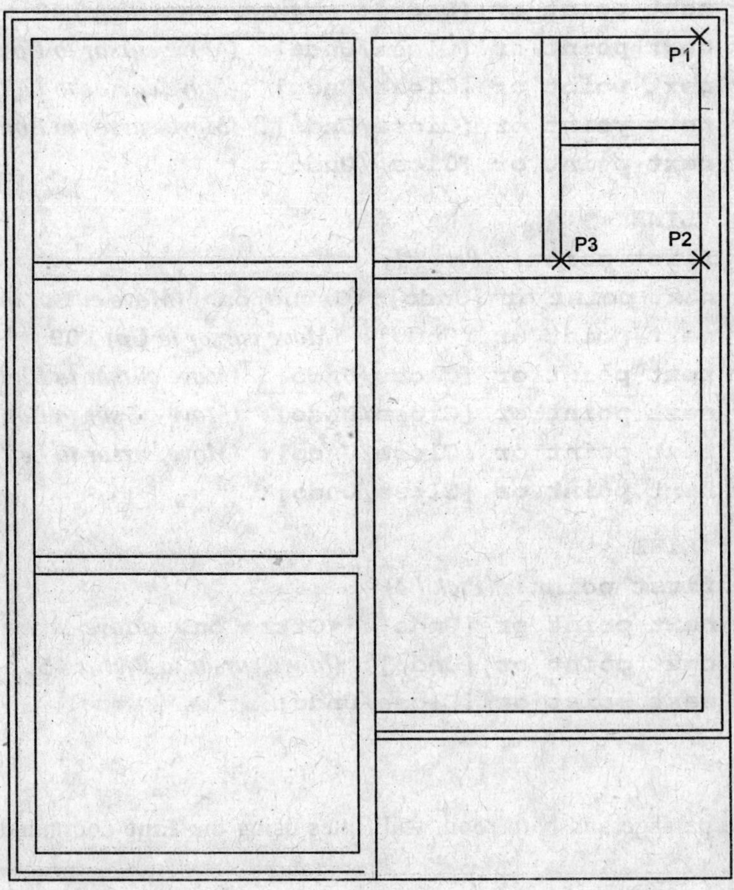

FIG. 5

Command: **LINE** ↵
Specify first point: (*Pick P3*)
Specify next point or [Undo]: <Ortho on> (*Move cursor to Up*) **15** ↵
Specify next point or [Undo]: (*Move cursor to Right*) **18** ↵
Specify next point or [Close/Undo]: (*Move cursor to Up*) **2.25** ↵
Specify next point or [Close/Undo]: (*Move cursor to Left*) **18** ↵
Specify next point or [Close/Undo]: ↵

See Fig. 5.

4. Using the **Erase** command, delete/remove the construction lines. Also, using the **Trim** command, cut the necessary lines in the plan.

5. Now, draw the lines to represent the doors using the **Line** command. Then, cut the in between lines using the **Trim** command. The command sequence is:

Command: **LINE** ↵
Specify first point: (*Pick P1*)
Specify next point or [Undo]: <Ortho on> (*Move cursor to Right*) **4** ↵
Specify next point or [Undo]: (*Move cursor to Up*) **3.5** ↵
Specify next point or [Close/Undo]: (*Move cursor to Right*) **10** ↵
Specify next point or [Close/Undo]: (*Move cursor to Bottom*) **3.5** ↵
Specify next point or [Close/Undo]:

Command: **LINE** ↵
Specify first point: (*Pick P2*)
Specify next point or [Undo]: (*Move cursor to Right*) **4** ↵
Specify next point or [Undo]: (*Move cursor to Up*) **2.25** ↵
Specify next point or [Close/Undo]: (*Move cursor to Right*) **10** ↵
Specify next point or [Close/Undo]: (*Move cursor to Bottom*) **2.25** ↵
Specify next point or [Close/Undo]: ↵

Command: **LINE** ↵
Specify first point: (*Pick P2*)
Specify next point or [Undo]: (*Move cursor to Bottom*) **4** ↵
Specify next point or [Undo]: (*Move cursor to Left*) **2.25** ↵
Specify next point or [Close/Undo]: (*Move cursor to Bottom*) **10** ↵
Specify next point or [Close/Undo]: (*Move cursor to Right*) **2.25** ↵
Specify next point or [Close/Undo]: ↵

```
Command: LINE ↵
Specify first point: (Pick P3)
Specify next point or [Undo]: (Move cursor to Up) 4 ↵
Specify next point or [Undo]: (Move cursor to Right) 2.25 ↵
Specify next point or [Close/Undo]: (Move cursor to Up) 10 ↵
Specify next point or [Close/Undo]: (Move cursor to Left) 2.25 ↵
Specify next point or [Close/Undo]: ↵

Command: LINE ↵
Specify first point: (Pick P4)
Specify next point or [Undo]: (Move cursor to Bottom) 4 ↵
Specify next point or [Undo]: (Move cursor to Right) 2.25 ↵
Specify next point or [Close/Undo]: (Move cursor to Bottom) 10 ↵
Specify next point or [Close/Undo]: (Move cursor to Left) 2.25 ↵
Specify next point or [Close/Undo]: ↵
```

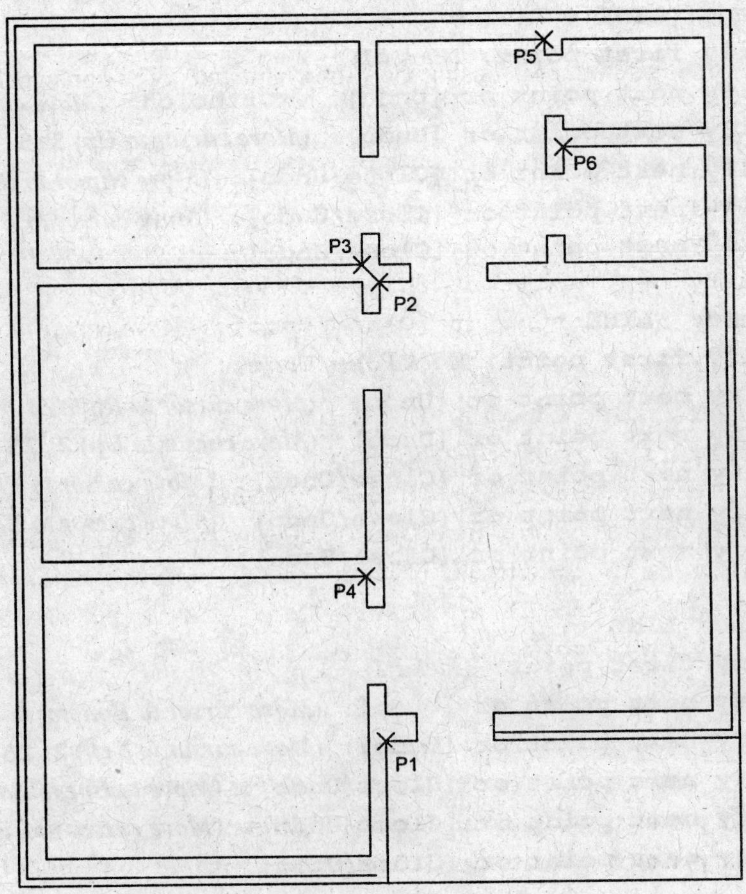

FIG. 6

Command: **LINE** ↵
Specify first point: *(Pick P5)*
Specify next point or [Undo]: <Ortho on> *(Move cursor to Bottom)* 2 ↵
Specify next point or [Undo]: *(Move cursor to Right)* 2.25 ↵
Specify next point or [Close/Undo]: *(Move cursor to Bottom)* 8 ↵
Specify next point or [Close/Undo]: *(Move cursor to Left)* 2.25 ↵
Specify next point or [Close/Undo]: ↵

Command: **LINE** ↵
Specify first point: *(Pick P6)*
Specify next point or [Undo]:<Ortho on> *(Move cursor to Bottom)* 3.5 ↵
Specify next point or [Undo]: *(Move cursor to Left)* 2.25 ↵
Specify next point or [Close/Undo]: *(Move cursor to Bottom)* 8 ↵
Specify next point or [Close/Undo]: *(Move cursor to Right)* 2.25 ↵
Specify next point or [Close/Undo]: ↵

See Fig. 6.

6. Draw the windows in the plan using the **Line** command. The command sequence is:

Command: **LINE** ↵
Specify first point: *(Pick P1)*
Specify next point or [Undo]: <Ortho on> *(Move cursor to Left)* 14 ↵
Specify next point or [Undo]: *(Move cursor to Bottom)* 3.5 ↵
Specify next point or [Close/Undo]: *(Move cursor to Left)* 15 ↵
Specify next point or [Close/Undo]: *(Move cursor to Up)* 3.5 ↵
Specify next point or [Close/Undo]: ↵

Command: **LINE** ↵
Specify first point: *(Pick P2)*
Specify next point or [Undo]: <Ortho on> *(Move cursor to Up)* 12 ↵
Specify next point or [Undo]: *(Move cursor to Left)* 3.5 ↵
Specify next point or [Close/Undo]: *(Move cursor to Up)* 12 ↵
Specify next point or [Close/Undo]: *(Move cursor to Right)* 3.5 ↵
Specify next point or [Close/Undo]: ↵

Command: **LINE** ↵
Specify first point: *(Pick P3)*
Specify next point or [Undo]: *(Move cursor to Up)* 12 ↵
Specify next point or [Undo]: *(Move cursor to Left)* 3.5 ↵
Specify next point or [Close/Undo]: *(Move cursor to Up)* 12 ↵

```
Specify next point or [Close/Undo]: (Move cursor to Right) 3.5 ↵
Specify next point or [Close/Undo]: ↵

Command: LINE ↵
Specify first point: (Pick P4)
Specify next point or [Undo]: (Move cursor to Up) 8 ↵
Specify next point or [Undo]: (Move cursor to Left) 3.5 ↵
Specify next point or [Close/Undo]: (Move cursor to Up) 12 ↵
Specify next point or [Close/Undo]: (Move cursor to Right) 3.5 ↵
Specify next point or [Close/Undo]: ↵

Command: LINE ↵
Specify first point: (Pick P5)
Specify next point or [Undo]: (Move cursor to Right) 15 ↵
Specify next point or [Undo]: (Move cursor to Up) 3.5 ↵
Specify next point or [Close/Undo]: (Move cursor to Right) 12 ↵
```

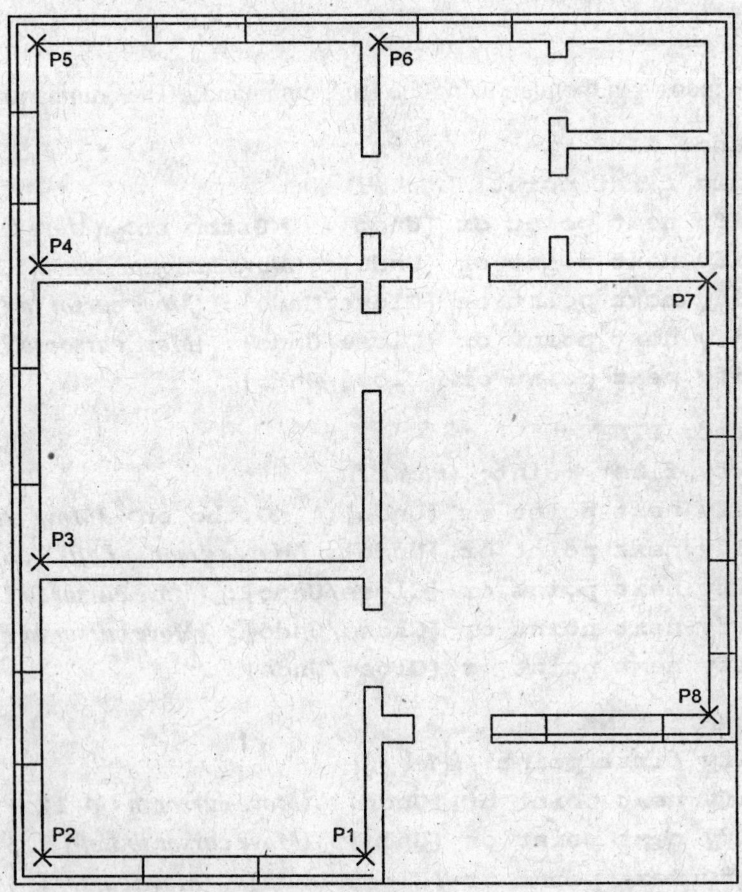

FIG. 7

Specify next point or [Close/Undo]: *(Move cursor to Bottom)* 3.5 ↵
Specify next point or [Close/Undo]: ↵

Command: **LINE** ↵
Specify first point: *(Pick P6)*
Specify next point or [Undo]: *(Move cursor to Right)* 5 ↵
Specify next point or [Undo]: *(Move cursor to Up)* 3.5 ↵
Specify next point or [Close/Undo]: *(Move cursor to Right)* 12 ↵
Specify next point or [Close/Undo]: *(Move cursor to Bottom)* 3.5 ↵
Specify next point or [Close/Undo]: ↵

Command: **LINE** ↵
Specify first point: *(Pick P7)*
Specify next point or [Undo]: *(Move cursor to Bottom)* 8 ↵
Specify next point or [Undo]: *(Move cursor to Right)* 3.5 ↵
Specify next point or [Close/Undo]: *(Move cursor to Bottom)* 12 ↵
Specify next point or [Close/Undo]: *(Move cursor to Left)* 3.5 ↵
Specify next point or [Close/Undo]: ↵

Command: **LINE** ↵
Specify first point: *(Pick P8)*
Specify next point or [Undo]: *(Move cursor to Up)* 8 ↵
Specify next point or [Undo]: *(Move cursor to Right)* 3.5 ↵
Specify next point or [Close/Undo]: *(Move cursor to Up)* 12 ↵
Specify next point or [Close/Undo]: *(Move cursor to Left)* 3.5 ↵
Specify next point or [Close/Undo]: ↵

Command: **LINE** ↵
Specify first point: *(Pick P8)*
Specify next point or [Undo]: *(Move cursor to Left)* 6 ↵
Specify next point or [Undo]: *(Move cursor to Bottom)* 3.5 ↵
Specify next point or [Close/Undo]: *(Move cursor to Left)* 15 ↵
Specify next point or [Close/Undo]: *(Move cursor to Up)* 3.5 ↵
Specify next point or [Close/Undo]: ↵

See Fig. 7.

7. Now, remove the construction lines using the **Erase** command. Also, cut the necessary lines using the **Trim** command. And, finish the window with a wide line using the **Width** option in the **Pline** command. The command sequence is:

Command: **PLINE** ↵
Specify start point:

Current line-width is 0.0000
Specify next point or [Arc/Halfwidth/Length/Undo/Width]: W ↵
Specify starting width <0.0000>: 1 ↵
Specify ending width <1.0000>: 1 ↵
Specify next point or [Arc/Halfwidth/
Length/Undo/Width]: ***(Pick a point on one end of the window)***
Specify next point or [Arc/Close/Halfwidth/
Length/Undo/Width]: ***(Pick a point on another end of the window)***

Similarly, draw wide lines in all the windows using the **Width** option of the **Pline** command.

8. Draw the ventilators of the plan using the **Line** command. Then, remove the construction lines using the Erase command. The command sequence is:

Command: **LINE** ↵
Specify first point: ***(Pick P1)***
Specify next point or [Undo]: <Ortho on> ***(Move cursor to Up)*** **4.5** ↵
Specify next point or [Undo]: ***(Move cursor to Right)*** **3.5** ↵

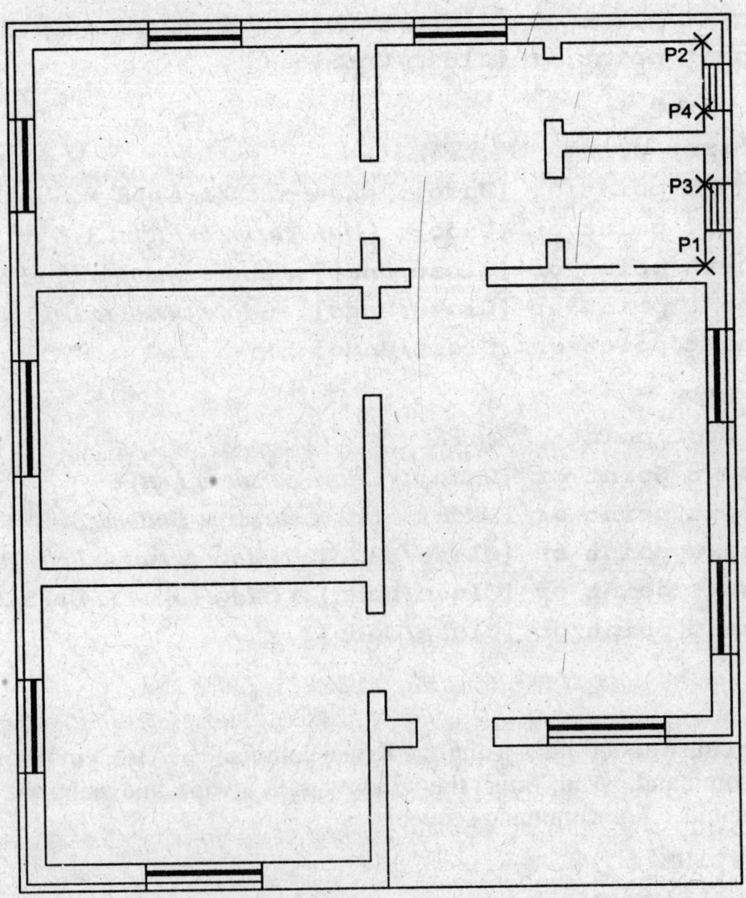

FIG. 8

```
Specify next point or [Close/Undo]: (Move cursor to Up) 6 ↵
Specify next point or [Close/Undo]: (Move cursor to Left) 3.5 ↵
Specify next point or [Close/Undo]: ↵

Command: LINE ↵
Specify first point: (Pick P2)
Specify next point or [Undo]: (Move cursor to Bottom) 3 ↵
Specify next point or [Undo]: (Move cursor to Right) 3.5 ↵
Specify next point or [Close/Undo]: (Move cursor to Bottom) 6 ↵
Specify next point or [Close/Undo]: (Move cursor to Left) 3.5 ↵
Specify next point or [Close/Undo]: ↵

Command: LINE ↵
Specify first point: (Pick P3)
Specify next point or [Undo]: (Move cursor to Right) .8 ↵
Specify next point or [Undo]: (Move cursor to Bottom) 6 ↵
Specify next point or [Close/Undo]: (Move cursor to Right).8 ↵
Specify next point or [Close/Undo]: (Move cursor to Up) 6 ↵
Specify next point or [Close/Undo]: ↵

Command: LINE ↵
Specify first point: (Pick P4)
Specify next point or [Undo]: (Move cursor to Right) .8 ↵
Specify next point or [Undo]: (Move cursor to Up) 6 ↵
Specify next point or [Close/Undo]: (Move cursor to Right) .8 ↵
Specify next point or [Close/Undo]: (Move cursor to Bottom) 6 ↵
Specify next point or [Close/Undo]: ↵
```

See Fig. 8.

9. Darken the necessary lines using the **Width** option of the **Pedit** command.

10. Draw the steps using the **Rectang** command. Also, draw the sunshade of the plan using the **Line** command. The command sequence is:

```
Command: RECTANG ↵
Specify first corner point or [Chamfer/
   Elevation/Fillet/Thickness/Width]: (Pick P1)
Specify other corner point or [Area/Dimensions/Rotation]: D ↵
Specify length for rectangles <10.0000>: 18 ↵
Specify width for rectangles <10.0000>: 3 ↵
Specify other corner point or [Area/Dimensions/Rotation]:(Pick P2)
```

```
Command: RECTANG ↵
Specify first corner point or [Chamfer/
  Elevation/Fillet/Thickness/Width]: (Pick P3)
Specify other corner point or [Area/Dimensions/Rotation]: D ↵
Specify length for rectangles <18.0000>: 18 ↵
Specify width for rectangles <3.0000>: 3 ↵
Specify other corner point or [Area/Dimensions/Rotation]:(Pick P4)

Command: LINE ↵
Specify first point: (Pick P5)
Specify next point or [Undo]:  <Ortho on> (Move cursor to Left) 2 ↵
Specify next point or [Undo]: (Move cursor to Bottom) 5 ↵
Specify next point or [Close/Undo]: (Move cursor to Right) 19 ↵
Specify next point or [Close/Undo]: (Move cursor to Up) 5 ↵
Specify next point or [Close/Undo]: ↵
```

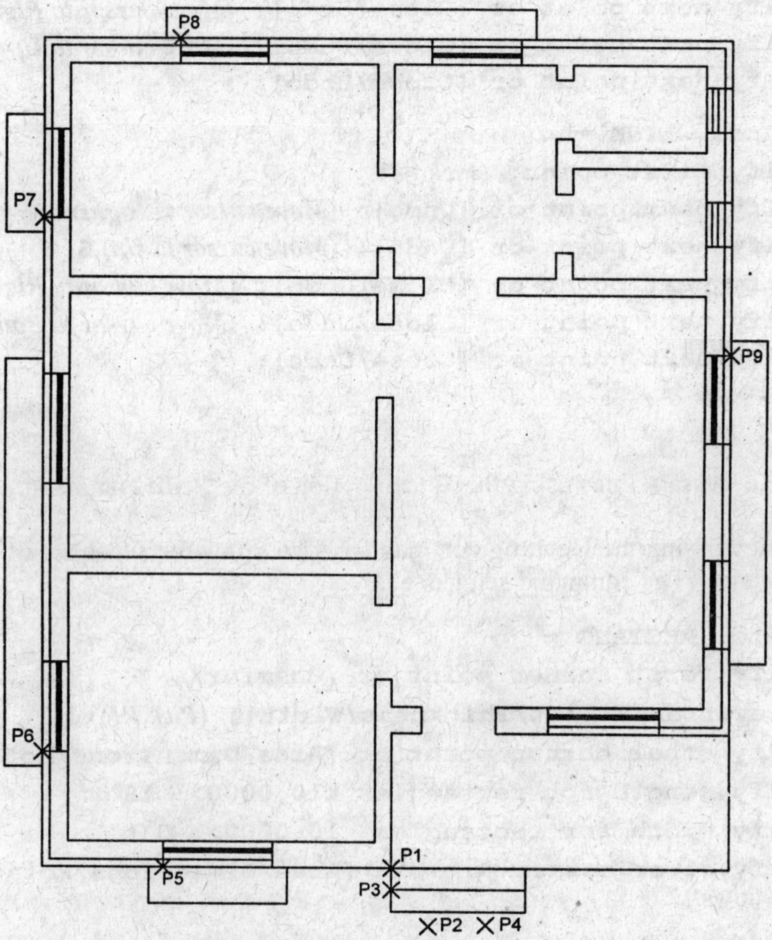

FIG. 9

Command: **LINE** ↵
Specify first point: (*Pick P6*)
Specify next point or [Undo]: **<Ortho on>** (*Move cursor to Bottom*) 2 ↵
Specify next point or [Undo]: (*Move cursor to Left*) 5 ↵
Specify next point or [Close/Undo]: (*Move cursor to Up*) 55.25 ↵
Specify next point or [Close/Undo]: (*Move cursor to Right*) 5 ↵
Specify next point or [Close/Undo]: ↵

Command: **LINE** ↵
Specify first point: (*Pick P7*)
Specify next point or [Undo]: **<Ortho on>** (*Move cursor to Bottom*) 2 ↵
Specify next point or [Undo]: (*Move cursor to Left*) 5 ↵
Specify next point or [Close/Undo]: (*Move cursor to Up*) 16 ↵
Specify next point or [Close/Undo]: (*Move cursor to Right*) 5 ↵
Specify next point or [Close/Undo]: ↵

Command: **LINE** ↵
Specify first point: (*Pick P8*)
Specify next point or [Undo]: (*Move cursor to Left*) 2 ↵
Specify next point or [Undo]: (*Move cursor to Up*) 5 ↵
Specify next point or [Close/Undo]: (*Move cursor to Right*) 50.25 ↵
Specify next point or [Close/Undo]: (*Move cursor to Bottom*) 5 ↵
Specify next point or [Close/Undo]: ↵

Command: **LINE** ↵
Specify first point: (*Pick P9*)
Specify next point or [Undo]: **<Ortho on>** (*Move cursor to Up*) 2 ↵
Specify next point or [Undo]: (*Move cursor to Right*) 5 ↵
Specify next point or [Close/Undo]: (*Move cursor to Bottom*) 44 ↵
Specify next point or [Close/Undo]: (*Move cursor to Left*) 5 ↵
Specify next point or [Close/Undo]: ↵

See Fig. 9.

11. In the plan, the sunshade is drawn as dashed lines. Also, the inner lines of the ventilators are also drawn as dashed one. Select the lines to be dashed one and click the **Linetype control** option on the **Properties** tool bar and choose the **Dashed** linetype.

12. Name the rooms including dimensions using the **Text** command. Also, mark doors as D or D_1, windows W or W_1, ventilators as V and steps as S using the **Text** command.

13. Draw the column at the right bottom of the sit-out as a rectangle using the **Rectang** command. Mark the Column and Sunshade using the **Text** command.
14. Below the plan, draw a rectangle using the **Rectang** command and write abbreviations and their dimensions using the **Text** command. Also, place the text "ALL DIMENSIONS ARE IN mm ONLY" at the bottom using the **Text** command.
15. Finally save drawing. **Fig. 10** shows the final view of the plan as shown in **Fig. 2.**

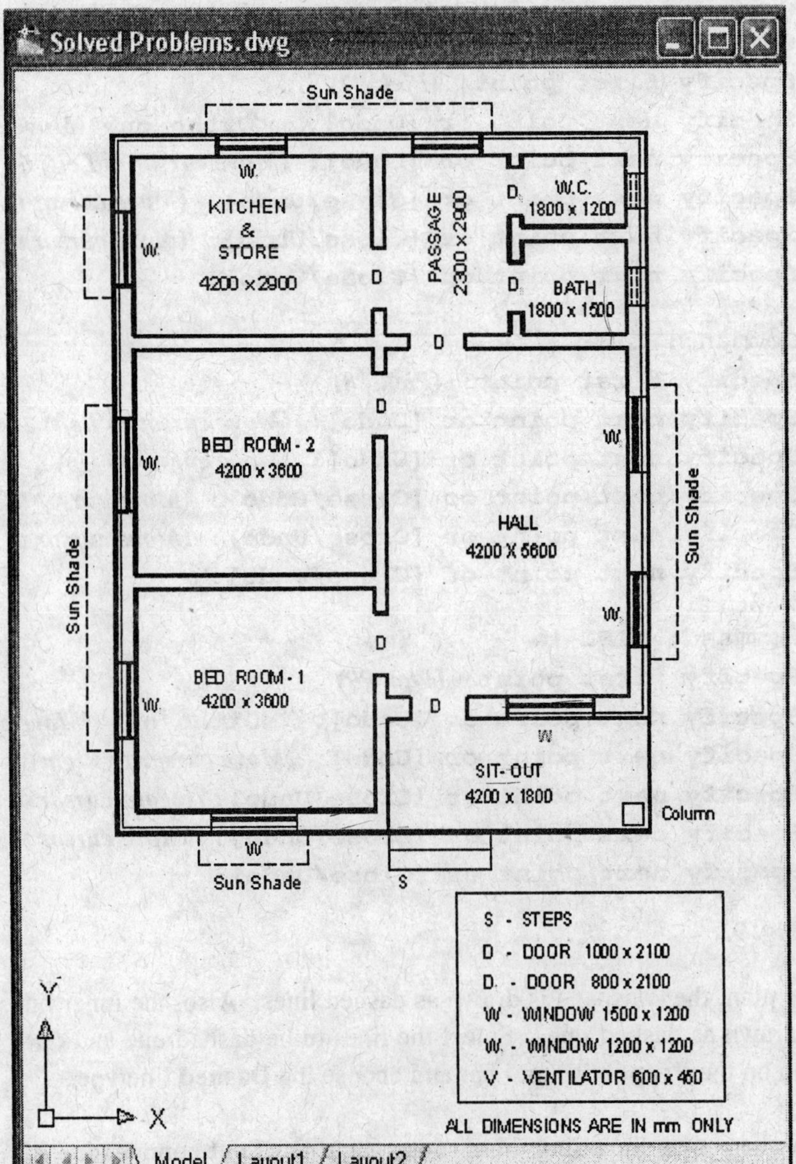

FIG. 10

Ex. No. : 1 Date :	*Ch.20* - **SIMPLE STEEL TRUSS**

AIM : To *draw the **Simple Steel Truss** shown in **Fig.1**, using Auto CAD.*

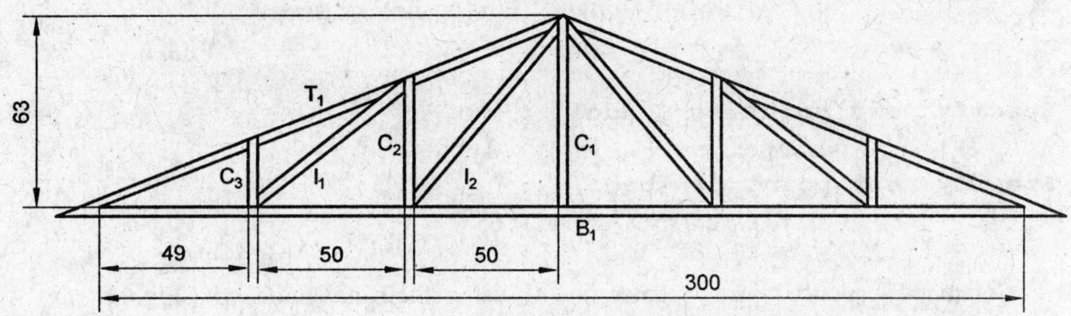

FIG. 1 SIMPLE STEEL TRUSS

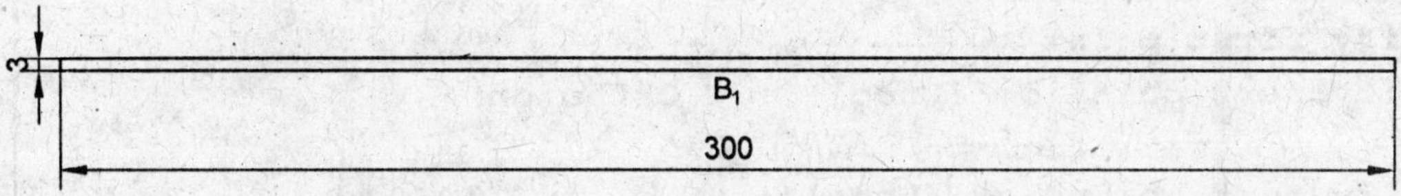

FIG. 2

STEP 1 : Command sequence to draw the Base line B_1 using the **Line** command : (**Fig.2**)

Command : **LINE**

```
Specify first point :
Specify next point or [Undo]   : < Ortho on > ↵
              ( Move the cursor to right )  300 ↵
Specify next  point or [Undo] :
              ( Move the cursor to up )     3 ↵
Specify next point or [Undo]   :
              ( Move the cursor to left )   300 ↵
Specify next point or [Undo]   :
              ( Move the cursor to down )   3 ↵
```

STEP 2 : Command sequence to draw center line C_1 using the **Line** command : (**Fig.3**)

Command : **LINE**

```
Specify first point :
Specify next point or [Undo]   : < Ortho on > ↵
              ( Move the cursor to right )  3 ↵
Specify next  point or [Undo] :
              ( Move the cursor to up )     63 ↵
```

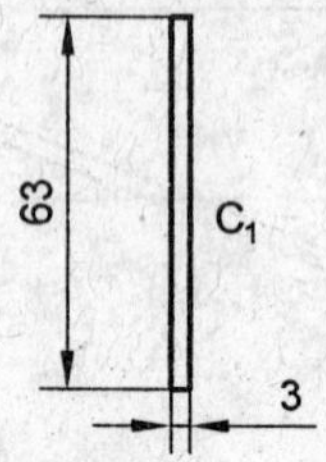

FIG. 3

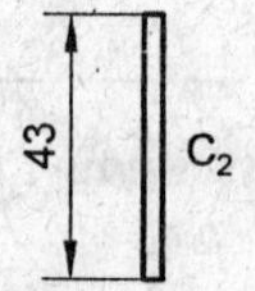

FIG. 4

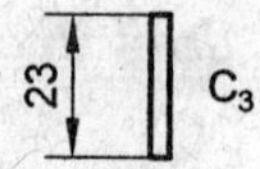

FIG. 5

Specify next point or [Undo] :
(*Move the cursor to left*) 3 ↵
Specify next point or [Undo] :
(*Move the cursor to down*) 63 ↵

STEP 3 : Command sequence to draw center line C_2 using the **Line** command: (**Fig.4**)

Command : **LINE**

Specify first point :
Specify next point or [Undo] : < Ortho on > ↵
(*Move the cursor to right*) 3 ↵
Specify next point or [Undo] :
(*Move the cursor to up*) 43 ↵
Specify next point or [Undo] :
(*Move the cursor to left*) 3 ↵
Specify next point or [Undo] :
(*Move the cursor to down*) 43 ↵

STEP 4 : Command sequence to draw center line C_3 using the **Line** command : (**Fig.5**)

Command : **LINE**

Specify first point :
Specify next point or [Undo] : < Ortho on > ↵
(*Move the cursor to right*) 3 ↵
Specify next point or [Undo] :
(*Move the cursor to up*) 23 ↵
Specify next point or [Undo] :
(*Move the cursor to left*) 3 ↵
Specify next point or [Undo] :
(*Move the cursor to down*) 23 ↵

STEP 5 : Command sequence to draw the truss line T_1 using the **Line** command : (**Fig.6**)

Command : **LINE**

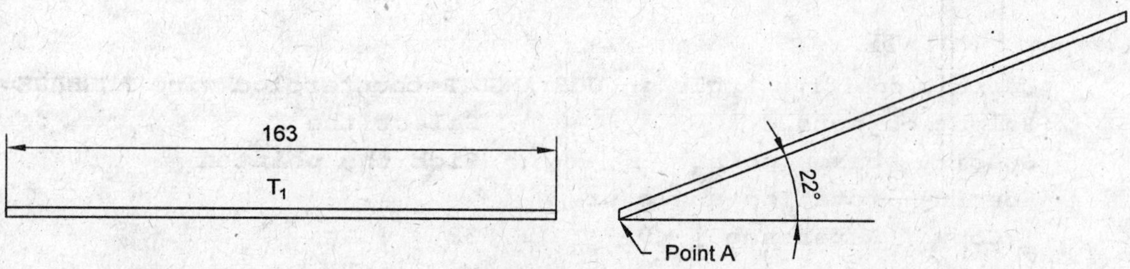

FIG. 6

```
Specify first point :
Specify next point or [Undo]   : < Ortho on > ↵
            ( Move the cursor to right )  163 ↵
Specify next  point or [Undo] :
            ( Move the cursor to up )     3 ↵
Specify next point or [Undo]   :
            ( Move the cursor to left )   163 ↵
Specify next point or [Undo]   :
            ( Move the cursor to down )   3 ↵
```

Command : **ROTATE**

```
Current positive angle in UCS:
ANGDIR=counterclockwise ANGBASE=0
Select objects                 : Select the  T
Specify  base  point           : Pick the point A
Specify  rotation angle or
[ Copy / Reference ] <0>       :  22
```

STEP 6 : Command sequence to draw the inclined line I_1 using the **Line** command : (**Fig.7**)

Command : **LINE**

```
Specify first point :
Specify next point or [Undo]   : < Ortho on > ↵
            ( Move the cursor to right )  66 ↵
Specify next  point or [Undo] :
            ( Move the cursor to up )     3 ↵
Specify next point or [Undo]   :
            ( Move the cursor to left )   66 ↵
Specify next point or [Undo]   :
            ( Move the cursor to down )   3 ↵
```

Command : **ROTATE**

Current positive angle in UCS:ANGDIR=counterclockwise ANGBASE=0
Select objects : Select the I_1
Specify base point : Pick the point A
Specify rotation angle or
[Copy / Reference] <0> : 39

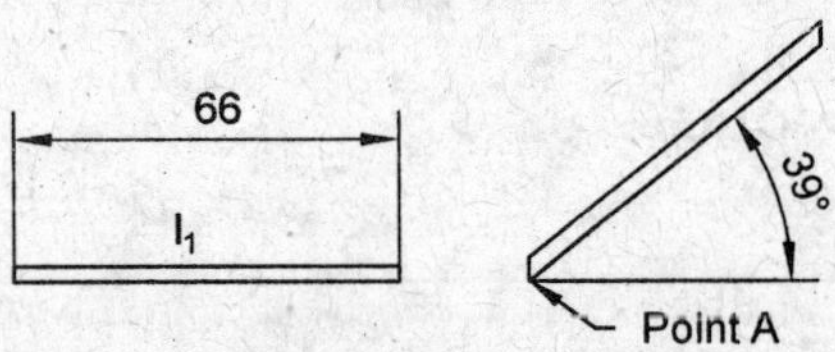

FIG. 7

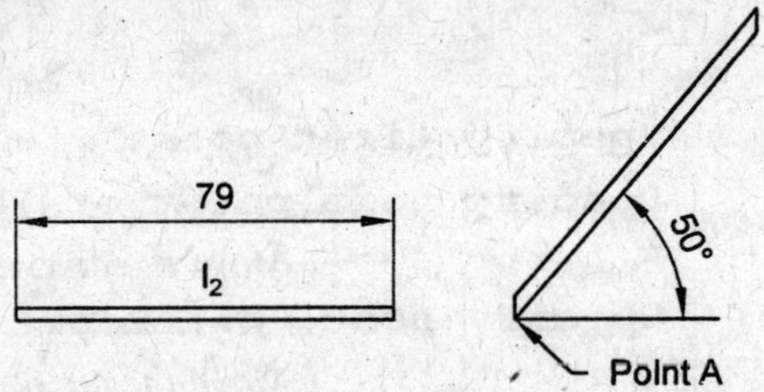

FIG. 8

STEP 7 : Command sequence to draw the inclined line I_2 using the **Line** command : (**Fig.8**)

Command : **LINE**

Specify first point :
Specify next point or [Undo] : < Ortho on > ↵
(*Move the cursor to right*) 79 ↵
Specify next point or [Undo] :
(*Move the cursor to up*) 3 ↵
Specify next point or [Undo] :
(*Move the cursor to left*) 79 ↵
Specify next point or [Undo] :
(*Move the cursor to down*) 3 ↵

Command : **ROTATE**

Current positive angle in UCS:
ANGDIR=counterclockwise ANGBASE=0
Select objects : Select the I_2
Specify base point : Pick the point A
Specify rotation angle or
[Copy / Reference] <0> : 50

STEP 8 : Command sequence to join C_1 and B_1 using the **Move** command : (**Fig.9**)

Command : **MOVE**

Select objects : C_1
Specify base point or [Displacement] : C_1 Center point

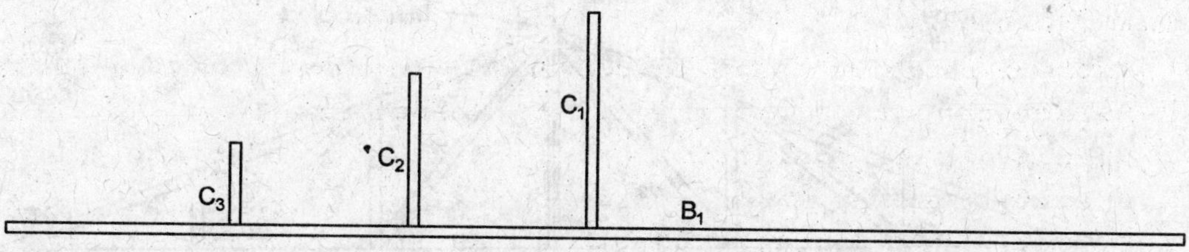

FIG. 9

```
<Displacement>:
Specify second point or
<use first point as displacement>:          : B1  Center point
```

*Similarly, use **MOVE** command for C_2 & C_3 to fix on B_1 with distances 50 & 50 as in **Fig.9**.*

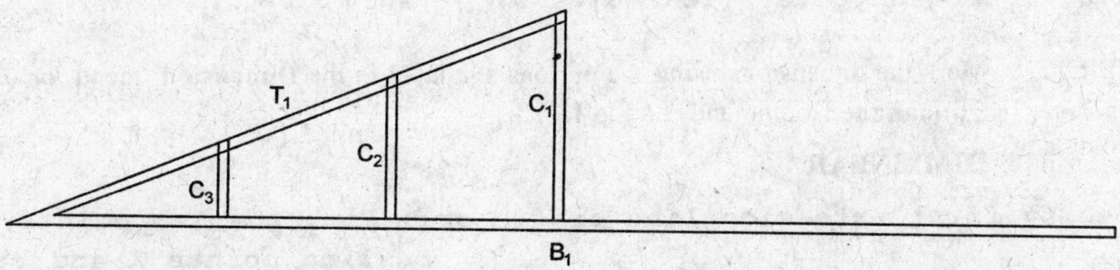

FIG. 10

STEP 9 : Command sequence to join C_1 and T_1 using the **Move** command : (**Fig.10**)
Command : **MOVE**

```
Select objects                               : T1
Specify base point or [Displacement]         : T1  Start point
<Displacement>:
Specify second point or
<use first point as displacement>:           : C1  End point
```

*Similarly, use **MOVE** command to join I_1 with C_2 and I_2 with C_1 as shown in **Fig.10.***

STEP 10 : Use TRIM command for trimming the joint in the Truss : **See Fig.11.**

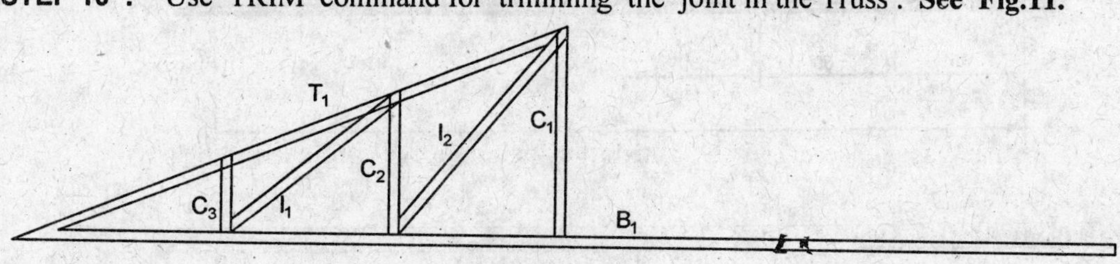

FIG. 11

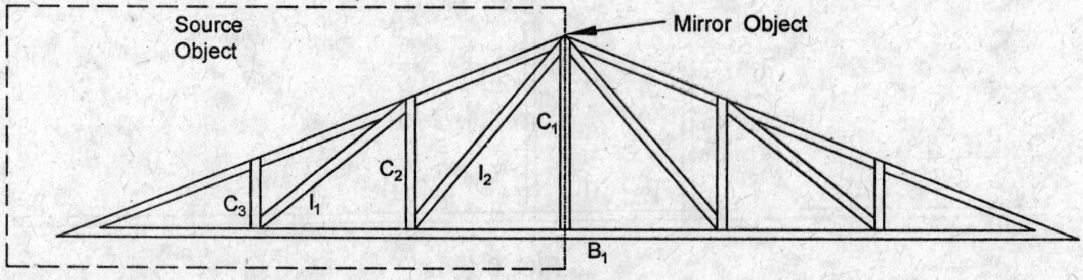

FIG. 12

STEP 11 : Command sequence using the **Mirror** command : (**Fig.12**)

Command : **MIRROR**

```
Select objects                          :  Select all
Specify first point of mirror line  :  pick the mirror line bottom
Specify second point of mirror line :  pick the mirror line top
Erase source objects? [Yes/No] <N>  :  No
```

STEP 12 : Mark the dimensions using the options available in the **Dimension** menu *or* using the **dimlinear** *or* **dimaligned** commands : (**Fig.13**)

Command : **DIMLINEAR**

```
Specify first extension line origin or : Pick the two points, say,
                                         line points X and Y, drag
                                         and left click by mouse.
```

Note : Following the above procedure, create the other dimensions of the given Steel Truss.

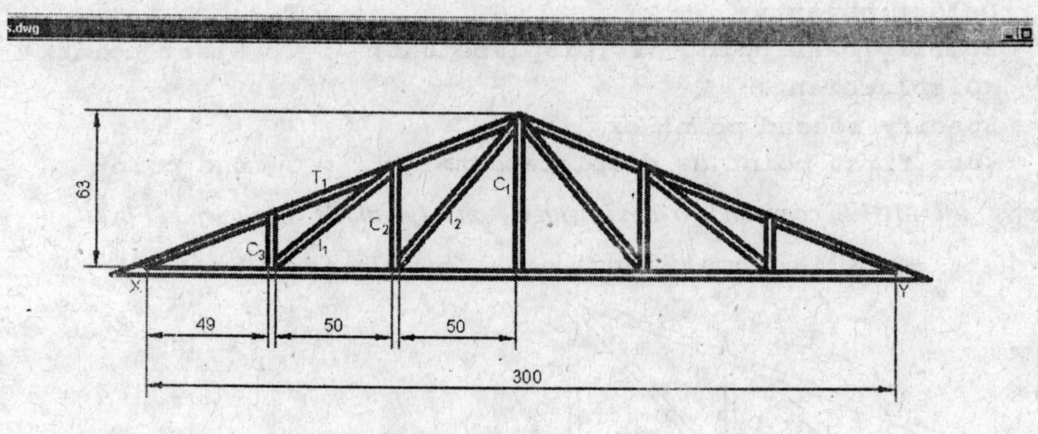

FIG. 13

Ch.21 - SECTIONAL VIEWS OF SIMPLE SOLIDS

HATCHING THE DRAWINGS
THEORY

1. HATCHING

While drawing sections of solids, the sectioned area needs to be filled with some pattern. Filling objects with a pattern is known as **Hatching**. The **Hatching** process is accomplished by using the **Hatch** tool. Before learning the **Hatch** tool, understand some terms that are used while hatching. They are: **Hatch Patterns** and **Hatch Boundary**.

1.1 HATCH PATTERNS

AutoCAD provides a variety of hatch patterns. Every hatch pattern is composed of one or more hatch lines of a solid fill. The lines are placed at specified angle and spacing. User can change the angle and the spacing between the hatch lines.

AutoCAD provides a solid fill and more than 50 industry-standard hatch patterns that user can use to differentiate the components of objects or represent object materials. AutoCAD also provides 14 hatch patterns that conform to the ISO (International Standards Organization) standards. When an ISO pattern is selected, specify a pen width, which determines the line weight in the pattern.

1.2 HATCH BOUNDARY

You can hatch an enclosed area or hatch within a specified boundary using the **Hatch** tool. By default, **Hatch** tool creates associative hatches that are updated when the boundary is changed. A hatch can be created by selecting an object to hatch or by defining a boundary and then specifying an internal point. A **Hatch Boundary** can be any combination of objects, such as lines, arcs, circles, and polylines, that forms an enclosed area.

Enclosed areas within the hatch area are referred to as islands. Hatch them or leave them un-hatched depending on the Islands setting in the **Hatch and Gradient** dialog box. If you are hatching a small area in a complex drawing, you can use boundary sets to speed the process.

Objects can be hatched only if they are in a plane parallel to the *XY* plane of the current UCS. Note that if you want to hatch an area that is not completely enclosed, you can set a gap tolerance. Any gaps equal to or smaller than the value you specify in the gap tolerance are ignored and the boundary is treated as closed.

2. HATCH TOOL

The **Hatch** tool fills an enclosed area or selected objects with a predefined hatch pattern, solid fill or gradient fill. The **Hatch** command can be invoked using any one of the following methods:

1. Type **HATCH** or **H** in the command prompt and press Enter.
2. Choose the **Hatch** tool from the **Draw** panel in the **Home** tab.
3. Choose the **Hatch** tool from the **Draw** menu.
4. Choose the **Hatch** tool from the **Draw** toolbar.

Enter ***-hatch*** at the Command prompt to display the options in the **Hatch** command. If the **Hatch** command is invoked, then the **Hatch and Gradient** dialog box is displayed as shown in **Fig. 1.** It defines the boundaries, pattern type, pattern properties and other parameters for hatch and gradient fill objects.

The **Hatch and Gradient** dialog box includes the following:

- Hatch tab
- Gradient tab
- More Options section
- Add: Pick Points
- Add: Select Objects
- Remove Boundaries
- Recreate Boundary
- View Selections
- Select Boundary Objects
- Options
- Inherit Properties
- Preview

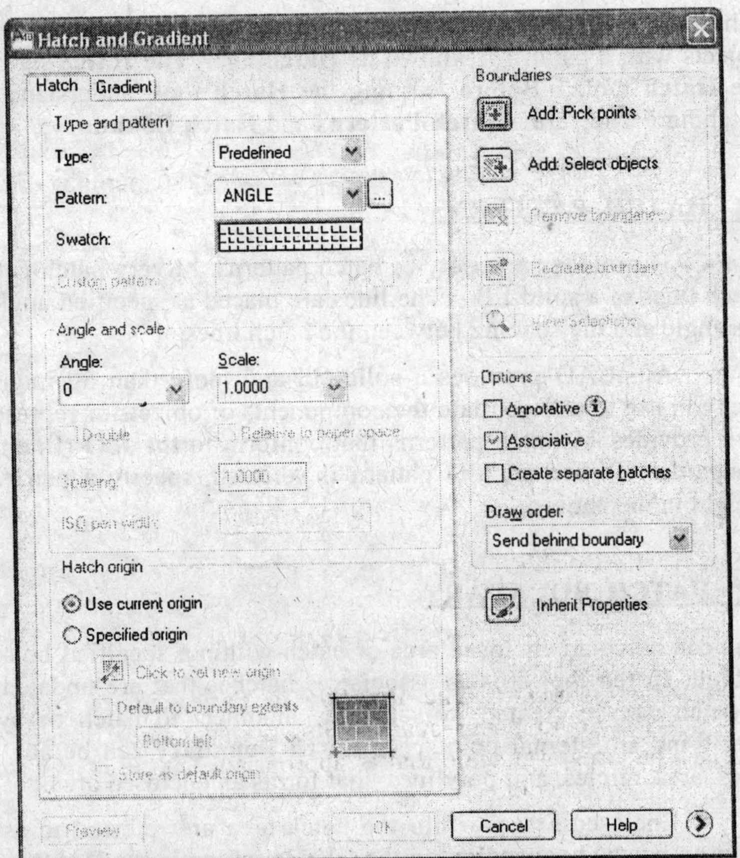

FIG. 1

2.1 HATCH TAB

Type and Pattern

The **Type and Pattern** area specifies the type of hatch and the pattern.

Type: The **Type** textbox sets the pattern type. User-defined patterns are based on the current linetype in the drawing.

A custom pattern is a pattern that is defined in any custom PAT files that user has added to the search path. User can control the angle and scale of any pattern.

Pattern: The **Pattern** textbox lists the available predefined patterns. The six most recently used predefined patterns appear at the top of the list. The Pattern option is available only if user sets Type to Predefined.

[...] Button: The ... button displays the **Hatch Pattern Palette** dialog box, in which user can view preview images for all predefined patterns at once to help us to make a selection.

Swatch: The **Swatch** textbox displays a preview of the selected pattern. Click the swatch to display the **Hatch Pattern Palette** dialog box. When the SOLID pattern is selected, user can click the right arrow to display a list of colors or the Select Color dialog box.

Custom Pattern: The **Custom Pattern** text box lists the available custom patterns. The six most recently used custom patterns appear at the top of the list. The name of the selected pattern is stored in the HPNAME system variable. The **Custom Pattern** option is available only if user sets **Type to Custom**.

[...] Button: The ... button displays the **Hatch Pattern Palette** dialog box, in which user can view preview images for all custom patterns at once to help to make a selection.

Angle and Scale

The **Angle and Scale** area specifies an angle and a scale for the selected hatch pattern.

Angle: The **Angle** textbox specifies an angle for the hatch pattern relative to the *X* axis of the current UCS. HATCH stores the angle in the HPANG system variable.

Scale: The **Scale** textbox expands or contracts a predefined or custom pattern. HATCH stores the scale in the HPSCALE system variable. This option is available only if user sets Type to Predefined or Custom.

Double: The **Double** checkbox is used for user-defined patterns. It draws a second set of lines positioned at 90° to the original lines, creating a crosshatch. This option is available only if user sets **Type to User Defined** on the **Hatch** tab.

Relative to Paper Space: The **Relative** to **Paper Space** checkbox scales the hatch pattern relative to paper space units. Using this option, user can easily display hatch patterns at a scale that is appropriate for the layout. This option is available only from a layout.

Spacing: The **Spacing** textbox specifies the spacing of lines in a user-defined pattern. HATCH stores the spacing in the HPSPACE system variable. This option is available only if user sets Type to User Defined.

ISO Pen Width: The ISO Pen Width textbox scales an ISO predefined pattern based on the selected pen width. This option is available only if user sets Type to Predefined and set Pattern to one of the available ISO patterns.

Hatch Origin
The Hatch Origin area controls the starting location of hatch pattern generation. Some hatches, such as brick patterns, need to be aligned with a point on the hatch boundary. By default, all hatch origins correspond to the current UCS origin.

Use Current Origin: The Use Current Origin radio button uses the setting stored in the HPORIGINMODE system variable. The origin is set to 0,0 by default.

Specified Origin: The Specified Origin radio button specifies a new hatch origin. Click this option to make the following options available.

Click to Set New Origin: The Click to Set New Origin button specifies the new hatch origin point directly.

Default to Boundary Extents: The Default to Boundary Extends checkbox calculates a new origin based on the rectangular extents of the boundary for the hatch object. Choices include each of the four corners of the extents and its center.

Store as Default Origin: The Store as Default Origin checkbox stores the value of the new hatch origin in the HPORIGIN system variable.

Origin Preview: The Origin Preview option shows the current location of the origin.

2.2 GRADIENT TAB

The Gradient Tab defines the appearance of the gradient fill to be applied. **See Fig. 2.**

Color
The Color area controls the color, shade and gradient pattern for the selected hatch pattern.

One Color: The One Color radio button specifies a fill that uses a smooth transition between darker shades and lighter tints of one color. When One Color is selected, HATCH displays a color swatch with Browse button and a Shade and Tint slider.

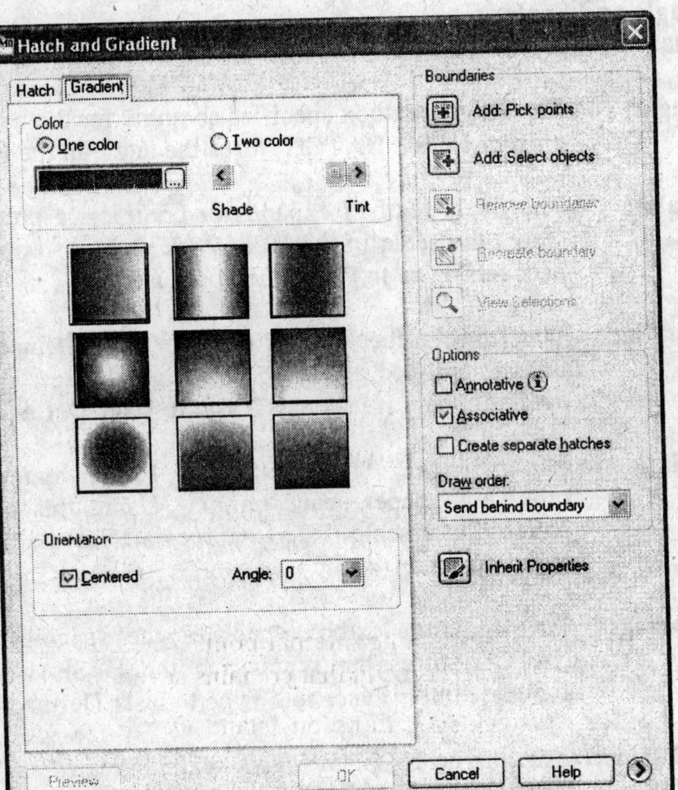

FIG. 2

Two Color: The Two Color radio button specifies a fill that uses a smooth transition between two colors. When Two Color is selected, HATCH displays a color swatch with a Browse button for color 1 and for color 2.

Color Swatch: The Color Swatch specifies the color for the gradient fill. Click the Browse button [...] to display the Select Color dialog box, where user can select an AutoCAD Color Index (ACI) color, true color or color book color. The default color displayed is the current color in the drawing.

Shade and Tint Slider: The Shade and Tint Slider specifies the tint (the selected color mixed with white) or shade (the selected color mixed with black) of a color to be used for a gradient fill of one color.

Gradient Patterns

The Gradient Patters displays nine fixed patterns for gradient fills. These patterns include linear sweep, spherical and parabolic.

Orientation

The Orientation area specifies the angle of the gradient and whether it is symmetrical.

Centered: The Centered checkbox specifies a gradient configuration that is symmetrical. If this option is not selected, the gradient fill is shifted up and to the left, creating the illusion of a light source to the left of the object.

Angle: The Angle option specifies the angle of the gradient fill. The specified angle is relative to the current UCS. This option is independent of the angle specified for hatch patterns.

2.3 Add: Pick Points Button

The **Add: Pick Point** button determines a boundary from existing objects that form an enclosed area around the specified point. The dialog box closes temporarily and the user is prompted to pick a point. The prompt displayed is:

> Pick internal point or [Select objects/remove Boundaries]: *Click within the area to be hatched or filled, specify an option, enter u or undo to undo the last selection or press* ENTER *to return to the dialog box*

While picking internal points, the user can right-click in the drawing area at any time to display a shortcut menu that contains several options.

If the user turns on Island Detection, objects that enclose areas within the outermost boundary are detected as islands. How HATCH detects objects using this option depends on which island detection method the user select in the More Options area of the dialog box.

2.4 Add: Select Objects Button

The **Add: Select Objects** button determines a boundary from selected objects that form an enclosed area. The dialog box closes temporarily and the user is prompted to select objects. The prompt displayed is:

Select objects or [picK internal point/remove Boundaries]: *Select objects that define the area to be hatched or filled, specify an option, enter u or undo to undo the last selection or press* ENTER *to return to the dialog box*

When the user uses the Select Objects option, HATCH does not detect interior objects automatically. User must select the objects within the selected boundary to hatch or fill those objects according to the current island detection style.

Each time Select Objects is clicked, the previous selection set is cleared. While selecting objects, the users can right-click at any time in the drawing area to display a shortcut menu. The users can undo the last selection or all selections, change the selection method, change the island detection style or preview the hatch or gradient fill.

2.5 Remove Boundaries

The **Remove Boundaries** button removes from the boundary definition any of the objects that were added previously. When the user clicks Remove Boundaries, the dialog box closes temporarily and displays a prompt as shown below:

Select Objects or [Add boundaries]: *Select objects to be removed from the boundary definition, specify an option or press* ENTER *to return to the dialog box*

Select Objects
The Select Objects option removes temporary boundary objects for hatching or filling as the user selects them.

Add Boundaries
The Add Boundaries option adds temporary boundary objects for hatching or filling as the user selects them.

2.6 Recreate Boundary

The Recreate Boundary button creates a polyline or region around the selected hatch or fill and optionally associates the hatch object with it. When the user clicks Recreate Boundary, the dialog box closes temporarily and displays a prompt as shown below:

Enter type of boundary object [Region/Polyline] <*current*>: ***Enter r to create a region or p to create a polyline***

Reassociate hatch with new boundary? [Yes/No] <*current*>: ***Enter y or n***

2.7 View Selections

The View Selections button temporarily closes the Hatch and Gradient dialog box and displays the currently defined boundaries with the current hatch or fill settings. This option is unavailable when no boundary has been defined.

2.8 Select Boundary Objects

The Select Boundary Objects button displays boundary grip controls for selected hatch and closes the Hatch and Gradient dialog box. This option is unavailable when no boundary has been defined for an existing hatch. Note that this option is only available in the Hatch Edit dialog box and replaces the View Selections option.

When the user manually selects or uses the Select Boundary Objects option to select a non-associative hatch, the boundary of the hatch displays grips. When the user manually selects an associative hatch, it displays only a single grip point of the hatch.

To display the boundary grip controls of the objects associated to the hatch, use the Select Boundary Objects option. The user can only edit an associative hatch by grip editing the objects it is associated with.

2.9 Options

The Options area controls several commonly used hatch or fill options.

Annotative: The Annotative checkbox specifies that the hatch is annotative. Click the information icon to learn more about annotative objects.

Associative: The Associative checkbox controls whether the hatch or fill is associative or non-associative. A hatch or fill that is associative is updated when user modifies its boundaries.

Create Separate Hatches: This checkbox controls whether a single hatch object or multiple hatch objects are created when several separate closed boundaries are specified.

Draw Order: The Draw Order options assign the draw order to a hatch or fill. User can place a hatch or fill behind all other objects, in front of all other objects, behind the hatch boundary or in front of the hatch boundary.

2.10 Inherit Properties

Inherit Properties option hatches or fills specified boundaries using the hatch or fill properties of a selected hatch object. After selecting the hatch object whose properties the user want the hatch to inherit, the user can right-click in the drawing area and use the options on the shortcut menu to switch between the Select Objects and Pick Internal Point options to create boundaries.

When the user clicks Inherit Properties button, the dialog box closes temporarily and the prompt displayed is as shown below:

`Select hatch object:` ***Click within a hatched or filled area to select the hatch whose properties are to be used for the new hatch object***

2.11 Preview

The Preview button dismisses the dialog box and displays the currently defined boundaries with the current hatch or fill settings. Click in the drawing or press ESC to return to the dialog box. Right-click or press ENTER to accept the hatch or fill. This option is not available when the user has not yet specified points or selected objects to define the boundaries.

2.12 More Options

The **More Options** button expands the dialog box to display more options. The **More Options** section controls the operation of islands and boundaries.

Problem 1: *Hatch an enclosed area of an object using the Hatch command.*

The command sequence to hatch the enclosed area of an object using the Hatch command is as follows:

Command: **HATCH** ↵

(The Hatch and Gradient dialog box is displayed on the screen. On this, click on the Add: Pick Points option button to close the Hatch and Gradient dialog box temporarily.)

Pick internal point or [Select objects/remove Boundaries]: ***(Pick P1)***

Selecting everything...

Selecting everything visible...

Analyzing the selected data...

Analyzing internal islands...

Pick internal point or [Select objects/remove Boundaries]: ***(Pick P2)***

Analyzing internal islands...

Pick internal point or [Select objects/remove Boundaries]: ↵

(Now, the Hatch and Gradient dialog box is appears on the screen again. Select the required Hatch Type and Pattern and then click OK.)

See Fig. 4.

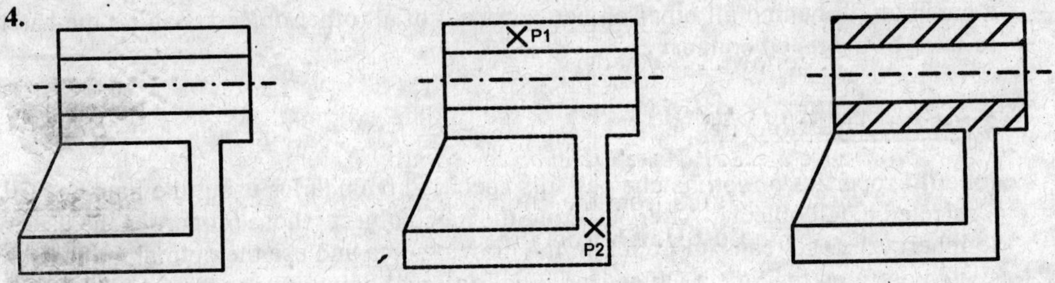

Objects before Hatch　　Boundaries Selected to Hatch　　Objects after Hatch

FIG. 4

Problem 2: *Hatch the outermost enclosed object using the Hatch command.*

See Fig. 5. The command sequence to hatch the outermost enclosed object using the Hatch command is as follows:

Command: **HATCH** ↵

(The Hatch and Gradient dialog box is displayed on the screen. On this, click on the Add: Pick Points option button to close the Hatch and Gradient dialog box temporarily.)

Pick internal point or [Select objects/remove Boundaries]: ***(Pick P1)***

Selecting everything...

Selecting everything visible...

Analyzing the selected data...

Analyzing internal islands...

Pick internal point or [Select objects/remove Boundaries]: ↵

(Now, the Hatch and Gradient dialog box is appears on the screen again. Select the required Hatch Type and Pattern. Click on the More Options button at the bottom right corner of the Hatch and Gradient dialog box to display the More Options. Select the Outer option in the Islands area and then click OK.)

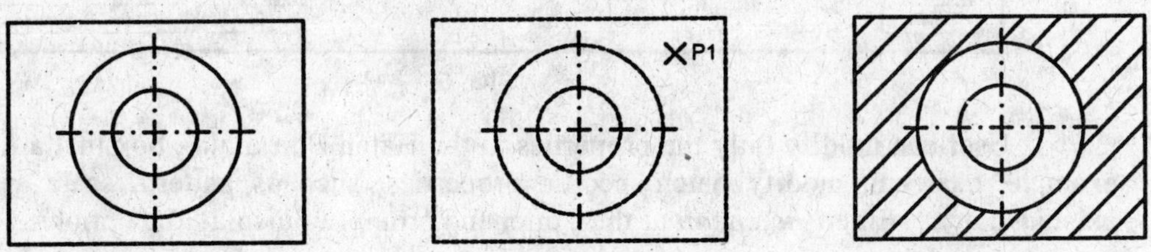

Objects before Hatch | Boundaries Selected to Hatch | Objects after Hatch

FIG. 5

3. EDITING HATCH PROPERTIES (EDIT HATCH TOOL)

The **Edit Hatch** tool is used to edit a hatch pattern. The Edit Hatch tool can be invoked using any one of the following methods:

1. Type **HATCHEDIT** or **HE** in the command prompt and press Enter.
2. Choose the **Edit Hatch** icon on the **Modify** panel in the **Home** tab.
3. Choose the **Hatch** from the **Object** in the **Modify** menu.
4. Choose the **Edit Hatch** from the **Modify II** toolbar.

When the **Hatchedit** command is invoked, AutoCAD prompts to select a hatch object. Select a hatched area using any one of the object selection methods. Then, the **Hatch Edit** dialog box is displayed on the screen as shown in **Fig. 6.** The **Hatch Edit** dialog box displays the current properties of the selected hatch or fill object.

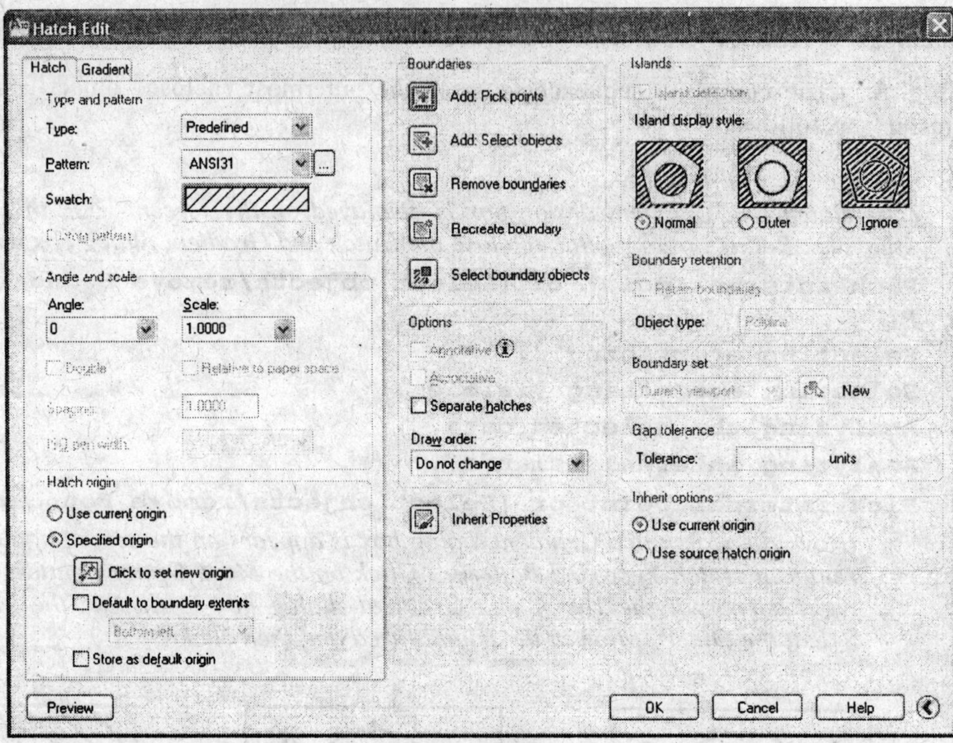

FIG. 6

User can modify only the properties in the Hatch Edit dialog box that are available. For example, user can modify hatch-specific properties, such as pattern, scale and angle for an existing hatch. Enter *-hatchedit* at the Command prompt to display the options.

Hatch Tab: In the **Hatch Tab,** the hatch pattern properties are modified. For information about these options, see the Hatch Tab in the Hatch and Gradient dialog box as shown in **Fig. 1.**

Gradient Tab: This tab provides options to modify the gradient fill properties. For information about these options, see the Gradient tab in the Hatch and Gradient dialog box as shown in **Fig. 2.**

Problem 3: *Edit the hatching using the Hatchedit command.*

See Fig. 7. The command sequence to edit the hatching using Hatchedit command is as follows:

Command: **HATCHEDIT** ↵

Select hatch object: ***(Select the hatch area)***

(The Hatch Edit dialog box is displayed on the screen. On this, click on the Scale text box and select the 0.5000 as the scale. Click the Preview button to close the Hatch Edit dialog box and see the result.)

Pick or press Esc to return to dialog or <Right-click to accept hatch>:

(Press Esc to return to the Hatch Edit dialog box. Click the OK button.)

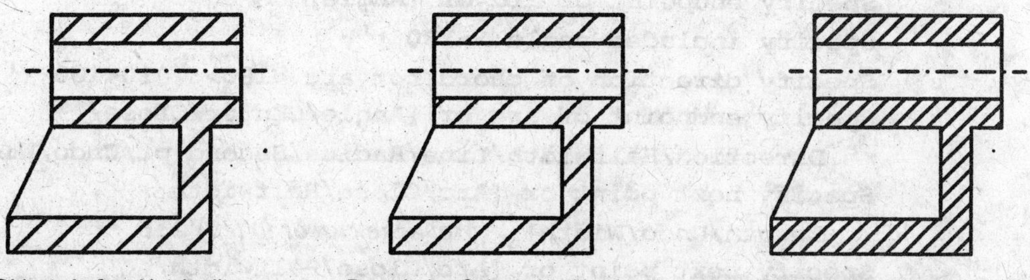

FIG. 7

4. CAD EXERCISES - Step-by-Step Solutions

Example 1: *Draw the diagram shown in* ***Fig. 8*** *using the Pline and Line commands. Also, mark the dimensions and center point.*

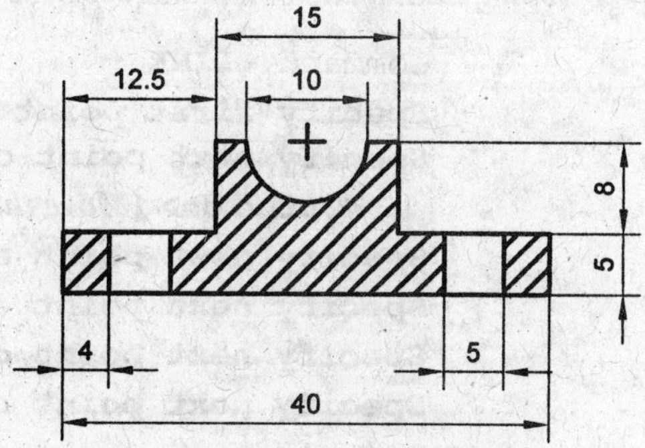

SECTIONAL VIEW OF AN OBJECT

FIG. 8

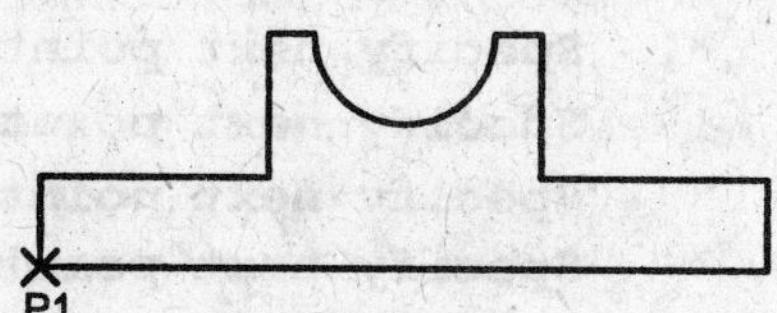

FIG. 9

The procedure and command sequence to draw the diagram shown in **Fig. 8** is given below:

STEP 1 : First draw the outline of the object using the Pline command. The command sequence is given below:

Command: **PLINE** ↵

Specify start point: *(Pick P1)*

Current line-width is 0.0000

Specify next point or [Arc/Halfwidth/Length/Undo/Width]: *(Move the cursor to right)* **40** ↵

Specify next point or [Arc/Close/Halfwidth/Length/Undo/Width]: *(Move the cursor to up)* **5** ↵

Specify next point or [Arc/Close/Halfwidth/Length/Undo/Width]: *(Move the cursor to left)* **12.5** ↵

Specify next point or [Arc/Close/Halfwidth/Length/Undo/Width]: *(Move the cursor to up)* **8** ↵

Specify next point or [Arc/Close/Halfwidth/Length/Undo/Width]: *(Move the cursor to left)* **2.5** ↵

Specify next point or [Arc/Close/Halfwidth/Length/Undo/Width]:A ↵

Specify endpoint of arc or [Angle/CEnter/CLose/Direction/Halfwidth/Line/Radius/Secondpt/Undo/Width]: R ↵

Specify radius of arc: 5 ↵

```
Specify endpoint of arc or [Angle]: A ↵
Specify included angle: -180 ↵
Specify direction of chord for arc <180>: @10<180 ↵
Specify endpoint of arc or [Angle/CEnter/CLose/
   Direction/Halfwidth/Line/Radius/Second pt/Undo/Width]: L ↵
Specify next point or [Arc/Close/Halfwidth/
   Length/Undo/Width]: (Move the cursor to left) 2.5 ↵
Specify next point or [Arc/Close/Halfwidth/
   Length/Undo/Width]: (Move the cursor to down) 8 ↵
Specify next point or [Arc/Close/Halfwidth/
   Length/Undo/Width]: (Move the cursor to left) 12.5 ↵
Specify next point or [Arc/Close/Halfwidth/Length/Undo/Width]:C ↵
```

See Fig. 9.

STEP 2 : Draw the lines in the diagram using the Line command. The command sequence is given below:

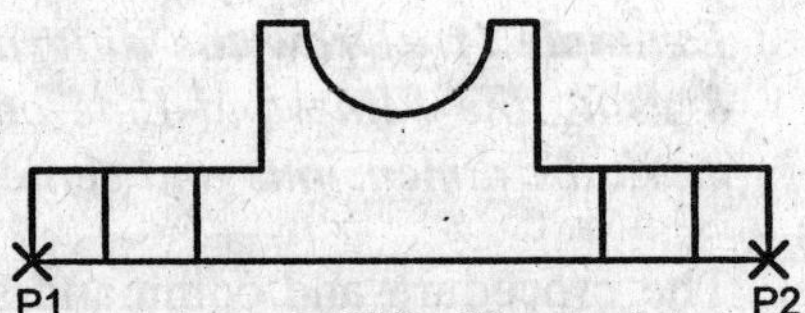

FIG. 10

```
Command: LINE ↵
Specify first point: (Pick P1)
Specify next point or [Undo]:
   <Ortho on> (Move the cursor to right) 4 ↵
Specify next point or [Undo]: (Move the cursor to up) 5 ↵
Specify next point or [Close/Undo]: (Move the cursor to right) 5 ↵
Specify next point or [Close/Undo]: (Move the cursor to down) 5 ↵
Specify next point or [Close/Undo]: ↵

Command: LINE ↵
Specify first point: (Pick P2)
Specify next point or [Undo]: (Move the cursor to left) 4 ↵
Specify next point or [Undo]: (Move the cursor to up) 5 ↵
Specify next point or [Close/Undo]: (Move the cursor to left) 5 ↵
Specify next point or [Close/Undo]: (Move the cursor to down) 5 ↵
Specify next point or
   [Close/Undo]: ↵
```

See Fig. 10.

STEP 3 : Mark the center point of the arc using the Dimcenter command.

STEP 4 : Mark all the dimensions using the Dimlinear command.

STEP 5 : Also, place the text SECTIONAL VIEW OF AN OBJECT using the Text command.

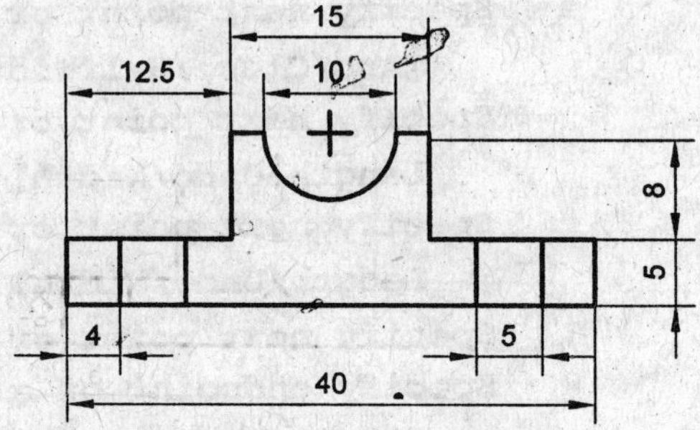

SECTIONAL VIEW OF AN OBJECT

FIG. 11

See Fig. 11. It shows the final view of the diagram shown in **Fig. 8** except hatching.

STEP 6 : To hatch the drawing, first invoke the Hatch command. The **Hatch and Gradient** dialog box will display on the screen as shown in **Fig. 12.**

In this dialog box, choose the **Add: Pick points** button. Now, the **Hatch and Gradient** dialog box disappears temporarily and AutoCAD prompts to pick internal point.

Pick the points P1, P2 and P3 by left-clicking the mouse. After picking the points, press **Esc** or **Spacebar** to display the **Hatch and Gradient** dialog box.

Now, choose the down arrow in the **Pattern** text box in the **Type and pattern** area of the **Hatch and Gradient** dialog box.

A list of available patters is displayed here. In this list, choose the **LINE** pattern.

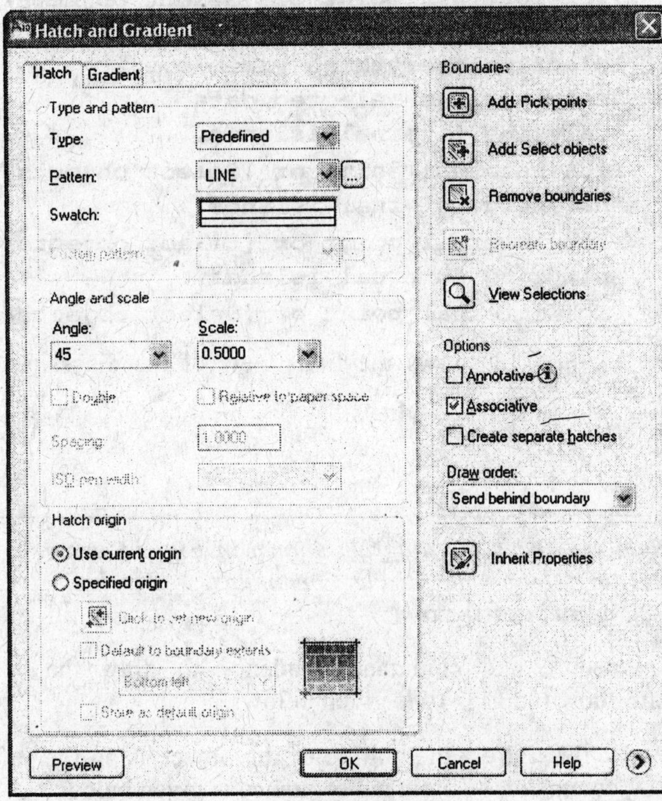

FIG. 12

At the **Angel and scale** area, select **45** in the **Angles** text box and select **0.5000** in the **Scale** text box. To view the result, click the **Preview** button. Press **Esc** or **Spacebar** to return to the **Hatch and Gradient** dialog box. Click **OK** button to accept the hatching.

See Fig. 13 for final result.

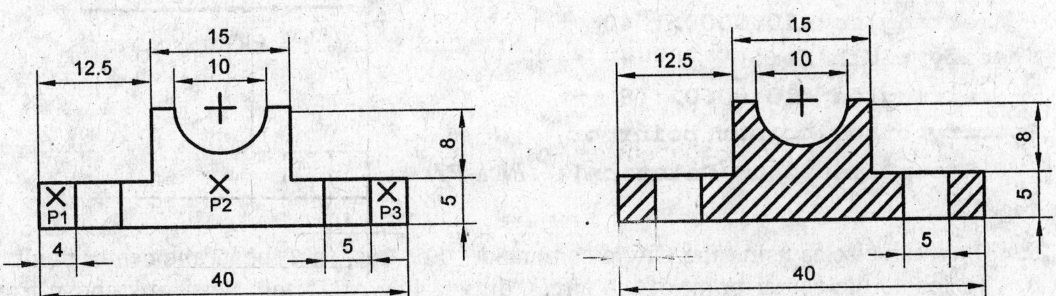

SECTIONAL VIEW OF AN OBJECT
Before Hatching

SECTIONAL VIEW OF AN OBJECT
After Hatching

FIG. 13

The command sequence while hatching is given below:

```
Command: HATCH ↵
Pick internal point or [Select objects/remove Boundaries]:
Selecting everything...
Selecting everything visible...
Analyzing the selected data...
Analyzing internal islands...
Pick internal point or [Select objects/remove Boundaries]:(Pick P1)
Analyzing internal islands...
Pick internal point or [Select objects/remove Boundaries]: Pick P2)
Analyzing internal islands...
Pick internal point or [Select objects/remove Boundaries]: Pick P3)
```

STEP 7 : Fig. 13 shows the final view of the diagram shown in **Fig. 8.** Finally save the drawing.

---

*Example 2: Draw the diagram shown in **Fig. 14** using the Rectang, Line and Circle commands. Mark the dimensions and center point.*

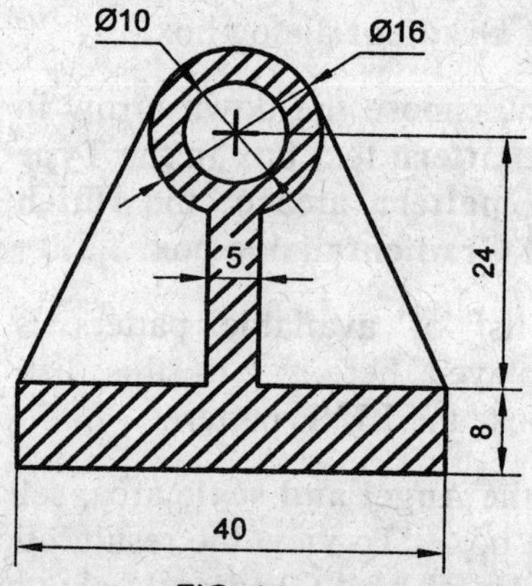

FIG. 14

The procedure and command sequence to draw the diagram shown in **Fig. 14** is given below:

STEP 1 : First draw the outline of the object using the Rectang command. Command sequence is given below:

```
Command: RECTANG ↵
Specify first corner point or
   [Chamfer/Elevation/Fillet/
   Thickness/Width]: (Pick P1)
Specify other corner point or
   [Area/Dimensions/Rotation]: D ↵
Specify length for
   rectangles <10.0000>: 40 ↵
Specify width for
   rectangles <10.0000>: 8 ↵
Specify other corner point or
   [Area/Dimensions/Rotation]: (Pick P2)
```

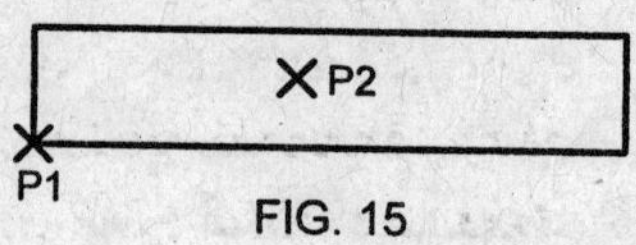

FIG. 15

See Fig. 15.

STEP 2 : Draw the circles using the Circle command. For this, first locate the center point of the circle. To locate the center point of the circle, draw a line of 24 mm vertically above from the mid-point of the top edge of the rectangle. The command sequence is given below:

```
Command: LINE ↵
```

Specify first point: *(Pick P1)*
Specify next point or [Undo]:
  <Ortho on> *(Move the cursor to up)* **24** ↵
Specify next point or [Undo]: ↵

Command: **CIRCLE** ↵
Specify center point for circle or
  [3P/2P/Ttr (tan tan radius)]: *(Pick C1)*
Specify radius of circle or [Diameter]:D ↵
Specify diameter of circle: 10 ↵

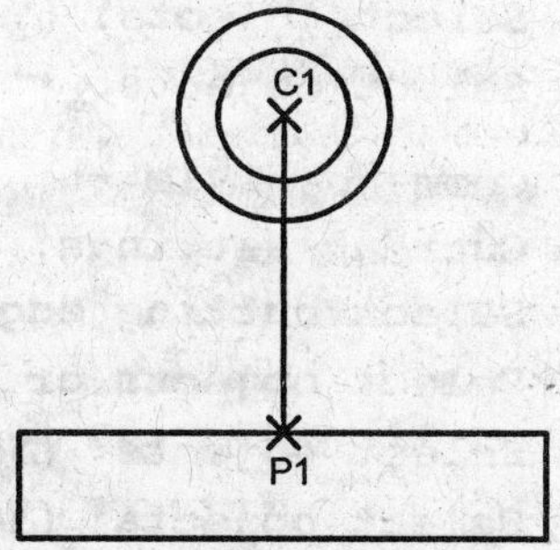

FIG. 16

Command: **CIRCLE** ↵
Specify center point for circle or
  [3P/2P/Ttr (tan tan radius)]: *(Pick C1)*
Specify radius of circle or [Diameter] <5.0000>: D ↵
Specify diameter of circle <10.0000>: 16 ↵

See Fig. 16.

STEP 3 : Draw the lines using the Copy command. The command sequence is given below:

Command: **COPY** ↵
Select objects:
  (Select the vertical line) **1 found**
Select objects: ↵
Current settings:
  Copy mode = Multiple
Specify base point or
  [Displacement/mOde]
  <Displacement>: *(Pick P1)*
Specify second point or <use first point as
  displacement>: <Ortho on> *(Move the cursor to right)* **2.5** ↵
Specify second point or [Exit/Undo]
  <Exit>: *(Move the cursor to left)* **2.5** ↵
Specify second point or [Exit/Undo] <Exit>: ↵

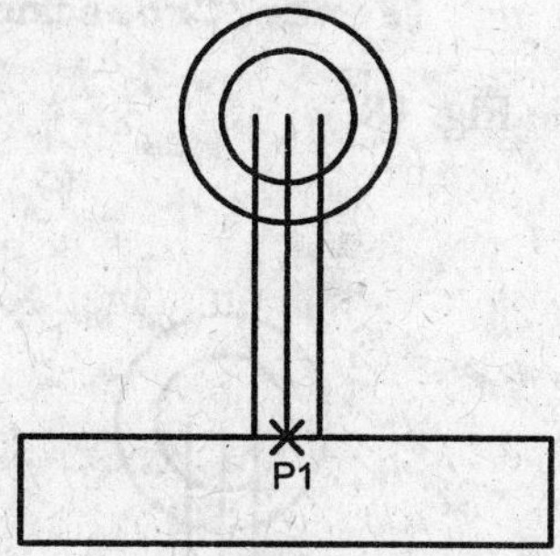

FIG. 17

See Fig. 17.

STEP 4 : Using the Erase command, erase the line that is drawn through the mid-point of the top edge of the rectangle. Trim the unwanted lines and arc segment using the Trim command. The command sequence is given below:

Command: **ERASE** ↵

```
Select objects: (Select the L1 line) 1 found
Select objects: ↵

Command: TRIM ↵
Current settings: Projection=UCS, Edge=None
Select cutting edges ...
Select objects or <select all>: (Select Line-1) 1 found
Select objects: (Select Line-2) 1 found, 2 total
Select objects: (Select the circle C1) 1 found, 3 total
Select objects: ↵
Select object to trim or shift-select to extend or
   [Fence/Crossing/Project/Edge/eRase/Undo]: (Pick P1)
Select object to trim or shift-select to extend or
   [Fence/Crossing/Project/Edge/eRase/Undo]: (Pick P2)
Select object to trim or shift-select to extend or
   [Fence/Crossing/Project/Edge/eRase/Undo]: (Pick P3)
Select object to trim or shift-select to extend or
   [Fence/Crossing/Project/Edge/eRase/Undo]: (Pick P4)
Select object to trim or shift-select to extend or
   [Fence/Crossing/Project/Edge/eRase/Undo]: ↵
```

See Fig. 18.

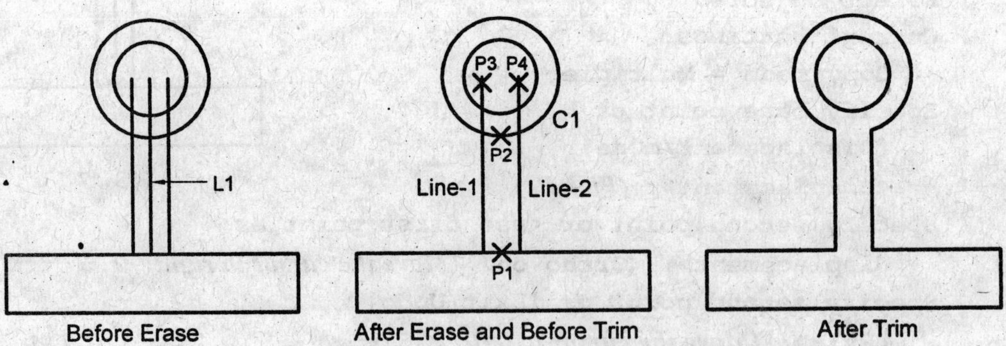

FIG. 18

STEP 5 : Draw the two extreme lines using the Line command. The command sequence is:

```
Command: LINE ↵
Specify first point: (Pick P1)
Specify next point or [Undo]: (Move the cursor to toward the left extreme point
of the circle until the Tangent symbol appears. Click when the tangent symbol appears.)
Specify next point or [Undo]: ↵
```

Command: **LINE** ↵

Specify first point: *(Pick P2)*

Specify next point or [Undo]: *Move the cursor to toward the right extreme point of the circle until the Tangent symbol appears. Click when the tangent symbol appears.*

Specify next point or [Undo]: ↵

See Fig. 19.

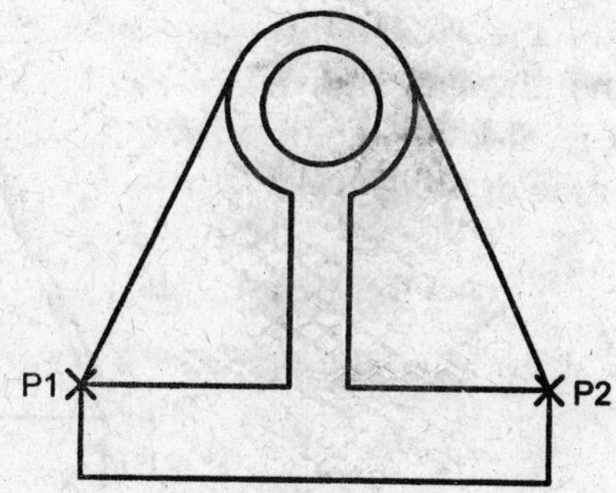

FIG. 19

STEP 6 : Mark the center point using the **Dimcenter** command. Mark the linear dimensions with the dimension values 40, 5, 8 and 24 using the **Dimlinear** command.

STEP 7 : Mark the diameters of the circles using the **Dimdiameter** command. See Fig. 20. It shows the final view of the diagram shown in Fig. 14 except hatching.

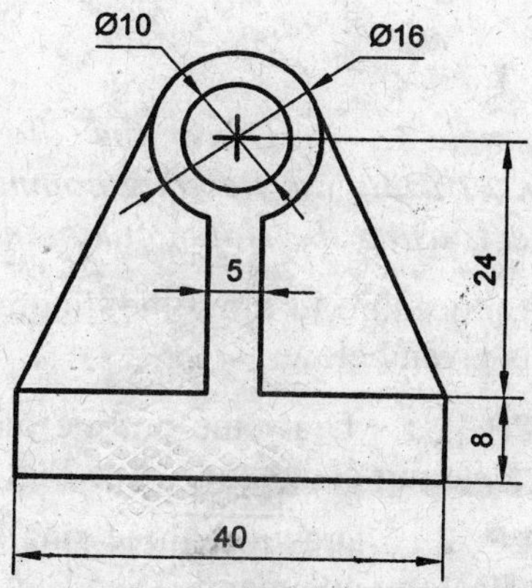

FIG. 20

STEP 8 : To hatch the drawing, first invoke the **Hatch** command. The **Hatch and Gradient** dialog box will display on the screen.

In this dialog box, choose the **Add: Pick points** button. Now, the **Hatch and Gradient** dialog box disappears temporarily and AutoCAD prompts to pick internal point.

Pick the points P1, P2 and P3 by left-clicking the mouse. After picking the points, press **Esc** or **Spacebar** to display the **Hatch and Gradient** dialog box. Now, choose the down arrow in the **Pattern** text box in the **Type and pattern** area of the **Hatch and Gradient** dialog box. A list of available patters is displayed here. In this list, choose the **LINE** pattern.

At the **Angel and scale** area, select **45** in the **Angles** text box and select **0.5000** in the **Scale** text box. To view the result, click the **Preview** button. Press **Esc** or **Spacebar** to return to the **Hatch and Gradient** dialog box. Click **OK** button to accept the hatching. The command sequences that are displayed at the Command prompt during the Hatching operation is given below:

Command: **HATCH** ↵

Pick internal point or [Select objects/remove Boundaries]:

Selecting everything...

Selecting everything visible...

Analyzing the selected data...

Analyzing internal islands...

Pick internal point or [Select objects/remove Boundaries]: *(Pick P1)*

Analyzing internal islands...

STEP 9 : **Fig. 21** shows the final view of the diagram shown in **Fig. 14.** Finally save the drawing.

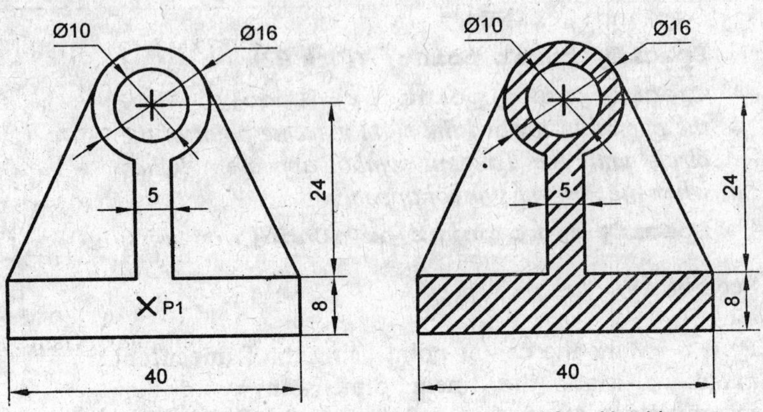

Before Hatching FIG. 21 After Hatching

Example 3: *Draw the diagram shown in Fig. 22 using the Rectang command. Hatch the objects using the Hatch command.*

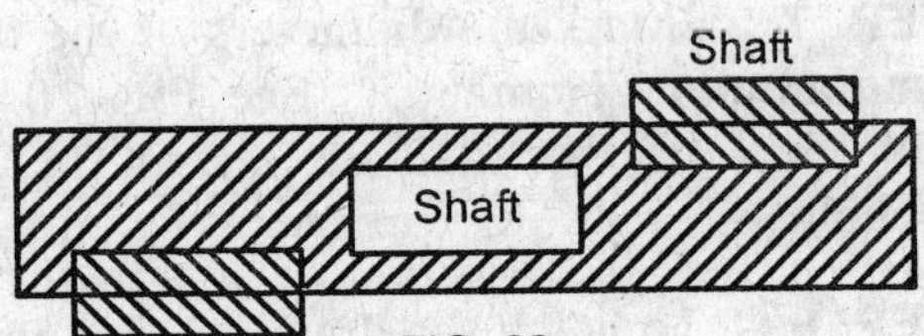

FIG. 22

The procedure to draw the diagram shown in **Fig. 22** is given below:

FIG. 23

STEP 1 : Draw the outline of the object using the **Rectang** command. **See Fig. 23.**

STEP 2 : Draw the three small rectangles using the **Rectang** command. **See Fig. 24.**

STEP 3 : Place the text **Shaft** at two places using the **Text** command. **See Fig. 25.**

STEP 4 : Hatch the big rectangle using the **Hatch** command. **See Fig. 26.**

STEP 5 : Hatch the two small rectangles using the Hatch command. **See Fig. 27.**

STEP 6 : **Fig. 27** shows the final view of the object shown in **Fig. 22.**

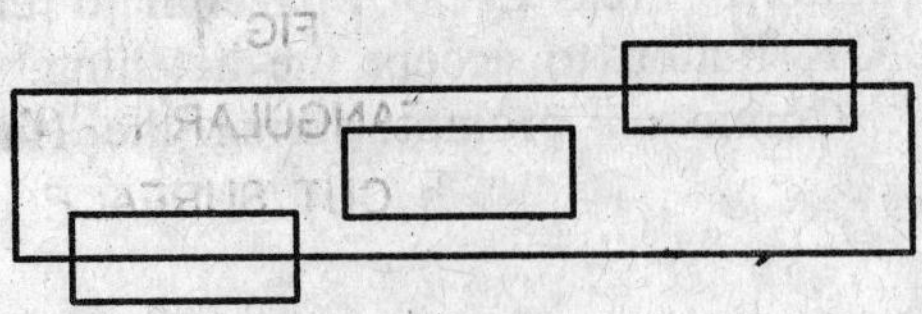

FIG. 24

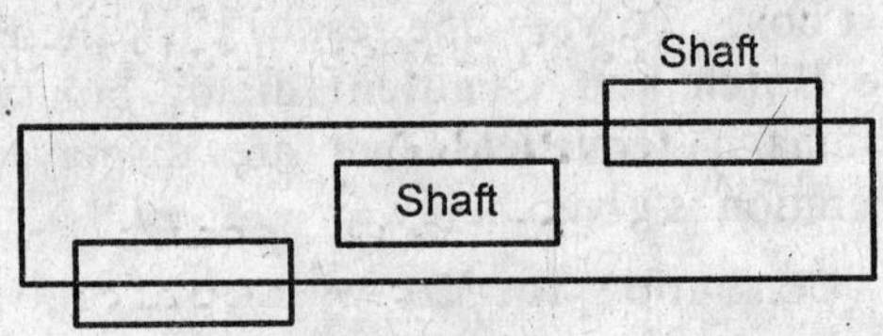

FIG. 25

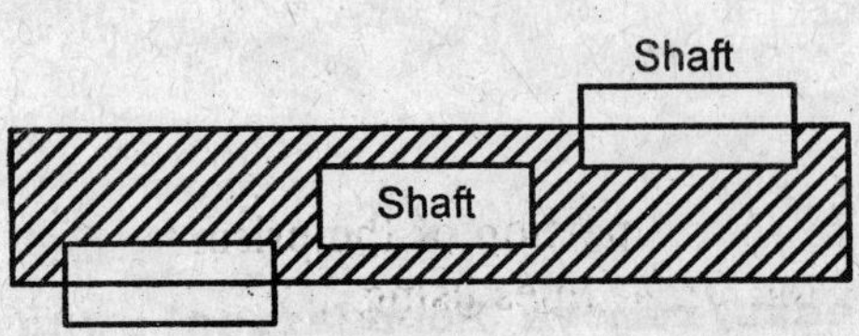

FIG. 26

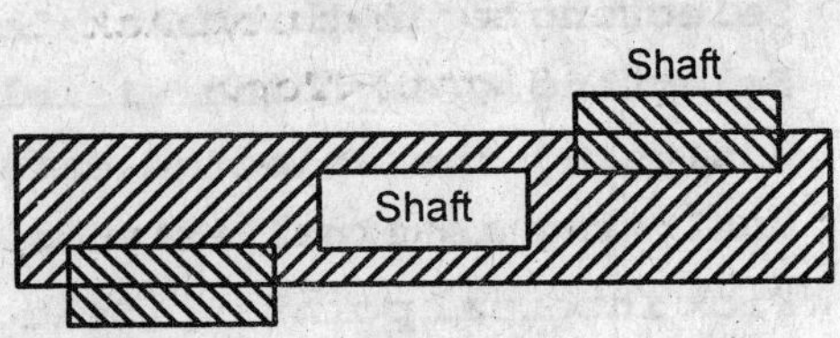

FIG. 27

Ex. No. : 1 Date :	*Ch.21* - **SECTIONAL VIEWS OF SIMPLE SOLIDS**

AIM : *A **Rectangular Prism**, side of base 40 mm x 25 mm and height 60 mm, rests with its base on HP such that one of its larger rectangular faces is parallel to VP.*

A Section Plane perpendicular to HP and parallel to VP cuts the prism into two equal halves. Draw its top view and sectional front view, using CAD Software.

STEP 1 : To draw the 3-D view of the given Rectangular Prism : **(Fig. 1)**

Command : **VPOINT**

Specify a view point or[Rotate]<display compass and tripod>:1,-1,1

Command : **SHADEMODE**

Enter an option [2dwireframe/3dwire frame/3dHidden/ Realistic/ Conceptual/Other] <2dwireframe> : 3D

Command: **RECTANG**

Specify first corner point or [Chamfer/Elevation/Fillet/Thickness/Width]:

: **(Pick a point below XY line)**

Specify other corner point or [Area/Dimensions/ Rotation] : D

Specify length for rectangles <10.0000> : 40

Specify width for rectangles <10.0000> : 25

Specify other corner point or [Area/Dimensions/ Rotation] : enter

Command : **EXTRUDE**

Select objects to extrude : 1 found

Select objects to extrude :

Specify height of extrusion or [Direction/Path/Taper angle] <70.0000>:60

Command : **SECTIONPLANE**

Select face or any point to locate section line or [Draw section/ Orthographic] : O

Align section to:[Front/bAck/Top /Bottom/Left/Right]<Top> : T

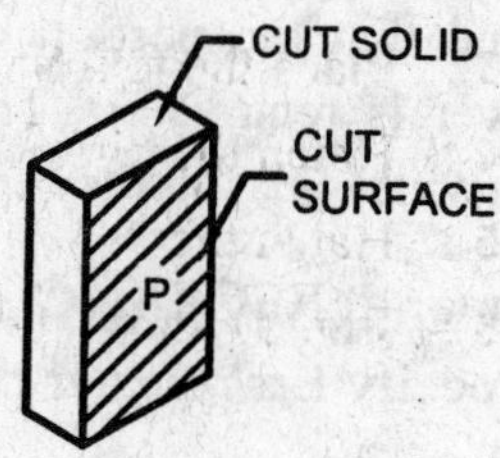

FIG. 1

RECTANGULAR PRISM with CUT SURFACE

TEP 2 : Then, draw the sectional front view for the remaining portion of the prism by *thick* nes (H). In this view, the cut surface is shown by hatching (*thin*) lines using 2H.

Command: **HATCH** ↵

Pick internal point or [Select objects/remove Boundaries]: Selecting everything...
Selecting everything visible...
Analyzing the selected data...
Analyzing internal islands...
Pick internal point or [Select objects/remove Boundaries]: *Pick P*
Analyzing internal islands...

STEP 3 : (Fig. 2)

Draw a line arbitrarily using the LINE command. Name it as **XY** using the TEXT command.

Note: *(i)* *Within the solid portion, the S.P. coincides with the cut surface which is to be shown by full wide line necessarily.*

(ii) *When S.P. is parallel to HP or VP, the Sectional Front View or Sectional Top View of the cut surface itself shows the* ***True Shape of Section****.*

STEP 4 : Top View (Fig. 2)

To draw rectangular prism of *side of base 40 mm x 25 mm* with one of the sides parallel to XY, use the RECTANG command. Hence, draw the top view of S.P. as a line (*long-dashed dotted wide lines* at ends) parallel to XY and passing through the axis. Assume that the portion of the prism between the S.P. and the observer is removed. The remaining portion is then shown by *thick* (wide) lines in the top view. The prompt sequence is:

FIG. 2

Command: **RECTANG**

Specify first corner point or [Chamfer/Elevation/Fillet/Thickness/Width]:
: **(Pick a point below XY line)**
Specify other corner point or [Area/Dimensions/Rotation] : **D**
Specify length for rectangles <10.0000> : **40**
Specify width for rectangles <10.0000> : **25**
Specify other corner point or [Area/Dimensions/Rotation] : enter

Mark corner points of top face as S,P using TEXT command.

Command : **TEXT**

Current text style: "Standard" Text height : 2.5
Specify start point of text or [Justify/Style] :
Specify rotation angle of text <0> : 0

STEP 5 : Front View (Fig. 3)

Using LINE command, draw the vertical projectors from top view to meet XY at two points.

Command : **LINE**

```
Specify first point :
Specify next point or [Undo]   :
```
(Move the cursor to right) 40
```
Specify next  point or [Undo]:
```
(Move the cursor to up) 60
```
Specify next point or [Undo]  :
```
(Move the cursor to left) 40
```
Specify next point or [Undo]  :
```
(Move the cursor to down) 60

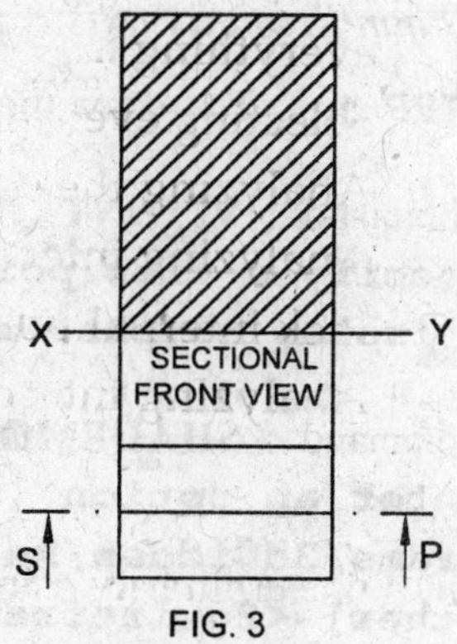

FIG. 3

NOTE: Use **narrow (thin)** lines for XY line, construction lines and dimension lines. Use **wide (thick)** lines for top & front views from **Properties** toolbar. Choose appropriate line thicknesses.

STEP 6 : Dimensioning

Mark the dimensions using the options available in the **Dimension** menu, or using the **dimlinear, dimaligned** or **dimangular** commands. To edit the dimension text, select the dimension and use the DDEDIT or ED command. Finally, save the file.

Command : **DIMLINEAR** ↵

```
Specify first extension line origin or <select object> (Pick S)
Specify second extension line origin : (Pick P )
Specify dimension line location or
[Mtest/Text/Angle/Horizontal /Vertical/
Rotated] :
Dimension text =  40
```

NOTE : ***Following the above procedure, create the other dimensions of the given Rectangular Prism.***

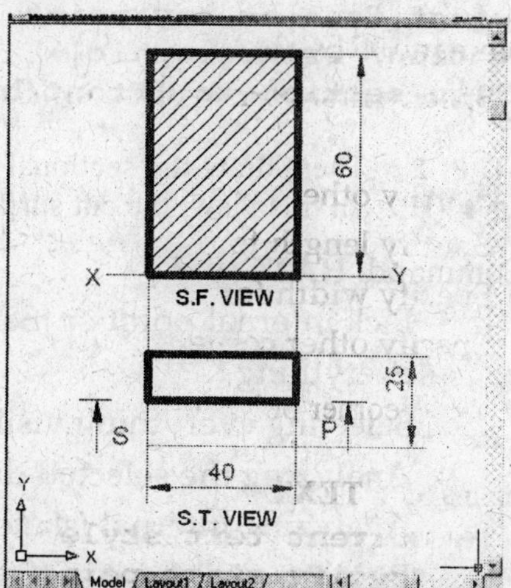

FIG. 4 RECTANGULAR PRISM

Ex. No. : 2 - *A **Hexagonal Prism**, side of base 30 mm and axis 60 mm long, rests with its base on HP such that one of its rectangular faces is parallel to VP.*

*A **S.P.** perpendicular to HP and parallel to VP cuts the prism at a distance of 10 mm from its axis. Draw its top and sectional front views, using CAD Software.*

STEP 1 : To draw the 3-D view of the given Hexagonal Prism: (**Fig. 1**)

Command : **VPOINT**
```
Specify a view point or [Rotate]
<Display compass and tripod>            :   1,-1,1
```

Command : **SHADEMODE**
```
Enter an option [2dwireframe/3dwire
frame/3dHidden/Realistic/Conceptual/
Other] <2dwireframe>                     :3D
```

Command : **POLYGON**
```
Enter number of sides <4>                : 6
Specify center of polygon or [Edge]      : 0
Enter an option [Inscribed in
circle/Circumscribed about circle] <I>: I
Specify radius of circle                 : 30
```

Command : **EXTRUDE**
```
Select objects to extrude          :1 found
Select objects to extrude               :
Specify height of extrusion or
[Direction/Path/Taper angle] <70.0000> :   60
```

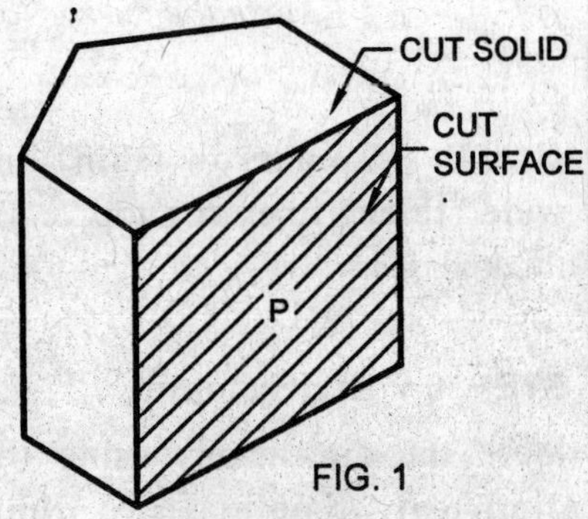

FIG. 1
HEXAGONAL PRISM with CUT SURFACE

Command : **SECTIONPLANE**
```
Select face or any point to locate section line or [Draw
section/ Orthographic]                                    : O
Align section to:[Front/bAck/Top/Bottom/Left/Right]<Top>  : T
```

STEP 2 : Then, draw the sectional front view for the remaining portion of the prism by *thick* lines (H). In this view, the cut surface is shown by hatching (*thin*) lines using 2H.

Command: HATCH ↵

Pick internal point or [Select objects/remove Boundaries]: Selecting everything...

Selecting everything visible...

Analyzing the selected data...

Analyzing internal islands...

Pick internal point or [Select objects/remove Boundaries]: *Pick P*

STEP 3 : (Fig. 2)

Draw a line arbitrarily using the LINE command. Name it as **XY** using the TEXT command. Mark VP above the XY line and HP below the XY line using the TEXT command.

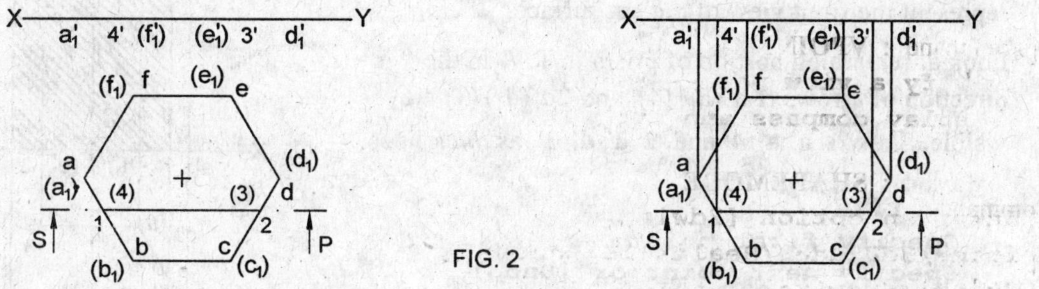

FIG. 2

STEP 4 : Top View (Fig. 2)

Name the section points 1 and 2 where the S.P. cuts the visible edges ab and cd respectively. Name the points (3) and (4) where the S.P. cuts the invisible edges $(d_1)(c_1)$ and $(b_1)(a_1)$ respectively. Show remaining portion of the prism as *thick* lines.

Command: **POLYGON** ↵

```
Enter number of sides <4>               : 6
Specify center of polygon or[Edge]      : E ↵
Specify first endpoint of  Edge      :(Pick a point below XY
line)
Specify second endpoint of  Edge    :(move cursor to the up)30↵
```

Mark corner points of top face as a, b, c, d and e using TEXT command. Similarly, mark bottom face corners as (a_1), (b_1), (c_1), (d_1) & (e_1).

Command : **TEXT**

```
Current text style:  "Standard"  Text
height                          : 2.5
Specify  start  point  of  text  or
[Justify/Style]                 :
Specify rotation angle of text <0>: 0
```

STEP 5 : Front View (Fig. 3)

Using LINE command, draw the vertical projectors from top view to meet XY at the points a′, b′, (f′), c′, (e′) and d′.

Cut surface: Project the above section points on the corresponding edges in the front view. From 1(4) draw a projector to cut a′ b′ at 1′ and a_1' b_1' at 4′. Similarly mark 2′ and 3′ in the front view.

Join 1′ 2′ 3′ 4′ by *thick* lines and hatch this area to represent the front view of the cut surface.

Look at remaining portion of prism in T.V. in the direction of arrows. 1 a (a_1) (4) and 2d (d_1) (3) are visible. Show 1′ a′ a_1' 4′ and 2′ d′ d_1' 3′ as *thick* lines.

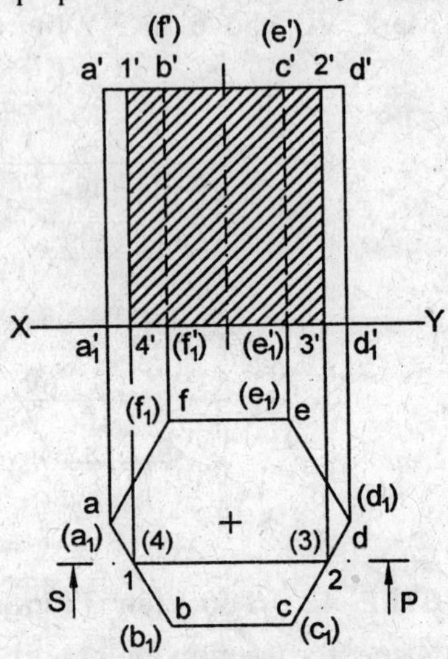

FIG. 3

Command : **LINE**

```
Specify first point :
Specify next point or [Undo]   :
                    (Move the cursor to right) 30 ↵
Specify next  point or [Undo] :
                    (Move the cursor to up) 60 ↵
Specify next point or [Undo]   :
                    (Move the cursor to left) 30 ↵
Specify next point or [Undo]   :
                    (Move the cursor to down) 60 ↵
```

Mark these points using TEXT command and join them using the LINE command. At these points, draw vertical lines of 60 mm height using LINE command. Mark the points a′, b′, (f′), c′ , (e′), and d′ using TEXT command and join them using LINE command.

Draw the axis line of the hexagon using the LINE command. Select this line and choose the required **Linetype** from **Properties** toolbar.

Note: (i) Use **narrow (thin)** lines for XY line, construction lines & dimension lines. Use **wide (thick)** lines for top and front views. (ii) Use **dashed** lines for the invisible lines from the **Properties** toolbar. Choose appropriate line thicknesses.

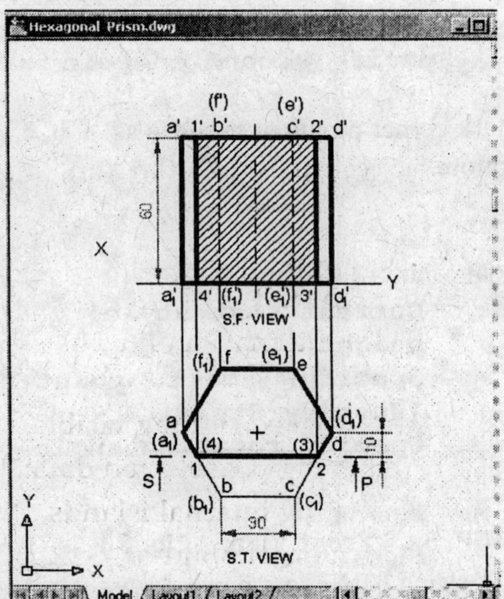

FIG.4 HEXAGONAL PRISM

<u>**Ex. No. : 3**</u> - *A* ***Cylinder*** *of 50 mm diameter and 60 mm height stands vertically with its base on HP.*

It is cut by a ***Section Plane*** perpendicular to HP, parallel to VP *and 30 mm from the axis. Draw its top and sectional front views, using CAD Software.*

NOTE : In this Problem, S.P. does not cut any of the Cylinder generators. Hence, top view circle is not divided into the usual number of 12 equal parts to represent the generators.

STEP 1 : To draw the 3-D view of the given Cylinder: (**Fig. 1**)

Command : **VPOINT**

Specify a view point or[Rotate]<display compass and tripod> :1,-1,1

Command : **SHADEMODE**

Enter an option [2dwireframe/3dwire frame/3dHidden/Realistic/Conceptual/ Other] <2dwireframe> : 3D

Command : **CYLINDER**

Specify center point of base or [3P/2P/ Ttr/Elliptical] : Pick any point

Specify base radius or [Diameter] :D

Specify diameter :50

Specify height or [2Point/Axis endpoint]:60

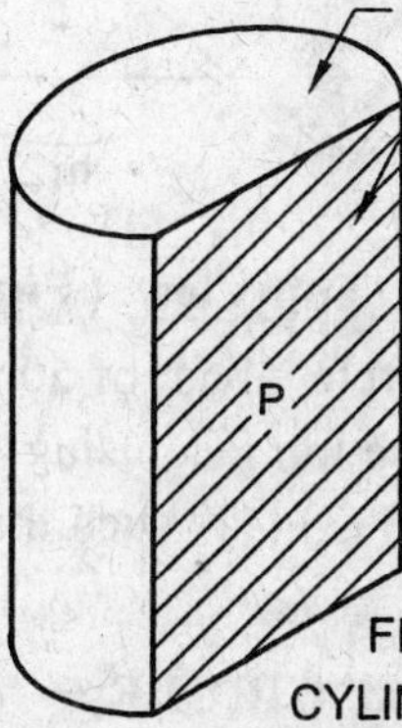

FIG. 1
CYLINDER
with CUT SURFACE

Command : **SECTIONPLANE**

Select face or any point to locate section line or [Draw section/Orthographic] : O

Align section to:[Front/bAck/Top/Bottom/Left/Right]<Top> : T

STEP 2 : Then, draw the sectional front view for the remaining portion of the prism by *thick* lines (H). In this view, the cut surface is shown by hatching (*thin*) lines using 2H.

Command: **HATCH** ↵

Pick internal point or [Select objects/remove Boundaries]: Selecting everything...

Selecting everything visible...

Analyzing the selected data...

Analyzing internal islands...

Pick internal point or [Select objects/remove Boundaries]: *Pick P*

Analyzing internal islands...

STEP 3 : (Fig. 2)

Draw a line arbitrarily using the LINE command. Name it as **XY** using the TEXT command. Mark VP above the XY line and HP below the XY line using the TEXT command.

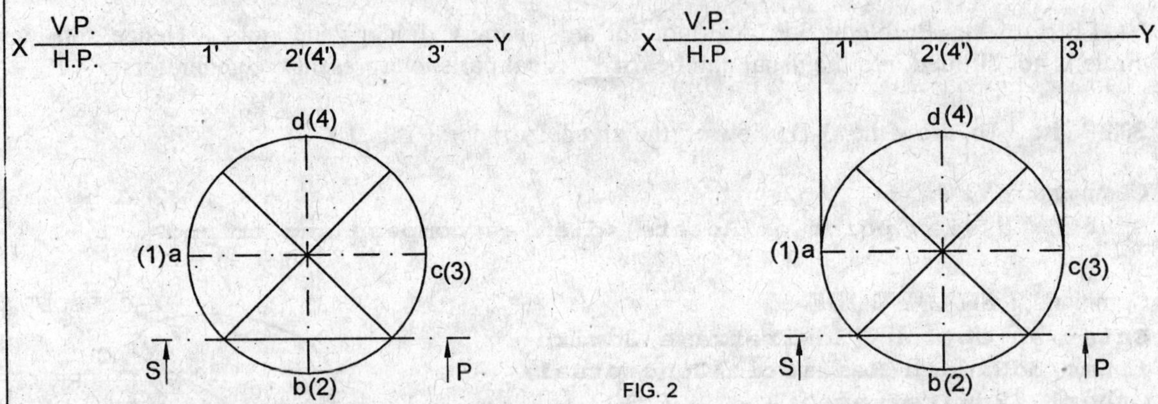

FIG. 2

STEP 4 : Top View (Fig. 2)

Draw a circle abcd of 50 mm diameter such that center is 30 mm below XY to represent the top view of the top face using CIRCLE command. Base 1234 is hidden. Hence mark its top view as (1) (2) (3) (4) such that (1) and a coincide using TEXT command, etc.

Command: **CIRCLE** ↵

```
CIRCLE Specify center point for
circle or [3P/2P/Ttr (tan tan radius)]    : 0
Specify radius of circle or [Diameter]    : D
Specify diameter of circle                : 50
```

Mark corner points of top face as S,P using TEXT command.

Command : **TEXT**

```
Current text style: "Standard" Text height          : 2.5
Specify start point of text or [Justify/Style]      :
Specify rotation angle of text <0>                  : 0
```

STEP 5 : Front View (Fig. 3)

Using LINE command, draw the vertical projectors from top view to meet XY at the points 1′, 2′, (4′) and 3′.

Command : **LINE**

```
Specify first point :
Specify next point or [Undo]   :
```

(Move the cursor to right) 50

```
Specify next  point or [Undo] :
```

(Move the cursor to up) 60

```
Specify next point or [Undo]   :
```

(Move the cursor to left) 50

```
Specify next point or [Undo]   :
```

(Move the cursor to down) 60

Mark these points using TEXT command and join them using the LINE command. At these points, draw vertical lines of 60 mm height using LINE command. Mark the points a′, b′ (d′), and c′ using TEXT command and join them using LINE command.

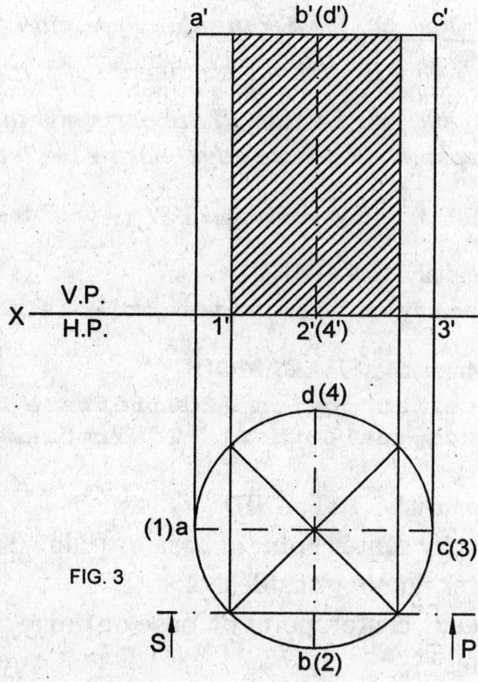

FIG. 3

NOTE: Use **narrow (thin)** lines for XY line, construction lines and dimension lines. Use **wide (thick)** lines for top & front views from **Properties** toolbar. Choose appropriate line thicknesses.

STEP 6 : Dimensioning

Mark the dimensions using the options available in the **Dimension** menu, or using the **dimlinear, dimaligned** or **dimangular** commands. To edit the dimension text, select the dimension and use the DDEDIT or ED command. Finally, save the file.

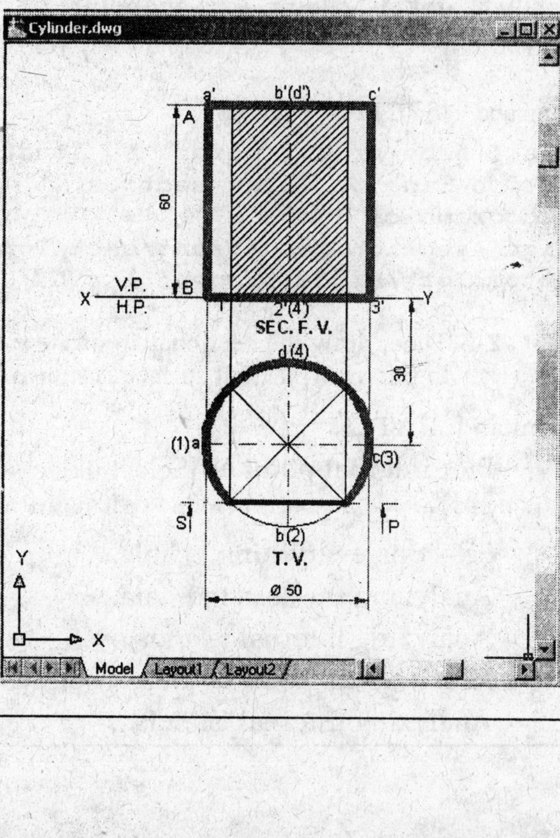

FIG. 4 CYLINDER

Ex. No. : 4 - *A* ***Triangular Pyramid*** *is resting on one its base corners on the ground, such that its 30mm base side on top is parallel to HP. Its 65mm long axis is ⊥ to VP. It is cut by a* ***Section Plane*** *perpendicular to VP and inclined to HP at 60° such that it bisects the top base edge. Draw the top and front views, using CAD Software.*

STEP 1 : To draw the 3-D view of the given Triangular Pyramid: (**Fig. 1**)

Command : **VPOINT**
Specify a view point or[Rotate]<display compass and tripod>:1,-1,1

Command : **SHADEMODE**
Enter an option [2dwireframe/3dwire frame/3dHidden/ Realistic/ Conceptual/Other] <2dwireframe> : 3D

Command : **PYRAMID**
Specify center point of base or [Edge/Sides] : S
Enter number of sides <4> : 3
Specify center point of base or [Edge/ Sides] : Pick any point
Specify base radius or [Inscribed] : I
Specify base radius or [Circumscribed] : 30
Specify height or [2Point/Axis endpoint/ Top radius] : 65

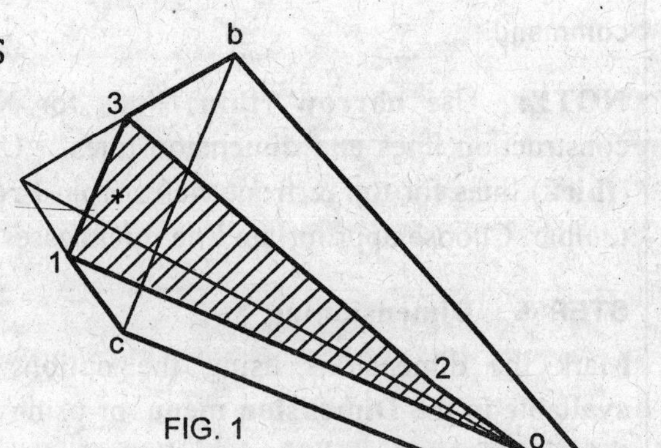

FIG. 1
TRIANGULAR PYRAMID
with CUT SURFACE

Command : **SECTIONPLANE**
Select face or any point to locate section line or [Draw section/ Orthographic] : O
Align section to: [Front/bAck/Top/ Bottom/Left/Right]<Top> : L

STEP 2 : Then, draw the sectional front view for the remaining portion of the prism by *thick* lines (H). In this view, the cut surface is shown by hatching (*thin*) lines using 2H.

Command: **HATCH** ↵

Pick internal point or [Select objects/remove Boundaries]: Selecting everything...
Selecting everything visible...
Analyzing the selected data...
Analyzing internal islands...
Pick internal point or [Select objects/remove Boundaries]: *Pick P*
Analyzing internal islands...

STEP 3 : Draw a line arbitrarily using the LINE command. Name it as **XY** using the TEXT command.

STEP 4 : Top View (Fig. 2)

To draw the Line use the LINE command. Locate the points 1, 2, 3 cutting edges a-c, o-a and a-b respectively. Project these points on their corresponding edges in the Top View.

Join the points 1, 2, 3 and hatch the area. Draw the remaining portion as mentioned in the earlier *e.g.* to get the Sectional View.

(Here also, some portion of the solid is removed and lies outside the section, so it is represented by dashed double dotted lines.)

Command : **LINE**
Specify first point :
Specify next point or [Undo] : (*Move the cursor to right*) 30
Specify next point or [Undo] : (*Move the cursor to down*) 65
Specify next point or [Undo] : (*Move the cursor to down*) 65 (Join the point o)

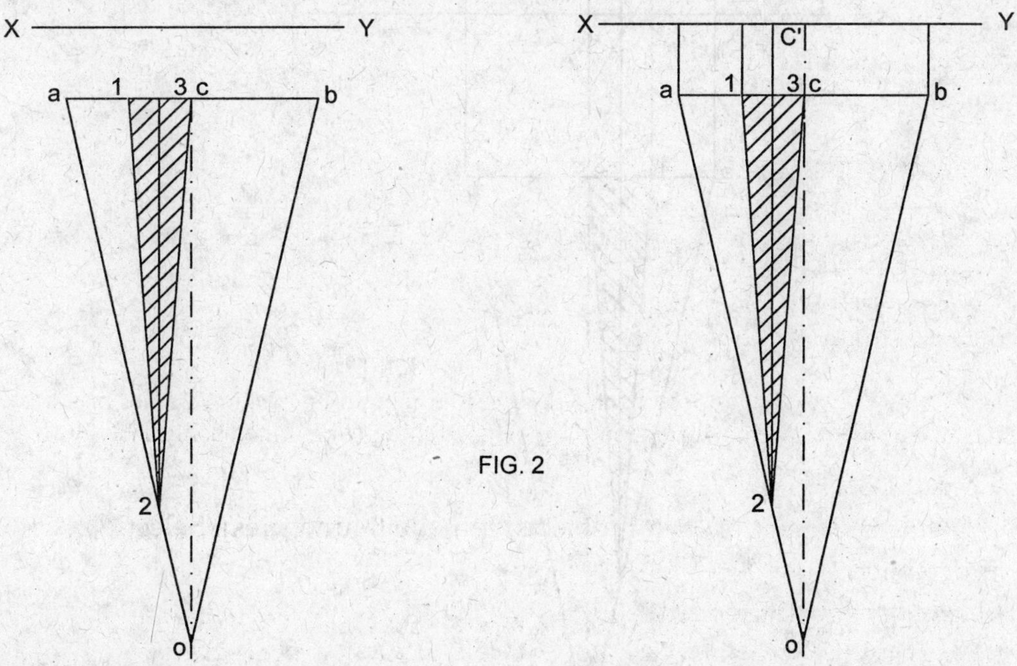

FIG. 2

Command : **TEXT**
Current text style: "Standard" Text height : **2.5**
Specify start point of text or [Justify/Style] :
Specify rotation angle of text <0> : **0**

STEP 5 : Front View (Fig. 3)

Draw tetrahedron front view. In front view, locate the points a′-c′, o′-a′ and a′-b′ cutting edges 1′, 2′, 3′ respectively. Draw line S.P. in the front view meeting the midpoint of edge a′, b′ and inclined at 60° to HP.

Command: **POLYGON**

```
Enter number of sides <4>                 : 3
Specify center of polygon or[Edge]        : E ↵
Specify first endpoint of  Edge           :(Pick a point below XY line)
Specify second endpoint of  Edge          :(move cursor to the up)30↵
```

Mark corner points of front face as S.P. using TEXT command.

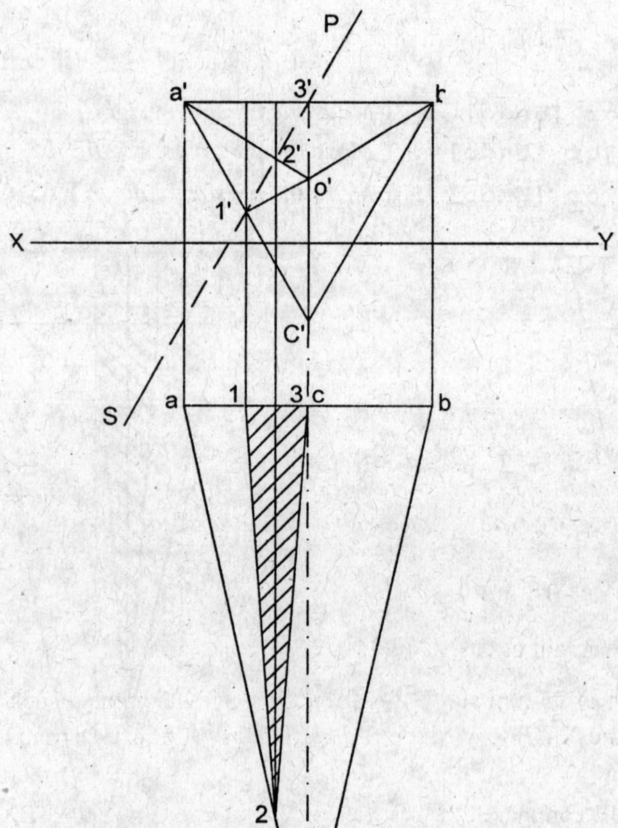

FIG. 3

NOTE: Use **narrow (thin)** lines for XY line, construction lines and dimension lines. Use **wide (thick)** lines for top & front views from **Properties** toolbar. Choose appropriate line thicknesses.

STEP 6 : Dimensioning

Mark the dimensions using the options available in the **Dimension** menu, or using the **dimlinear, dimaligned** or **dimangular** commands. To edit the dimension text, select the dimension and use the DDEDIT or ED command. Finally, save the file.

Command : **DIMLINEAR** ↵

Specify first extension line origin or
<select object> : *(Pick A)*
Specify second extension line origin
: *(Pick B)*
Specify dimension line location or
[Mtest/Text/Angle/Horizontal /Vertical/
Rotated] :
Dimension text = 40

NOTE : *Following the above procedure, create the other dimensions of the given Triangular Pyramid.*

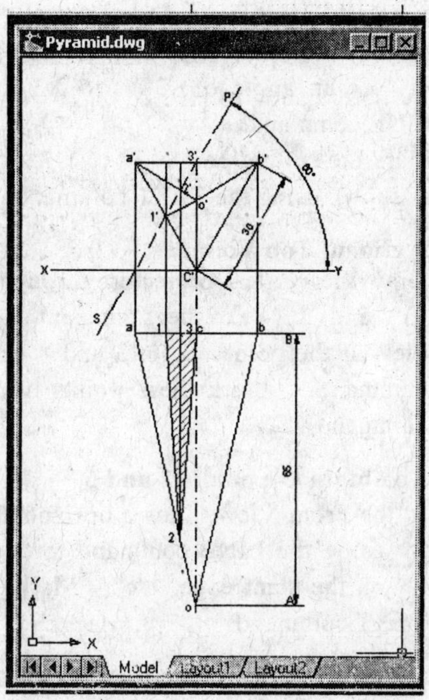

FIG.4 TRIANGULAR PYRAMID

<u>**Ex. No. : 5**</u> - *A **Hexagonal Pyramid**, side of base 25 mm and axis 50 mm long, rests with its base on HP and an edge of its base is perpendicular to VP.*

It is cut by a S.P. perpendicular to VP, inclined at 30° to HP and passing through a point on the axis 20 mm below the apex. Draw the sectional top view, using CAD Software.

1. Start the **AutoCAD Software**. Open and setup a new drawing sheet. Draw a line arbitrarily using the LINE command. Name it as **XY** using the TEXT command.

2. **Top View:** Draw a hexagon of 25 mm side using the POLYGON command such that an edge of its base is perpendicular to the XY line. Name the corners as a, b, c, d, e and f using TEXT command.

   Join the diagonals using LINE command. Mark the center point o using the TEXT command.

3. **Front View:** Draw the vertical projectors from the top view to meet the XY line using the LINE command. Mark the points as a′, (f′), b′, (e′), c′ and (d′) using the TEXT command.

   From b′ draw a vertical line of height 50 mm using the LINE command. Mark the apex o′ using the TEXT command. Join the slant edges o′ a′ and o′ c′ using the LINE command.

4. **Section Plane:** Mark a point 20 mm below o′. Through this point, draw a line (*long-dashed dotted wide line* to represent the Section Plane) at an angle of 30° to XY line using the LINE command.
Mark the cutting points 1′, (6′), 2′, (5′), 3′ and (4′) as shown using the TEXT command.

5. **Sectional Top View**
Draw the vertical projectors through the points 1′ (6′) and 3′ (4′) to meet the slant edges in the top view at the points 1, 6, 3 and 4 using the LINE command. Mark these points using the TEXT command.

To obtain the points 2 and 5
In the Front View, draw a horizontal line through 2′ using the LINE command to obtain the point p′ on the slant edge o′c′. Mark p′ using the TEXT command.

6. Through p′, draw a vertical projector to meet the slant edges c o and d o at the points p_1 and p_2 using the LINE command. Mark the points p_1 and p_2 using the TEXT command.

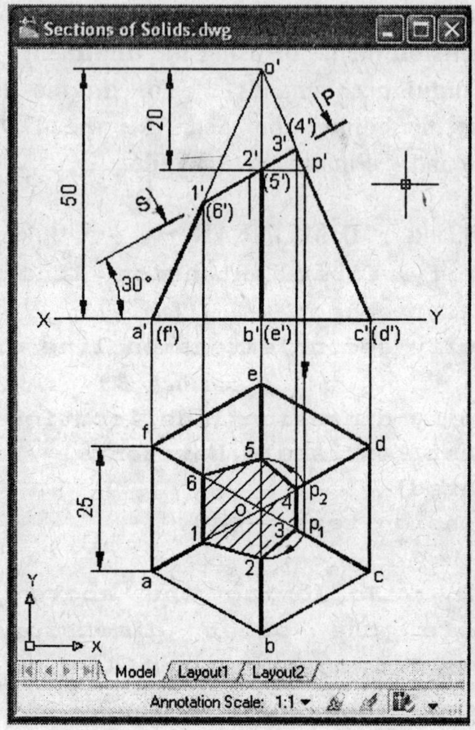

FIG. 13

o as center and o p_1 as radius, draw an arc using the ARC command to meet the line o b to obtain the point 2. Mark the point 2 using the TEXT command.

Similarly, o as center and o p_2 as radius, draw an arc using the ARC command to meet the line o e to obtain the point 5. Mark the point 5 using the TEXT command.

Now, joint the points 1, 2, 3, 4, 5 and 6 using the LINE command.

7. **Hatching:** Hatch the polygon 1 2 3 4 5 6 using the HATCH command as shown.

Note: Use **narrow (thin)** lines for XY line, construction lines and dimension lines. For hatching lines, use thinner lines. Use **wide (thick)** lines for the top and front views. Choose appropriate line thicknesses.

8. **Dimensioning:** Mark the dimensions using the options available in the **Dimension** menu, or using the **dimlinear, dimaligned** or **dimangular** commands.

9. Draw necessary arrows at the appropriate places to show the direction of section plane, using the PLINE command and setting the width for arrowhead. Finally, save the file.

Ex. No. : 6 - *A **Cone** of base 50 mm diameter and 65 mm height is resting on its base on HP.*

*It is cut by a **Section Plane** such that the true shape produced is a parabola of base 35 mm. Draw the sectional top view using the CAD software. Also, find its true shape.*

Note: *When a cone is cut by a Section Plane, parallel to an end generator, the section produced is a Parabola. Size of parabola depends on the position of S.P.*

---

1. Start the **AutoCAD Software**. Open and setup a new drawing sheet. Draw the XY line using the LINE and TEXT commands.
2. Draw the top of the cone as a circle of 50 mm diameter using the CIRCLE command.
3. Draw one vertical / horizontal radial line using the LINE command. Divide the top view circle into 8 equal parts using the ARRAY command.
4. Name the division points as 1, 2, ..., 8 and the center point as o using the TEXT command.
5. To draw the front view, draw vertical projectors upwards from the division points using the LINE command to meet the XY line. Name the corresponding points 1′, 2′, ..., 8′ using the TEXT command.
6. Mark o′ at a height of 65 mm from XY using the TEXT command. Join o′ with the division points on the XY line using the LINE command.
7. In the top view, locate the chord aj of length 35 mm perpendicular to XY. For this, using the LINE command, draw horizontal lines 17.5 mm above and below the center of the top view circle.
8. Name the intersecting points as a and j on the circumference of the circle using the TEXT command. Join a and j using the LINE command.
9. Through aj, draw a projector upwards to meet XY at a′(j′) using the LINE command.

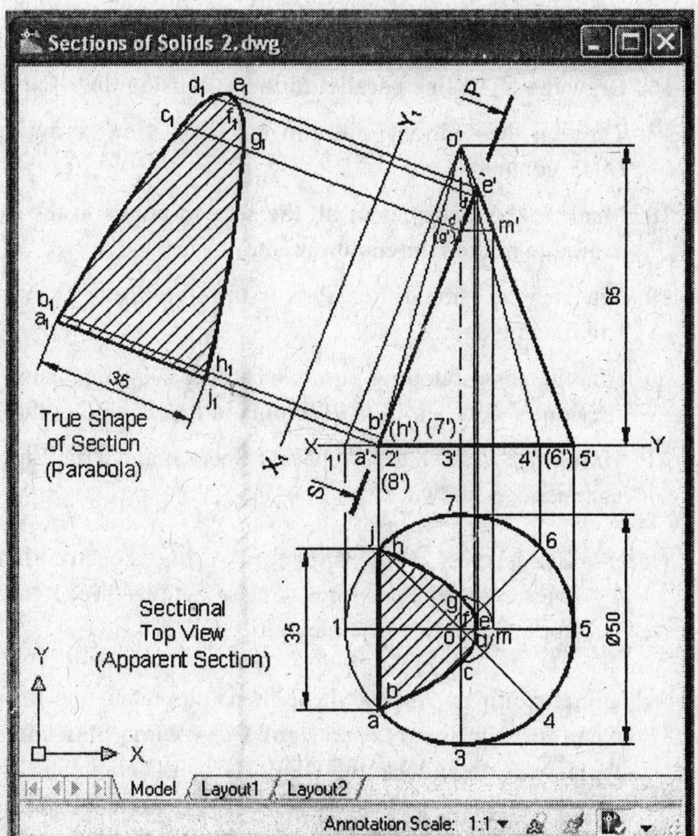

FIG. 14

10. Through a′(j′), draw the section plane parallel to the extreme generator 1′o′ using the LINE command as shown. Use **dashdot** lines from the **Properties** toolbar to represent the section plane line as *long-dashed dotted wide line.*
11. Mark the section points a′, b′, ..., j′ in the front view using the TEXT command.
12. From these section points, draw vertical projectors downwards to meet the corresponding points in the top view. Mark the intersecting points as a, b, ..., j using the TEXT command.
13. To obtain the points c and g, draw a horizontal line from c′(g′) in the front view to cut the extreme generator o′5′ at m′ using the LINE and TEXT commands. At m′, draw a vertical line downwards to meet the radial line o5 at m using the LINE and TEXT commands.
14. With o as center and om as radius, draw a semi-circle using the CIRCLE command to cut the radial lines o3 and o7 at the points c and g respectively.
15. Draw a smooth curve through these points using the SPLINE command to obtain the Apparent Section.

True Shape of Section

16. Draw the X_1Y_1 line parallel to the S.P. using the LINE and TEXT commands.
17. Through the section points in the front view, draw projectors perpendicular to X_1Y_1 using the LINE command.
18. Measure the distances of all the section points in the top view from the XY line using the options available in the **Dimension** menu.
19. Transfer the same dimensions with reference to X_1Y_1 on the corresponding projectors using the LINE command.
20. Join the corresponding points in proper sequence using the LINE and SPLINE commands. Name the points using the TEXT command and complete the True Shape of Section.
21. **Hatching:** Hatch the Apparent Section and True Shape of Section (parabola) using the HATCH command as shown.

Note: Use **narrow (thin)** lines for XY line, construction lines and dimension lines. For hatching lines, use thinner lines. Use **wide (thick)** lines for the top and front views. Choose appropriate line thicknesses.

1. **Dimensioning:** Mark the dimensions using the options available in the **Dimension** menu, or using the **dimlinear, dimaligned** or **dimangular** commands. To edit the dimension text, select the dimension and use the DDEDIT or ED command.
2. Draw necessary arrows at the appropriate places to show the direction of section plane, using the PLINE command and setting the width for arrowhead.
3. Using the TEXT command, name the views of the cone at the appropriate locations.
4. Finally, save the file.

Ch.22 - ISOMETRIC PROJECTION OF SIMPLE OBJECTS

THEORY

1. CONCEPT OF ISOMETRIC DRAWINGS

Isometric Drawings are used to help visualize the shape of an object.

For example, **Fig. 1** shows the Orthographic Views of an object. It takes time to visualize the shape of the object. If an Isometric Drawing is given as shown in **Fig. 2,** it is much easier to conceive the shape of the object. Therefore, isometric drawings are widely used in industry to understand the shape and size of the products.

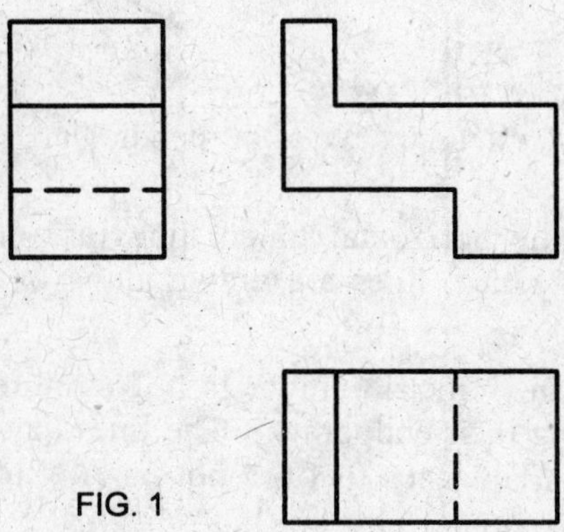

FIG. 1

FIG. 2

An isometric drawing is a two-dimensional (2D) representation of a 3D drawing on a 2D plane. In other words, an isometric drawing is a 3D drawing on a 2D plane, whereas as 3D drawing is a true 3D model of the object. To model can be rotated and viewed from any direction. A 3D model can be a wireframe model, surface model or solid model.

1.1 ISOMETRIC PROJECTION

The word *Isometric* means *equal measure*, because the angles between three principle axes of an Isometric Drawing are each 120°. Isometric Drawing is a 2D drawing representing a 3D object. Isometric drawings are always drawn to a full scale because their purpose is to help the user to visualize the shape of the object.

Isometric drawings are not meant to describe the actual size of the object. The actual dimensions and feature symbols must be shown in the orthographic views. Also, avoid showing any hidden lines in the isometric drawings, unless they show an important feature of the object or help in understanding its shape.

1.2 ISOMETRIC AXES

Isometric drawings have three isometric axes, namely, Right Horizontal Axis (R.H.A.), Vertical Axis (V.A.) and Left Horizontal Axis (L.H.A.). **See Fig. 3.** The two horizontal axes are inclined at 30° to the horizontal or X axis. The vertical axis is at 90°.

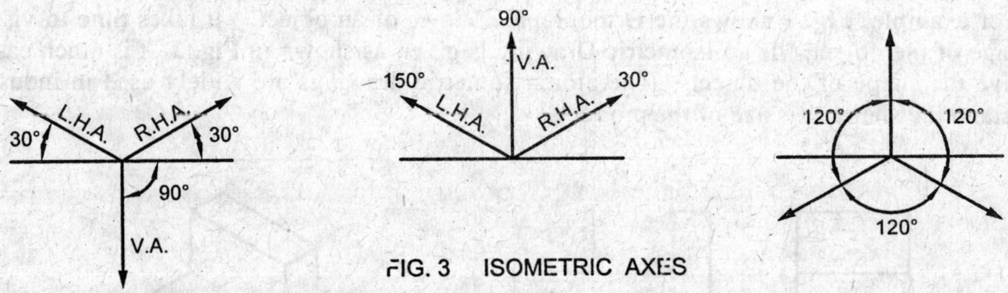

FIG. 3 ISOMETRIC AXES

When an isometric drawing is drawn, the horizontal object lines are drawn along or parallel to the horizontal axis. Similarly, the vertical lines are drawn along or parallel to the vertical axis.

Note that the angles do not appear true in isometric drawings. Therefore, the edges or surfaces that are at an angle are drawn by locating their endpoints. The lines that are parallel to the isometric axes are called **Isometric Lines**. The lines that are not parallel to the isometric axes are called **Non-Isometric Lines**.

1.3 ISOMETRIC PLANES

Isometric Planes have three principal planes. They are Isoplane Right, Isoplane Top and Isoplane Left. The three isometric planes are shown in **Fig. 4.**

If we look at each of the isometric axis, we can identify a plane lying between each axis. These are referred to as Isoplane Right, Isoplane Top and Isoplane Left as shown.

The Isoplane Right is defined by the vertical axis and the right horizontal axis. The Isoplane Top is defined by the right and left horizontal axes. Similarly, the Isoplane Left is defined by the vertical axis and the left horizontal axis.

Similar to the lines, the planes can be isometric planes or non-isometric planes.

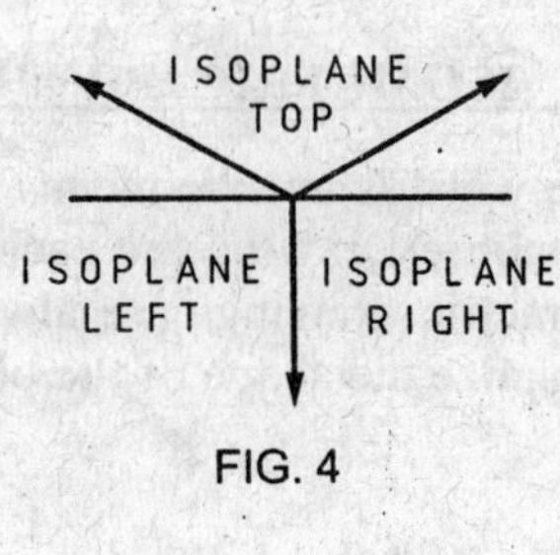

FIG. 4

2. SETTING ISOMETRIC GRID AND SNAP

Use the **SNAP** command to set the isometric grid and snap. The STYLE (S) option permits you to select the style of the snap grid, viz., Standard or Isometric.

Isometric grid lines are arranged to draw 30, 90, 150, 210, 270 and 360 degree lines. The distance between the grid lines is determined by the Vertical Spacing, which is specified by using the **GRID** or **SNAP** command. The grid lines coincide with three isometric axes, which make it easier to create isometric drawings.

Problem 1: *Set the isometric grid and snap of 1 unit each using the **Snap** command.*

See Fig. 5. The command sequence to set the isometric grid and snap of 1 unit each using the **Snap** command is as follows:

Command: **SNAP** ↵
Specify snap spacing or [ON/OFF/Aspect/Style/Type] <0.2500>: **S** ↵
Enter snap grid style [Standard/Isometric] <S>: **I** ↵
Specify vertical spacing <0.2500>: **1** ↵

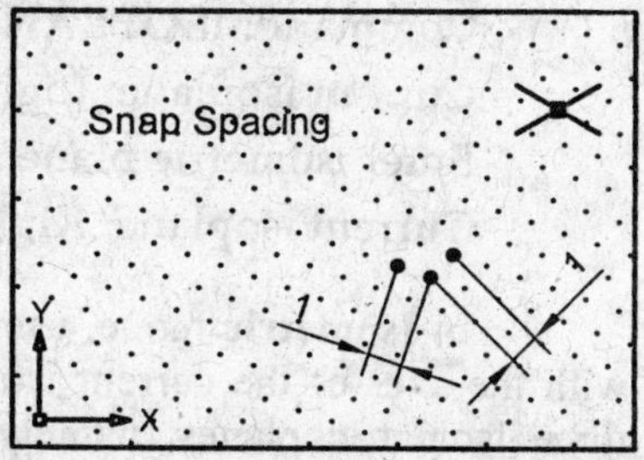

FIG. 5

Note that the <default> entries enclosed in brackets are the default values for the current command. The default value will be executed if you press ENTER.

The isometric grid and snap can be set by using the **Drafting Settings** dialog box. This can be invoked by entering **DSETTINGS** at the command prompt. The **Drafting Settings** dialog box is shown in **Fig. 6.**

The **Drafting Settings** dialog box can also be invoked by right-clicking the **Snap, Grid, Polar** or **Osnap** button available in the **Status Bar** and choosing **Settings** from the shortcut menu.

Choose the **Grid On (F7)** check box located in the **Snap and Grid** tab of the **Drafting Settings** dialog box to turn on/off the display of the isometric snap and grid.

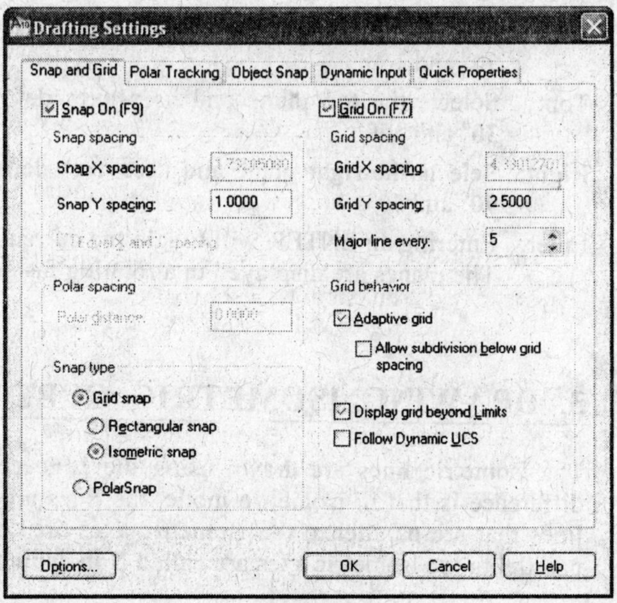

FIG. 6

2.1 ISOPLANE COMMAND

When the isometric grid is set, the display of crosshairs also changes. The crosshairs are displayed at an isometric angle and their orientation depends on the current isoplane. It is possible to toggle between isoplane right, isoplane left and isoplane top by pressing the **Ctrl** and **E** keys (**Ctrl + E**) simultaneously or using the function key **F5**. It is also possible to toggle between different isoplanes by using the **Drafting Settings** dialog box.

Also, user can toggle between the three isometric planes using the **ISOPLANE** command. Enter **ISOPLANE** command at the **Command** prompt to select the current isoplane and the pair of axes.

Command: **ISOPLANE** ↵
Current isoplane: Right
Enter isometric plane setting [Left/Top/Right] <Left>: **R** ↵
Current isoplane: **Right**

In **Isometric** mode, use the **Ortho** mode to align with the axes of the current isoplane. **Fig. 7** shows the three isometric planes, namely Isoplane Left, Isoplane Top and Isoplane Right. The options in the **ISOPLANE** command are explained as follows:

Left: Selects the left plane and uses axes defined by 90° and 150°.

Top: Selects the top plane and uses axes defined by 30° and 150°.

Right: Selects the right plane and uses axes defined by 90° and 30°.

Enter: Entering an ENTER will toggle the current plane. The planes are displayed in a rotating fashion.

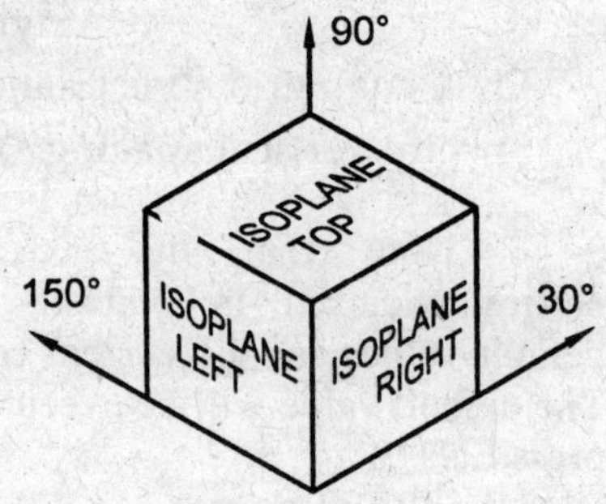

FIG. 7

3. DRAWING ISOMETRIC CUBE

The isometric lines are drawn using the **Line** command similar to orthographic lines. Only difference is that in isometric mode, the lines are drawn only through the isometric axes. The lines that are parallel to the isometric axes are called **Isometric Lines**. The lines that are not parallel to the isometric axes are called **Non-Isometric Lines**.

Problem 2: *Draw a cube of side 30 mm using the Line command in Isometric Mode.*

The procedure and command sequences to draw a cube of 30 mm side using the Line command in the Isometric Mode is explained below:

1. Start the AutoCAD software and setup a new drawing sheet.
2. Right-click the **SNAP** button on the **Status Bar** and choose **Settings**. On the **Snap and Grid** tab, in the **Snap type** section, choose **Grid snap** (if not already selected) radio button, and then choose the **Isometric snap** radio button.
3. Press **F5** to toggle between the planes Isoplane Left, Isoplane Right and Isoplane Top. Press **F8** until you see the <Ortho On> message at the command prompt.
4. ***See Fig. 8.*** Draw a square in isometric mode using the following command sequence:

Command: **LINE** ↵
Specify first point: (*Pick P1*)
Specify next point or [Undo]:
(*Move the cursor to top*) **30** ↵
Specify next point or [Undo]:
(*Move the cursor to left*) **30** ↵
Specify next point or [Close/Undo]:
(*Move the cursor to bottom*) **30** ↵
Specify next point or [Close/Undo]:
(*Move the cursor to right*) **30** ↵
Specify next point or [Close/Undo]: ↵

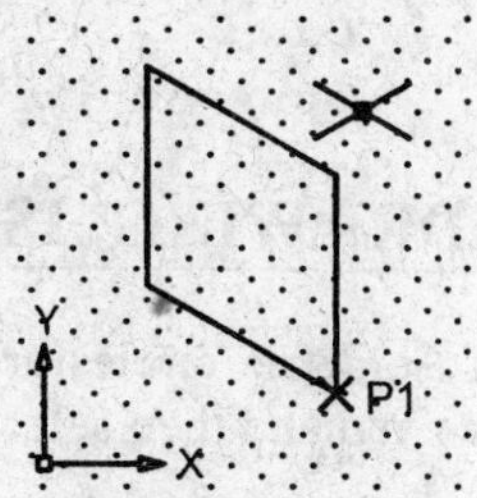

FIG. 8

5. ***See Fig. 9.*** Draw the other set of lines of the cube in isometric mode using the following command sequence:

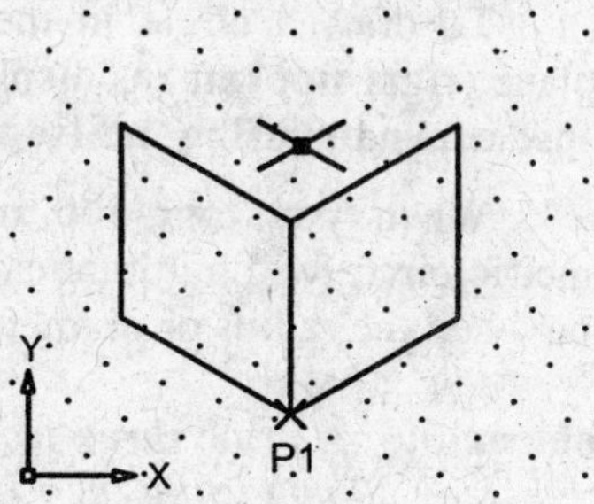

FIG. 9

Command: **LINE** ↵
Specify start point: (*Pick P1*)
Current line-width is 0.0000
Specify next point or [Arc/Halfwidth/
Length/Undo/Width]: <Isoplane Right>
(*Move the cursor to right*) **30** ↵
Specify next point or [Arc/Close/Halfwidth/
Length/Undo/Width]: <Isoplane Top> (*Move the cursor to top*) **30** ↵
Specify next point or [Arc/Close/Halfwidth/Length/Undo/Width]:
<Isoplane Top> (*Move the cursor to left*) **30** ↵
Specify next point or [Arc/Close/Halfwidth/Length/Undo/Width]: ↵

6. ***See Fig. 10.*** Draw the last set of lines of the cube in isometric mode using the following command sequence:

Command: **LINE** ↵

Specify first point: (*Pick P2*)
Specify next point or [Undo]: <Isoplane Top>
(*Move the cursor to right*) **30** ↵
Specify next point or [Undo]:
(*Move the cursor to down*) **30** ↵
Specify next point or [Close/Undo]: ↵

7. Finally, save the drawing.

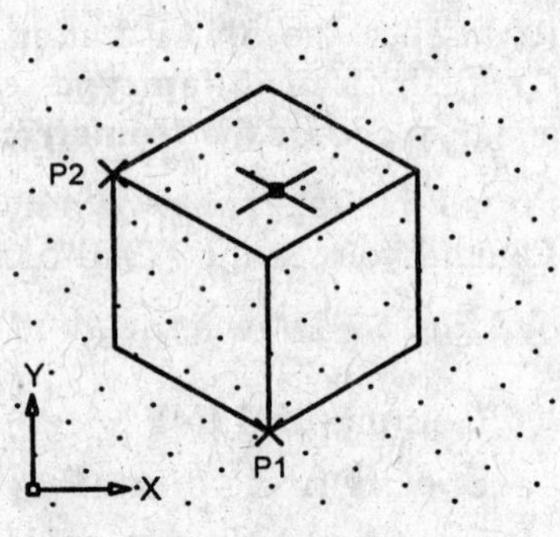

FIG. 10

4. DRAWING ISOMETRIC CIRCLES

The isometric circles are drawn using the **Ellipse** command. For this, first invoke the **Ellipse** command and then select the Isocircle option.

You must have isometric snap ON, to display the Isocircle option in the **Ellipse** command. If isometric snap is not ON, you cannot draw isometric circle. Before entering radius or diameter of the isometric circle, make sure that it is in the required isoplane.

To draw a circle in the right isoplane, toggle through the isoplanes until the required isoplane (right isoplane) is displayed. Also, set the required isoplane current before entering the **Ellipse** command using the **Isoplane** command.

When you toggle through different isoplanes, the crosshairs and the shape of the isometric circle will automatically change. AutoCAD draws the isometric circle in the selected plane when the radius or diameter of the circle entered.

Problem 3: *Draw three isometric circles of radius 5 mm at the centers of three planes of a cube of side 30 mm using the Ellipse command in the Isometric Mode.*

The procedure and command sequences to draw a cube of 30 mm side using the Line command in the Isometric Mode is explained in the **Problem 2**. The command sequences draw three isometric circles of radius 5 mm using the Ellipse command is as follows:

1. Command sequence to draw the isocircle in the left isoplane is as follows:

Command: **ELLIPSE** ↵
Specify axis endpoint of ellipse or
[Arc/Center/Isocircle]: **I** ↵
Specify center of isocircle: (*Pick P1*)
Specify radius of isocircle or [Diameter]:
<Isoplane Right> <Isoplane Left> **5** ↵

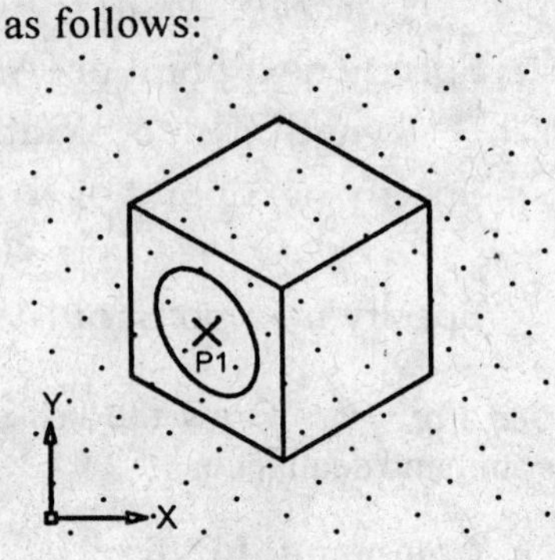

FIG. 11

See Fig. 11.

2. Command sequence to draw the isocircle in the right isoplane is as follows:

   Command: **ELLIPSE** ↵
   Specify axis endpoint of ellipse or
   [Arc/Center/Isocircle]: **I** ↵
   Specify center of isocircle: (*Pick P2*)
   Specify radius of isocircle or [Diameter]:
   <Isoplane Top> <Isoplane Right> **5** ↵

   See Fig. 12.

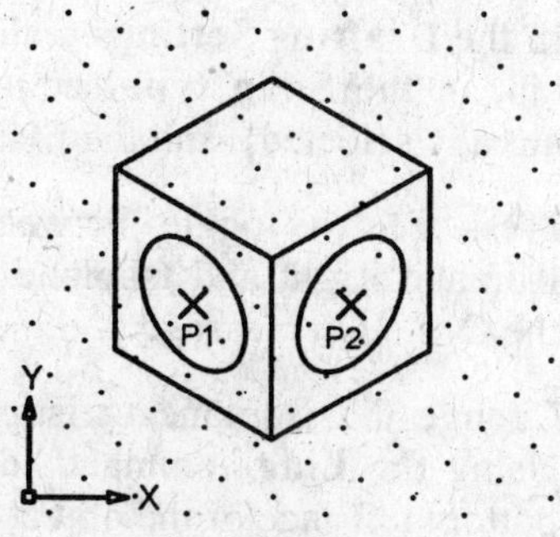

FIG. 12

3. Command sequence to draw the isocircle in the top isoplane is as follows:

   Command: **ELLIPSE** ↵
   Specify axis endpoint of ellipse or
   [Arc/Center/Isocircle]: **I** ↵
   Specify center of isocircle: (*Pick P3*)
   Specify radius of isocircle or [Diameter]:
   <Isoplane Left> <Isoplane Top> **5** ↵

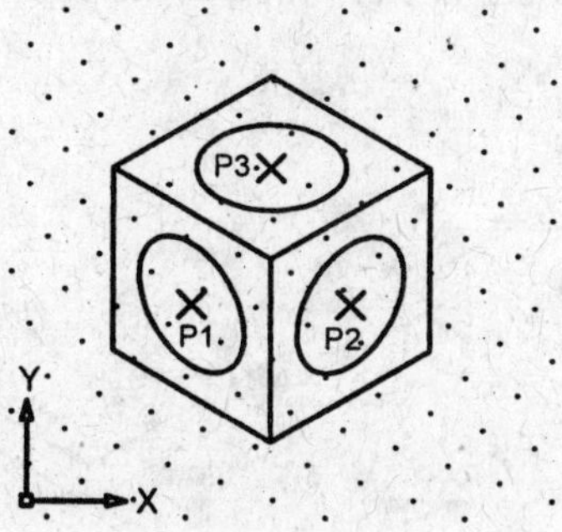

FIG. 13

4. **See Fig. 13.** Finally save the drawing.

Ex. No. : 1 **Date :**	**DRAWING OBJECTS IN ISOMETRIC MODE**

AIM : *To draw the Isometric Projection of the object in* ***Fig. 14.***

Procedure to draw Isometric Projection of the object shown in **Fig. 14** :

1. Start the **AutoCAD** Software and setup a new drawing sheet.

2. Right-click the **SNAP** button on the **Status Bar** and choose **Settings**. The **Drafting Settings** dialog box will be displayed on the screen.

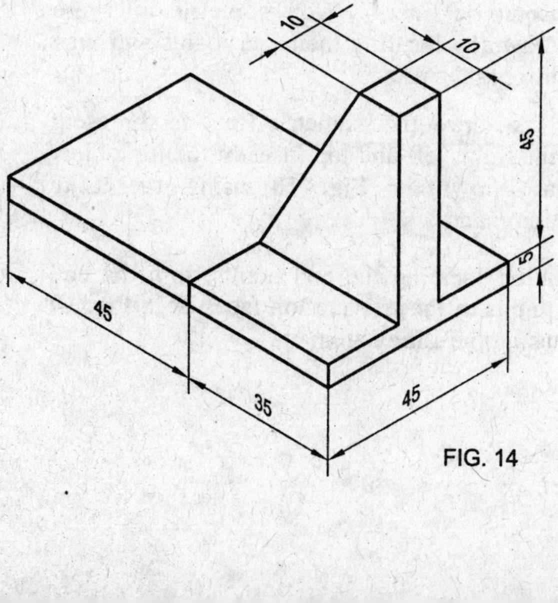

FIG. 14

3. In the **Drafting Settings** dialog box, on the **Snap and Grid** tab, in the **Snap type** section, choose **Grid snap** (if not already selected), and then **Isometric snap**.

4. Press **F5** to toggle between the planes Isoplane Left, Isoplane Right and Isoplane Top. Press **F8** until you see the Ortho On message at the command prompt.

5. Change the isoplane to isoplane left by pressing F5 key. Using the **Line** command, draw the lines to represent the bottom left face of the object as shown in **Fig. 15.**

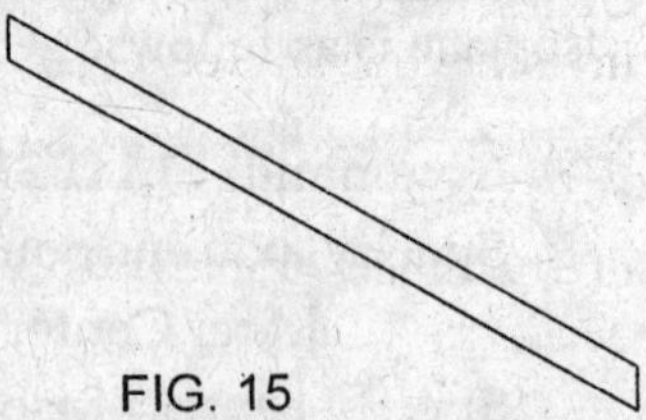

FIG. 15

6. Change the isoplane to isoplane right by pressing F5 key. Draw the lines to represent the bottom right face of the object as shown in **Fig. 16** using the **Line** command.

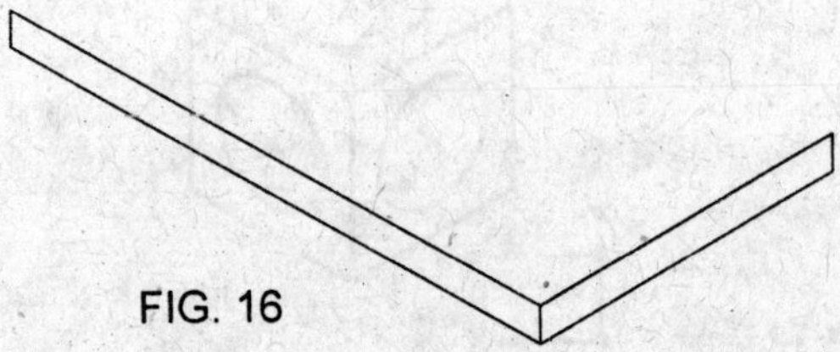

FIG. 16

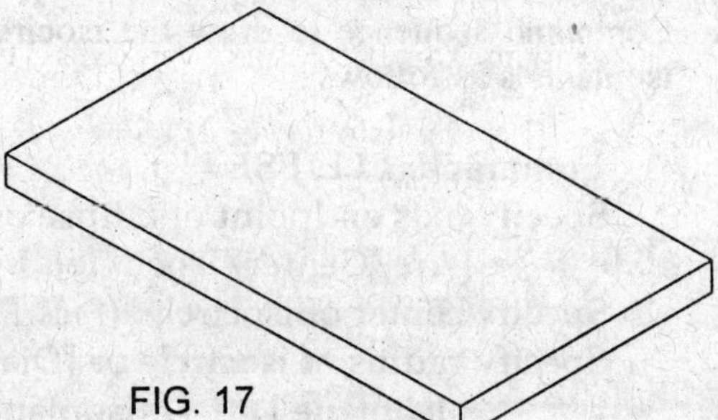

FIG. 17

7. Change the isoplane to isoplane top by pressing F5 key. Draw the lines to represent the top face of the object as shown in **Fig. 17** using the **Line** command.

8. In the top tapered portion of the object, non-isometric lines are present. Non-isometric lines cannot be drawn similar to isometric lines. Non-isometric lines are drawn by locating their end points and then joining them.

   First, draw the isometric lines to represent the right, left and top faces of the top object as shown in **Fig. 18** using the **Line** command.

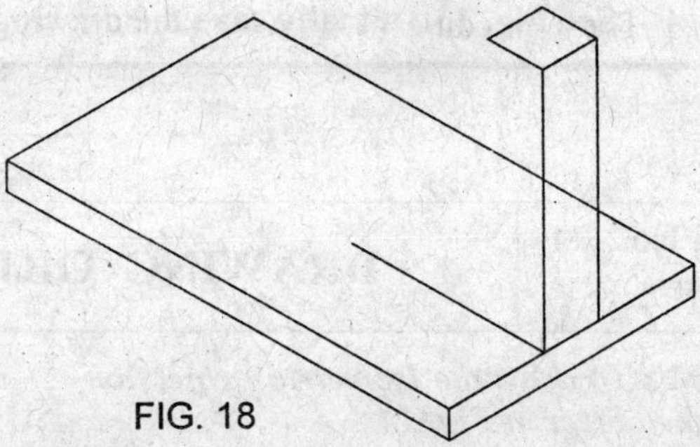

FIG. 18

9. After locating the end points, join the end points of the left and top faces as in **Fig. 19** using the **Line** command.

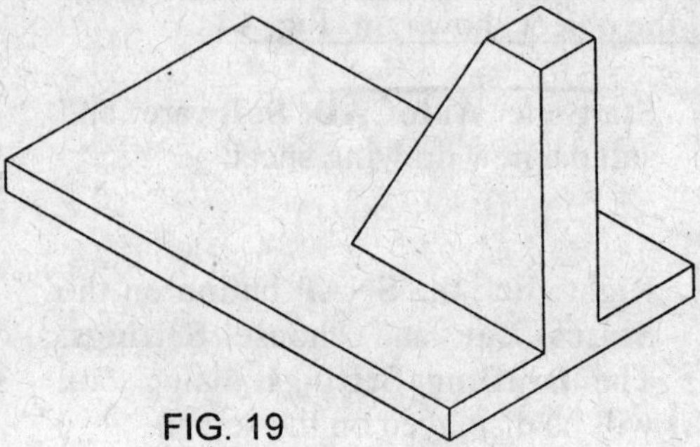

FIG. 19

10. Using the **TRIM** command, trim the invisible lines. **See Fig.19.**
11. Reduce **Fig. 19** to 82% using Scale Command. Thus, the Isometric Projection of the object is obtained as shown in **Fig. 20.**
12. Finally, save the drawing.

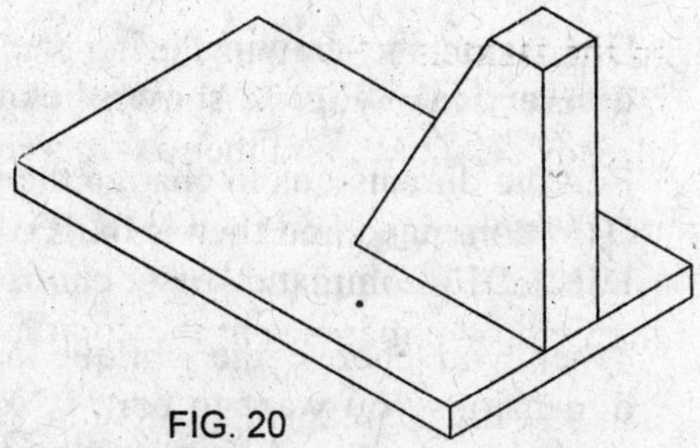

FIG. 20

5. DIMENSIONING THE OBJECTS IN ISOMETRIC MODE

Dimensioning an isometric object involves Two Steps:

First Step: Dimension the drawing using the standard dimensioning commands such as **dimaligned** or **dimvertical**.

Second Step: Edit the dimensions to change them to oblique dimensions. The dimensions are edited using the **Oblique** option in the **Dimedit** command.

Problem 4: *Draw the Isometric Projection of the object given in* ***Fig. 21.*** *Also, mark the dimensions in Isometric Mode.*

Note : The procedure to draw the Isometric *Projection* of the object as shown in **Fig. 20** is already explained in **Problem 4.** Procedure and Command Sequence to mark the dimensions for the object in isometric mode is explained as follows:

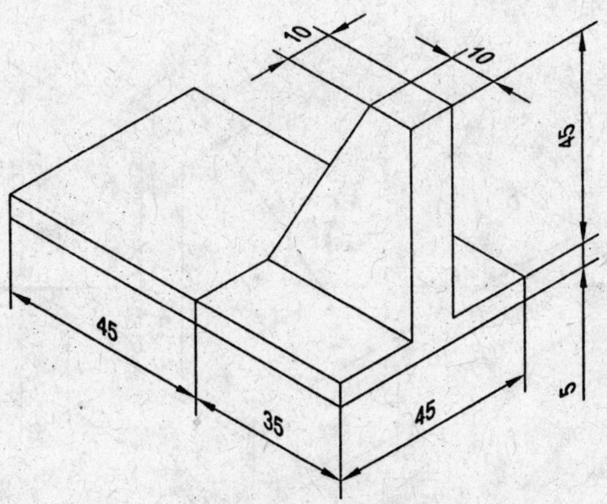

FIG. 21 (Given)

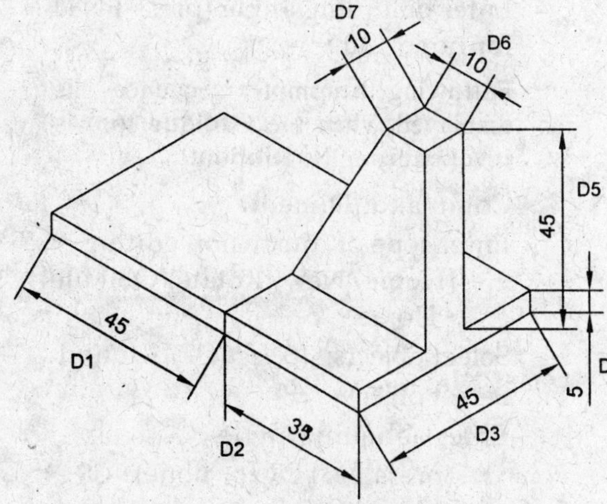

FIG. 22

1. Dimension the drawing using the standard dimensioning commands such as **dimaligned** or **dimvertical**. **Fig. 22** shows the object with dimensions.

2. Edit the dimensions to change them to oblique dimensions. To edit the dimensions, enter the **DIM** command and then **OBLIQUE** at the command prompt or use the **Oblique** option in the **DIMEDIT** command. Also, choose **Oblique** tool in the **Dimensions** panel in **Annotate** tab.

   When you choose the oblique option, AutoCAD prompts to select objects. Select the dimensions you want to edit. Now, AutoCAD prompts to enter the obliquing angle. The obliquing angle is determined by the angle that the extension line of the isometric dimension makes with the positive X axis.

   The prompt sequences to edit the dimensions are given below:

   Command: **DIM** ↵
   Dim: **OBLIQUE** ↵
   Select objects: (*Select D1*) 1 found
   Select objects: (*Select D2*) 1 found, 2 total
   Select objects: (*Select D3*) 1 found, 3 total
   Select objects: ↵
   Enter obliquing angle (press ENTER for none): **90** ↵
   Dim: (*Press Esc to exit the Dim tool*)

   Command: **DIMEDIT** ↵
   Enter type of dimension editing [Home/New/Rotate/Oblique] <Home>: **O** ↵
   Select objects: (*Select D4*) 1 found
   Select objects: (*Select D5*) 1 found, 2 total
   Select objects: (*Select D6*) 1 found, 3 total
   Select objects: ↵
   Enter obliquing angle (press ENTER for none): **30** ↵

   Following prompt sequence is displayed when the **Oblique** tool is invoked from the **Ribbon**:

   Command: **Dimedit**
   Enter type of dimension editing [Home/New/Rotate/Oblique] <Home>: o
   Select objects: (*Select D7*) 1 found
   Select objects: ↵
   Enter obliquing angle (press ENTER for none): **-30** ↵

3. **See Fig. 23** for completed dimensioning.

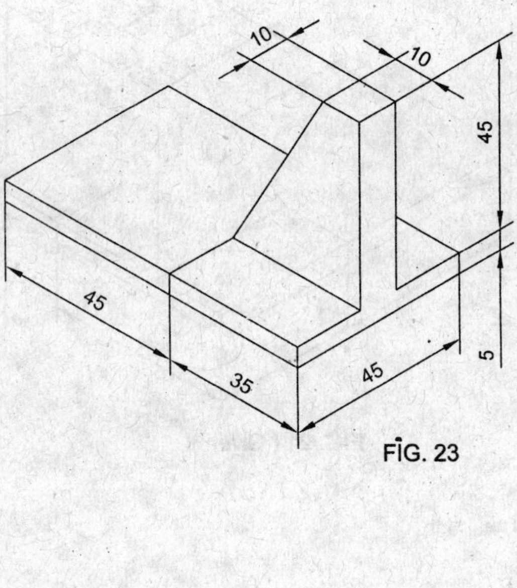

FIG. 23

6. CREATING TEXTS IN ISOMETRIC MODE

The text in an isometric drawing is oblique at a positive or negative 30°. However, use regular text when placing the text in an isometric drawing.

Now, create two text styles with oblique angles of 30° and negative 30°. To create a new text style, use the **-STYLE** command or the **Text Style** dialog box.

Fig. 24 shows the **Text Style** dialog box. In this dialog box, create a new text style **Iso-Text1** with a 30° oblique angle.

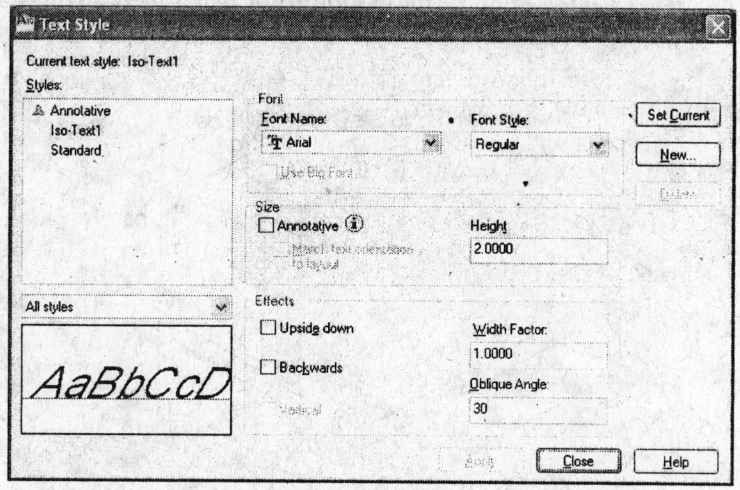

FIG. 24

Similarly, create another text style, with the name Iso-Text2, with a -30° oblique angle.

When placing the text in an isometric drawing, you must specify the rotation angle of the text. **See Fig. 25.**

The text style and the rotation angle depend on the placement of the text in the isometric drawing.

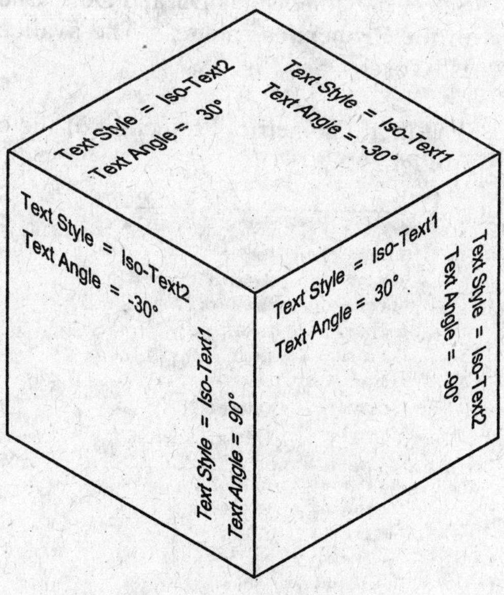

FIG. 25

Problem 5: *Draw the Isometric Projection of the object shown in* ***Fig. 21*** *and mark the Dimensions in Isometric Mode. Also, place the Text in Isometric Mode.*

The procedure to draw the Isometric *Projection* of the object is already explained above.

The procedure and command sequence to mark the dimensions for the object in **Isometric Mode** as shown in **Fig. 23.**

<u>Procedure to place the **TEXTS** in Isometric Mode is explained below:</u>

1. **See Fig. 26.** Select the dimensions D1, D2, D4, D5 and D7. Choose the down-arrow in the **Text Style** option in the **Annotation** panel of the **Home** tab. The available text styles are listed. Choose the text style Iso-Text2. **See Fig. 27.**

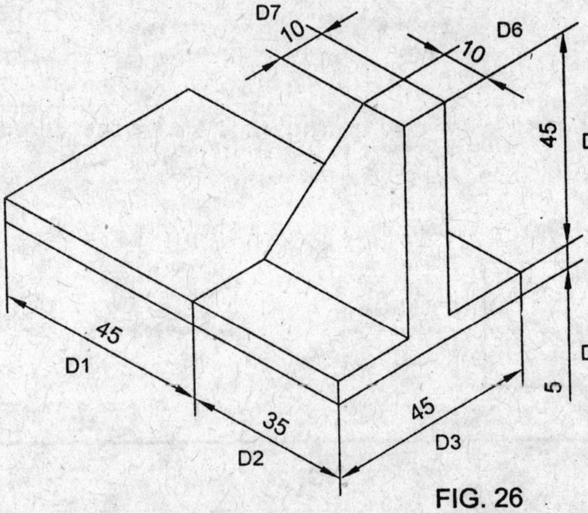

FIG. 26

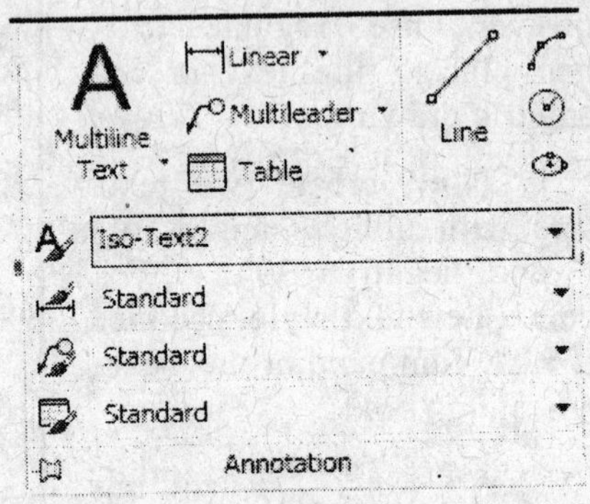

FIG. 27

2. Select the dimensions D3 and D6. Choose the down-arrow in the **Text style** in the **Text** tab of the **Properties** palette. The available text styles are listed here. Choose the text style Iso-Text1. **See Fig. 28.**

3. The final Isometric Projection of the object with dimensions in **Isometric Mode** is shown in **Fig. 29.**

Text	
Fill color	None
Fractional type	Horizontal
Text color	ByBlock
Text height	2.0000
Text offset	1.0000
Text outside align	Off
Text pos hor	Centered
Text pos vert	Above
Text style	Iso-Text1
Text inside align	On
Text position X	36.9492
Text position Y	5.5575
Text rotation	0
Text view direction	Left-to-Right
Measurement	25.5150
Text override	45

FIG. 28

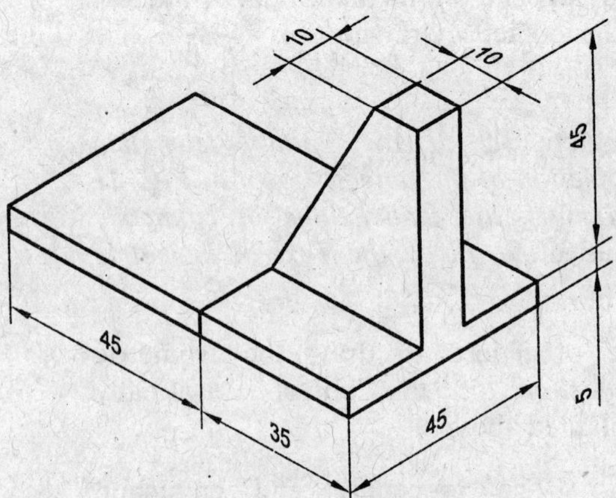

FIG. 29

4. Finally save the drawing.

Ex. No. : 2 Date :	ISOMETRIC PROJECTION OF DOOR STEPS

RULE

"Reduce the Isometric View to 82% using Scale Command to obtain the Isometric Projection of the object".

AIM: To create the Isometric Projection of the **DOOR STEPS** shown in **Fig.1.**

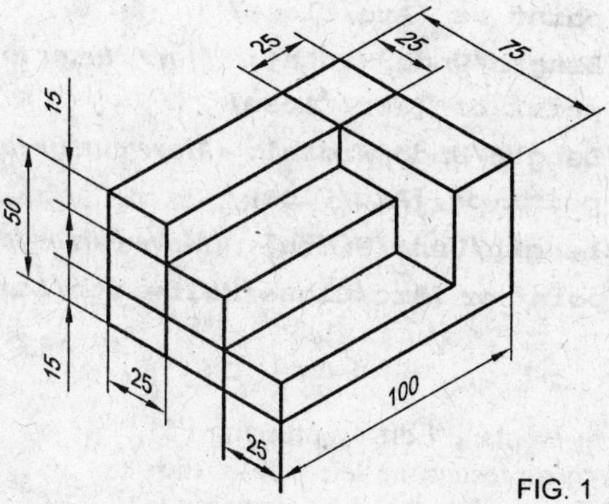

FIG. 1 DOOR - STEPS

1. Right-click the **SNAP** button on the **Status Bar** and choose **Settings**. The **Drafting Settings** dialog box will be displayed on the screen.

   [Another method is, type **DS** at the command prompt to display the Drafting Settings dialog box.]

2. In the **Drafting Settings** dialog box, on the **Snap and Grid** tab, in the **Snap type** section, choose **Grid snap** (if not already selected), and then **Isometric snap.**

3. Press **F5** to toggle between the planes **Isoplane Left, Isoplane Right** and **Isoplane Top.** Press **F8** until the `<Ortho On>` message displayed at the command prompt.

4. Change the isoplane to Isoplane Right by pressing F5 key. Draw the lines to represent the right face of the steps using the **PLINE** command. The command sequence is:

```
Command:  <Isoplane Right>
Command: PLINE ↵
```

4. Change the isoplane to Isoplane Right by pressing F5 key. Draw the lines to represent the right face of the steps using the **PLINE** command. The command sequence is:

Command: <Isoplane Right>

Command: PLINE ↵

Specify start point: (*Pick P1*)

Current line-width is 0.0000

Specify next point or
[Arc/Halfwidth/Length/
Undo/Width]: <Ortho on>
(*Move cursor to Right*) 100 ↵

Specify next point or
[Arc/Close/Halfwidth/
Length/Undo/Width]: (*Move cursor to Up*) 50 ↵

Specify next point or [Arc/Close/
Halfwidth/Length/Undo/Width]: (*Move cursor to Left*) 25 ↵

Specify next point or [Arc/Close/
Halfwidth/Length/Undo/Width]: (*Move cursor to Down*) 35 ↵

Specify next point or [Arc/Close/
Halfwidth/Length/Undo/Width]: (*Move cursor to Left*) 75 ↵

Specify next point or [Arc/Close/Halfwidth/Length/Undo/Width]: C ↵

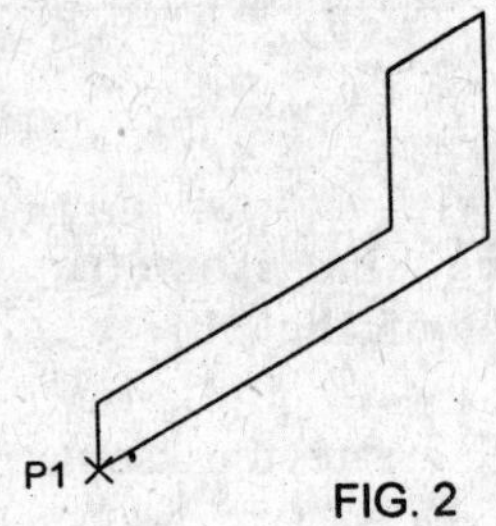

FIG. 2

See Fig. 2.

5. Change the isoplane to Isoplane Left by pressing F5 key. Draw the lines to represent the left face of the steps using the **PLINE** command. The command sequence is:

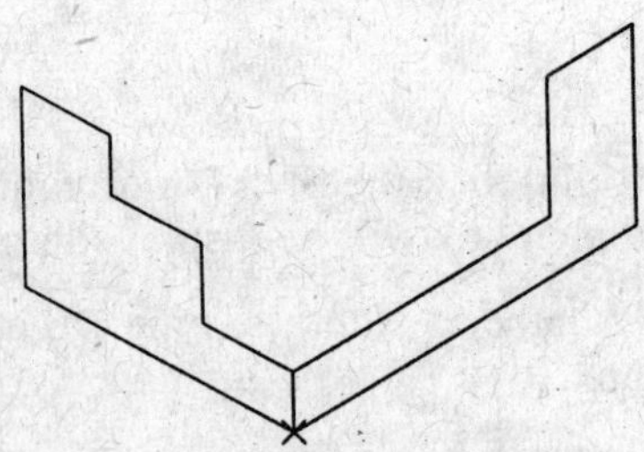

FIG. 3

Command: <Isoplane Left>

Command: PLINE ↵

Specify start point: (*Pick P1*)

Current line-width is 0.0000

Specify next point or
[Arc/Halfwidth/Length/
Undo/Width]: <Ortho on> (*Move cursor to Left*) 75 ↵

Specify next point or [Arc/Close/Halfwidth/
Length/Undo/Width]: (*Move cursor to Up*) 50 ↵

Specify next point or [Arc/Close/Halfwidth/
Length/Undo/Width]: (*Move cursor to Right*) 25 ↵

Specify next point or [Arc/Close/Halfwidth/
Length/Undo/Width]: (*Move cursor to Down*) 15 ↵

```
Specify next point or [Arc/Close/Halfwidth/
   Length/Undo/Width]: (Move cursor to Right) 25 ↵
Specify next point or [Arc/Close/Halfwidth/
   Length/Undo/Width]: (Move cursor to Down) 20 ↵
Specify next point or [Arc/Close/Halfwidth/
   Length/Undo/Width]: (Move cursor to Right) 25 ↵
Specify next point or [Arc/Close/Halfwidth/Length/Undo/Width]: ↵
```

See Fig. 3.

6. Change the isoplane to Isoplane Top by pressing F5 key. Draw the lines to represent the top face of the steps using the **PLINE** command. The command sequence is:

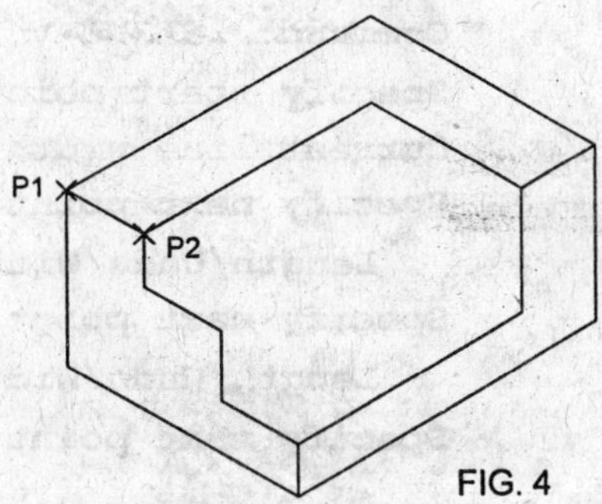

FIG. 4

```
Command: <Isoplane Top>
Command: PLINE ↵
Specify start point: (Pick P1)
Current line-width is 0.0000
Specify next point or [Arc/
   Halfwidth/Length/Undo/Width]:
   <Ortho on> (Move cursor to Right) 100 ↵
Specify next point or [Arc/Close/Halfwidth/
   Length/Undo/Width]: (Move cursor to Right-bottom) 75 ↵
Specify next point or [Arc/Close/Halfwidth/Length/Undo/Width]: ↵

Command: PLINE ↵
Specify start point: (Pick P2)
Current line-width is 0.0000
Specify next point or [Arc/Halfwidth/
   Length/Undo/Width]: (Move cursor to Right) 75 ↵
Specify next point or [Arc/Close/Halfwidth/
   Length/Undo/Width]: (Move cursor to Right-bottom) 50 ↵
Specify next point or [Arc/Close/
   Halfwidth/Length/Undo/Width]: ↵
```

See Fig. 4.

7. Change the isoplane to Isoplane Right by pressing F5 key. Draw the lines to represent the right and top face of the top step using the **PLINE** command. The command sequence is:

```
Command: <Isoplane Right>
Command: PLINE ↵
```

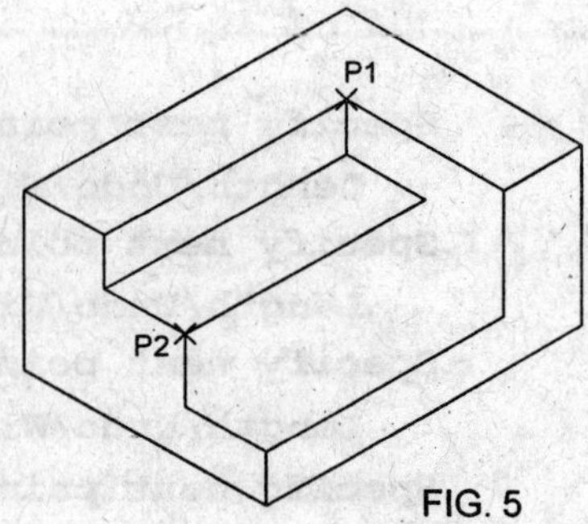

FIG. 5

```
Specify start point: (Pick P1)
Current line-width is 0.0000
Specify next point or [Arc/
   Halfwidth/Length/Undo/Width]:
   <Ortho on> (Move cursor to Down) 15 ↵
Specify next point or [Arc/Close/
   Halfwidth/Length/Undo/Width]:
   (Move cursor to Left) 75 ↵
Specify next point or [Arc/Close/
   Halfwidth/Length/Undo/Width]: ↵

Command: PLINE ↵
Specify start point: (Pick P2)
Current line-width is 0.0000
Specify next point or [Arc/Halfwidth/
   Length/Undo/Width]: (Move cursor to Right) 75 ↵
Specify next point or [Arc/Close/Halfwidth/
   Length/Undo/Width]: <Isoplane Left> (Move cursor to Upper-left) 25 ↵
Specify next point or [Arc/Close/Halfwidth/Length/Undo/Width]: ↵
```

See Fig. 5.

8. Change the isoplane to Isoplane Right by pressing F5 key. Draw the lines to represent the right and top face of the bottom step using the **PLINE** command. The command sequence is:

```
Command: <Isoplane Right>
Command: PLINE ↵
Specify start point: (Pick P1)
Current line-width is 0.0000
Specify next point or [Arc/
   Halfwidth/Length/Undo/Width]:
   <Ortho on> (Move cursor to Right) 75 ↵
Specify next point or [Arc/Close/
   Halfwidth/Length/Undo/Width]:
   (Move cursor to Up) 20 ↵
Specify next point or [Arc/Close/
   Halfwidth/Length/Undo/Width]: ↵

Command: PLINE ↵
Specify start point: (Pick P2)
Current line-width is 0.0000
Specify next point or [Arc/Halfwidth/
```

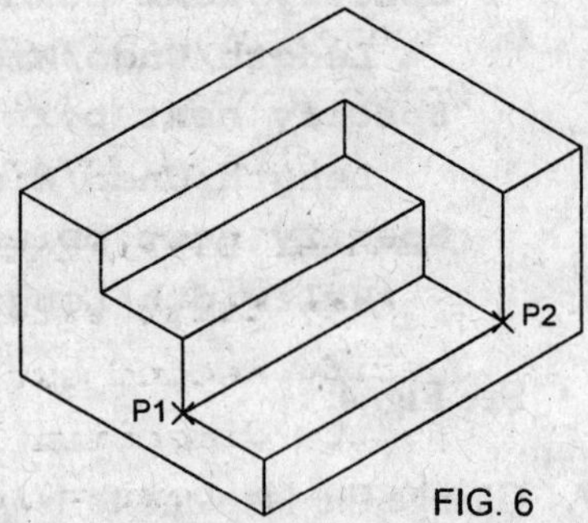

FIG. 6

Length/Undo/Width]: **<Isoplane Left>** (*Move cursor to Left*) **25** ↵
Specify next point or [Arc/Close/Halfwidth/Length/Undo/Width]: ↵

See Fig. 6.

9. Change the lineweight of the object using **Chprop** command. Mark the dimensions using the **Dimaligned** command. The command sequence is:

Command: CHPROP ↵
Select objects: (*Select L1*) **1 found**
Select objects: (*Select L2*)
1 found, 2 total
Select objects: (*Select L3*)
1 found, 3 total
Select objects: (*Select L4*)
1 found, 4 total
Select objects: (*Select L5*)
1 found, 5 total
Select objects: (*Select L6*)
1 found, 6 total
Select objects: (*Select L7*)
1 found, 7 total
Select objects: (*Select L8*)
1 found, 8 total
Select objects: ↵

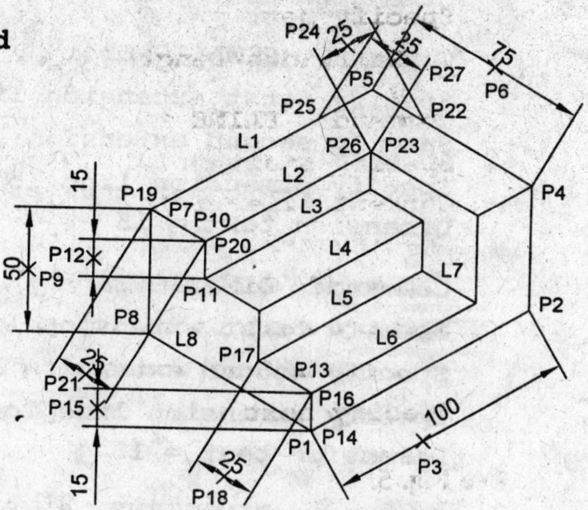

FIG. 7

Enter property to change [Color/LAyer/LType/ltScale/LWeight/ Thickness/Material/Annotative]: LW ↵
Enter new lineweight <ByLayer>: .45 ↵
Lineweight rounded to nearest valid value of 0.40 mm
Enter property to change [Color/LAyer/LType/ltScale/LWeight/ Thickness/Material/Annotative]: ↵

Command: DIMALIGNED ↵
Specify first extension line origin or <select object>: (*Pick P1*)
Specify second extension line origin: (*Pick P2*)
Specify dimension line location or [Mtext/Text/Angle]: (*Pick P3*)
Dimension text = 100

Command: DIMALIGNED ↵
Specify first extension line origin or <select object>: (*Pick P4*)
Specify second extension line origin: (*Pick P5*)

Specify dimension line location or [Mtext/Text/Angle]: *(Pick P6)*
Dimension text = 75

Command: DIMALIGNED ↵
Specify first extension line origin or <select object>: *(Pick P7)*
Specify second extension line origin: *(Pick P8)*
Specify dimension line location or [Mtext/Text/Angle]: *(Pick P9)*
Dimension text = 50

Command: DIMALIGNED ↵
Specify first extension line origin or <select object>: *(Pick P10)*
Specify second extension line origin: *(Pick P11)*
Specify dimension line location or [Mtext/Text/Angle]: *(Pick P12)*
Dimension text = 15

Command: DIMALIGNED ↵
Specify first extension line origin or <select object>: *(Pick P13)*
Specify second extension line origin: *(Pick P14)*
Specify dimension line location or [Mtext/Text/Angle]: *(Pick P15)*
Dimension text = 15

Command: DIMALIGNED ↵
Specify first extension line origin or <select object>: *(Pick P16)*
Specify second extension line origin: *(Pick P17)*
Specify dimension line location or [Mtext/Text/Angle]: *(Pick P18)*
Dimension text = 25

Command: DIMALIGNED ↵
Specify first extension line origin or <select object>: *(Pick P19)*
Specify second extension line origin: *(Pick P20)*
Specify dimension line location or [Mtext/Text/Angle]: *(Pick P21)*
Dimension text = 25

Command: DIMALIGNED ↵
Specify first extension line origin or <select object>: *(Pick P22)*
Specify second extension line origin: *(Pick P23)*
Non-associative dimension created.
Specify dimension line location or [Mtext/Text/Angle]: *(Pick P24)*
Dimension text = 25

Command: DIMALIGNED ↵
Specify first extension line origin or <select object>: *(Pick P25)*
Specify second extension line origin: *(Pick P26)*

Specify dimension line location or [Mtext/Text/Angle]: (*Pick P27*)
Dimension text = 25

See Fig. 7.

10. Now, change the dimension lines and extension lines in isometric dimensioning lines. This can be done using the **DIMEDIT** command. The command sequence is:

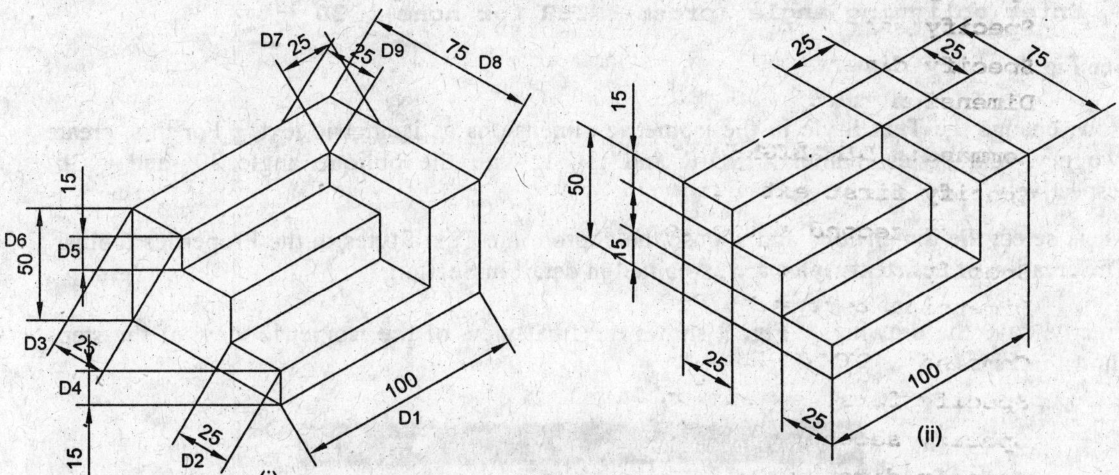

FIG. 8

Command: **DIMEDIT** ↵
Enter type of dimension editing
[Home/New/Rotate/Oblique] <Home>: O ↵
Select objects: (*Select D1*) **1 found**
Select objects: (*Select D2*) **1 found, 2 total**
Select objects: (*Select D3*) **1 found, 3 total**
Select objects: ↵
Enter obliquing angle (press ENTER for none): 90 ↵

Command: DIMEDIT ↵
Enter type of dimension editing
[Home/New/Rotate/Oblique] <Home>: O ↵
Select objects: (*Select D4*) **1 found**
Select objects: (*Select D5*) **1 found, 2 total**
Select objects: (*Select D6*) **1 found, 3 total**
Select objects: (*Select D7*) **1 found, 4 total**
Select objects: ↵
Enter obliquing angle (press ENTER for none): -30 ↵

```
Command:  DIMEDIT ↵
Enter type of dimension editing
   [Home/New/Rotate/Oblique] <Home>: O ↵
Select objects: (Select D8) 1 found
Select objects: (Select D9) 1 found, 2 total
Select objects: ↵
Enter obliquing angle (press ENTER for none): 30 ↵
```

See Fig. 8.

11. Now, change the Text Style in the isometric dimensions as isometric text. For this, create two new text styles, namely, ISO-R and ISO-L with the oblique angle 30° and – 30° respectively.

    Then, select the dimensions and choose the appropriate Text Styles in the Properties toolbar. The creation of new text styles are explained in detail in Section 7.

12. Finally, save the drawing. **Fig. 9** shows the final view of the isometric view of the steps shown in **Fig. 1.**

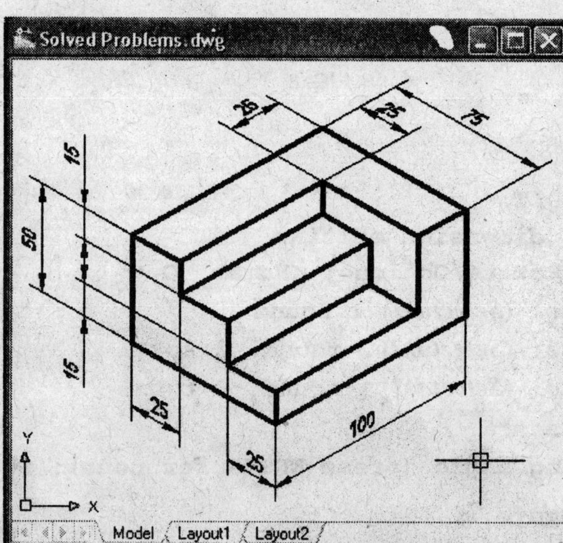

FIG. 9

Ex. No. : 3 - To draw the Isometric Projection of the Square Headed Bolt shown in **Fig. 1.**

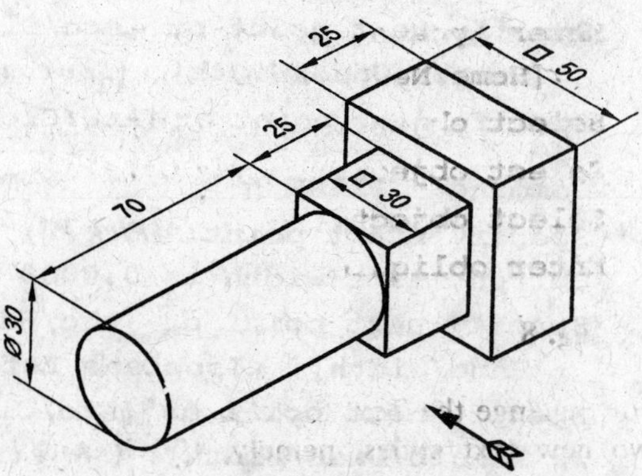

FIG. 1 SQUARE-HEADED BOLT

1. Right-click the **SNAP** button on the **Status Bar** and choose **Settings.** The **Drafting Settings** dialog box will be displayed on the screen.

   [Another method is, type **DS** at the command prompt to display the Drafting Settings dialog box.]

2. In the **Drafting Settings** dialog box, on the **Snap and Grid** tab, in the **Snap type** section, choose **Grid snap** (if not already selected), and then **Isometric snap.**
3. Press **F5** to toggle between the planes **Isoplane Left**, **Isoplane Right** and **Isoplane Top.** Press **F8** until the `<Ortho On>` message displayed at the command prompt.

4. Draw the lines to represent the big square of the square-headed bolt using the **PLINE** command. The command sequence is:

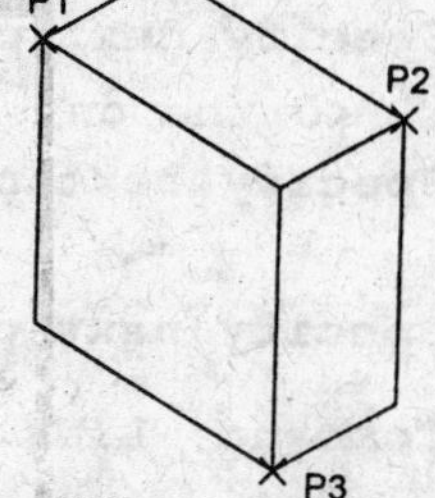

FIG. 2

```
Command: PLINE ↵
Specify start point: (Pick P1)
Current line-width is 0.0000
Specify next point or
[Arc/Halfwidth/Length/Undo/Width]:
(Move cursor to Right-bottom) 50 ↵
Specify next point or
   [Arc/Close/Halfwidth/Length/
   Undo/Width]:  <Isoplane Top> (Move cursor to Right-up) 25 ↵
Specify next point or [Arc/Close/Halfwidth/
   Length/Undo/Width]: (Move cursor to Left-up) 50 ↵
Specify next point or [Arc/Close/
   Halfwidth/Length/Undo/Width]: C ↵

Command:  PLINE ↵
Specify start point: (Pick P2)
Current line-width is 0.0000
Specify next point or [Arc/Halfwidth/Length/
   Undo/Width]:  <Isoplane Right> (Move cursor to bottom) 50 ↵
Specify next point or [Arc/Close/Halfwidth/
   Length/Undo/Width]: (Move cursor to Left-bottom) 25 ↵
```

Specify next point or [Arc/Close/Halfwidth/
Length/Undo/Width]: *(Move cursor to Up)* **50** ↵
Specify next point or [Arc/Close/Halfwidth/Length/Undo/Width]: ↵

Command: PLINE ↵
Specify start point: *(Pick P3)*
Current line-width is 0.0000
Specify next point or [Arc/Halfwidth/Length/
Undo/Width]: <Isoplane Left> *(Move cursor to Left-up)* **50** ↵
Specify next point or [Arc/Close/Halfwidth/
Length/Undo/Width]: *(Move cursor to Up)* **50** ↵
Specify next point or
[Arc/Close/Halfwidth/Length/Undo/Width]: ↵

See Fig. 2.

5. Draw the lines to represent the small square of the square-headed bolt using the **LINE** command. The command sequence is:

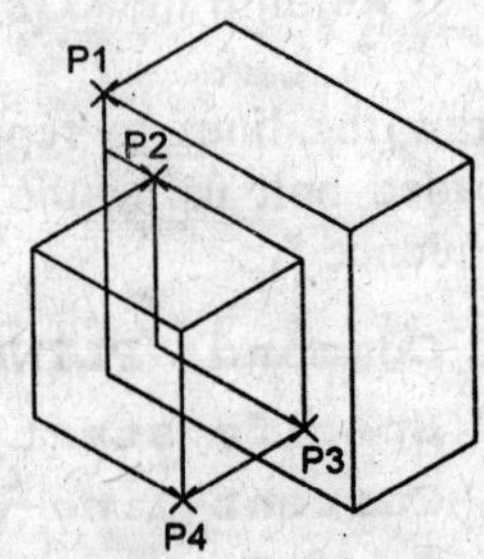

FIG. 3

Command: **LINE** ↵
Specify first point: *(Pick P1)*
Specify next point or [Undo]:
<Ortho on> *(Move cursor to Bottom)* **10** ↵
Specify next point or [Undo]:
(Move cursor to Right) **10** ↵
Specify next point or [Close/Undo]: ↵

Command: LINE ↵
Specify start point: *(Pick P2)*
Current line-width is 0.0000
Specify next point or [Arc/Halfwidth/
Length/Undo/Width]: *(Move cursor to Right)* **30** ↵
Specify next point or [Arc/Close/
Halfwidth/Length/Undo/Width]: *(Move cursor to Bottom)* **30** ↵
Specify next point or [Arc/Close/
Halfwidth/Length/Undo/Width]: *(Move cursor to Left)* **30** ↵
Specify next point or [Arc/Close/
Halfwidth/Length/Undo/Width]: *(Move cursor to Up)* **30** ↵
Specify next point or [Arc/Close/Halfwidth/Length/
Undo/Width]: <Isoplane Top> *(Move cursor to Left-bottom)* **25** ↵
Specify next point or [Arc/Close/Halfwidth/
Length/Undo/Width]: *(Move cursor to Right-bottom)* **30** ↵
Specify next point or [Arc/Close/
Halfwidth/Length/Undo/Width]: *(Move cursor to Right-up)* **25** ↵

Specify next point or [Arc/Close/
Halfwidth/Length/Undo/Width]: ↵

Command: LINE ↵
Specify start point: (*Pick P3*)
Current line-width is 0.0000
Specify next point or [Arc/Halfwidth/
Length/Undo/Width]: (*Move cursor to Left-bottom*) 25 ↵
Specify next point or [Arc/Close/Halfwidth/Length/
Undo/Width]: <Isoplane Right> (*Move cursor to Up*) 30 ↵
Specify next point or [Arc/Close/Halfwidth/Length/Undo/Width]: ↵

Command: LINE ↵
Specify start point: (*Pick P4*)
Current line-width is 0.0000
Specify next point or [Arc/Halfwidth/
Length/Undo/Width]: <Isoplane Left> (*Move cursor to Left-up*) 30 ↵
Specify next point or [Arc/Close/
Halfwidth/Length/Undo/Width]: (*Move cursor to Up*) 30 ↵
Specify next point or [Arc/Close/
Halfwidth/Length/Undo/Width]: ↵

See Fig. 3.

6. Now, erase the unwanted lines using the **Erase** command. Also, cut the hidden lines using the **Trim** command. The command sequence is:

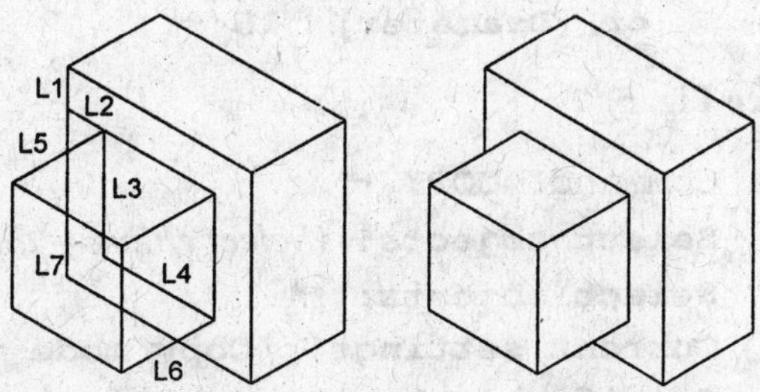

FIG. 4

Command: ERASE ↵
Select objects:
(*Select L1*) **1 found**
Select objects:
(*Select L2*) **1 found, 2 total**
Select objects:
(*Select L3*) **1 found, 3 total**
Select objects: (*Select L4*) **1 found, 4 total**
Select objects: ↵

Command: TRIM ↵
Current settings: Projection=UCS, Edge=None
Select cutting edges ...
Select objects or <select all>: (*Select L5*) **1 found**
Select objects: (*Select L6*) **1 found, 2 total**

Select objects: ↵
Select object to trim or shift-select to extend or
[Fence/Crossing/Project/Edge/eRase/Undo]: (*Select L7*)
Select object to trim or shift-select to extend or
[Fence/Crossing/Project/Edge/eRase/Undo]: ↵

See Fig. 4.

7. Now, the cylindrical part of the square-headed bolt is to be drawn using the **ELLIPSE** and **LINE** commands. Here, the **Isocircle** option of the **Ellipse** command is used. The command sequence is:

Command: LINE ↵
Specify first point: (*Pick P1 – the mid-point*)
Specify next point or [Undo]: (*Pick P2 – the mid-point*)
Specify next point or [Undo]: ↵

Command: ELLIPSE ↵
Specify axis endpoint of ellipse
or [Arc/Center/Isocircle]: I ↵
Specify center of isocircle:
(*Pick P3 – the mid-point*)
Specify radius of isocircle
or [Diameter]: 15 ↵

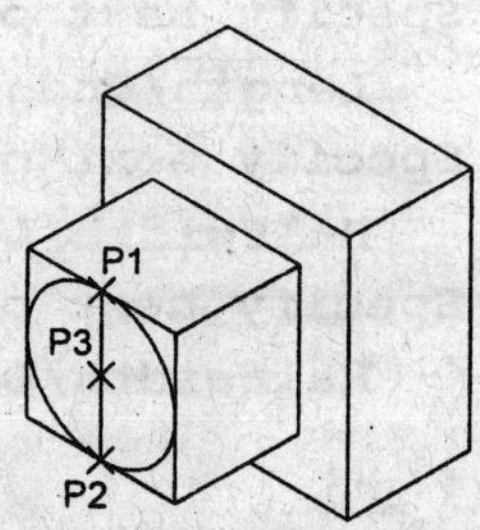

FIG. 5

See Fig. 5.

Command: **COPY** ↵
Select objects: (*Select ellipse – the isocircle*) **1 found**
Select objects: ↵
Current settings: Copy mode = Multiple
Specify base point or [Displacement/
mOde] <Displacement>: (*Pick P1*)
Specify second point or <use first
point as displacement>:
<Ortho on> <Isoplane Left>
(*Move cursor to Left-bottom*) **70** ↵
Specify second point
or [Exit/Undo] <Exit>: ↵

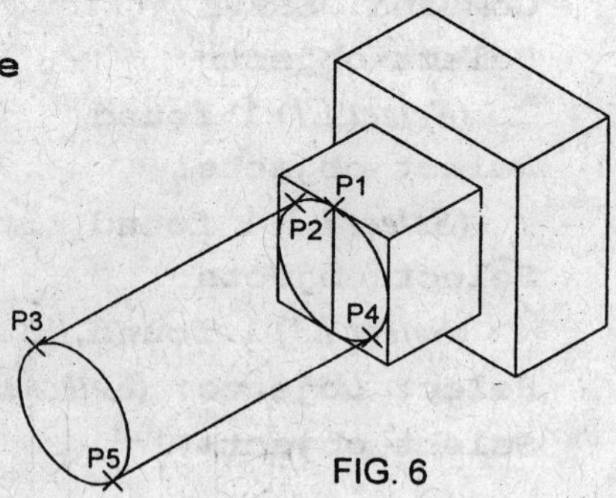

FIG. 6

Command: **LINE** ↵
Specify first point: (*Pick P2*)
Specify next point or [Undo]: (*Pick P3*)

```
Specify next point or [Undo]: ↵

Command:  LINE ↵
Specify first point: (Pick P4)
Specify next point or [Undo]: (Pick P5)
Specify next point or [Undo]: ↵
```

See Fig. 6.

8. Now, remove the unwanted line using the **Erase** command. Also, cut the necessary lines using the **Trim** command. The command sequence is: **See Fig. 7.**

```
Command: ERASE ↵
Select objects: (Select L1) 1 found
Select objects: ↵

Command: TRIM ↵
Current settings: Projection=UCS, Edge=None
Select cutting edges ...
Select objects or <select all>: (Select L2) 1 found
Select objects: (Select L3) 1 found, 2 total
Select objects: ↵
Select object to trim or shift-select to extend or
   [Fence/Crossing/Project/Edge/eRase/Undo]: (Select L4)
Select object to trim or shift-select to extend or
   [Fence/Crossing/Project/Edge/eRase/Undo]: (Select L5)
Select object to trim or shift-select to extend or
   [Fence/Crossing/Project/Edge/eRase/Undo]: (Select E1)
Select object to trim or shift-select to extend or
   [Fence/Crossing/Project/Edge/eRase/Undo]: ↵
```

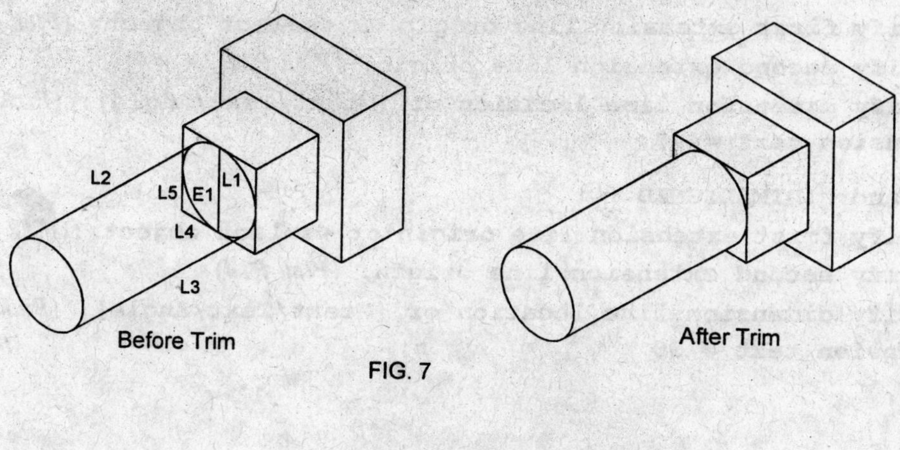

FIG. 7

9. Now, change the lineweight of the object using the **Chprop** command. Also, mark the dimensions using the **Dimaligned** command. The command sequence is:

```
Command: CHPROP ↵
Select objects: All   17 found
Select objects: ↵
Enter property to change [Color/LAyer/LType/ltScale/
   LWeight/Thickness/Material/Annotative]: LW ↵
Enter new lineweight <ByLayer>: .4 ↵
Enter property to change [Color/LAyer/LType/ltScale/
   LWeight/Thickness/Material/Annotative]: ↵

Command: DIMALIGNED ↵
Specify first extension line origin or <select object>: (Pick P1)
Specify second extension line origin: (Pick P2)
Specify dimension line location or [Mtext/Text/Angle]: (Pick P3)
Dimension text = 50

Command:  DIMALIGNED ↵
Specify first extension line origin or <select object>: (Pick P4)
Specify second extension line origin: (Pick P5)
Specify dimension line location or [Mtext/Text/Angle]: (Pick P6)
Dimension text = 25

Command:  DIMALIGNED ↵
Specify first extension line origin or <select object>: (Pick P7)
Specify second extension line origin: (Pick P8)
Specify dimension line location or [Mtext/Text/Angle]: (Pick P9)
Dimension text = 25

Command:  DIMALIGNED ↵
Specify first extension line origin or <select object>:(Pick P10)
Specify second extension line origin: (Pick P11)
Specify dimension line location or [Mtext/Text/Angle]: (Pick P12)
Dimension text = 70

Command:  DIMALIGNED ↵
Specify first extension line origin or <select object>:(Pick P13)
Specify second extension line origin: (Pick P14)
Specify dimension line location or [Mtext/Text/Angle]: (Pick P15)
Dimension text = 30
```

```
Command: DIMALIGNED
Specify first extension
   line origin or
   <select object>: (Pick P16)
Specify second extension
   line origin: (Pick P17)
Specify dimension line
   location or [Mtext/
   Text/Angle]: (Pick P18)
Dimension text = 30
```

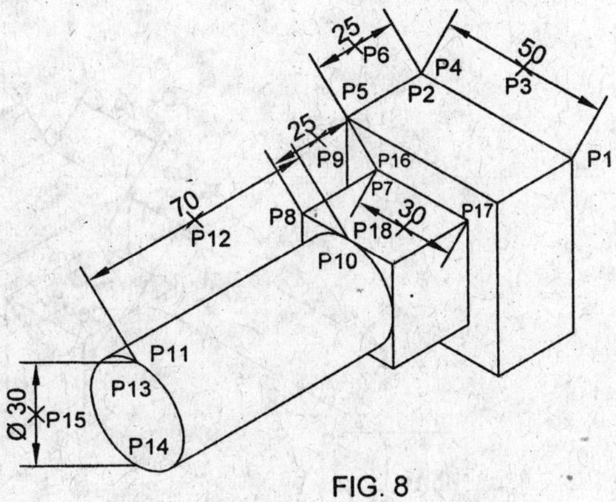

FIG. 8

See Fig. 8.

10. Now, change the dimension lines and extension lines as isometric dimensioning lines. This can be done using the **DIMEDIT** command. The command sequence is:

```
Command: DIMEDIT ↵
Enter type of dimension editing
   [Home/New/Rotate/Oblique] <Home>: O ↵
Select objects: (Select D1) 1 found
Select objects: (Select D2) 1 found, 2 total
Select objects: (Select D3) 1 found, 3 total
Select objects: (Select D4) 1 found, 4 total
Select objects: ↵
Enter obliquing angle (press ENTER for none): -30 ↵

Command: DIMEDIT ↵
Enter type of dimension editing
   [Home/New/Rotate/Oblique] <Home>: O ↵
Select objects: (Select D5) 1 found
Select objects: ↵
Enter obliquing angle (press ENTER for none): 30 ↵

Command: DIMEDIT ↵
Enter type of dimension editing
   [Home/New/Rotate/Oblique] <Home>: O ↵
Select objects: (Select D6) 1 found
Select objects: ↵
Enter obliquing angle (press ENTER for none): 30 ↵
```

See Fig. 9.

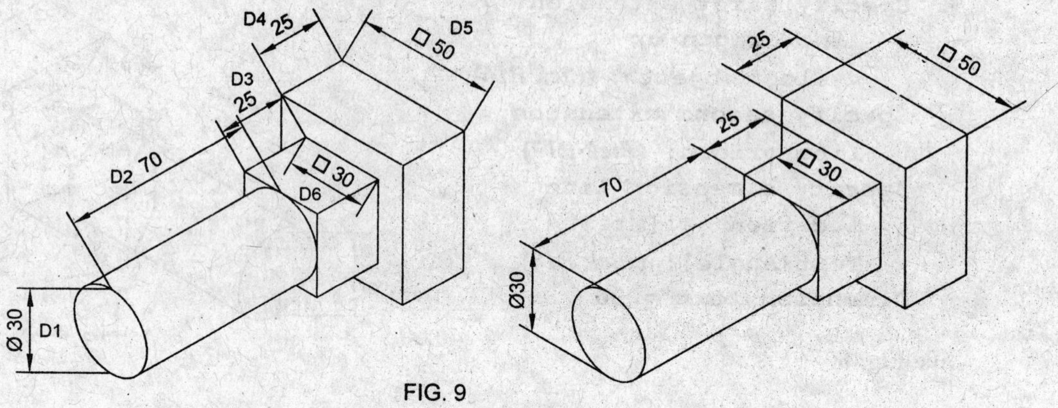

FIG. 9

11. Now, change the Text Style in the isometric dimensions as isometric text. For this, create two new text styles, namely, ISO-R and ISO-L with the oblique angle 30° and – 30° respectively.

    Then, select the dimensions and choose the appropriate Text Styles in the Properties toolbar. The creation of new text styles are explained in detail in Section 7.

12. Finally, save the drawing. **Fig. 10** shows the final view of the isometric view of the steps shown in **Fig. 1.**

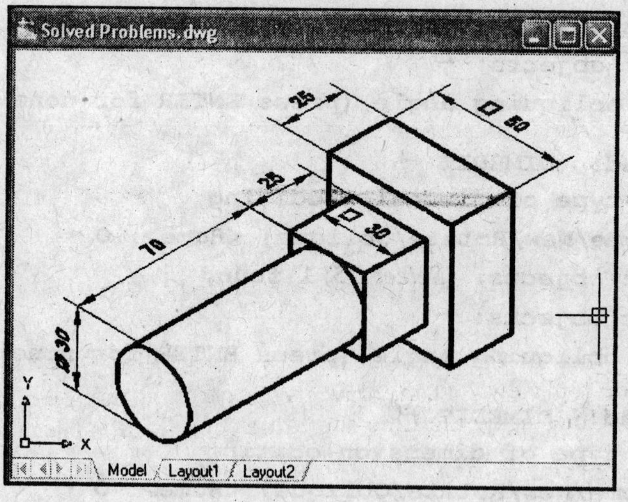

FIG. 10

Ex. No. : 4 - To draw the Isometric Projection of the Hexagonal Nut shown in **Fig. 1.**

1. In the **Fig. 1,** non-isometric lines are present. It is difficult to draw non-isometric lines in isometric mode directly. Therefore, first draw the top view of the hexagonal nut and enclose it in a rectangle. Then, draw the rectangle in isometric mode and transfer the distances. **Fig. 2** shows the top view of the Hexagonal Nut.

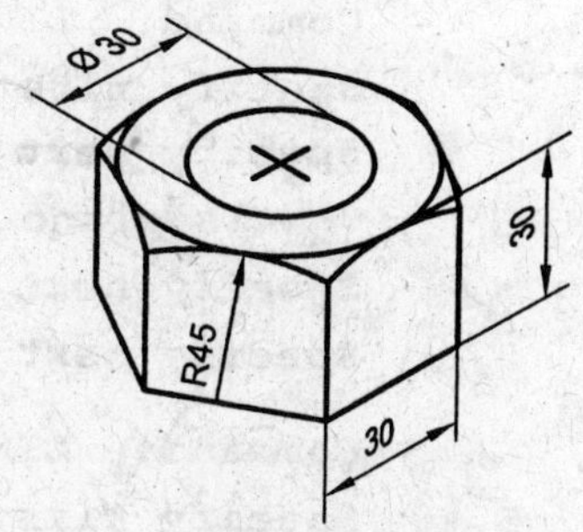

FIG. 1 HEXAGONAL NUT

2. Right-click the **SNAP** button on the **Status Bar** and choose **Settings. Drafting Settings** dialog box will be displayed on the screen. [Another method is, type **DS** at the command prompt to display the Drafting Settings dialog box.]

3. In the **Drafting Settings** dialog box, on the **Snap and Grid** tab, in the **Snap type** section, choose **Grid snap** (if not already selected), and then **Isometric snap**.

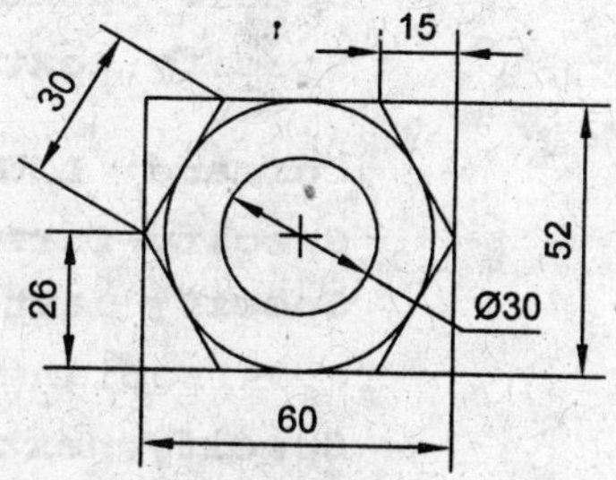

TOP VIEW

FIG. 2

4. Press **F5** to toggle between the planes **Isoplane Left, Isoplane Right** and **Isoplane Top.** Press **F8** until the `<Ortho On>` message displayed at the command prompt.

5. Draw the lines to represent the rectangle using the **LINE** command. The command sequence is: **See Fig. 3.**

```
Command: LINE ↵
Specify first point: (Pick P1)
Specify next point or [Undo]: <Ortho on>
    <Isoplane Top> (Move cursor to Right-top) 60 ↵
Specify next point or [Undo]:
    (Move cursor to Left-top) 52 ↵
Specify next point or [Close/Undo]:
    (Move cursor to Left-bottom) 60 ↵
Specify next point or [Close/Undo]: C ↵
```

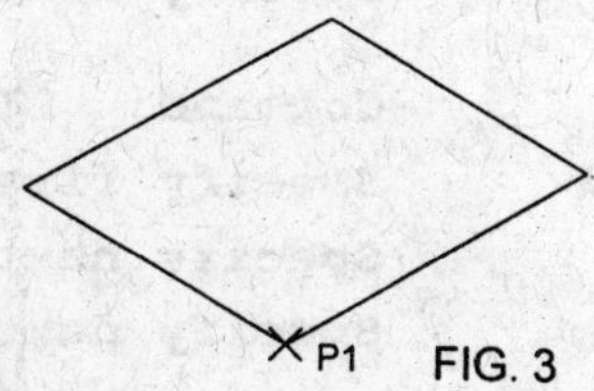

FIG. 3

6. Draw vertical lines of the hexagonal nut by measuring distances from the corners of the rectangle in the top view. Then, draw the hexagon at the top and bottom of these vertical lines. Draw the lines using the **Line** and **Pline** commands. The command sequence is:

```
Command: LINE ↵
  Specify first point: (Pick P1)
  Specify next point or [Undo]:<Ortho on>
                         (Move cursor to Right-top) 15 ↵
  Specify next point or [Undo]:<Isoplane Left>
```

```
   (Move cursor to Left-top) 52 ↵
Specify next point or [Close/Undo]: ↵

Command:  LINE ↵
Specify first point: (Pick P2)
Specify next point or [Undo]:
   <Isoplane Top> (Move cursor to Left-Bottom) 15 ↵
Specify next point or [Undo]: (Move cursor to Left-top) 52 ↵
Specify next point or [Close/Undo]: ↵

Command:  LINE ↵
Specify first point: (Pick P1)
Specify next point or [Undo]: (Move cursor to Left-top) 26 ↵
Specify next point or [Undo]: (Move cursor to Right-top) 60 ↵
Specify next point or [Close/Undo]: ↵

Command: LINE ↵
Specify first point: (Pick P3)
Specify next point or [Undo]:
   <Isoplane Right> (Move cursor to Up) 30 ↵
Specify next point or [Undo]: ↵

Command:  LINE ↵
Specify first point: (Pick P4)
Specify next point or [Undo]: (Move cursor to Up) 30 ↵
Specify next point or [Undo]: ↵

Command:  LINE ↵
Specify first point: (Pick P5)
Specify next point or [Undo]: (Move cursor to Up) 30 ↵
Specify next point or [Undo]: ↵

Command:  LINE ↵
Specify first point: (Pick P6)
Specify next point or [Undo]: (Move cursor to Up)  30 ↵
Specify next point or [Undo]: ↵

Command:  LINE ↵
Specify first point: (Pick P7)
Specify next point or [Undo]: (Move cursor to Up) 30 ↵
Specify next point or [Undo]: ↵
```

```
Command:  LINE ↵
Specify first point: (Pick P8)
Specify next point or [Undo]: (Move cursor to Up) 30 ↵
Specify next point or [Undo]: ↵
```

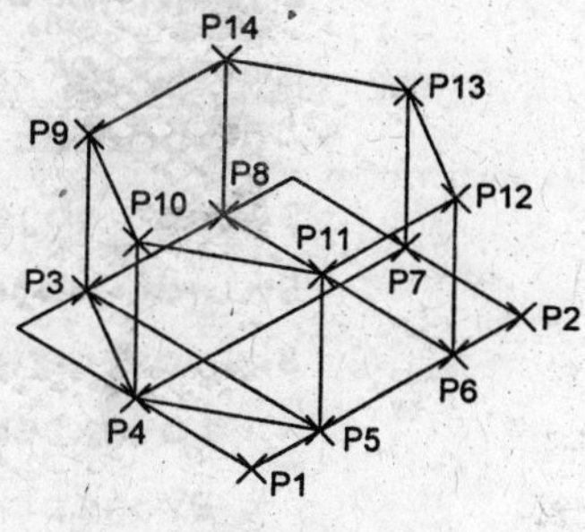

FIG. 4

```
Command:  PLINE ↵
Specify start point: (Pick P9)
Current line-width is 0.0000
Specify next point or [Arc/Halfwidth/
   Length/Undo/Width]: (Pick P10)
Specify next point or [Arc/Close/
   Halfwidth/Length/Undo/Width]: (Pick P11)
Specify next point or [Arc/Close/
   Halfwidth/Length/Undo/Width]: (Pick P12)
Specify next point or [Arc/Close/
   Halfwidth/Length/Undo/Width]: (Pick P13)
Specify next point or [Arc/Close/
   Halfwidth/Length/Undo/Width]: (Pick P14)
Specify next point or [Arc/Close/Halfwidth/Length/Undo/Width]: C ↵

Command:  PLINE ↵
Specify start point: (Pick P3)
Current line-width is 0.0000
Specify next point or
   [Arc/Halfwidth/Length/Undo/Width]: (Pick P4)
Specify next point or [Arc/Close/
   Halfwidth/Length/Undo/Width]: (Pick P5)
Specify next point or [Arc/Close/
   Halfwidth/Length/Undo/Width]: (Pick P6)
Specify next point or [Arc/Close/Halfwidth/Length/Undo/Width]: ↵
```

See Fig. 4.

7. Now, remove the hidden lines and unnecessary lines using the **Erase** command. Also, cut the hidden lines using the **Trim** command. The command sequence is:

```
Command: ERASE ↵
Select objects: (Select L1) 1 found
Select objects: (Select L2) 1 found, 2 total
Select objects: (Select L3) 1 found, 3 total
Select objects: (Select L4) 1 found, 4 total
Select objects: (Select L5) 1 found, 5 total
```

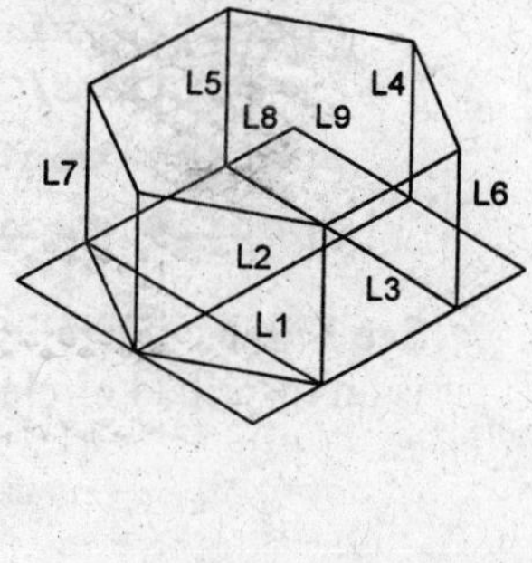

```
Select objects: ↵
Command: TRIM ↵
Current settings: Projection=UCS, Edge=None
Select cutting edges ...
Select objects or
   <select all>: (Select L6) 1 found
Select objects: (Select L7) 1 found, 2 total
Select objects: ↵
Select object to trim or shift-select
   to extend or[Fence/Crossing/
   Project/Edge/eRase/Undo]: (Select L8)
Select object to trim or shift-select to extend or
   [Fence/Crossing/Project/Edge/eRase/Undo]: (Select L9)
Select object to trim or shift-select to extend or
   [Fence/Crossing/Project/Edge/eRase/Undo]: ↵
```

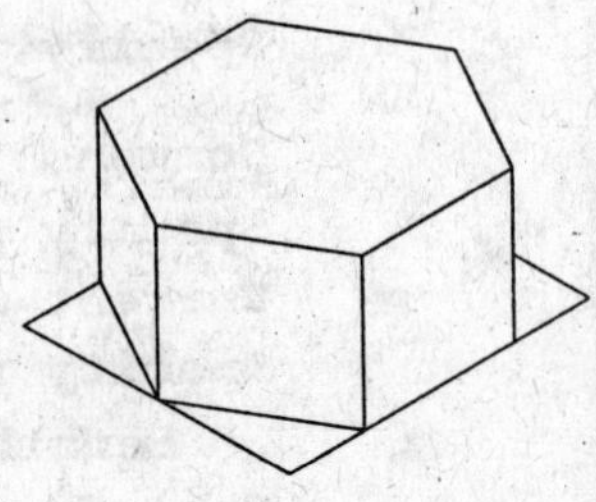

FIG. 5

See Fig. 5.

8. Draw the top circles of the hexagonal nut using the **Isocircle** option of the **Ellipse** command. For this, first locate the center point of the top face. This can be done by drawing a line between opposite corners of the top face of the hexagon. The command sequence is:

```
Command: LINE ↵
Specify first point: (Pick P1)
Specify next point or [Undo]: (Pick P2)
Specify next point or [Undo]: ↵
Command: ELLIPSE ↵
Specify axis endpoint of ellipse or
   [Arc/Center/Isocircle]: I ↵
Specify center of isocircle: (Pick P3)
Specify radius of isocircle or
   [Diameter]:  <Isoplane Top> 15 ↵
Command: ELLIPSE ↵
Specify axis endpoint of ellipse
   or [Arc/Center/Isocircle]: I ↵
Specify center of isocircle: (Pick P3)
Specify radius of isocircle or [Diameter]: 26 ↵
```

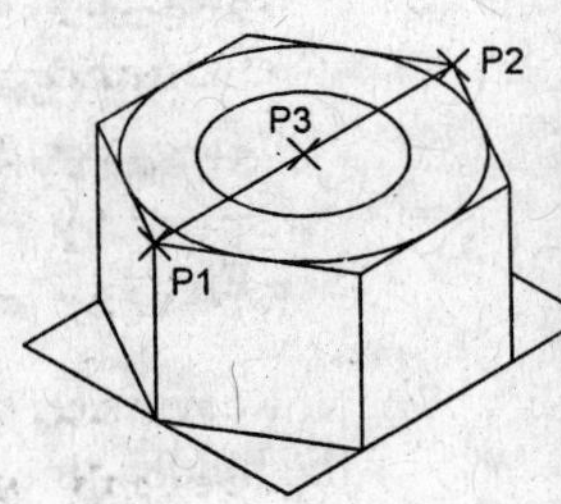

FIG. 6

See Fig. 6. Here, the radius of the circle is 26 mm. This is because, the top circle (ellipse) is an inscribed circle (ellipse) inside the hexagon of side 30 mm.

9. Now, draw the arcs in all the six side faces of the hexagon using the **Arc** command. The command sequence is:

```
Command: LINE ↵
Specify first point: (Pick P1)
Specify next point or [Undo]: <Ortho on> (Move cursor to Bottom) 3 ↵
Specify next point or [Undo]: ↵

Command: LINE ↵
Specify first point: (Pick P2)
Specify next point or [Undo]: (Move cursor to Bottom) 3 ↵
Specify next point or [Undo]: ↵

Command: ARC ↵
Specify start point of arc
   or [Center]: (Pick A1)
Specify second point of arc
   or [Center/End]: (Pick A2)
Specify end point of arc: (Pick A3)

Command: LINE ↵
Specify first point: (Pick P3)
Specify next point or [Undo]: (Move cursor to Bottom) 3 ↵
Specify next point or [Undo]: ↵

Command: ARC ↵
Specify start point of arc or [Center]: (Pick A3)
Specify second point of arc or [Center/End]: (Pick A4)
Specify end point of arc: (Pick A5)
Command: LINE ↵
Specify first point: (Pick P4)
Specify next point or [Undo]: (Move cursor to Bottom) 3 ↵
Specify next point or [Undo]: ↵

Command: ARC ↵
Specify start point of arc or [Center]: (Pick A5)
Specify second point of arc or [Center/End]: (Pick A6)
Specify end point of arc: (Pick A7)

Command: COPY ↵
Select objects: (Select arc A1-A2-A3) 1 found
Select objects: ↵
Current settings:  Copy mode = Multiple
Specify base point or [Displacement/mOde] <Displacement>:(Pick A3)
```

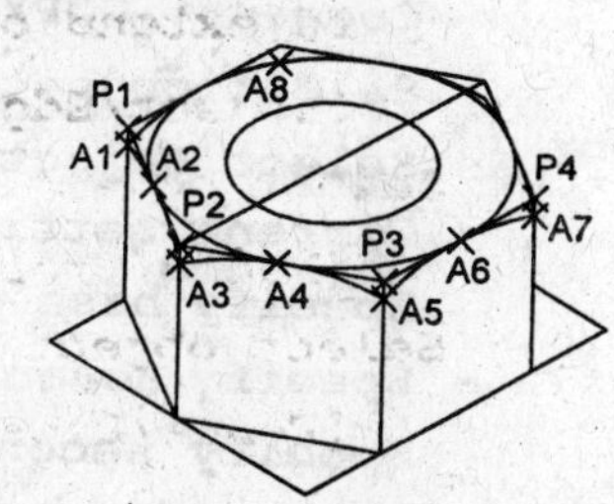

FIG. 7

```
Specify second point or <use first point as displacement>: (Pick A7)
Specify second point or [Exit/Undo] <Exit>: ↵

Command: COPY ↵
Select objects: (Select arc A5-A6-A7) 1 found
Select objects: ↵
Current settings:  Copy mode = Multiple
Specify base point or [Displacement/mOde] <Displacement>:(Pick A5)
Specify second point or <use first point as displacement>: (Pick A1)
Specify second point or [Exit/Undo] <Exit>: ↵

Command: COPY ↵
Select objects: (Select arc A3-A4-A5) 1 found
Select objects: ↵
Current settings:  Copy mode = Multiple
Specify base point or [Displacement/mOde] <Displacement>:(Pick A3)
Specify second point or <use first point as displacement>: (Pick A8)
Specify second point or [Exit/Undo] <Exit>: ↵
```

See Fig. 7.

10. Now, remove the unwanted lines using the **Erase** command. Also, cut the unnecessary lines using the **Trim** command. The command sequence is:

```
Command: ERASE ↵
Select objects: (Select L1) 1 found
Select objects: (Select H1) 1 found, 2 total
Select objects: ↵

Command: TRIM ↵
Current settings:
   Projection=UCS,
   Edge=None
Select cutting edges...
Select objects or
   <select all>:
   (Select A1) 1 found
Select objects: (Select A2)
   1 found, 2 total
Select objects: (Select A3) 1 found, 3 total
Select objects: ↵
Select object to trim or shift-select to extend or
   [Fence/Crossing/Project/Edge/eRase/Undo]: (Pick L2)
```

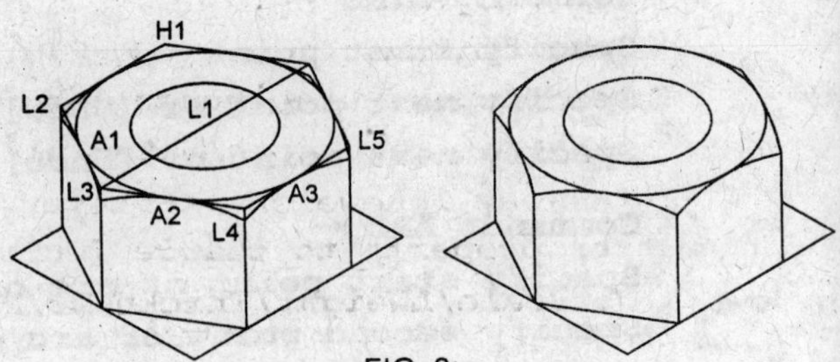

FIG. 8

Select object to trim or shift-select to extend or
[Fence/Crossing/Project/Edge/eRase/Undo]: *(Pick L3)*

Select object to trim or shift-select to extend or
[Fence/Crossing/Project/Edge/eRase/Undo]: *(Pick L4)*

Select object to trim or shift-select to extend or
[Fence/Crossing/Project/Edge/eRase/Undo]: *(Pick L5)*

Select object to trim or shift-select to extend or
[Fence/Crossing/Project/Edge/eRase/Undo]: ↵

See Fig. 8.

11. Darken the necessary lines using the **LWeight** option of the **Chprop** command. Also, draw the axis for the top circle (ellipse) of the hexagonal nut using the **Line** command. The command sequence is:

Command: CHPROP ↵

Select objects: *(Select L1)* 1 found

Select objects: *(Select L2)* 1 found, 2 total

Select objects: *(Select L3)* 1 found, 3 total

Select objects: *(Select L4)* 1 found, 4 total

Select objects: *(Select L5)* 1 found, 5 total

Select objects: *(Select A1)* 1 found, 6 total

Select objects: *(Select A2)* 1 found, 7 total

Select objects: *(Select A3)* 1 found, 8 total

Select objects: *(Select A4)* 1 found, 9 total

Select objects: *(Select A5)* 1 found, 10 total

Select objects: *(Select A6)* 1 found, 11 total

Select objects: *(Select E1)* 1 found, 12 total

Select objects: *(Select E2)* 1 found, 13 total

Select objects: ↵

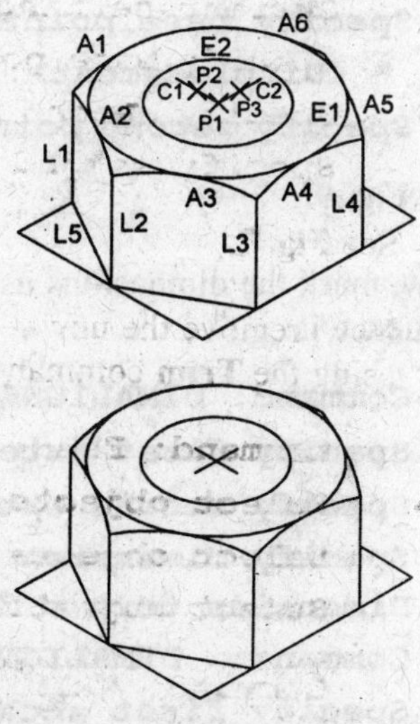

FIG. 9

Enter property to change [Color/LAyer/LType/ltScale/
LWeight/Thickness/Material/Annotative]: LW ↵

Enter new lineweight <ByLayer>: .4 ↵

Enter property to change [Color/LAyer/LType/
ltScale/LWeight/Thickness/Material/Annotative]: ↵

Command: LINE ↵

Specify first point: *(Pick P1, which is the center point of the ellipse)*

Specify next point or [Undo]: <Ortho on>*(Move cursor to Right-up)* 12 ↵

Specify next point or [Undo]: ↵

```
Command:  LINE ↵
Specify first point: (Pick P1)
Specify next point or [Undo]:
   <Isoplane Left> (Move cursor to Left-up) 12 ↵
Specify next point or [Undo]: ↵

Command: MOVE ↵
Select objects: (Select line C1) 1 found
Select objects: ↵
Specify base point or [Displacement]
   <Displacement>: (Pick P2, which is the mid-point of the line C1)
Specify second point or <use first point as displacement>:(Pick P1)

Command:  MOVE ↵
Select objects: (Select line C2) 1 found
Select objects: ↵
Specify base point or [Displacement]
   <Displacement>: (Pick P3, which is the mid-point of the line C2)
Specify second point or <use first point as displacement>:(Pick P1)
```

See Fig. 9.

12. Now, mark the dimensions using the **Dimaligned** and **Dimradius** commands. The command sequence is:

```
Command: DIMALIGNED ↵
Specify first extension line origin or <select object>: (Pick P1)
Specify second extension line origin: (Pick P2)
Specify dimension line location or [Mtext/Text/Angle]: (Pick P3)
Dimension text = 30
Command:  DIMALIGNED ↵
Specify first extension line origin or <select object>: (Pick P4)
Specify second extension line origin: (Pick P5)
Specify dimension line location or [Mtext/Text/Angle]: (Pick P6)
Dimension text = 30

Command:  DIMALIGNED ↵
Specify first extension line origin or <select object>: (Pick P5)
Specify second
   extension line origin: (Pick P7)
Specify dimension line location
   or [Mtext/Text/Angle]: (Pick P8)
Dimension text = 30
```

```
Command: DIMRADIUS ↵
Select arc or circle: (Pick A1)
Dimension text = 45
Specify dimension line location or
    [Mtext/Text/Angle]: (Pick P9)
```

See Fig. 10.

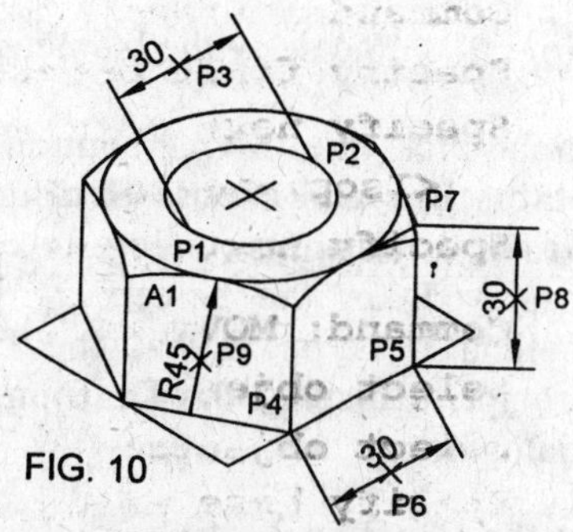

FIG. 10

13. Now, change the dimension lines and extension lines to isometric lines using the **Oblique** option in the **Dimedit** command. The command sequence is: **See Fig. 11.**

```
Command: DIMEDIT ↵
Enter type of dimension editing
    [Home/New/Rotate/Oblique] <Home>: O ↵
Select objects: (Pick D1) 1 found
Select objects: ↵
Enter obliquing angle
    (press ENTER for none): -30 ↵
Command:  DIMEDIT ↵
Enter type of dimension editing
    [Home/New/Rotate/Oblique] <Home>: O ↵
Select objects: (Pick D2) 1 found
Select objects: ↵
Enter obliquing angle
    (press ENTER for none): 30 ↵
Command:  DIMEDIT ↵
Enter type of dimension editing
[Home/New/Rotate/Oblique] <Home>: O
Select objects: (Pick D3) 1 found
Select objects: ↵
Enter  obliquing  angle  (press
ENTER for none): 90 ↵
```

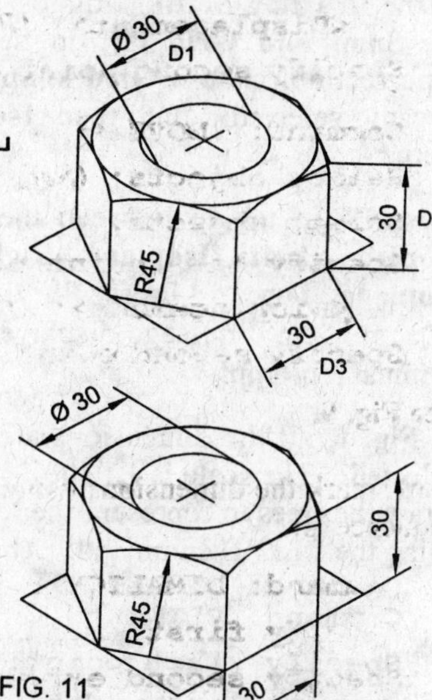

FIG. 11

14. Now, change the Text Style in the isometric dimensions as isometric text. For this, create two new text styles, namely, ISO-R and ISO-L with the oblique angle 30° and – 30° respectively.

Then, select the dimensions and choose the appropriate Text Styles in the Properties toolbar. The creation of new text styles are explained in detail in Section 7. **See Fig. 12.**

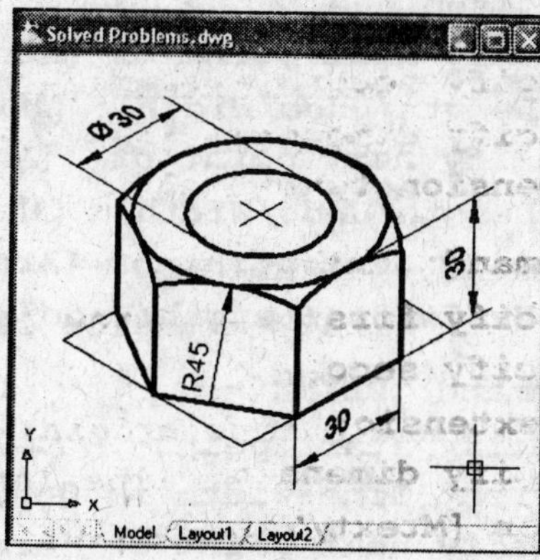

FIG. 12

Ex. No. : 5 - To draw the Isometric Projection of the Stage shown in **Fig. 1.**

1 Right-click the **SNAP** button on the **Status Bar** and choose **Settings.** The **Drafting Settings** dialog box will be displayed on the screen. [Another method is, type **DS** at the command prompt to display the Drafting Settings dialog box.]

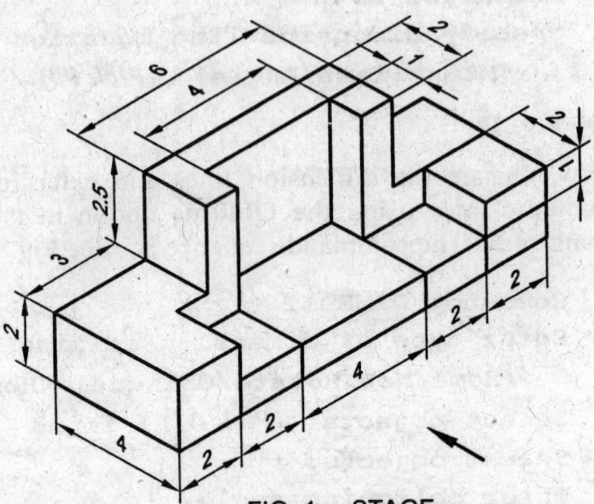

FIG. 1 STAGE

2 In the **Drafting Settings** dialog box, on the **Snap and Grid** tab, in the **Snap type** section, choose **Grid snap** (if not already selected), and then **Isometric snap.**

3 Press **F5** to toggle between the planes **Isoplane Left, Isoplane Right** and **Isoplane Top.** Press **F8** until the <Ortho On> message displayed at the command prompt.

4 In **Fig. 1**, all the dimensions are in m (meter). Therefore, a suitable scale is needed to be selected. The scale is 1 : 100.

5 Draw the lines to represent the left and top face of the stage using the **PLINE** command. The command sequence is:

Command: PLINE ↵
Specify start point: *(Pick P1)*
Current line-width is 0.0000
Specify next point or [Arc/Halfwidth/ Length/Undo/Width]: <Ortho on> <Isoplane Left> *(Move cursor to Left)* **40 ↵**
Specify next point or [Arc/Close/Halfwidth/ Length/Undo/Width]: *(Move cursor to Up)* **20 ↵**
Specify next point or [Arc/Close/Halfwidth/ Length/Undo/Width]: *(Move cursor to Right)* **40 ↵**
Specify next point or [Arc/Close/ Halfwidth/Length/Undo/Width]: C ↵

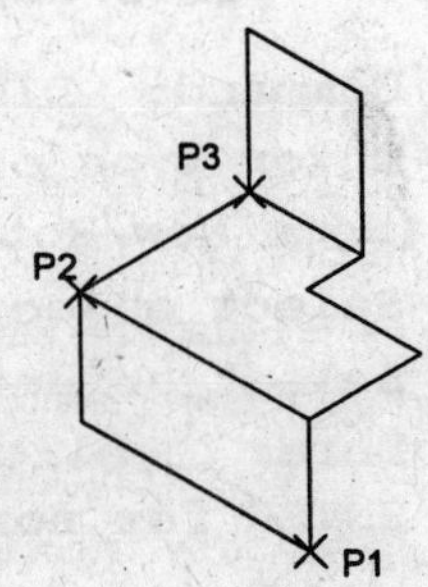

FIG. 2

Command: PLINE ↵
Specify start point: *(Pick P2)*
Current line-width is 0.0000
Specify next point or [Arc/Halfwidth/Length/ Undo/Width]: <Isoplane Top> *(Move cursor to Right-up)* **30 ↵**

```
Specify next point or [Arc/Close/
   Halfwidth/Length/Undo/Width]: (Move cursor to Right-bottom) 20 ↵
Specify next point or [Arc/Close/Halfwidth/
   Length/Undo/Width]: (Move cursor to Left-bottom) 10 ↵
Specify next point or [Arc/Close/Halfwidth/
   Length/Undo/Width]: (Move cursor to Right-bottom) 20 ↵
Specify next point or [Arc/Close/Halfwidth/
   Length/Undo/Width]: (Move cursor to Left=bottom) 20 ↵
Specify next point or [Arc/Close/Halfwidth/Length/Undo/Width]: ↵

Command:   PLINE ↵
Specify start point: (Pick P3)
Current line-width is 0.0000
Specify next point or [Arc/Halfwidth/Length/
   Undo/Width]:   <Isoplane Right> (Move cursor to Up) 25 ↵
Specify next point or [Arc/Close/Halfwidth/Length/
   Undo/Width]: <Isoplane Left> (Move cursor to Right-bottom) 20 ↵
Specify next point or [Arc/Close/Halfwidth/
   Length/Undo/Width]: (Move cursor to Bottom) 25 ↵
Specify next point or [Arc/Close/Halfwidth/Length/Undo/Width]: ↵
```

See Fig. 2.

6 Draw the lines to represent the top face of the Stage using the **PLINE** command. The command sequence is:

```
Command:   PLINE ↵
Specify start point: (Pick P1)
Current line-width is 0.0000
Specify next point or [Arc/Halfwidth/
   Length/Undo/Width]: (Move cursor to Right-Up) 60 ↵
Specify next point or [Arc/Close/Halfwidth/
   Length/Undo/Width]: (Move cursor to Right-bottom) 20 ↵
Specify next point or [Arc/Close/Halfwidth/
   Length/Undo/Width]: (Move cursor to Left-Bottom) 10 ↵
Specify next point or [Arc/Close/Halfwidth/
   Length/Undo/Width]: (Move cursor to Left-up) 10 ↵
Specify next point or [Arc/Close/Halfwidth/
   Length/Undo/Width]: (Move cursor to Left-bottom) 40 ↵
Specify next point or [Arc/Close/Halfwidth/
   Length/Undo/Width]: (Move cursor to Right-bottom) 10 ↵
Specify next point or [Arc/Close/Halfwidth/Length/Undo/
```

Width]: *(Move cursor to Left-bottom)* 10 ↵
Specify next point or [Arc/Close/
Halfwidth/Length/Undo/Width]: ↵

Command: PLINE ↵
Specify start point: *(Pick P2)*
Current line-width is 0.0000
Specify next point or [Arc/Halfwidth/
Length/Undo/Width]: <Isoplane Right>
(Move cursor to Bottom) 35 ↵
Specify next point or [Arc/Close/
Halfwidth/Length/Undo/Width]:
(Move cursor to Left-bottom) 10 ↵
Specify next point or [Arc/Close/
Halfwidth/Length/Undo/Width]: ↵

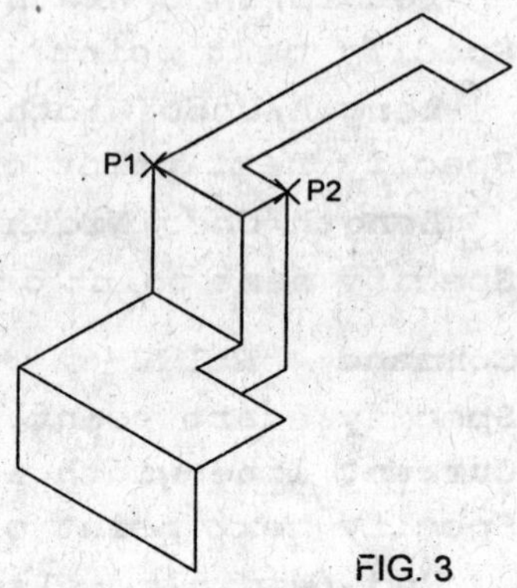

FIG. 3

See Fig. 3.

7 Draw the lines to represent the right side face of the Stage using the **PLINE** command. The command sequence is:

Command: PLINE ↵
Specify start point: *(Pick P1)*
Current line-width is 0.0000
Specify next point or [Arc/Halfwidth/Length/Undo/Width]:
<Ortho on> <Isoplane Right> *(Move cursor to Right)* 120 ↵
Specify next point or [Arc/Close/Halfwidth/
Length/Undo/Width]: *(Move cursor to Up)* 20 ↵
Specify next point or [Arc/Close/Halfwidth/
Length/Undo/Width]: *(Move cursor to Left-bottom)* 20 ↵
Specify next point or [Arc/Close/Halfwidth/
Length/Undo/Width]: *(Move cursor to Bottom)* 10 ↵
Specify next point or [Arc/Close/Halfwidth/
Length/Undo/Width]: *(Move cursor to Left-bottom)* 80 ↵
Specify next point or [Arc/Close/Halfwidth/
Length/Undo/Width]: *(Move cursor to Up)* 10 ↵
Specify next point or [Arc/Close/Halfwidth/Length/Undo/Width]: ↵

Command: PLINE ↵
Specify start point: *(Pick P2)*
Current line-width is 0.0000
Specify next point or [Arc/Halfwidth/

Length/Undo/Width]: *(Move cursor to Bottom)* 25 ↵
Specify next point or [Arc/Close/Halfwidth/
Length/Undo/Width]: *(Move cursor to Right-bottom)* 10 ↵
Specify next point or [Arc/Close/Halfwidth/
Length/Undo/Width]: *(Move cursor to Bottom)* 10 ↵
Specify next point or [Arc/Close/Halfwidth/
Length/Undo/Width]: *(Move cursor to Left-bottom)* 20 ↵
Specify next point or [Arc/Close/Halfwidth/
Length/Undo/Width]: *(Move cursor to Up)* 35 ↵
Specify next point or [Arc/Close/Halfwidth/Length/Undo/Width]: ↵

Command: PLINE ↵
Specify start point: *(Pick P3)*
Current line-width is 0.0000
Specify next point or
[Arc/Halfwidth/Length/
Undo/Width]: <Isoplane Left>
(Move cursor to Left-up) 10 ↵
Specify next point or
[Arc/Close/Halfwidth/
Length/Undo/Width]:
(Move cursor to Up) 35 ↵
Specify next point or [Arc/Close/Halfwidth/Length/Undo/Width]: ↵

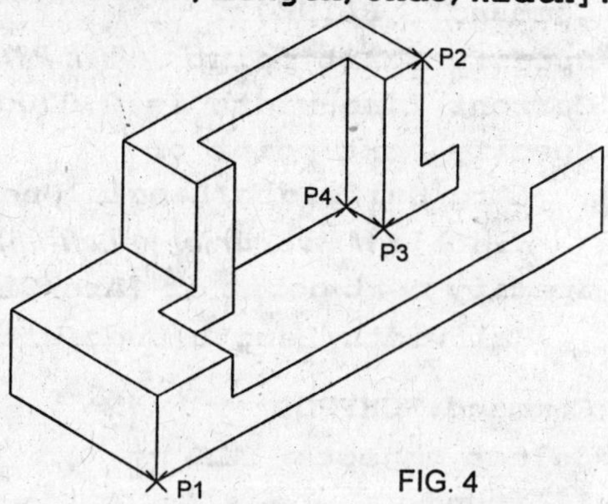

FIG. 4

Command: PLINE ↵
Specify start point: *(Pick P4)*
Current line-width is 0.0000
Specify next point or [Arc/Halfwidth/Length/
Undo/Width]: <Isoplane Top> *(Move cursor to Left-bottom)* 30 ↵
Specify next point or [Arc/Close/Halfwidth/Length/Undo/Width]: ↵

See Fig. 4.

8 Draw the remaining lines of the Stage using the PLINE command. Darken the lines using the LWeight option of the Chprop command. The command sequence is:

Command: PLINE ↵
Specify start point: *(Pick P1)*
Current line-width is 0.0000
Specify next point or [Arc/Halfwidth/Length/
Undo/Width]: *(Move cursor to Left-up)* 40 ↵
Specify next point or [Arc/Close/Halfwidth/

Length/Undo/Width]: *(Move cursor to Left-bottom)* 10 ↵
Specify next point or [Arc/Close/Halfwidth/Length/Undo/Width]: ↵

Command: PLINE ↵
Specify start point: *(Pick P2)*
Current line-width is 0.0000
Specify next point or [Arc/Halfwidth/
Length/Undo/Width]: *(Move cursor to Left-up)* 20 ↵
Specify next point or [Arc/Close/Halfwidth/Length/Undo/Width]: ↵

Command: PLINE ↵
Specify start point: *(Pick P3)*
Current line-width is 0.0000
Specify next point or
[Arc/Halfwidth/Length/Undo/
Width]: *(Move cursor to Left-up)* 20 ↵
Specify next point or [Arc/Close/
Halfwidth/Length/Undo/Width]: ↵

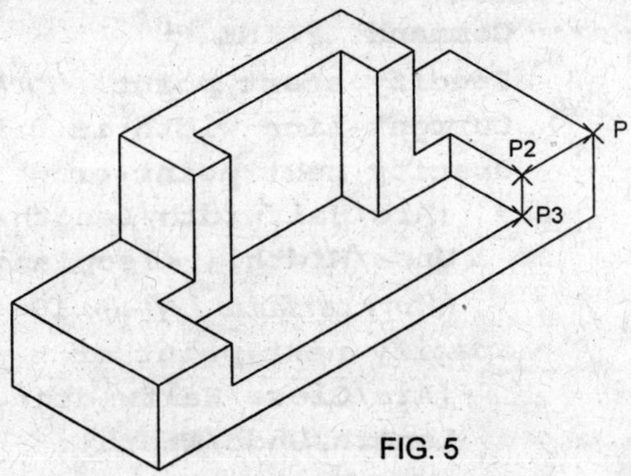

FIG. 5

Command: CHPROP ↵
Select objects: ALL ↵
12 found
Select objects: ↵
Enter property to change [Color/LAyer/LType/
ltScale/LWeight/Thickness/Material/Annotative]: LW ↵
Enter new lineweight <ByLayer>: .4 ↵
Enter property to change [Color/LAyer/LType/
ltScale/LWeight/Thickness/Material/Annotative]: ↵

See Fig. 5.

9 Now, mark the dimension using the **Dimaligned** command. The command sequence is:

Command: DIMALIGNED ↵
Specify first extension line origin or <select object>: *(Pick P1)*
Specify second extension line origin: *(Pick P2)*
Specify dimension line location or [Mtext/Text/Angle]: *(Pick P3)*
Dimension text = 40

Command: DIMALIGNED ↵
Specify first extension line origin or <select object>: *(Pick P2)*
Specify second extension line origin: *(Pick P4)*
Specify dimension line location or [Mtext/Text/Angle]: *(Pick P5)*

Dimension text = 20

Command: DIMALIGNED ↵
Specify first extension line origin or <select object>: *(Pick P4)*
Specify second extension line origin: *(Pick P6)*
Specify dimension line location or [Mtext/Text/Angle]: *(Pick P7)*
Dimension text = 30

Command: DIMALIGNED ↵
Specify first extension line origin or <select object>: *(Pick P6)*
Specify second extension line origin: *(Pick P8)*
Specify dimension line location or [Mtext/Text/Angle]: *(Pick P9)*
Dimension text = 25

Command: DIMALIGNED ↵
Specify first extension line origin or <select object>: *(Pick P8)*
Specify second extension line origin: *(Pick P10)*
Specify dimension line location or [Mtext/Text/Angle]: *(Pick P11)*
Dimension text = 60

Command: DIMALIGNED ↵
Specify first extension line origin or <select object>: *(Pick P10)*
Specify second extension line origin: *(Pick P12)*
Specify dimension line location or [Mtext/Text/Angle]: *(Pick P13)*
Dimension text = 20

Command: DIMALIGNED ↵
Specify first extension line origin or <select object>: *(Pick P14)*
Specify second extension line origin: *(Pick P15)*
Specify dimension line location or [Mtext/Text/Angle]: *(Pick P16)*
Dimension text = 10

Command: DIMALIGNED ↵
Specify first extension line origin or <select object>: *(Pick P15)*
Specify second extension line origin: *(Pick P17)*
Specify dimension line location or [Mtext/Text/Angle]: *(Pick P18)*
Dimension text = 40

Command: DIMALIGNED ↵
Specify first extension line origin or <select object>: *(Pick P19)*
Specify second extension line origin: *(Pick P20)*
Specify dimension line location or [Mtext/Text/Angle]: *(Pick P21)*
Dimension text = 20

Command: DIMALIGNED ↵
Specify first extension line origin or <select object>: *(Pick P20)*
Specify second extension line origin: *(Pick P22)*
Specify dimension line location or [Mtext/Text/Angle]: *(Pick P23)*
Dimension text = 10

Command: LINE ↵
Specify first point: *(Pick P22)*
Specify next point or [Undo]: <Ortho on>
<Isoplane Right> *(Move cursor to Down)* 10 ↵
Specify next point or [Undo]: ↵

Command: LINE ↵
Specify first point: *(Pick P24)*
Specify next point or [Undo]:
<Isoplane Left> *(Move cursor to Right-down)* 20 ↵
Specify next point or [Undo]: *(Move cursor to Down)* 10 ↵
Specify next point or [Close/Undo]: ↵

Command: LINE ↵
Specify first point: *(Pick P25)*
Specify next point or [Undo]: *(Move cursor to Right-down)* 20 ↵
Specify next point or [Undo]: *(Move cursor to Down)* 10 ↵
Specify next point or [Close/Undo]: ↵
Command: LINE ↵
Specify first point: *(Pick P26)*
Specify next point or [Undo]: *(Move cursor to Down)* 10 ↵
Specify next point or [Undo]: ↵

Command: DIMALIGNED ↵
Specify first extension line origin or
<select object>: <Isoplane Right> *(Pick P1)*
Specify second extension line origin: *(Pick P27)*
Specify dimension line location or [Mtext/Text/Angle]: *(Pick P28)*
Dimension text = 20

Command: DIMALIGNED ↵
Specify first extension line origin or
<select object>: *(Pick P27)*
Specify second extension line origin: *(Pick P29)*
Specify dimension line location or [Mtext/Text/Angle]: *(Pick P30)*
Dimension text = 20

```
Command: DIMALIGNED ↵
Specify first extension line origin or
   <select object>: (Pick P29)
Specify second extension line origin: (Pick P31)
Specify dimension line location or [Mtext/Text/Angle]: (Pick P32)
Dimension text = 40
```

```
Command:  DIMALIGNED ↵
Specify first extension
   line origin or
   <select object>:
   (Pick P31)
Specify second
   extension line
   origin: (Pick P33)
Specify dimension
   line location or
   [Mtext/Text/Angle]:
   (Pick P34)
Dimension text = 20
```

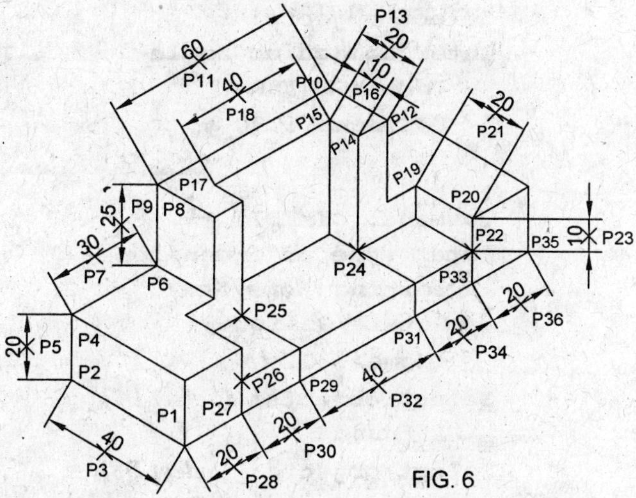

FIG. 6

```
Command: DIMALIGNED ↵
Specify first
   extension line origin or <select object>: (Pick P33)
Specify second extension line origin: (Pick P35)
Specify dimension line location or [Mtext/Text/Angle]: (Pick P36)
Dimension text = 20
```

See Fig. 6.

Now, change the dimension lines and extension lines to isometric lines using the **Oblique** option in the **Dimedit** command. The command sequence is:

```
Command: DIMEDIT ↵
Enter type of dimension editing
   [Home/New/Rotate/Oblique] <Home>: O ↵
Select objects:
   (Select D1) 1 found
Select objects: (Select D2)
   1 found, 2 total
Select objects: (Select D3)
   1 found, 3 total
```

```
Select objects: (Select D4)
   1 found, 4 total
Select objects: (Select D5)
   1 found, 5 total
Select objects: (Select D6)
   1 found, 6 total
Select objects: ↵
Enter obliquing angle
   (press ENTER
   for none): 90 ↵

Command: DIMEDIT ↵
Enter type of dimension
   editing [Home/New/
   Rotate/Oblique]
   <Home>: O ↵
Select objects: (Select D7)
   1 found
Select objects: (Select D8)
   1 found, 2 total
Select objects: (Select D9)
   1 found, 3 total
Select objects: (Select D10)
   1 found, 4 total
Select objects: (Select D11)
        1 found, 5 total
Select objects: ↵
Enter obliquing angle (press ENTER for none): -30 ↵

Command:  DIMEDIT ↵
Enter type of dimension editing
   [Home/New/Rotate/Oblique] <Home>: O ↵
Select objects: (Select D12) 1 found
Select objects: (Select D13) 1 found, 2 total
Select objects: (Select D14) 1 found, 3 total
Select objects: (Select D15) 1 found, 4 total
Select objects: ↵
Enter obliquing angle (press ENTER for none): 30 ↵
```

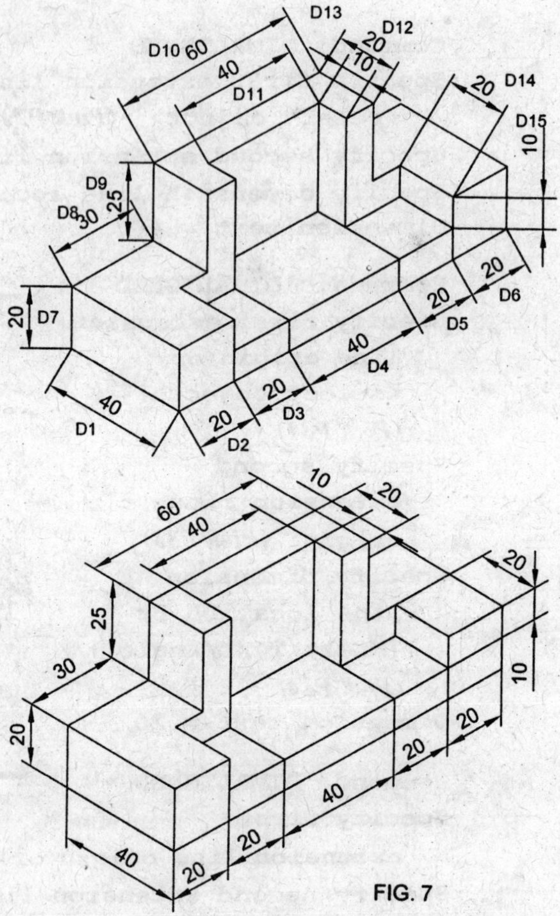

FIG. 7

See Fig. 7.

11 In this Stage diagram, a scale of 1 : 100 is used. Therefore, value of the dimension is to be changed in all the dimensions. For this, use **DDEDIT** command to change dimension value.

`Command: DDEDIT ↵`

`Select an annotation object or [Undo]:` *(Select D1 and type 4)*

`Select an annotation object or [Undo]:` *(Select D2 and type 2)*

`Select an annotation object or [Undo]:` *(Select D3 and type 2)*

`Select an annotation object or [Undo]:` *(Select D4 and type 4)*

`Select an annotation object or [Undo]:` *(Select D5 and type 2)*

`Select an annotation object or [Undo]:` *(Select D6 and type 2)*

`Select an annotation object or [Undo]:` *(Select D7 and type 2)*

`Select an annotation object or [Undo]:` *(Select D8 and type 3)*

`Select an annotation object or [Undo]:` *(Select D9 and type 2.5)*

`Select an annotation object or [Undo]:` *(Select D10 and type 6)*

`Select an annotation object or [Undo]:` *(Select D11 and type 4)*

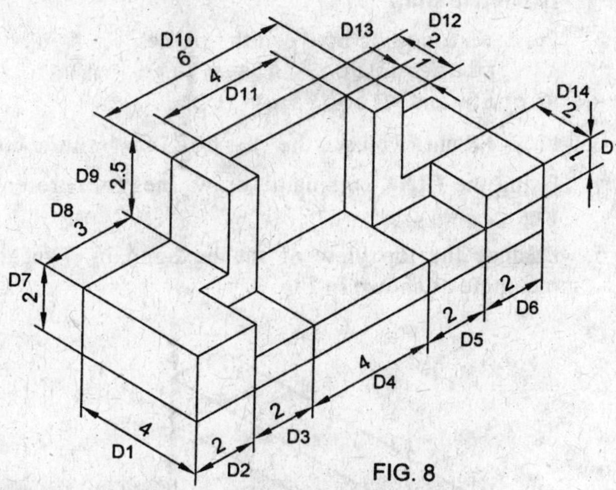

FIG. 8

`Select an annotation object or [Undo]:` *(Select D12 and type 2)*

`Select an annotation object or [Undo]:` *(Select D13 and type 1)*

`Select an annotation object or [Undo]:` *(Select D14 and type 2)*

`Select an annotation object or [Undo]:` *(Select D15 and type 1)*

`Select an annotation object or [Undo]: ↵`

See Fig. 8.

12 Now, change the Text Style in the isometric dimensions as isometric text. For this, create two new text styles, namely, ISO-R and ISO-L with the oblique angle 30° and – 30° respectively. Then, select the dimensions and choose the appropriate Text Styles in the Properties toolbar. The creation of new text styles are explained in detail in Section 7.

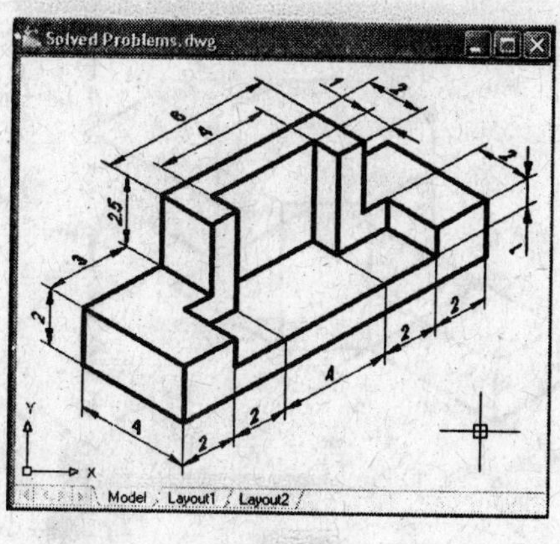

FIG.9

<u>Ex. No. : 6</u> *Draw the isometric projection for the orthographic views shown in* ***Fig. 1*** *using the CAD Software.*

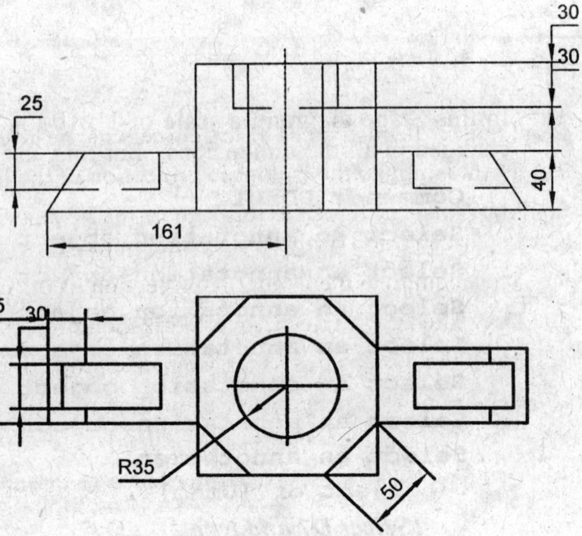

FIG. 1

1. Start the **AutoCAD Software**. Open and setup a new drawing sheet.
2. Right-click the **SNAP** button on the status bar and choose **Settings**.

   On the **Snap and Grid** tab, in the **Snap type** section, choose **Grid snap** (if not already selected), and then **Isometric snap.**
3. Press **F5** to toggle between the planes `<Isoplane Left>`, `<Isoplane Right>` and `<Isoplane Top>`.

   Press **F8** until you see the `<Ortho On>` on the command prompt.
4. Using the **LINE** command, draw lines to represent the rectangular base of the object as shown in **Fig. 2.**
5. Enclose the top view of the hexagon in a rectangle. Draw the isometric projection of this rectangle as shown in **Fig. 3.**

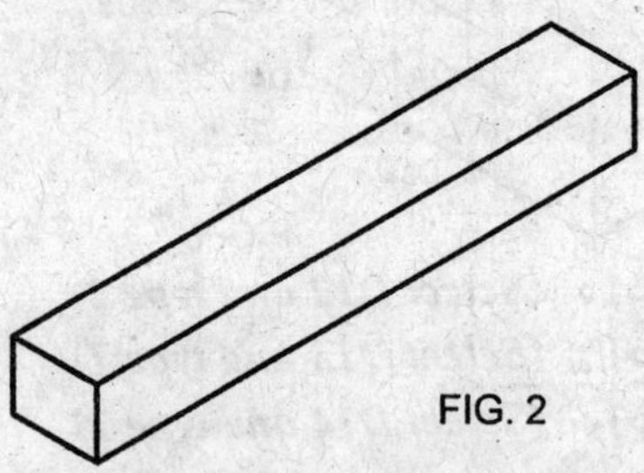

FIG. 2

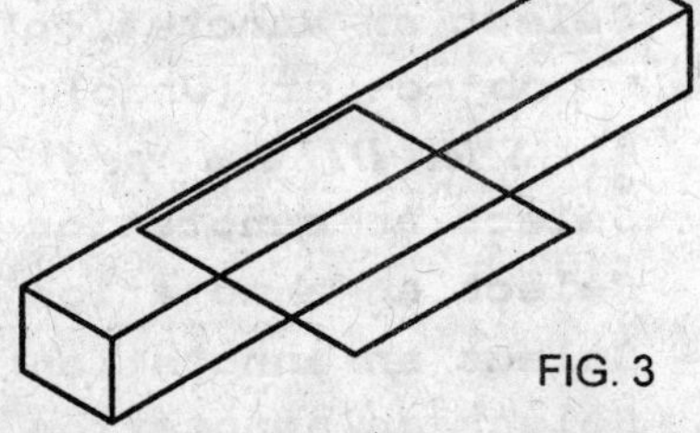

FIG. 3

FIG. 4

FIG. 5

6. Transfer the distances of the corners of the hexagon in the top view to the isometric projection.
7. Then complete the isometric projection of the hexagon as shown in **Fig. 4.**
8. Mark the center of the top face of the hexagon. Using this as center, draw an isocircle using the Isocirlce option of the ELLIPSE command.
9. Then complete the isometric projection of the circular hole as shown in **Fig. 5.**
10. Draw the non-isometric lines corresponding to the slots of the base.
11. Mark the dimensions in the isometric projection of the object and save the file.

See Fig.6 for the isometric projection of the given object.

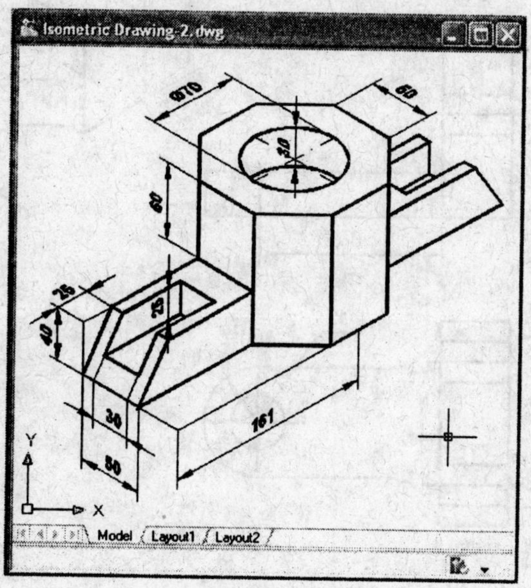

FIG. 6

Ex. No. : 7 *- The Isometric Projection for the orthographic views shown in* ***Fig. 1*** *using the CAD software.*

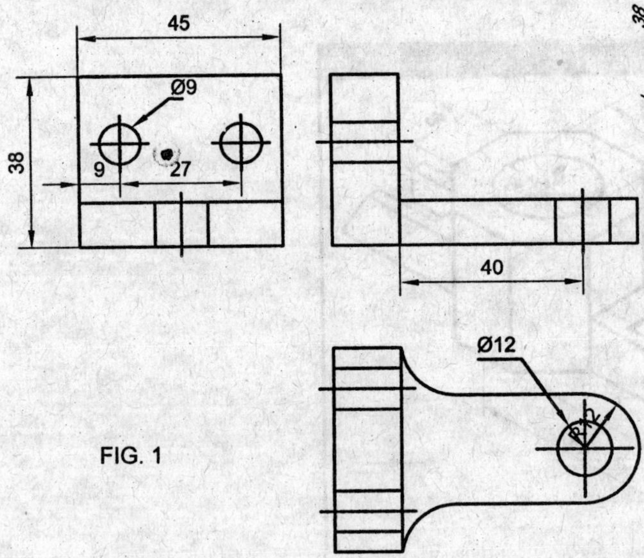

FIG. 1

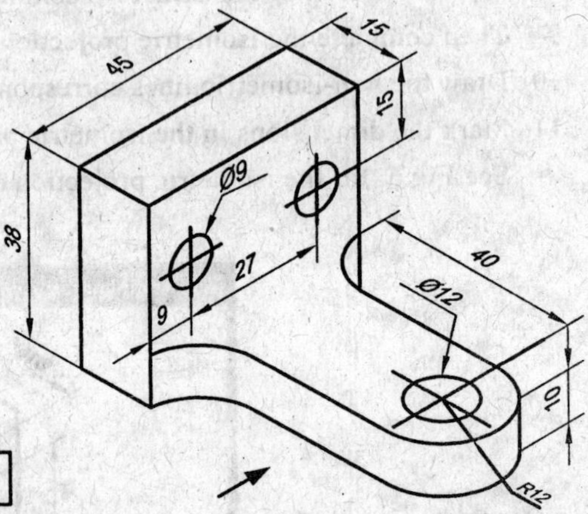

FIG. 2

3-D MODELING

and

CREATION of MULTI-VIEW DRAWINGS

Ch.23 - 3-D MODELING and CREATION of MULTI-VIEW DRAWINGS

THEORY

A Model is a mathematical representation of a geometric form, which is stored in the computer memory. 2D Models are recognized by the system as flat frameworks bounded by a number of points, which are defined by X and Y Cartesian coordinates. A 3D Model may be held in computer memory by specifying points with a third Z coordinate.

How to approach 3D? It is first assumed that you have a good working knowledge of 2D drawing functions of AutoCAD. Using AutoCAD 3D requires expertise in many of the commands learned so far. Coordinate System (UCS), used to create and view the 3D drawings.

STARTING 3D MODELING IN AutoCAD

In AutoCAD, 3D modeling can be started in a separate workspace. In this workspace, all the tools required to create the 3D design are displayed in this workspace.

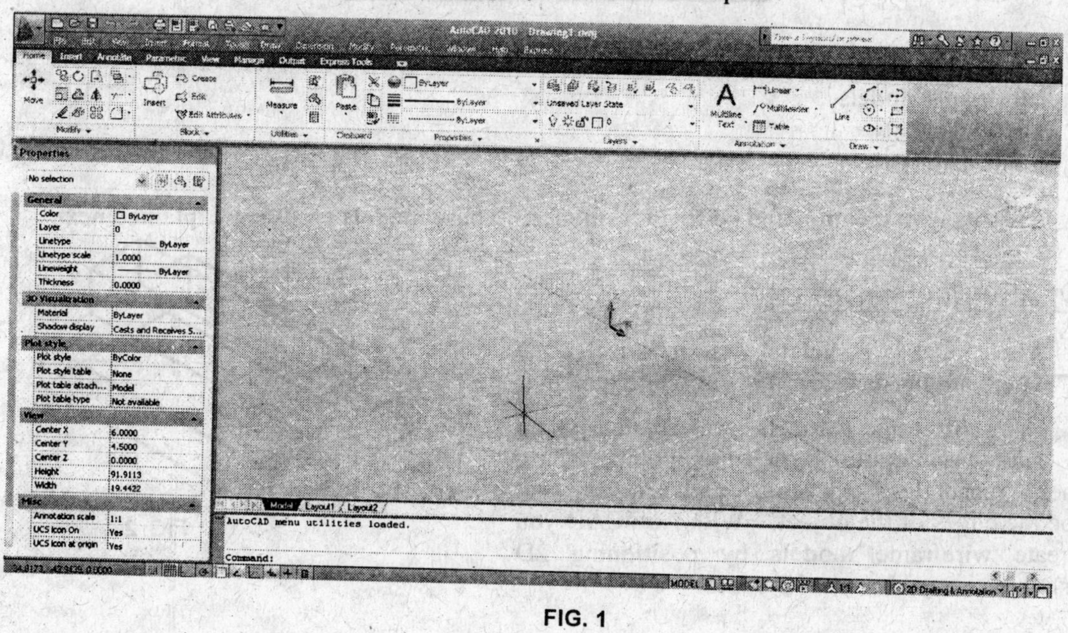

FIG. 1

Start a new file in the 3D workspace by invoking the **Select template** dialog box and selecting the Acad3d.dwt template. This template file supports the 3D environment. Now, select the 3D modeling option from the Workspace drop-down list available at the top-left corner of the title bar. Fig. 1 shows the 3D Modeling workspace of AutoCAD.

USES OF 3D MODELING

In computer, a 3D object can be created using the CADD technology. In this technology, user can create models with the third coordinate called the Z coordinate, in addition to the X and Y coordinates. One of the most exciting features of AutoCAD is 3D. AutoCAD contains the capabilities to produce 3D models. These capabilities are used interactively with 2D drawings. Modeling in 3D has several advantages. They are:

- **Drawing Views:** User can view the model from any vantage point. Viewing an object in 3 dimensions helps to get a sense of its true shape and form.
- **Reliable:** User can generate reliable standard and auxiliary 2D views automatically
- **Sectioned Drawings:** User can create sections and 2D drawings
- **Realistic Effect:** User can remove hidden lines and do realistic shading
- **Interferences:** User can check interferences and perform engineering analysis
- **Realistic Effect:** User can add lighting and create realistic rendering
- **Navigate:** User can navigate through the model
- **Animation:** Use the model to create an animation

2. TYPES OF 3D MODELS

AutoCAD supports three types of 3D models. They are:

1. Wireframe Models
2. Surface Models
3. Solid Models

Each type has its own creation and editing techniques. These models types are explained next.

2.1 WIREFRAME MODELS

A wireframe model is a skeletal description of a 3D object. There are no surfaces in a wireframe model.

The Wireframe Models are created using simple AutoCAD entities such as points, lines, polylines, rectangles, polygons and curves that describe the edges of the object. With AutoCAD you can create wireframe models by positioning 2D (planar) objects anywhere in 3D space.

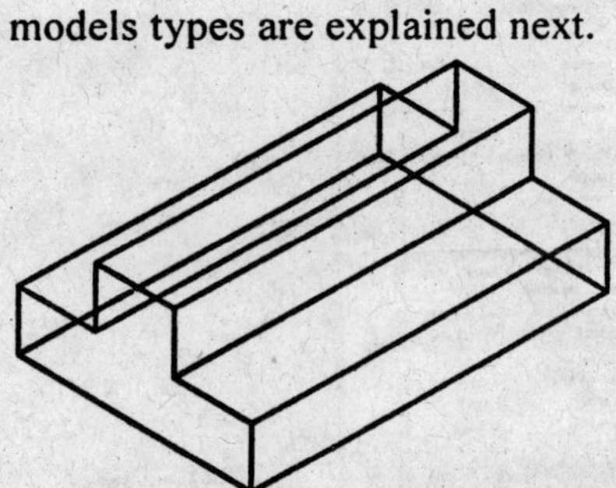

FIG. 2

Because each object that makes up a wireframe model must be independently drawn and positioned, this type of modeling can be the most time-consuming. Wireframe models are generally used in the bodybuilding of the vehicles. Fig. 2 shows a wireframe model.

2.2 SURFACE MODELS

Surface models are made up of one or more surfaces. It is more sophisticated than wireframe modeling. It defines not only the edges of a 3D object, but also its surfaces.

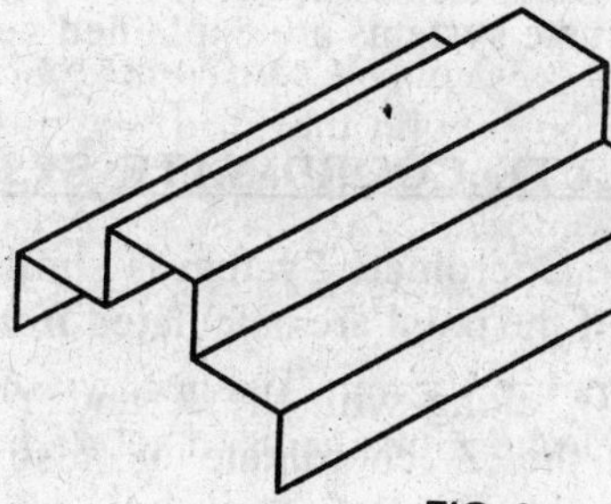

FIG. 3

The 3D object is made up of opaque surfaces called 3D faces. The inner portion of the object is hollow. The details available behind the surfaces are hidden. Fig. 3 shows a surface model.

The AutoCAD surface modeler defines faceted surfaces using a polygonal mesh. Because the faces of the mesh are planar, the mesh can only approximate curved surfaces.

In engineering analysis, surface modeling is not sufficient to get more information like volume, mass, moment of inertia, etc.

.3 SOLID MODELS

Solid Model is a solid filled model having properties such as mass, volume, center of gravity and moments of inertia. It is the easiest type of 3D modeling to use. To understand a solid mode, consider a model made up of metal or wood.

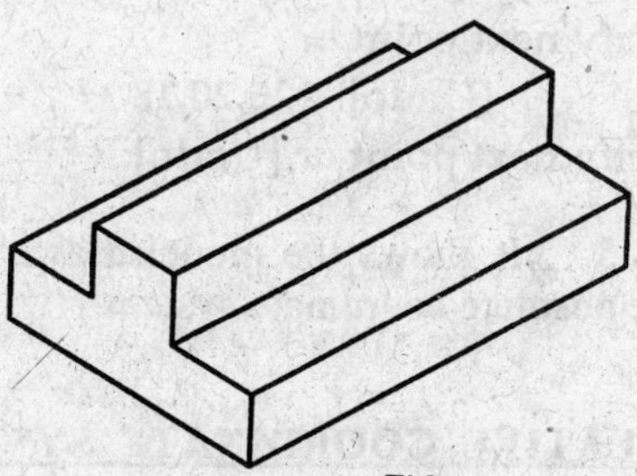

FIG. 4

With the AutoCAD solid modeler, user can make 3D objects by creating primitive solids such as box, cone, dish, dome, mesh, pyramid, sphere, torus (donuts), wedge and cylinder. Fig. 4 shows a solid model.

User can then combine these shapes to create more complex solids by joining or subtracting them or finding their intersecting (overlapping) volume. User can also create solids by sweeping a 2D object along a path or revolving it about an axis. With Mechanical Desktop, user can also define solids parametrically and maintain associativity between 3D models and the 2D views that user generate from them.

Draw a custom polysolid extrusion or use various sweeping operations to create solids whose shapes conform to a path you specify. Then modify or recombine objects to create new solid shapes. Complex solid shapes are easier to construct and edit than legacy wireframe models. However, if needed, user can explode a solid to break it down to regions, bodies, surfaces, and wireframe objects.

3. 3D COORDINATE SYSTEMS

In AutoCAD, there are two main types of coordinate system. They are:

1. Absolute Coordinate System
2. Relative Coordinate System

These coordinate systems are explained next.

3.1 ABSOLUTE COORDINATE SYSTEM

The Absolute Coordinate System is similar to the 2D Absolute Coordinate System. In 2D, the coordinates of the point are calculated from the origin (0,0).

In 3D, along with the X and Y coordinates, the Z coordinate is also included.

For example, draw a line in 3D space starting from the origin to a point, say, 25,20,18. The command sequences to draw this lines is given below:

Command: **LINE** ↵
Specify first point: **0,0,0** ↵
Specify next point or
[Undo]: **#25,20,18** ↵
Specify next point or [Undo]: ↵

See Fig. 5. It shows the model drawn using the absolute coordinate system.

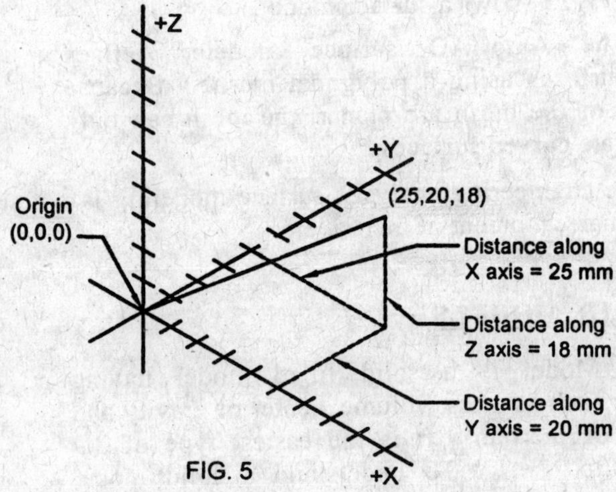

FIG. 5

3.2 RELATIVE COORDINATE SYSTEM

In 3D, there are three types of relative coordinate systems. They are explained next.

1. **Relative Rectangular Coordinate System**
   The Relative Rectangular Coordinate System is similar to the relative rectangular coordinate system of 2D. The only difference is that in 3D user also have to enter the Z coordinate along with the X and Y coordinates. The syntax for the relative rectangular system in 3D is **@X coordinate, Y coordinate, Z coordinate.**

2. **Relative Cylindrical Coordinate System**
   In the Relative Cylindrical Coordinate System, the point can be located by specifying its distance from the reference point, the angle in the XY plane and its distance from the XY plane.

The syntax for the relative cylindrical coordinate system in 3D is **@Distance from the reference point in the XY plane < Angle in the XY plane from the X axis, Distance from the XY plane along the Z axis**. Fig. 6 shows the components of the relative cylindrical coordinate system.

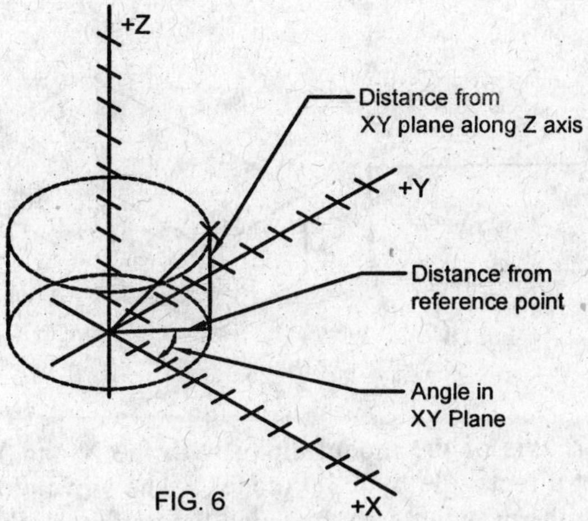

FIG. 6

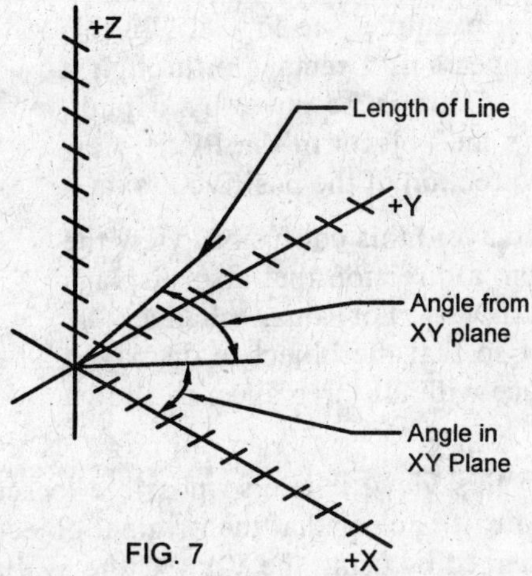

FIG. 7

3. **Relative Spherical Coordinate System**
   In the Relative Spherical Coordinate System, the point can be located by specifying its distance from the reference point, the angle in the XY plane and the angle from the XY plane. The syntax of the relative spherical coordinate system is **@ Length of the line from the reference point < Angle in the XY plane from the X axis < Angle from the XY plane.** Fig. 7 shows the components of the relative spherical coordinate system.

3.3 DIRECT DISTANCE ENTRY METHOD

In AutoCAD, user can create models in 3D space. This is similar to thc direct distance entry followed in 2D. Using the Direct Distance Entry method, it is easy to draw a model using the **Line** tool in 3D space.

Turn on the Dynamic Input option button in the Status Bar before drawing a model using this method. Then, invoke the **Line** tool. AutoCAD prompts to specify the first point. Enter the coordinate value and press Enter. Now, AutoCAD prompts to specify the next point. Here, move the cursor along the direction in which the line need to be drawn. Then enter the absolute length of the line and its angle in the corresponding text boxes with respect to the previous point. Use the Tab key to toggle between the text boxes.

To draw a line along the Z axis, move the cursor along the Z axis. Note that the tooltip displays **Ortho: (current length) < +Z,** if the Ortho mode is on. Type the absolute distance and the angle and press Enter. If the Ortho mode is off, position the cursor at the desired angle, type the length at the Command prompt and then press Enter.

4. CHANGING THE VIEWPOINT TO VIEW 3D MODELS

Before attempting to create 3D model, one must be familiar with the view setting commands, which enable the objects drawn to appear in 3D space. View setting must be drawn before starting 3D drawing practice.

For example, see Fig. 8. In this view, it appears as a rectangle through it is a box. This is because, by default, user views the objects in the Plane view from the direction of the positive Z axis.

To avoid this confusion, view the object from a direction that also displays the Z axis. For this, change the viewpoint so that the object is displayed in the space with all three axes, as shown in Fig. 9.

FIG. 8

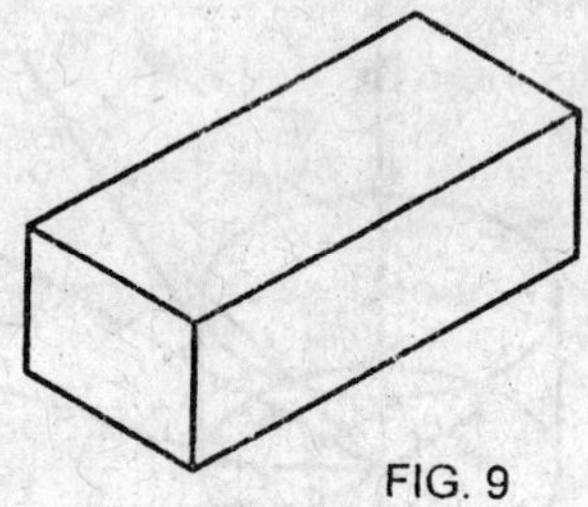

FIG. 9

In this view, it is also possible to see the Z axis of the model along with the X and Y axes. Now, it is clear that the original object is not a rectangle by a 3D model. The viewpoint can be changed by using the **View Cube** available in the drawing area, by using the options in the **View** panel, **DDVPOINT** command or the **VPOINT** command. These are explained next.

4.1 CHANGING THE VIEWPOINT USING THE VIEW CUBE

Using the **ViewCube**, the view of the models can be changed easily and quickly. The **ViewCube** is displayed when the **3D Modeling** workspace is enabled. It allows user to switch between the standard and isometric views, roll the current view or return to the Home view of a model.

The ViewCube consists of Cube, Home, Compass and WCS menu. Move the cursor over the ViewCube to activate it and the area at the point tip gets highlighted. The highlighted area may be a face, a corner or an edge of the View Cube. These highlighted areas are called **Hotspots**.

There are 8 corners, 6 faces and 12 edges on a cube as shown in Fig. 10. So, using the ViewCube, you can get 26 views.

User can select the required hotspot to restore a view. Also, user can go back to the Home view by clicking on the **Home** icon of the ViewCube.

It is also possible to set any existing view as the Home view. This can be done by choosing the **Set Current View as Home** option from the shortcut menu that is displayed on right-clicking on the ViewCube.

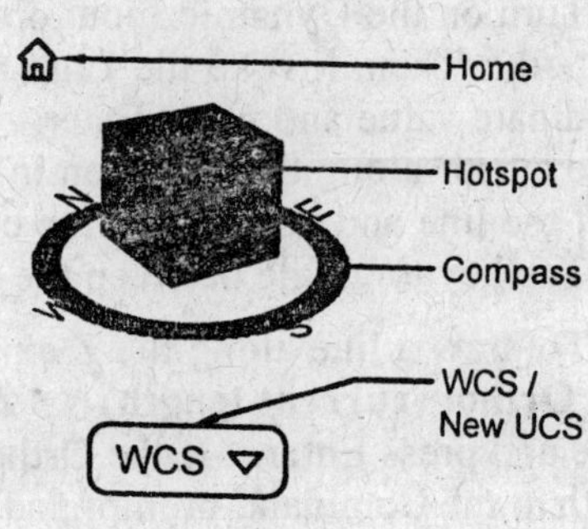

FIG. 10

In AutoCAD, by default a model is displayed in the perspective view. User can change the display model by right-clicking on the ViewCube and then choosing the Parallel from the shortcut menu.

User can choose between the UCS and WCS from the WCS menu and even create a new UCS from the menu. Right-click on the ViewCube to display a shortcut menu.

Choose the ViewCube settings option from the shortcut menu. The ViewCube settings dialog box is displayed on the screen as shown in Fig. 11.

Using this dialog box, user can adjust the display of the compass ring and UCS menu, size, appearance and location of the ViewCube.

The compass of the ViewCube indicates the geographic location of a model.

The alphabets N, E, S, and W on the compass indicate the North, East, South and West directions of a 3D model. Pick and drag the compass ring to rotate the current view in the same plane.

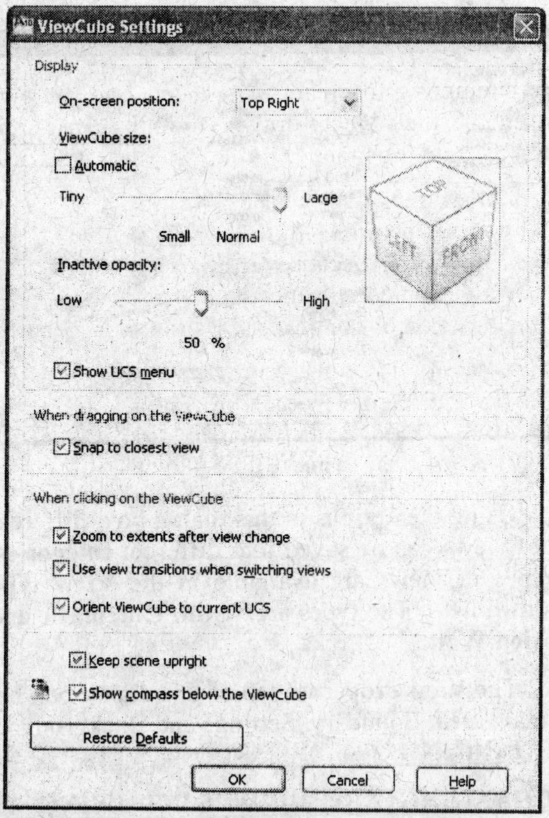

FIG. 11

4.2 CHANGING THE VIEWPOINT USING THE RIBBON OR THE TOOLBAR

The viewpoint can be set either by using the **Views** panel in the **View** tab of the **Ribbon** or by using the **View** toolbar. The **View** drop-down list in the **View** panel is shown in Fig. 12. It contains six present orthographic views, namely, Top, Bottom, Left, Right, Front and Back and four preset isometric views, namely, SW Isometric, SE Isometric, NE Isometric and NW Isometric.

It is also possible to retrieve the previously set views or any previously created named views using the View panel. All the above-stated controls are also available in the **View Manager** dialog box. Select the **View Manager** option from the **View** drop-down list to display the **View Manager** dialog box as shown in Fig. 13.

To create a new view, in the **View Manager** dialog box, choose the New button. The **New View / Shot Properties** dialog box is displayed on the screen as shown in Fig. 14. In the **View name** edit box, enter a name to save the view.

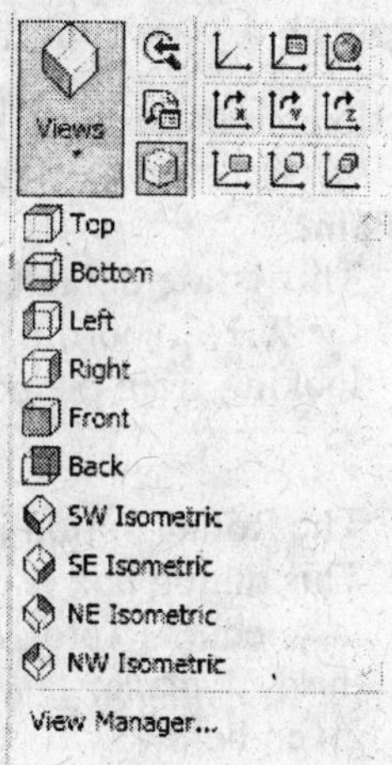

FIG. 12

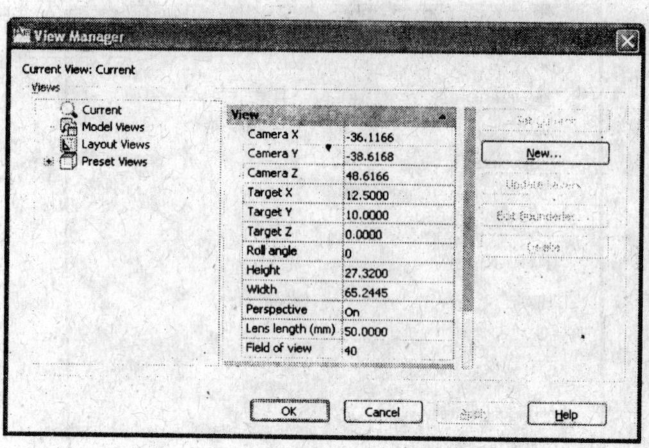

FIG. 13

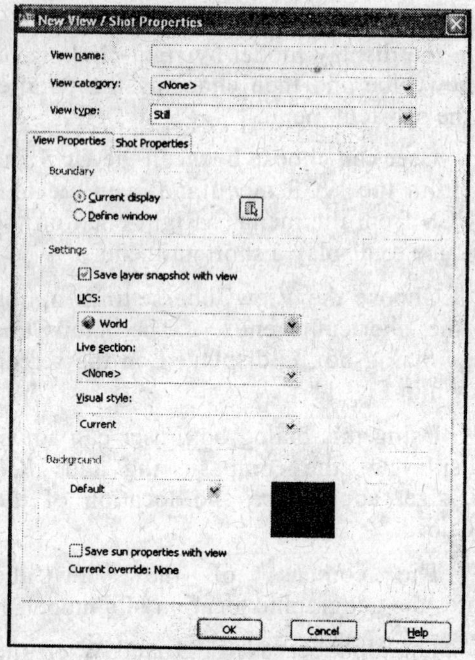

FIG. 14

Using the options in this dialog box, different types of views can be saved into different categories. The types of views are available in the **View type** drop-down list. The types are: **Still, Cinematic** and **Recorded Walk.**

The View Properties tab of this dialog box has three main area, Boundary, Settings and Background.

4.3 CHANGING THE VIEWPOINT USING THE VPOINT COMMAND

The VPOINT command is used to define a viewpoint for viewing the 3D models. When the Vpoint command is invoked, the prompt sequence that will follow is given below:

> Current view direction: VIEWDIR=0.0000,0.0000,1.0000
> Specify a view point or [Rotate] <display compass and tripod>:

The options in the Vpoint command are explained next.

View Point

This is the default option. It is used to set a viewpoint by specifying its location using the *X,Y,Z* coordinates of that particular point. The view defined is as if the viewer is looking from the point back at the origin (0,0,0).

Rotate

The Rotate option is similar to setting the viewpoint in the **Viewpoint Presets** dialog box. This dialog box is displayed when the DDVPOINT command invoked. When this option is selected, AutoCAD prompts to specify the angle in the XY plane and the angle from the XY plane. When the Rotate option is selected, then the next prompt displayed is given below:

> Enter angle in XY plane from X axis <*current*>: *Specify an angle*
> Enter angle from XY plane <*current*>: *Specify an angle*

Compass and Axis Tripod

The Compass and Axis Tripod option displays a compass and axis tripod, which you use to define a viewing direction in the viewport.

Press Enter at the **Specify a viewpoint or [Rotate] <display compass and tripod>** prompt to display the compass and the axis tripod as shown in Fig. 15.

Using this compass, user can directly set the viewpoint. The crosshairs appear on the compass. Select any point on this compass to specify the viewpoint.

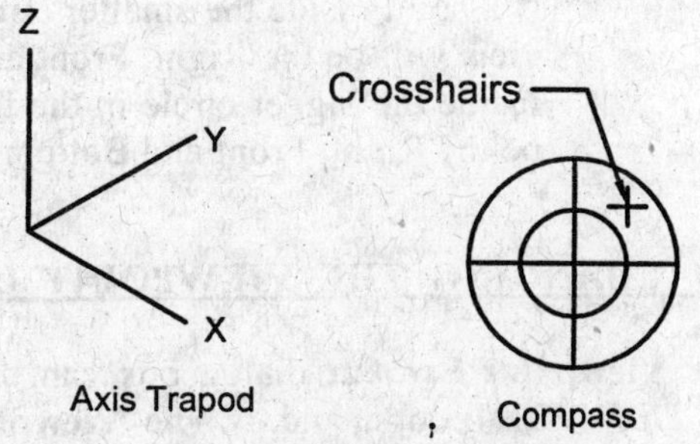

FIG. 15

The compass consists of two circles, a smaller circle and the bigger circle. These two circles are divided into four quadrants, First, Second, Third and Fourth. The resultant view will depend upon the quadrant and the circle, on which user selects the point.

The directions of the compass are shown in Fig. 16. These directions are explained below:

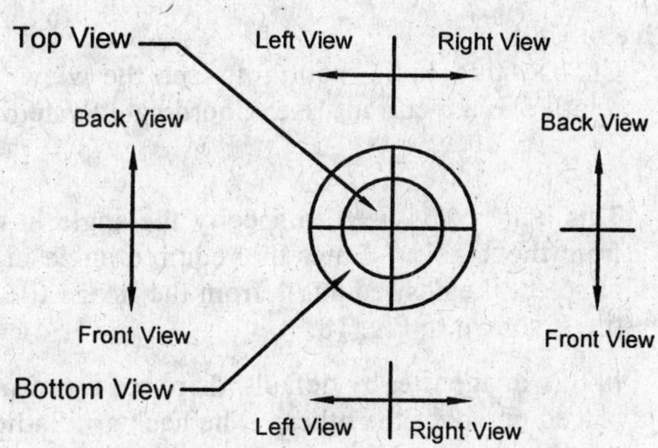

FIG. 16

1. If a point inside the smaller circle in the first quadrant is selected, then the resultant view will be the Right, Back and Top view. If a point outside the smaller circle and inside the bigger circle in the first quadrant is selected, then the resultant view will be the Right, Back and Bottom view.

2. If a point inside the smaller circle in the second quadrant is selected, then the resultant view will be the Left, Back and Top view. If a point outside the smaller circle and inside the bigger circle in the second quadrant is selected, then the resultant view will be the Left, Back and Bottom view.

3. If a point inside the smaller circle in the third quadrant is selected, then the resultant view will be the Left, Front and Top view. If a point outside the smaller circle and inside the bigger circle in the third quadrant is selected, then the resultant view will be the Left, Front and Bottom view.

4. If a point inside the smaller circle in the fourth quadrant is selected, then the resultant view will be the Right, Front and Top view. If a point outside the smaller circle and inside the bigger circle in the fourth quadrant is selected, then the resultant view will be the Right, Front and Bottom view.

4.4 CHANGING THE VIEWPOINT USING VIEWPOINT PRESETS DIALOG BOX

The **Viewpoint Present** dialog box can be invoked by using the DDVPOINT command. The **Viewpoint Present** dialog box is shown in Fig. 17. This dialog box is used for setting the viewpoint to view 3D models. Using this dialog box, the viewpoint is set with respect to the angle from the X axis and the angle from the XY plane.

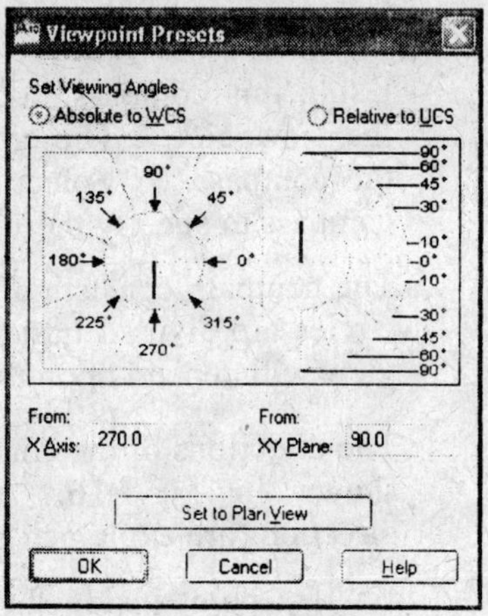

FIG. 17

Options in the Viewpoint Present dialog box

Absolute to WCS

Choose this radio button to set the view direction relative to the World Coordinate System (WCS).

Relative to UCS

Choose this radio button to set the view direction relative to the current User Coordinate System (UCS).

From: X Axis

This edit box is used to specify the angle in the XY plane from the *X* axis. Enter the required angle in this edit box or select the desired angle from the image tile. The image tile is shown in Fig. 18.

In this image tile, by default, there are two arms. They are placed one over the other. The back arm indicates the new viewing angle. The gray arm indicates the current viewing angle. When a new angle from the image tile is selected, then it is automatically displayed in the X Axis edit box.

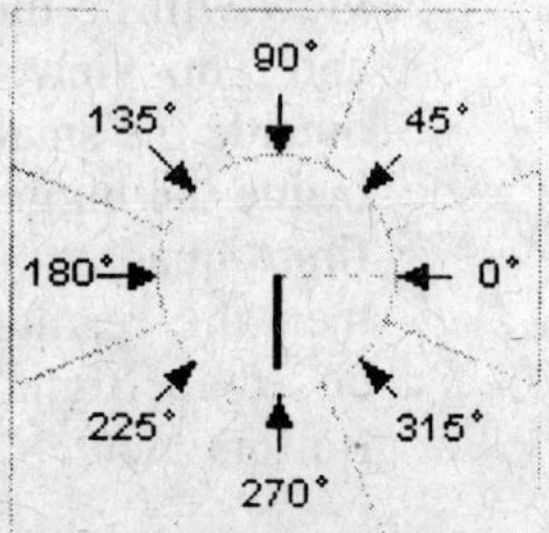

FIG. 18

From: XY Plane

This edit box is used to specify the angle from the *XY* plane. Enter the required angle in this edit box or select the angle from the image tile. The image tile is shown in Fig. 19.

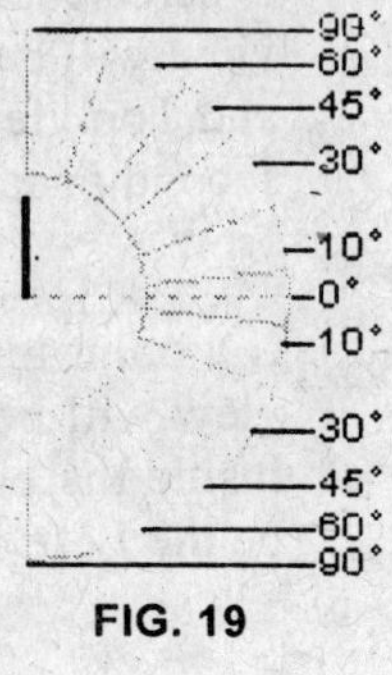

FIG. 19

Set to Plan View

This button is used to set the viewing angles to display the Plan View (*XY* plane) relative to the selected coordinate system.

Problem 1: Draw the 3D wireframe model shown in Fig. 20. The dimensions are given in Fig. 21.

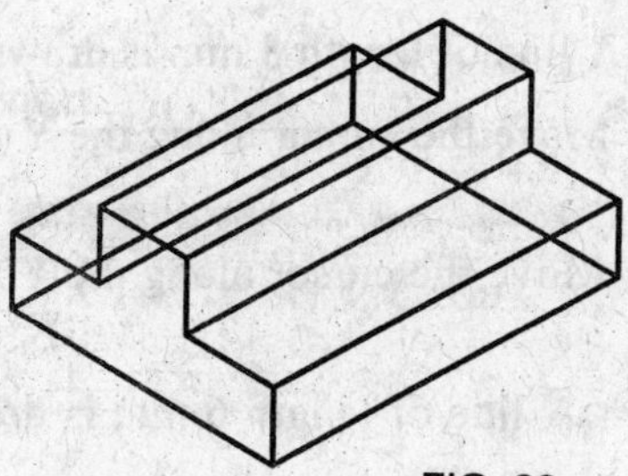

FIG. 20

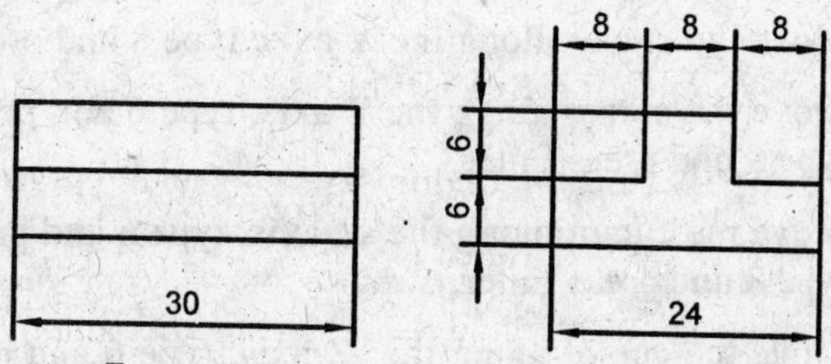

Front View

Left Side View

FIG. 21

The procedure and command sequence to draw the 3D wireframe model shown in Fig. 20 is given below:

1. Start a new file in the *Acad3d.dwt* template. Make sure that the **Ortho Mode** and **Dynamic Input** buttons are chosen.
2. Choose the **SW Isometric** option from the **View** list in the **View** tab. On the other hand, select the Southwest top corner hotspot on the **ViewCube.**
3. Invoke the **Line** tool from the **Draw** panel or enter **LINE** at the command prompt. Specify the start point of the line, here, any point P1.
4. Move the cursor along the X axis, type 30 and press Enter. A line of length 30 mm is drawn along the X axis.
5. Move the cursor along the positive Y axis, type 24 and press Enter. A line of length 24 mm is drawn along the Y axis.
6. Similarly, draw the other two lines to create the closed profile at the bottom of the model. The command sequence is given below:

   Command: **LINE** ↵
   Specify first point: *Pick P1*
   Specify next point or [Undo]: **30** ↵
   Specify next point or [Undo]: **24** ↵
   Specify next point or [Close/Undo]: **30** ↵
   Specify next point or [Close/Undo]: **24** ↵
   Specify next point or [Close/Undo]: ↵

See Fig. 22.

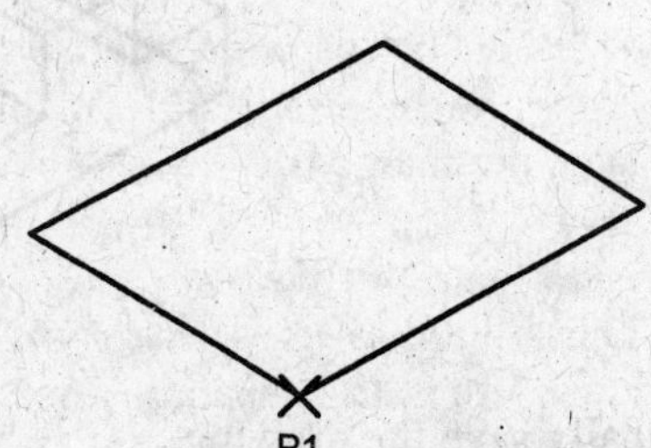

FIG. 22

7. Invoke the **Line** tool from the **Draw** panel or enter **LINE** at the command prompt. Specify the start point of the model (here, P1). From the start point of the model, move the cursor along the positive Z axis. Note that the tooltip displays **Ortho: (current length) < +Z.**

8. Type 6 at the command prompt and press Enter. A line of length 6 mm is drawn.

9. Move the cursor along the Y axis, type 8 and press Enter. A line of length 8 mm is drawn.

10. Move the cursor along the Z axis, type 6 and press Enter. Move the cursor along the Y axis, type 8 and press Enter.

11. Move the cursor along the -Z axis, type 6 and press Enter. Move the cursor along the Y axis, type 8 and press Enter.

12. Move the cursor along the -Z axis, type 6 and press Enter. A line of length 6 mm is drawn. The command sequence is given below:

    Command: **LINE** ↵
    Specify first point: *Pick P1*
    Specify next point or [Undo]: **6** ↵
    Specify next point or [Undo]: **8** ↵
    Specify next point or [Close/Undo]: **6** ↵
    Specify next point or [Close/Undo]: **8** ↵
    Specify next point or [Close/Undo]: **6** ↵
    Specify next point or [Close/Undo]: **8** ↵
    Specify next point or [Close/Undo]: **6** ↵
    Specify next point or [Close/Undo]: ↵

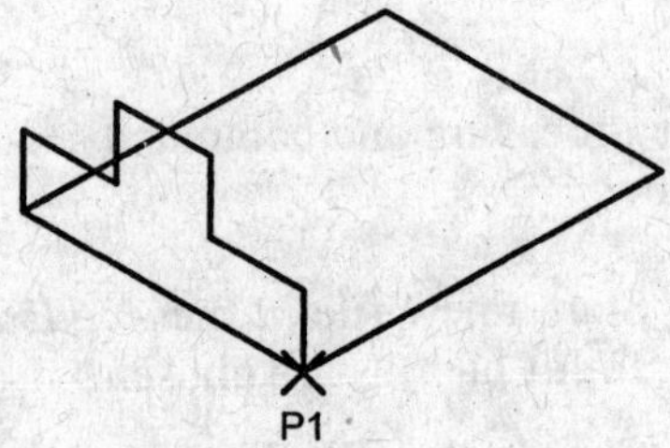

FIG. 23

    See Fig. 23.

13. Similarly, draw other lines to complete the model. The final model is shown in Fig. 24.

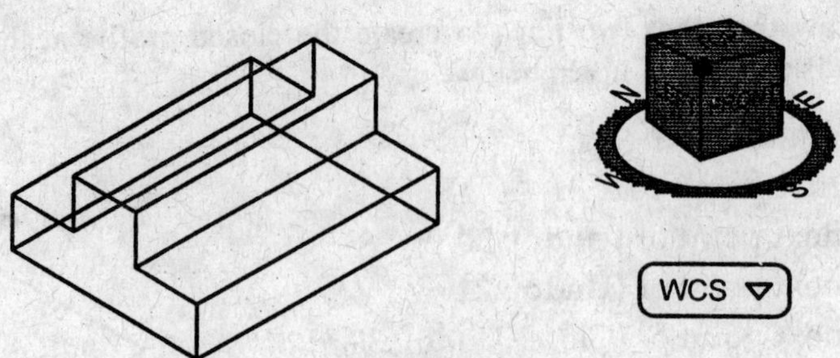

FIG. 24

14. Finally save the drawing.

5. CONVERTING WIREFRAME MODELS INTO SURFACE MODELS

A Wireframe Model can be converted into a Surface Model using the 3DFACE command and the PFACE command.

5.1 3DFACE COMMAND

The **3DFACE** command is used to create 3D faces in space. Using this command, user can create three-sided or four-sided faces. Invoke the **3DFACE** command either by selecting **Draw > Modeling > Meshes > 3D Face** or by entering **3DFACE** at the command prompt.

When the 3DFACE command is invoked, AutoCAD prompts to specify the first, second, third and fourth points of the 3D face. Specify the first four points. AutoCAD again prompts to specify the third and fourth point. Here, specify the third and fourth points as the first and second points respectively. This process will continue until Enter is pressed at the **Specify third point or [Invisible] <exit>** prompt.

5.2 PFACE COMMAND

The PFACE command is similar to the 3DFACE command. Using the PFACE command, a mesh of any desired surface shape can be created by specifying the coordinates of the vertices and assigning the vertices to the faces in the mesh.

The difference between the 3DFACE and PFACE commands is that in 3DFACE command, user won't select the vertices that joint another face twice. However, in PFACE command, it is necessary to select all the vertices of a face, even if they are coincident with the vertices of another face. Like this, user can avoid generating unrelated 3D faces that have coincident vertices. Here, there is no restriction on the number of faces and vertices the mesh can have.

5.3 SUPPRESSING THE HIDDEN EDGES

When a surface or a solid mode is created, the edges that lie at the back are also visible. As a result, the model appears like a wireframe model. Using the **Hide** command, user can manually suppress the hidden lines in the 3D model. When the Hide command is invoked, all the objects on the screen are regenerated. And 3D models are displayed with the hidden edges suppressed.

5.4 EXTRUDE COMMAND

The **Extrude** command extends the dimensions of a 2D object or 3D face into 3D space. In most cases, if you extrude a closed object, the result is a new 3D solid. If you extrude an open object, the result is a surface. When user selects a mesh face, the resulting extrusion distorts the face, but the extruded face continues to be part of the original object.

When user selects the face of a 3D solid to extrude, a new 3D solid object is created. If a selected polyline has width, the width is ignored and the polyline is extruded from the center of the polyline path. If a selected object has thickness, the thickness is ignored.

6. SETTING THICKNESS AND ELEVATION FOR THE NEW OBJECTS

The **ELEV** command sets elevation and extrusion thickness of new objects. The Elev command can be invoked by typing ELEV at the command prompt. When the Elev command is invoked, the next prompts displayed is given below:

Specify new default elevation <current>: *Specify a distance or press Enter*
Specify new default thickness <*current*>: *Specify a distance or press Enter*

The current Elevation is the default *Z* value for new objects when user specifies only *X* and *Y* values for a 3D point. The elevation setting is the same for all viewports regardless of their user coordinate systems (UCSs). New objects are created at the specified *Z* value relative to the current UCS in the viewport. The elevation option sets the elevation only for the new objects and the existing objects are not modified using this option.

The Thickness sets the distance to which a 2D object is extruded above or below its elevation. A positive value is extruded along the positive *Z* axis; a negative value is extruded along the negative *Z* axis. The Thickness option sets the thickness only for the new objects and the existing objects are not modified.

ELEV controls only new objects; it does not affect existing objects. The elevation is reset to 0.0 whenever user changes the coordinate system to the world coordinate system (WCS).

7. DRAWING POLYFACE MESHES

In AutoCAD 3D space, user can create some standard polygon meshes, meshes, and polyface meshes like box, cone, dish dome, pyramid, torus, sphere, mesh and wedge. These standard surface primitives can be created using the **3D** command. Invoke the **3D** command and select the required surface using the Command prompt. When the **3D** command is invoked, the following prompt sequences are displayed:

Command: 3D ↵
Initializing... 3D Objects loaded.
Enter an option
[Box/Cone/DIsh/DOme/Mesh/Pyramid/Sphere/Torus/Wedge]:

The options in the 3D command are explained next.

7.1 BOX OPTION

The **Box** option is used to create a 3D polygon mesh in the shape of a rectangular or square box. Fig. 25 shows a rectangular box-shaped surface mesh. When this option is selected, AutoCAD prompts to specify the corner of the box. Specify the corner of the box. Now, AutoCAD prompts to specify the length, width and height of the box.

After specifying the length, width and height of the box, AutoCAD prompts to specify the rotation angle of the box. Specify the rotation angle by directly or by using the **Reference** option. The prompt sequence to draw a rectangular box as shown in Fig. 25 is given below:

Command: **3D** ↵
Enter an option [Box/Cone/DIsh/DOme/
  Mesh/Pyramid/Sphere/Torus/Wedge]: **B** ↵
Specify corner point of box: **0,0,0** ↵
Specify length of box: **30** ↵
Specify width of box or [Cube]: **13** ↵
Specify height of box: **10** ↵
Specify rotation angle of box
  about the Z axis or [Reference]: ↵

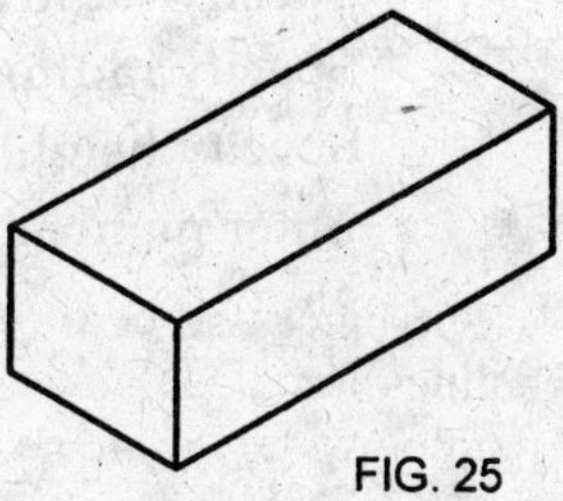

FIG. 25

7.2 CONE OPTION

The **Cone** option is used to create a polygon mesh model of a pointed cone or a truncated cone. If the MESHTYPE system variable is set to 1, the resulting surface is a mesh. If the MESHTYPE system variable is set to 0, the resulting surface is a polygon mesh.

1. Pointed Cone

To draw a pointed cone, three parameters are needed. They are: (1) Center point of the base of the cone, (2) Diameter/Radius of the base of the cone and (3) Height of the cone. The prompt sequence to draw a pointed cone is given below:

Command: **3D** ↵
Enter an option [Box/Cone/DIsh/DOme/Mesh/
  Pyramid/Sphere/Torus/Wedge]: **C** ↵
Specify center point for base of cone: *Pick a point*
Specify radius for base of cone or [Diameter]: **10** ↵
Specify radius for top of cone or [Diameter] <0>: ↵
Specify height of cone: **30** ↵
Enter number of segments for
  surface of cone <16>: **14** ↵

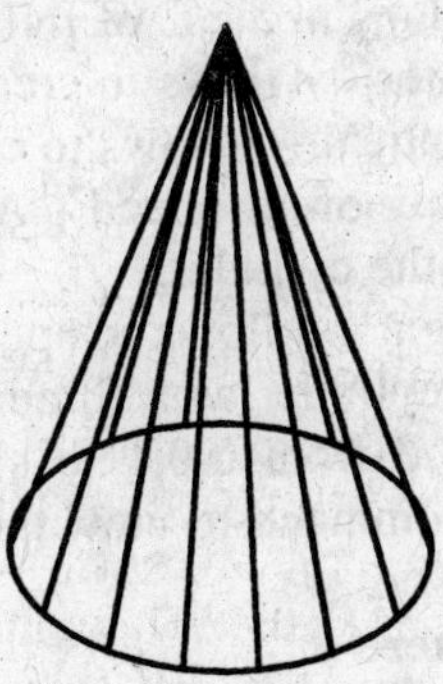

FIG. 26

See Fig. 26.

2. Truncated Cone

To draw a truncated cone, there are four parameters needed. They are: Center point of the base of the cone, Diameter/radius of the base of the cone, Diameter/radius of the top of the cone and Height of the cone. The prompt sequence to draw a truncated cone is given below:

Command: **3D** ↵
Enter an option [Box/Cone/DIsh/DOme/
Mesh/Pyramid/Sphere/Torus/Wedge]: **C** ↵
Specify center point for base of cone: *Pick a point*
Specify radius for base of cone or [Diameter]: **10** ↵
Specify radius for top of cone or [Diameter] <0>: **5** ↵
Specify height of cone: **30** ↵
Enter number of segments for surface of cone <16>: **14** ↵

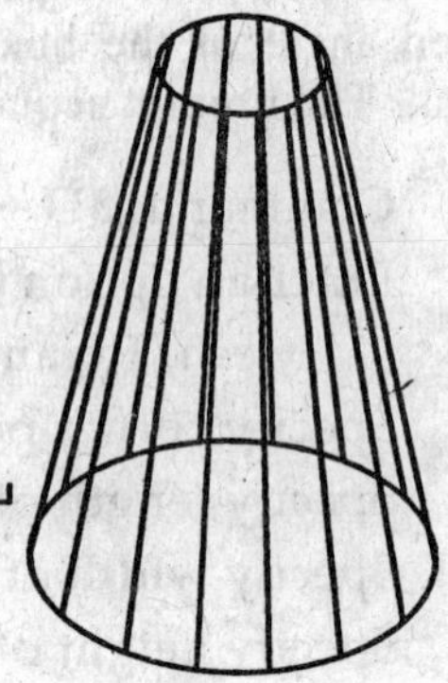

FIG. 27

See Fig. 27.

7.3 CYLINDER OPTION

The **Cylinder** option is used to create a solid cylinder. The base of the cylinder lies on the current XY plane and the height or extrusion of it is obtained along Z axis. The prompt sequence is:

```
Command: CYLINDER ↵
Current wire frame density:  ISOLINES=4
Specify center point for base of cylinder or [Elliptical] <0,0,0>: ↵
Specify radius for base of cylinder or [Diameter]: 10 ↵
Specify height of cylinder or
          [Center of other end]: 20 ↵
```

The options in the CYLINDER command are:

Center – Allows to create a cylinder with a circular base.
Elliptical – Allows to create a cylinder with an elliptical base.
Center of other end – Allows to specify top end of the cylinder.
Height – Allows to specifying the height of the cylinder. To see the cylinder as a three dimensional object, viewpoint should be altered from 0,0,1 to some other point, say, 1,1,1. Use the **HIDE** command to view the required shape as shown in Fig. 28.

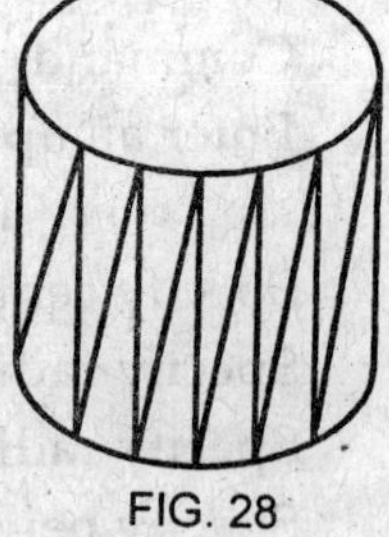

FIG. 28

1. **Sphere**
   The SPHERE command is used to draw a three-dimensional solid sphere. The SPHERE command can also be selected from the options available in the 3D command. The prompt sequence is:

```
Command: SPHERE ↵
Current wire frame density:  ISOLINES=4
Specify center of sphere <0,0,0>: ↵
Specify radius of sphere or [Diameter]: 10 ↵
```

- **Extrude**

The EXTRUDE command is used to add thickness to 2D objects. The 2D objects can be extruded along a specified path or with a height value and a tapered angle. The prompt sequence is:

```
Command: EXTRUDE ↵
Current wire frame density:  ISOLINES=4
Select objects: (Select the rectangle) 1 found
Select objects: ↵
Specify height of extrusion or [Path]: 20 ↵
Specify angle of taper for extrusion <0>: ↵
```

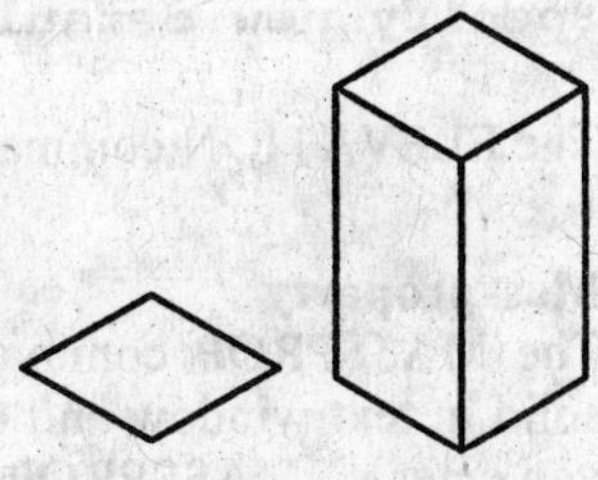

FIG. 29

Use **HIDE** command to view required shape as shown in Fig. 29.

- **Union**

The UNION command is used to combine several solids. If the solids are touching, you get a new, unified solid. If the solids are not touching, but rather completely separate, using UNION command is like grouping. The prompt sequence is:

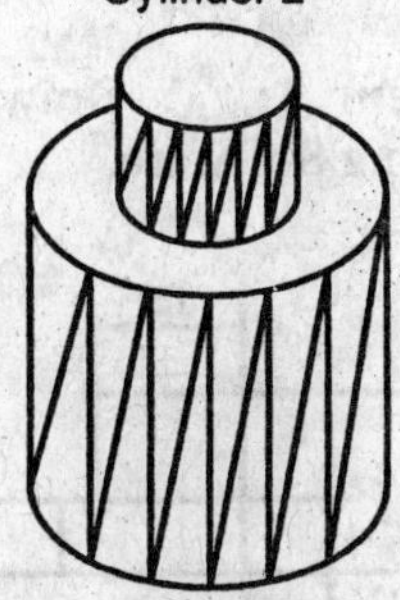

FIG. 30

```
Command: UNION ↵
Select objects: (Selection Cylinder 1) 1 found
Select objects: (Selection Cylinder 2) 1 found, 2 total
Select objects: ↵
Command: HIDE ↵
Regenerating model.
```

Fig. 30 shows the union of two cylinders after a **HIDE**.

- **Subtract**

The SUBTRACT command is used to subtract one solid from another. This command is most commonly used to create holes. The prompt sequence is:

```
Command: SUBTRACT ↵
Select solids and regions to subtract
                                  from..
Select objects: (Selection Cylinder 1) 1 found
Select objects: ↵
Select solids and regions to subtract ..
Select objects: (Selection Cylinder 2) 1 found
Select objects: ↵
```

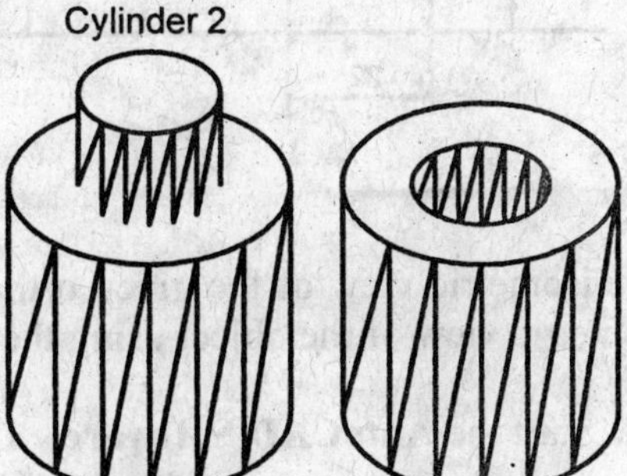

FIG. 31

Fig. 31 shows the result of subtracting a small cylinder from a larger one and performing a **HIDE**.

- **Elevations and Thickness**

The ELEVATION command is used to set elevation and

extrusion thickness of new objects. The default value in the AutoCAD prototype drawings is zero for each, resulting in a flat entity in 3D. The prompt sequence is:

`Command:` **`ELEVATION`** (or **ELEV** for transparent use) ↵
`Specify new default elevation <current>:` Specify a distance or press ENTER
`Specify new default thickness <current>:` Specify a distance or press ENTER

The ELEVATION command controls only new objects; it does not affect existing objects.

6. **Massproperty**
The MASSPROP command automatically calculates and displays various properties of a solid in text window and then asks if you want to write the mass properties to a text file. If you enter **y**, MASSPROP prompts you to enter a file name.

TYPICAL PROBLEMS

Problem 1: Draw the isometric view for the orthographic views shown in Fig. 32 using 3D Modeling Software.

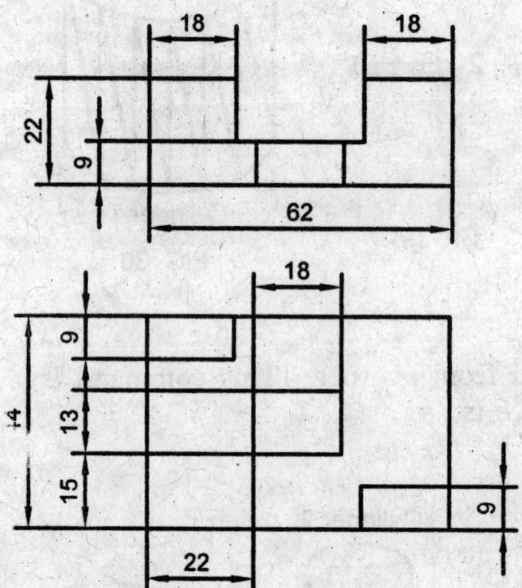

FIG. 32

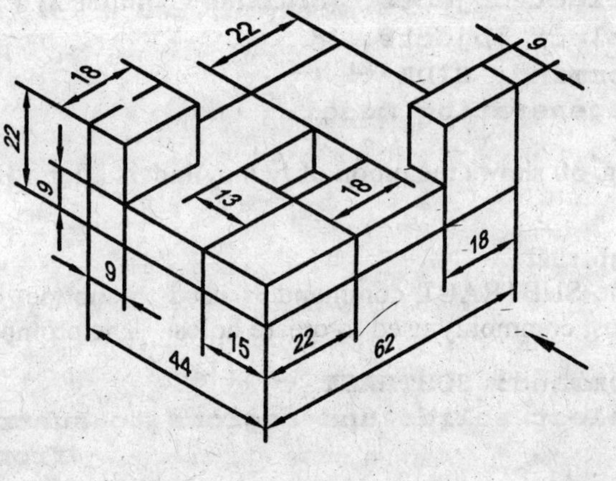

FIG. 33

The isometric view of the given orthographic views is shown in Fig. 33. The steps to draw the isometric view of the object using the 3D Modeling are explained as follows:

1. Start the **AutoCAD Software**. Open and setup a new drawing sheet.
2. Using the **RECTANG** command, draw a rectangle of size 62 x 44. The prompt sequence is:
`Command:` **`RECTANGLE`** ↵

```
Specify first corner point or [Chamfer / Elevation / Fillet /
Thickness / Width]: 0,0 ↵
Specify other corner point or [Dimensions]: @62,44 ↵
```

3. Using **EXTRUDE** command, provide height for the rectangle. The prompt sequence is:

```
Command: EXTRUDE ↵
Current wire frame density:  ISOLINES=4
Select objects: (Select the rectangle) 1 found
Select objects: ↵
Specify height of extrusion or [Path]: 9 ↵
Specify angle of taper for extrusion <0>: ↵
```

4. Using the **RECTANGLE** command, draw two rectangles 1 and 2 of size 18 x 9. The prompt sequence is:

```
Command: RECTANG ↵
Specify first corner point or [Chamfer / Elevation / Fillet /
Thickness / Width]: (Click on the top left corner of the rectangle)
Specify other corner point or [Dimensions]: @18,-9 ↵

Command: RECTANG ↵
Specify first corner point or [Chamfer / Elevation / Fillet /
Thickness / Width]: (Click on the bottom right corner of the rectangle)
Specify other corner point or [Dimensions]: @-18,9 ↵
```

5. Using the **RECTANGLE** command, draw a rectangle 3 of size 18 mm x 13 mm at the specified position of the first rectangle. The prompt sequence is:

```
Command: RECTANG ↵
Specify first corner point or [Chamfer /
      Elevation / Fillet / Thickness /
               Width]: 22,15 ↵
Specify other corner point or
              [Dimensions]: @18,13 ↵
```

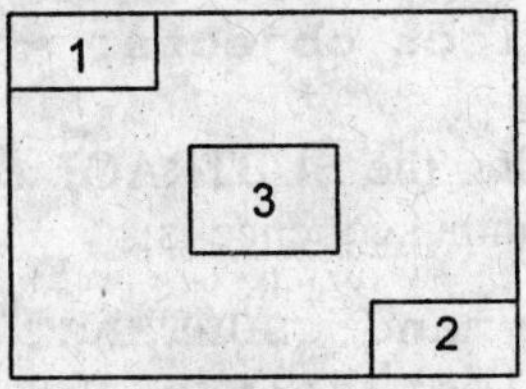

(i)

See Fig. (i), which shows the top view of the given object.

6. Using **EXTRUDE** command, provide height for the above three rectangles. The prompt sequence is:

```
Command: EXTRUDE ↵
Current wire frame density:  ISOLINES=4
Select objects: (Select the Rectangle 1) 1 found
Select objects: (Select the Rectangle 2) 1 found, 2 total
Select objects: ↵
Specify height of extrusion or [Path]: 22 ↵
Specify angle of taper for extrusion <0>: ↵
```

```
Command: EXTRUDE ↵
Current wire frame density:  ISOLINES=4
Select objects: (Select the Rectangle 3) 1 found
Select objects: ↵
Specify height of extrusion
          or [Path]: 9 ↵
Specify angle of taper for
          extrusion <0>: ↵
```

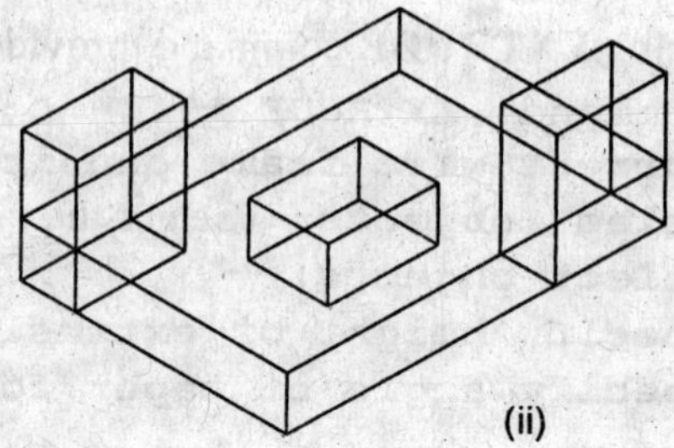

(ii)

7. Using the **VPOINT** command, change the viewpoint from 0,0,1 to 1,1,1 to view the object in isometric as shown in Fig. (ii). The prompt sequence is:

```
Command: VPOINT ↵
Current view direction:  VIEWDIR=0.0000,0.0000,1.0000
Specify a view point or [Rotate] <display compass and tripod>:
1,1,1 ↵
Regenerating model.
```

8. Using the UNION command, combine the base rectangle with the rectangles 1 and 2. The prompt sequence is:

```
Command: UNION ↵
Select objects: (Select the Base Rectangle) 1 found
Select objects: (Select the Rectangle 1) 1 found, 2 total
Select objects: (Select the Rectangle 2) 1 found, 3 total
Select objects: ↵
```

9. Using the SUBTRACT command, subtract the rectangle 3 from the base rectangle. The prompt sequence is:

```
Command: SUBTRACT ↵
Select solids and regions to subtract from ..
Select objects: (Select the Base Rectangle) 1 found
Select objects: ↵
Select solids and regions to subtract ..
Select objects: (Select the Rectangle 3) 1 found
Select objects: ↵
```

(iii)

10. Using the HIDE command, hide the invisible lines to view the required 3D view of the given object as shown in Fig. (iii). The prompt sequence is:

```
Command: HIDE ↵ Regenerating model.
```

11. Finally, save the file.

ANNA UNIVERSITY - CAD LAB EXERCISES

Ex. No. : 1

Create a 3-D Model of the I- BEAM shown, using 3-D Commands such as Region and Extrude.
Draw the 2-D Multi-Views from the above.

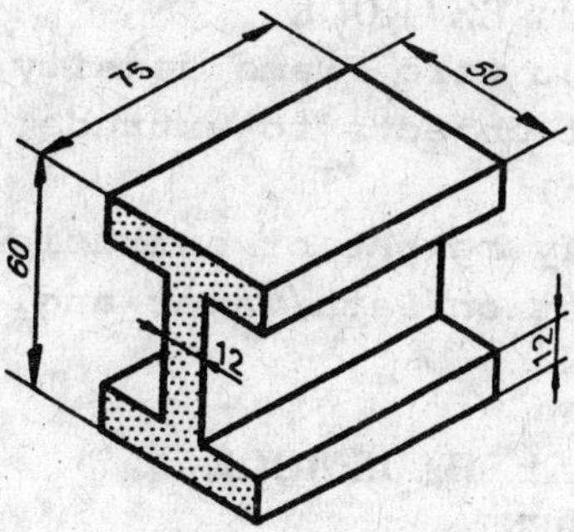

AIM :

To create 3-D Model of the I- BEAM :

Step-by-Step PROCEDURE:

Command: **LIMITS**

```
Reset Model space limits:
Specify lower left corner or [ON/OFF] <0.0000,0.0000>: 0,0
Specify upper right corner <12.0000,9.0000>: 210,297
```

Command: **LINE**

```
Specify first point: 0,0
Specify next point or [Undo]: @50,0
Specify next point or [Undo]: @0,12
Specify next point or [Close/Undo]: @-19,0
Specify next point or [Close/Undo]: @0,36
Specify next point or [Close/Undo]: @19,0
Specify next point or [Close/Undo]: @0,12
Specify next point or [Close/Undo]: @-50,0
Specify next point or [Close/Undo]: @0,-12
Specify next point or [Close/Undo]: @19,0
Specify next point or [Close/Undo]: @0,-36
Specify next point or [Close/Undo]: @-19,0
Specify next point or [Close/Undo]: C
```

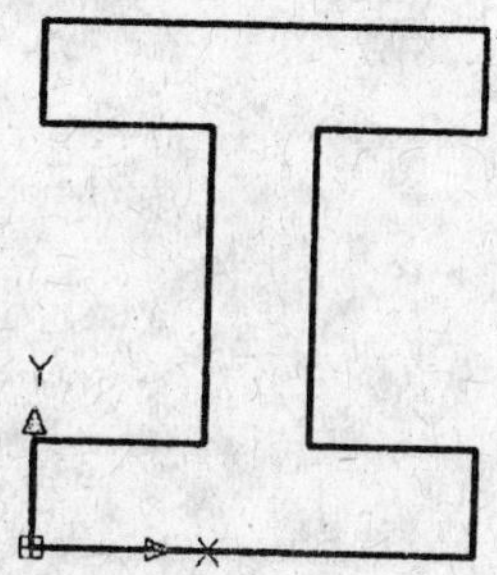

Command: **ZOOM**

```
Specify corner of window, enter a scale factor (nX or nXP), or
All/Center/Dynamic/Extents/Previous/Scale/Window/Object] <real
ime>: ALL
```

Command: **REGION**

```
Select objects: (select all lines)
1 loop extracted.
1 region created.
```

Command: **EXTRUDE**

```
Current wire frame density:  ISOLINES=4
Select objects to extrude:  (select the
region)
Specify height of extrusion or
[Direction/Path/Taper angle]: 75
```

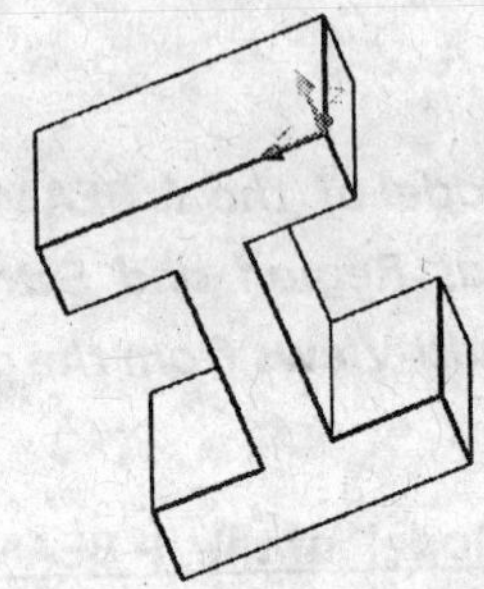

Command: **SHADEMODE**

```
VSCURRENT
Enter an option
[2dwireframe/3dwireframe/3dHidden/Realistic/Conceptual/Other]
<2dwireframe>: C
```

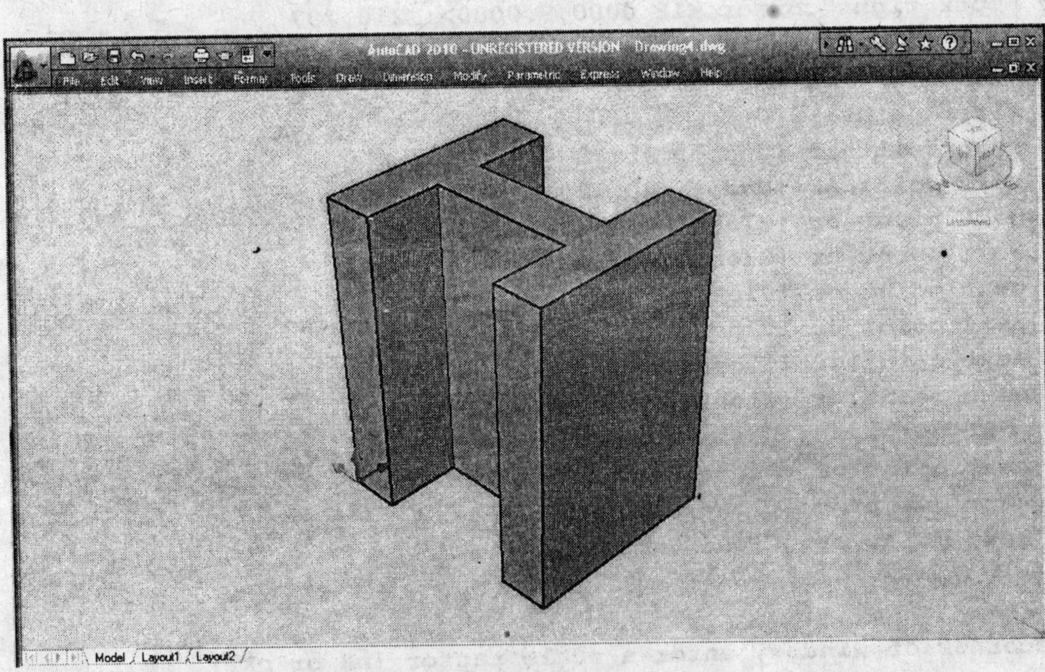

Create a New Viewport

Select View Menu ⟶ Viewports ⟶ New viewport

Give a name to the viewport
Select Four: Equal from Standard viewports menu
Change the Visual style to 3D hidden
The following screen appears:

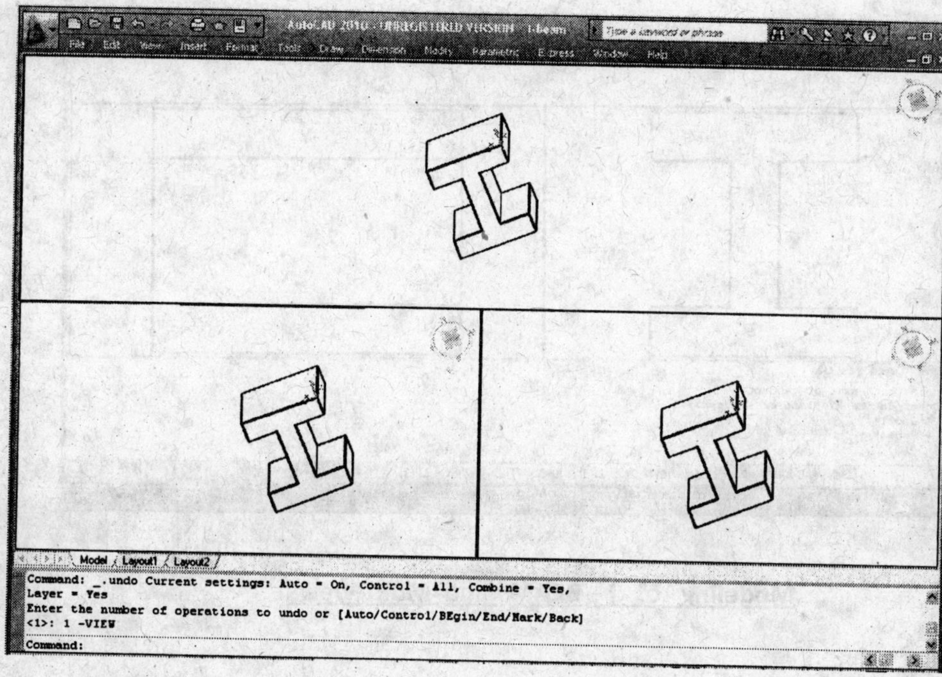

Select the lower left block
Command: **-VIEW**
Enter an option
[?/Delete/Orthographic/Restore/Save/sEttings/Window]: O
Enter an option [Top/Bottom/Front/BAck/Left/Right]<Top>: F

Select the lower right block
Command: **-VIEW**
Enter an option
[?/Delete/Orthographic/Restore/Save/sEttings/Window]: O
Enter an option [Top/Bottom/Front/BAck/Left/Right]<Top>: L

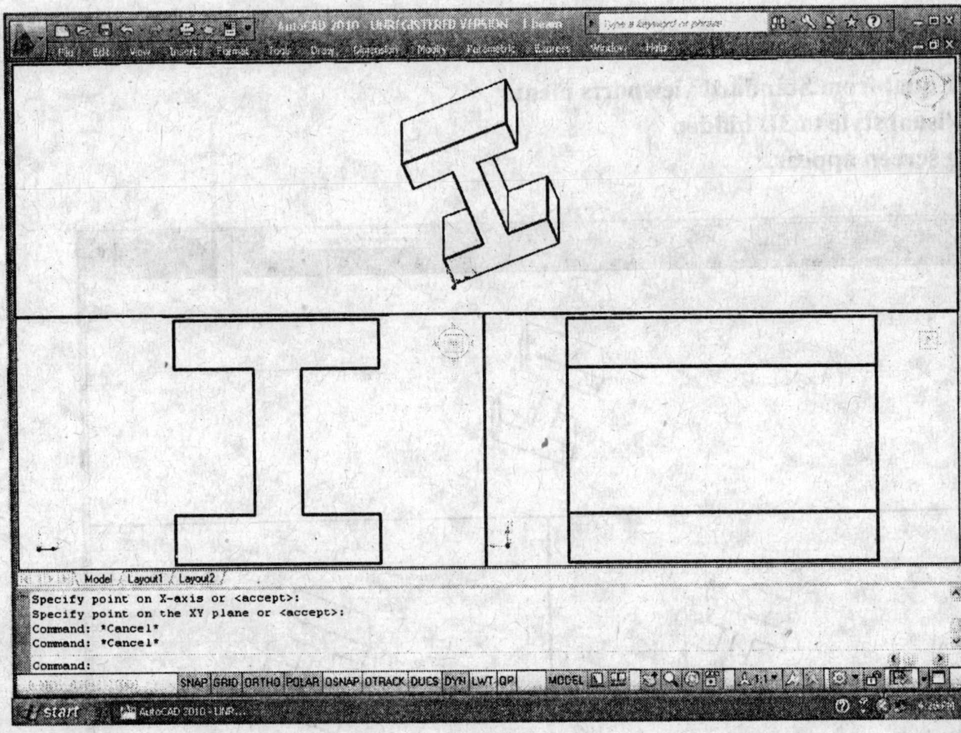

Modeling of I – BEAM and Multi-Views

Ex. No. : 2

Create a 3-D Model of the STEPS shown, using 3-D Commands such as Region and Extrude.
Draw the 2-D Multi-Views from the above.

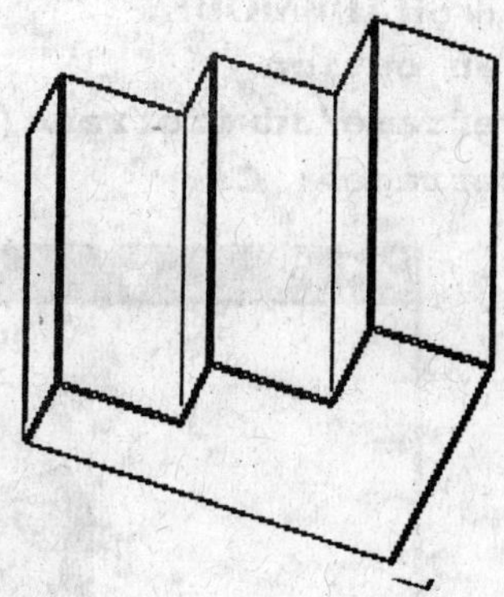

AIM :

To create 3-D Model of the STEPS:

Step-by-Step PROCEDURE:

Command: **LIMITS**

```
Reset Model space limits:
Specify lower left corner or [ON/OFF] <0.0000,0.0000>: 0,0
Specify upper right corner <12.0000,9.0000>: 210,297
```

Command: **LINE**

```
Specify first point: 0,0
Specify next point or [Undo]: @25,0
Specify next point or [Undo]: 0,@-20
Specify next point or [Close/Undo]: @25,0
Specify next point or [Close/Undo]: 0,@-15
Specify next point or [Close/Undo]: @25,0
Specify next point or [Close/Undo]: 0,@-15
Specify next point or [Close/Undo]: @-75,0
Specify next point or [Close/Undo]: C
```

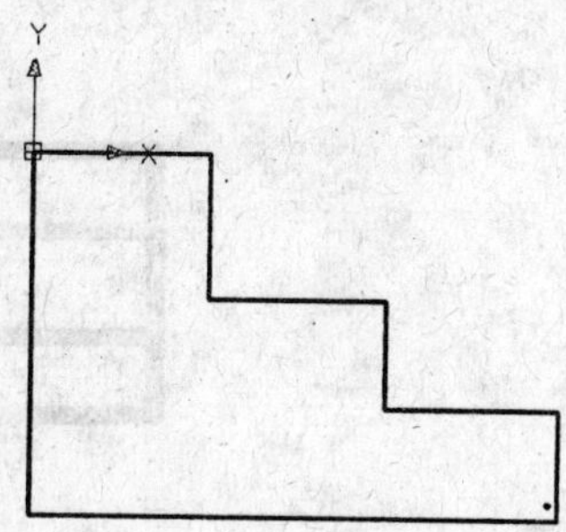

Command: **REGION**

```
Select objects: (Select all lines)
1 loop extracted.
1 Region created.
```

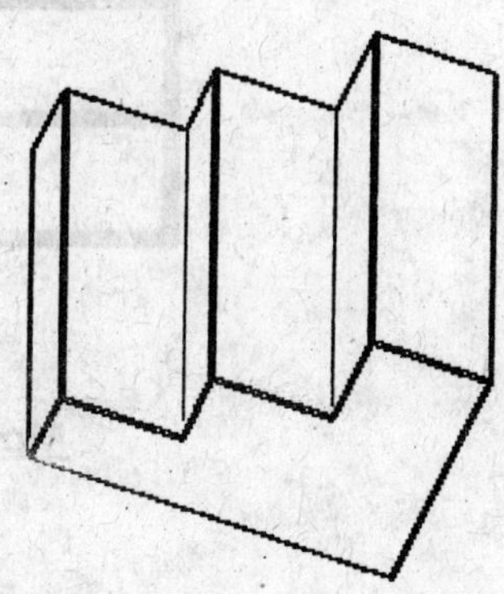

Command: **EXTRUDE**

```
Current wire frame density:  ISOLINES=4
Select objects to extrude: (select the
region)
```

Specify height of extrusion or [Direction/Path/Taper angle] : 100
Command: **SHADEMODE**
Enter an option
[2dwireframe/3dwireframe/3dHidden/Realistic/Conceptual/Other]
<2dwireframe>: C

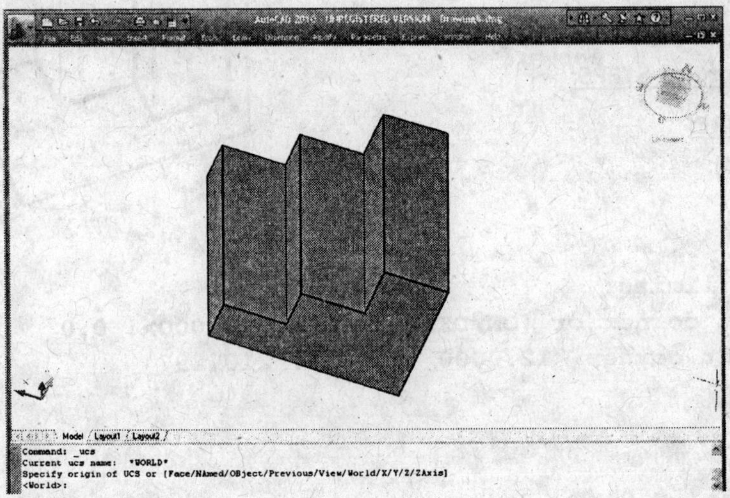

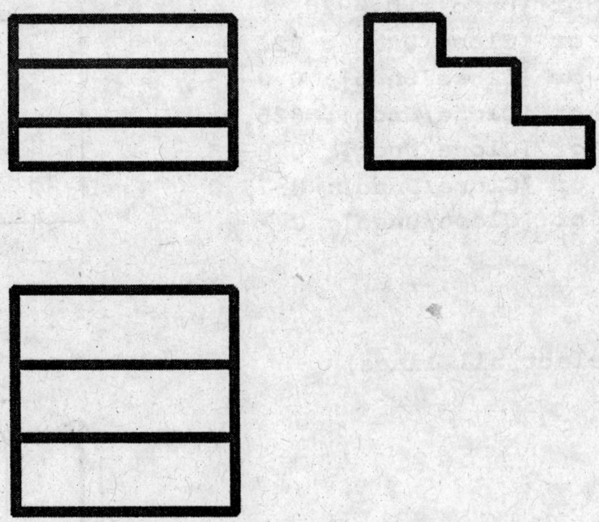

Modeling of STEPS and Multi-Views

Ex. No. : 3

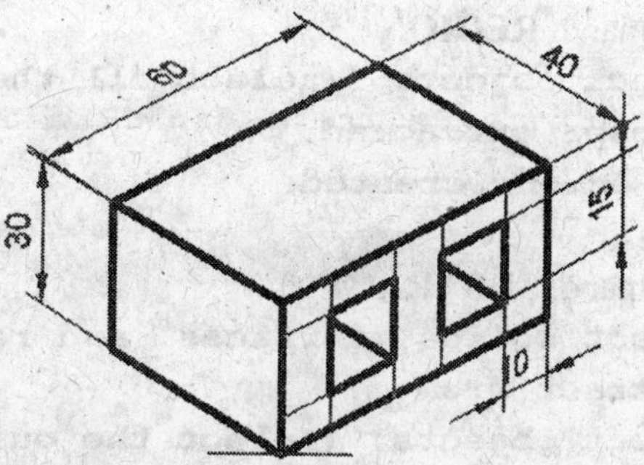

HOLLOW BLOCK

Create a 3-D Model of the HOLLOW BLOCK shown, using 3-D Commands such as Region, Extrude and Subtract.
Draw the 2-D Multi-Views from the above.

AIM :

To create 3-D Model of the *HOLLOW BLOCK* :

Step-by-Step PROCEDURE:

Command : **LIMITS**

```
Reset Model space limits:
Specify lower left corner or [ON/OFF] <0.0000,0.0000>: 0,0
Specify upper right corner <12.0000,9.0000>: 210,297
```

Command: **RECTANGLE**

```
Specify first corner point or
[Chamfer/Elevation/Fillet/Thickness/Width]:
0,0
Specify other corner point or
[Area/Dimensions/Rotation]: @60,40
```

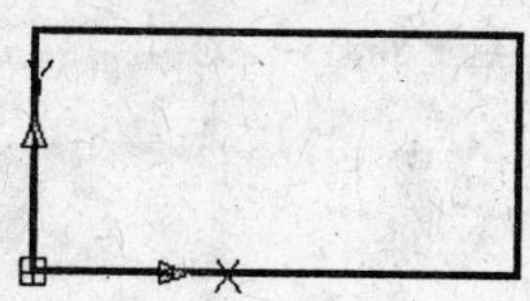

Command: **RECTANGLE**

```
Specify first corner point or
[Chamfer/Elevation/Fillet/Thickness/Width]:
10,7.5
Specify other corner point or
[Area/Dimensions/Rotation]: D
Specify length for rectangles <10.0000>: 15
Specify width for rectangles <10.0000>: 15
```

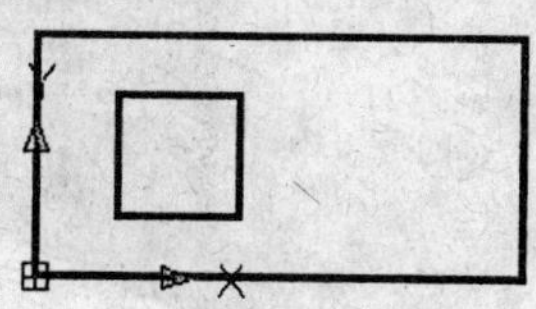

Command: **COPY**

```
Select objects:  (select the inner rectangle)
Specify base point or [Displacement/mOde]
<Displacement>: 10,7.5
Specify second point or <use first point as
displacement>: 35,7.5
```

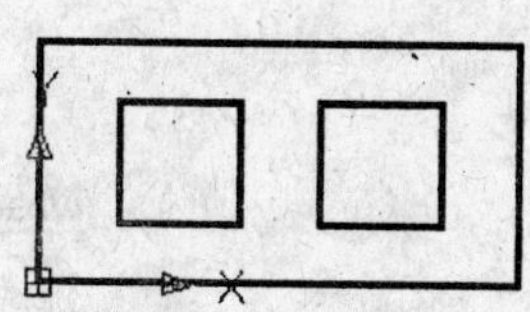

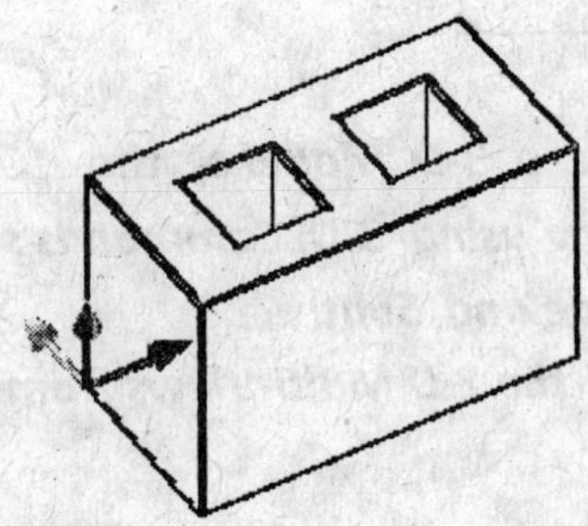

Command: **REGION**
Select objects: (select all the rectangles)
3 loops extracted.
1 Regions created.

Command: **SUBTRACT**
Select solids, surfaces, and regions to subtract from ..
Select objects: (select the outer rectangle)
Select solids, surfaces, and regions to subtract ..
Select objects: (select the two inner squares)

Command: **EXTRUDE**
Current wire frame density: ISOLINES=4
Select objects to extrude: (select the region)
Specify height of extrusion or [Direction/Path/Taper angle]: 40

Command: **SHADEMODE**
Enter an option
[2dwireframe/3dwireframe/3dHidden/Realistic/Conceptual/Other]
<2dwireframe>: **C**

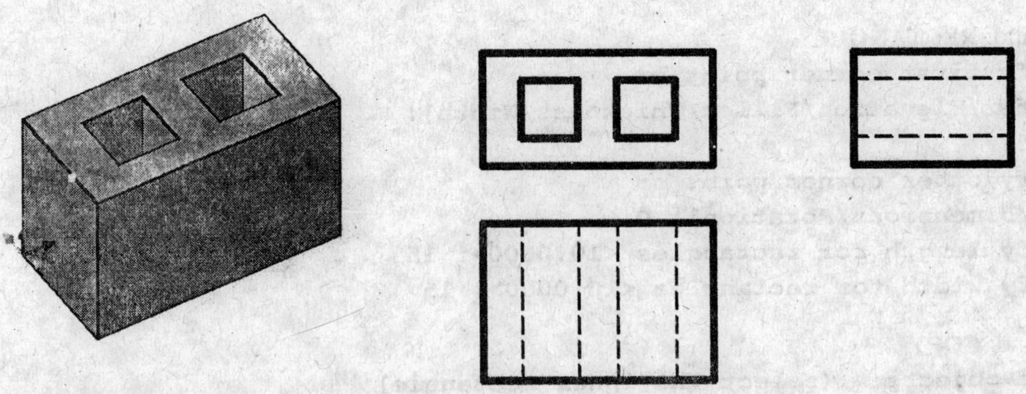

Modeling of HOLLOW BLOCK and Multi-Views

Ex. No. : 4

Create a 3-D Model of the V- BLOCK shown, using 3-D Commands such as Region ,Extrude and Subtract . Draw the 2-D Multi-Views from the above.

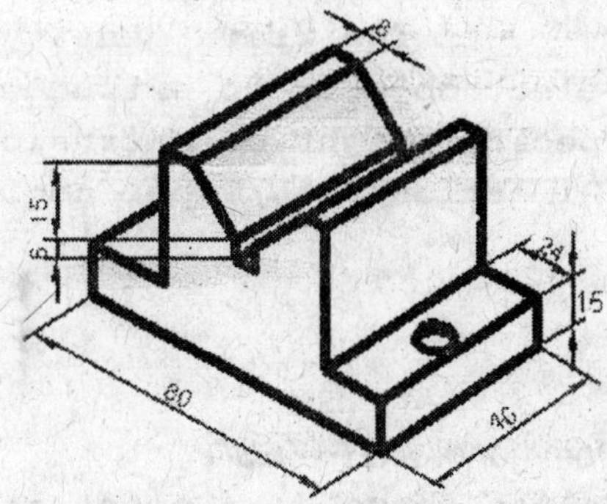

AIM :

To create 3-D Model of the *V- BLOCK* :

Step-by-Step PROCEDURE:

Command : **LIMITS**
Specify lower left corner or
[ON/OFF] <0.0000,0.0000>:
Specify upper right corner
<420.0000,297.0000>: 120,100

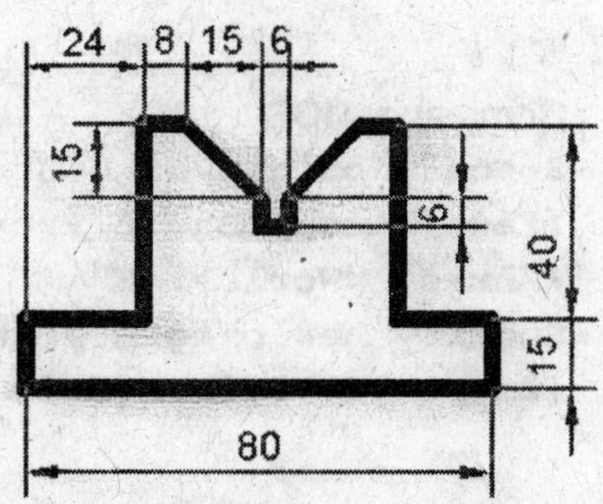

Command: **ZOOM**
[All/Center/Dynamic/Extents/Previous/Scale /Window/Object] <real time>: a

Create 2-D diagram using PLINE Command, take Coordinate of P1 as 0,0

Command: **VPOINT**
Specify a view point or [Rotate] <display compass and tripod> : 1,-1,1

Command: **REGION**
Select objects : (Select any Line)
Select objects : enter
1 loop extracted.
1 Region created.

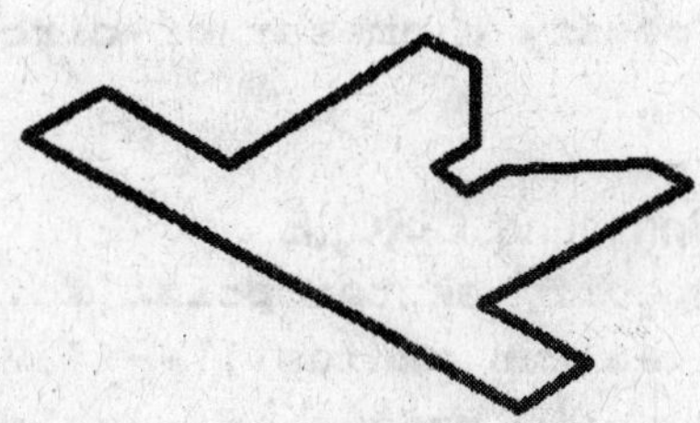

Command: **SHADEMODE**
Enter an option
[2dwireframe/3dwireframe/3dHidden/Realistic/Conceptual/Other]
<2dwireframe>: H

Command: **EXTRUDE**

Cu..ent wire frame density:ISOLINES=4
Select objects to extrude:
Specify height of extrusion or
[Direction/Path/Taper angle]: 40

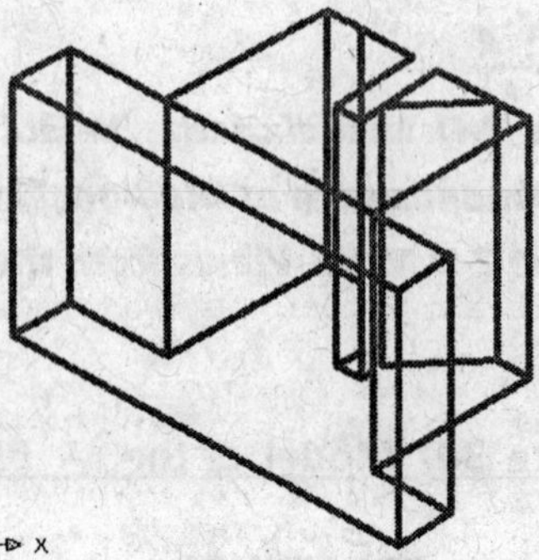

Command: **ROTATE3D**

Select objects: (Select any Line)
Specify first point on axis or define axis
by [Object/Last/View/Xaxis/Yaxis/Zaxis/
2points] : X
Specify a point on the X axis <0,0,0>:
Specify rotation angle or [Reference]: 90

Command: **UCS**

Specify origin of UCS or
[Face/NAmed/OBject/Previous/View/World/X/Y/Z
/ZAxis] <World>: M
Specify new origin point or
[Zdepth]<0,0,0>: (Select Point A1)

Command: CIRCLE

Specify center point for circle or [3P/2P/Ttr
(tan tan radius)]: 12,20
Specify radius of circle or [Diameter]: D
Specify diameter of circle: 16

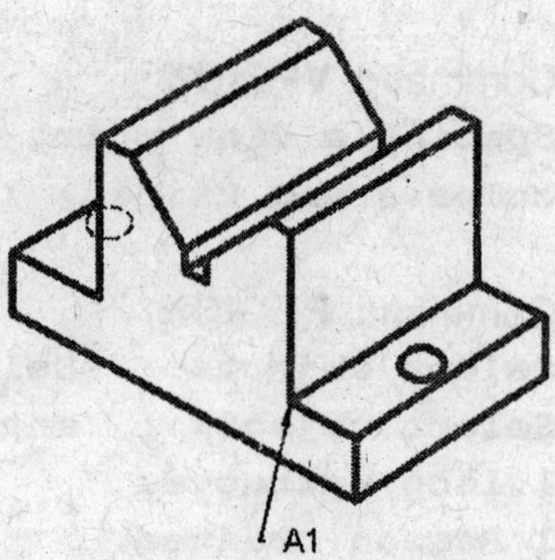

Command: **CIRCLE**

Specify center point for circle or [3P/2P/Ttr
(tan tan radius)]: -64,20
Specify radius of circle or [Diameter]: D
Specify diameter of circle: 16

Command: **EXTRUDE**

```
Current wire frame density:ISOLINES=4
Select objects to extrude:(Select
Circle C)
Select objects to extrude:(Select
Circle C1)
Select objects  : enter
Specify height of extrusion or
[Direction/Path/Taper angle]: -40
```

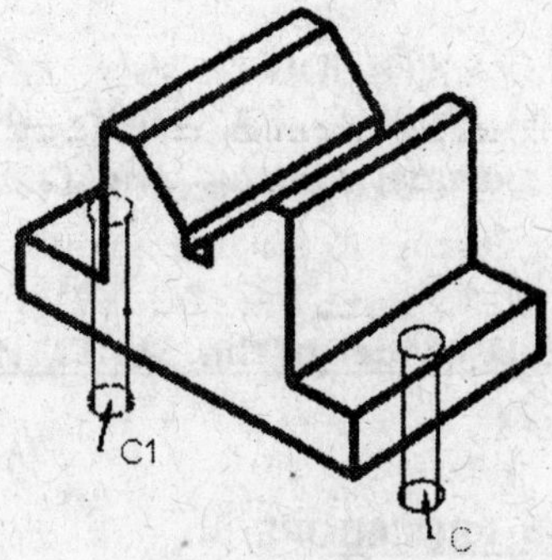

Command: **SUBTRACT**

```
Select objects: 1 found
Select objects
Select objects
```

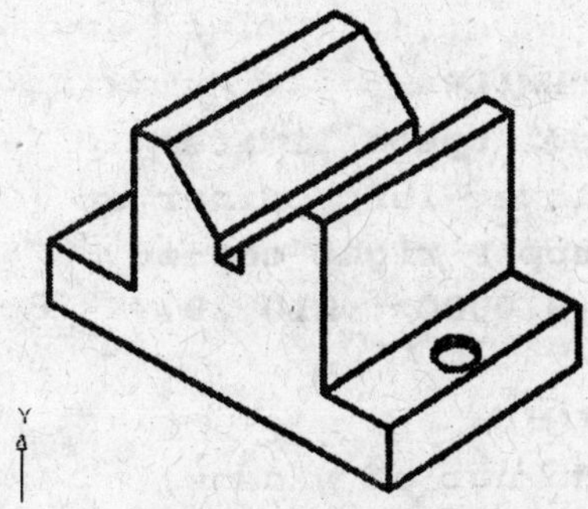

Command: **SHADEMODE**

```
Enter an option [2dwireframe/3dwireframe/3dHidden/Realistic/
Conceptual/Other] <2dwireframe>: C
```

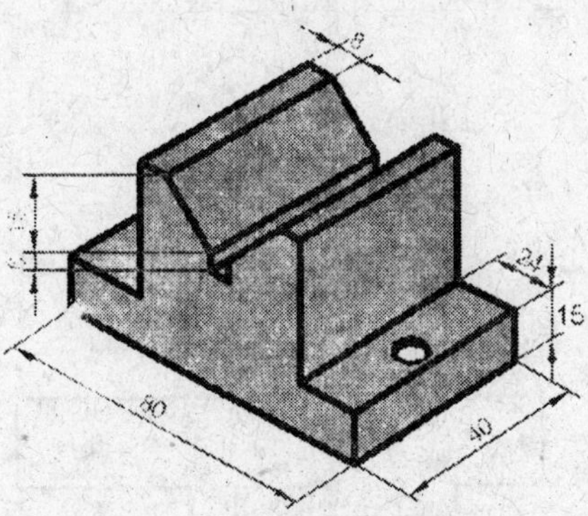

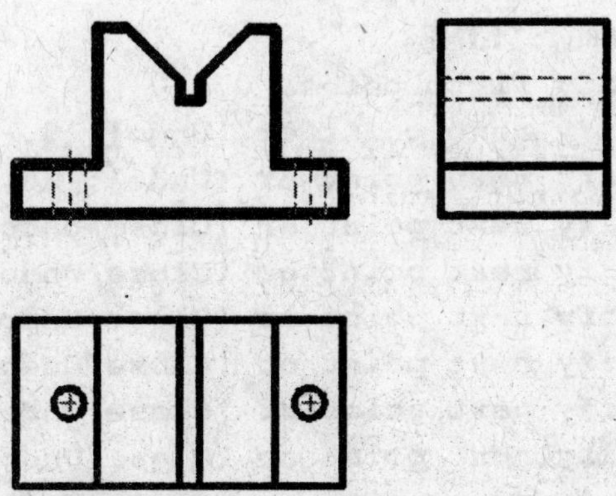

Modeling of V- BLOCK and Multi-Views

Ex. No. : 5

Create a 3-D Model of the SHAFT WITH MOUNTINGS shown, using 3-D Commands such as Region, Extrude, Revolve and Chamfer.

AIM :

To create 3-D Model of the *SHAFT WITH MOUNTINGS* :

Step-by-Step PROCEDURE:

Command: **LIMITS**
Reset Model space limits:
Specify lower left corner or [ON/OFF] <0.0000,0.0000>: 0,0
Specify upper right corner
<12.0000,9.0000>: 210,297

Command: **ZOOM**
Specify corner of window, enter a scale factor (nX or nXP), or [All/Center/Dynamic/Extents/Previous/Scale/Window/Object] <real time>: ALL

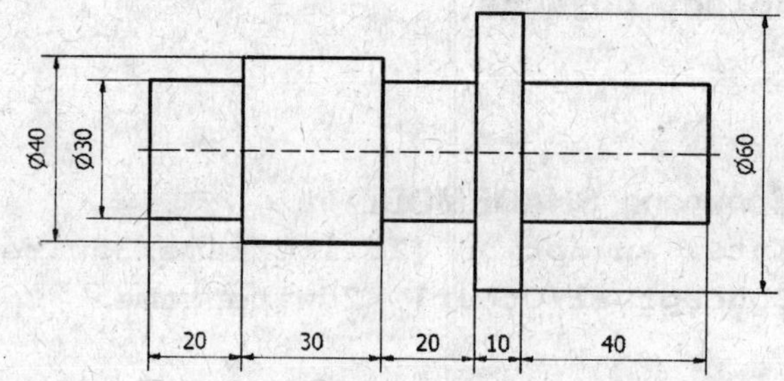

Command: **LINE**
Specify first point: 0,0,0
Specify next point or [Undo]: 0,-15
Specify next point or [Undo]: 20,-15
Specify next point or [Close/Undo]: 20,-20
Specify next point or [Close/Undo]: 50,-20
Specify next point or [Close/Undo]: 50,-15
Specify next point or [Close/Undo]: 70,-15
Specify next point or [Close/Undo]: 70,-30
Specify next point or [Close/Undo]: 80,-30
Specify next point or [Close/Undo]: 80,-15
Specify next point or [Close/Undo]: 120,-15
Specify next point or [Close/Undo]: 120,0
Specify next point or [Close/Undo]: 0,0
Specify next point or [Close/Undo]: C
Zero length line created at (0.0000, 0.0000, 0.0000)

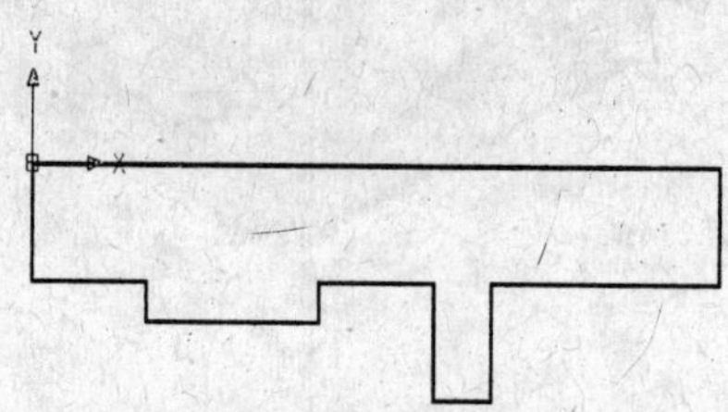

Command: REGION
Select objects: (select all lines)
1 loop extracted.
1 region created.

Command: **REVOLVE**
Current wire frame density: ISOLINES=4
Select objects to revolve: (select the region)
Specify axis start point or define axis by [Object/X/Y/Z] <Object>: X
Specify angle of revolution or [STart angle] <360>: 360

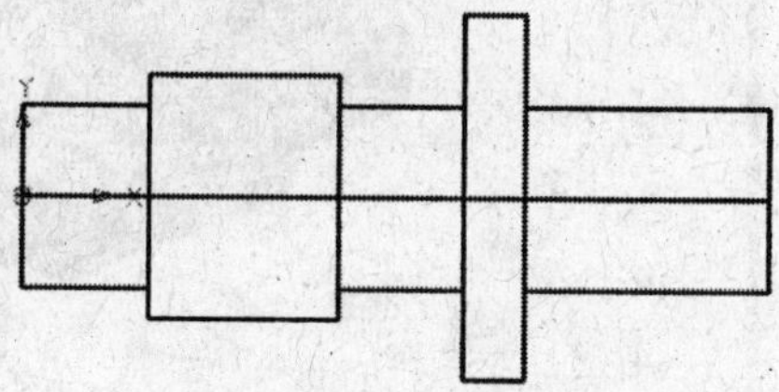

Command: **SHADEMODE**
Enter an option [2dwireframe/3dwireframe/3dHidden/Realistic /Conceptual/Other]<2dwireframe>: C

Command: **CHAMFER**
Select first line or [Undo/Polyline/Distance/Angle/Trim/mEthod/Multiple]: (select the edge)
Base surface selection...
Enter surface selection option [Next/OK (current)] <OK>: (Enter key)
Specify base surface chamfer distance: 1
Specify other surface chamfer distance <1.0000>:1
Select an edge or [Loop]: (select the edge again)

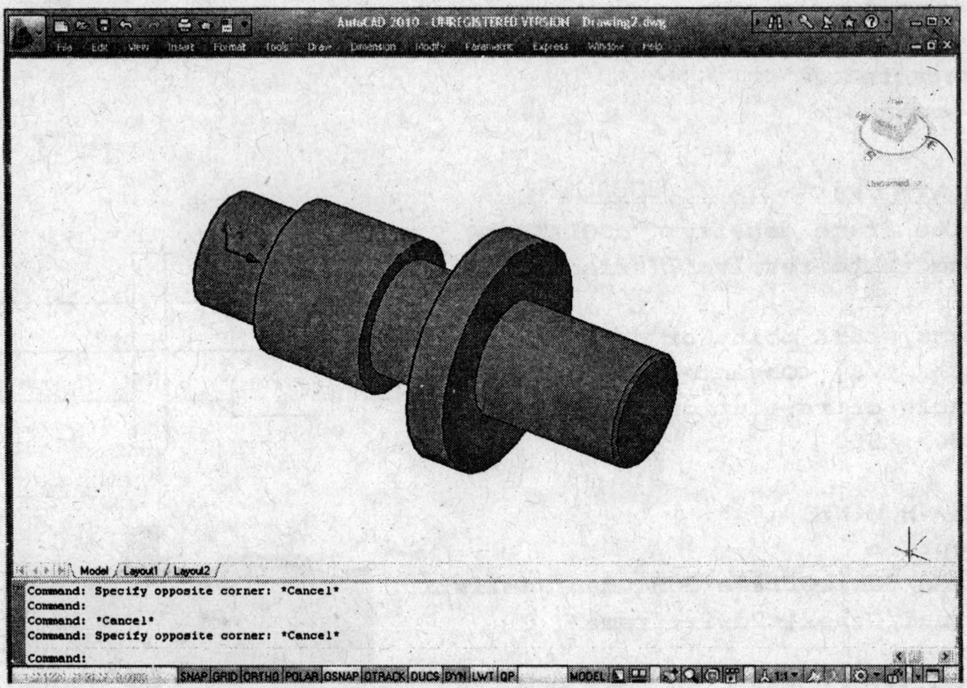

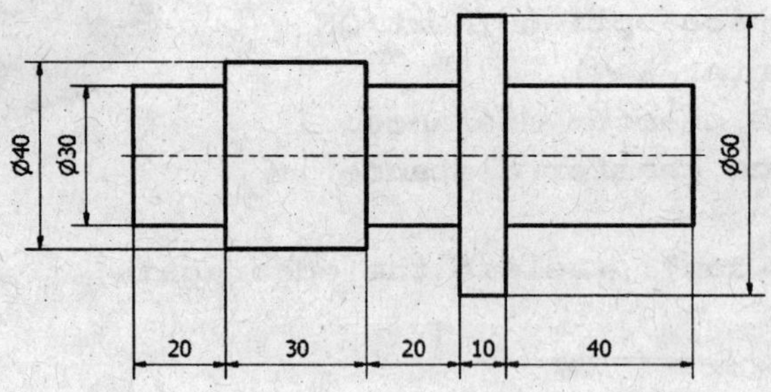

<u>**Modeling of SHAFT WITH MOUNTINGS and Front View**</u>

<u>**Ex. No. : 6**</u>

Create a 3-D Model of the FLANGE COUPLING shown, using 3-D Commands such as ***Region, 3D Array, Extrude and Subtract.***

<u>**AIM :**</u>

<u>**To create 3-D Model of the FLANGE COUPLING :**</u>

<u>**Step-by-Step PROCEDURE:**</u>

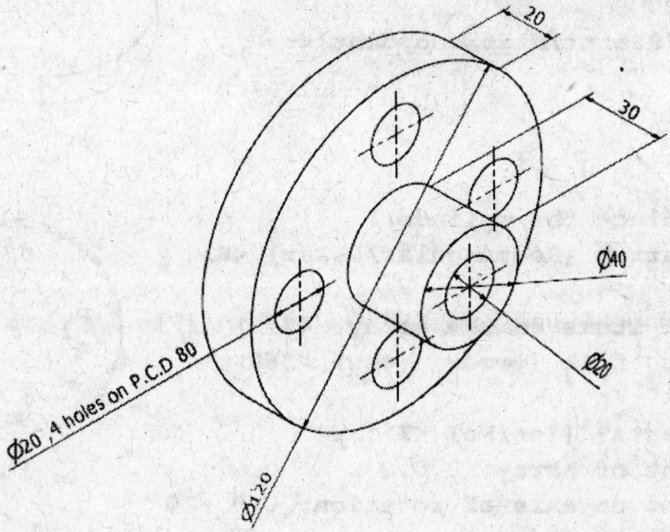

Command: **LIMITS**

```
Reset Model space limits:
Specify lower left corner or [ON/OFF]
<0.0000,0.0000>: 0,0
Specify upper right corner
<210.0000,297.0000>: 210,297
```

Command: **CIRCLE**

```
Specify center point for circle or
[3P/2P/Ttr (tan tan radius)]: 0,0,0
Specify radius of circle or [Diameter]: D
Specify diameter: 120
```

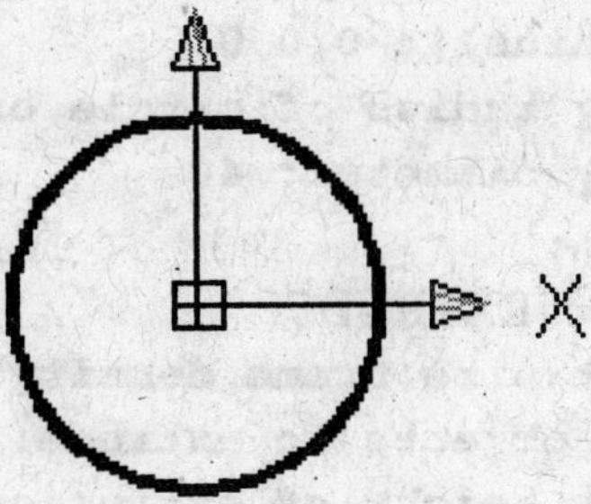

Command: **EXTRUDE**
Select objects to extrude: (select the circle)
Specify height of extrusion or
[Direction/Path/Taper angle] <20>: -20

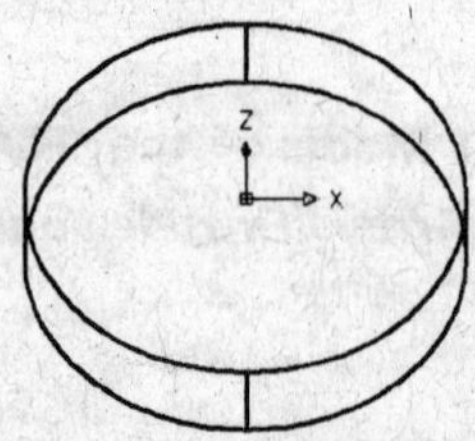

Command: **CYLINDER**
Specify center point of base or
[3P/2P/Ttr/Elliptical]: 40,0,0
Specify base radius or [Diameter]: D
Specify diameter: 20
Specify height or [2Point/Axis endpoint]<-
20>:-23

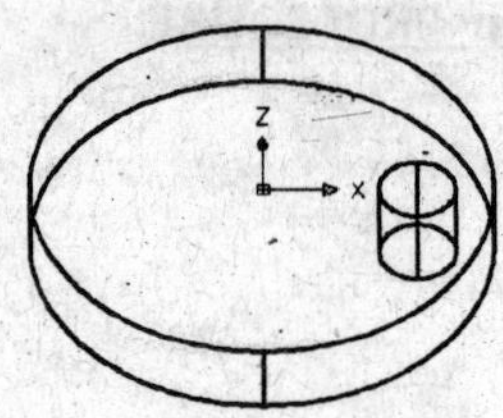

Command: **3DARRAY**
Select objects: (select the cylinder)
Enter the type of array [Rectangular/Polar] <R>:
P
Enter the number of items in the array: 4
Specify the angle to fill (+=ccw, -=cw) <360>:
360
Rotate arrayed objects? [Yes/No] <Y>: Y
Specify center point of array: 0,0,0
Specify second point on axis of rotation: 0,0,-20

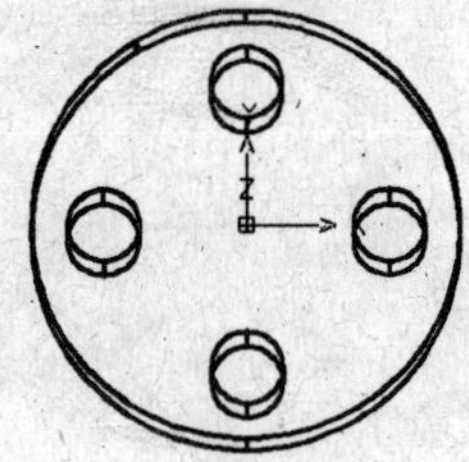

Command: **SUBTRACT**
Select objects: (select the outer cylinder)
Select objects: (select all inner cylinders)

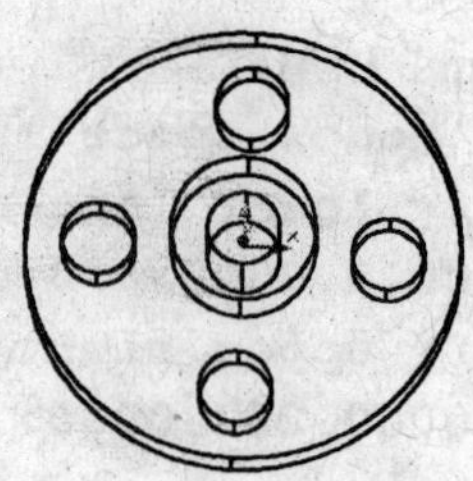

Command: **CIRCLE**
Specify center point for circle or [3P/2P/Ttr (tan tan radius)]: 0,0,0
Specify radius of circle or [Diameter] <60>: D
Specify diameter: 40

Command: **EXTRUDE**
Current wire frame density: ISOLINES=4
Select objects to extrude: (select the circle)
Specify height of extrusion or [Direction/Path/Taper angle] <30>: 30

Specify center point for circle or [3P/2P/Ttr (tan tan radius)]: 0,0,30
Specify radius of circle or [Diameter] <20>: D
Specify diameter: 20

Command: **EXTRUDE**
Current wire frame density: ISOLINES=4
Select objects to extrude: (select the inner circle)
Specify height of extrusion or [Direction/Path/Taper angle] <30>:-52

Command: **SUBTRACT**
Select objects: (select the cylinders of diameter 120 & 40)
Select objects: (select the inner cylinder (dia. 20))

Command: **SHADEMODE**
Enter an option
[2dwireframe/3dwireframe/3dHidden/Realistic/Conceptual/Other]
<2dwireframe>: c

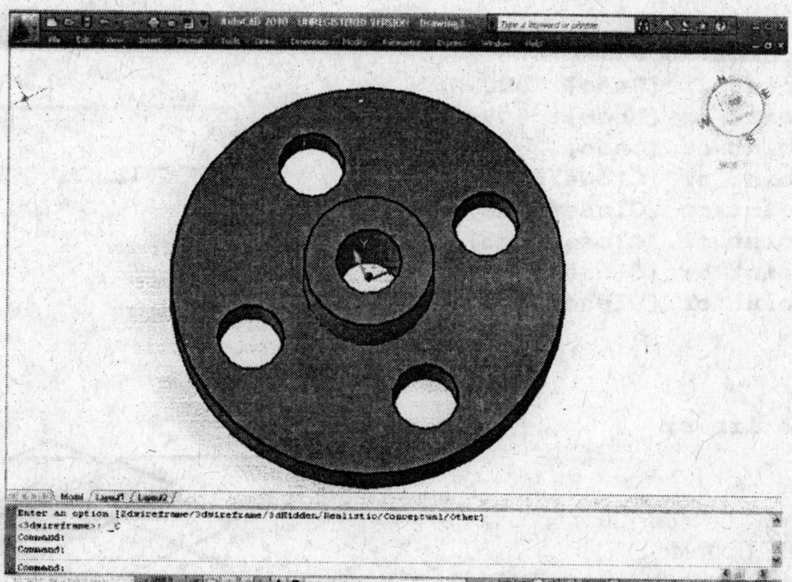

<u>Ex. No. : 7</u>

Create a 3-D Model of the TAIL STOCK shown, using 3-D Commands such as *Region, Extrude and Subtract.*

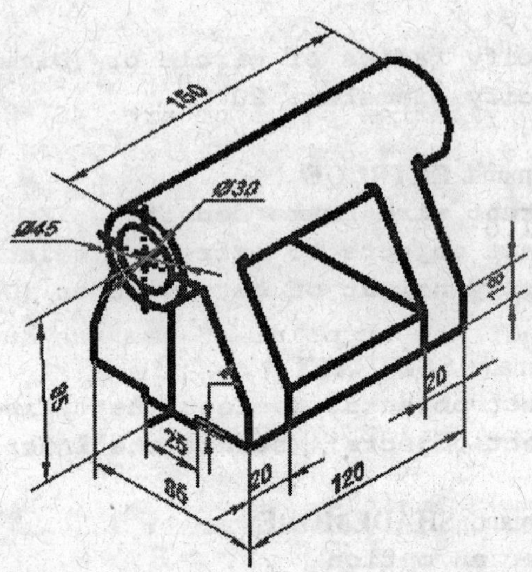

<u>AIM :</u>

<u>To create 3-D Model of the TAIL STOCK :</u>

<u>Step-by-Step PROCEDURE:</u>

Command: **LIMITS**

```
Specify lower left corner or
[ON/OFF] <0,0>: 0,0
Specify upper right corner <17,11>:210,297
```

Command: **LINE**

```
Specify first point: 0,0
Specify next point or [Undo]: @30,0
Specify next point or [Undo]: @0,-4
Specify next point or [Undo]: @25,0
Specify next point or [Close/Undo]: @0,4
Specify next point or [Close/Undo]: @30,0
Specify next point or [Close/Undo]: @0,18
Specify next point or [Close/Undo]: @-85,0
Specify next point or [Close/Undo]: @0,-18
```

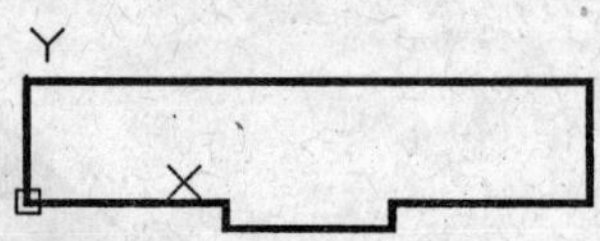

Command: **REGION**

```
(Select all the lines)
```

Command: **EXTRUDE** (Extrude 1)

```
Select objects to extrude or [MOde]: 1 found
Specify height of extrusion or
[Direction/Path/Taper angle/Expression] <-
20>: 120
```

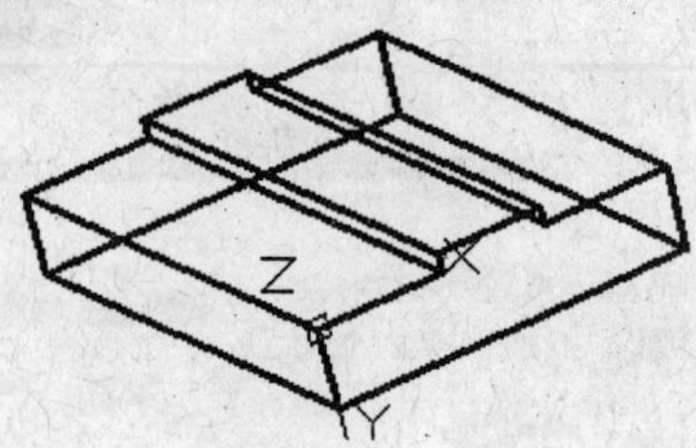

Command: **ARC**
Specify start point of arc or [Center]: c
Specify center point of arc: 42.5,81,0
Specify start point of arc: 20,81,0
Specify end point of arc or [Angle/chord Length]: 63,81,0

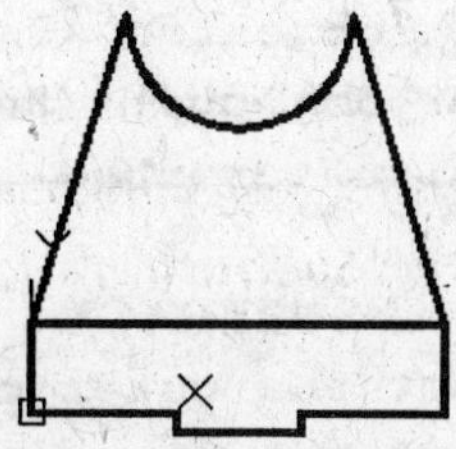

Command: **LINE**
(Select the endpoint of the arc and the base)

Command: **LINE**
(Select the other endpoint of the arc and the base)

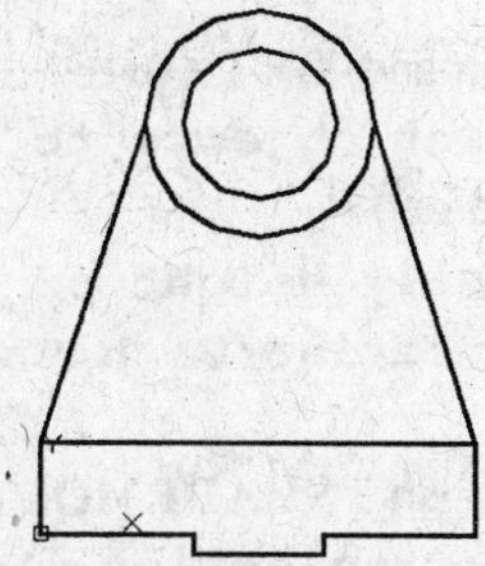

Command: **REGION**
Select objects :(select three lines and the arc)
1 loop extracted.
1 Region created.

Command: **EXTRUDE** (Extrude 2)
Select objects to extrude or [MOde]: 1 found
Specify height of extrusion or [Direction/Path/Taper angle/Expression] <-20>: 20

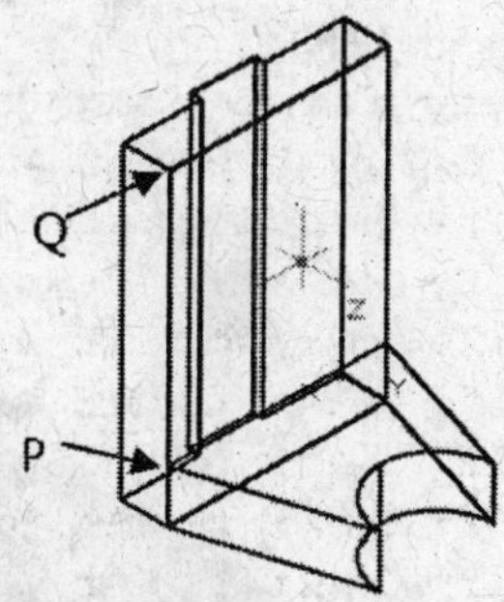

Command: **COPY**
Select objects to copy : (Select Extrude 2 object)
Specify base point or [Displacement/mOde] <Displacement>:
(Select the point P as the first base point)
Specify second point or <use first point as displacement>:
(Select the point Q as the second base point)

Command: **CIRCLE**
Specify center point for circle or [3P/2P/Ttr (tan tan radius)]: 42.5, 81,-15
Specify radius of circle or [Diameter] <23>: D
Specify diameter of the circle: 45

Command: **CIRCLE**
Specify center point for circle or [3P/2P/Ttr (tan tan radius)]: 42.5, 81,-15
Specify radius of circle or [Diameter] <23>: D
Specify diameter of the circle: 30

Command: **REGION**
Select objects: (Select the outer circle and click enter)
Select objects: (Select the inner circle and click enter)
2 Regions created.

Command: **SUBTRACT**
(Select the outer circle and press ENTER,
Select the inner circle and press ENTER)

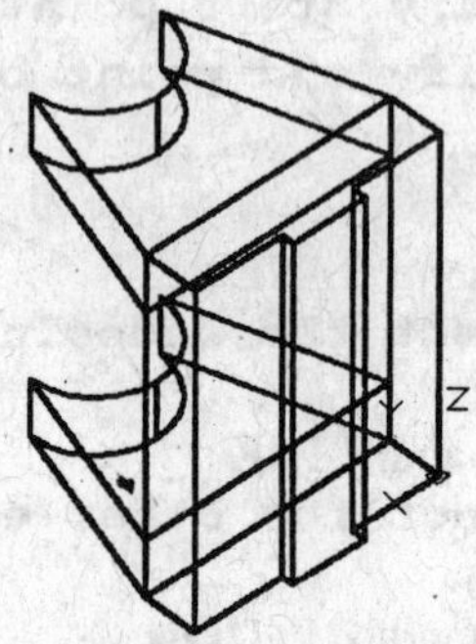

Command: **EXTRUDE** (Extrude 2)
Select objects to extrude or [MOde]: (select the region)
Specify height of extrusion or
[Direction/Path/Taper angle/Expression] <20>: 150

Command: **SHADEMODE**
Enter an option
[2dwireframe/Wireframe/Hidden/Realistic/Conceptual/Shaded/shaded with
Edges/shades of Gray/SKetchy/X-ray/Other] <2dwireframe>: C

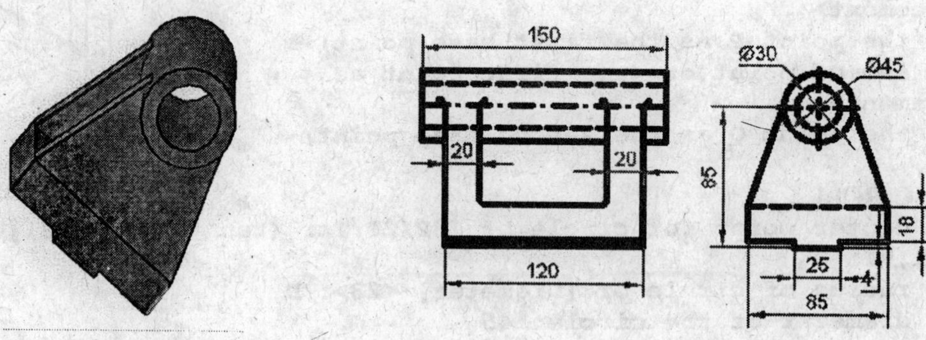

Modeling of TAIL STOCK and Multi - Views

<u>Ex. No. : 8</u> *Draw the 3D model of the given Object and obtain the 2-D multi-views.* (Anna University 2013)

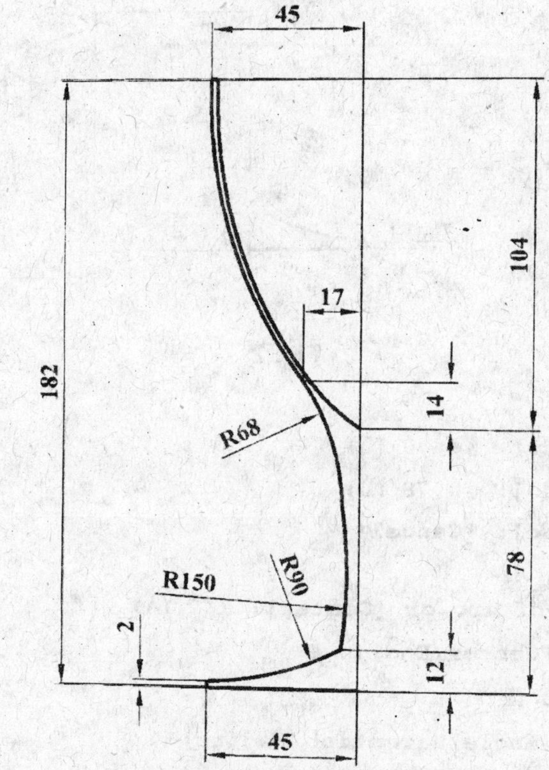

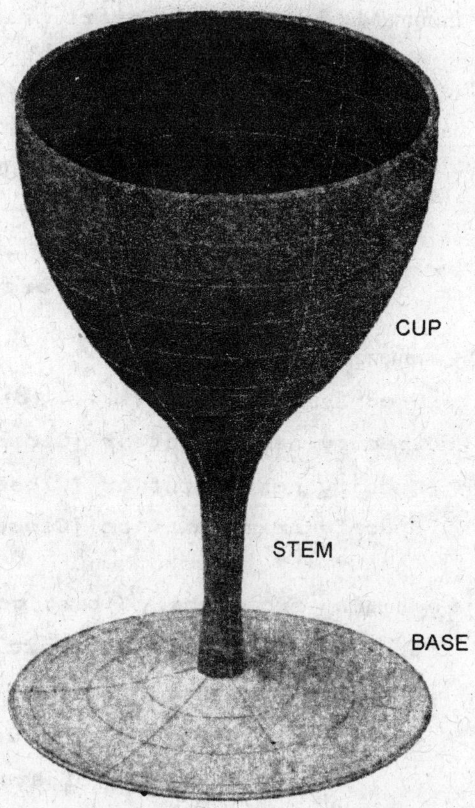

All dimensions are in mm.

Fig. 1

<u>AIM:</u>

To create the 3-D Model of the given OBJECT shown in Fig. 1 and obtain the 2-D multi-views.

<u>STEP-BY-STEP PROCEDURE:</u>

STEP 1: To set the LIMITS

Command: **LIMITS**

```
Specify lower left corner or [ON/OFF] <0,0>: 0,0
Specify upper right corner <17,11>: 210, 297
```

Command: **ZOOM**

```
Specify corner of window, enter a scale factor (nX or nXP), or
  [All/Center/Dynamic/Extents/Previous/Scale/Window/Object]
  <real time>: A
```

NOTE : Figs. 2 to 5 in STEPS 2 to 5 are SKELETON FIGURES only. Dimensions are shown just to check the Command Sequences.

STEP 2: To draw the BASE of the Object: (Fig. 2)

Command: _arc Specify start point of arc or [Center]: 1,2 **(A)**

Specify second point of arc or [Center/End]: _E

Specify end point of arc: @0,-2 **(B)**

Specify center point of arc or [Angle/Direction/Radius]:

_r Specify radius of arc: 1

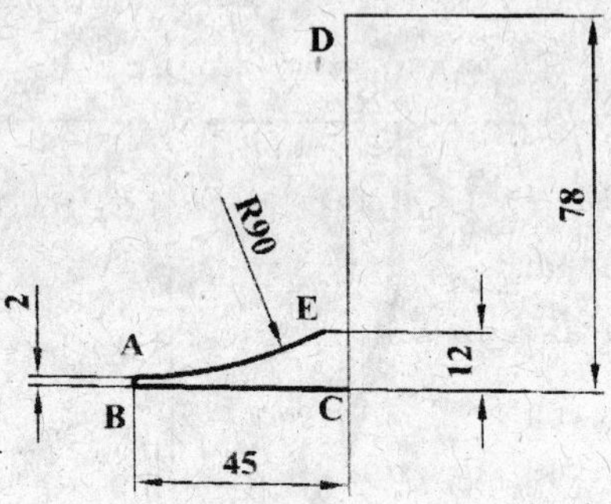

Fig. 2

Command: **LINE**

Specify first point:. 1,0 **(B)**

Specify next point or [Close/Undo]: @44,0 **(C)**

Specify next point or [Close/Undo]: @0,78 **(D)**

Specify next point or [Close/Undo]: *Cancel*

Command: _arc Specify start point of arc or [Center]: 1,2 **(A)**

Specify second point of arc or [Center/End]: _E

Specify end point of arc: @39,10 **(E)**

Specify center point of arc or [Angle/Direction/Radius]:

_r Specify radius of arc: 90

STEP 3: To draw the STEM of the object: (Fig. 3)

Command: _arc Specify start point of arc or [Center]: 40,12 **(E)**

Specify second point of arc or [Center/End]: _E

Specify end point of arc: @0,43 **(F)**

Specify center point of arc or [Angle/Direction/Radius]:

_r Specify radius of arc: 150

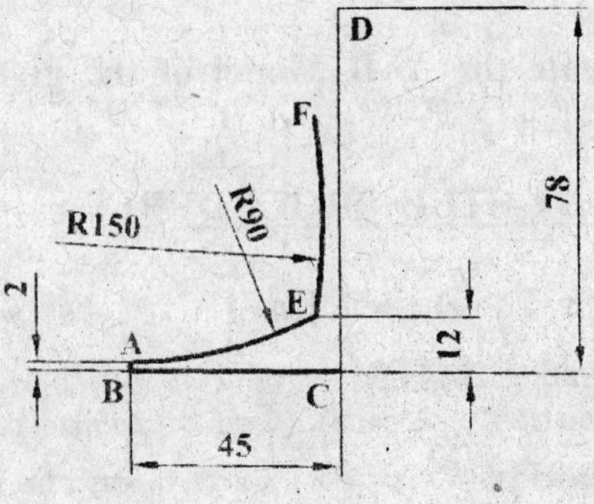

Fig. 3

Command: **FILLET**

Current settings: Mode = TRIM, Radius = 1

```
Select first object or [Undo/Polyline/Radius/Trim/Multiple]: _R
Specify fillet radius <1>: 1
Select first object or
    [Undo/Polyline/Radius/Trim/Multiple]: (AE)
Select second object or shift-select to apply corner: (EF)
```

STEP 4: To draw OUTER SURFACE of the Cup: (Fig. 4)

Command:

```
_arc Specify start point of arc or
    [Center]: 40,55 (F)
Specify second point of arc or
    [Center/End]: _E
Specify end point of arc:
    @-12,37 (G)
Specify center point of arc or
    [Angle/Direction/Radius]:
    _r Specify radius of arc: 68
```

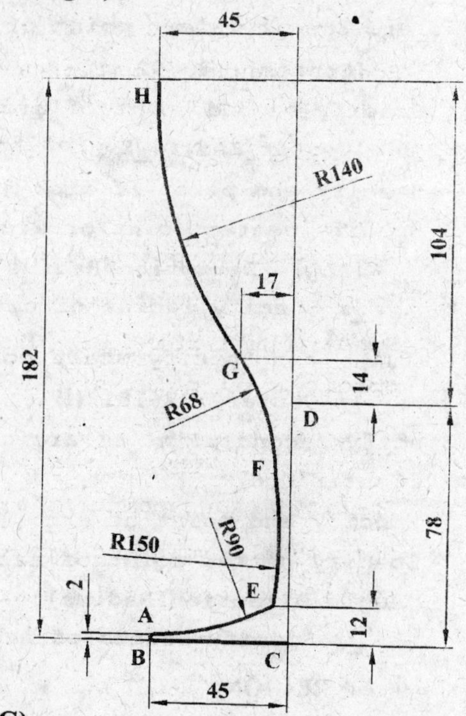

Fig. 4

Command:

```
_arc Specify start point of arc or
    [Center]: 0,181 (H)
Specify second point of arc or
    [Center/End]: _E
Specify end point of arc: @28,-89 (G)
Specify center point of arc or
    [Angle/Direction/Radius]:
    _r Specify radius of arc: 140
```

[Note: Missing Radius of OUTER ARC (HG), measured from the given Fig. 1 ≈ 140 mm]

STEP 5: To draw the INNER SURFACE of the Cup: (Fig. 5)

Command:

```
_arc Specify start point of arc or
    [Center]: 2,181 (I)
Specify second point of arc or
    [Center/End]: _E
```

```
Specify end point of arc: @28,-89 (J)
Specify center point of arc or
    [Angle/Direction/Radius]:
    _r Specify radius of arc: 138
```

[Note: Missing Radius of INNER ARC (IJ) ≈ 138 mm]

Command:

```
_arc Specify start point of arc or
    [Center]: 30,92 (J)
Specify second point of arc or
    [Center/End]: _E
Specify end point of arc: @15,-14 (D)
Specify center point of arc or
    [Angle/Direction/Radius]:
    _r Specify radius of arc: 68
```

Command: `_arc Specify start point of arc or[Center]: 2,181 (I)`

```
Specify second point of arc or
  [Center/End]: _E
  Specify end point of arc: @-2,0 (H)
  Specify center point of arc or
  [Angle/Direction/Radius]:
    _r Specify radius of arc: 1
```

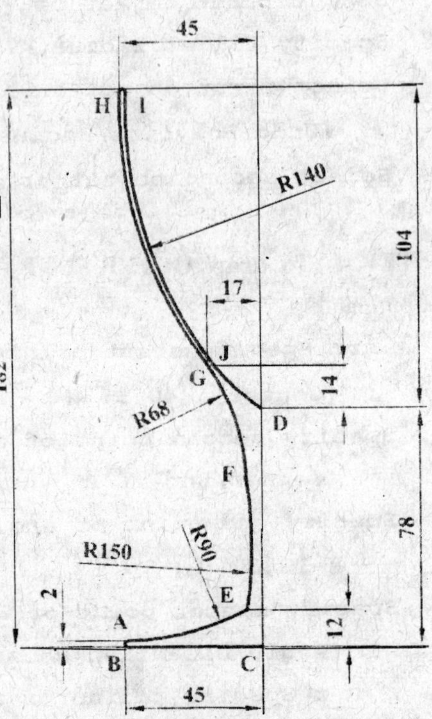

Fig. 5

HALF FRONT VIEW

Command: **REGION**

```
Select objects: all 11 found
Select objects: 1 loop extracted. 1 Region
created.
```

[NOTE : HALF FRONT VIEW in Fig. 5 is required for 2 purposes :
(1) For Revolving and Creating the 3-D Model without Dimensions &
(2) For Drawing the Full Front View with Dimensions.]

STEP 6: To COPY the HALF Front View: (Fig. 6)

Command: **COPY**

```
Select objects:
Specify base point or [Displacement]
<Displacement>: 45,0
Specify second point or [Exit/Undo] <Exit>: @180,0
```

Fig. 6

STEP 7: To REVOLVE the object to obtain 3-D MODEL: (Fig. 7)

Command: **REVOLVE**

```
Current wire frame density: ISOLINES=4
Select objects to revolve:
   1 found Select objects to revolve:
Specify axis start point or define axis by [Object/X/Y/Z]
   <Object>:45,0
   Specify axis endpoint: @0,78
Specify angle of revolution or
   [Start angle] <360>: 360
```

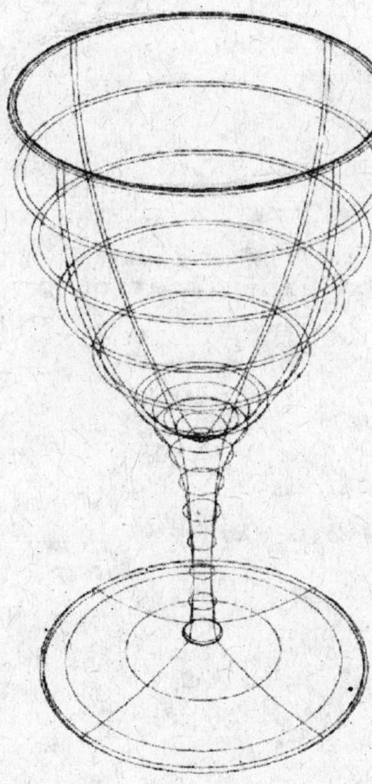

Fig. 7

Fig. 8

STEP 8: To create the SHADEMODE of the 3-D MODEL of the OBJECT: (Fig. 8)

Command: **SHADEMODE**

```
Enter an option
[2dwireframe/3dwireframe/
3dHidden/Realistic/Conceptual/Other]
<3dHidden>: C
```

STEP 9: To draw the 2-D MULTI-VIEWS : (Fig. 9)

NOTE : Refer Fig. 6. It shows the Skeleton HALF FRONT VIEW.

To Draw the Full Front View with Dimensions:

Command: **MIRROR**

```
Select objects: 1 found (Select the Skeleton Half Front View – Fig. 6)
Specify first point of mirror line: 45,0
Specify second point of mirror line: >>Enter new value for
  ORTHOMODE <1>:
  Resuming MIRROR command.
Specify second point of mirror line: @0,78 Erase source
  objects? [Yes/No] <N>: N
```

DIMENSIONING

BASE

Command: **_DIMRADIUS**

```
Select arc or circle: (AE)
  Dimension text = 90 Specify dimension line location or
  [Mtext/Text/Angle]:
```

Command: **_DIMLINEAR**

```
Specify first extension line origin or
  <select object>: 1,2
Specify second extension line origin: @-2,0 (B)
Non-associative dimension created.
Specify dimension line location or
  [Mtext/Text/Angle/Horizontal/Vertical/Rotated]:
  Dimension text = 2
```

Command: **_DIMLINEAR**

```
Specify first extension line origin or <select object>: 0,1
Specify second extension line origin: @45,-1 (C)
  Non-associative dimension created.
Specify dimension line location or
  [Mtext/Text/Angle/Horizontal/Vertical/Rotated]:
  Dimension text = 45
```

STEM

Command :**_DIMLINEAR**

```
Specify first extension line origin or <select object>:
```

```
Specify second extension line origin: @13,12
Specify dimension line location or
    [Mtext/Text/Angle/Horizontal/Vertical/Rotated]:
    Dimension text = 12
```

Command: **_DIMLINEAR**

```
Specify first extension line origin or <select object>: 45,0
Specify second extension line origin: @0,78 (D)
    Non-associative dimension
    created.
Specify dimension line location or
    [Mtext/Text/Angle/Horizontal/V
    ertical/Rotated]:
    Dimension text = 78
```

Command: **_DIMRADIUS**

```
Select arc or circle: Dimension
    text = 150
Specify dimension line location or
    [Mtext/Text/Angle]:
```

CUP

Similarly, mark the dimensions for the CUP using _DIMLINEAR and _DIMRADIUS commands as shown in Fig. 9.

TO DRAW THE TOP VIEW WITH DIMENSIONS:

- Draw the Top View using CIRCLE commands.
- Mark the Dimensions of the Circles using _DIMRADIUS Command.

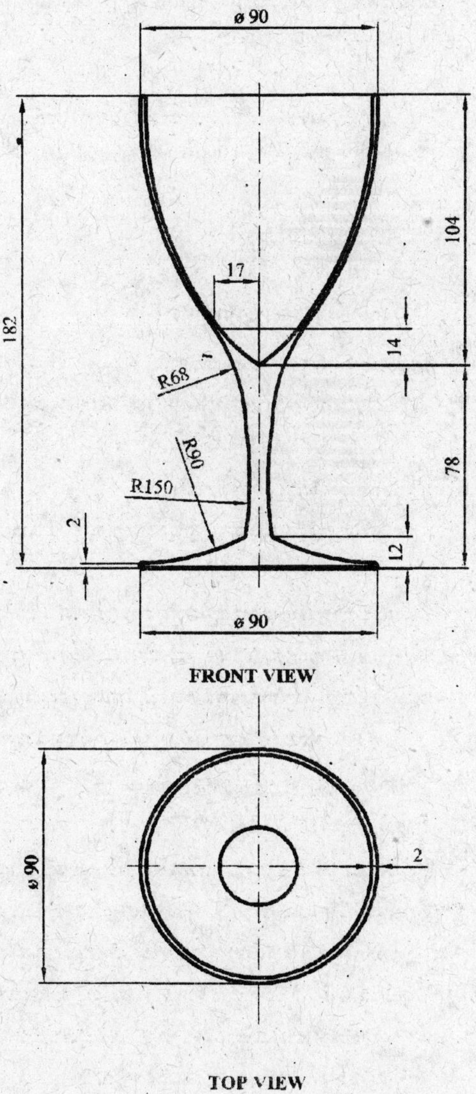

Fig. 9

VIVA-VOCE
QUESTIONS AND ANSWERS

OBJECTIVE QUESTIONS

1. A BYTE is made up of .... BITS. **[eight]**
2. Laser Printer uses .... beam for printing. **[laser]**
3. Micro-Computer is also known as .... **[Personal Computer]**
4. Commercial Computer - Aided Drafting was introduced in 1964 by the ....
[International Business Machines Corporation]
5. An engineer, using the CAD technique can try out different design ideas by just sitting at the terminal without making any .... **[prototype]**
6. .... has hit the technical world like a shock wave, revolutionizing the manner of drawing preparation. **[AutoCAD]**
7. .... are those commands which can tell the basic functions of AutoCAD.
[Utility Commands]
8. According to AutoCAD, an engineering drawing is considered to be made up of different drawing elements known as .... **[entities]**
9. To tell AutoCAD which entity to draw, type the required command on the keyboard in the .... area. **[command prompt]**
10. Command prompt means AutoCAD is ready for you to type a command name.
(T / F) **[True]**

11. Size of the Electronic Drawing sheet can be changed to any value by setting .... and .... **[Limits , Units]**

12. Drawing Aids are nothing but .... used for locating specific points on the Electronic Drafting Sheet. **[positioning tools]**

13. State the three positioning tools or Drafting Aids. **[Ortho , Grid and Snap]**

14. .... command allows you to draw lines at right angles only. **[Ortho]**

15. Snap mode is used to set .... for cursor movements. **[increments]**

16. GRID command is used to display .... lines on the screen at predefined spacing. **[dotted]**

17. Snap spacing is dependent of Grid spacing. **(T / F)** **[False]**

18. .... Boxes are similar to pull - down menus and are opened by selecting the items like Drawing Aids , Layers , etc. **[Dialogue]**

19. AutoCAD settings are called .... settings. **[default]**

20. State the three coordinate systems the AutoCAD uses to locate a point in XY plane. **[Absolute , Relative and Polar Coordinate System]**

21. In Absolute Coordinate System , points are located with respect to .... **[origin { 0, 0}]**

22. Define Relative Coordinate System.
[If the displacement along X and Y axes are measured with reference to the previous point, it is known as Relative Coordinate System]

23. In AutoCAD , the Relative Coordinate System is designated by the symbol .... and should precede any entry. **[@]**

24. Define Polar Coordinate System.
When a point is located by the distance of the point from the current point and the angle that the line between the two points makes with the positive X – axis, it is Polar Coordinate System

25. In AutoCAD, in the Polar Coordinate System, the angle is positive if measured in clockwise direction **(T / F)** **[False]**

26. The .... coordinates of a point are located with reference to the previous point. **[relative]**

27. The .... option of CIRCLE command can be used to draw a circle, if you want the circle to be tangent to two previously drawn objects. **[Tangent Tangent Radius]**

28. For drawing a circle, three point option can be used by three points on the of the circle. **[circumference]**

29. The prompt sequence for drawing a rectangle if the first and opposite corners are [6,6] and [12 , 10] is as follows :

    Command : ....

    First corner : ....

    Other corner : .... **[RECTANG , [6 ,6] , [12 , 10]]**

30. You can erase a previously drawn line using the ....option of the LINE command . **[Undo]**

31. The range of Rotation Angle used to draw an ellipse is 0 to 89.4 degree only, since a rotation angle of 0 degree produces a .... and an angle greater than 89.4 produces a .... **[Circle , Line]**

32. When you select the ERASE command , a small box known as the .... replaces the screen cursor. **[pick box]**

33. While using the Window option in the .... command, the objects to be erased must completely lie within the window. **[ERASE]**

34. The Polygon command constructs polygons of a specified number of sides. What is the minimum number of sides ? .... **[3]** ; The maximum ? .... **[1024]**

35. The rectangle generated on the screen is treated as a single object. **(T / F)** **[True]**

36. If you exit the LINE command after drawing a line and then select LINE command again, the ....option can be used to draw a line by grabbing the end point of the last line. **[Continue]**

37. If you have to remove more than one line, you can use the Undo option to undo only the most recent line drawn. **(T / F)** **[False]**

38. State any five significant EDIT commands. **[ERASE , UNDO , REDO , CHANGE and OFFSET]**

39. To establish which objects to edit, AutoCAD asks you to select one or more objects called .... **[Selection Set]**

40. When it needs a Selection Set, AutoCAD prompts : .... **[Select objects]**

41. When you select the EDIT / ERASE command , the screen cursor cross – hair is converted to a small box called .... **[Pick Box]**

42. AutoCAD confirms the object selection by temporarily changing the selected objects into .... lines. **[dashed]**

43. When using the Window option in the EDIT / ERASE command, the selected objects must .... lie within the window. **[completely]**

44. You can erase a previously drawn line using the .... option of the LINE command. **[Undo]**

45. Only one object is selected even if you use the .... option a number of times. **[Last]**

46. The .... selection option is used to select the most recently drawn object on the screen. **[Last]**

47. .... selection option brings a previously selected set of entities from a previous command for editing. **[Previous]**

48. Polygon selection option is similar to Window option except that you can define the .... selection option. **[an irregular polygon]**

49. The .... command restores objects that have been erased by the previous ERASE command. **[OOPS]**

50. With the help of the Previous selection option, you can edit the previous selection set by reselecting its objects individually. **(T / F)** **[False]**

51. Remove selection option removes the selected objects from the drawing. **(T / F)** **[False]**

52. The .... selection option is used to select objects by touching the objects to be selected with the selection line. **[Fence]**

53. The One option of the UNDO command restrains U and UNDO commands to a single operation. **(T / F)** **[True]**

54. The Control option lets you determine how many of the UNDO options you want active. **[T / F]** **[True]**

55. If the Auto option of the UNDO command is OFF, any group of commands that is used to insert an object is undone together. **[T / F]** **[False]**

56. .... command can be used to undo any previous command , or undo several commands at once. **[UNDO]**

57. The .... option of the UNDO command disables the UNDO and U command entirely. **[Control]**

58. To activate the UNDO options if they are disabled, you must enter .... option **[All]**

59. A group of commands is caused to be treated as a single command for the U and UNDO commands by the combined work of the .... and .... UNDO options. **[Begin , End]**

60. The Group option in the Undo screen menu is the same as the .... option **[Begin]**

61. You can use the Begin option only when the UNDO control is set to .... **[All]**

62. UNDO has the power to wipe out your entire drawing in one step, but if you catch it .... with REDO, you can save it. **[immediately]**

63. ZOOM command does not affect the actual size of the object **[T / F]** **[True]**

64. With the help of ZOOM All option, you can view the entire drawing in the current viewport. **[T / F]** **[True]**

65. Transparent commands cannot be used while another command is in progress. **[T /F]** **[False]**

66. An absolute magnification value is specified by a value followed by X. **[T / F]** **[False]**

67. The scale factor is a .... of the drawing scale. **[reciprocal]**

68. To scale a view relative to Paper Space units, the ZOOM .... option is used **[XP]**

69. After completion of a transparent command, AutoCAD returns you to the Command : prompt. **[T / F]** **[False]**

70. You can use the ZOOM command an indefinite number of times on a drawing. **[T / F]** **[False]**

71. While using the ZOOM Previous option, you can go back up to .... views for a viewport. **[10]**

72. You can view the entire drawing [even if it is beyond limits] with the help of the .... option of ZOOM command. **[All]**

73. In the ZOOM WINDOW option, the area inside the window is .... or .... to completely fill the display. **[magnified, reduced]**

74. The material the object is made of can be indicated by the hatch pattern. (T / F) **[True]**

75. The .... command automatically defines the boundary, whereas in the case of the .... command you have to define the boundary by selecting the objects that form the boundary of the hatch area. **[BHATCH, HATCH]**

76. Hatch boundary may be comprised of Line, Circle, Arc, Plines, 3Dface, or other objects and must be completely displayed on the screen or within the active viewport. (T / F) **[True]**

<u>Types of Modeling, View point, View ports, Cylinder, Cone, Box</u>

77. What are the axes in the Cartesian Coordinate System? **(X, Y, Z)**

78. A 3D Surfaced Wireframe model is described entirely in terms of ...., ... and .... **[PONTS, LINES, FACES]**

79. SOLID Modeling is the process of creating objects that have all the .... and .... of an actual solid object. **[qualities, properties]**

80. It is sufficient to define the .... and .... of an object, if you create a Surfaced Wireframe Model. **[shape, size]**

81. Solid Modeling requires not only the shape and size of the object, but also properties like ...., ..., ..., etc. **[mass, moment of inertia, density, Young's Modules, Poisson's ratio** - any three only **]**

82. Solid Modeling eliminates the need for making costlier .... and makes the product development cycle shorter. **[prototypes]**

83. Surfaced Wireframe Modeling is more error-prone than Solid Modeling. (T / F) **[True]**

84. The solid .... form the basic building blocks for any solid. **[primitives]**

85. You can use the .... command to construct a solid cylinder. **[CYLINDER]**

86. The CONE command creates a solid cone with a .... or .... base. **[circular, elliptical]**

87. The BOX command used to create a solid box has two options : Center and ....

[Corner]

88. What commands are used to generate a third dimension of a drawing ? [VPOINT and DVIEW]

89. The default viewpoint is located at .... and the view obtained with this viewpoint is called the Top View. [0, 0, 1]

90. For the Front View display, the VPOINT coordinate is to be set at .... [0, –1, 0]

91. To make it easier to draw a 3D object on a 2D screen, AutoCAD lets you split the screen into more than one view, called a .... [Viewport]

92. A .... is a rectangular part of the graphics area of the screen. [Viewport]

93. The AutoCAD drawing screen may be divided into several windows called .... [viewports]

94. Using VPORTS command, viewports are created to create a .... or layout [model]

95. When you use VPORTS command, you are in a mode called .... [Model Space]

96. Using VPORTS command, zooming can be performed in each viewport .... [independently]

97. "Port" means "................". [Opening]

98. You can edit your drawing in one viewport and immediately see the result in all viewports, each of which displays the same view of your drawing. (T / F) [False]

Union, Subtract, Mass property, Sectional View

99. Region Models are those .... any height while Solid Models are true shape 3D objects .... height. [without, with]

100. .... are created out of Lines, Polylines, Arcs, Circles and Ellipses. [Regions]

101. 3D Solids are created by ...., Revolving or Sweeping a profile. [Extruding]

102. Several Regions or Solids can be combined using the .... command. [UNION]

103. Solids cannot be combined with Regions using UNION command. (T / F) [True]

104. Since AutoCAD assigns a density of one to the solids, mass and volume are .... [equal]

105. The .... command can be used to analyze the properties of a solid model **[MASSPROP]**

106. Full sections are usually cut through the .... axis of the object, which is referred to as .... axis. **[longer, longitudinal]**

107. To obtain Half Sectional View, one quarter of the object has to be cut. **(T / F)** **[True]**

108. Can you show the Half Sectional view either with a solid line in the middle or center line itself ? **[Yes]**

109. .... command is used to draw Polylines of required width to represent the Cutting (Section) Plane Lines. **[PLINE]**

110. The spacing between the hatch lines is decided by the .... to be hatched . **[area]**

111. If the Scale Factor is one, the spacing between the Hatch Lines is the .... as given in the hatch pattern file for that particular hatch. **[same]**

112. If there are two .... parts to be hatched, change the direction of the hatch angle to have the hatched areas look .... **[adjacent, differently]**

113. Hatch angle may be changed from 45 degrees to 60 degrees, if the hatch lines happen to be parallel to an edge of the hatch area. **(T / F)** **[True]**

114. In AutoCAD, you can control the spacing between the hatch lines by specifying the .... at the time of hatching. **[Scale Factor]**

Isometric Drawing and Basic Dimension

115. Isometric Drawing is a 2D drawing representing a .... object. **[3D]**

116. "Isometric" means "................. ", because the three angles between the three principle axes of an Isometric Drawing are each .... degrees. **["equal measure" , 120]**

117. What command do you use to set the Isometric Grid and Snap ? **[SNAP command]**

118. Isometric Snap should be ON to display the Isocircle option with the ELLIPSE command **(T / F)** **[True]**

119. Isometric circles are drawn using .... command and then selecting the .... option. **[ELLIPSE, Isocircle]**

120. Isometric .... points are arranged to draw 30, 90, 150, 210, 270 and 360 degree lines. **[grid]**

121. The grid lines coincide with the three isometric axes, which makes it easier to make isometric drawings. **(T / F)** **[True]**

122. What command is used to enter Isometric mode ? **[SNAP]**

123. While dimensioning an object, settings such as space between the dimension text and the dimension line, ..., ..., etc are maintained and used.
[arrow size / text size / tick mark size]

124. The modification of dimensioning standards can be achieved through ....
[Dimension variables]

125. Different industries like Mechanical, Electrical, Civil, etc., adopt different or modified dimensioning standards. **(T / F)** **[True]**

126. You can specify dimension text of your own or accept the measured value computed by AutoCAD. **(T / F)** **[True]**

127. Dimension variables control most of the aspects of a dimension. **(T / F)** **[True]**

128. A dimension variable can be set by entering the variable name at the Command : Prompt. **(T / F)** **[True]**

129. Aligned Dimensioning is used to dimension an object that is inclined at an angle and parallel to X or Y axis. **(T / F)** **[False]**

130. The dimension created with the Aligned option is .... to the object being dimensioned. **[parallel]**

131. Rotated dimensioning is used when you want to place the dimension line at ....
[an angle]

132. The control sequence .... can be used to generate the degree symbol °. **[%% d]**

133. The control sequence .... is used to generate the diameter symbol ∅. **[%% C]**

134. A linear or Angular dimension should not exist already to use the Baseline Dimensioning **(T / F)** **[False]**

135. Continue Dimensioning is also known as .... Dimensioning. **[Chain]**

136. What is the shape of the dimension line in Angular Dimensioning ? **[Arc]**

137. In the Angular Dimensioning of angle between two non-parallel lines, the dimensioned angle should not be greater than .... degrees. **[180]**

138. In Aligned Dimensioning, the dimension text by default is aligned with the object being dimensioned. **(T / F)** **[True]**

139. Horizontal dimension measures displacement along the Y axis. **(T / F)** **[False]**

140. In Rotated Dimensioning, the dimension line is always aligned with the object being dimensioned. **(T / F)** **[True]**

141. The Rotated dimension can be specified to get the effect of Horizontal or Vertical dimension. **(T / F)** **[True]**

142. Polylines are thick lines having a uniform or .... width. **[Varying]**

143. For a Polyline, the longitudinal center line is taken as .... line for measurement, hatching, etc. **[reference]**

144. A .... width produces a polyline like the LINE command. **[zero]**

145. Width option of PLINE command lets you specify both the .... and .... widths of the polyline. **[starting, ending]**

146. .... means width from the center of a thick Pline to one of its edges. **[Halfwidth]**

147. Comments for width option of PLINE command are not applicable to Halfwidth option. **(T / F)** **[False]**

148. The function of PLINE Undo Option is the same as LINE Undo option. **(T / F)** **[True]**

149. PLINE Undo option can be invoked by entering .... or .... at the following prompt : .... **[Undo, U ; Arc / Close / Halfwidth / Length / Undo / Width / < Endpoint of line > : U]**

150. You can Undo any number of times, until there is just one .... left in the polyline segment. Further use of Undo option evokes the message : "................"

[point, "All segments already undone]